LAND USE AND LAND USE PLANNING IN BANGLADESH

Land Use and Land Use Planning in Bangladesh

Hugh Brammer

 The University Press Limited

The University Press Limited
Red Crescent Building
114 Motijheel C/A
GPO Box 2611
Dhaka 1000
Bangladesh
Fax: (88 02) 9565443
E-mail: upl@bttb.net.bd

First published 2002

Cover designed by Ashraful Hassan Arif

ISBN 984 05 1565 9

Published by Mohiuddin Ahmed, The University Press Limited, Dhaka. This book has been set in Times New Roman by MNS Computer Printers, Dhaka. Designer: Babul Chandra Dhar and produced by Abarton, 99 Malibagh, Dhaka. Printed at Akota Offset Press, 119 Fakirapool, Dhaka, Bangladesh.

Contents

PART I. ENVIRONMENT AND LAND USE

1. THE PHYSICAL BASIS OF LAND USE IN BANGLADESH

PART II. LAND USE STUDIES

2. TRADITIONAL AND MODERN METHODS OF INTENSIFYING CROP PRODUCTION

3. AGRICULTURE AND FOOD PRODUCTION IN POLDER AREAS

PART IV. TECHNICAL INFORMATION TO SUPPORT PLANNING

14. SOIL SURVEY AND LAND USE PLANNING

15. SELECTING SITES FOR FOOD-FOR-WORK SCHEMES

16. SELECTING SITES FOR SMALL-SCALE WATER DEVELOPMENT SCHEMES

17. USE OF TANKS FOR IRRIGATION AND FISH FARMING

List of Tables and Figures

Tables

Figures

Abbreviations and Acronyms

Ac	acre(s)
ADAB	Association of Development Agencies in Bangladesh
AEZ	agroecological zone
B/b	broadcast
BADC	Bangladesh Agricultural Development Corporation
BARC	Bangladesh Agricultural Research Council
BARD	Bangladesh Academy for Rural Development
BARI	Bangladesh Agricultural Research Institute
BAU	Bangladesh Agricultural University
BBS	Bangladesh Bureau of Statistics
BIP	Barisal Irrigation Project
BKB	Bangladesh Krishi Bank (Agricultural Development Bank)
BRDB	Bangladesh Rural Development Board
BRE	Brahmaputra Right Embankment
BRRI	Bangladesh Rice Research Institute
BS	Block Supervisor
BUET	Bangladesh University of Engineering and Technology
BWDB	Bangladesh Water Development Board
CEC	cation exchange capacity
CEP	Coastal Embankment Project
CHT	Chittagong Hill Tracts
cm	centimetre
DAE	Department of Agricultural Extension
DDA	Deputy Director of Agriculture
DDP	Delta Development Project
DEO	District Extension Officer
DND	Dhaka-Narayanganj-Demra (project)
DTW	deep tube-well
Ec	electrical conductivity
EPWAPDA	East Pakistan Water and Power Development Authority
FAO	Food and Agriculture Organization of the United Nations
g	gram
GIS	Geographical Information System
G-K	Ganges-Kobadak (project)

H	Highland
ha	hectare
HDB	Horticultural Development Board
HTW	hand tube-well
HYV	High-yielding variety
IECo	International Engineering Company
INA	Institute of Nuclear Agriculture
IRDP	Integrated Rural Development Programme
IRRI	International Rice Research Institute
KSS	Krishi Samay Samiti (farmers' cooperative group)
L	Lowland
LGED	Local Government Engineering Department
LIV	local improved variety
LLP	low-lift pump
LV	local variety
M	million
m	metre
MAF	Ministry of Agriculture and Forest
md	maund
meq	milli-equivalent
MH	Medium Highland
ML	Medium Lowland
mm	millimetre
mmhos	millimhos
MSL	mean sea-level
N	nitrogen
NGO	non-government organization
NPK	nitrogen, potash and phosphorus (fertilizers)
P	phosphorus
oz	ounce(s)
pH	(symbol used for acidity/alkalinity reaction)
ppm	parts per million
PWDD	Public Works Department datum
q-m	quick-maturing
RHD	Roads & Highways Department
SDAO	Subdivision Agricultural Officer
SMO	Subject Matter Officer
SMS	Subject Matter Specialist
SP	saturation percentage
SRDI	Soil Resources Development Institute

SSP	Single superphosphate (fertilizer)
STW	shallow tube-well
T/t	transplanted
T&V	Training and Visit system
TIP	Thana Irrigation Programme
Tk	Taka (Bangladesh's currency)
TSP	triple superphosphate (fertilizer)
TW	tube-well
UAA	Union Agricultural Assistant
UNDP	United Nations Development Programme
VEA	Village Extension Agent
VL	Very Lowland

Preface

The purpose of this volume is somewhat different from that of the earlier volumes of the author's collected works. Partly, it is historical: to bring together in one place papers describing various aspects of land use and agricultural development planning as those subjects were viewed in the 1970s and 1980s. Mainly, it is to encourage present-day officials and researchers to review the present status of land use and the thinking on agricultural development planning, using the chapters in this volume as a benchmark against which to measure and assess changes that have occurred over the past twenty years. To both those ends, an additional purpose is to make the information more readily available to researchers and students: most of the papers presented in this volume originally appeared as cyclostyled reports which had a limited circulation beyond the official recipients. The methods and information described in successive chapters provide material that could be used for practical training in agricultural universities, colleges and extension training institutes, rural development academies, and university geography and soil science departments.

The author is well aware that land use and the thinking on land use planning in Bangladesh have moved on since he was last directly involved in those subjects fifteen years ago. Land use in the country always was dynamic, as is described in Chapter 2. Official attitudes to rural land use planning also evolved and fluctuated over time, too, and appear to be quite different now from what they were during the 1960s and 1970s. The author feels fortunate to have served in East Pakistan/Bangladesh during the latter period, witnessing, in turn, the pioneering efforts of Akhter Hameed Khan and the Comilla Academy (now BARD) in Thana development planning during the 1960s, developing a model which had much in common with the Chinese commune system; various short-lived attempts made by politico-academics to introduce communal farming in the heady political aftermath of the independence struggle in 1971; the more Stalinist model of state planning introduced by the first Government after Independence, culminating in BAKSAL's 'compulsory cooperatives' in 1975; the enthusiastic efforts of Mahbubul Alam Chasi to promote *Swanirvar Bangladesh* (self-sufficient Bangladesh) in the mid-1970s; official efforts to promote local self-government later in the 1970s both through the *Gram Sarkar* (village government) movement and the devolution of development planning responsibilities to Thana and Union Councils; the effort of the then Secretary for Rural Development (Mr A.M. Anisuzzaman) to revive the Comilla model of Thana development planning in 1979; and that of the then Minister for Planning (Dr Fashiuddin Mahtab) to promote a Thana Land Use Development Programme in 1980-81. Simultaneously, efforts were being made to rationalize urban land use planning through the Dhaka (and other city) Improvement Trusts starting in the 1960s, and through national and urban physical plans prepared by the Urban Development Directorate in the 1970s.

The 1980s and 1990s saw dynamic changes in agriculture resulting from the spread of small-scale irrigation, fertilizer use and improved crop varieties. Those changes provided increases in food production far beyond the nightmare predictions of those who were deeply concerned about the country's burgeoning population (54 million when the author first arrived in East Pakistan in 1961, probably 130 million in 1999). The increases in production were not the result of planned land use. They were the outcome of national policy and planning decisions which encouraged farmers to use modern agricultural technology, initially through direct (and subsidized) distribution by Government of new seed, fertilizers, pesticides and irrigation equipment (and credit that was often not repaid). Through the 1980s, the collectivist approaches to agricultural development of the previous decade gradually gave way (under external pressure) to a free-market approach, manifested by a growing 'liberalization' of the supply of inputs to farmers, including the removal of surviving restrictions on the siting of irrigation equipment (which, in truth, had been widely circumvented). Modern land use studies could usefully examine the impact (and the possible implications for public policy) of these changes in three particular areas of concern:

a. on the size of land holdings, in view of the much higher economic threshold for farmers using costly production equipment and inputs compared with 'traditional' (or poor) low-input farmers; simultaneously, if and where any increasing trend in size of holdings is found, the knock-on impacts on displacement of small-holders, tenants and labourers could usefully be examined;

b. related to the latter, on any trend toward the consolidation of fragmented land holdings as a consequence of private ownership of small-scale irrigation equipment and/or power-tillers; and

c. on soil fertility and the sustainability of agricultural production at present levels of input use, farm incomes and market prices; (also at projected levels required to meet future population needs).

The 1980s and 1990s also saw a considerable withdrawal of Government involvement in rural land use planning. The enthusiastic efforts of some development activists and politicians in the 1970s to devolve responsibility for food production and rural employment to village level, involving the preparation of village food production and other development plans, eventually petered out, essentially because of the lack of commitment of Government agencies and officials to support them (and possibly because of the recognition that Government funds would not be adequate to meet the development aspirations of the people consulted in this way). Thana development planning also stumbled on the same obstacle: the opposition of central government agencies and officials to working 'under', as they saw it, local government councils. Such planning was also frustrated by central government departments operating independent, even mutually-conflicting, rural development programmes, and by agencies such as BWDB organizing regional work areas so that they did not conform with Thana or District administrative units. BWDB's large-scale water development projects always were 'blue-printed' over the heads of local governments, other development agencies and the people with minimal consultation (and consequent minimal willingness on the part of the 'beneficiaries' to pay for the improvements). A change of Government around 1990 reduced the independent powers of Thana Councils. Thus, the trend in the 1990s was to re-centralize both political and bureaucratic planning authority, while at the same time releasing the natural independence and entrepreneurial talents of farmers and traders — (and the devil take the hindmost?).

What is the role of land use planning in the year 2000? There are two aspects to land use planning, both of which are exemplified in this book. One is that of *regulation*, such as may be required for soil conservation, the rational use of irrigation water in areas where it is scarce, or to prevent the indiscriminate sprawl of settlement over valuable agricultural land. The other aspect — often unrecognized — is that of *enabling:* i.e., through government policies and fund allocations, planning to facilitate optimum land use rather than to control it. Both kinds of planning are needed; and both central government and local governments have roles to play in such planning.

The author remains sympathetic to the Comilla model of local-level, participatory planning, involving a dialogue between the people, their elected representatives and technical officials, and the resolution of conflicts through local negotiation. He is now less sympathetic to the cooperative society component of the Comilla model: experience showed that credit-and-loan cooperatives did not suit the individualistic character of the people (though he wonders whether marketing cooperatives might have been more successful). He believes that local governments could play a vital role in identifying subjects for land use regulation, and in enforcing such regulations; and that the role of officials is to help farmers to overcome perceived obstacles and to make the best use of their physical and economic resources, not, as it appeared to be in the past, to tell farmers what to do. In that respect, the various chapters on agricultural planning in this book should not be seen as providing a prescription for what farmers should do but, rather, as presenting a supermarket of opportunities for crop selection and management from which extension officials (including NGOs) can help farmers choose items to suit their specific physical and economic environments. Additionally, like land use itself, land use planning will need to change with the times, addressing actual needs rather than providing a strait-jacket which might hinder economic progress.

In that respect, it is relevant to note the recurrent theme of achieving national foodgrain self-sufficiency which runs through this book. That reflects the national obsession of politicians and officials during the 1970s and 1980s with meeting that objective. But already by 1985 it was recognized that agriculture alone could not employ more than 30 percent of the annual incremental growth in the rural labour supply, implying an urgent need to expand other sectors of the economy to provide employment and incomes; and, in fact, the share of the agriculture sector in the national GDP fell from around 60 percent to less than 30 percent between 1970 and 1999, reflecting the growing importance of the other sectors (especially services). Bangladesh does not need to be self-sufficient in foodgrain supply. It could produce goods and services for export which it could exchange for food imports. And although in several chapters of this book the loss of agricultural land to settlement and industry is deprecated, it now needs to be recognized that, whereas one acre of agricultural land might produce five or more tons of rice and provide 200 person-days of employment annually, the same area under industry or commerce might employ several hundred persons on an annual basis and produce goods or services worth many times that of the rice production displaced. The implications of this for land use policy deserve to be examined by the author's successors.

The book is arranged in five parts, of which Part I comprises an introductory chapter describing Bangladesh's physical and land use characteristics to provide readers with background information for understanding the technical contents of subsequent chapters.

Part II includes nine chapters covering a wide range of land use studies made in the 1970s and 1980s, (including studies by consultants initiated by the author). The subjects range from the ways in which farmers have intensified crop production (Chapter 2), through descriptions of various changes in land use and settlement that have taken place (Chapters 3-7) and of the needs for soil conservation and mango orchard rehabilitation (Chapters 8-9), to a review of the legal aspects of land use regulation (Chapter 10).

Part III contains three chapters describing the land use policies and principles which underlie the contents of Parts IV and V: nine principles of national policy (Chapter 11); policy aspects of biomass production (Chapter 12); and the principles of land management in Bangladesh's hill areas (Chapter 13).

The five chapters in Part IV describe the technical information which is available to support the planning of more intensive land use. Chapter 14 describes the kinds of information which can be obtained from soil survey reports; Chapters 15-17 provide guidelines for selecting small-scale land and water development schemes; and Chapter 18 describes how waste land and fallow land could be brought into productive use.

Part V comprises six chapters dealing with local-level planning. Chapter 19 summarizes points relevant for Bangladesh made at an international workshop on land use planning in the tropics. Chapter 20 describes a method for making village agricultural development plans, while Chapters 21-23 deal comprehensively with Thana land use planning. The final chapter (24) illustrates how soil survey information can be used for land use zoning.

Because of the different purposes for which the original papers were written and the fact that the papers were written over a period of several years, there inevitably is some overlap and repetition of information between chapters. That has the advantage of making each chapter self-sufficient, reducing the need for readers to cross-refer to other chapters for relevant information; also, of reinforcing important points that are made, which can be useful in teaching. In general, the contents of the original papers have been reproduced as they were written, but with some abbreviation and editing where relevant. Footnotes have been used to provide additional information and comments.

Cambridge, September 1999   *H. Brammer*

PART I
ENVIRONMENT AND LAND USE

Bangladesh is fortunate in having a great deal of information on its land and water resources which can be used for planning rational land use development at national, regional and local levels. Chapter 1 provides a summary description of Bangladesh's main physical and land use characteristics in order to help readers to better understand the concepts and practices described in subsequent parts of this volume.

Chapter 1

THE PHYSICAL BASIS OF LAND USE IN BANGLADESH[1]

An understanding of physical environmental conditions is essential for understanding land use and cropping practices in Bangladesh. It is essential also for sound land use planning. This chapter briefly describes Bangladesh's physical environments and how land use is related to specific environmental conditions. It provides the basis for understanding the principles and practices of land use and land use planning which are described in subsequent chapters.

1.1 LOCATION AND EXTENT

Bangladesh lies between 20°25' and 26°38'N latitude and between 88°01 and 92°40'E longitude. The total area is 144,862 km² (55,931 sq, miles), of which about 9,700 km² is occupied by the country's main rivers and estuaries. Figure 1.1 shows the old (pre-1982) administrative Districts into which the country is divided and which are referred to in the text of this and subsequent chapters.

1.2 CLIMATE

Land use in Bangladesh is strongly influenced by its tropical monsoon climate with the associated seasonal differences in rainfall, temperatures and risk of extreme weather-related events. Four main seasons are recognized, viz.

- *Pre-monsoon* (March-May), the hot or 'summer' season, with the highest temperatures and evaporation rates. This season is characterized by the occurrence of occasional line-squalls (nor'-westers) with thunderstorm rainfall, strong wind, occasionally hail and, exceptionally, tornadoes. Tropical cyclones (typhoons) with associated storm surges are liable to affect coastal areas.
- *Monsoon* (June-September), the period of highest rainfall, humidity and cloudiness. This also is the season when floods are most likely to occur following heavy rainfall within the country or in the catchment area of rivers flowing into Bangladesh.
- *Post-monsoon* (October-November), a hot and humid period with decreasing rainfall, but sunny and with heavy dew at night. Tropical cyclones are again liable to affect coastal areas.
- *Dry season (or winter)*, (December-February), the coolest, driest and sunniest period of the year.

---

[1] *This chapter has been adapted from Chapter 1 in Brammer (1999). Bangladesh's physical environments are described in more detail in Brammer (1996).*

FIGURE 1.1

Old (pre-1982) Administrative Districts

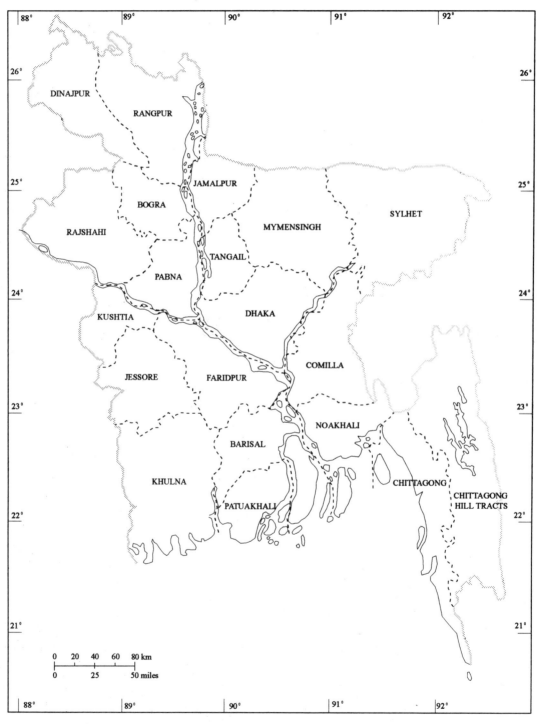

Mean annual temperature everywhere is about 25°C. Mean monthly temperatures range between about 18°C in winter and 30°C in the pre-monsoon season. Extreme temperatures range between about 5°C in winter and 43°C in the pre-monsoon season, except near the coast where the range is narrower. There are significant differences in seasonal temperatures across the country: for instance, the cool winter period lasts longer in the north than near the coast, and the highest pre-monsoon temperatures occur in the west.

Mean annual rainfall is lowest in the west (1250-1500 mm; 50-60 inches) and highest in the north, east and south (>2500 mm; over 100 inches); it exceeds 5000 mm (200 inches) in the extreme north-east of Sylhet District. In general, about 85-90 percent of the annual total occurs between April and September (the 'rainy season'), though the duration of this period is longer in the north-east than in the west. However, rainfall is variable from year to year, both in total amount and in the time of onset and ending of the rainy season. This variability provides problems of drought, excessive or untimely rainfall, and flooding. Tropical cyclones, tornadoes and hail are also variable in occurrence and location between years.

Rainfall everywhere exceeds evapo-transpiration rates in the monsoon season and for the year as a whole, even in dry years. However, evapo-transpiration rates exceed rainfall during winter and in the first part of the pre-monsoon season. Evapo-transpiration rates also exceed rainfall, of course, during droughts, most significantly during the pre-monsoon season when temperatures and evaporation rates are highest.

The possible impacts of greenhouse warming on future land use are described below in Section 1.7.

1.3 PHYSIOGRAPHY AND RELIEF

Bangladesh comprises hill, terrace and floodplain areas. The Northern and Eastern Hills occupy about 12 percent of the country, the so-called terrace areas (the Madhupur and Barind Tracts, and the Akhaura Terrace)[2] about 8 percent, and floodplains the remaining 80 percent. The main features of each of these areas are described briefly below. The location of the main physiographic units recognized in Bangladesh — referred to throughout this volume as agroecological regions — is shown on Figure 1.2 and the area of the individual units is shown in Table 1.1. It should be realized that, because of the small scale of the map in Figure 1.2, the boundaries of the units shown are highly generalized.

Bangladesh lies in an active tectonic zone (Brammer, 1996). District Gazetteers record several severe earthquakes occurring in past centuries. A major earthquake in 1897 caused widespread damage to structures throughout the country; it also caused liquefaction of floodplain sediments and ejection of sand from fissures in the north and east. The 1950 Assam earthquake caused extensive landslides on mountain ranges in the Brahmaputra catchment area which greatly increased the sediment load of the Brahmaputra-Jamuna river for several years afterwards. In turn, this additional sediment load may have been responsible for the increased rate of bank-erosion and widening of the Brahmaputra-Jamuna river channel in Bangladesh in recent decades; more beneficially, it created a large area of new land on the Noakhali coast.

Hills. The Northern and Eastern Hills (Region 29 on Figure 1.2) are underlain by sandstones, siltstones and shales of Tertiary and Quaternary ages. The rocks have been folded,

---

[2] *These physiographic units are actually uplifted fault blocks, not river or marine terraces.*

TABLE 1.1

Area of agroecological regions

Agroecological region	Area	
	Sq. miles	Sq. km
1. Old Himalayan Piedmont Plain	1,549	4,008
2. Active Teesta Floodplain	323	836
3. Teesta Meander Floodplain	3,658	9,468
4. Karatoya-Bangali Floodplain	994	2,572
5. Lower Atrai Basin	329	851
6. Lower Purnabhaba Floodplain	50	129
7. Active Brahmaputra-Jamuna Floodplain	1,233	3,190
8. Young Brahmaputra and Jamuna Floodplains	2,289	5,924
9. Old Brahmaputra Floodplain	2,794	7,230
10. Active Ganges Floodplain	1,288	3,334
11. High Ganges River Floodplain	5,103	13,205
12. Low Ganges River Floodplain	3,079	7,968
13. Ganges Tidal Floodplain	6,594	17,066
14. Gopalganj-Khulna Beels	867	2,247
15. Arial Beel	56	144
16. Middle Meghna River Floodplain	600	1,555
17. Lower Meghna River Floodplain	351	909
18. Young Meghna Estuarine Floodplain	3,581	9,269
19. Old Meghna Estuarine Floodplain	2,991	7,740
20. Eastern Surma-Kusiyara Floodplain	1,786	4,622
21. Sylhet Basin	1,767	4,573
22. Northern and Eastern Piedmont Plains	1,560	4,038
23. Chittagong Coastal Plains	1,437	3,720
24. St Martin's Coral Island	3	8
25. Level Barind Tract	1,591	5,049
26. High Barind Tract	618	1,600
27. North-eastern Barind Tract	417	1,079
28. Madhupur Tract	1,640	4,244
29. Northern and Eastern Hills	7,021	18,171
30. Akhaura Terrace	44	113
Total area	**55,931**	**144,836**

Source: FAO (1988).

faulted and uplifted, then deeply dissected by rivers and streams. Hill slopes generally are steep or very steep. Steep slopes over shaley rocks are subject to landslides, even under natural forest. There are only a few exposures of hard rock suitable for use as building material.

Terraces. The Madhupur Tract, Barind Tract and Akhaura Terrace (Regions 25-28 and 30) are underlain by the unconsolidated Madhupur Clay, which may be of Tertiary age. These regions have been uplifted and broken into several fault blocks, the surfaces of which generally lie a few metres higher than adjoining floodplain land. The Madhupur Tract and

FIGURE 1.2
Agroecological regions

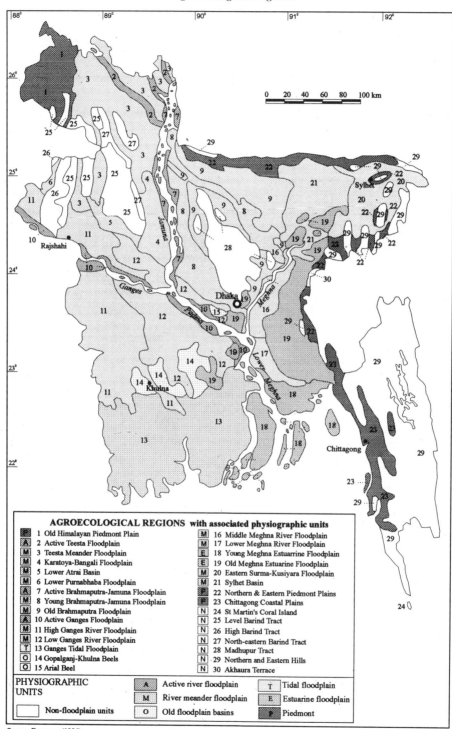

Akhaura Terrace have been more dissected by rivers and streams than the Barind Tract, and have more complex relief and soil patterns (Brammer, 1996).

Floodplains. Five main kinds of floodplain are recognized.

  a. *Active river floodplains* (Regions 2, 7, 10; 16,17):[3] the youngest alluvial land within and alongside the main rivers which is subject to alternate deposition of new sediments and erosion by shifting channels within the main river course. The temporary alluvial formations (known as *chars* in Bangladesh) have an irregular relief with stratified sandy and silty deposits.

  b. *Meander floodplains* (Regions 3, 4, 6, 8, 9, 11, 12, 20; parts of 21, 23): relatively older parts of the Teesta, Atrai, Brahmaputra-Jamuna, Karatoya-Bangali, Ganges and Surma-Kusiyara river floodplains, away from the present main river channels. They have relatively stable landscapes with complex patterns of curved ridges (former river banks), basins (back-swamps) and cut-off channels, crossed by a few active river channels (tributary or distributary channels of the main rivers). Differences in elevation between ridge crests and adjoining depression centres generally are 2-3 metres, but are up to 5-6 metres in parts of the Sylhet Basin (Region 21). Sediments and soils generally are sandy or silty on ridges, grading into heavier silts and clays in depressions. Most older floodplain land no longer receives regular additions of new alluvium from the rivers, but some young floodplain land near to active channels (especially on the Jamuna Floodplain) receives new deposits during high floods.

  Enclosed within the meander floodplains are ***old floodplain basins***, the largest of which (Regions 5, 6, 14, 15; parts of 21) are shown separately on Figure 1.2. These generally are subject to deep flooding, and basin centres stay wet for part or all of the dry season. Heavy clay soils predominate, but Peat Soils occur extensively in Region 14.

  c. *Piedmont plains* (Regions 1, 22; parts of 23): gently-sloping land at the foot of hills where colluvial and alluvial sediments are (or were) deposited by rivers and streams subject to flash floods. They include the Old Himalayan Piedmont Plain at the foot of the Himalayas and active alluvial fans at the foot of the Northern and Eastern Hills (including parts of the Chittagong Coastal Plains). The Old Himalayan Piedmont Plain (a former alluvial fan of the river Teesta which was probably abandoned by that river several thousand years ago) mainly lies above present-day flood levels, but flash floods occur along valleys in the north. This region has the complex ridge and channel relief of a former braided river landscape, and predominantly deep, loamy soils. The Northern and Eastern Piedmont Plains have gently sloping relief which is locally irregular. Local differences in elevation between ridge tops and neighbouring depressions generally are small. The sediments grade from sands near the hills through loams over most of the plains to heavy clays in basins where the plains merge into the adjoining river or tidal floodplains.

  d. *Estuarine floodplains* (Regions 18, 19): smooth, almost-level land with few or no river channels.[4] Differences in elevation between adjoining ridges and depression

---

[3] *Regions 16 and 17 are included in this group for convenience. However, Region 16 (the Middle Meghna Floodplain) is actually the former active floodplain of the Brahmaputra river which has been only thinly covered with Meghna sediments since the Brahmaputra abandoned this course about two hundred years ago; and Region 17 (the Lower Meghna River Floodplain) is transitional between the Active Ganges River Floodplain (Region 10) and the Young Meghna Estuarine Floodplain (Region 18). Regions 16 and 17 receive only very small increments of new alluvium during annual floods (in areas where they have not been protected by embankments), and they are less subject to change by river-bank erosion than the other active floodplain regions.*

[4] *Parts of the Old Meghna Estuarine Floodplain have a network of small, man-made khals.*

centres usually are less then 2 metres over a distance of 0.5-1 km. The deep silty sediments were laid down in the Meghna estuary as it extended southwards over a period of several thousand years. These floodplains are divided into the young part (Region 18) adjoining the Meghna estuary which is still subject to tidal flooding (where not embanked) and to new accretion and erosion by shifting estuarine channels, and the stable, old part (Region 19) which no longer receives new alluvial sediments and is no longer flooded by tidal water.

e. *Tidal floodplains* (Region 13; parts of 23): almost-level clay plains crossed by innumerable tidal rivers and creeks which often are interconnected. Differences in elevation between river banks and basin centres usually are about 1 metre. Under natural conditions, the land is subject to flooding with silty water at high tides during at least a part of the year, but many areas have been embanked and thus cut off from tidal flooding and sedimentation. On the Ganges Tidal Floodplain, tidal water is saline throughout the year in the south-west and fresh throughout the year in the north-east; in between is a zone where the floodwater is fresh in the monsoon season and saline for part or all of the dry season.

1.4 HYDROLOGY

River-flow, floods and flooding. Heavy rainfall occurring within the Ganges-Brahmaputra-Meghna catchment area, together with summer snow-melt in the Himalayas, causes the main rivers to rise rapidly in May-June, reach peak levels in July-August and then gradually recede to low levels in March-April. Generally, the Brahmaputra and Meghna rivers begin to rise earlier and peak earlier than the Ganges. However, significant variations occur from year to year: peak levels in the main rivers occasionally coincide, causing extensive overland flooding; and late floods (in September) occur occasionally in the Brahmaputra-Jamuna and can be particularly damaging for agriculture. Rivers and streams flowing from the Northern and Eastern Hills are subject to flash floods in all parts of the rainy season. Storm surges associated with tropical cyclones periodically flood coastal land with sea-water; more rarely, they flood land along the Lower Meghna, Middle Meghna and Ganges rivers with fresh river water.

Most floodplain and piedmont land is subject to seasonal flooding; so are some interior terrace areas as well as valleys in hill and terrace areas. The extent of flooding varies from year to year according to flood levels in the main rivers and the intensity of rainfall within Bangladesh. The high river levels during the monsoon season are mainly caused by water flowing into Bangladesh from surrounding territories.

High river levels block the drainage of rainwater falling on adjoining floodplain land. Therefore, most of Bangladesh's floodplain areas are flooded by clear rainwater, not (as is popularly supposed) by silty river water depositing annual increments of new alluvium. Flooding with silty river water mainly occurs on active floodplains, the Northern and Eastern Piedmont Plains, and unembanked parts of the Young Meghna Estuarine Floodplain and the Ganges Tidal Floodplain. Only during abnormally high river floods does silty water extend over parts of meander floodplains adjoining the main rivers and their distributaries. Some old floodplain areas, such as the Old Brahmaputra Floodplain, the High Ganges River Floodplain and especially the Old Meghna Estuarine Floodplain, appear not to have been flooded by river water for several centuries, and perhaps even longer, not even in major floods such as that in 1988. The distinction between areas that are flooded by silty river water bringing new alluvium to floodplain land, and areas that are flooded by rainwater which does not contain new alluvium, is important in designing flood protection schemes and in assessing the potential impacts of such schemes on soil fertility.

It is useful to distinguish between floods (*bonna* in Bengali) and flooding (*barsha*). The term 'flood' implies abnormal submergence of land, such as may cause damage or loss of crops, property and/or lives. Crops can be damaged or destroyed by abnormally early or late inundation, abnormally high water levels, or unusually rapid rates of rise or flow of water on the land. The term 'flooding', on the other hand, merely implies submergence of land by water, such as floodplain inhabitants expect in 'normal' years (i.e., in perhaps three years out of four or five). In most floodplain and terrace areas, it is normal flooding conditions on which farmers base their cropping patterns. The distinction is between floodwater (whether from rivers, rainwater or the sea) which is liable to cause damage and floodwater that does not damage crops.[5]

The depth and duration of seasonal flooding determine the crops which farmers grow on their different kinds of land. The information given in Table 1.2 has been standardized from Bangladeshi farmers' own classification of land types in relation to 'normal' seasonal flooding. In general, normal seasonal flooding is shallow in the north-west, west, east and south of the country, and is deep in the centre and north-east: Table 1.3 shows how the proportions of the different land types vary between regions. However, it is important to understand that flooding depths also vary within areas as small as villages, because of the ridge and basin relief of most floodplain areas, and many farmers cultivate fields on several of the land types shown in Table 1.2; (see also Figure 1.3). It is also important to understand that natural flooding depths and duration have been changed in flood protection and drainage project areas.

TABLE 1.2
Classification of depth-of-flooding land types

Land type	Description
Highland (H)	Land which is above normal flood level.
Medium Highland (MH)	Land which normally is flooded up to about 90cm deep during the monsoon season.
Medium Lowland (ML)	Land which normally is flooded up to between 90cm and 180cm during the monsoon season.
Lowland (L)	Land which normally is flooded up to between 180cm and 300cm during the monsoon season.
Very Lowland (VL)	Land which normally is flooded deeper than 300cm during the monsoon season.
Bottomland	Depression land in any of the above land types which remains wet throughout the year.

Note: This classification was amended after the introduction of HYVs of rice in the late 1960s. Medium Highland was split into MH-1 (flooded up to 30 cm deep, and suitable for HYV aman), and MH-2 (flooded up to 30-90 cm deep, and suitable only for local varieties of transplanted aman).

---

[5]*A map showing the broad distribution of the different types of flood and flooding in Bangladesh is given in Brammer (1999), Figure 8.3.*

TABLE 1.3
Depth-of-flooding land types in agroecological regions

Region	Highland %	Medium Highland %	Medium Lowland %	Lowland %	Very Lowland %	Settlm't + water %
1	58	34	1	–	–	7
2	2	72	–	–	–	26
3	35	51	4	1	–	9
4	23	44	14	4	1	14
5	2	8	21	65	–	4
6	–	–	10	60	*	30
7	5	37	20	8	–	30
8	18	42	19	9	–	12
9	28	35	20	7	–	10
10	12	33	18	4	–	33
11	43	32	12	2	–	11
12	13	29	31	14	2	11
13	2	78	2	–	–	18
14	3	13	41	28	11	4
15	–	–	13	73	*	14
16	–	8	29	25	11	27
17	14	28	31	–	–	27
18	<1	451	7	–	–	47
19	2	24	33	21	3	17
20	5	25	20	36	<1	14
21	<1	4	19	43	23	11
22	33	31	16	9	1	10
23	17	43	13	–	–	27
24	33	63	2	–	–	2
25	30	55	4	2	–	9
26	93	1	<1	<1	–	6
27	36	56	1	–	–	7
28	56	18	7	9	–	10
29	92	2	<1	<1	<1	5
30	55	11	10	15	3	6
Bangladesh	**29**	**35**	**12**	**8**	**1**	**15**

Notes: 1. Source: FAO (1988).

2. Very Lowland = Bottomland + Lowland flooded >300 cm.

3. * = Very Lowland and Lowland not differentiated.

Groundwater. Monsoon rainfall is everywhere sufficient to recharge groundwater annually where aquifer conditions are suitable, except possibly in the extreme west during years when severe drought occurs. Recharge from rainfall is considerably supplemented by the seasonal flooding of floodplain and valley land, and through river beds. In many floodplain areas, the groundwater-table is sufficiently shallow that suction pumps (hand pumps and shallow tube-wells) can be used for domestic water supplies and irrigation. Elsewhere, force-mode pumps need to be used (in so-called deep tube-wells and deep-set shallow tube-wells).

Aquifer conditions generally are very good on the Old Himalayan Piedmont Plain, the Teesta and Brahmaputra-Jamuna Floodplains, and most parts of the Ganges (River) Floodplain. Aquifers are mainly poor on the Eastern Surma-Kusiyara Floodplain, in the north of the Madhupur Tract and the west of the Barind Tract, and in and near to the Northern and Eastern Hills. Groundwater is saline near the coast and in some southern parts of the Ganges River Floodplain and the Old Meghna Estuarine Floodplain, but fresh water occurs in deep aquifers (>300m) in some coastal areas.

1.5 Soils

Bangladesh has a wide diversity of soils, and they often occur in complex patterns. Superimposed over this diversity and complexity are:

- differences in the depth and duration of seasonal flooding on different parts of floodplain, terrace and valley relief;
- differences in moisture-holding capacity of floodplain soils due to local differences in the thickness of subsurface layers with different textures; and
- differences caused by differences in soil management: e.g., whether soils are puddled or not for transplanted paddy cultivation; differences between fields in the amounts of fertilizers, manures and tank silt used; local removal of topsoil for various construction purposes or during field levelling; whether fields are irrigated or not; and the cultivation of a wide diversity of wetland and dryland crops during the three main growing seasons.

This diversity of soil conditions — between and within regions, within villages, between neighbouring fields and even within individual fields — provides diverse and complex patterns of land use, crop suitability, soil fertility and agronomic practices in many parts of Bangladesh. The diversity and complexity have important implications for land use planning, agricultural research, agricultural extension and the collection of crop statistics. They also mean that the impact of natural disasters can vary considerably between regions, within regions, and on different land and soil types within a village.

The soils of Bangladesh have been classified in 21 General Soil Types. This is a non-technical grouping of soils which have formed in the same way and which have a broadly similar appearance. Table 1.4 gives summary descriptions of these soil types and indicates their relative proportions within Bangladesh. More detailed descriptions of these soils are given in Brammer (1996). The main characteristics of hill, terrace and floodplain soils are summarized below.

Hill soils. Most hill soils are yellow, brown or red, loamy and very strongly acid. Most of the soils occupy steep or very steep slopes, have a low moisture-holding capacity and are low in natural fertility. Over soft rocks, soils usually are deep and resistant to erosion. Over hard rocks, soils are shallow, and some are susceptible to landslides. Valley soils range from acid, sandy or loamy piedmont soils to loamy or clayey, less-acid, floodplain soils.

Terrace soils. Considering that they have all developed over or from the uniform Madhupur Clay, a surprising diversity of soils occurs on the Madhupur and Barind Tracts and on the related Akhaura Terrace. They range from red to grey, deep to shallow, level to sloping, well drained to very poorly drained, and from calcareous to very strongly acid. Most have a low moisture-holding capacity, so they are easily prone to drought, and natural fertility generally is low. The proportions in which the different soils occur vary greatly between the three tracts: Deep and Shallow Red-Brown Terrace Soils predominate on the Madhupur Tract and the Akhaura Terrace, and there are significant proportions of valley soils, whereas Deep and Shallow Grey Terrace Soils predominate on the Barind Tract, with only small areas of valley soils. Soil patterns often are complex, especially on the Madhupur Tract.

Floodplain soils. In broad terms, six different kinds of soil profile are found in Bangladesh's floodplain and piedmont soils; (details of the general soil types referred to are given in Table 1.4).

a. *Noncalcareous Alluvium, Calcareous Alluvium and Acid Sulphate Soils* have stratified alluvium from the surface or from below the cultivated topsoil. They occur on active river floodplains, the Young Meghna Estuarine Floodplain and in some permanently wet sites elsewhere (including Sunderbans mangrove forest in the case of Acid Sulphate Soils). These young soils generally are slightly or moderately alkaline in reaction, but Acid Sulphate Soils are actually or potentially extremely acid;

b. *Noncalcareous and Calcareous Grey and Dark Grey Floodplain Soils* are the most extensive soils on river, estuarine and tidal floodplains. Grey soils generally occur on relatively young floodplains, and dark grey soils on old floodplains. Calcareous soils occur on the Ganges and Lower Meghna River Floodplains, and on some river banks on the Ganges Tidal Floodplain. Floodplain soils typically have three contrasting layers (horizons):

   • *the topsoil* (10-15 cm thick) which has a compacted *ploughpan* at the base in most cultivated soils;
   • *the subsoil* (extending to 30 cm or more) with structure, oxidized mottles, and often shiny surfaces (coatings) on the faces of cracks and pores; and
   • *the substratum* (underlying the soil proper) which often is stratified alluvium, but sometimes is an older, buried soil.

   Subsoil textures generally range from sandy or loamy on ridge tops to clay in depressions, but the proportions between light-textured and heavy-textured soils vary between different floodplain regions. Topsoils generally are moderately to very strongly acid, except on young floodplains which occasionally receive increments of new alluvium (which generally is neutral or alkaline in reaction). Subsoils generally are neutral to moderately alkaline in reaction; in calcareous general soil types, either the whole or part of the soil profile contains lime.

c. *Grey Piedmont Soils* resemble Noncalcareous Grey Floodplain Soils, but their subsoils tend to be less strongly structured, more prominently mottled, and slightly to strongly acid in reaction. They occur mainly on the Northern and Eastern Piedmont Plains and parts of the Chittagong Coastal Plains.

d. *Noncalcareous and Calcareous Brown Floodplain Soils, and Black Terai Soils*, are permeable loams with yellow-brown to olive-brown subsoils. Calcareous soils occur on the Ganges River Floodplain; elsewhere, the soils are moderately to strongly acid. Black Terai Soils are similar to noncalcareous brown soils except that they have a thick, black or very dark grey topsoil which sometimes extends sufficiently deep to obscure the brown subsoil colour. Brown soils occur on floodplain ridges which are

TABLE 1.4

Summary descriptions of General Soil Types

General Soil Type (%)[1]	Diagnostic properties
Floodplain soils	
1. Noncalcareous Alluvium (3.9)	Raw or stratified alluvium; not containing lime and not extremely acid (actually or potentially) within 125 cm from the surface; (generally, such soils are neutral to moderately alkaline in reaction throughout).
2. Calcareous Alluvium (4.1)	Raw or stratified alluvium; calcareous throughout or in some layer within 125 cm from the surface.
3. Acid Sulphate Soils (1.6)	Poorly or very poorly drained, grey or dark grey soils, with or without a developed subsoil, and containing sufficient sulphur compounds that they are actually or potentially extremely acid ($pH < 3.5$) within 125 cm from the surface; mainly saline. (Associated with present or former Sunderbans mangrove forest.)
4. Peat Soils (0.9)	Very poorly drained soils in which organic matter (peat or muck) comprises more than half of the uppermost 80 cm.
5. Noncalcareous Grey Floodplain Soils (23.4)	Seasonally-flooded soils with a developed subsoil which is dominantly grey or has prominent grey coatings on the faces of subsoil cracks and pores; not calcareous within 125 cm from the surface. Topsoil generally is slightly to strongly acid in reaction (when not submerged); lower layers generally are between slightly acid and moderately alkaline.
6. Calcareous Grey Floodplain Soils (1.2)	Seasonally-flooded soils with a developed subsoil which is dominantly grey or has prominent grey coatings on the faces of subsoil cracks and pores; contains lime in some or all layers within 125 cm from the surface.
7. Grey Piedmont Soils (1.5)	Imperfectly to poorly drained soils in piedmont alluvium, similar to Noncalcareous Grey Floodplain Soils, but generally more strongly mottled and medium to strongly acid in reaction in the subsoil.
8. Noncalcareous Dark Grey Floodplain Soils (11.0)	Seasonally-flooded soils similar to Noncalcareous Grey Floodplain Soils, but either dominantly dark grey or with dark grey coatings on the faces of subsoil cracks and pores.
9. Calcareous Dark Grey Floodplain Soils (0.9)	Similar to Noncalcareous Dark Grey Floodplain Soils, but containing lime in some layer within 125 cm from the surface. (Many basin soils on the Ganges River Floodplain have a neutral or acid topsoil and a noncalcareous upper subsoil layer.)
10. Acid Basin Clays (2.4)	Poorly or very poorly drained, grey or dark grey, heavy clays with a developed subsoil; very strongly or extremely acid ($pH < 5$ but > 3.5) to 50 cm or more, and not calcareous within 125 cm from the surface.
11. Noncalcareous Brown Floodplain Soils (2.6)	Moderately well to imperfectly drained soils with a yellow-brown or olive-brown subsoil; not calcareous within 125 cm from the surface. Topsoil and upper subsoil generally are medium or strongly acid, lower layers less acid or neutral. Soils transitional to Black Terai Soils in Region 1 have a thick dark brown topsoil.
12. Calcareous Brown Floodplain Soils (3.3)	Moderately well to imperfectly drained floodplain soils with a yellow-brown or olive-brown subsoil; calcareous throughout or in some layer within 125 cm from the surface.

(Contd.)

(Continued)

General Soil Type (%)[1]	Diagnostic properties
13. Black Terai Soils (0.6)	Imperfectly to poorly drained soils with a black or very dark brown topsoil more than 25 cm thick. In soils where the topsoil is less than about 90 cm thick, there is a brown subsoil. Medium to strongly acid in the topsoil and upper subsoil; less acid to neutral below.
Hill Soils	
14. Brown Hill Soils (10.8)	Moderately well to excessively drained soils with a yellow-brown to strong brown subsoil, mainly overlying soft or fragmented rock at 50-100 cm. Most are very strongly or extremely acid throughout; some are less acid in the surface layer and in weathering rock.
Terrace Soils	
15. Deep Red-Brown Terrace Soils (1.3)	Moderately well to well drained soils with a red to yellow-brown subsoil overlying a strongly red-mottled, pervious, clay substratum. Strongly or very strongly acid throughout.
16. Shallow Red-Brown Terrace Soils (0.5)	Moderately well to imperfectly drained soils with a red to yellow-brown subsoil overlying grey, heavy, Madhupur Clay at 25-60 cm. Mainly strongly or very strongly acid, but very shallow soils contain lime nodules at an irregular depth.
17. Brown Mottled Terrace Soils (0.3)	Imperfectly drained soils with a strongly mottled pale brown and red subsoil overlying a strongly red-mottled, pervious, clay substratum. Mainly strongly or very strongly acid throughout.
18. Deep Grey Terrace Soils (2.4)	Poorly drained, grey, porous, silty soils with a strongly mottled grey and red (or brown) subsoil overlying a dominantly red-mottled, pervious, clay substratum. Mainly medium to strongly acid throughout.
19. Shallow Grey Terrace Soils (1.8)	Poorly drained soils similar to Deep Grey Terrace Soils in the topsoil and upper subsoil, but less strongly mottled in the subsoil and overlying grey, heavy, Madhupur Clay at 20-60 cm. Slightly to strongly acid in the silty topsoil and subsoil, becoming less acid (and locally calcareous) in the clay substratum.
20. Grey Valley Soils (0.8)	Poorly drained, deep, grey, porous, silty soils occurring in terrace valleys. Most are medium to strongly acid throughout; some on the Barind Tract contain lime layers.
Man-made land	
21. Made-land (0.7)	Soils on artificially raised cultivation platforms; better drained and more permeable than the floodplain soil materials from which they are derived, but broadly similar to them in colour and other properties.

Note: 1. The percentage figures represent the proportion of the whole country. Soils occupy 85 percent of the total area. Settlements and water together occupy the remaining 15 percent.

rarely or only intermittently flooded. Black Terai Soils occur on both flooded and non-flooded land in the north of the Old Himalayan Piedmont Plain.

e. ***Acid Basin Clays*** are grey to dark grey, heavy clays which are very strongly acid in reaction to at least 50 cm below the surface. They occur in old floodplain basins.

f. ***Peat Soils*** are dark-coloured soils in which peat or muck occupies the greater part of the profile down to at least 80 cm. They occupy some perennially-wet depressions in old floodplain areas. They occur most extensively in the Gopalganj-Khulna Beels.

1.6 LAND USE

Land use in Bangladesh is determined mainly by the monsoon climate and the seasonal flooding which affects the greater part of the country. These physical determinants are reinforced by high population pressure and, increasingly, by alterations to the natural environment through flood protection, drainage and irrigation interventions.

Agriculture dominates both land use and the national economy. Arable land occupies about 22 million (M) acres (9 M ha), forest about 5 M acres (2 M ha), and settlements plus water about 7.5 M acres (3 M ha). Floodplain settlements typically are concentrated on the highest land available, on river banks or ridges (old river banks). They are surrounded by agricultural land extending down to the lowest land which is most deeply flooded in the monsoon season. Thus, the agricultural land in a typical village comprises a range of soil and depth-of-flooding land types, and so do the farmers' fragmented land holdings.[6]

Bangladesh's climate makes conditions suitable for growing tropical crops such as rice and jute in the warm rainy season, temperate crops such as wheat and potato in the cool winter months, and subtropical crops such as sugarcane and banana throughout the year. More than fifty different crops are grown in Bangladesh. However, the high rainfall and seasonal flooding make conditions particularly suitable for paddy cultivation, and rice (the staple cereal crop) occupies about 80 percent of the cropped area.[7]

There are two main cropping seasons (*kharif* and *rabi*) and three rice-growing seasons (*aus*, *aman* and *boro*). The kharif season comprises an early part (pre-monsoon and early monsoon) when aus paddy and jute are the principal crops, and a later part (second half of the monsoon season and early post-monsoon) when transplanted aman paddy is the principal crop; deepwater aman paddy is sown pre-monsoon and harvested post-monsoon. High-yielding varieties (HYVs) of aus and aman paddy are grown mainly on Highland and Medium Highland-1: (see Table 1.2, footnote). The rabi (dry) season includes the cool winter months when temperate dryland crops such as wheat, pulses and oilseeds are grown (mainly on residual soil moisture), and the hot pre-monsoon months when so-called summer fruits and vegetables are grown; boro paddy is sown in seedbeds in winter, but mainly grows and matures in the field in the hot pre-monsoon season (mainly with irrigation). Much land produces two crops a year, and some produces three (even four) crops. The main cropping patterns on depth-of-flooding land types are shown in Table 1.5.

Figure 1.3 shows how the growing seasons relate to climate, seasonal flooding and major kinds of natural disaster. All the seasons overlap. Their beginning and end dates also differ across the country: the rainy season starts earliest in the north-east and latest in the west; and the cool winter period starts earlier and ends later in the north than in the south. However, as was indicated in Section 1.2, there is considerable variation between years in

---

[6] *The average farm holding of about 2.5 acres (1 ha) is divided into an average of about ten separate plots (some of which may be divided into two or more fields). Typically, a farmer's plots are located in different parts of a village and sometimes in neighbouring villages. There is also much renting in and renting out of plots or fields. Thus, even small farmers usually cultivate fields on different land and soil types. This provides them with opportunities for crop diversification (including the cultivation of different rice varieties) and reduces the risk that all their crops will be lost when natural disasters occur.*

[7] *In Bangladesh, the term 'paddy' is used for both the rice crop in the field and the unhusked grain, and the term 'rice' for the milled grain. Yields and production are reported as rice (i.e., milled grain), whereas international crop statistics (including those of FAO) are reported as 'brown rice' (i.e., unhusked grain). Milled rice is equivalent to about two-thirds the weight of unhusked grain.*

FIGURE 1.3
Cropping patterns in relation to seasonal flooding, climate and natural disasters

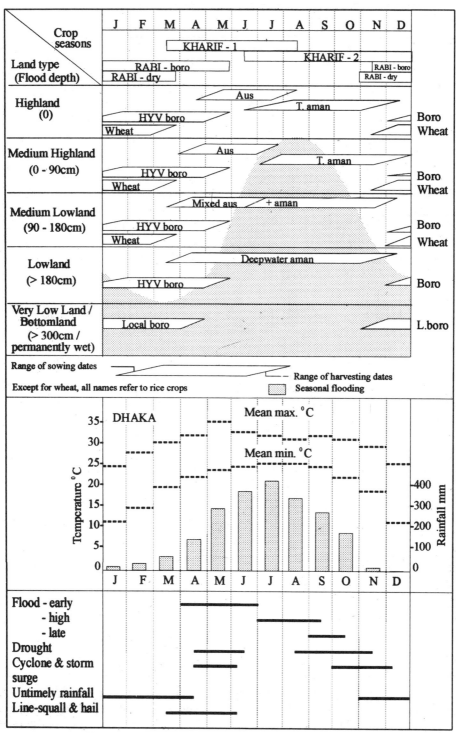

TABLE 1.5
Main cropping patterns on floodplain land types

Land/soil type	Crops/crop rotation Without irrigation	Crops/crop rotation With irrigation
Highland		
Permeable	Tree crops; sugarcane; kharif vegetables, spices, fruits. B.aus-rabi crops Jute/mesta-rabi crops	Similar to non-irrigated, but more emphasis on wheat and rabi cash crops (vegetables, spices, tobacco, cotton)
Impermeable	HYV/LV t.aman HYV/LV t.aus-HYV/LV t.aman (in eastern Districts)	HYV boro/aus-HYV t.aman
Medium Highland-1		
Permeable	Similar to Highland, but no tree crops	Similar to Highland, permeable
Impermeable	Similar to Highland	Similar to Highland, impermeable
Medium Highland-2		
Permeable	B.aus/jute-rabi crops B.aus/jute-LV t.aman	Similar to Highland, permeable
Impermeable	HYV/LV t.aman HYV/LV t.aus-LV t.aman (except western Districts)	HYV boro-LV t.aman
Medium Lowland		
Permeable	Mixed b.aus+b.aman-rabi crops Jute-rabi crops	Similar to Highland, permeable
Impermeable	Similar to permeable, but less jute	HYV boro HYV boro-t.deepwater aman
Lowland		
Permeable & impermeable	B.aman-rabi pulses/oilseeds B.aman-rabi fallow	HYV boro
Very Lowland		
Permeable & impermeable	LV boro Uncultivated grassland/reed swamp	LV boro

Notes: 1. Excludes saline areas where salinity may prevent cultivation of rabi crops (including boro paddy), and hill areas where *jhum* cultivation is practised..

2. Rotations vary regionally with differences in annual rainfall, winter temperatures, risk of flash floods near hills, and speed of drainage of depressions after rainy season.

3. HYV = high yielding varieties. LV = local varieties. B = broadcast. t = transplanted. – = followed by.

the start and end dates of the main growing seasons; also, normal cropping patterns can be disrupted by natural disasters.

1.7 GREENHOUSE WARMING

Current climatic projections suggest that, in and around Bangladesh, monsoon rainfall could increase by 10-15 percent by 2030 and dry-season rainfall by 5-10 percent. Such changes could increase the frequency and severity of floods and keep some basin land wet longer into the dry season than occurs at present. Higher temperatures ($+1$-1.25^0C in the monsoon season; $+1.25$-1.5^0C in the dry season) would reduce the suitability of the climate for wheat, potato and other temperate crops grown in the rabi season, but they might benefit boro paddy and kharif crops.

The projected rise in sea-level by 14-24 cm by 2030 would mainly affect interior floodplain areas in the south-centre of the country. Along the coast and on the banks of tidal and estuarine rivers, silt deposition by river and tidal flooding is expected to raise land-levels concurrently with the rise in sea-level. Annual flooding by rainwater ponded on the land behind the raised coastal land and higher river levees would be deeper and more prolonged than at present. That could reduce the areas suitable for aus, jute, transplanted aman and possibly boro paddy, but it could increase the area suitable for deepwater aman. Arrangements would need to be made to allow silty tidal or river water to enter embanked areas near the coast periodically so that siltation could maintain the land surface at the same level as at present relative to sea-level.

It is wholly uncertain what the impact of a rising sea-level might be on existing salt-water limits. That is partly because the impact of the increased river flows which may result from the predicted increase in rainfall in the region cannot be predicted. However, it is mainly due to the uncertainty regarding future human interventions in the flow of the major rivers which pass through Bangladesh due to increasing rates of abstraction of water for domestic, industrial and irrigation use in the catchment area, the construction of more dams, barrages and flood embankments, and the possibly increased rates of run-off and erosion in hill and mountain areas due to increasing degradation of the natural vegetation with growing population pressure.

A detailed review of the possible impacts of greenhouse warming on future land use is given in Warrick & Ahmad (1996) and is summarized in Ahmad *et al.* (1994).

PART II
LAND USE STUDIES

The nine chapters in this part cover a wide range of topics related to land use and land use planning in Bangladesh. Chapter 2 analyses the ways in which farmers intensified their cropping systems over a period of one century, enabling national food production to keep pace broadly with population growth. Chapter 3 examines how farmers actually responded to the crop intensification opportunities provided in major flood control, drainage and irrigation project areas.

The remaining chapters are based on reports by consultants who were commissioned in the early-1980s to investigate specific topics of relevance for national or local-level planning. Chapter 4 describes the changes in land use and soils — positive and negative — which had taken place in five major water-control project areas, while Chapter 6 describes the extent and influence on land use of natural changes in flood-levels which had occurred in some areas since the 1960s. Chapter 5 assesses the extent of agricultural land consumed by the spread of human settlements and infrastructure, and Chapter 7 assesses the extent of land made derelict, especially by brickyards, and the possibilities of restoring such land (and derelict tanks) to productive use. Chapters 8 and 9 respectively describe the need for soil conservation interventions in Bangladesh's hill areas and for rehabilitation of mango orchards in western Districts. The possible legal or administrative measures which central government or local governments could use to prevent undue loss or waste of the country's scarce land resources are reviewed in Chapter 10.

Chapter 2

TRADITIONAL AND MODERN METHODS OF INTENSIFYING CROP PRODUCTION[1]

This chapter reviews the various means by which farmers have intensified crop production in Bangladesh. The three-fold increase in foodgrain production achieved in the century 1881-1981 came mainly from small farmers following intensification pathways appropriate for their environmental and economic conditions. Seven pathways and three stages of intensification are described, and the implications for agricultural development planning are examined.

2.1 PREFACE

If history provides the best guide for the future, then a study of the ways in which farmers have intensified their production techniques during the past century — during which time foodgrain production in the country probably increased three-fold — can provide useful lessons for agricultural planners, researchers and extensionists to guide them in helping farmers to speed up the rate of intensification in the future. This chapter aims to provide some of those lessons.

The view from Dhaka appears to be simple: Bangladesh has seven 'soil tracts'; is part Highland and part flooded land (some of which is 'flood-prone'); has a wet season and a dry season, which are divided into three crop seasons; has abundant water for irrigation; and has small peasant farmers who are ignorant, conservative and dependent on Government for inputs, technical advice and motivation for change.

The reality is somewhat different. Bangladesh has a highly complex environment: five main land types related to seasonal flooding; many hundreds of different soils; important regional differences in climate and hydrology; and with varying degrees of risk of disastrous floods, drought and cyclones. Almost every village — perhaps almost every farmer — has two or more agroecological environments, and farmers' cropping patterns are very finely adapted to them. In this respect, it is the farmers who are the 'experts' within their own villages.

Also, only half the agricultural land in Bangladesh is owned by small farmers (farmers with less than 5 acres). Those farmers, like the big farmers, may be conservative: i.e., reluctant

---

[1] *This chapter is an edited version of a review paper prepared for the Ministry of Agriculture in July 1981 (Brammer, 1981b). Footnotes which appeared in the original paper are given in normal font. Footnotes that have been added are given in italics. As in other chapters, the Districts referred to are the pre-1982 Districts shown on Figure 1.1.*

to change from well-tried and proven methods. But unlike the big farmers, the small farmers have proved themselves to be remarkably innovative and adaptive. It is mainly through the intensive methods and cropping patterns which they have discovered or adopted that agricultural production in the country has increased three-fold in the past century. In the areas of big land-holdings, agriculture is still predominantly in its most simple stage, producing a single, unimproved crop in a year with minimum inputs (even without weeding in some cases).

These observations have important implications for agricultural planners, researchers and extensionists. The first is that national production, research and extension plans need to be made with greater awareness of the complex reality of Bangladesh's physical and socio-economic environments. 'Top-down' plans are likely to succeed only where they touch that reality. The large gaps left between the points of contact, where the plans are irrelevant, can produce results which are far below plan targets.

For agricultural plans to be more relevant, they must be well adapted to the real environment. Since no-one at the centre can expect (or be expected) to be familiar with all the local environments in the country — or even in a District; perhaps even in a Thana — that means that there must be considerable decentralization of planning authority and implementation. And since the farmers are the experts on the environments in their own locality, it also means that plans are likely to be more realistic and successfully implemented if they include a strong element of 'bottom-up' planning. The introduction of the Village Development Planning and Thana Land Use Development Planning Programmes are promising steps in this direction.[2]

The second important implication of the observations made above is that, since it is the small farmers who have proved themselves most progressive and productive, Government's objectives of achieving national self-sufficiency in foodgrain production within a short period can only be met if agricultural policies, programmes, research and extension are concentrated on providing support and assistance to those small farmers. The alternative would be to adopt policies and programmes which would bring the fifty percent of the land owned by big farmers into intensive production. However, the agrarian reform or rapid mechanization which that would require are unlikely to occur sufficiently quickly to meet short-term production targets. In fact, the social upheaval which either of those measures could cause would likely be counter-productive in the short term.

For a rapid increase in agricultural production, therefore, there is no practical alternative but to concentrate attention on the 77 percent of the farmers who own less than 5 acres of land.[3] These farmers are unequally distributed about the country. The areas where they predominate need to be defined. Staff and funds then need to be allocated to those areas in relation to their needs and potentials for rapid progress.

Those needs and potentials can best be identified by making policies and production, research and extension programmes which provide for a continuous and genuine dialogue between officials with their modern technical knowledge and farmers (or their representatives)

---

[2] *Neither of these proposed programmes actually got off the ground: see Chapters 20 and 22. Essentially, they were defeated by the reluctance of administrators and technical officials — and later politicians — to give up their central control.*

[3] The upper limit will vary from place to place according to climate, land quality, water resources and considerations of social status.

with their detailed local experience. In that way, the best elements of top-down and bottom-up planning can be combined. This manual has been prepared to assist that dialogue by providing top-down planners with a better understanding of the bottom-up potentials for intensifying agricultural production. In that sense, it is complementary to the manual entitled 'Seventeen possible ways to increase agricultural production in Bangladesh' (Brammer, 1981a).[4]

2.2 INTRODUCTION

The population of the territory which is now called Bangladesh increased almost four-fold during the century between 1881 and 1981: from about 24 million in 1881 to almost 90 million in 1981. In order to feed the increased population, foodgrain production probably increased almost three-fold. Additionally, there were increasing food imports (which averaged 1.74 million tons in the nine years 1971-72 to 1980-81) and some degree of belt-tightening (which probably decreased the average daily foodgrain intake from more than 16 oz per head to the present 15.5 oz per head assumed in national foodgrain budgeting).[5]

How was this three-fold increase in production achieved? Even in 1881, the population density of this territory was more than 400 per square mile, which is higher than that in many developing countries today. In 1981, the average density was 1,618 per square mile. An analysis of the ways in which agricultural production has been increased in the past can provide useful lessons for the future.

The process of intensification is a continuous one. It has advanced further in some places than in others. Experience gained in one area may provide a useful guide for speeding up the pace of intensification in less advanced areas. Also, an analysis of the factors which contribute to rapid intensification can help to identify critical points where Government policies and programmes could intervene to speed up progress more widely in the future.

The following account is to some extent conjectural. That is partly due to the difficulty in making statistical comparisons throughout the period because of the boundary changes which took place during the partition and reunification of Bengal early in the 1900s and again on the partition of the Indian subcontinent in 1947. It is partly due, also, to the lack of reliable agricultural statistics during the earlier and later parts of the period.[6]

The account depends greatly on field observations made by the author in different parts of Bangladesh over the past 20 years (i.e., 1961-81). Because of the author's background as a Geographer and Soil Surveyor, the account particularly emphasizes the environmental factors which have induced and allowed farmers in different areas to take different pathways in seeking to increase their production. Although these pathways are described separately, it should be realized that different pathways can be followed concurrently in different parts of the country. For national and regional planners, and for aid donors, this is an important point to understand. Bangladesh is far from being uniform — physically, demographically or socio-economically.

---

[4] *It is intended to include this manual in a future volume of the author's collected works: Brammer (in press).*

[5] *The population in 1997 was estimated to be 125 million. Foodgrain production in 1997-98 was 20.65 million tons and imports were 1.93 million tons. National food budgets now (1999) assume a daily foodgrain requirement of 16 oz (455 g) per head.*

[6] *For comments on the questionable reliability of modern agricultural statistics, see Section 2.3.1 below and Brammer (1997), Sections 10.11.3 and 12.3.10.*

For example, the opportunities for further crop intensification in Comilla District, where the population density in 1981 was 2,742 per square mile, obviously are different from those in Dinajpur District where the 1981 population density was 1,267 per square mile. Increased production in Dinajpur District in recent years has come partly from the immigration of small farmers from more densely-populated eastern Districts such as Comilla. Between 1961 and 1981, the population of Dinajpur District increased by 3.18 percent per annum compared with 2.26 percent in Comilla District. The immigrant farmers in Dinajpur introduced double cropping in place of the single crop mainly produced by local 'big' land-owners from whom they have bought the land; (similar trends are apparent in other western Districts and in coastal Districts). On the other hand, progressive small farmers in parts of the Comilla Kotwali Thana are moving from double cropping to triple and quadruple cropping with the help of irrigation and new, quick-maturing, high-yielding varieties (HYVs) of paddy.[7]

Even within the same village, different intensification pathways may be followed simultaneously on different kinds of land, perhaps even by the same farmer. For example, on Highland,[8] a farmer may change from growing two or three traditional subsistence crops a year (e.g., broadcast aus followed by rabi pulses) to intensive, year-round, vegetable cultivation with hand irrigation. On neighbouring Lowland, the same farmer may change from growing traditional deepwater aman in the rainy season to growing HYV boro paddy with pump irrigation in the dry season.[9]

Intensification of production, it should be noted, does not necessarily mean growing more crops in a year on the same area of land. An overall national cropping intensity of 200 percent is not necessarily better than an intensity of 150 percent. Intensity should refer to the intensity of effort and inputs used — which, on economic grounds, one expects will be reflected in increased value of outputs — not merely on the number of crops grown in a year. In one of the examples given above, the replacement of a single traditional crop of deepwater aman by a single crop of irrigated HYV boro paddy represents a considerable degree of intensification, which is reflected in the four-fold increase in production expected, but not in the cropping intensity index which remains the same. Similarly, the substitution of sugarcane or banana for the traditional rotation of broadcast aus followed by rabi crops can represent a considerable degree of intensification, even though it reduces the cropping intensity by half.

The output of most interest to the farmer is takas (Bangladesh's currency). This accounts for farmers in Lowland areas of Comilla District preferring to grow a single crop of HYV boro paddy when subsidized irrigation from low-lift pumps and deep tube-wells is introduced instead of the traditional mixed aus+aman paddy followed by wheat, for which the soils are equally well suited and which could produce more grain per acre, but apparently less profit.

---

[7] *An example of a quadruple cropping pattern using traditional crop varieties on non-irrigated land is given below in Section 2.3.3.*

[8] *The main land types related to seasonal flooding are defined in Table 1.2.*

[9] *The 1983-84 Agricultural Census (BBS, 1984) showed that farm holdings were divided into an average of 9.6 fragments. These fragments (plots) typically are scattered over most or all the land types in a village. Where farmers do not own plots on particular land types, they commonly rent in fields on those land types from other farmers. This spread of an individual farmer's plots over several land types enables him to diversify his production, spread his labour inputs and reduce the risk of total crop losses from natural disasters and pest/disease epidemics.*

This example shows that intensification of technology can sometimes result in a reduction in cropping intensity: in this case, from 300 to 100 percent.[10]

These few examples indicate that population pressure, land quality, water resources, available technology, Government policies and programmes (e.g., subsidies, irrigation development), markets, relative crop prices, socio-economic conditions and cultural traditions can all be involved in determining the pathways suitable and used for increasing agricultural production in a particular area.

2.3 PATHWAYS OF INTENSIFICATION

2.3.1 Introduction

Bangladeshi farmers have used various methods for increasing production: e.g., opening up new land; growing more crops in a year on the same piece of land; improving yields by better land or crop management; and providing irrigation and drainage. These changes are reflected in the expansion of the three main paddy crops and wheat since 1947, shown in Table 2.1.[11]

TABLE 2.1

Area and production of paddy and wheat 1947-48 and 1980-81

Crop	Area (million acres)		Increase %	Production (million tons)		Increase %
	1947-48	1980-81		1947-48	1980-81	
Aus	4.9	7.7	57	1.4	3.2	129
Aman	13.3	14.1	6	5.0	7.8	56
Boro	0.8	3.00	275	0.3	2.6	767
Wheat	0.1	1.7	1600	0.02	1.4	6900
Total	**19.1**	**26.5**	**39**	**6.72**	**15.0**	**123**

Notes: 1. Paddy production is reported as milled rice (= 0.66 percent of unmilled 'brown' rice).

2. Aman includes both broadcast and transplanted aman.

3. Data for 1980-81 are preliminary estimates of the Bangladesh Bureau of Agricultural Statistics.

There have also been changes in the acreage and production of other crops, especially potato and vegetables. On the other hand, the acreage and production of pulses and oilseeds may have decreased in the face of competition from HYV wheat and paddy crops. However, it is difficult to be certain of this because of the apparent unreliability of the official statistics for these crops.[12]

---

[10]*Mixed aus+aman apparently is regarded as a single crop in the Bangladesh Agricultural Statistics. However, although seed of the two crops are sown together, the crops are harvested separately and they occupy the land during the kharif-1 and kharif-2 seasons respectively. Accordingly, it seems preferable to consider mixed aus+ aman as two crops (with a cropping intensity of 200 percent).*

[11]*By 1996-97, the acreage and production of paddy crops and wheat had changed to the following levels: aus 3.93 M acres, 1.87 M tons; aman 14.34 M acres, 9.55 M tons; boro 6.88 M acres, 7.46 M tons; wheat 1.75 M acres, 1.45 M tons; total 26.90 M acres, 20.34 M tons. In addition, there were 220,000 acres of minor cereals, producing 66,000 tons of grain.*

[12]*The 1983-84 Agricultural Census indicated a considerably greater area of rabi pulses and oilseeds than had been reported in the annual statistics.*

The various methods by which crop production has been intensified are described in the following sections and in Tables 2.3 to 2.13 (at the end of this chapter).

2.3.2 New land

In 1901, when the population was around 29 million, there were apparently considerable areas of land not used for crop production, especially in the tidal areas of Khulna, Barisal and Patuakhali Districts, in some low-lying river floodplain areas inland, and in parts of Dinajpur District in the north. Up to about 1950, the rate of population growth was relatively slow, and part of the population increase could be accommodated and fed by extending settlements into new areas and by bringing more land under the plough in settled areas.

For example, the net cropped area of what is now Bangladesh (minus Kushtia, Sylhet and Chittagong Hill Tracts Districts, for which pre-1947 statistics are not readily available) increased from 19.53 million acres in 1901-02 to 20.8 million acres in 1978-79. In Barisal-Patuakhali, the cropped area increased from 1.69 million acres to 2.21 million acres between 1901-02 and 1940-41. Even in Comilla District, the cropped area increased from 1.3 to 1.5 million acres during that period, probably by reclamation of low-lying land in the north of the District.

This expansion phase has not entirely ceased. It is continuing under three main circumstances, as is described below.

New char areas. The huge amounts of sediment brought down by the Brahmaputra river and deposited in the Meghna estuary following the 1950 Assam earthquake created approximately half-a-million acres of new land in Noakhali District. This was quickly settled and brought under cultivation. Accretion of new land in the estuary is still continuing, but at a slower rate than in the few years after that catastrophic event. As new *char* land appears and becomes consolidated, it is first occupied seasonally for growing transplanted aman paddy.[13] If the new land increases in area so that it is considered less likely to be quickly eroded by changing currents in the estuary, it may eventually be permanently settled (usually by tenants of absentee big land-owners living on the mainland).

Reclamation of 'culturable waste land'. The spread of small-scale pump and tube-well irrigation since the early 1960s has probably brought under cultivation about a quarter-of-a-million acres of land previously used as dry-season grazing land, mainly in low-lying floodplain areas, such as some *haor* areas of Sylhet and Mymensingh Districts, the *barani* lands of Pabna District (in Region 5), and on a smaller scale in some other Districts.

Clearing of forest. It is more difficult to estimate the area cleared from forest and brought under cultivation during the past century. That is partly because Sylhet District and the Chittagong Hill Tracts were not part of Bengal before 1947, and some western Districts such as Dinajpur were divided at partition in 1947: statistics for these areas are not readily available in Dhaka. It is partly also because of the nature of cultivation in some of the hill areas (*jhum*, or shifting cultivation) in which land may revert to forest after cultivation.

The Bangladesh crop statistics show the cultivated area in the Chittagong Hill Tracts District decreasing from 186,000 acres in 1947-48 to 179,399 acres in 1979-80. Those figures probably do not take into account illegal encroachment into forest areas, which may

---

[13]*The first stage on emerging estuarine char land, in fact, seems to be use for grazing by herds of water buffaloes in the dry season. Cultivation and settlement follow when continuing siltation has raised the land to levels suitable for transplanting aman paddy in July-August and making houses.*

have been considerable. The rapid increase in population in the Chittagong Hill Tracts suggests that, in fact, much new land must have been cleared for cultivation to feed the expanding population. Some land also went under tea, rubber, cashew and other tree crops. The population of this District increased almost six-fold between 1901 and 1981, and almost three-fold between 1947 and 1981. That growth rate is much higher than in any other District, and almost twice the national average.

2.3.3 Multiple cropping

The most widespread method used for intensifying production has been to increase the number of crops grown on the land in a year. That may involve sequence cropping, relay cropping or intercropping, and it may be achieved either with or without altering the natural environment (e.g., by providing irrigation or drainage). Examples under traditional conditions are given below.

a. Add dry-season pulses or oilseeds after harvesting aus paddy on permeable Highland and Medium Highland soils, or following deepwater aman on lower land. The dry-season crops use moisture stored in the soil following the rainy season or seasonal flooding.

b. Add broadcast or transplanted aus before transplanted aman on slowly-permeable, level Highland and Medium Highland soils. On the Teesta floodplain in Rangpur District, and on parts of the Noakhali char land, aus is sown on residual soil moisture in February, without waiting for pre-monsoon rainfall.

c. On Medium Lowland, add aus to deepwater aman, by sowing them mixed together. Jute, various millets (*kaon*, *bhurra*, *shama*), or sesamum are sown mixed with deepwater aman in some areas.

d. Intensify the mixed aus+aman pattern further by intersowing dry-season pulses or oilseeds through the standing aman crop 1-2 weeks before the latter crop is harvested, or sowing wheat, barley, maize, potato, sweet potato, pulses or oilseeds after harvesting the aman.

e. The mixed aus+aman-rabi crops pattern was still further intensified in western parts of Comilla District which have deep silty soils with a high moisture-holding capacity. Mixed aus+deepwater aman were followed by dry-season pulses or mustard intersown through the aman crop before it was harvested; the pulse crops were grazed off by cattle and the mustard harvested in late-January or early-February; then — after ploughing the land (for the only time in the year) — foxtail millet (*kaon*) or sesamum were sown or chilli seedlings transplanted at the end of the cold weather, in February; the following mixed aus+aman crops were intersown through the latter crops when the first pre-monsoon showers fell in March-April; and the late dryland rabi crops were harvested by pulling them from the soil in May or early June, as floodwater began to cover the land. Weeds cut and used (or sold) for fodder in the pre-monsoon period provided yet another harvest from this intensive traditional cropping pattern. (Around the end of the 1970s, rainfed wheat or irrigated HYV boro paddy largely replaced the traditional dry-season crops.)

f. Sow rabi pulses between sugarcane rows; sow aus, kharif pulses or early rabi crops in young mango (or other fruit tree) orchards; and plant aus or kharif vegetables between raised beds of ginger. These practices are mainly found in the drier western parts of Bangladesh.

g. Intersow or relay-sow kharif or rabi vegetables, spices, gourds, etc. The author once counted as many as 15 different rabi crops growing together in the same small plot in Gabtali Thana of Bogra District. (Multi-crop mixtures of subsistence crops — including aus paddy, sesamum, beans, gourds, hill cotton, and sometimes several other crops — are also found in *jhum* cultivation.)

With modern technology, the main methods of intensification through multiple cropping have been by means of irrigation and drainage, viz.

i. With irrigation, HYV boro (or transplanted aus) was added to traditional transplanted aman in some former single-cropped areas of Barisal and Patuakhali Districts, over large areas of the Barind Tract and locally elsewhere.

ii. In Comilla Kotwali Thana, some farmers changed from traditional rainfed broadcast aus followed by transplanted aman, first to irrigated HYV boro followed by HYV aman, then to three quick-maturing HYVs of boro, aus and aman. In 1979, the author observed some farmers to be experimenting with four crops in a year: HYV boro, HYV or local aus, HYV aman, then wheat or mustard.

iii. In parts of Comilla District and the east of Dhaka District, and probably elsewhere, some farmers started to transplant deepwater aman after harvesting irrigated HYV boro in the late-1970s.[14]

iv. In some areas protected by the Coastal Embankment, farmers added broadcast aus or sesamum to the traditional transplanted aman, without irrigation.

v. In pump-drained and irrigated areas such as the Dhaka-Narayanganj-Demra (DND) project area, areas which formerly grew a single crop of deepwater aman now produce HYV boro and HYV aman. In the late-1970s, some farmers started to add mustard or wheat grown on residual soil moisture after harvesting the aman crop.

Tables 2.3 to 2.13 show the stages of intensification by multiple cropping under traditional and modern cropping systems on different land and soil types.

2.3.4 Change in land management

Three examples are given below of changes in land management which farmers introduce in order to intensify their production. The first two methods (soil puddling; making ridges or beds) are mostly used on impermeable soils. The third method (dibbling) is most appropriate on moderately permeable, loamy soils.

Puddling. Since the early-1970s, there has been an increasing tendency for farmers to transplant aus instead of broadcast sowing it, even on non-irrigated land. This practice involves puddling the soil instead of preparing it for dry sowing. It may also involve levelling the fields and making bunds around them to retain rainwater. Transplanting of aus is most extensive on slowly-permeable Highland and Medium Highland soils in high-rainfall areas in eastern Districts, but the practice spread to the Tongi-Joydebpur area of Dhaka District around 1970 and, later in the 1970s, to parts of Mymensingh and Tangail Districts

---

[14]*This practice subsequently became more widespread, and in several areas — especially on the Jamuna Floodplain in Tangail and Dhaka Districts — farmers then added a crop of mustard (or rape-seed) growing on residual soil moisture after harvesting the aman.*

and the eastern half of the Barind Tract in Bogra District. This practice provides three advantages:

   a. greater security against pre-monsoon drought, because the aus is transplanted in late-May or early-June when the rainfall is heavier and more reliable than in March-April when aus is broadcast sown;

   b. better conditions for harvesting and drying aus in late-August or early-September than in the cloudier and wetter period of July or early-August when broadcast aus normally matures; and

   c. higher yields, because of better weed control and more uniform spacing.

Also, because of the more secure growing conditions, the change from broadcast sowing of aus to transplanting the crop often is accompanied by a change from local varieties to HYVs and greater use of fertilizers, both of which can greatly increase yields. Short-term varieties (especially Purbachi in the late 1970s) usually are grown so that aman can be transplanted after the aus has been harvested.[15]

Ridges and beds. Soils puddled for transplanted paddy cultivation usually are in an unsuitable physical condition for sowing a following dryland rabi crop, with or without irrigation. Farmers on such soils in Bogra District, both on floodplain land and on the Barind Tract, found a way to overcome this problem. After harvesting transplanted aman (or late aus), they hand-cultivate the soil to make ridges or narrow beds, such as are usually used on permeable soils for cultivating potato or vegetables. Then they plant potato, spices or vegetables, which they hand-irrigate with frequent small applications of water from tanks, road-side ditches, dug wells or hand pumps.[16] After the rabi crops have been harvested, the fields are levelled for the next kharif paddy crop.

Dibbling. The practice of dibble-sowing aus paddy instead of broadcast sowing the seed was observed to be spreading in the late-1970s. Local information indicated that the practice probably started in the 1940s in Ramgati Thana of Noakhali District where some of the deep, silty soils become slightly saline at the surface during the dry season. Most soils in this area are used for a single crop of transplanted aman, but some farmers started to dibble-sow local aus varieties on residual soil moisture in February, and then transplant their aman crop later, in the monsoon season. This practice spread not only to other parts of the Noakhali char land, but also to Sandwip and Bhola islands elsewhere in the Meghna estuary, and onto the Noakhali mainland (where the soils are not saline). With Extension advice, dibble-sowing later spread to several inland Districts, although mainly as a substitute

---

[15]*This change was interesting because, contrary to the author's assumptions made in assessing the potential for growing HYVs of rice under rainfed conditions in 1974 (see Brammer 1997, Chapter 10), farmers chose to grow an HYV paddy in the aus season rather than in the aman season. That was because, in central parts of the country, the rainy season is not long enough for two HYV rice crops to be grown without irrigation, and (with varieties existing in the 1970s and 1980s) it would still be too late to transplant HYV aman after harvesting transplanted aus, even if a local aus variety was used. On the other hand, a photoperiod-sensitive local aman variety could be transplanted in September after harvesting transplanted HYV aus. In practice, farmers often chose to grow a locally-improved variety (LIV) of aman (e.g., Nigersail) which gave them grain of a quality they preferred to eat and for which they could obtain a higher price in the market than for aus or HYV aman grain.*

[16]*In the late-1970s, farmers on the Barind Tract west of Bogra town started to sow wheat on similar ridges or narrow beds and irrigate the crop by hand.*

for broadcast sowing of aus, not in order to grow an extra crop. As practised on Noakhali char land, dibble-sowing has three interesting features:

a. the land is only roughly ploughed (or hand-cultivated) since it is not necessary to prepare the fine tilth that is needed for broadcast sowing seed;

b. holes for dibbling the seed are made by hand using a strong stick 4-5 feet long, which is less laborious than making holes with a small hand tool (such as normally is used for transplanting chilli seedlings); the work is suitable for old men and boys, therefore; and

c. the holes are left open after sowing 7-8 seeds in each hole; the farmers say that this is done so that salty soil does not cover the seed and prevent germination or damage seedlings.

Dibbling — and line-sowing behind the plough, which is practised in some other parts of the country: e.g., for sowing wheat and *kaon* in Thakurgaon (in the north of Dinajpur District) — has the advantage that the seeds are placed in contact with moist soil. Therefore, germination is immediate, and the seedlings do not suffer from drought if there is no rainfall in the first 2-3 weeks following sowing, as can happen to broadcast aus germinating on or near the soil surface. Because the crop is planted in lines, too, weeding is easier than with broadcast aus, and plant development can be better because of more uniform spacing. The yield potential is increased, therefore; at the same time, a lower seed-rate can be used.[17]

2.3.5 Change of land or soil type

Two traditional methods of changing soil and land types are widely used in Bangladesh. One method is to make raised soil platforms which change Medium Highland, Medium Lowland, Lowland or Bottomland into Highland (or sometimes to a higher type of seasonally-flooded land). The other method is to bury the existing soils with alluvium or tank silt from another area. In modern times, pump or tidal drainage has also had the effect of changing land types: e.g., changing former Lowland into Medium Highland or Highland in the DND project area.

Soil platforms. In some deeply-flooded areas, there are many raised platforms which are used for intensive crop production, especially of vegetables. These platforms may originally have been made to provide housing sites. This seems to be the case in the Munshiganj and Baidya Bazar areas of Dhaka District, on the sites of the ancient cities of Vikrampur and Sonargaon. Elsewhere, especially on Medium Highland, the soil platforms appear to have been made deliberately to raise field levels above flood-level, as a means of intensifying crop production. Such platforms are common in parts of the Teesta Floodplain adjoining the Barind Tract in Rangpur and Bogra Districts, in Puthia Thana of Rajshahi District, and west of the Lalmai Hills in Comilla District. Some platforms in western Districts appear to be old, and may at one time have been used for growing indigo or mulberry (for silk worms).

---

[17]*Sown in February, quick-maturing aus varieties could be harvested in May or early-June, before the period of heavy monsoon rains and leaving plenty of time to prepare the land for the following transplanted aman crop. While most farmers (in the late-1970s) used local aus varieties which they said were somewhat salt-tolerant, some farmers in Noakhali District were also observed to be trying IR-8, a long-maturing HYV.*

Whatever their origin, raised platforms usually are intensively cultivated, often with the help of hand-irrigation. Commonly, they are used for banana, *pan* (betel leaf) or mango, or to produce three or four subsistence and cash crops in a year (e.g., aus paddy, jute, aman paddy seedlings, wheat, potato, melon, pumpkin, kharif and rabi vegetables and spices, in various combinations). Intercropping and relay cropping are common practices, so that the land can produce crops all through the year.

Change of soil type. The construction of raised platforms or beds may also involve a change of soil type. For instance, farmers on perennially-wet land in the Satla-Baghda and Swarupkati areas of Barisal District, where the natural peaty soils are too soft for cultivation, mix alluvial material with the peat to make raised beds on which they grow guava, sugarcane, vegetables and aus paddy. Water-filled ditches between the beds provide access by boat, as well as water for hand irrigation of the crops in the dry season. The alluvial material is either taken from layers below the peat or it is carried by boat or in baskets from neighbouring river-banks or river-beds.

Elsewhere, in some deeply-flooded basins — for example, around Arial Beel in the south of Dhaka District — farmers dig canals to bring in floodwater from neighbouring rivers. Especially near to big rivers and hill areas, the floodwater leaves behind silty deposits which bury the natural heavy basin clay. The deposits also quickly raise the land level from Bottomland or Lowland to Medium Lowland or Medium Highland. This change of soil and land types makes it possible for farmers to grow two or three crops in a year (e.g., mixed aus+aman or jute, followed by dryland rabi crops) in place of a single, often flood-prone, crop of local boro or deepwater aman.[18]

Flood protection and drainage. Modern flood-protection and drainage projects also have the effect of changing land types. The exclusion of river water and pumping out of rainwater has reduced flood-levels within the DND and Chandpur Irrigation Project areas, converting land which formerly was Medium Lowland and Lowland into Highland and Medium Highland. Together with the provision of irrigation, this has enabled farmers to grow two transplanted HYV paddy crops in a year (boro-t.aman) in place of the former broadcast aman or mixed aus+aman.

Although such large-scale projects are not without their problems — they are costly to provide and operate; they may increase hydrological problems due to channelization of rivers between embankments; and they may allow settlements to sprawl wastefully over good agricultural land after the deep-flooding constraint is removed (see Chapter 5) — there would seem to be no long-term alternative to their widespread adoption in Bangladesh as a means of making most floodplain land suitable for intensive, high-yielding, crop production throughout the year.

2.3.6 Irrigation

Traditional methods of irrigation have been widely used to intensify agricultural production in Bangladesh. The methods used include carrying water in pitchers, using open wells and operating various simple, manual devices (*dons*, swing baskets) for lifting water a few feet from rivers or tanks. In hill areas, seasonal dams on small rivers are used to divert water

---

[18]*Subsequently, in the 1980s, the author observed farmers in Arial Beel were making mounds of water hyacinth plants mixed with local basin clay on which to grow winter vegetables for sale in Dhaka city, to which they were transported by boat.*

onto adjoining land. In some tidal areas, cross-dams are built across small rivers and streams after the rainy season to retain fresh water which can be used for small-scale irrigation in the dry season.

From the 1960s, there was a widespread expansion of irrigation by means of low-lift pumps (LLPs), deep tube-wells (DTWs), shallow tube-wells (STWs) and hand pumps. The LLPs and tube-wells, which irrigate 5-100 acres, differ from most traditional forms of irrigation in that they require cooperation in the use of water among neighbouring farmers. So do the larger canal irrigation projects, such as the Ganges-Kobadak (G-K) Irrigation Project; but in such projects, the cooperation is enforced by the project authority which controls the supply of water, not by the farmers themselves.

Traditionally, irrigation was used to grow boro paddy in the dry season on land which is too deeply flooded for safe cultivation in the rainy season. On higher land, irrigation was used to grow small areas of vegetables and spices around homesteads or on soil platforms, also in the dry season. Increasingly, in recent years, irrigation — by both traditional and modern methods — has been provided so as to:

a. grow a crop of HYV boro on land which previously stayed fallow in the dry season;

b. substitute HYV boro or wheat, or cash crops such as tobacco, potato, vegetable or spices, for subsistence crops of pulses, oilseeds or older varieties of wheat and barley;

c. substitute a perennial crop such as banana for both kharif and rabi subsistence crops;

d. ensure reliable crops of transplanted aus and transplanted aman in drier western Districts and on light soils, such as in the BWDB G-K and Thakurgaon Deep Tube-well project areas; and

e. intensify cropping patterns in densely-populated areas, such as the HYV boro-HYV (or local) aus-HYV aman-wheat/mustard patterns in Comilla Kotwali Thana referred to in Section 2.3.3.

With rising fuel and equipment costs, and given the difficulty of maintaining cooperation among economically and socially competitive farmers, traditional and small-scale methods of irrigation can be expected to continue to expand, at least until large areas are commanded by large-scale irrigation and drainage projects.[19]

Although easily-usable surface-water supplies are by now almost fully utilized, there remains considerable scope to improve the efficiency of irrigation so that greater crop production could be obtained with the same amount of water. There remains, also, considerable scope to increase the efficiency of use of groundwater for irrigation.

In many parts of the country, good-quality groundwater is available only a few feet below the ground surface during the rainy season and during the cool winter months which follow. In parts of Bogra, Rangpur and Jamalpur Districts, many thousands of shallow dug wells and hand pumps came into use in the 1970s for irrigating boro or aus paddy, wheat, potato, vegetables and spices. Their number could be increased many-fold in these and several other Districts. Even where DTWs or STWs exist, it may be more economical for farmers to use dug wells or hand pumps for supplementary irrigation of transplanted aman paddy during the rainy season and for irrigation of wheat, potato and vegetables during the

---

[19]*Even in large-scale projects — e.g., the Chandpur Irrigation Project — the trend since 1971 has been to provide irrigation by low-lift pumps rather than directly by canal distribution systems, as in the G-K project.*

cool winter months than to use DTWs or STWs during those periods. The latter would be more appropriate for use to grow boro or early aus paddy during the hot pre-monsoon months, when the groundwater is deeper and the quantity of water required per acre is much greater than in the winter months.

Production could be increased in many areas by using these easily-available surface-water and groundwater resources to eliminate the risk of drought in the rainy season. (The same applies to DTWs, STWs and LLPs, where they exist.) The readiness to use irrigation when drought threatens to occur could make the cultivation of HYV aus and aman — as well as sugarcane and other kharif cash crops — more secure. The greater security of production provided by supplementary irrigation when needed could also encourage farmers to use more fertilizers and increase the efficiency of fertilizer use, thus increasing yields and production still further.[20]

2.3.7 Manure and fertilizers

In traditional agriculture, soil fertility and productivity are maintained by ploughing crop residues and weeds into the soil, by biological nitrogen fixation by blue-green algae and leguminous crops and weeds, and by the addition of generally small amounts of cattle manure, oil-cake or humus-rich tank silt. These means are sufficient to sustain modest yields of one or two subsistence crops a year. For more intensive crop production under traditional conditions, especially of cash crops, more organic manure or tank silt is given.

The introduction of chemical fertilizers in the 1950s paved the way for a rapid increase in agricultural production in the 1960s and 1970s. This rapid increase in production could not have occurred without a corresponding increase in the use of fertilizers. The use of organic materials could not so easily have been increased at the same rate in the face of growing competition for the use of crop residues, dung and leaves as fuel and of weeds as fodder. The fact that chemical fertilizers were cheap when first introduced, were more convenient and cheaper to apply because of their 100-fold greater concentration of nutrients, and were more suitable for use in wet paddy soils than equivalent amounts of organic matter, also contributed to their rapid substitution for organic manures.

Fertilizer use in Bangladesh reached approximately 870,000 tons in 1980-81 (equivalent to about 375,000 nutrient tons).[21] That quantity is equivalent to about 90 lbs of fertilizer per acre of cultivated land per annum (or 38 lbs of fertilizer nutrients). Spread over three crop seasons, that is a very low level compared with that in, for example, Japan where the average rate in 1977 was 345 lbs of fertilizer nutrients per acre, used mainly on one paddy crop per annum.[22]

None-the-less, essential though their use may be, fertilizers do not provide a panacea for increasing crop production. Fertilizers are expensive to provide, both for the national

---

[20]*Travelling in North Bengal in the mid-1990s, the author observed many STWs being used for supplementary irrigation of transplanted aman. It is more difficult to organize the large number of farmers in the command area of DTWs to provide the fuel and operator costs at short notice to provide supplementary irrigation when there is a threat of drought in the rainy season.*

[21]*By the mid-1990s, fertilizer use in Bangladesh exceeded 2 million tons.*

[22]However, the figures for Bangladesh are higher than those for the Philippines and Indonesia. In 1977, these were: Bangladesh 31 lbs nutrients per cropped acre; Philippines 26 lbs/acre; Indonesia 18 lbs/acre. Fertilizer usage in these countries was similar on a *per caput* basis: Bangladesh 9.7 lbs; Philippines 12.8 lbs; Indonesia 9.3 lbs. In Japan, usage in 1977 was 41.2 lbs per head of population.

economy and for farmers, especially small farmers. The increased use of concentrated fertilizers such as urea and triple superphosphate (TSP), coupled with the depletion of organic matter and the increased rate of removal of nutrients from the soils because of higher crop yields and cropping intensities, can lead to deficiencies of other essential nutrients such as sulphur and zinc, as became evident in some parts of the country in the late-1970s. These deficiencies must, in turn, be overcome by using other kinds of fertilizers, some of which may be expensive.

Therefore, there is an urgent need to reduce the relative cost of using fertilizers by using them more efficiently. Probably only 25-50 percent of the urea used in farmers' fields actually benefits the crops. This is due to improper timing and methods of application, unbalanced use in relation to other fertilizers, and unsatisfactory water use and control, both under irrigated and rainfed conditions.

Apart from improvements in crop, soil and water management, dryland crops (especially legumes) need to be introduced into paddy rotations, the use of blue-green algae and Azolla needs to be maximized, and more organic matter needs to be returned to the soil by way of crop residues, cattle manure and well-made compost. For small farmers, at least, increased use of organic materials will be possible only if cheap alternatives to cattle dung and crop residues as household fuel can be developed and provided (e.g., solar cookers).

2.3.8 Change of crop variety

Modern technology has enabled farmers to increase production by substituting high-yielding varieties for traditional varieties, especially in the case of paddy. Both aus and aman HYVs spread rapidly in the 1970s, even under rainfed conditions, and HYVs of boro paddy have spread rapidly in irrigated areas. New varieties of wheat, potato, mustard, fruit and winter vegetables have also spread rapidly. Obviously, the new varieties have contributed greatly to increased agricultural production and incomes in recent decades, but it is impossible to isolate their specific contribution because their higher yields are also associated with an increased use of fertilizers, more intensive management and, over large areas, the provision of more secure growing conditions through irrigation and flood-protection.

Although HYVs normally are introduced, tested and demonstrated by Government research and extension organizations, their expansion thereafter is mainly by way of farmer-to-farmer extension and seed distribution.[23] Thus, the Pajam paddy variety (called Masori elsewhere in S.E. Asia) spread to almost all parts of Bangladesh in the 1960s and 1970s since it was introduced by the Comilla Rural Development Academy about 1960.

---

[23]*While monitoring intensive crop production programmes in the 1970s, the author frequently observed farmers testing new varieties in a corner of a field — sometimes no more than a square metre — using a few seed or seedlings they had obtained from other farmers. Surprised to see small plots of the Pajam paddy variety in the north of Dinajpur in 1974, the author was told that a farmer had brought back a small amount of seed he had obtained from farmers near Comilla while he was attending a training course at the Comilla Rural Development Academy. Also, following the 1974 flood disaster, farmers (or their representatives) in some areas were reported to have travelled long distances to obtain transplanted aman seedlings from non-affected areas; and in 1977, when early flash floods destroyed most of the boro paddy crop in Sylhet District but flood-levels later in the rainy season were much below average, farmers in south Sylhet obtained aman seedlings from as far away as India in order to grow a crop on basin land which the oldest farmers said had not been used for transplanted aman for fifty years. The two latter examples provide a means for the spread of new crop varieties without official intervention (and even without official recognition!).*

In the mid-to-late1970s, Pajam became the most popular improved paddy variety grown in the country, despite official disapproval of the variety on the grounds of its greater disease susceptibility and lower yield potential than IRRI-BRRI varieties. Obviously, these limitations and its longer growing season were outweighed in the farmers' opinion by Pajam's better grain and straw quality, and by its satisfactory response to modest fertilizer inputs. This example indicates that farmers may be more concerned with optimizing returns on inputs than with maximizing yields and production.

Apart from changing crop varieties, farmers are constantly seeking to improve their local varieties. This they do by collecting and saving seed from the best plant heads. In Bangladesh, the selection and care of seed usually is women's work (which may seem surprising, considering the fact that most women do not visit the fields). By this continuous process of selection, many thousands of paddy varieties have been developed which are adapted to specific agroecological conditions. Farmers have even made selections within HYVs such as IR-8.[24]

2.4 STAGES OF INTENSIFICATION

Table 2.2 shows the successive stages of crop intensification, as observed in various parts of Bangladesh. Tables 2.3 to 2.13 give details of the successive stages on particular land and soil types. The sequences shown in these tables should be regarded as indicative rather than specific. That is because, as is discussed later, many factors are involved in determining the actual sequence followed by an individual farmer or by farmers in a particular area.

Also, under certain conditions (such as the provision of irrigation or drainage in a particular area), farmers may omit one or more steps in the normal sequence: e.g., by changing from subsistence cultivation of broadcast deepwater aman to intensive cultivation of HYV boro paddy. In fact, in order to speed up the rate of increasing agricultural production, employment and incomes, it must be one of the objectives of agricultural planners and Extension officials to identify places in Table 2.2 or in Tables 2.3 to 2.13 where appropriate measures can be taken which will induce or enable farmers to omit steps: that is, to move to a higher stage of intensification without passing through all the usual evolutionary steps.

Three main stages of intensification can be identified, viz.

1. *Simple traditional*: subsistence production of one or more crops of local varieties, without irrigation or use of fertilizers.

2. *Intensive traditional*: cultivation of crops for all of the natural growing season, possibly extended by the use of hand irrigation and construction of soil platforms, and including at least one cash crop or improved crop variety (LIV), but not using modern technical inputs such as HYVs, fertilizers or motorized pump (or Government-provided canal) irrigation.[25]

3. *Modern intensive*: cultivation of one or more crops, including at least one cash crop or HYV crop, for all of the natural growing season, possibly extended by the use of

---

[24]*Interestingly, Bangladeshi farmers' selections were for longer seedlings. This reflected their perception that the first dwarf IRRI varieties, designed for irrigated conditions, were not well adapted to uncontrolled water levels in fields when the crop was grown in the monsoon season.*

[25]*Cash crops are those which are produced primarily for sale. However, it needs to be kept in view that even small subsistence farmers need to sell a proportion of their produce (e.g., paddy or pulses) in order to obtain cash with which to purchase their other food or household needs.*

irrigation or drainage, and using one or more modern technical inputs such as HYVs, fertilizers, motorized or canal irrigation, flood protection, etc.

The boundaries between the main stages are not absolute, of course. For example, jute — included under 'intensive traditional' — is sometimes grown by non-intensive methods similar to those used for subsistence crops in a farmer's other fields.[26] At the other boundary of 'intensive traditional', jute (and other cash crops) may receive a modest dose of fertilizers, without cultivation being in any other ways intensified or modernized. In such cases, the boundaries should be regarded as transitional.

Within each of the main stages, there usually are a number of successive steps of increasing intensification. At each successive step, production and/or income are increased by increasing the number of crops grown in a year, increasing the inputs used (e.g., irrigation, fertilizers), or increasing the value of the crops grown (e.g., by changing from low-value wheat to high-value vegetables). The reason for a farmer moving from one step or stage to the next one may be economic pressure to produce more food or income from his small land holding, or it may be the recognition of an opportunity to increase his production or income as a result of new information received, a new market opened up by the provision of a new road, or the arrival of new technology (e.g., the inclusion of his land within an irrigation and drainage project area).

At certain points, farmers must take critical decisions regarding the future pathway they will follow in order to increase production or income from their land. However, in some cases, the decision is made for them by, for example, the inclusion of their land within an irrigation or drainage project area. Three particularly critical points are:

a. the change from subsistence crop production to the cultivation of one or more cash crops;

b. the change from rainfed production to irrigated production; and

c. the time when, on seasonally-flooded land or Bottomland, production can only be increased further by changing the land type, either by an individual farmer making a raised soil platform or raised beds, or by Government, a community or a group of farmers providing flood protection and drainage to an area.

These critical points are not necessarily reached or passed in that order or even separately. For example, the construction of a soil platform may simultaneously provide the opportunity for irrigation with water which fills the adjoining excavation, or it may necessitate the provision of irrigation (e.g., by hand pump) in order to ensure high-yielding crop production on the platform which will pay for the construction and maintenance of the platform. Similarly, the inclusion of an area in a Government flood protection project (such as the DND project) may allow some farmers to change within one year from simple subsistence production of broadcast deepwater aman to intensive production of one or two,

---

[26] *Jute is not grown entirely as a cash crop. The sticks and a small proportion of the fibre were always retained for domestic use. Also, farmers continued to grow substantial areas of jute even in years when prices for jute fibre were low. In the 1970s, that was partly because they could obtain Government loans to purchase inputs for this crop, but also because jute was often grown as a cleaning crop once in three or four years: when weeding, jute seedlings are easier to differentiate from weed rices and sedges than aus or deepwater aman seedlings. Farmers also recognized the value for soil fertility of leaf-fall from jute plants; later, the dense canopy of a mature jute crop shades out weeds.*

TABLE 2.2
Stages in the intensification of crop production

A. Simple traditional

    1. First clearing of natural vegetation; or first cultivation of new alluvial land.

    2. Grow a single, non-irrigated, subsistence crop: usually in the rainy season, but in the dry season in some depression sites.

    3. Where the growing season is long enough, add a second, non-irrigated, subsistence crop, where possible.

    4. Add a third, non-irrigated, subsistence crop to the annual rotation, where possible.

B. Intensive traditional

    1. Substitute or add one improved crop (LIV), cash crop or improved traditional practice.

    2. Substitute or add a second improved crop, cash crop or traditional practice; or intercrop one or more subsistence or cash crops with a perennial or long-term cash crop.

    3. Where possible, substitute a third (and later perhaps a fourth) cash crop or improved crop; or change to one or more cash crops of higher value.

    4. Where necessary, improve field drainage for dryland crops by making ditches, ridges or raised beds.

    5. Where needed and possible, provide hand irrigation so as to increase production in the dry season.

    6. Where necessary and possible, make a soil platform or raised beds so as to increase production throughout the growing season (without irrigation) or throughout the year (with irrigation). Alternatively, make raised beds on Bottomland or seasonally-flooded land so as to grow cash crops in the dry season.

C. Modern intensive

    1. Substitute or add one or more HYVs for LIV or subsistence crops; or use balanced doses of appropriate fertilizers to increase yields of traditional subsistence or cash crops.

    2. Where necessary, improve field drainage for dryland crops by making ditches, ridges or beds.

    3. Where needed and possible, provide irrigation; or change from hand irrigation to motorized or canal irrigation.

    4. Where necessary and possible, change land or soil type: either make a soil platform or raised beds; or provide flood protection and pump or tidal drainage.

    5. After 2, 3 or 4 above, add one or more cash crops or HYVs.

    6. Use quicker-maturing varieties, relay sowing or intersowing so as to increase the number of crops grown in a year; or change to one or more crops of higher value.

Note: Throughout the main stages B and C, there also is an increase in intensity of management so as to increase individual crop yields or total crop production: e.g., by increasing the use of manure or fertilizers; by better crop, soil and water management; and by changing from broadcast sowing to dibble-sowing, line-sowing or transplanting. Simultaneously, there usually is more intensive use of homestead land, banks of tanks and *ails* (small bunds between fields), mainly for growing vegetables, spices, fruits and gourds, and for paddy seed-beds.

irrigated, HYV paddy crops a year.[27] Elsewhere, the sequence may be different from that shown above: e.g., where soil platforms are used first for rainfed production of kharif subsistence and cash crops, and only later are provided with irrigation in order to grow additional or higher-value cash crops such as fruit or vegetables throughout the year.

2.5 CHOICE OF PATHWAY

Fundamentally, the choice of pathways for intensification depends on environmental factors: i.e., the length and duration of the rainy season; land type and risk of natural disasters; and

---

[27] *Farmers are not always quick to make such changes: see Chapter 3, Section 3.3.2.*

soil type. It depends also on whether the influence of these factors can be changed by irrigation, flood protection and/or drainage.

Intensification also implies that part of the increased production must be sold off the farm to pay for the additional inputs used. In intensive traditional agriculture, the additional inputs may have been mainly hired labour. In modern intensive agriculture, cash inputs such as fertilizers are also used. Therefore, the choice of crop or crops to be grown depends on the availability of a market for them, which can be affected by Government pricing and procurement policies, by communications and by competition between farmers.

A particular farmer's choice of one pathway or another — including a decision *not* to intensify his production — can depend, also, on the size of his holding, his economic resources (including family labour and draught animals) and the alternative opportunities which exist for investment or employment.

The farmer's decision may not be a simple one, therefore. It is complicated further by the fact that most farmers — even small farmers — have fragmented holdings, with plots scattered on different soil and land types in different parts of the village, or even in different villages. Bari (1974) describes a progressive farmer in the Comilla Kotwali Thana who, in 1974, had a holding of 3.10 acres, of which 2.51 acres were cropped, divided into 17 plots ranging in size from 0.04 to 0.32 acres. On those 17 plots, the farmer had 17 different crop rotations in 1973, including 9 HYVs of paddy and 6 local paddy varieties with specific properties or qualities. Over a five-year period, a total of 54 rotations were used, and none of them was repeated twice on the same plot. In part, the changes in rotations were responses to different weather and flooding conditions experienced in each year. The complexity of the management decisions which this fragmentation of holdings implies belies the popular image of the simple, ignorant peasant. It raises important questions, too, regarding methods of applied research and extension in such complex management situations.[28]

Regarding options available to the farmer, the following general observations can be made.

a. Level Highland and Medium Highland provide a wider range of options for intensification than do more-deeply-flooded land types. Deep flooding in the kharif season or permanent wetness generally limits the kinds of crops that can be grown.

b. Permeable loamy soils provide a wider range of options, especially regarding choice of cash crops, than do sands and clays. The latter soil types have a lower moisture-holding capacity and, in the case of clays, may provide tillage and waterlogging problems for growing dryland crops.

c. Without irrigation, the relatively wetter eastern and central parts of Bangladesh are generally better suited for double and triple cropping patterns (except in deep depressions) than are the drier western Districts.

d. With or without irrigation, the drier climate of western Districts makes them generally more suitable for dryland crops than the wetter eastern and central Districts, especially for crops such as cotton, cigarette tobacco, wheat, maize, sorghum, pulses, soya bean and groundnut which are sensitive to temporary waterlogging after heavy rainfall.

e. The wetter eastern Districts are correspondingly better suited than western Districts for transplanted paddy (on land where flooding depths in the growing period are suitable).

[28]*See Brammer 2000, Chapter 6.*

Under dire economic circumstances, small farmers may grow crops or use practices which might seem impractical or uneconomic. Examples are:

- using hand methods of irrigation (e.g., hand pumps) for growing boro paddy, which may require round-the-clock pumping in the hot dry season;[29]
- using intensive horticultural techniques for growing wheat on soils that had previously been puddled for transplanted paddy cultivation: that is, making ridges or beds by hand, and irrigating almost daily by hand, as widely practised on the Barind Tract in Bogra District in the late-1970s;
- making raised cultivation platforms.

Such practices may be feasible only where the opportunity cost of labour is close to zero.

Tables 2.3 to 2.13 give an outline of the stages of agricultural intensification on different land and soil types and indicate possible future intensification possibilities. The tables provide a guide to planners, researchers and extensionists to help them in identifying appropriate methods of assisting farmers to intensify production using traditional and modern techniques on particular land and soil types. More detailed information is given in the manual '17 possible ways to increase agricultural production' (Brammer, 1981a).[30]

2.6 SOCIAL CONSTRAINTS

Not unexpectedly, the most intensive practices generally are used by small farmers, probably mainly those owning about 1-3 acres. Very small farmers who own less than about 1 acre may lack the resources (including draught cattle) to cultivate their land intensively, or they may not like to take the risk of doing so. Often, such very small farmers prefer to cultivate low-input subsistence crops and sell their spare labour time to other farmers or employers. Those who own only a small fraction of an acre may prefer to lease it out to relatively bigger farmers and use all their labour time for cash employment.

On the other hand, farmers owning more than about 5 acres usually do not farm their land intensively; (the lower limit probably varies from place to place with land quality and with considerations of social status.)[31] Typically, 'big' farmers use share-croppers or hired labour to farm their land, and they take 50 percent of the gross output without investing anything in production (other than perhaps loans which they may make to their tenants, the interest on which may further increase the proportion of the harvest which they take). With 5 acres of land, an owner can therefore obtain the production equivalent of 2.5 acres virtually cost-free. In the Highland and Medium Highland areas in the north-west and south-east of Bangladesh where big land-holdings are most widespread, 2.5 acres growing a single crop of local transplanted aman can produce about 1.25 tons of milled rice in a year. That is more than sufficient to feed an average family for a year.

Many land-owners in these areas apparently possess much more than 5 acres. In fact, these areas provide two of the three traditional rice-surplus areas of the country, despite the

---

[29] *In Jamalpur District in the late-1970s, hand pumps were observed to be operated by men and boys during daylight hours and —for reasons of* purdah *— by women and girls during the night.*

[30] *See footnote 4 above.*

[31] *During field trips in the 1970s, the author observed that, whereas 'big' farmers in Comilla District would work alongside their labourers in the field, those owning as little as 1 acre in Kushtia District considered themselves as* maliks *(managers) and would only supervise field labour.*

prevalent single cropping of local varieties without the use of fertilizers or other modern inputs. (The third major rice-surplus area is the Sylhet-Kishoreganj haor areas, which also is an area of big land-holdings and single cropping of local paddy varieties, in this case boro.)[32] A report in 1979 estimated that holdings of 5 acres and above occupy more than 48 percent of the total agricultural land in Bangladesh, and they are owned by only 13 percent of rural households, which have an average holding of 10.3 acres (Januzzi & Peach, 1979). Add to this the land which is share-cropped on behalf of absentee urban land-owners with holdings less than 5 acres — a common practice among Government and commercial employees and small businessmen — and the implication is that more than half the agricultural land in Bangladesh is presently not available for intensive cultivation because of land-tenure constraints.[33]

2.7 DANGEROUS DIRECTIONS

There are signs that the situation described at the end of the last section may be beginning to change. The catalyst generally is the introduction of LLP or tube-well irrigation, but Gill (1981) reported similar trends where tractors or power-tillers had been introduced. In areas of big land-holdings, such machines tend to be controlled by a single influential person or family, even where they are not owned directly. Where they are owned, they seem often to be used to gain control of a larger holding or a consolidated holding, either by eviction of former tenants, the leasing in of additional land for direct farming, or the judicious use of loans for irrigation or cultivation services leading eventually to the acquisition of the debtors' plots.

The introduction of irrigation can undoubtedly lead to increased crop production. However, it does not always provide a higher cropping intensity or generate more employment. Clay (1978) reported the example of a single, irrigated, HYV boro crop employing 109 man-days per acre displacing a rotation of mixed aus+aman followed by a rabi pulse crop which employed 125 man-days per acre per annum.

In the case of mechanized tillage, Gill (*op.cit.*) found no evidence that the use of tractors or power-tillers increased either cropping intensity or crop production. What it did was increase the operators' profits and the size of their operational holdings. However, a single power-tiller used only for land preparation could displace as many as 700 man-days of labour in a year. That labour displacement effect could increase much further in future if, as seems probable, tractors or power-tillers were to be used for mechanizing other operations

---

[32]*Both in the coastal zone and in the haor areas, a considerable amount of migrant labour is used for crop harvesting. In the haor areas, the traditional system was to use contract labour gangs (mainly from Faridpur District), who received around 10 percent of the harvest in payment.*

[33]*Twenty years after the original paper was written, the land-tenure situation deserves re-examination to investigate the possible impact of modern agricultural technology on land holdings and land management. Two aspects deserve particular attention. 1. Has the spread of modern technology (especially HYVs and irrigation) made it more economic for 'big' land-owners to farm the land themselves instead of through share-croppers? There were indications in Barisal District in the 1970s that some big land-owners were growing irrigated HYV boro (or aus) directly (or through a relative) but using share-croppers to grow a following local transplanted aman crop. 2. Has the spread of STWs and power-tillers into areas of big land holdings in the 1980s and 1990s led to consolidation of fragmented holdings? Such a change would have considerable operational advantages for land and crop management, but it could have adverse implications for the tenant cultivators it would displace. This subject is discussed in Section 2.7.*

presently carried out manually, such as sowing, transplanting, weeding, harvesting, transportation and threshing, as has happened in several countries of south-east Asia and in China.

The mechanization pathway to intensification is therefore fraught with the danger of adverse social consequences. Also, increasing production by means which reduce employment, or which provide only a small increase in employment, must eventually bring about a situation where there is not enough purchasing capacity in rural areas to absorb the increased production. Therefore, Government policies aiming to increase agricultural production need to be framed with an awareness of their wider implications for employment and incomes. An indiscriminate policy of mechanization or of motorized irrigation provides a panacea only for the manufacturers, the middlemen and the investors. It does not benefit the national economy if it leads to increased unemployment and pauperization; nor does it benefit the machine owners if, due to lack of consumer purchasing capacity, it depresses crop prices below the costs of production.

Especially is this the case where Governments heavily subsidize the purchase and operation of such equipment. In poor and densely-populated countries such as Bangladesh, subsidies deserve to be used, if at all, only for measures which will directly increase production, employment and incomes in the areas where they are used. Such could be the case with tractors or irrigation equipment owned and operated by genuine village cooperatives within which the benefits would be shared by all the members. However, where socio-political conditions prevent the formation or operation of genuine cooperatives, then it would seem preferable to phase out the subsidies on motorized equipment.[34] Subsidies could then be transferred, if needed, to the provision of small-scale equipment or improvements which could increase the production and employment of small farmers and agricultural labourers. Examples are:

- hand pumps or dug wells for irrigation;
- the construction of raised cultivation platforms in flood-prone areas;
- seed or planting material of new or improved crop varieties;
- more rural roads to improve access to markets and services;
- more crop purchase centres to stabilize prices;
- more crop processing facilities to enlarge markets and employment opportunities.

The provision of large-scale flood-protection and drainage projects in densely-populated, deeply-flooded, floodplain areas with predominantly small land-holdings (as in the Chandpur Irrigation Project area) would achieve the same objectives.

2.8 PLANNING DOWN OR PLANNING UP?

As was indicated in Section 2.2, many factors may be involved in intensifying agricultural production in any particular area: pressure of population on the land; land quality; water resources; available technology; Government development policies and programmes; markets; relative crop prices; socio-political and socio-economic conditions; and cultural traditions.

This complexity has often been overlooked by Government agencies (and aid donors) in designing top-down, national or regional development plans. Often, there seems to be an

---

[34] *Subsidies on fertilizers were gradually reduced during the 1980s, and direct subsidies on irrigation equipment and power-tillers were removed in 1988.*

aversion to recognizing or accepting complexity, lest it delay the start of a project or require coordination between a number of agencies. Complexity equally is apt to be overlooked in framing top-down agricultural research and extension programmes; (has anyone, for example, considered what are the appropriate research and extension methods for areas with big land-owners plus share-croppers?; also, whether methods used in areas with resident big land-owners, as in Dinajpur District, are suitable in areas of absentee land-owners, as in parts of Noakhali, Barisal, Patuakhali and Khulna Districts?). The frequent failure or disappointing progress of such development plans is probably due to bureaucratic (and aid-donor) ignorance of actual development opportunities and constraints at the micro level, or a reluctance to adapt plans to complex realities.

These failures compare unfavourably with the record of achievement by the farmers themselves. Obviously, it is largely through the farmers' own innovations that foodgrain production has apparently tripled over the past 100 years.[35] This record of achievement strongly suggests that planners should not plan *for* the farmers but should plan *with* the farmers. And since small farmers in the 1-5 acres class apparently are the most innovative and progressive, policies should be framed so as to provide this class of farmers with incentives and security for investments in increased production. Policies should equally be framed to increase employment opportunities for small farmers and landless labourers.

Such policies would be more likely to succeed if they included a large element of bottom-up planning. Development plans might then be better adapted to locally-perceived resources, opportunities and needs. Government's Village Development Planning Programme and the Thana Land Use Development Planning Programme indicate a promising move in this direction.[36]

2.9 CROP INTENSIFICATION TABLES

2.9.1 How to use Tables 2.3 to 2.13

1. Identify the land type (i.e., Highland, Medium Highland, etc.) and the soil type (i.e., permeable or impermeable) of interest. Definitions of the land and soil types are given below in Section 2.9.2.
2. Turn to the relevant table for the land and soil type identified. The tables are presented in the sequence from Highland to Bottomland.
3. Identify the present stage of crop intensification and read the relevant column in order to identify the present level of intensification in the area of interest. Definitions of the column headings are given in Section 2.9.2.
4. In the same column, read the 'possible improvements' section. Decide which of the steps suggested is most suitable for the area of interest. If further information is needed about these steps, refer to the relevant land and soil type table in the manual 'Seventeen possible ways to increase crop production in Bangladesh' (Brammer, 1981a).[37]

---

[35]*This statement now needs to be qualified. The considerable increases in paddy and wheat production which have occurred since the 1970s have largely been due to Government policies which promoted the use of HYVs, fertilizers and irrigation.*

[36]*Those programmes were soon abandoned: see footnote 2 above.*

[37]*See footnote 4 above.*

5. In general, the sequence of intensification is as follows.

   a. Use more manure, tank silt or fertilizers in order to increase yields of present crops.

   b. Improve management in other ways: e.g., use recommended seed rates, plant spacing, weeding times, etc.

   c. If possible, increase the number of crops grown within the available growing season. If necessary, intersow or relay-sow crops, or use quicker-maturing varieties.

   d. Increase production or income by growing a higher-yielding variety or cash crop.

   e. If necessary, and if possible, provide irrigation in order to lengthen the growing season.

   f. If necessary, and if possible, change the land or soil type in order to lengthen the growing season; (this usually is accompanied by step d).

   g. Continue to increase production or profits by increasing the number of crops grown in a year, or by growing one or more crops of higher value, and using recommended intensive management practices.

2.9.2 Explanation of terms used

1. Land types

Highland is land above normal flood-level. It is divided in the tables into *level* and *sloping*. Sloping Highland needs protection against erosion if it is cleared from forest or grassland: see Chapter 13.

Medium Highland is land which normally is flooded up to about 3 feet deep in the rainy season. Land which is shallowly flooded for a few hours at high tide each day is included. Where the soils are suitable, aus and transplanted aman can be grown on this land type.[38]

Medium Lowland is land which normally is flooded up to 3-6 feet deep in the rainy season. On suitable soils, mixed aus+aman can be grown on this land type.

Lowland is land which normally is flooded deeper than 6 feet in the rainy season, but which becomes dry for all or most of the dry season. Lowland is not suitable for growing aus paddy, but it may be suitable for deepwater aman.

Bottomland is land in depressions which normally stays wet for all or most of the dry season. Local boro paddy is usually the only suitable crop. Most Bottomland is deeply flooded in the rainy season, but some is only moderately deeply or shallowly flooded. The important difference between Bottomland and other land types is that it stays wet for all or most of the dry season, so cannot be used for dryland rabi crops (or for broadcast sowing aus or deepwater aman paddy), whereas other land types become dry for most or all of the dry season (except where they are kept wet artificially by irrigation).

2. Soil types

Permeable soils allow water to enter and pass through rapidly. Water does not stay on the surface for more than a few hours after heavy rainfall or irrigation. These soils are not suitable for transplanted paddy unless they are naturally flooded or stay wet because of a high water-table during the rainy season. Permeable soils usually are:

- sands;
- light loams which have not been puddled for transplanting paddy;

[38] *For subdivisions of Medium Highland, see Table 1.2.*

- deep red and brown clays on the Madhupur and Barind Tracts (such as those which are used for jackfruit trees).

Impermeable soils do not allow water to enter and pass through rapidly. Water may stay on the surface for several days after heavy rainfall or irrigation. Where there is sufficient rainfall or irrigation, these soils are better suited for transplanted paddy than they are for dryland crops. If dryland crops are grown, drains are needed and careful irrigation is required to prevent waterlogging the topsoil. Impermeable soils include:

- heavy clays (except on the Ganges River Floodplain, where most clays are of a cracking type which is moderately permeable);
- loams and clays puddled for transplanted paddy.

Peat soils consist of decayed organic matter which stays wet all through the year. If drained and allowed to become dry, peat quickly shrinks and decomposes, thus lowering the land level close to the water-table again.

3. Column headings

Natural vegetation is the vegetation which it is believed covered the soils before they were brought under cultivation. In the case of new alluvium which is brought under cultivation as soon as it is deposited, there is no natural vegetation and the term *bare alluvium* is used.

Simple traditional means unimproved methods of cultivation using local crop varieties, mainly for subsistence use.

Intensive traditional means the cultivation of crops for all of the natural growing season using local or locally-improved varieties, hand irrigation (where needed), and organic manures. (Since about 1950, it may also have included the use of fertilizers, but often insufficiently or inefficiently.) Usually, at least one of the crops is a cash crop.

Modern intensive means the cultivation of crops for all of the natural growing season, or for the whole of the year with irrigation and/or drainage, using modern technical inputs: e.g., HYVs (where available for the crop); fertilizers; pest/disease management; irrigation (by motorized or hand methods); flood protection and drainage (where relevant and available). All or a substantial part of the crop production is for sale.

Possible improvements are methods by which crop production could possibly be increased, depending on the present intensity of cultivation, the farmers' resources, technical feasibility (e.g., provision of flood protection or irrigation), and soil-crop suitability. Possible improvements under 'simple traditional' and 'intensive traditional' may follow either the traditional intensive or the modern intensive pathway.

4. Abbreviations and symbols

HYV	=	high yielding variety
LIV	=	locally improved variety
LV	=	local (traditional) variety
/	=	or; e.g., aus/mesta means that either aus or mesta can be grown on the same piece of land in different years
–	=	followed by: e.g., B.aus-rabi pulses means b.aus followed by rabi pulses in the annual crop rotation
±	=	with or without

B.aus	=	broadcast aus; (includes also line-sown and dibble-sown)
B.aman	=	broadcast (deepwater) aman
T.aman	=	transplanted aman; (t.deepwater aman = transplanted deepwater aman)
LLP	=	low-lift pump
TW	=	tube-well (either deep or shallow, but not including hand pump).

TABLE 2.3

Stages in crop intensification on level Highland, permeable soils[1]

Natural vegetation	Simple traditional	Intensive traditional	Modern intensive
Forest; (sometimes replaced by grassland, bamboo or scrub after deforestation)	1. B.aus, kaon, mesta, kharif pulses or oilseeds, arum 2. B.aus-rabi pulses or oilseeds 3. Tree crops: jackfruit, mango, coconut, betelnut or others; (usually around homesteads and on field boundaries)	1. B.aus or groundnut-rabi tobacco, vegetables, spices, etc. 2. Sugarcane, ginger, turmeric, arum, pineapple 3. Same as 2, but intercropped with kharif or rabi pulses, vegetables, etc. 4. Two, three or four successive kharif and rabi vegetables ± aus, jute, wheat, kaon, etc. 5. Betel leaf (*pan*), banana 6. Improved orchards (e.g., mango) ± intercropped b.aus, pulses, barley, etc.	1. HYV b.aus-cotton, tobacco, wheat, potato, rabi vegetables 2. Same as 1, but HYV kharif crops (pulses, soyabean, vegetables) substituted for aus 3. HYV sugarcane or banana, intercropped with kharif or rabi vegetables, pulses, soyabean 4. Same as 'Intensive traditional', but with use of fertilizers, pest management and/or HYVs ± group irrigation
	Possible improvements[2]	**Possible improvements[2]**	**Possible improvements[2]**
	a. Use more manure or fertilizer b. Introduce new varieties (LIV/HYV) c. Grow one or more cash crops d. Grow an extra crop: e.g., change from 1 to 2 above; or from 1 above to 1 under 'Intensive traditional' or 'Modern intensive' e. Use irrigation: either hand irrigation or group irrigation f. For share-croppers, improve tenancy terms so as to provide an incentive for investment in extra inputs	a. Use more compost or manure b. Make ridges or beds, if necessary, to prevent waterlogging of kharif crops c. Provide hand irrigation (where not used already) d. Improve water use and management e. Grow one or more additional crops, where feasible, by relay cropping, intercropping or mixed cropping f. Increase the value of production by growing one or more high-value crops: e.g., banana, betel leaf, vegetables g. Introduce HYVs, fertilizers and/or group irrigation: see 'Modern intensive'	a. Use recommended methods of crop, soil and water management b. Grow one or more additional kharif or rabi crops by relay cropping or intercropping, where possible c. Introduce new HYVs as they become available d. Introduce new crops: e.g., maize, sorghum, soyabean, HYV mustard, HYV pulses, etc. e. Increase the value of production by introducing one or more high-value crops: e.g., quick-growing fruit and vegetables

Notes: 1. Includes raised platforms.

2. For saline soils, try to prevent salt from coming to the surface during the dry season by:

   a. covering the surface with a mulch of straw or leaves after the last kharif crop;

   b. making drains between the fields in the kharif season;

   c. providing irrigation (where feasible).

   Where irrigation is not feasible, try to grow a quick-maturing rabi crop after harvesting the last kharif crop, if the soil is not too dry or too wet for sowing at that time.

TABLE 2.4

Stages in crop intensification on level Highland, impermeable soils

Natural vegetation	Simple traditional	Intensive traditional	Modern intensive
Acacia forest or savannah woodland	1. LV t.aman 2. LV b.aus-LV t.aman	1. LIV t.aman 2. LV/LIV b.aus-LIV t.aman 3. LV/LIV t.aus-LIV t.aman 4. Same as 2 or 3, plus rabi pulses 5. Same as 2 or 3, plus hand-irrigated rabi crops on ridges or beds (e.g., LV potato, vegetables, spices, wheat) 6. On raised platforms: one or two paddy seedbeds; or one, two or three kharif and rabi vegetables, spices or oilseeds	1. HYV t.aus or HYV t.aman (rainfed) 2. HYV t.aus-LIV/HYV t.aman (rainfed) 3. HYV boro-LIV/HYV t.aman (irrigated) 4. Same as 2 or 3, plus HYV wheat, potato, vegetables or spices (on ridges or beds, with irrigation) 5. HYV boro-LIV/HYV t.aus-LIV/HYV t.aman 6. Same as 5, plus HYV wheat, potato, vegetables, mustard, soyabean
	Possible improvements[1] a. Use more manure or fertilizer b. Introduce new varieties (LIV/HYV) c. Grow one or more cash crops: e.g., paddy for seed; rabi crops d. Grow an extra crop: e.g., change from 1 to 2 above; or from 1 above to 2, 3, 4, 5 or 6 under 'Intensive traditional' or 'Modern intensive' e. Use irrigation: either hand irrigation or group irrigation f. For share-croppers, improve tenancy terms so as to provide an incentive for investment in extra inputs	**Possible improvements[1]** a. Use more compost or manure b. Provide hand irrigation (where not used already) c. Improve water use and management d. After t.aus or t.aman, make ridges or beds so as to grow rabi cash crops (with irrigation) e. Introduce HYVs, fertilizers and/or group irrigation: see 'Modern intensive'	**Possible improvements[1]** a. Use recommended methods of crop, soil and water management b. Introduce new HYVs as they become available c. Grow one or more additional kharif or rabi crops: e.g., change from 1 to 2 or 3 above; from 3 to 4 or 5; or from 4 or 5 to 6 d. Make raised beds or platforms and provide hand irrigation: grow banana, guava, pineapple, kharif and rabi vegetables, spices. Protect soil surface against heavy rainfall by mulching with straw or leaves

Notes: 1. For saline soils, try to prevent salt from coming to the surface during the dry season by:
a. covering the surface with a mulch of straw or leaves after the last kharif crop;
b. making drains between the fields in the kharif season;
c. providing irrigation (where feasible).
Where irrigation is not feasible, try to grow a quick-maturing rabi crop after harvesting the last kharif crop, if the soil is not too dry or too wet for sowing at that time.

TABLE 2.5

Stages in crop intensification on sloping Highland, permeable soils[1]

Natural vegetation	Simple traditional	Intensive traditional	Modern intensive
Forest; (sometimes replaced by grassland, bamboo or scrub after deforestation)	1. *Jhum* (shifting) cultivation: mixed b.aus, maize, kharif pulses, sesamum, gourds, etc.; locally with hill cotton, banana, cassava 2. Tree crops: banana or jackfruit 3. (Madhupur and Barind Tracts, homestead platforms, embankments): b.aus, kharif vegetables, spices, pulses, etc. **Possible improvements** a. Use recommended soil conservation practices: • avoid steep slopes • clear only small areas at a time • make narrow fields along the contour • cultivate crops on the contour • keep the soil surface covered with crops or mulch • use manure or fertilizers where possible b. Grow fodder crops (grasses, legumes) c. Plant trees or bamboo as cash crops for firewood, poles, pulp or fruit. Use recommended practices d. Return steep or eroded slopes to forest	1. Intensive *jhum* cultivation: arum, pineapple, ginger 2. (Moist hill-foot sites): betel leaf or banana gardens 3. (Madhupur and Barind Tracts, homestead platforms, embankments): kharif and rabi vegetables, spices, tobacco, etc. (usually with hand-irrigation) **Possible improvements** Same as for 'Simple traditional'	1. Tree crops: tea, coffee, rubber, cashew, etc. 2. Soil conservation cultivation: pineapple, hill cotton, fodder legumes 3. Forest plantations: • bamboo (for pulp, poles) • quick-growing trees (for firewood, poles, matches) • timber trees (e.g., teak) **Possible improvements** Same as for 'Simple traditional', but with more emphasis on producing cash crops (e.g., firewood, fruit)

Notes: 1.   Includes sloping land in hill areas, in the red soil areas of the Madhupur and Barind Tracts, and on homestead platforms, embankments, etc.

TABLE 2.6
Stages in crop intensification on sloping Highland, impermeable soils[1]

Natural vegetation	Simple traditional	Intensive traditional	Modern intensive
Acacia forest or scrub	1. Grazing land 2. B.aus, kharif pulses, groundnut or vegetables. (Growth usually is poor, yields very low and soil damaged by erosion, leading to early abandonment.) **Possible improvements** a. Do not overgraze grassland b. Grow fodder grasses or legumes c. Plant trees suitable for clay soils (for firewood, charcoal, poles, lac culture, etc.) Use recommended practices d. Make terraces: see 'Intensive traditional' and 'Modern intensive' columns e. Use more manure or fertilizers f. Provide irrigation, if possible, for improved paddy cultivation on terraces	1. On terraced fields: LV t.aman (rainfed) **Possible improvements** a. Same as for 'Simple traditional', but with more emphasis on: • using more manure or compost • maintaining terraces • providing irrigation • using recommended soil conservation practices b. Introduce HYVs, fertilizers, group irrigation: see 'Modern intensive'	1. On terraced fields: LIV/HYV t.aman 2. On terraced fields with irrigation: HYV t.aus-HYV t.aman 3. Same as 2, plus HYV wheat, potato, vegetables, spices on ridges or beds 4. On sides of platforms: intensive vegetables (with hand irrigation) 5. On embankments: fodder grasses, legumes; seedbeds **Possible improvements** Same as for 'Intensive traditional', but with more emphasis on: • using balanced fertilizer doses and more organic matter • using recommended methods of crop, soil and water management, including soil conservation methods • growing crops all through the year (with irrigation): e.g., change from 1 to 2 above, or from 2 to 3

Notes: 1.   Includes sloping clay soil on the Madhupur and Barind Tracts, and on the sides of homestead platforms, embankments, etc.

TABLE 2.7

Stages in crop intensification on Medium Highland, permeable soils

Natural vegetation	Simple traditional	Intensive traditional	Modern intensive
Swamp grassland or bare alluvium	1. B.aus or kaon 2. B.aus-rabi pulses or oilseeds 3. T.aman (in wet areas) 4. B.aus or kaon-t.aman (in wet areas) **Possible improvements[1]** a. Use more manure or fertilizer b. Introduce new varieties (LIV/HYV) c. Grow one or more cash crops d. Grow an extra crop: e.g., change from 1 to 2 above; or from 3 to 4 e. Use irrigation: either hand irrigation or group irrigation f. Make soil platforms so as to grow Highland cash crops: see Table 2.3 g. For share-croppers, improve tenancy terms so as to provide an incentive for investment in extra inputs	1. B.aus or jute-rabi pulses or oilseeds 2. B.aus or jute-rabi cash crop (vegetables, spices, tobacco, LV potato) 3. Sugarcane 4. Sugarcane intercropped with rabi pulses, vegetables, etc. 5. (In wet areas): LV/LIV b.aus or jute-LV/LIV t.aman ± rabi pulses/oilseeds **Possible improvements[1]** a. Use more compost or manure b. Provide hand irrigation (where not used already) c. Improve water use and management d. Make drains, ridges or beds for rabi crops to prevent waterlogging by winter rains or irrigation e. Grow one or more additional crops, where feasible, by relay cropping, intercropping or mixed cropping f. Make soil platforms so as to grow Highland cash crops: see Table 2.3 g. Introduce HYVs, fertilizers and/or group irrigation: see 'Modern intensive'	1. HYV b.aus-one or two rabi cash crops 2. Sugarcane intercropped with irrigated rabi vegetables, potato 3. (In wet areas): LIV/HYV t.aus-LIV/HYV t.aman 4. Same as 3, plus HYV wheat, potato, vegetables, spices **Possible improvements[1]** a. Use recommended methods of crop, soil and water management b. Introduce new HYVs as they become available c. Introduce new rabi or early kharif crops: e.g., maize, sorghum, soyabean d. Grow one or more additional kharif or rabi crops by relay cropping or intercropping, where possible e. Grow Highland crops (see Table 2.3) by: • making soil platforms and providing hand irrigation; or • providing flood protection and pump or tidal drainage ± modern irrigation

Notes: 1. For saline soils, try to prevent salt from coming to the surface during the dry season by:

a. covering the surface with a mulch of straw or leaves after the last kharif crop;

b. making drains between the fields in the kharif season;

c. providing irrigation (where feasible).

Where irrigation is not feasible, try to grow a quick-maturing rabi crop after harvesting the last kharif crop. if the soil is not too dry or too wet for sowing at that time.

TABLE 2.8

Stages in crop intensification on Medium Highland, impermeable soils

Natural vegetation	Simple traditional	Intensive traditional	Modern intensive
Swamp grassland or bare alluvium	1. LV t.aman 2. LV b.aus-LV t.aman 3. (In wet areas): LV t.aus-LV t.aman	1. LIV t.aman 2. LV/LIV b.aus or jute-LV/LIV t.aman 3. Same as 1 or 2, plus khesari/other rabi pulses 4. LV/LIV t.aus-LV/LIV t.aman 5. Same as 2, 3 or 4, plus irrigated potato, wheat, vegetables, spices (on ridges or beds)	1. HYV t.aus or HYV t.aman (rainfed) 2. HYV t.aus-LIV t.aman (rainfed) 3. HYV boro-LIV/HYV t.aman (irrigated) 4. Same as 2 or 3, plus irrigated HYV potato, wheat, vegetables or spices (on ridges or beds) 5. HYV boro-LIV/HYV t.aus-LIV/HYV t.aman 6. Same as 5, plus irrigated HYV wheat, potato or vegetables, or mustard or soyabean on residual soil moisture

Simple traditional — Possible improvements[1]

a. Use more manure or fertilizer
b. Introduce new varieties (LIV/HYV)
c. Grow one or more cash crops: e.g., paddy for seed; rabi crops
d. Grow an extra crop: e.g., change from 1 to 2 or 3 above; or from 1, 2 or 3 above to rotations under 'Intensive traditional' or 'Modern intensive'
e. Use irrigation: either hand irrigation or group irrigation
f. Make soil platforms so as to grow Highland cash crops: see Table 2.4
g. For share-croppers, improve tenancy terms so as to provide an incentive for investment in extra inputs

Intensive traditional — Possible improvements[1]

a. Use more compost or manure
b. Provide hand irrigation (where not used already)
c. Improve water use and management
d. After t.aus or t.aman, make ridges or beds so as to grow rabi cash crops (with irrigation)
e. Make soil platforms so as to grow Highland cash crops: see Table 2.4
f. Introduce HYVs, fertilizers and/or group irrigation: see 'Modern intensive'

Modern intensive — Possible improvements[1]

a. Use recommended methods of crop, soil and water management
b. Introduce new HYVs as they become available
c. Grow one or more additional kharif or rabi crops: e.g., change from 1 to 2 or 3 above; from 3 to 4 or 5; or from 5 to 6
d. Grow Highland crops (see Table 2.4) by:
- making soil platforms and providing hand irrigation; or
- providing flood protection and pump or tidal drainage ± modern irrigation

Notes: 1. On saline soils:

a. provide embankments (with sluices) to keep out saline water;
b. provide irrigation (where feasible) so as to grow a quick-maturing boro crop.

Where irrigation is not feasible, try to grow a quick-maturing rabi crop as soon as possible after harvesting the last kharif crop, if the soil is not too dry or too wet for sowing at that time.

TABLE 2.9

Stages in crop intensification on Medium Lowland, permeable soils

Natural vegetation	Simple traditional	Intensive traditional	Modern intensive
Swamp grassland or bare alluvium	1. B.aman 2. Mixed b.aus+aman 3. Mixed b.aus+aman-khesari, maskalai, mustard	1. Mixed b.aus+aman or jute-rabi pulses or oilseeds 2. Mixed b.aus+aman or jute-LV/LIV rabi cash crop (potato, vegetables, spices) 3. Same as 1 or 2 above, but with kaon, *bhurra, shama* or sesamum substituted for aus 4. Mixed b.aus+aman or jute-rabi pulses, mustard-kaon, sesamum or chilli; (the following kharif crops are sown through the standing kaon, sesamum or chilli)	1. Mixed b.aus+aman or jute-HYV wheat, potato, vegetables, spices 2. Mixed b.aus+aman or jute-two rabi crops (e.g., two vegetables, two crops of potato, potato-melon or pumpkin) 3. Transplanted deepwater aman-irrigated HYV boro 4. Transplanted deepwater aman-mustard-irrigated HYV boro
	Possible improvements	**Possible improvements**	**Possible improvements**

	a. Use more manure or fertilizer
	b. Introduce new varieties (LIV/HYV)
	c. Grow one or more cash crops: e.g., jute, potato
	d. Grow an extra crop: e.g., change from 1 to 2 above; or from 2 to 3; or from 2 or 3 above to 2 under 'Modern intensive'
	e. Use irrigation (if needed): either hand irrigation or group irrigation
	f. Make soil platforms so as to grow Highland cash crops: see Table 2.3
	g. For share-croppers, improve tenancy terms so as to provide an incentive for investment in extra inputs
		a. Improve soil, crop and water management
		b. Use more compost or manure
		c. Provide hand irrigation (where not used already)
		d. Grow an extra crop, where feasible: e.g.. change from 1 to 2 above; from 2 to 4; or from 1 or 2 above to 2 under 'Modern intensive'
		e. Make soil platforms so as to grow Highland cash crops: see Table 2.3
		f. Introduce HYVs, fertilizers and/or group irrigation: see 'Modern intensive'
			a. Use recommended methods of crop, soil and water management
			b. Introduce new HYVs as they become available. Also, introduce better varieties of aus and deepwater aman from other areas
			c. Introduce new rabi or early kharif crops: e.g., maize, vegetables, melon
			d. Grow an additional crop, if possible: e.g.. change from 1 to 2 or 4 above
			e. Grow Highland crops (see Table 2.3) by:
			  • making soil platforms and providing hand irrigation; or
			  • providing flood protection and pump or tidal drainage ± modern irrigation

TABLE 2.10

Stages in crop intensification on Medium Lowland, impermeable soils

Natural vegetation	Simple traditional	Intensive traditional	Modern intensive
Swamp grassland or bare alluvium	1. B.aman 2. Mixed b.aus+aman 3. Mixed b.aus+aman-khesari	1. Mixed b.aus+aman or jute-rabi pulses or oilseeds 2. Mixed b.aus+aman or jute-LV/LIV rabi cash crop (wheat, potato, vegetables, spices) grown on ridges or beds, with hand irrigation 3. Same as 1 above, but with kaon, *bhurra, shama* or sesamum substituted for aus or jute 4. LV/LIV boro (with hand irrigation)	1. HYV boro 2. HYV boro-transplanted deepwater aman 3. Mixed b.aus+aman or jute-HYV wheat, potato, vegetables or spices (on ridges or beds, with hand irrigation)
	Possible improvements a. Use more manure or fertilizer b. Introduce new varieties (LIV/HYV) c. Grow one or more cash crops: e.g., jute, rabi vegetables d. Grow an extra crop: e.g., change from 1 to 2 or 3 above; or from 1 or 2 above to 1, 2 or 3 under 'Intensive traditional' e. Use irrigation (if needed): either hand irrigation or group irrigation f. Make soil platforms so as to grow Highland cash crops: see Table 2.4 g. For share-croppers, improve tenancy terms so as to provide an incentive for investment in extra inputs	**Possible improvements** a. Improve soil, crop and water management b. Use more compost or manure, especially on cash crops c. Provide hand irrigation (where not used already) d. Grow an extra crop or a better cash crop, where feasible: e.g., change from 1 to 3 above; or from 1 or 3 above to 2 or 3 under 'Modern intensive' e. Make soil platforms so as to grow Highland cash crops: see Table 2.4 f. Introduce HYVs, fertilizers and/or group irrigation: see 'Modern intensive'	**Possible improvements** a. Use recommended methods of crop, soil and water management b. Introduce new HYVs as they become available. Also, introduce better varieties of deepwater aman from other areas c. Grow an additional crop, if possible: e.g., change from 1 to 2 above d. After harvesting aman or jute, make ridges or beds and provide irrigation: grow two potato or rabi vegetable crops; or potato or vegetables-melon, pumpkin, chilli, etc. e. Grow Highland or Medium Highland crops by: • making soil platforms and providing hand irrigation (see Table 2.4); or • providing flood protection and pump or tidal drainage ± modern irrigation (see Tables 2.4 and 2.6)

TABLE 2.11

Stages in crop intensification on Lowland, permeable soils

Natural vegetation	Simple traditional	Intensive traditional	Modern intensive
Swamp grassland or bare alluvium	1. B.aman 2. B.aman-rabi pulses or oilseeds	1. B.aman or jute-rabi pulses or oilseeds 2. B.aman or jute-LV/LIV rabi cash crop (potato, vegetables, spices) 3. Same as 1 or 2 above, but with kaon, *bhurra, shama* or sesamum intersown with aman	1. B.aman or jute-HYV wheat, potato, vegetables, spices, etc. 2. B.aman or jute-two rabi crops (e.g., two vegetable or potato crops, or potato-melon, pumpkin, etc.)

	Possible improvements
	a. Use more manure or fertilizer
	b. Introduce new varieties (LIV/HYV)
	c. Grow one or more cash crops: e.g., jute, potato
	d. Grow an extra crop: e.g., change from 1 to 2 above; or from 1 or 2 above to 3 under 'Intensive traditional' or to 2 under 'Modern intensive'
	e. Use irrigation (if needed): either hand irrigation or group irrigation
	f. Make soil platforms so as to grow Highland cash crops: see Table 2.3
	g. For share-croppers, improve tenancy terms so as to provide an incentive for investment in extra inputs
		Possible improvements
		a. Improve soil, crop and water management
		b. Use more compost or manure, especially on cash crops
		c. Provide hand irrigation (where not used already)
		d. Grow an extra crop, where feasible: e.g., change from 1 to 2 above; or from 2 above to 2 under 'Modern intensive'
		e. Make soil platforms so as to grow Highland cash crops: see Table 2.3
		f. Introduce HYVs, fertilizers and/or group irrigation: see 'Modern intensive'
			Possible improvements
			a. Use recommended methods of crop, soil and water management
			b. Introduce new HYVs as they become available. Also, introduce better varieties of deepwater aman from other areas
			c. Introduce new rabi or early kharif crops: e.g., maize, vegetables, melon
			d. Grow an additional crop, if possible: e.g., change from 1 to 2 above
			e. Grow Highland or Medium Highland crops by:
			  • making soil platforms and providing hand irrigation (see Table 2.3); or
			  • providing flood protection and pump or tidal drainage ± modern irrigation (see Tables 2.3 and 2.5)

TABLE 2.12

Stages in crop intensification on Lowland, impermeable soils

Natural vegetation	Simple traditional	Intensive traditional	Modern intensive
Swamp grassland (sometimes replaced by grazed *doub* grassland)	1. B.aman 2. B.aman-khesari	1. B.aman or jute-gram (or other pulses), barley 2. LV/LIV boro (with hand irrigation)	1. HYV boro 2. HYV boro-transplanted deepwater aman 3. B.aman-HYV wheat, potato, vegetables or spices (on ridges or beds, with hand irrigation)
	Possible improvements a. Use improved methods of crop, soil and water management b. Introduce new varieties (LIV/HYV): e.g., better varieties of deepwater aman from other areas c. Grow an extra crop: e.g., change from 1 to 2 above; or from 1 above to 1 under 'Intensive traditional' or to 2 under 'Modern intensive' d. Use irrigation (if needed): either hand irrigation or group irrigation e. Make soil platforms so as to grow Highland crops all through the year: see Table 2.4. Alternatively, make lower platforms so as to grow one or two rabi cash crops (e.g., vegetables) f. For share-croppers, improve tenancy terms so as to provide an incentive for investment in extra inputs	**Possible improvements** a. Improve soil, crop and water management for b.aman and rabi crops b. Provide hand irrigation (where not used already) c. Grow a quick-maturing boro variety in areas subject to early floods; also where deepwater aman could be transplanted after boro d. Grow an extra crop, where feasible: e.g., change from 2 above to 2 under 'Modern intensive' e. Make soil platforms: see e under 'Simple traditional' f. Introduce HYVs, fertilizers and/or group irrigation: see 'Modern intensive'	**Possible improvements** a. Use recommended methods of crop, soil and water management b. Introduce new HYVs as they become available. c. After harvesting aman, make ridges or beds and provide irrigation: grow one or two rabi cash crops (e.g., potato, vegetables, spices, melon, pumpkin) e. Grow Highland or Medium Highland crops by: • making soil platforms and providing hand irrigation (see Table 2.4); or • providing flood protection and pump or tidal drainage ± modern irrigation (see Tables 2.4 and 2.6)

TABLE **2.13**

Stages in crop intensification on Bottomland[1,2]

Natural vegetation	Simple traditional	Intensive traditional	Modern intensive
Swamp grassland or aquatic plants	1. LV boro or arum	1. LV/LIV boro with improved management; possibly also with hand irrigation, flood embankments, (where needed)	1. LV/LIV boro with use of fertilizers, pest management and/or irrigation (where needed)
		2. (On sandy and loamy soils): rabi vegetables, spices, potato, tobacco, etc., (on raised beds)	2. Same as 2 under 'Intensive traditional' with use of fertilizers, pest management and/or irrigation (where needed)
		3. (On shallowly or moderately-deeply flooded land): LV/LIV boro-LV t.aman or transplanted deepwater aman	3. Same as 3 under 'Intensive traditional' with use of better varieties, fertilizers, pest management and/or irrigation (where needed)
	Possible improvements	**Possible improvements**	**Possible improvements**
	a. Change to methods described under 'Intensive traditional' or 'Modern intensive'	a. Improve soil, crop and water management	a. Use recommended methods of crop, soil and water management
	b. For share-croppers, improve tenancy terms so as to provide an incentive for investment in extra inputs	b. Grow a quick-maturing boro variety in areas subject to early floods	b. Make embankments to protect boro from early floods (if feasible)
		c. Make soil platforms so as to grow one or two rabi cash crops: see 2 above	c. Make raised beds, and use methods for 2 above
		d. Make soil platforms so as to grow Highland cash crops: see Tables 2.3 and 2.4. Alternatively, make lower platforms so as to grow one or two rabi cash crops: see Tables 2.5 and 2.6	d. Grow Highland, Medium Highland or Medium Lowland crops (according to depth of flooding) by: • making soil platforms and providing hand irrigation: see Tables 2.3–2.10; or • providing flood protection and pump or tidal drainage (if feasible)±modern irrigation: see Tables 2.3–2.10

Notes: 1. Includes permeable, impermeable and peat soils.

2. Peat soils often are too soft to be cultivated. They can also provide fertility and weed problems. These soils should not be drained, if possible. The best way to improve peat soils is to make raised beds or platforms with alluvial material dug from below the peat or carried from a neighbouring river; then grow cash crops (e.g., vegetables, fruits).

Chapter 3

AGRICULTURE AND FOOD PRODUCTION IN POLDER AREAS[1]

The environmental and agricultural setting of polder development in Bangladesh is described and problems which led to project achievements falling below targets are reviewed. Recommendations include adopting more multi-disciplinary, participatory planning, more rigorous economic assessment, environmental impact assessment and monitoring, and land use regulation to preseve valuable agricultural land against encroachment of settlements and industry.

3.1 INTRODUCTION

The organizers of the Symposium on Polders of the World originally requested the author to present a paper giving an overview of agricultural aspects of polder development outside The Netherlands.[2] That task proved to be impossible within the time and resources available to the author in Bangladesh. Instead, the author chose to speak on polder development in Bangladesh. The objective was not to provide a detailed description of polder development in Bangladesh but rather to use Bangladeshi examples as a means to illustrate principles, experience and issues of wider relevance.

3.2 ENVIRONMENTAL SETTING

3.2.1 Environment and demography

Bangladesh has both the physical and the demographic environments where polders are most needed. Alluvial floodplains occupy 80 percent of the total land area of 145,000 km^2.

---

[1] *This chapter is an edited version of a keynote paper presented at The International Symposium on Polders of the World in Lelystad, Netherlands, October 1982 (Brammer, 1982). An abbreviated version of the paper was published in the Symposium proceedings. Population and agricultural production data used in the original paper have been retained, but in view of the time-lapse since 1982, statements originally made in the present tense have been converted to the past tense to make the situation clear. Up-dating comments have been added in footnotes. Nearly 20 years after the original paper was prepared, it is interesting to see the progress in agricultural development that has occurred, mainly by small-scale irrigation development, not by major water-control projects. However, the author's experience on the Bangladesh Flood Action Plan 1989-94 indicated that engineers' attitudes had progressed little in the meantime. Footnotes which appeared in the original paper are given in normal font. Footnotes that have been added are given in italics. The Districts referred to are the pre-1982 Districts shown on Figure 1.1*

[2] *Polder is a Dutch term for the land enclosed within an embankment which is used to exclude external water, usually with the help of pump or tidal drainage.*

It is estimated from soil surveys that about 75 percent of the floodplain area is flooded deeper than 30 cm for 3-5 months in the rainy season. In addition, before embankments were built, about 1 million hectares near the coast were subject to tidal flooding with saline water.

Most of the country's population of over 90 million lives in floodplain areas.[3] The average population density is 628/km^2. Regionally, it varies from more than 1,000/km^2 in Comilla, the most densely settled District, to less than 500/km^2 in two coastal Districts. Considering the fact that more than 80 percent of the country's total population is rural, that is a very high population density.

Unlike The Netherlands, Bangladesh does not have major areas where new land for settlement or agricultural production could be reclaimed from the sea by empolderment. The purpose of making polders in Bangladesh is mainly to protect existing settled agricultural land from deep flooding or from tidal flooding with saline water, so that improved crops can be grown in the monsoon season. Often, irrigation is provided at the same time, partly so as to compensate farmers for the loss of soil moisture derived from seasonal flooding under natural conditions, partly to enable farmers also to grow improved crops in the dry season.

3.2.2 Agriculture and food production

Bangladesh's economy is predominantly agricultural. In 1980, Agriculture contributed about 55 percent of the GNP and supported, directly or indirectly, about 75 percent of the work force. The major cash crop, jute, provided about 70 percent of the country's export earnings.[4]

Rice is the principal crop, occupying about 80 percent of the net cropped area, spread over three growing seasons. The two rainy-season rice crops are mainly dependent on rainfall and seasonal flooding, but almost all the dry-season rice crop is irrigated. (In 1980), almost 2 million hectares of the rainy-season crop were occupied by deepwater rice varieties which can withstand flooding depths greater than 30 cm. Average rice yields were low: 1.35 tons/ha. That reflected the relatively low adoption rate of modern technology, as illustrated by average fertilizer rates (for all crops) of around 100kg/ha (= <50kg/ha nutrients) per annum, spread over three seasons.[5]

The average size of farm holdings in 1983-84 was 1.4 ha. However, it would be wrong to infer from this that Bangladesh is a country of predominantly small peasant farmers. In 1978, the 8.5 percent of rural land-owners who possessed 2 ha or more held 48.4 percent of the land. On the other hand, 50.4 percent of rural households owned less than 0.2 ha (including those with no agricultural land at all) (Januzzi & Peach, 1980). Land-owners with more than about 2 ha generally use share-croppers or hired labour to cultivate their land; often, they are absentee owners. In the past, such 'big' owners have generally shown little interest in using modern technology to increase production, although there are

[3] *Bangladesh's population in 1999 is estimated to be 127 million.*

[4] *By 1996-97, the agriculture sector contributed 32.4 percent of GNP, and garments, shrimps and remittances from overseas employment had superseded jute as major earners of foreign exchange.*

[5] *By 1996-97, the area of deepwater rice had decreased to 0.83 M ha and average rice yields had increased to 1.88 tons/ha. Average fertilizer rates (for the total cropped area) had increased to 290 kg/ha per annum in 1992-93 (the latest year for which statistics are available).*

indications that a change may be taking place in some areas. Progressive small farmers are found mainly in the south-east and centre of the country.

(In 1980), Bangladesh produced 14-15 million tons of foodgrains annually, depending on whether harvests were good or bad. The population of 92 million needed an estimated 14.5 million tons. A further 1.5 million tons were needed to cover seed, feed and waste. That left a deficit of 1-2 million tons. Each year, too, population growth added a further 400,000 tons to the requirement.[6]

In its Second Five-year Plan (1980-81 to 1984-85), the Government of Bangladesh aimed to achieve national self-sufficiency in foodgrain production and to expand the production of other food and cash crops, including sugarcane, banana, jute, cotton, pulses, oilseeds, potato, vegetables and spices. The foodgrain production target by 1984-85 was 18-20 million tons, including provision for building up a reserve food stock. In order to achieve these ambitious targets, it was planned to double the area under irrigation, from 1.47 million ha in 1980 to 2.88 million ha in 1984-85, and to provide flood protection and drainage to an additional 600,000 ha. Therefore, although priority was given to small-scale irrigation, polders also had an important role to play in this planned development.[7]

3.2.3 Physiography and soils

Most of the country comprises the combined delta of the Ganges, Brahmaputra and Meghna rivers. This area can be divided into six broad physiographic types (Figure 3.1).

a. *Active and very young floodplains* along the major river channels (700,000 ha). This land is subject to bank erosion and deposition of new sandy or silty alluvium each flood season, so is not suitable for embankment projects.

b. *Young and old river meander floodplains* of the major rivers (5.7 million ha), These areas are characterized by a ridge-and-basin topography with 2-5 m local differences in relief. Predominant soils are heavy silts to clays with developed profiles 30-120 cm deep over a stratified substratum. Such land is suitable for polder projects so long as embankments are set well back from active river channels and there are suitable sites for irrigation/drainage headworks on stable tributary (or distributary) channels. The Ganges-Kobadak (G-K) project, referred to later, is on the Ganges river meander floodplain.

c. *Young and old estuarine floodplains*, occurring mainly east of the Meghna estuary (3.1 million ha). These areas are characterized by almost-level local relief (<2 m), few or no natural channels, and deep silty deposits in which soil profiles 20-120 cm deep have developed. Such land is suitable for polder projects, provided that embankments and irrigation/drainage headworks can be sited away from active river channels. The Chandpur (CIP) and Dhaka-Narayanganj-Demra (DND) projects, referred to later, occupy parts of the old and young Meghna estuarine floodplains.

d. *Tidal floodplains*, occurring mainly in the south-west, locally in the south-east, (1 million ha). Tidal floodplains are characterized by almost-level, saucer-shaped basins

---

[6] *Foodgrain production in 1997-98 was 20.66 million tons. The population of 125 million in that year needed an estimated 20.37 million tons (at 16 oz per head per year), plus another 2.04 million tons for seed, feed and waste, leaving an annual deficit of 1.75 million tons needing to be imported. Imports in 1997-98 were 1.93 million tons.*

[7] *The irrigated area in 1996-97 was 3.65 million ha, of which 3.50 million ha was small-scale (including traditional) and 0.15 million ha in large-scale project areas.*

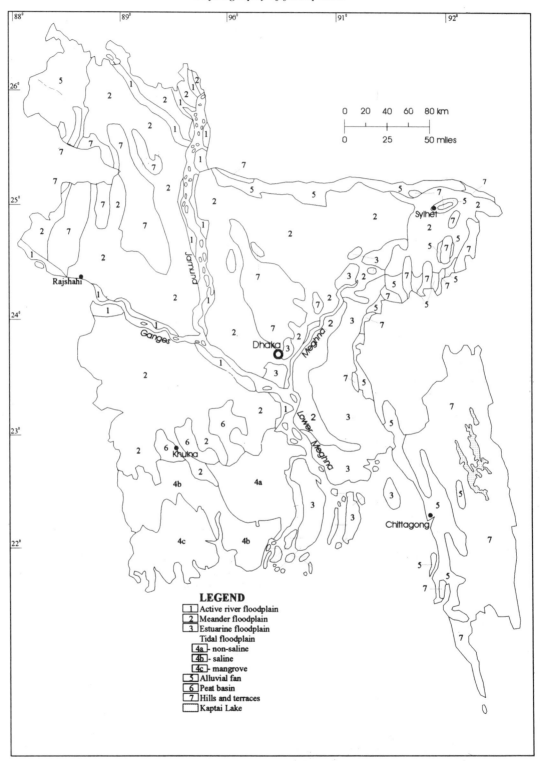

FIGURE 3.1

Physiography of floodplains

LEGEND
1 Active river floodplain
2 Meander floodplain
3 Estuarine floodplain
   Tidal floodplain
4a - non-saline
4b - saline
4c - mangrove
5 Alluvial fan
6 Peat basin
7 Hills and terraces
   Kaptai Lake

with <1 m local difference in elevation, and numerous tidal creeks. Clay soils predominate. About 400,000 ha is non-saline; about 600,000 ha is saline (most of it only in the dry season). The Coastal Embankment Project occupies most of the saline area, and the Barisal Irrigation Project (which includes embankments) occupies a part of the non-saline Ganges Tidal Floodplain.

e. ***Alluvial fans and piedmont plains*** (1.1 million ha), occurring partly in the north-west near the foot of the Himalayas, the rest mainly adjoining the Northern and Eastern Hills. Local relief often is irregular, and soils range from sands to clays. The embankment of hill-foot rivers provides difficult problems because of the deposition of sediments in river-beds between the embankments following flash floods and the constant risk of embankments being breached. The Manu, Muhuri and Karnafuli projects occupy hill-foot sites.

f. ***Peat basins*** (200,000 ha) occur most extensively in the transition zone between the Ganges meander and tidal floodplains in the south-west. The empolderment of peat basins is suitable only so long as they are not deeply drained. The land should be kept permanently wet or moist in order to prevent the peat from shrinking and thus lowering land levels.

On all floodplains, there is a characteristic pattern of permeable, usually loamy, soils on the highest parts of the relief and impermeable, usually clay, soils on the lower parts. The proportions between light and heavy soils differ both between the major floodplains and within them. Generally, heavy soils occupy most of the landscape. Rapidly permeable soils occur mainly on high floodplain ridges, some piedmont fans (especially in the north-west), and some temporary islands (*chars*) on active river floodplains. The most extensive soils are Fluvaquentic Haplaquepts (Eutric and Calcaric Fluvisols in the FAO/Unesco system).[8]

Ganges river alluvium contains lime; so does young Meghna estuarine alluvium, although only in small amounts. Ganges tidal, Brahmaputra river and old Meghna estuarine alluvia are neutral to moderately alkaline in reaction, but not calcareous. Alluvial fans and Meghna river deposits usually are slightly to moderately acid in reaction.

Because of the seasonal cycle of flooding and drying out, soil development is rapid. The seasonal changes cause rapid development of structure (where textures are suitable) and the development of iron-oxidation mottles. Alluvial stratification is quickly broken up by biological activity down to the permanently-saturated zone. Biological activity (roots, soil fauna) also increases subsoil porosity, aeration, permeability and moisture-holding capacity. On the other hand, cultivation tends to destroy topsoil structure and to create a slowly-permeable ploughpan, especially in soils deliberately puddled for transplanting rice.

3.2.4 Soil fertility

The seasonal reduction and oxidation of the topsoil — which usually is cultivated, and often puddled — quickly decalcifies and acidifies this layer in most floodplain soils. Exceptions occur in areas where the deposition of new alluvium neutralizes such changes and in some older, light-textured soils where biological activity constantly brings subsoil material to the surface to neutralize the changes. However, whether topsoils are acid or alkaline in

---

[8]*Later reclassified as Typic and Aeric Haplaquepts (USDA) and Eutric Gleysols (FAO/Unesco) (Brammer, 1996).*

the dry season, they all become neutral in reaction when submerged and reduced in the rainy season.

The rapid leaching of most floodplain topsoils confirms field observations that most river and estuarine floodplains are not flooded by river water. They are flooded with rainwater or the raised groundwater table derived from the heavy monsoon rainfall which is ponded on the land by high monsoon-season river levels. Silty floodwater mainly deposits new alluvium on active floodplains and the immediately adjoining young meander floodplains, on unembanked tidal floodplains, and on alluvial fans (piedmont plains) at the foot of the Northern and Eastern Hills.[9]

This observation has important implications for embankment projects. Farmers (and lay officials) believe that the fertility of floodplain soils is maintained by an annual deposit of alluvium from the seasonal floods. Since most floodplains do not receive such annual deposits, and yet clearly are at least as productive as those that do — e.g., under traditional farming conditions, large areas of the Brahmaputra and Ganges floodplains were triple cropped, without irrigation and with little or no use of fertilizers — the self-evident fertility of these soils must be derived from some other source.

The ready availability of phosphorus and potash can be accounted for by the seasonal cycle of reduction and oxidation in these mineral-rich soils. However, this phenomenon cannot provide nitrogen, and many cultivated soils contain little organic matter as a nitrogen source. It now appears certain that the nitrogen fertility of Bangladesh's floodplain soils is provided by biological activity in the floodwater itself, especially that of blue-green algae. It is probable that such organisms can provide up to 30 kg/ha of nitrogen annually, perhaps even more on deeply-flooded land where deepwater aman paddy is grown. Since these organisms are dependent on light for photosynthesis, it is probable that they produce more nitrogen in clear rainwater than in silty floodwater. Therefore the construction of polder embankments will not necessarily cut off farmers from these sources of plant nutrients, at least on land where wetland rice continues to be grown.[10]

That should not be taken to imply that Bangladesh's floodplain soils do not need or respond to fertilizers. Without fertilizers or manure, the natural fertility maintains production at only a low or moderate equilibrium level. For increased yields, particularly for HYVs and irrigated crops, it is necessary to add nitrogen and phosphorus fertilizers regularly, and sometimes potash as well. Also, as will be described later, there is increasing evidence of zinc and sulphur deficiencies in some places.

3.2.5 Cropping patterns

Under natural conditions — i.e., without artificial drainage or irrigation — farmers' cropping patterns on floodplain land are determined largely by the length of the rainy season and the depth and duration of seasonal flooding. Soil permeability, soil moisture-holding capacity and the presence or absence of salinity are also important, particularly for dry-season crops grown with or without irrigation. Because of the characteristic floodplain relief of ridges and basins, variations in soils, depth of flooding and flood

---

[9] *Most of the Old Himalayan Piedmont Plain in the north-west, abandoned long ago by the Teesta river which formed it, is flooded by rainwater.*

[10]*For a more detailed account of the contribution of biological activity to seasonally-flooded soils, see Brammer 2000, Chapter 8.*

duration occur on a local scale, even within the area of a village. Cropping patterns often are complex, therefore.

Rice occupies about 10 million ha, which is about 80 percent of the cropped area. It can be grown in three seasons:

- *aus*, sown in the pre-monsoon season and harvested in the monsoon season;
- *aman* (traditional varieties of which are photoperiod-sensitive), sown before or in the monsoon season and harvested after the monsoon season; and
- *boro*, sown in seed-beds in the first half of the dry season, transplanted at the end of the cool winter period and harvested just before or early in the monsoon season.

Aus and aman are mainly grown without irrigation, although use of irrigation is expanding in both seasons, either in order to increase security or to allow both crops to be grown in western areas where the 4-month rainy season is insufficient to support more than one rainfed crop. Boro traditionally was grown in depressions which stay wet for most or all of the dry season, but it is now also widely grown with irrigation on relatively higher land.

Within the three broad rice groups, farmers have selected many thousands of rice varieties to suit their specific micro-environmental conditions, especially for the aman crop. Aman includes varieties with different maturity periods, tolerant of different degrees of salinity, zinc deficiency and iron toxicity, and adapted to different depths and durations of seasonal flooding. Some deepwater aman varieties can elongate their stems to as much as 4-5 metres.

High-yielding varieties (HYVs) of rice introduced since the late-1960s are not adapted to a wide range of Bangladesh's environments. In order to give high yields, they require good water control to provide a very shallow water depth, and relatively high fertilizer doses. The farmer will only invest in the latter where he feels there is sufficient security to ensure a reliable return on his investment. For that reason, by 1980, the HYVs had spread to only an estimated 15 percent of the total rice area. About half the HYV area is boro, grown with irrigation in the dry season. The rest is about equally divided between aus and aman, grown both with and without irrigation on relatively heavy soils in areas where the risk of damage by floods is low.[11]

It is in this context that polders are important for agricultural development in Bangladesh. About 75 percent of the floodplain land — about 8.5 million ha gross — is too deeply flooded for existing HYVs of rice to be grown reliably in the monsoon season. Also, some of the land cannot be used for irrigated HYV boro in the dry season, either because floodwater recedes too slowly or because the risk of early, pre-monsoon, floods is too high. A further area of shallowly-flooded tidal land near the coast has soils or water which are too saline in the dry season for boro rice to be grown.

3.3 POLDER DEVELOPMENT AND EXPERIENCE

3.3.1 Master Plan

The Master Plan for water development drawn up by the erstwhile East Pakistan Water and Power Development Authority (EPWAPDA, now BWDB) in 1964 envisaged polder

---

[11]*By 1996-97, HYVs of rice were grown on 5.05 million ha: 2.46 M boro; 2.12 M aman; 0.47 M aus.*

development extending eventually over a gross area of 5.8 million hectares (IECo, 1964). Three kinds of project were envisaged:

- flood embankments with gravity drainage in meander floodplain and piedmont plain areas;
- flood embankments with tidal sluice drainage in tidal areas; and
- flood embankments with pump drainage.

For most of the projects, provision of irrigation was also envisaged, sometimes as a second stage. Priority was given to flood protection.

By 1982, only seven of the 35 major flood-protection and irrigation projects envisaged in the Master Plan had been wholly or mainly completed. For a variety of reasons, it is difficult to quantify the benefits which they have provided.

One major reason for that derives from the meaning of the word 'completed'. Project authorities tend to use the term to indicate that construction works have been completed. That does not necessarily mean that project benefits have been brought to all the project command area. A particular problem arises in the case of the 'completed' Coastal Embankment project, which supposedly protects 1.08 million ha from saline tidal flooding. Many sections of embankments have been eroded or breached since they were built, and many sluices either were not installed or have subsequently been damaged, so that many polders are now polders only in name. It is probable that only about one-third (or possibly less) of the 'completed' project area is, in fact, receiving the full project benefits of protection from saline floodwater.

A further problem is provided by the lack of reliable crop production statistics. Even where project authorities make estimates of crop area and production within project command areas, it is difficult to estimate the net increase in production attributable to the project, especially in the case of relatively older projects. That is because, for most project areas, it cannot be assumed that, without the project, land use would have remained in the pre-project condition. In the case of the G-K project, for example, where transplanted improved aus and aman varieties have replaced the former broadcast traditional aus and aman varieties (and some jute), the comparison should be made with areas of similar land adjoining the project. Undoubtedly, there have been significant changes in land use outside the project area during the years since the project started: in addition to the traditional aus and aman still grown in the monsoon season, there has been a considerable expansion of wheat, tobacco, cotton and sugarcane production, part of it with small-scale irrigation. Because of the difference in crops grown, a realistic comparison could be made only on the basis of economic returns per hectare. Unfortunately, reliable data are not available for this purpose. Moreover, analysis would be complicated by different level of input subsidies provided within and outside the project area.

On the basis of existing information, the author's best guess is that flood protection may actually have been provided by major projects to about half-a-million hectares and irrigation to about 85,000 ha. The direct benefits in terms of increased foodgrain production may be about 1 million tons annually (net). In addition, because of the greater security which flood protection provides, farmers have been able to provide or obtain small-scale irrigation from surface-water or groundwater sources, as well as to grow additional or better dry-season crops without irrigation in some areas. Unfortunately, reliable data are not available to enable such benefits to be quantified.[12]

3.3.2 Plan defects

Important though the direct benefits from embankment projects have been, they have been much less than was envisaged when the Master Plan was prepared. It is instructive to examine the reasons why polder development has been so slow. There are lessons to be learnt from this not only for Bangladesh but probably also for other countries.

The first reason undoubtedly is because the Master Plan and its component projects were too narrow in concept and focus. The Master Plan is primarily a civil engineering plan.[13] It is not an agricultural development plan as such. With the benefit of hindsight, one can understand why that should be so. The origin of the Water Development Board and the Master Plan lie in serious floods which ravaged what is now Bangladesh in the 1950s. Flood protection was then seen as a priority for providing security to crop production. Irrigation usually was a secondary consideration. Alternative possibilities for agricultural development were not considered at all. The engineering projects in the Master Plan were considered to provide a panacea for the country's agricultural development.

Three main factors have combined to delay implementation of the Plan. The major cause has been the reluctance of international aid donors to finance some of the major proposed projects because of the technical difficulties of siting headworks on such major rivers as the Ganges and the Brahmaputra, whose banks can erode or recede by as much as 600 metres in a single year, and where intake and outlet canals can silt up in a single flood season. On the G-K project, for example, it can take six dredgers up to three months to desilt the 1,000 m long intake canal to the main pump-house before irrigation can begin each year; and on the Chandpur project, 20 km of river embankments had to be rebuilt before the project had even been completed, because of actual or threatened breaches in the original embankment by the Lower Meghna river. Reservations have been expressed, also, on the advisability of double-embanking rivers as big and as active as the Brahmaputra and the Ganges. The lack of international agreements on water use in rivers originating outside the country was a further constraint on obtaining funds for projects involving irrigation as well as flood protection.

A second factor — and one which also influenced donor funding — was the growing recognition during the second half of the 1960s that there were alternative (and cheaper) ways to increase crop production than through costly embankment and canal irrigation projects. By 1970, about 24,000 small low-lift pumps and 1,000 tube-wells had been installed, irrigating an estimated 370,000 ha. By 1981-82, those numbers had grown to about 40,000 low-lift pumps, 12,000 deep tube-wells and over 50,000 shallow tube-wells, as well as more than 200,000 hand pumps, together irrigating an estimated 1.27 million ha. That figure compares with only about 85,000 ha irrigated within major irrigation projects

---

[12] *By 1997-98, official figures indicated that major water development projects (excluding the Coastal Embankment Project) covered 402,000 ha. The FAP12/13 review reported that substantial areas in some project areas were not receiving benefits (FPCO, 1992a). See also Chapter 4 of this volume.*

[13] In Bangladesh, as in many developing countries, such projects generally are planned, executed and operated by engineers with a background in civil or mechanical engineering, not in agricultural or irrigation engineering.

in 1981-82.[14] Although the limit of easily-available surface water usable by small pumps has almost been reached, there remains considerable scope to expand irrigation from groundwater. The development of small-scale irrigation has greatly expanded crop production in the dry season, thus reducing the urgency for flood protection and drainage in many seasonally-flooded areas. The emphasis in crop production has been switched from the hazardous monsoon season to the relatively safe dry season.

A third delaying factor has been the difficulty and expense of acquiring land for the construction of embankments and irrigation/drainage canals. In a country where the average farm size is only 1.4 ha and where the average population density is more than 600 /km^2 — and exceeds 1,000/km in some floodplain areas — the reluctance of farmers to give up their land, and for them to sell it only for a high price, is understandable. This factor also has influenced donors' decisions, and it has led to changed designs which minimize the amount of land needed for irrigation distribution systems. Preference now is given to the use of small pumps along existing or improved internal channels rather than to the construction of new, gravity-flow, channels.

3.3.3 Farmers' alternatives

During the years that have intervened since the Master Plan was prepared, there has been a growing recognition that technical and physical factors are not the only considerations to be taken into account in planning agricultural development. In the Master Plan, it was rather naively assumed that land which remained uncultivated in the dry season did so because it was too dry; some planners and policy-makers still express such views (see Chapter 18). Planners also naively assumed that, with the provision of flood-protection and irrigation, farmers would quickly adopt improved methods of cultivation and grow two or three high-yielding crops a year. Project planners — and assertive aid-donors — calculated benefit:cost ratios accordingly, showing attractive rates of return on proposed investments.

Two things have happened to upset those early assumptions. One is that there has been a considerable increase in double-cropping and triple-cropping of land, even without flood-protection, drainage or irrigation. The second is that, in irrigation and drainage project areas, farmers have either not adopted the cropping patterns designed for them by the project planners, or they have done so more slowly than was projected.

In the first case, soil surveyors have confirmed what farmers obviously knew already: namely, that many floodplain soils store sufficient moisture after the floods and the rainy season to support a satisfactory crop of wheat, pulses or oilseeds without irrigation during the cool winter months. The changes from single to double cropping, and from double to triple cropping, have resulted more from population pressure — and hence economic pressure — than from the provision of modern technology: see Chapter 2. In areas with relatively low population density, much land still remains fallow in the dry season or in the first half of the rainy season, even though conditions may be suitable for growing crops during those periods. Big farmers using share-croppers can obtain a sufficient surplus from

---

[14]*Recent figures for numbers of tubewells installed are not available to the author, but the 1996-97 agricultural statistics give the following figures for the areas under different types of irrigation in that year (converted to ha): LLP 687,204; DTW 669,839; STW 1,748,221; HTW 31,607; traditional 358,736; canal 154,114.*

one crop per year, with little or no management or investment, so that there is little incentive for them to grow a second crop or to invest in increased production. That is particularly so in the case of absentee land-owners.

In the second case, farmers have been much slower to adopt intensive cropping patterns and HYVs than project planners assumed. Figure 3.2 gives examples of the rates of adoption of HYVs in the boro/aus and aman seasons in the DND and G-K project areas. Both areas have controlled drainage and irrigation, and have soils which are suitable for HYV rice with irrigation. Yet, in the G-K project (Phase-I), it took more than 10 years for HYVs to cover even 30 percent of the area, although the trend has been continuously upward. In the DND area, it took only two years to reach 50 percent in the boro season and eight years to reach 90 percent HYV coverage, at which level the proportion seems to have plateaued; however, in the aman season, progress has been erratic, and seems to have plateaued at 70 percent.

Two lessons can be drawn from this experience. One is that drainage and irrigation projects should be regarded primarily as agricultural development projects, not as engineering projects. Therefore, agronomists and soil scientists need to be given a stronger voice in the planning and implementation of such projects — and that voice should be listened to!

The second lesson is that agricultural development involves farmers. Therefore, farmers should be consulted about the practicality and acceptability of the plans being prepared for them. It is the policy-makers or planners, not the farmers or Extension officials, who should be blamed if ambitious project targets are not met. In the case of both the G-K and the DND projects in Bangladesh, the project authority — comprising administrators and engineers — planned three HYV cereal crops a year for the project, without finding out whether that was what the farmers wanted to do or whether such cropping patterns were practical for them to adopt.

Recent investigations indicate that such intensive cereal cropping patterns do not suit all farmers. In the G-K project area, for example, the average size of farm holding is 2 ha, and the majority of farmers are dependent on hired, migrant labour for transplanting and harvesting the aus and aman rice crops.[15] Harvesting and threshing (by bullock treading) takes about 1-2 months or more, which prevents the quick turn-around which the addition of a third HYV rice crop per year would require. Moreover, the production of two HYV rice crops per year gives farmers owning 2 ha or more a huge grain surplus, about five or six times their family consumption needs. There is no incentive for them to grow a third crop per year merely to satisfy the plans of the project authority.[16, 17]

---

[15] *See the comment made in Chapter 2, footnote 31. The G-K project lies mainly in Kushtia District.*

[16] *There is less economic incentive for them to do so because the farmers receive the irrigation water very nearly free. The project authority was never able to collect more than a minor percentage of the irrigation charge, already highly subsidized. It was estimated in the mid-1980s that farmers were paying only about 5 percent of the actual cost of irrigation. One could justifiably ask why should they pay? They had not requested the project. They had even been opposed to it: the author recalls that, on his first visit to the G-K project in October 1961, the 11-mile embankment between Kushtia and Bheramara had been cut in more than 90 places by farmers fearful of the embankment preventing floodwater from spreading over their land. The project was blue-printed over their heads — obviously with good top-down intentions — but without consultation. One EPWAPDA Chairman, addressing a public gathering in the area in the late-1960s, even complained about the 'ungrateful' farmers not growing three crops a year, the implication being that the farmers were supposed to be growing crops to satisfy project needs, not that the project was intended to serve the farmers' needs.*

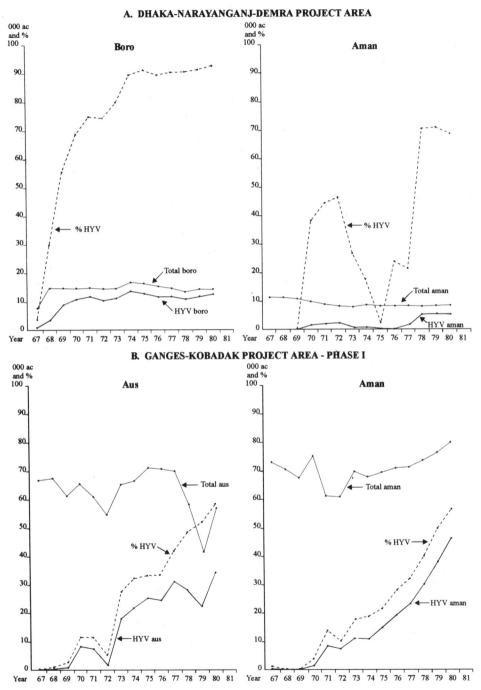

FIGURE 3.2

Spread of HYV rice in two flood-protected and irrigated project areas

[17]*In practice, irrigation could not be provided for a third HYV rice crop in the G-K project because of the time taken to de-silt the intake canal after the flood season and, after 1975, because of the Indian diversion of dry-season flow in the Ganges river at the Farakka barrage.*

The experience of the G-K project and the Chandpur project illustrates another common weakness in planning: i.e., ignoring soil factors which influence farmers' choice of crops. In the former case, the soil survey report carried out for the G-K project indicated 20 percent of the area as being unsuitable for irrigated rice because of rapidly permeable soils (FAO, 1959). Even if that were not apparent from the soil survey report — which, admittedly, like many reports of its time was more descriptive than prescriptive — it should have become obvious from site examinations along the proposed canal alignments. Yet the irrigation layout and cropping pattern adopted totally ignored that information. The main distribution channels are aligned along the most permeable soils — because they occupy the highest part of the landscape, as is required for a gravity distribution system — but they are unlined. Also, two transplanted rice crops a year are irrigated, even on permeable soils, mainly because the very low (or no) irrigation charges do not give farmers any incentive to use water more efficiently. Not surprisingly, water does not reach tail-end areas, and only about 55 percent of the supposed command area actually receives irrigation.[18]

The Chandpur project plan expected farmers to grow two (or three) HYV rice crops a year. In fact, within the command area of almost 30,000 ha, farmers grew only 18,783 ha of boro rice in the 1981-82 dry season. They grew 3,507 ha of irrigated wheat and other dry-season crops; and a further 6,347 ha of dry-season crops (mainly chilli) were grown without irrigation. This reflects the fact — known to the farmers, and described in the soil survey reports — that a substantial area within the project boundaries has light-textured, permeable soils which are not well suited to irrigated rice cultivation in the dry season. Under pre-project conditions, some of those soils were intensively used for dry-season crops without irrigation, especially for chilli, which formed the area's most important cash crop. Obviously, farmers find it more economic to continue growing chilli (and other dryland crops) on such soils, without using irrigation, rather than to follow project plans blue-printed over their heads from Dhaka (or from a donor's headquarters).[19]

3.3.4 Agro-socio-economic surveys

In this, the farmers are right. Projects should be tailored to suit farmers, not vice versa. However, it often appears as though project planners first calculate an economic rate of return which will justify investment in a project, and then fabricate an intensive cropping pattern to provide that rate of return.[20] Admittedly, the planner's task is difficult. But it could be made easier if agricultural and socio-economic surveys were made in advance, and if project plans were then based on a realistic assessment of the findings. Project planners raise no questions regarding the need for detailed site surveys when dams and headworks are being designed. There needs to be a similar recognition of the need for

---

[18]*See Chapter 4, Section 4.6, for a detailed description and discussion of physical conditions in the G-K project area.*

[19]*See Chapter 4, Section 4.3, for a detailed description and discussion of physical conditions in the Chandpur Irrigation Project area.*

[20]*The author witnessed another example of 'top-down planning', where a Chief Engineer simply crossed out the word 'not' from the recommendation that certain soils were 'not suitable for irrigation' in the draft report on a detailed soil survey of a proposed irrigation project area. The authority was successful in obtaining funds from the donor to implement the project — which was an unmitigated disaster.*

detailed agricultural and socio-economic site surveys to be made before costly agricultural projects are designed.[21]

Agricultural surveys should provide information on the following subjects:

a. soil patterns in relation to topography and hydrology, because most floodplain land is neither level nor uniform in soils;

b. physical soil properties (actual or predicted) in relation to irrigation, drainage and natural moisture storage;

c. crops and cropping patterns in relation to soils, including evidence from crops presently grown in the area with irrigation;

d. farm size and tenancy conditions;

e. seasonal availability and cost of labour;

f. preferred staple and cash crops, crop price relationships (including HYV versus traditional varieties), and relative production costs and returns, etc.;

g. opinions of big, medium and small farmers on which crops they would prefer to grow with the proposed project improvements, and what additional inputs or services might be needed;

h. opinions, if any, from those whose livelihoods might suffer as a result of project implementation: e.g., fishermen; farmers on relatively high land who might suffer from the prevention of seasonal flooding; and farmers in depressions which might become perennially waterlogged after installation of irrigation canals

If the findings of such a survey indicate that the proposed project would not be economic, then so much the better: the funds can be better spent elsewhere. How many projects must there be around the world by now that present a drain on national economies because their plans were not based on a realistic study and appraisal of the agro-socio-economic factors! In such a situation, project planners (or Government policy-makers) have four alternatives:

a. accept the findings that the proposed project would not be economic, and divert the proposed fund allocations to a more economic investment (preferably within the same area);

b. accept the findings, and design (or re-design) the project to suit the physical, social and economic conditions found;

c. accept the findings, and consider whether intensive extension activity, price incentives, improved markets, etc., would persuade farmers within a reasonable period to adopt cropping patterns which would make the proposed project economic; in this respect, a pilot scheme can be useful, both for the farmers and the project planners;

d. accept the findings that the project, as proposed, will not be profitable, but proceed with it in the knowledge that it will need to be subsidized, temporarily or permanently, in the national interest.

---

[21] *Such surveys face a problem similar to that described in the previous footnote, namely acceptability to the project authority (or the aid-donor). Bangladeshi consultants hired to carry out such surveys (and also project appraisals) were aware that 'happiness reports' were more likely to ensure them future business than strictly objective reports on their findings.*

3.4 PROBLEMS

3.4.1 First-generation problems

The low irrigation coverage in the G-K project area due to seepage losses, and the erosion of the original embankments in the Chandpur and Brahmaputra Right Bank Embankment projects, can be regarded as first-generation problems: i.e., they result directly from the project design itself. Another example is the cutting of embankments by farmers or fishermen who feel that the project is adversely affecting their livelihoods. In the latter case, advance public education about the effects of a proposed project could help to avoid the problem.

Another example is provided by project designs which, in seeking to optimize economic rates of return, prevent project benefits from being provided to substantial numbers of farmers within the project boundaries. Both the DND and the Chandpur projects provide examples of this, viz.

- In the DND area, the optimum economic pump drainage design left about 10 percent of the polder area, in depression sites, subject to deep flooding for periods of a week or more after sustained heavy monsoon rainfall, such that farmers on such land cannot risk growing transplanted aman (including HYVs) or using costly production inputs on their monsoon-season crops.[22]

- In the Chandpur project area, also, sustained heavy pre-monsoon rainfall in 1980-81 caused flooding which destroyed about one-third of the HYV boro crop and prevented farmers from growing HYV aus in low-lying areas.

The solution to this problem would seem to be to design projects so that they optimize the benefits to farmers, even if this requires accepting a lower rate of return on project investment. That principle would seem to be particularly important in areas where small farmers predominate; (in the Chandpur project area, for example, the average size of farm holding is only 0.4 ha).[23, 24]

The difficulty of satisfying the needs of all farmers within the Coastal Embankment Project polders can also be regarded as a first-generation problem which could have been anticipated. The tidal landscape comprises shallow basins with raised rims (levees) along rivers and creeks. Although the differences in elevation between the higher margins and the basin centres may be no more than 60-100 cm, such differences can be critical for rice farmers, especially for those who wish to grow dwarf HYVs. Tidal sluices in the embankments provide drainage of local run-off following monsoon-season rainfall. The problem is, how to regulate the drainage? If the basins are drained to leave the optimum depth of water on the land for transplanted aman seedlings, the higher fields do not retain

---

[22]*See Chapter 4, Section 4.2, for a detailed description and discussion of physical conditions in the DND project area.*

[23]*This argument would be stronger, of course, if farmers were prepared to pay a reasonable fee for the undoubted benefits which they (or most of them) receive from such projects.*

[24]*A different kind of example of farmers being deprived of benefits occurred in the G-K area where the project authority prevented farmers from obtaining tube-wells to irrigate their land, even in parts of the area where canal irrigation could not be provided. This was possible because, until the late-1980s, farmers could only obtain tube-wells either through BADC or with loans from the Agricultural Development Bank, both of them Government agencies which BWDB was able to influence.*

enough water. On the other hand, if water is retained to satisfy the needs of farmers on the higher margins, then the basin land stays too deeply flooded. A possible solution would be to construct low interior embankments within polders to retain water on the land at different levels to satisfy the requirements of farmers on high, intermediate and low land. However, experiments to test or demonstrate this practice proved unsuccessful, because of lack of cooperation from big land-owners.[25]

3.4.2 Second-generation problems

A number of problems has arisen in embankment projects after they have become operational. These can be regarded as second-generation problems which it may or may not have been possible to predict during project design.

The first such problem of which the author became aware was the rapid siltation of creeks outside some of the Coastal Embankment polders. Under natural conditions, tidal water flooding the land twice a day flows slowly off the land again as the tide falls, thus keeping the creeks flushed. After embankments have been completed, sluice-gates prevent tidal water from entering the polder at high tide. Therefore, water in the creek stagnates at high tide and drops some of its silt load, which the slow flow of the ebbing tide is insufficient to pick up again. Some creeks in the north-west of the Coastal Embankment Project area silted up within three years of embankments being closed.[26] That not only restricted navigation in the creeks, which formerly had been important. It also caused waterlogging in the adjacent polders because of the restricted outflow of drainage water during the monsoon season, rendering large areas of former agricultural land unsuitable for crop production. Hydraulic studies are needed to provide a solution to this problem.

A second early problem to develop was perennial waterlogging of some depression sites in the G-K project area. That resulted from excessive seepage losses from neighbouring irrigation channels located, as was described earlier, on permeable floodplain ridges. This problem could become more serious and extensive if full-scale irrigation were to be introduced in the dry season; (so far, the project has mainly provided supplementary irrigation in the pre-monsoon and monsoon seasons, allowing the water-table to fall during the first half of the dry season). If the problem were to become more serious — and it is, of course, already serious for the farmers whose land is affected — it might be necessary to introduce two measures to reduce waterlogging: line irrigation canals along sections where seepage losses are most serious; and if this does not provide a sufficient alleviation, install tube-wells to lower the water-table (as has been done in some canal-irrigated areas of Pakistan and northern India).

Since the late-1970s, there has been a growing awareness of zinc (and sometimes sulphur) deficiency in rice crops growing in the DND, Chandpur, Barisal and G-K project areas. Recent studies suggest that sulphur deficiency might eventually become the more widespread of the two. The symptoms develop where the rate of removal of soil nutrients has been increased due to the cultivation of one or more HYV crops per year and where the provision of irrigation for growing boro rice keeps the soils wet for most or all of the dry

---

[25] *Opposition led to one project engineer being killed in 1970.*

[26] *The author witnessed this phenomenon on his first visit to BWDB's Benerapota agricultural research station near Satkhira in October 1961. Station staff said that bed-levels in the neighbouring Betna river had risen by 10 feet (3+ m) in the previous three years.*

season in addition to the monsoon season. Farmers have found two solutions. One is to grow a quick-maturing winter crop — e.g., mustard or pulses — before planting boro rice. That helps the topsoil to dry out and become oxidized for a time, which increases zinc and sulphur availability. The second solution is to add zinc sulphate fertilizer. The use of this fertilizer increased remarkably within the first 18 months of it being made available, to the extent that a consultant examining the problem early in 1982 was able to find little visible evidence of zinc deficiency in the DND and Chandpur project areas: most farmers appeared to be using the fertilizer (Andriesse, 1982: see Chapter 4). Farmers clearly are much less conservative about adopting new practices that they are popularly condemned as being, at least when there are obvious and simple remedies available.

Acid Sulphate Soils, fortunately, provide a relatively minor problem in Bangladesh. Such soils occur patchily on saline tidal floodplains. The acidity problem is most severe and extensive in the south-east (around the Chakaria Sunderbans), where some soils have gone out of cultivation. However, a substantial area of such empoldered soils is highly productive for making salt. On the Ganges Tidal Floodplain, the acid sulphate problem is less serious because Ganges silt in the rivers during the flood season contains lime which could be used to neutralize the acidity, if necessary.

Peat basins in the transition zone between the Ganges river and tidal floodplains have not been empoldered, so problems of subsidence of the land surface due to drainage have not yet arisen on a large scale. However, extensive parts of these peat basins are included within the proposed Satla-Baghda and Faridpur projects. Problems from subsidence can be expected to develop in these project areas unless the original plans for draining the basins are modified so as to keep the peat wet (or to bury it with alluvium dredged from adjoining rivers).

3.4.3 Land use regulation

Two other second-generation problems have been identified: the encroachment of settlement onto flood-protected land; and the conversion of polders from agricultural use to shrimp farming.

A consultant's study of seven, scattered, rural areas showed that, in general, settlement and related non-agricultural land use expanded by only 0.8 percent (in total) between 1952 and 1974, even though the human population expanded by an average of 58 percent during that period (Serno, 1981: see Chapter 5). Examination of airphotos showed that the population had expanded almost entirely within existing settlements, by reducing the area under trees and waste land. That was partly explained by the seasonal flooding, which makes it costly to build a new earthen platform above flood-level, and partly by the farmers' natural inclination to preserve their land for agricultural production. However, in the first 10 years following the completion of the DND polder on the periphery of Dhaka, the area under settlement and industry doubled, and the trend obviously has continued as farmers (and suburban non-farmers) build individual houses scattered over the whole area instead of within existing settlements. Within the next 10-20 years, it is probable that the polder will no longer be a viable agricultural project: it will be a suburb of Dhaka.[27]

---

[27]*That prediction was correct. By the mid-1990s, more than half the DND polder had gone under houses and factories, and agriculture was confined to a small area in the east. The situation was aggravated by a new alignment of the Dhaka-Chittagong highway which was built across the centre of the polder, dividing the*

There is a danger that a similar sprawl of settlement could eventually negate the objectives of other polder projects. (Even pre-project, 28 percent of the Chandpur project area was occupied by settlements.) There is the risk, too, that the spread of settlement on the flat (i.e., without making high platforms) could lead to catastrophic loss of life and property if, for any reason, a polder embankment were to be breached during the flood season. It seems essential, therefore, that the spread of settlement (and industry) within flood-protected areas should be regulated so that the minimum amount of valuable agricultural land is transferred to non-agricultural uses, and so as to minimize the risk of catastrophic casualties and property damage occurring if an embankment is breached (or the drainage pumps fail).[28] At present, the Government of Bangladesh has no practical legal means to regulate land use. That is an omission which needs to be rectified without delay: see Chapter 10.

The same lack of land use regulation has permitted powerful businessmen and land-owners to convert parts of agricultural polders in parts of the Coastal Embankment Project area to shrimp farms. The process is simple. The embankment is breached, allowing brackish water to flood the land and shrimps to enter for breeding and growth. The subsequent soil salinity either prevents cultivators from growing their traditional, single, aman crop or it greatly reduces aman yields and production. It was estimated that, up to 1981, more than 4,000 ha of land had been lost to agriculture in this way in south-western polders; no figures are readily available for losses in the south-east.

Shrimp farming is highly profitable to the powerful individuals who control it. Shrimp exports also earn the country valuable foreign exchange. But the effect on small farmers and agricultural labourers can be disastrous, and the breaching of the embankments negates the purpose for which they were constructed. A thorough socio-economic study is needed to determine the net social and economic gains and losses. Technical studies also are needed to determine whether shrimp farming and crop production can be combined or can be practised on separate areas within a polder.[29] Whatever the findings, a locally-elected council or central government should have the power to regulate land use in the polders in the greater public interest.[30]

3.5 FUTURE NEEDS

To-date, major embankment projects have contributed an estimated one million tons (net) to annual foodgrain production. That is much less than was expected when the projects were planned. It also is much less than the 2.5 million tons (net) annually which small-scale pump and tube-well irrigation schemes have contributed.[31]

---

remaining agricultural area in two and considerably improving access to the central part of the polder for new settlement and industry. The main purpose of the project embankment and pumps is now to protect urban land.

[28] *See Chapter 24. For a discussion of emergency evacuation procedures needed in settled polder areas, see Brammer (1999), Chapter 8..*

[29] *Shrimp cultivation is discussed further in Chapter 4, Section 4.7.5.*

[30] *The situation might be different if shrimp farmers (and cultivators) were willing to pay charges for the benefits they derive from the polder project, but they do not. Also, it has to be acknowledged that the situation might not be any different if local government councils were empowered to regulate land use: such councils tend to be dominated by big land-owners.*

[31] *See footnote 14 above for recent figures on small-scale irrigation coverage.*

The major embankment projects included in the 1964 Master Plan have been slow to attract donor investment. Apart from technical problems described above, donors have been reluctant to take up such projects because of the high capital costs and the long gestation period before benefits appear. Small-scale projects have therefore attracted more support because of the lower investment cost per hectare, the quicker returns and the more widespread distribution of benefits. Included in those small projects are a number of so-called early implementation projects, usually providing flood protection and/or irrigation (but usually not polders) to areas of up to 6,000 ha.

Undoubtedly, if the country's population continues to grow at current rates — doubling in about 30 years — then major polder projects (perhaps including estuary closures) will eventually be needed so as to enable high-yielding transplanted aus and aman rice varieties to be grown on most of the country's floodplain land, 70 percent of which is too deeply flooded under natural conditions for such varieties to be grown reliably during the monsoon season. Irrigation will also be needed to expand HYV crop cultivation in the dry season and to make production more reliable in the monsoon season. By the year 2,000, it is estimated that annual foodgrain production must increase to 25 million tons to satisfy the population's consumption needs.[32]

Regarding such projects, the period in the immediate future while attention is concentrated on small-scale methods needs to be used to make an exhaustive study of experience gained from polder projects which have been completed. Those studies should include not only engineering considerations, but — at least equally important — agricultural, social and economic considerations: what has succeeded; what has failed. Armed with more comprehensive information, planners should then be able to design more realistic and profitable projects which are better tailored to the farmers' needs. That will require the recognition that engineering works are not an end in themselves. They are a means to an end. In Bangladesh, that end is agricultural development, as reflected in optimum improved land use and a well-fed population.[33]

3.6 CONCLUSIONS

Bangladesh's experience with major embankment projects suggests a number of principles which may be of wider relevance, especially in developing countries.

1. Where embankment projects are undertaken primarily to increase agricultural production, they should be regarded primarily as agricultural development projects rather than primarily as engineering projects. That implies that:

    a. soil scientists, agronomists, agro-economists and agricultural extension specialists should be given a more responsible role in project identification, design, appraisal and implementation;

---

[32] *See footnote 6 above.*

[33] *After the original paper was drafted, Government prepared a Master Plan for Water Resources Development with UNDP and World Bank assistance (MPO, 1985). The report focussed more on irrigation development and allocation of water between sectors than on flood-protection and polder development. Following severe floods in 1987 and 1988, Government (with widespread donor assistance) carried out wide-ranging studies under the Flood Action Plan (FPCO, 1995), but to-daie (early-1999), these have not led to further investment in major embankment projects (largely because of donor reservations regarding Government's institutional capacity to operate and maintain large-scale projects). Amongst the Flood Action Plan studies was a comprehensive review of experience with existing water-control projects (FPCO, 1992a, b; Sultana et al., 1995).*

b. in areas which already are cultivated, the opinions of a representative range of farmers in proposed project areas should be sought in advance regarding feasible cropping patterns with proposed project inputs;

c. where a project would greatly alter existing agroecological conditions (as usually will be the case with embankment projects), possible new crops or cropping patterns should be tested and demonstrated in pilot areas before the full project is implemented; and

d. objections from those whose livelihoods might suffer as a result of project implementation should be considered with a view either to modifying the project design so as to remove their objections or to provide them with adequate alternatives or compensation.

2. Because embankment projects usually are expensive, especially when they include pump drainage and irrigation, they should be regarded as a development of last resort. That means that Government should examine and use alternative, cheaper, agricultural development modes wherever possible, until embankment, etc., becomes the most economic mode remaining available.

3. Geomorphological, hydrological and hydraulic studies should be made to determine the optimum location of project embankments and irrigation/drainage headworks along active river channels and in tidal floodplains, taking into account the predicted effects of project works on river-flow and sedimentation outside embankments and on drainage within embankments.

4. Irrigation channels should be sited and designed so as to minimize seepage losses which might cause waterlogging and prevent irrigation benefits from being provided to tail-end areas.

5. Especially in areas where small farmers predominate, projects should be designed so as to minimize land acquisition for project works and so as to maximize the number of farmers who benefit, even if that means accepting a suboptimum rate of return.

6. Soil and crop conditions on different agroecological land types within project areas should be monitored regularly so as to provide early warnings of any physical, chemical or biological problems which may develop under the changed hydrological and cropping regimes. Relevant studies should be made to find practical solutions, including solutions which might require modification of project design or operation. Similarly, agro-economic surveys should be made regularly and, where necessary, appropriate changes should be made in project design, operation or charges so as to ensure that both farmers and project authorities can achieve profitable returns.

7. Either at national or at project level, land use regulations should be made — and enforced — which will ensure that settlement and industry do not spread unnecessarily onto valuable agricultural land or onto sites where disastrous losses of life and property might occur in the event of an embankment being breached by floods; also, so as to prevent or control forms of land use which conflict with project objectives.

Chapter 4

CHANGES IN LAND USE AND SOILS IN MAJOR WATER DEVELOPMENT PROJECT AREAS[1]

This study assessed the beneficial and adverse changes which had occurred in land use and soils in five major irrigation and drainage project areas. Particular attention was paid to assessing increases in foodgrain production that had been achieved, identifying reasons for shortfalls in project targets and examining the circumstances under which zinc and sulphur deficiencies occurred. Remedial actions were recommended where project design deficiencies or adverse environmental changes were identified.

4.1 BACKGROUND

Major flood protection, drainage and irrigation projects have been implemented in East Pakistan and Bangladesh since the mid-1950s in the framework of successive Governments' policies to increase food production so as to keep pace with the increasing population. The contribution that could be made by such projects was recognized as early as 1951 when, with the assistance of FAO specialists, plans were formulated that later provided the basis for the first project of this kind, the Ganges-Kobadak (G-K) project. The so-called Master Plan prepared by EPWAPDA (now BWDB) in 1964 envisaged the development of 35 polder projects including flood-control embankments for a gross area of approximately 13.5 million acres of land (IECo, 1964). Generally, the plans also included the provision of irrigation.

By 1982, seven of those embankment and polder projects had been completed: Dhaka-Narayanganj-Demra (DND) project; Chandpur Irrigation Project (CIP); Barisal Irrigation Project (BIP), Phase I; G-K project, Kushtia Unit, Phases I & II; Brahmaputra Right Bank Embankment (BRE) project; Manu River Project; and Coastal Embankment Project (CEP). All these project areas have benefited from flood protection. All but the BRE and CEP areas have been provided with irrigation facilities, also. The benefits, as expressed in increased annual rice production since project implementation, range from 30 percent (BIP) to 300 percent (DND). This increase was achieved by the introduction of an extra rice

---

[1] *This chapter is an edited and abbreviated version of the report on a study carried out by W. Andriesse, Land Use Consultant, under the FAO/UNDP Agricultural Development Adviser Project (Andriesse, 1982). Background information given on the environment, agriculture and population has been omitted: relevant information is given in Chapters 1-3. Except where stated otherwise, the information relates to the time of the study, April-June 1982. Footnotes which appeared in the original document are given in normal font. Footnotes that have been added are given in italics.*

crop (DND, CIP) — in which areas cropping intensity increased by 80 and 100 percent respectively — and by the introduction of high-yielding varieties (IIYVs) of rice.

However, in most cases, the benefits have been less than were envisaged in the original plans. A large number of factors — technical as well as socio-economic — have contributed to constrain production. This study concentrates on the physical factors which may have limited production.

Five project areas were studied: DND; CIP; BIP; G-K, Kushtia unit, Phase I; and Polder 22 of the CEP: see Figure 4.1. These areas were selected on the basis of their developed status — most had been operational for several years — and their performance. The selection includes 'successful' projects such as DND,[2] as well as problematic projects such as BIP and G-K. Polder 22 was selected as an example of the CEP area which has specific physical factors (salinity) to cope with.

FIGURE 4.1

Location of study areas

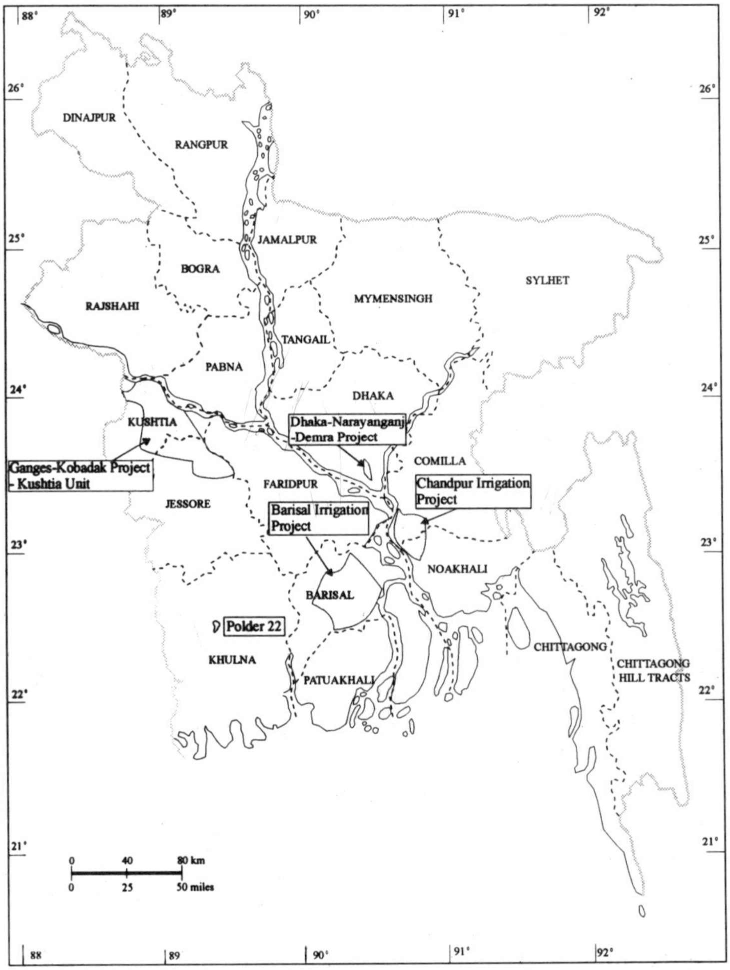

---

[2] *For comments on subsequent developments in the DND project area, see Chapter 5, Section A8.*

The findings in the five selected project areas are described separately in the following sections. A final section discusses specific soil problems related to wetland paddy cultivation.

4.2 DHAKA-NARAYANGANJ-DEMRA PROJECT

4.2.1 Physical characteristics

The DND project comprises flood protection, internal drainage and irrigation on 20,600 acres of land (gross) just south-east of Dhaka, between the Buriganga and Sitalakhya rivers (Figure 4.2).[3] The project area lies within three main physiographic units: Madhupur Tract; Old Meghna Estuarine Floodplain; and Young Brahmaputra (Jamuna) Floodplain.

The outliers of the Madhupur Tract in the north-west of the project area consist of down-warped, little-weathered, Madhupur Clay that has been shallowly dissected by broad valleys. The terrace soils in this area are mainly grey, mottled olive-grey and olive-yellow, heavy clays. The soils in the valleys dissecting the terrace are mainly very dark grey, heavy clays. Local height differences are up to 3 feet.

The Old Meghna Estuarine Floodplain occupies most of the project area. The soils of this unit occur in a pattern of broad ridges and basins, with grey, mottled yellowish brown, silt loams or silty clay loams on the higher parts and grey to dark grey, mottled yellowish brown, silty clays and dark grey, very heavy clays in the basins. The height differences between adjoining ridges and basins generally do not exceed 1.5-2 feet.

The low-lying Young Brahmaputra Floodplain deposits occur in a narrow strip along the western boundary. They include grey silty clay soils on smooth, low ridges, and grey and dark grey heavy clays in basins.

4.2.2 Project characteristics

The project area is divided into two units. Unit I (gross area 14,500 ac), occurring south of the Dhaka-Demra road, comprises flood protection by means of a heightened road embankment surrounding the area. Internal drainage is regulated by means of four reversible pumps, with a total capacity of 600 cusecs, and a system of drainage canals. Irrigation water is pumped from the Sitalakhya river by the same pumping station, from where it is gravity-fed into the area through two main canals (16 miles total length) and six lateral canals (32 miles). The total irrigable area is 10,500 ac. The remainder of the land in this unit consists of cultivable land above irrigation command level (terrace hillocks and high parts of floodplain ridges) estimated at 8 percent of the gross area, plus roads, embankments and water bodies (500 ac; 3.5 percent), and homesteads (2,325 ac; 16 percent).

Unit II (gross area 6,100 ac) lies north of the Dhaka-Demra road. This unit has no flood protection or internal drainage component, but part of it can be irrigated from two laterals taking off from the northern main canal in Unit I. The irrigable area is 4,700 ac. A relatively larger proportion of the land in Unit II is above irrigation command level, mainly due to the relative abundance of elevated hillocks and river levees (total area about 1,000 ac; 16 percent of the gross area of Unit II). The levees occur mainly along the Balu river. The area occupied by roads and water bodies is estimated at 100 ac (1.5 percent) and the area of homesteads at 300 ac (5 percent).

---

[3] *Figure 4.2 has been reduced in scale from the original in Andriesse (1982). Figures 4.1, 4.4, 4.6, 4.8 and 4.10 have also been reduced in scale to suit the format of this volume.*

FIGURE 4.2

Dhaka-Narayanganj-Demra project area

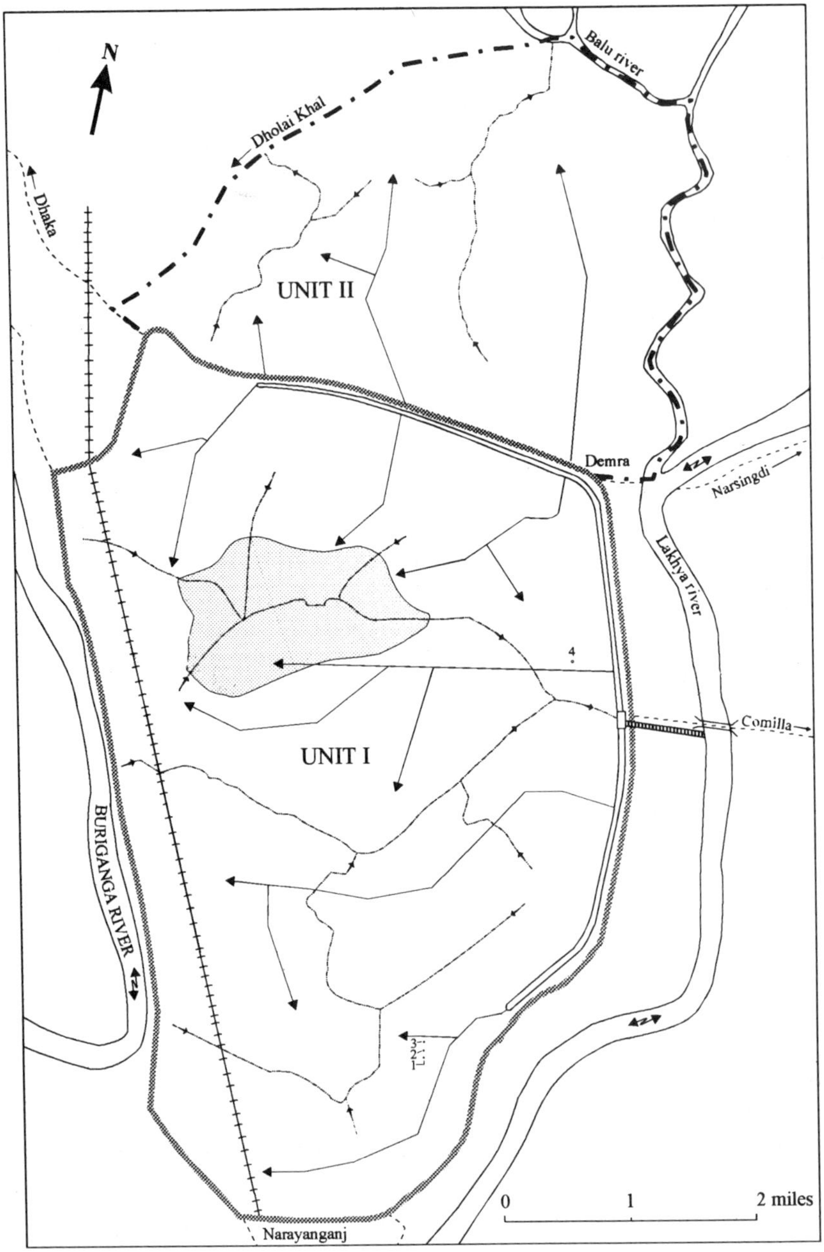

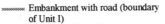

LEGEND

xxxxx Embankment with road (boundary of Unit I)	- - - - Road
— · Boundary of Unit II	+++++ Railway
⬭ Main area with inadequate drainage after heavy rainfall	——▸ Irrigation canal
▭ Pumping plant	- - -▸ Drain
· 1 Observation site	▥▥▥ Intake canal
	⬯ Main distribution canal
	⬌➤ River (tidal)

Before project implementation, practically all of the area was subject to annual flooding by accumulated rainwater which could not drain into the adjoining rivers when they were at high flood levels. Under project conditions, flooding has been virtually eliminated from Unit I due to the provision of a flood embankment and drainage pumps. However, seasonal flooding still occurs in Unit II. The depth and duration of flooding in that area depend on the topographic position. Terrace hillocks and floodplain ridges are mainly flooded up to about 3 feet for 4-6 months (May-October), whereas the deeper basin centres are flooded up to 6-12 feet for up to 8 months (April-November).

4.2.3 Land use

Before project implementation, almost all of the land except homestead land was flooded during the monsoon season. Also, rainfall in the dry season is very low: the mean total in the months November-April is less than 2.5 inches. Therefore, the main land use formerly consisted of the cultivation of a single crop of broadcast deepwater aman paddy, and the land was left fallow in the dry season. Local paddy varieties were used, adapted to the various flood levels occurring in the area. In the deepest basins, these included the so-called long-stemmed floating paddy varieties which can keep growing with quickly-rising floodwater. On some of the higher ridges and on terrace land, mainly in the north of the area, dryland rabi crops were grown (mainly mustard, pulses, khesari), using residual moisture stored in the soils after the rainy/flood season. On Medium Lowland, mixed broadcast aus+aman or single crops of jute or broadcast aman were grown. However, the overall cropping intensity was low (approximately 110-120 percent) and so were average yields: b.aman 15 md/ac; b.aus 12 md/ac; jute 12 md/ac (IECo, 1964).[4]

After irrigation water became available in 1967, farmers in the DND area quickly took to growing boro paddy and, to a lesser extent, aus. The total area of boro and aus — which had been less than 1,500 ac before the project started — increased to about 8,000 ac in 1967 and to about 15,000-18,000 ac in the years thereafter (Figure 4.3). Boro is the more important of the two crops, presently covering 10,000-13,000 ac annually. In another development, HYVs became available from 1966-67, and were quickly adopted by farmers. In 1982, about 90 percent of all the boro and aus paddy grown in the area was HYVs. On average, the HYVs produce 45-50 md/ac with modest applications of fertilizers.

Boro paddy is usually transplanted from December to February and harvested in June.[5] In Unit I, which is flood-protected, boro generally is followed by a short fallow period before transplanted aman is grown (July-December). Where HYV aus is grown, it is transplanted in March and harvested in July, and followed immediately by t. aman. Preceding aus, dryland rabi crops are sometimes grown: mustard, pulses, oilseeds. Such rabi crops are also grown on the higher parts of the project area that are beyond the reach of irrigation (2,175 ac in total). In the rainy season, t. aman is also grown on those ridges and low hillocks.

The total area of aman has decreased considerably, from approximately 12,000 ac in 1967 to less than 10,000 ac annually since 1971 (Figure 4.3). The decrease has mainly taken place in Unit II where deep seasonal flooding still occurs. HYV aman cannot be grown in that area. Even in Unit I, HYVs occupy only about 70 percent of the t. aman area.

---

[4] *1 maund (md) = 82.29 lbs = 37.3261 kg. 1 md/ac = 92.24 kg/ha.*

[5] *The first HYV released, IR-8, was a long-maturing variety.*

FIGURE 4.3

*Area of boro, aus and aman rice grown in the Dhaka-Narayanganj-Demra project
area 1967-80*

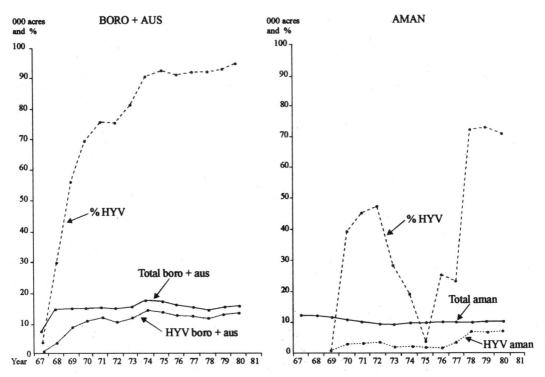

HYV aman is not suited to about 10-15 percent of the cultivable land in Unit I, in deep basins subject to rapid and deep flooding for a week or more following heavy rainfall. The pumping capacity of the project (600 cusec) is not sufficient to carry off the water sufficiently rapidly from these basin sites. Farmers cultivating these low areas prefer to grow longer-stemmed t. aman varieties (Pajam, Kartiksail) which yield 25-30 md/ac *versus* 35-40 md/ac for HYVs. Broadcast aman, grown on about 500-1,000 ac mainly in Unit II, gives yields of approximately 20 md/ac.

The overall cropping intensity in the DND following project implementation is estimated at 160 percent. Cropping intensity is much higher in Unit I (190 percent) than in Unit II (110 percent). The combined effect of increased cropping intensity and the introduction of HYVs has more than quadrupled paddy production since 1967. Pre-project annual grain production was estimated to be 8,700 metric tonnes (mt), and present (1981) production is approximately 37,500 mt. The original project plan aimed at a production of 15,350 mt: the introduction of HYVs was not foreseen at that time.

Another considerable change in land use which has occurred post-project is the encroachment of settlement. A recent study (Serno, 1981: see Chapter 5) has shown that, since project implementation, there has been a marked increase in the area occupied by homesteads and industry (e.g., brick factories) in Unit I, which is flood-protected. That study showed that homestead land increased from approximately 900 ac in 1968 to 1985 ac in 1977. At the present rate of expansion, the area could be converted into a suburb of Dhaka by the year 2000. Meanwhile, the area of settlements in Unit II has changed little and, in the absence of any planned flood-control measures, it will not do so in the future, either.[6]

Developments that have taken place on similar land outside the DND project area include the introduction of irrigation using small pumps. Low-lift pumps (LLPs, mainly 2 cusec, irrigating 30-50 ac) take water from the Sitalakhya river and smaller streams to irrigate areas east of the former river. Thirty-five deep tube-wells of similar capacity are used in the CARE-Demra project. Irrigation is mainly applied to HYV boro paddy. Dryland rabi crops include wheat, tobacco, chilli, mustard, and vegetables, mainly grown using residual soil moisture. Wet-season crops in these flooded areas are mainly broadcast aman and jute. Field observations suggest that the cropping intensity in these areas is 130-150 percent.[7]

4.2.4 Soil conditions affecting land use and productivity

Permeability, tillage and relief. The physical properties of most of the soils — i.e., those occurring in the basins and on the lower slopes of ridges — are well suited to irrigated paddy cultivation. They generally have a medium to fine texture, can easily be puddled and have low natural permeability. Under such conditions, water losses by percolation are low, made even more so because a ploughpan is easily formed under cultivation, which further reduces downward water movement. The soils on the ridges have lighter textures which, because of their favourable moisture-holding capacity and moderate to rapid permeability, make them well suited to the cultivation of irrigated or rainfed dryland rabi crops.

Both the low and the high parts of the project area have their own specific problems. The high floodplain ridges and the Madhupur Tract hillocks which occupy about 10 percent of the cultivable area (weighted average for Units I and II) are beyond the reach of gravity irrigation and can only be used in the dry season for rabi crops using residual soil moisture. In exceptional cases, the ridges have coarse-textured droughty soils that are unsuited to dryland rabi crops. Deep basins occupying approximately 10 percent of the cultivable area in Unit I are unsafe for HYV aman cultivation because the project's pump-drainage capacity is insufficient to control the depth of flooding adequately in these sites following heavy rainfall. Farmers grow local, long-stemmed, aman varieties instead in such sites.

Fertility. Soil fertility, or the ability of soils to supply adequate amounts of nutrients for good plant performance, is generally relatively high in the project area. In the past, under low-intensity management, the soils were capable of sustaining moderate yields of mainly a single crop of deepwater aman per year. The alternating wet (reduced) and dry (oxidized) conditions accounted for the ready availability of phosphorus and potash. In cropping systems involving wetland paddy cultivation, nitrogen supply can partly be attributed to biological activity, especially by blue-green algae which can provide nitrogen equivalent to approximately 0.5 md/ac of urea per year.

Under project conditions, with a much higher cropping intensity (190 percent in Unit I) and crop yields that have doubled since 1967, much larger amounts of plant nutrients are now removed from the soils annually than formerly. These losses have to be compensated

---

[6] *These predictions were broadly correct. Settlement and industry continued to expand rapidly in Unit I through the 1980s and 1990s, so that the Unit I area did become virtually a suburb of greater Dhaka. There has been some expansion of housing and industry in Unit II, mainly alongside the Dhaka-Demra road.*

[7] *A pump-drainage and irrigation project was subsequently provided on the east bank of the Sitalakhya area opposite the DND project area.*

if high crop yields are to be obtained and sustained. Manure and chemical fertilizers can serve this purpose, if supplied in adequate amounts. Average N, P and K applications in the project area (in 1982) are 1 md/ac urea (usually divided between a basal dose and one top-dressing), 1.5 md/ac triple superphosphate (TSP) (basal) and 0.5 md/ac muriate of potash (MP) (basal).

As a consequence of the increased cropping intensity and production, but also because of the prevailing chemically-reduced conditions in topsoils that are kept wet by the irrigation of boro and aman paddy, some nutrient deficiencies have developed in the project area, notably of zinc and sulphur. In fact, zinc and sulphur deficiencies are common disorders in continuous paddy cultivation that have been reported from many rice-producing countries. In the DND area, zinc deficiency was typically reported in aman and boro paddy crops in Unit I where the cropping intensity is high and reduced soil conditions occur almost throughout the year. Zinc deficiency can easily be corrected by the application of zinc sulphate, or by dipping the seedlings into a zinc oxide suspension before transplantation. In 1981, zinc sulphate became available to farmers, and a dramatic recovery of zinc-deficient rice plants was observed in the DND area. Unfortunately, the limited research data available do not reflect such high yield increases (Table 4.1). Application of zinc sulphate to suspected zinc-deficient plots increased the yields over controls by 17 and 13 percent respectively for boro and aman paddy. However, the relatively high average yields on the control plots seems to suggest that zinc deficiency was not acute. In the same experiment, the effect of applying gypsum (calcium sulphate) was tested, with yield increases of only 6 percent over control. The combined effect of zinc sulphate and gypsum on boro paddy was not higher than the single effect of zinc, but aman yields increased by 16 percent.

A few soil and plant samples were taken for laboratory analysis from sites suspected to be deficient in zinc and sulphur, but the results did not show a clear zinc deficiency: see Table 4.4 at the end of this chapter. A more detailed discussion of zinc and sulphur deficiency is given in Section 4.8.

4.3 CHANDPUR IRRIGATION PROJECT

4.3.1 Physical characteristics

The CIP comprises an area of 133,000 ac on both sides of the South Dakatia river south of Chandpur in parts of Comilla and Noakhali Districts (Figure 4.4). The soils in the area have developed in three main physiographic units:

a. Old Meghna Estuarine Floodplain, occupying only a relatively small area in the north-east of the project area;

b. Lower Meghna River Floodplain, occupying most of the project area; and

c. Young Meghna Estuarine Floodplain in the south-west.[8]

Both the Old Meghna Estuarine Floodplain and the Lower Meghna River Floodplain have an alluvial landscape consisting of low ridges (present or former levees) and shallow basins. The ridges are the more elevated sites with lighter-textured soils: mainly olive to olive-grey silt loams. The basins are slightly lower areas with moderate to fine-textured

---

[8] Units a and c were originally mapped as the Lower Meghna Tidal Floodplain.

TABLE 4.1

Effect of sulphur and zinc applications on yields of HYV boro and HYV aman in the DND project area

Crop (No of plots)	Yield (md/ac) and yield increase over control (%) due to fertilizer application			
	Control	$CaSO_4$ 60 lbs/ac	$ZnSO_4$ 11 lb/ac	$CaSO_4$ (60 lb/ac) + $ZnSO_4$ (11 lb/ac)
HYV boro (9)	29	31 (6)	34 (17)	33 (14)
HYV aman (7)	32	34 (6)	36 (13)	37 (16)

Note: Trials were carried out on 16 superphosphate trial plots.

soils: mainly grey to very dark grey silty clay loams and clay loams. In the Old Meghna Estuarine Floodplain, ridges and basins occur in a smooth, very gently undulating relief with local height differences of only 1-2 feet. In the Lower Meghna River Floodplain, the gently undulating relief is more irregular, with height differences of up to 4 feet locally. The soils in the Lower Meghna Estuarine Floodplain are relatively young and little-developed: mainly finely-stratified, slightly calcareous, olive to olive-grey, silt loams.

4.3.2 Project characteristics

The CIP, which effectively started in 1975, includes flood protection, drainage and irrigation, as well as other infrastructural improvements such as navigation facilities, roads, agricultural extension services, etc. The project area is protected from flooding from the Meghna and Dakatia rivers by 63 miles of flood-control embankments rising 10-14 feet above ground level. Drainage is provided by two regulators. The northern regulator (Char Baghadi) has reversible pumps, with a total capacity of 1,200 cusec, that can be used for drainage and for irrigation. The southern regulator (Hajimara), with a capacity of 23,000 cusec, serves for drainage only. Other drainage improvements included loop-cutting and dredging in the South Dakatia river, re-excavation of existing khals, and the construction of sluice-gates in the flood-control embankment.

Irrigation is by means of double lifting. At Char Baghadi pump-house, irrigation water is first lifted into the South Dakatia river which then serves as the main irrigation canal feeding water into tributary khals and a number of newly-constructed irrigation canals. Secondly, water is lifted by means of 2-cusec diesel LLPs which are hired out by the project to farmers' groups forming irrigation units of approximately 40 ac each. The project has 1,200 LLPs. A small part of the project area is irrigated with water from two irrigation canals that take off from the Char Baghadi pump-house and run parallel to the flood-control embankment. They have a total length of 10 miles and a planned command area of 5,000 ac. According to project statistics, the total irrigable area in the CIP is 72,000 ac, out of a gross cultivable area of 90,000 ac. The total area occupied by rivers, khals, roads and embankments is 5,000 ac.

The total population of the project area was estimated at 658,000 persons in 1976. The area then had 102,000 farm families. Approximately 77 percent of the farmers owned their cultivated land, 17 percent were owner-cum-tenants, and about 6 percent were purely tenants. The average gross farm area reportedly was 1.1 ac, of which 0.8 ac was cultivable. In 1976, about 50 percent of the farms were smaller than 0.5 ac, 20 percent were between 0.5 and 1 ac, and 15 percent were between 1 and 1.5 ac.

FIGURE 4.4

Chandpur Irrigation Project area

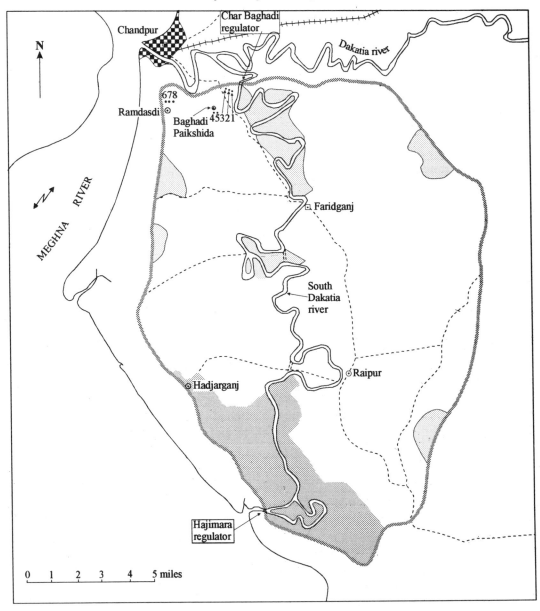

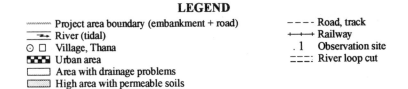

LEGEND

ᨡᨡᨡ	Project area boundary (embankment + road)	‒ ‒ ‒ ‒ Road, track
➤	River (tidal)	+‒+‒+ Railway
⊙ □	Village, Thana	. 1 Observation site
▨▨	Urban area	⹀⹀⹀ River loop cut
▭	Area with drainage problems	
▨	High area with permeable soils	

Earlier statistics, from a soil and agricultural survey carried out pre-project in 1967, showed average farm sizes that were considerably larger. The average farm size at that time was 1.9 ac and the net cultivated area was 1.5 ac per farm. Only 20 percent of the farms were smaller than 0.5 ac, and almost 60 percent were between 0.5 and 2 ac. The decreasing farm sizes not only reflect the subdivision of holdings due to the division of land amongst children, but they also reflect a process of consolidation of land into larger holdings. Big farmers often act as money-lenders to small farmers and, in such transactions, land usually is mortgaged. If a farmer fails to pay back his loan, he either loses his land to the money-lender, or he is forced to sell his land to another party. This consolidation is illustrated by statistics on the large farm sizes: in 1967, only 12 percent of all farms were larger than 2.5 ac, but in 1976 the proportion was 21 percent.

Due to the high population density in the project area (approximately 3,200 persons per sq. mile), a large proportion of the land consists of homesteads, tanks, etc., which occupy 38,000 ac, approximately 25 percent of the total project area.

4.3.3   Land use

Before project implementation, seasonal flooding allowed the cultivation of at least one paddy crop on most of the land (except homestead land). On the relatively high land that was subject to shallow flooding (1-3 feet) — mainly in the south-west and also on high ridges in other parts — t. aman was grown, preceded by b. aus and usually followed by dryland rabi crops such as chilli, pulses and millet (*kaon*) or by fallow. Local crop varieties were used. It is estimated that this cropping pattern prevailed on approximately 30 percent of the cultivable area. The winter fallow was predominantly practised on the highest and somewhat droughty land in the south-west (10 percent of the cultivable area). In addition to the droughtiness of those soils, the late harvesting of t. aman would make it impossible to plant dryland rabi crops so as to use residual soil moisture optimally.

Medium Lowland and Lowland, on which flood levels used to reach depths between 3 and 7 feet, were mainly used for mixed aus+aman in the rainy season, followed by dryland rabi crops in the winter. This cropping pattern prevailed on an estimated 60 percent of the cultivable area. Within this cropping pattern, jute was grown instead of aus on about 10 percent of the cultivable area. In areas that did not drain quickly after the flood season, mainly deep basins on the Old Meghna Estuarine Floodplain, b. aman was the main crop, and the soils usually were left fallow in the dry season (5 percent of the cultivable area). Basins near the northern part of the South Dakatia river were almost continuously wet throughout the year. No crops were grown in such areas, which were largely overgrown with reeds and tall grasses (5 percent of the cultivable area).

The overall cropping intensity pre-project was about 160 percent.[9] Yield records from the survey in 1964-66 indicate average aus yields then of 12-15 md/ac (paddy). Similarly, aman yields were low: 7.5-13 md/ac for b. aman and 5.5-16 md/ac for t. aman.

Since project implementation, and more particularly since the fielding of LLPs started, there has been an enormous increase in boro paddy cultivation (Figure 4.5). Before 1975, boro paddy was virtually non-existent in the project area. In 1977-78, when the first batch of 250 LLPs became operational, 9,940 ac were irrigated. In 1980-81, the boro paddy area

---

[9] Following BWDB custom, mixed aus+aman is considered as one crop.

FIGURE 4.5

Area of boro, aus and aman rice and dryland rabi crops grown in the Chandpur Irrigation Project area 1975-81

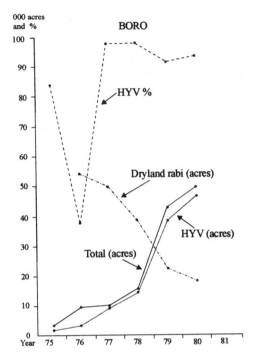

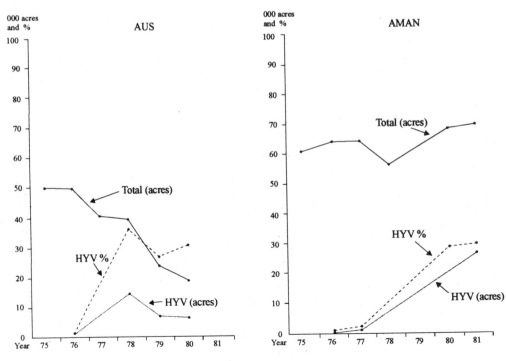

reached over 50,000 ac, with 930 pumps fielded.[10] Almost all the boro paddy grown consists of HYVs, mainly BR-3. In 1980-81, the average boro paddy yield was almost 50 md/ac (paddy). However, average boro paddy yields were much higher in previous years: 67-70 md/ac in 1977-80. The lower yields in 1980-81 probably were related to irrigation problems due to the reported late fielding of many LLPs.

The increase in the boro paddy area has clearly taken place at the cost of dryland rabi crop cultivation. In the period between 1976 and 1981, the area of dryland rabi crops decreased from approximately 54,000 ac to 19,000 ac. The main crops affected by this decrease were chilli (down from 21,000 ac in 1976-77 to 4,500 ac in 1980-81) and pulses (16,000 down to 3,000 ac). However, the area cultivated with wheat, Irish potato and vegetables increased from 1,200 ac (total) in 1976-77 to 6,600 ac in 1980-81.

The total area of aus paddy cultivated decreased from almost 50,000 ac in 1975-76 to 18,000 ac in 1980-81. Although the proportion of HYV aus relative to the total aus area increased from 1976, it had only reached 30 percent by 1981, suggesting that farmers feel little attracted to this crop. The cropping system in which HYV boro is transplanted in January-February and harvested in May-June leaves practically no time to cultivate an aus crop before the generally-more-profitable aman crop should be transplanted in July-August. Also, supplementary irrigation might be needed for land preparation for HYV transplanted aus, and farmers will be reluctant to hire LLPs for this limited purpose. The average yield of HYV aus (in 1980-81) was over 32 md/ac (paddy). Locally-improved varieties produced 17-20 md/ac, and local varieties 14-18 md/ac.

The jute area also decreased: from almost 9,000 ac in 1975-76 to 2,500 ac in 1980-81. However, there were about 13,000 ac under jute in 1977-79.

The total area cultivated with aman — 60-70,000 ac — has not changed much since project implementation (Figure 4.5). Also, the area of HYVs as a proportion of the total aman area has remained relatively low, not exceeding 30 percent in 1980-81. This low figure might be explained by drainage problems that still occur over considerable areas within the polder. In such areas, the longer-stemmed local varieties (plus Pajam) are more suitable than the short-stemmed HYVs. Another reason for the predominance of local varieties is their more useful straw and higher market value of the grain. HYV yields in 1980-81 averaged 59 md/ac (paddy); Pajam produced about 40 md/ac on average, and local varieties 20-30 md/ac.

The overall cropping intensity in 1980-81 (according to CIP statistics) was 177 percent. The total cropped area was 160,000 ac, and the cultivable area 90,000 ac.[11] Therefore, only a 10 percent increase over the pre-project cropping intensity of 160 percent was achieved. However, total grain production increased by much more: from 71,500 mt in 1975-76 to 206,500 mt in 1980-81 (paddy and wheat), an increase of about 290 percent. In spite of the reduction in the dryland rabi crop area, total dryland rabi crop production also increased: from 51,000 mt in 1976-77 to 67,000 mt in 1980-81.

---

[10]Area and yield data are based on CIP statistics. The boro area includes approximately 1,000 ac of gravity-irrigated land from the two canals in the north of the polder.

[11]The cropping intensity figure is considerably lower than that given in the World Bank's completion report in 1980. However, the World Bank's reported rabi crop area is much higher (40,240 ac in 1980-81), and it calculated the cropping intensity over a net cultivated area of 79,000 ac. In both calculations, mixed aus+aman was considered as one crop.

Changes in land use and the higher production would also have occurred in the project area even without project implementation. In order to assess these changes, land use outside the project area was examined. Changes that occurred there involved the (limited) introduction of HYV boro cultivation with LLP irrigation, and a sharp increase in the area of chilli, pulses and oilseeds. Although specific yield data are not available, it might be assumed that rabi crop yields increased as much in areas outside the project as within the project area, where the yields of pulses and oilseeds almost doubled. Therefore, it may be estimated that total dryland rabi crop production outside the project area increased considerably, too, probably up to 300 percent of pre-project production levels.[12]

4.3.4 Soil conditions affecting land use and productivity

Permeability/tillage. Some of the higher parts of the project area, occupying about 10 percent of the total cultivable area, include soils that are droughty in the dry season due to their elevated position and their relatively rapid permeability. These characteristics render such soils less suitable for irrigated paddy cultivation because of the high and frequent water applications that would be required. However, in the rainy season, local t. aman varieties can be (and usually are) grown on these soils, but late harvesting of that crop prevents dryland rabi crops from being sown, especially in the south-west of the project area. Also, the lower settlement density in the south-west suggests that there is a high incidence of absentee land-owners on these soils. Big absentee land-owners are traditionally not much interested in dryland rabi crop cultivation, as they earn sufficient income from one aman crop per year.

Poor drainage. In spite of the drainage facilities and improvements by the project, adverse drainage conditions still prevailed in some parts of the polder. These areas comprised an estimated total of 6,000 ac, notably the basins along the northern part of the South Dakatia river and some large depressions near the project boundary where natural drainage was blocked by the construction of the main embankment (see Figure 4.4). Throughout the rest of the polder, local depressions surrounded by higher ridges also impeded drainage, mainly due to the inflow of rainfall run-off from the ridges.

In the rainy season, the depressions are too deeply flooded to allow the cultivation of HYV paddy. They are used for the cultivation of local t. aman paddy varieties or for deepwater aman. Most such sites remain too wet for dryland rabi crops to be grown successfully. Some of the depressions along the South Dakatia river are not cultivated at all, but farmers cut the reeds and grasses growing there to use for roof-thatching.

In order to solve the drainage problems in depressions near the main embankment, the project is presently (1982) constructing three sluice-gates. Along the South Dakatia river, proposed improvement of drainage conditions consists of constructing low embankments which should prevent river flooding of these areas. However, the physiography of these low-lying areas suggests that the present flooding results from a combination of river flooding, run-off from adjacent higher land and a high water-table. Therefore, the construction of embankments alone will probably not be adequate to solve the drainage problem in these areas. Additional pumping might still be required. Project proposals to include fish ponds

---

[12]Later in the 1980s, there was a considerable expansion of tube-well irrigation in the area to the east of the CIP, used predominantly for HYV boro production.

in these areas have reportedly not attracted much interest from the farmers. Some of the small local depressions that occur scattered over the project area, and which are flooded mainly from local run-off, could possibly be drained sufficiently by the excavation of small ditches crossing the ridge barriers.

Fertility. In the reconnaissance soil survey report covering the area (SRDI, 1970b), the fertility levels of most floodplain soils were considered to be moderate. The exceptions were the soils occurring on the highest topographical positions which were lighter in texture and had lower organic mater contents, giving them a lower cation exchange capacity (CEC 10-15 meq/100g soil) compared with the CEC of basin soils (15-20 meq/100g soil).

With the increase in cropping intensity since project implementation and even more so with the increase in yields, large amounts of plant nutrients are being extracted from the soil, especially when crop residues such as rice straw are being harvested as well. Therefore, in these intensive cropping patterns, soil fertility has to be maintained by applying fertilizers and/or manure. Clear responses to applications of urea, TSP and MP to t. aman were reported on the soils of Tippera, Paikpara and Ramgati series in the project area (SRDI, 1970b). Fertilizer effects ranged from a minimum increase of 16 percent over control for a combined N and P application on fine-textured Paikpara soils to 81 percent increase for N, P plus K applications on the lighter-textured Ramgati soils.

Zinc deficiency was a rather widespread disorder in the 1981 aman crop shortly after it was transplanted. On the advice of BRRI scientists, farmers applied zinc sulphate, with apparent success. Field reports indicated that, in most cases, the crops recovered and 'reasonable' yields were obtained. Zinc deficiency was also observed in the 1982 boro crop, but not to a large extent. It was reported that most farmers who successfully applied zinc sulphate to the previous aman crop made a similar application to the boro crop. Analytical data for soil and plant samples that were taken generally confirm the field observations regarding zinc deficiency in rice: see Table 4.4 at the end of this chapter. In addition, however, the analyses showed that several of the plants sampled had low levels of sulphur, some even below critical levels. Therefore, application of gypsum (calcium sulphate) is recommended. A more detailed discussion on the occurrence of zinc and sulphur deficiency is given in Section 4.8.1.

Field trials on boro paddy (IR-8, BR-3) in 1981 also showed the incidence of zinc and sulphur deficiencies. On 24 randomly-selected plots, zinc sulphate, gypsum and zinc sulphate + gypsum were applied at rates equivalent to 8 kg/ac of $ZnSO_4$, 80 kg of $CaSO_4$ and 8 kg $ZnSO_4$ + 80 kg $CaSO_4$. The average increases over control were: 10 percent for sulphur, 22 percent for zinc, and 28 percent for sulphur + zinc. The average yield on the control plots was 40 md/ac. On five of the control plots, yields were only 12-20 md/ac, and at these sites the zinc and sulphur applications were very effective, giving yield increases of 44-48 percent for sulphur, 66-244 percent for zinc, and 100-276 percent for sulphur + zinc (Table 4.2). The results show that, at least in the lowest-yielding control plots, zinc and sulphur were both deficient. However, applications of zinc sulphate increased yields more than applications of gypsum.

Salinity. The reconnaissance soil survey (SRDI, 1970b) reported slight topsoil salinity in some soils in the Young Meghna Estuarine Floodplain due to sea-water flooding during past storm surges. Since the completion of the project embankment, such floods have not occurred, and the salt has apparently been washed out by rainwater: no salinity problems were reported by the project. It is noted that saline (deep) groundwater still occurs in the

TABLE 4.2

Effect of sulphur and zinc applications on yield of HYV boro in the Chandpur Irrigation Project area

Plot No	Yield (md/ac) and yield increase over control (%) due to fertilizer application			
	Control	CaSO₄ 80 kg/ac	ZnSO₄ 8 kg/ac	CaSO₄ (80 kg.ac) + ZnSO₄ (8 kg/ac)
1	18	26 (44)	30 (66)	38 (111)
2	20	32 (60)	36 (80)	40 (100)
11	13.5	22 (63)	45 (233)	48 (256)
12	12.5	18.5 (48)	32 (156)	35.5 (184)
Average of 24 plots	40	44 (10)	49 (22)	51 (28)

Notes: 1. Source: CIP Agricultural Research Officer.

2. Results are selected from 24 plots where the applications indicated were superimposed on NPK trial plots. Figures have been rounded.

south of the polder: water from domestic deep tube-wells in Raipur has a distinctly salty taste. Such water should not be used for irrigation in the dry season.

4.4 BARISAL IRRIGATION PROJECT

4.4.1 Physical characteristics

The BIP (Phase I) comprises approximately 180,000 ac of land in Barisal District (Figure 4.6). The project area comprises three physiographic units:

a. Ganges Tidal Floodplain, occupying about two-thirds of the area;[13]

b. Young Ganges Meander Floodplain; and

c. Old Ganges Meander Floodplain.

The two latter units occupy equal areas in the eastern part of the project area. All three units comprise ridges (levees) in a rather narrow strip along river and tidal channels, and basins further away from these channels. Throughout the basins, remnants of old ridges contribute to local relief. Due to differences in river flood levels, relief in the meander floodplains is more pronounced than in the tidal floodplain. Local elevation differences in the meander floodplains are up to 3-5 feet, whereas in the tidal floodplain they do not exceed 1-3 feet. The tidal floodplain deposits also are finer textured. A further characteristic difference between the two landscapes is that, in the tidal areas, rivers and streams typically have angular bends (zig-zag), whereas meander floodplain rivers have curved loops. All three physiographic units are interlaced with a network of creeks, especially the tidal floodplain.

The soils of the Ganges Tidal Floodplain are mainly olive-grey silt loams and silty clay loams on the levees, and grey silty clays and clays in the basins. In basin centres, very poorly drained soils may occur, with very dark grey to dark greenish grey colours. Peaty layers sometimes occur in the basin soils, generally below 18 inches. The meander floodplain soils comprise olive-brown to grey-brown silt loams on the levees, and grey to

---

[13]*This unit was originally classified as the Old Lower Meghna Tidal Floodplain.*

FIGURE 4.6
Barisal Irrigation Project area

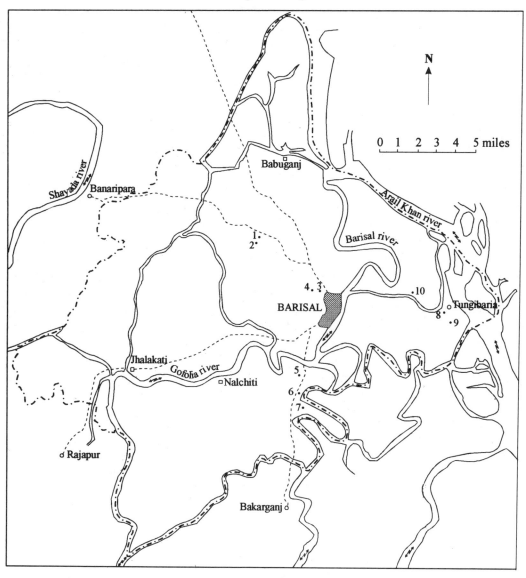

LEGEND

- ·`.·` Project area boundary
- —— Road
- ·1 Observation site

- River (tidal)
- o ▢ ◉ Village, Thana, District HQ

dark grey silty clay loams and silty clays in the basins. These soils contain lime, whereas only the thin strip of levee soils on the tidal floodplain contains lime.

In the wet season, when river levels are high, rainwater accumulates in the basins of the meander floodplains and may eventually cover the levees as well. The depth of flooding generally is 1-3 feet. It is directly related to the river flood level obstructing drainage off the land, and also by position on the relief. Flooding in the tidal floodplain is different: water carrying alluvium flows onto the land at high tide, ranging from 1-3 feet in depth. Saline water does not intrude into the project area, either in the wet season or in the dry season.

4.4.2 Project characteristics

The objective of the BIP is to provide irrigation facilities. Flood control and internal drainage are not project components. The BIP plan calls for the establishment of 59 primary pumps, each with a capacity of 25 cusecs, to lift water from perennial rivers and streams into semi-perennial streams which normally only contain water at high tide in the dry season. The latter streams would be converted into reservoirs by means of cross-dams and sluice-gates. Lock-gates would be constructed so as allow for navigation. The plan called for 2,500 LLPs of 1 and 2-cusec capacity to lift water from the reservoirs or directly from perennial water-courses onto the fields. It was intended that irrigation would mainly be applied to HYV boro. A total area of 141,000 ac was aimed at, out of a total cultivable area of 152,000 ac.[14] Non-irrigable cultivable land comprises high ridges and raised cultivation platforms (mainly near the western boundary of the project area) that are mainly used for guava orchards. Their total area was estimated at 10,000 ac. Homesteads, including betel-vine gardens, occupied approximately 20,500 ac. The area of water and roads was estimated at 7,500 ac.

4.4.3 Land use

Land use in the BIP before project implementation largely followed a simple pattern related to the physiography and flooding. In the basins, a single crop of local t. aman varieties generally was grown. Broadcast aus was grown before t. aman on the slightly higher basin edges and on the lower slopes of ridges. On higher areas, b. aus or jute was followed by t. aman, and this was followed by dryland rabi crops (chilli, mustard, tobacco, sweet potato). Some of the rabi crops were hand-irrigated. LLPs which farmers could obtain from BADC lifted water from perennial streams to irrigate HYV boro on about 5-10 percent of the cultivable area. Clearly, however, aman was the main crop, covering 80 percent of the cultivable area. Yields of t. aman were approximately 15-20 md/ac. Aus (LV), grown on about 30 percent of the cultivable area, yielded 10-15 md/ac. HYV boro yielded 40-50 md/ac. The overall cropping intensity was 120-130 percent.

As was stated above, the objective of the BIP was the large-scale introduction of irrigated HYV boro cultivation and the conversion of traditional t. aman to HYV aman cultivation. Up to 1982, those objectives had not been achieved. In 1980, HYV boro covered only about

---

[14]Consultant's estimates. Various figures are given in the several appraisal reports that have been written on the project.

5,000 ac, while hardly any change to HYV aman cultivation was noticeable. There were a number of reasons to explain the poor performance.

a. Project implementation was slow. Project plans aimed for the technical works (primary pumps, sluice-gates, etc.) to be completed in five years and for farmers to receive full benefits one year after that. However, four years after the start of construction, no LLPs had been fielded. It was only in 1978-79 that, through BADC, 680 LLPs were fielded, which together irrigated approximately 19,000 ac. Partly, the intended number of LLPs could not be fielded because several primary pump-houses had not been completed.

b. Irrigation was mainly applied to HYV aus, partly because of late fielding of LLPs and partly because of the farmers' preference. Probably the main reason for the latter is that the aus crop only needs supplementary irrigation, so it can be grown more economically than HYV boro paddy.

c. Physical conditions in the rainy season are largely unsuitable for HYVs of aman. Generally, flooding in the basins is too deep for short-stemmed HYVs.

Figure 4.7 shows the targeted and achieved areas under HYV paddy in the three growing seasons. Obviously, the achievements are well below the targets. The figure illustrates that the main achievement has been with HYV aus cultivation. Due to the low overall achievement, cropping intensity hardly changed, and total production did not increase appreciably after the project started.

4.4.4 Soil factors affecting land use and productivity

Physiography. Physiography rather than soil conditions is the most important factor determining the possibilities for introducing irrigated boro or HYV aman paddy in the project area. The ridge-and-basin topography has higher and lower parts on which flooding depths range between 1 and 3 feet during the rainy season. Traditionally, local varieties of aman are grown on almost all the flooded land.

The variety that a farmer chooses to grow on a particular site is selected for stem length to match the expected local flood level. The BIP design (which does not include a drainage component) failed to recognize that protracted flooding deeper than about 6 inches precludes the cultivation of HYV aman.[15] The farmers, however, recognized this limitation and therefore continue to grow local varieties.

Physiography also affects the possibilities for HYV boro paddy cultivation. Irrigation of HYVs requires a high degree of water management, implying provision of bunds and drains, as well as field levelling. In the tidal floodplain, local differences in elevation do not exceed 3 feet and levelling would be relatively easy. However, the more pronounced relief in meander floodplain areas — up to 5 feet locally, and occurring within short distances (100-300 feet) — seriously reduces farmers' willingness to undertake field levelling. Rather, farmers prefer to grow dryland rabi crops in these areas, followed by local varieties of b. aus and t. aman.

Permeability. A specific soil factor that may influence the HYV boro paddy area in the future is rapid soil permeability. According to the Barisal soil survey report (SRDI, 1968),

---

[15]One appraisal report (IBRD, 1975) explicitly stated "wet season flooding levels over much of the area do not inhibit the cultivation of high yielding rice varieties in the monsoon season".

FIGURE 4.7

Targets and actually achieved area of HYV boro, aus and aman in the Barisal Irrigation Project area 1978-81

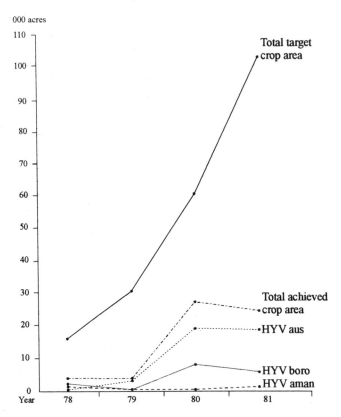

approximately 10-15 percent of the area has silt loam ridge soils. Although no measured permeability data are available, it may be assumed from field observations that considerable water losses will occur on such soils if they are put under irrigated paddy, and that farmers will be unable to maintain a continuous water layer on the soils. Therefore, farmers will probably be inclined to grow a dryland rabi crop on such soils, with or without irrigation, as they have been doing for many years.

Fertility. The reconnaissance soil survey report on the area (SRDI, 1968) states that the fertility of the floodplain soils is moderate but sustained. It has been sufficient to produce fair crops for many decades with little or no use of fertilizers. If, in future, cropping intensity and crop yields will increase, larger amounts of plant nutrients will be removed from the soil annually and these must be replaced. Fertilizer trials on double-cropped land in the area reportedly showed good response to N, P and K applications on t.aman. Also, applications of zinc sulphate and gypsum increased yields considerably. Unfortunately, detailed data were not available to the consultant.

Zinc deficiency was widespread in the 1981 aman crop, but it was much less in the 1982 aus crop. It appeared that the practice of applying zinc sulphate had not then been adopted in the BIP area. Analytical results for soil and plant samples taken from a number of plots showing symptoms of zinc or sulphur deficiency, as well as from some seemingly healthy plots, did not confirm the field diagnoses in all cases: (see Section 4.8.1, Table 4.4). In some cases, the zinc content was high in plants that looked to be deficient, while the soil sample taken on the same site was low in zinc. Plant condition and low plant sulphur content showed a better correlation, although soil sulphur was high in all samples. Detailed information on zinc and sulphur deficiency is given in Section 4.8.1.

4.5 GANGES-KOBADAK PROJECT

4.5.1 Physical characteristics

The G-K project was the first and largest water-control project on which the erstwhile EPWAPDA embarked (in 1955). The original plans included three units: Kushtia, Jessore, and Khulna. To-date, only the technical works in Kushtia unit have been implemented. This unit is located in the relatively dry western part of Bangladesh, comprising parts of Kushtia and Jessore Districts. It comprises a total area of 179,000 ac (gross) in the Young and Old Ganges Meander Floodplains.

The meander floodplains are built up of ridges and basins. The relief generally is gently undulating, with height differences of 2-4 feet over distances of 100-200 feet. Locally, mainly near the Gorai, Kumar and Nabaganga rivers, there is an irregular relief of high ridges and infilled channels. In the latter areas, local elevation differences of 2-4 feet occur over distances of 30-50 feet.

The soils in the basins generally are dark greyish brown to very dark grey clays and heavy clays. Middle slopes of the ridges have somewhat browner soils with lighter textures: olive-brown to dark greyish brown silty clays. On the tops of the ridges, the lightest-textured soils occur: olive to olive-brown loams and silt loams. All the soils are calcareous, either throughout or in subsurface layers.

The reconnaissance soil survey reports on the area (SRDI 1973a, 1977) do not refer to coarse or moderately-coarse textured soils. However, such soils were observed on an earlier soil survey (FAO, 1959), by a project review mission (Horst, 1978) and by this consultant. These soils are loamy fine sands, fine sandy loams, and silt loams to silty clay loams overlying sandy substrata at less than 10 inches. The occurrence of these coarse-textured soils has important implications for the G-K project's performance: see Section 4.5.4.

4.5.2 Project characteristics

The G-K project, Kushtia Unit, includes flood protection, internal drainage and irrigation components. Flooding by overflow from the Gorai river is prevented by the locally-heightened outer embankment of the northern main irrigation canal and by several cross-dams cutting off the Gorai river from its tributaries. Drainage comprises the original rivers and khals together with some newly-excavated canals that drain into the Kumar river (Phase I area) and Nabaganga river (Phase II area), then eventually through sluice-gates near Magura into the Madhumati river south-east of the project area.

Water from the Ganges river is lifted from a 3,000-feet-long intake channel near Bheramara in the north-west of the project area (Figure 4.8). The pumping station is located this far from the river in order to safeguard it against river-bank erosion. The main pump-house has three pumps with a total capacity of 3,000 cusec at 26 feet static head. A subsidiary pump-house next to the main pump-house has 12 pumps of 1,400 cusec total

FIGURE 4.8
Ganges-Kobadak Project, Kushtia Unit

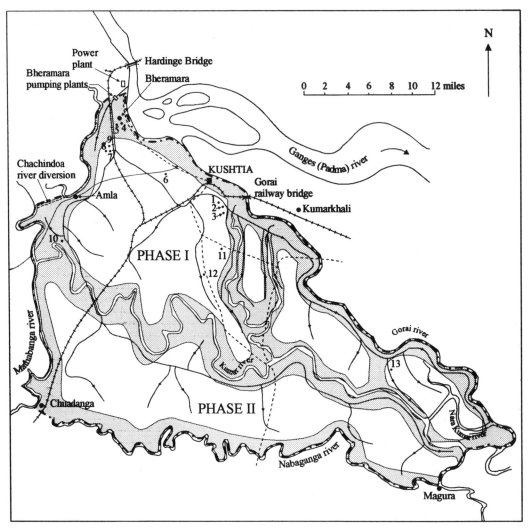

LEGEND

—·— Project area boundary
→ Main and secondary irrigation canals
▨ Areas with permeable soils
     (approximate location)
.1 Observation site and number

≈ River
---- Main road
—+— Railway
■ ● District HQ; town/village

capacity at 31 feet static head. The irrigation water is distributed through three main canals: the Ganges canal (25 miles), from which the Kushtia canal (39 miles, Phase I) and Alamdanga canal (38 miles, Phase II) branch off. Further distribution of irrigation water occurs through 35 secondary canals with lengths varying from 1 to 7 miles, and tertiary canals which, in some cases, take off directly from the main canals. According to the design, tertiary canals should each cover 300-800 ac. Field channels convey the water to farmers' plots. Roads were constructed along all the main and secondary canals, most of them un-metalled, but one of the roads along the top of embankments usually is brick-paved.

Phase I of the project, located north of the Kumar river, comprises a gross area of 208,000 ac. Implementation of works started in 1955 and was completed in 1969-70. The total cultivable area is 145,000 ac. Villages, homesteads, etc., are estimated to occupy 25 percent of the gross area (53,000 ac), and roads and water bodies 5 percent (10,000 ac). The planned irrigable area was 120,000 ac, leaving approximately 25,000 ac above irrigation command level.

Phase II of the project, located between the Kumar and Nabaganga rivers, comprises a gross area of 270,000 ac. Construction works started in 1960 and had not been completed by 1982. The total cultivable area is 206,000 ac. Settlements occupy 54,000 ac (20 percent), and roads, water, etc., about 13,500 ac (5 percent). The planned irrigable area was 150,000 ac, leaving about 56,000 ac above irrigation command level.

The total population of the project area (Phases I and II) is over 1 million. Overall population density (1,600 per sq. mile) is about the national average, but the density in the Phase I area is higher (1,900 per sq. mile) than in the Phase II area (1,400 per sq. mile). An estimated 170,000 households (i.e., 90 percent of the total number of households) are 'farm families' which depend for their livelihood on agricultural activities. However, land tenure conditions are highly skewed: about 35 percent of farm families are landless, and another 10 percent have not more than 0.5 ac. On the other hand, the average farm size in the project area is about 5 ac, which is much higher than the national average of approximately 2.5 ac (in 1977).[16]

4.5.3 Land use

Before project implementation, land use largely followed a pattern dictated by land elevations in relation to seasonal flooding. Highland, comprising the higher ridges which remained above flood-level, occupied approximately 30-35 percent of the project area and was used for broadcast aus paddy or jute in the rainy season and for dryland rabi crops (tobacco, chilli, pulses) in the dry season. Perennial crops were also grown: sugarcane and fruit trees (mango, jackfruit). Medium Highland, comprising low ridges and basin margins subject to shallow flooding (1-3 feet), occupied an estimated 45 percent of the total area. Cropping on this land included mixed aus+aman followed by dryland rabi crops.[17] Medium

---

[16]*The author (HB) was told by project agricultural extension staff in 1979 that relatively big land-owners (> ca 5 ac) farming through share-croppers tend to invest their surplus income from farming in urban property, trade and education of their children, thereby quickly reducing their primary dependence on agriculture.*

[17]*Despite the shallow flooding depth, aman was sown broadcast in western parts of the Ganges River Floodplain instead of being transplanted, as it is in other parts of the country on Medium Highland. The reason appeared to be because Medium Highland ridge soils on the Ganges River Floodplain generally are permeable and do not retain water well for t. aman under rainfed conditions; also, because Ganges river*

Lowland and Lowland, comprising basin edges and centres subject to deeper flooding (3-6 feet or more) and occupying 20 percent of the area, mainly grew b. aman (5-10 percent of the total area). Some deep basin centres occupying 2-3 percent of the area remained wet throughout the year and were mainly under reeds and grasses.

In summary, before project implementation, most of the land was double-cropped. The main cropping patterns were: aus/jute and rabi crops; b. aman and rabi crops; and mixed aus+aman and rabi crops or rabi fallow. The estimated cropping intensity in the area was about 175 percent. All the paddy grown was of local varieties. Paddy yields ranged from 10-13 md/ac (aus) to 10-15 md/ac for b. aman. Introduction of HYVs of paddy began from 1966-67.

With project, irrigation provides supplementary water to aus and aman crops between April and December. For both irrigated crops, either HYVs or LIVs are now mainly used. They are transplanted on levelled fields, and receive moderate doses of fertilizers and pesticides (i.e., below the levels recommended by project extension staff). HYVs of aus are transplanted in April-May and harvested in August, yielding on average 40-50 md/ac. LIVs of aus produce 20-25 md/ac. HYV aman is transplanted in August and harvested in November or December. Average yields are 45-50 md/ac. LIV aman is transplanted in August-September, harvested in December and yields 25-30 md/ac.[18]

Figure 4.9 shows how aus and aman HYVs have gradually gained importance over local and locally-improved varieties since they were first introduced. However, in 1980, not more than 60 percent of the aus and aman area was yet used for HYVs, and area targets had not been met. During the 1980 wet season, only about 50 percent of the irrigable area was actually irrigated in the aus season and only 70 percent in the aman season. This low project performance, more than 10 years after project completion (Phase I), is caused by a complex of problems that have affected the project. These problems are related to:

a. the socio-economic structure of the project area:

- land tenure conditions and related power structure in villages (and in irrigation units);
- unattractive share-cropping systems;
- lack of funds and/or credit facilities for small farmers;
- distrust by farmers of the reliability of the irrigation supply.

b. water management:

- siltation in the intake canal, requiring dredging by six dredgers for three months after the end of each flood season;

---

floods generally occur in late-August or September when aman normally is transplanted, which might make water levels on fields too high for transplanting or might drown newly-planted seedlings. The author recalls being told by the FAO agricultural team on the G-K project at the time of his first visit to the area in October 1961 that farmers were having to be taught transplanting techniques. Later, during soil surveys of Kushtia and Jessore Districts, it was found that many settlers had entered the area from Comilla and Noakhali Districts and had introduced intensive cropping practices, including transplanting aman under rainfed conditions.

[18]*Aman harvesting is often late in this area because big farmers mainly depend on migrant labour which is not available until after the labourers have harvested the aman crop in their home areas. Threshing (by bullock treading) may continue until January-February. These reasons were given to the author (HB) in 1979 as a reason for farmers not growing wheat or other rabi crops (other than some broadcast pulses) in the project area.*

FIGURE 4.9

Area of aus and aman rice grown in the Ganges-Kobadak project area, Kushtia Unit, 1967-80

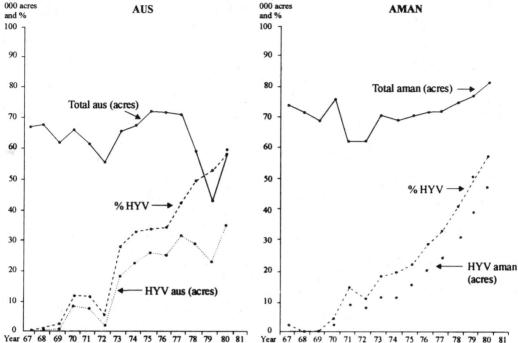

- late start of the irrigation season due to the dredging operations;
- power failures frequently interrupting operation of the pump stations, thus interrupting irrigation supply;
- unauthorized operation of irrigation structures by farmers;
- seepage losses from the main and secondary canals;
- high field water losses.

A discussion of the socio-economic and engineering problems is beyond the scope of this study. However, the occurrence of seepage and percolation losses from canals and fields is relevant for this study, and this is discussed in Section 4.5.4.

In contrast to the project area, changes in land use outside the G-K area have mainly occurred in the dry season. On similar land and soils to the south-west of the project area, wheat has become an important crop. It is sown in November and harvested in March-April. Yields obtained with use of fertilizers and irrigation are approximately 35 md/ac. Other common rabi crops outside the project area are sugarcane, tobacco, chilli, millet (*kaon*), pulses and vegetables. Orchard crops (especially mango, jackfruit) are also common. All these dryland crops are grown on the relatively higher floodplain ridges. In the rainy season, little change has taken place: b.aus and t.aman are grown on the Medium Highland, and b. aman is grown in the basins.[19]

---

[19]*In fact, transplanting of aman had become more widespread since the 1950s: see footnote 17 above. Subsequently, HYV boro paddy cultivation became widespread on basin soils, using irrigation from deep or shallow tube-wells.*

4.5.4 Soil factors affecting land use and productivity

Soil texture/permeability. As described earlier, the project area includes a considerable area of land with sandy loam and loamy sand soils. These occur on high ridges on both the Old and the Young Ganges Meander Floodplains, mainly along the Kumar, Kaliganga and lower part of the Nabaganga rivers. These soils were classified as Kumar and Bhairab series respectively by the FAO soil survey (FAO, 1959), mapped together in soil associations: Kumar association; Bhairab association; and Bhairab complex.

The Kumar association, occupying approximately 60 percent of the project area, comprises the Kumar series (relatively undeveloped, greyish brown to brown, sandy loams to silt loams and silts) and small amounts (not specified) of Eral series (grey to dark greyish brown, silty clay loams and clay loams in basins). The Bhairab association and Bhairab complex both comprise the dominant soils of Bhairab series (yellowish brown loamy sand over sand) with subordinate proportions of Kumar and Kobadak series. Permeability of the Bhairab soils is moderately to very rapid. The Bhairab association and Bhairab complex each occupy about 5 percent of the project area.

The FAO soil survey report gives a clear assessment of the irrigability of the Kumar association (p.161), Bhairab association (p.163) and Bhairab complex (p. 163-64), viz.

> "The irrigability of the soils of the Kumar association varies from moderate to poor, depending on the relief. The unconsolidated, structureless character of the very fine sandy to silty soils of the Kumar series is less favourable with respect to irrigation because of erosion hazards. A distinction should be made between areas with an irregular relief and those with a [smooth] relief. In several places, alternating former river channels and natural levees cause an irregular relief. The position of various elevated and isolated ridges will not permit their irrigation, whereas drainage problems in the old channels are complicated, involving the hazard of erosion by uncontrolled discharges of drainage water through bottlenecks. Levelling of these areas as a whole will be very expensive and not in proportion to eventual profits. For these reasons, the irrigability of areas with an irregular relief must be classified as poor."

> "[In Bhairab association], the arability of the soils of the Bhairab series is extremely poor. The soils are deficient in plant nutrients, soil moisture and organic matter, and are not suitable for satisfactory crop production, except for jackfruit. The soils are non-irrigable due to their elevated position and permeability".

> "[In Bhairab complex], the very poor soils of the Bhairab series are unsuitable for crop production ... Moisture deficiencies due to rapid external drainage, sandy soils and deep groundwater levels are not uncommon ... The great variability of the conditions of the complex as a whole is a serious drawback for development plans. The irrigability of the Bhairab complex varies from moderate to very poor, according to the relief."

The report estimated that, excluding homestead land, about 17 percent of the gross area in Phase I of the project area and about 15 percent in the Phase II area comprised land that was poorly suited or unsuited for irrigation. Irregular relief was considered the main limiting factor. However, based on his own field observations and a re-interpretation of both the FAO and SRDI soil survey reports on the area, the consultant considered that areas with light-textured soils and rapid permeability might cover as much as 25-30 percent of the total cultivable area. If that assessment were correct, such a high proportion of non-irrigable soils would seriously reduce project production potential: in fact, this constraint is actually shown in the field. Four aspects deserve mention, viz.

a. The main and secondary canals were constructed on the highest parts of the area: i.e., the high ridges, levees and infilled channels adjoining the Gorai river (Kushtia canal), Kaliganga river (secondary canals 85K and S6K), and Alamdanga river (Alamdanga canal). Therefore, they have been constructed on the most permeable soils in the area. Their location on high parts is, of course, correct with a view to maintaining the maximum irrigation head. However, the seepage losses resulting from this location should have been taken into account and the canals should have been lined. Seepage losses have been estimated to be about 40 percent at the beginning of the irrigation season, decreasing to about 8 percent in November. However, the period of highest water requirements (for HYV aus in April-May) coincides with the time of highest seepage losses.

b. The fields adjoining the main and secondary canals generally have permeable soil, also. These fields close to the canals have an ample water supply. However, due to their very rapid permeability, they have extremely high water requirements. Water applications every two days are not unusual. Nevertheless, yields are poor: not only as a result of inadequate water management, but also because of the low natural fertility of these light-textured soils. Applications of fertilizers are hardly recommendable because of the high leaching losses.

c. Good to moderately good irrigable land, such as the silty clay loams, silty clays and clays on ridge slopes and basin margins frequently suffer from lack of irrigation water. To a large extent, these shortages are caused by excessive seepage and percolation losses from canals and fields on higher land, referred to in a and b above.

d. Seepage and percolation water cause waterlogging or flooding in the deep broad basins throughout the area. This prevents HYVs of paddy from being cultivated in such sites; some sites cannot be cultivated at all. During field visits in May 1982, the total area of waterlogged land was estimated at about 3-4 percent of all the cultivable land. However, part of this waterlogging might have been due to local run-off because, during the previous week, local rain-showers had occurred almost daily in the late afternoon.

Seepage losses in the canals could, of course, still be reduced by canal lining. According to estimates made by Nedeco (1980), clay lining in the main canals would cost about Tk.370,000 per mile. A shallow soil layer would be removed from inside the embankment and replaced (by hand) in layers, and compacted. Nedeco estimated that at least 10-20 percent of the main canals (about 102 miles) needed to be lined.

Water losses in farmers' fields would not be high if farmers were charged according to actual water use. In the G-K project, as in most BWDB irrigation projects, water rates are calculated at only 3 percent of the production increase due to irrigation. However, BWDB has no real power to force farmers to pay these charges or, alternatively, it lacks the practical means to exclude farmers who refuse to pay for irrigation water. Additionally, regulator structures are sometimes operated by farmers on their own initiative, and embankments are sometimes breached or canals cross-dammed by farmers, in order to divert water onto their own fields (free of charge). High water rates would force the farmers in permeable areas to opt for more water-economical crops than transplanted paddy, such as kharif vegetables. However, irrigated rabi crops could only be grown if the irrigation season could start in November.[20]

Reduction of seepage and percolation losses on the higher land would also reduce the waterlogging problem in basin sites. Additional drainage ditches might need to be provided in some sites, which could be difficult and costly (due to land acquisition and deep drain cutting).

Fertility. The natural fertility of the soils of the Old and Young Ganges Meander Floodplains usually is high and well sustained. The soils are mainly rich in calcium, magnesium and potassium due to the abundance of weathering minerals such as feldspars and biotite. The base saturation of the soils generally is high (>80 percent). However, they have low contents of organic matter, especially in the light-textured soils on the higher ridges. Phosphate-fixation may occur in calcareous topsoils, which occur mainly in the floodplain ridge soils. In lower soils, lime usually has been leached from the topsoil (and sometimes from the subsoil as well). Under intensified cropping with high crop yields, applications of fertilizers are required.

Zinc deficiency was reported to be common in the 1981 t. aman crop. The application of zinc sulphate by farmers was not as widespread in the G-K project area as was found in the DND and CIP areas. The consultant collected several plant samples for zinc and sulphur analysis during a field visit in May 1982. The results are included in Table 4.4 (given at the end of this chapter). They show critical and below-critical levels of zinc and sulphur in almost all the samples, whether they were taken as 'controls' (healthy-looking plants) or from plants appearing to show zinc and/or sulphur deficiency symptoms. Low sulphur levels could be related to the low soil organic matter contents. Low zinc levels could be caused by the prevailing high *p*H levels of the soils which are (or recently were) calcareous.

4.6 COASTAL EMBANKMENT PROJECT, POLDER 22

4.6.1 Physical characteristics

CEP Polder 22 encompasses approximately 3,500 ac of land on the Ganges Tidal Floodplain about 30 miles south-west of Khulna (Figure 4.1). It consists of a low-lying, almost-level basin surrounded by slightly higher (2-3 feet) ridges which are the levees of tidal streams zig-zagging their way downstream to the Sunderbans and the Bay of Bengal. The soils on the levees are greyish brown silt loams and silty clay loams which locally overlie a coarser-textured substratum of (loamy) very fine sand: unit 1 on Figure 4.10.[21] The basins within

---

[20] *In the 1950s when the G-K project was planned (and even in the 1964 Master Plan), water-control development was mainly envisaged to safeguard and increase kharif crop production. A much bigger pumping capacity would have been required if the G-K project had been designed for dry-season cropping. The dry-season flow in the Ganges river might not have been sufficient to supply irrigation water to the whole of the G-K project area as originally envisaged, including the Jessore and Khulna units, even before the time when the diversion of Ganges water at the Farraka barrage needed to be considered.*

[21] The soil boundaries indicated on Figure 4.10 are schematic. They are based on interpretation of airphotos, a limited number of field observations and general physiographic information given in the reconnaissance soil survey report on Khulna District (SRDI, 1973b). Therefore, the soils information should not be used for detailed interpretation. In the SRDI soil survey report, the soil association covering Polder 22 describes mainly grey to dark grey silty clays or clays, but the Consultant encountered soils that were (dark) greyish brown silt loams, silty clay loams and silty clays.

FIGURE 4.10
Coastal Embankment Project, Polder 22

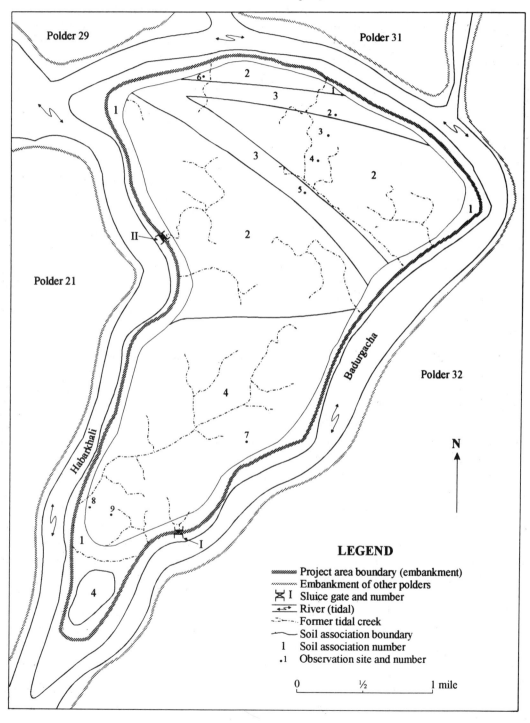

LEGEND

━━━ Project area boundary (embankment)
┄┄┄ Embankment of other polders
✕ I Sluice gate and number
━s→ River (tidal)
┄·┄· Former tidal creek
⌒ Soil association boundary
1 Soil association number
.1 Observation site and number

0   ½   1 mile

the levees comprise an association (unit 2) of (dark) greyish brown, fine to medium-textured soils (silty clays and silty clay loams) in the lower parts and — mainly on scattered, somewhat elevated parts (degraded former levees 1-2 feet high) — greyish brown, medium-textured soils (silt loams and silty clay loams) which overlie coarser-textured substrata (very fine sandy loam to loamy very fine sand). In the northern part of the polder, the latter soils occupy two distinct ridges (unit 3) which, due to their 2-3 feet higher elevation, are used for human settlements. The origin of these ridges is not clear. They were described as levees of a former river floodplain in the G-K soil survey report (FAO, 1959), but they could also have formed more recently as tidal deposits similar to the levees that presently surround the polder.

In the southern part of the polder, the basin soils overlie dark brown to very dark brown peat and clayey peat layers at depths of 2 feet or more (unit 4). The occurrence of these layers suggests a period (or periods) when the area was under forest (perhaps Sunderbans) in which alluvial sedimentation was absent or slow. Buried layers also occur locally in the basin soils at depths generally below 18 inches, in which acid sulphate conditions have developed. These layers are rich in pyrites (FeS_2). If soil drainage exposed these layers to the air, the pyrites would oxidize to form ferric hydroxide ($Fe(OH)_3$) and sulphuric acid (H_2SO_4), rendering the soils extremely acid. In the field, pH values of 4 to 5 were observed. Samples taken from wet reduced subsoils showed, upon drying, pH values decreasing from 7.5-8.0 to 3.7-4.0: see Table 4.3.

4.6.2 Project characteristics

CEP Polder 22 is one of 92 polders in the CEP. The main objective of the CEP is, by means of embankments and sluice-gates, to control flooding, tidal incursion and drainage on more than 3 million acres of land in the Ganges Tidal Floodplain and the Young Meghna Estuarine Floodplain. In Polder 22, on a pilot project basis, the embankments are being raised to a level 1.4 feet above PWD datum (PWDD), in order to safe-guard the land inside the polder against extreme river levels (1:50 year occurrence).[22]

Numerous creeks of various sizes occur throughout the polder. Their outlets have partly been blocked by the polder embankment. At present, two sluice-gates provide drainage from the area. Under the DDP, it was proposed to provide a number of small irrigation inlets.

Before the CEP embankment was constructed, the area was subject to shallow tidal flooding during the monsoon season. The mean surface level of the polder is approximately 3 feet (PWDD), ranging from 3-4 feet in the north to 1-2 feet in the south. River levels measured at sluice-gate II presently range between 7 feet PWDD at high tide in August, when river discharges are highest, to 3 feet at low tide. In the dry season (January-February), river levels range between +4.5 and -5 feet. In the monsoon season (mid-July to end-October), water in the Habarkhali and Badargacha rivers which surround Polder 22 is fresh, with an electrical conductivity (ECe) of less than 2,000 mmhos. However, with decreasing discharges in the dry season, saline sea-water gradually intrudes into the area so that, by mid-November, conductivity levels rise above 4,000 mmhos at high tide as well as at low tide, and extreme values above 20,000 mmhos occur towards the end of the dry season (April).

---

[22]*This improvement was carried out under the Delta Development Project (DDP) funded by The Netherlands. Further references in this section to 'the project' refer to the DDP, except where otherwise stated.*

TABLE 4.3
Selected analytical data for soils in CEP polder 22

Obs No	Depth (cm)	Texture	ECe	pH moist/wet	pH dry	SO₄-S ppm	CaCO₃
1	0-10	SiC	13.2	6.5	6.6	–	0
2A	0-10	SiCL	14.0	6.5	5.6	–	0
2B	80-90	SiC	16.8	8.0	5.3	–	2
3	0-10	SiCL	14.5	4.5	4.4	1286	0
4A	0-10	SiCL	9.5	7.5	6.6	–	0
4B	40-50	SiCL	13.0	5.5	4.8	–	2
5A	0-10	SiCL	6.5	6.0	4.9	476	0
5B	50-60	SiL	10.0	4.5	3.9	547	0
5C	90-100	vfSL	19.0	8.0	3.7	495	0
6	0-10	SiCL	17.5	7.5	6.8	–	2
7A	0-10	SiC	9.6	8.0	7.5	–	0
7B	90-100	pSiC	15.9	7.5	5.7	–	0
8A	0-10	SiC	12.9	6.5	5.8	–	1
8B	80-90	pSiC	11.0	8.0	5.2	–	1
9	80-90	p	15.4	8.0	6.1	–	0

Notes: 1. Observation numbers correspond with the sites indicated in Table 4.5 and on Figure 4.10.

2. Texture abbreviations: vfSL = very fine sandy loam. SiL = silt loam. SiCL = silty clay loam. SiC = silty clay. pSiC = peaty silty clay. p = peat.

3. – = not determined.

4. Methods: ECe values were calculated from EC^2 1:2 values as determined in the laboratory: (see text). pH (moist/wet) was determined in the field with a Hellige-Truog test kit. pH (dry) and SO₄-S were determined as explained in Annexe 1. Free CaCO₃ was determined on dry samples with 10% HCl: 0 = no effervescence; 1 = slight effervescence; 2 = strong effervescence.

Saline flooding from the rivers no longer occurs in the polder. However, saline soil conditions continue to prevail in the dry season. This is due to the capillary rise of saline water from the groundwater and also to the continuing practice of farmers cutting the embankment so as to artificially flood their aman crop with brackish river water if dry spells occur towards the end of the aman-growing season. Samples taken from topsoils and subsoils in the first week of May 1982 showed moderate to very high salinity levels, with ECe values in topsoils ranging from 6.9 to 17.5 mmhos: (see Table 4.3).[23]

The total population of Polder 22 is estimated at about 5,800 (DDP, 1982b), but it is growing at a high rate (over 4 percent per annum) due to immigration of tenant farmers and labourers. The population density of approximately 1,600 per square mile is low in comparison to that of Khulna District as whole (2,500/sq. mile). The population is predominantly Hindu (80 percent), whereas Khulna District as a whole is predominantly Muslim. Homesteads and tanks occupy approximately 325 ac in the polder.

Due to the relatively low population density, the average farm size of 3.5 ac is larger than the national average (2.5 ac). Even so, about two-thirds of all farms are less than 3 ac,

---

[23]In the laboratory, EC^2 was determined in a 1:2 soil-water extract. ECe figures were calculated from the EC^2 figures by means of the formula ECe = (200 ÷ SP) X EC^{2} which is generally applicable to marine saline conditions. SP (Saturation Percentage) was estimated as follows: very fine sandy loam 20%; silt loam 30%; silty clay loam 40%; silty clay and peat 70%.

and one-third are smaller than 1 ac. On the other hand, about 8 percent of the farms are larger than 10 ac, and these big farms occupy almost one-third of the farmland. Twenty percent of the households own no cultivable land other than their homesteads. There is evidence of concentration of land into larger holdings at the cost of small farmers (DDP, 1982b).

4.6.3 Land use

Before the CEP, the main land use in Polder 22 and similar land in the Ganges Tidal Floodplain was the cultivation of a single crop of t. aman, followed by fallow in the dry season during which cattle were grazed on the stubble and weeds remaining in the fields. Aman seed-beds were prepared and sown by mid-July. Land preparation of the main fields started in June-July, by when salts which accumulated during the dry season had been washed out of the soils by pre-monsoon and monsoon rainfall. Five or six ploughings were normally given, because of the weak draught power of the cattle. Transplanting was done in August, and harvesting of the photoperiod-sensitive varieties used took place between November and January, depending on the variety used.[24]

Short-duration paddy varieties were mainly planted on the higher land and harvested by mid-November. These varieties (e.g., Kartiksail) had low yields (10-16 md/ac), but they fetched high prices because of their preferred grain quality and early arrival in the market. Medium-duration varieties harvested later in November produced 15-25 md/ac. Late-maturing varieties grown in low areas and harvested in December-January yielded 20-35 md.ac. These high yields, obtained without the use of fertilizers, can be attributed to the low cropping intensity.[25]

As farmers often had to apply brackish water during late growth stages of the aman crop, the soils generally were too saline for the cultivation of a following rabi crop. Sometimes, farmers tried to grow mustard, but usually with poor results. Moreover, rabi crops suffered considerably from grazing by cattle. The density of cattle in the polder was (and still is) extremely high: 1.5 head per acre. Cattle feed problems occur annually at the end of the dry season, reflected in the skimpy conditions of most of the cows. The cattle are used for draught power, milking, production of cow-dung and as a capital investment. In the predominantly Hindu community, beef is not consumed.

Despite the efforts of BWDB and DDP agronomists to increase agricultural production, little change had resulted and cropping patterns in 1982 are still as described above. Dry spells in the later growth-stages of aman, particularly the late varieties, tempt farmers to cut openings in the embankment to let in (brackish) water at high tide. In order to prevent excessive damage to the embankment, the project decided to construct small irrigation inlet structures. The gates in such structures also serve as drainage outlets.

---

[24]*Because of longer day-length and the continuation of high night temperatures longer near the coast, aman traditionally was harvested about two weeks later in coastal Districts than further inland. Also, as was described for the G-K project area, it often took big farmers two months to harvest their crop: see footnote 18.*

[25]*A more likely reason for the higher yields in basin sites is the higher organic matter content of basin soils, their more assured moisture supply throughout the growing season, and possibly the greater amount of nitrogen provided by blue-green algae and other biological activity in such wet sites.*

Possible changes in crops and cropping patterns considered by the project include those described below.

a. Introduction of HYV aman (BR-10, BR-11). In view of the relatively high yields which the farmers presently obtain from their local paddy varieties without the use of fertilizers, it seems unlikely that the farmers will be willing to adopt the more intensive management needed for HYV paddy cultivation (field levelling, puddling, water management, use of fertilizers and pesticides, etc.). Moreover, the supply of fertilizers in the area has been very irregular, and farmers prefer the local varieties over HYVs because of their better grain quality and the higher prices they fetch in the market. The local differences in elevation between ridges and basins also make good water management very difficult in most of the area. Better water control would either require the construction of low embankments along the higher parts within the polder to retain water on those higher parts without flooding the basins or, as a very costly alternative, the provision of pump drainage for the lower area.

b. Introduction of an HYV aus crop. This is considered almost impossible because of the relatively low and unreliable pre-monsoon rainfall in this western area (mean May rainfall at Khulna 5 ins) and the fact that non-saline water suitable for irrigation is not available in the rivers until mid-July.

c. Introduction of rabi crops. The cultivation of dryland rabi crops is mainly restricted by the late harvesting of paddy. Late sowing of rabi crops generally results in low yields due to the increase in soil salinity as the dry season progresses. Intersowing rabi crops such as khesari in the aman before it is harvested might help to overcome this problem, but the uncontrolled grazing of cattle poses a serious problem.

4.6.4 Soil conditions affecting land use and productivity

Salinity. The main soil factor limiting cropping in Polder 22 is salinity. Saline soil conditions are caused mainly by capillary rise of saline groundwater to the surface in the dry season. Leaching of salts only starts in May-June with the onset of the rains, and the river water only becomes fresh and potentially usable for irrigation by mid-July. A possible solution could be the construction of cross-dams in rivers and creeks to store fresh water accumulated during the monsoon season for the irrigation of rabi crops. However, such reservoirs would only have a limited capacity and further hydrological and economic studies are required to ascertain their effectiveness and cost.

Topography and drainage. The ridge-and-basin topography in the polder gives a gently undulating relief with local differences in elevation of 2-3 feet. This creates water-control problems for paddy cultivation under both irrigated and non-irrigated conditions. With irrigation for HYV paddy cultivation, the basins would need drainage. Alternatively, low internal embankments would need to be constructed to retain water on the higher land without flooding the basins. However, local farmers have resisted suggestions for making such embankments, indicating that they do not regard the existing situation as a major constraint.[26]

An engineering drainage problem exists near sluice-gate I in the eastern embankment, which is inadequate to drain all the land in the south of the polder. A more logical location

---

[26] *See also Chapter 3, Section 3.4.1.*

for this sluice-gate would have been in the western embankment, at the mouth of the large creek which drains almost 75 percent of the southern area.[27]

Fertility. Although limited in number, fertilizer trials by the DDP have shown responses of local paddy varieties (Patnai Balam and Kartiksail) to applications of nitrogen, phosphorus and sulphur (DDP, 1982a). Application of zinc apparently did not increase yields. The trial plots were located in unit 2 on Figure 4.10, but no details of the soils were reported. Sustained yields of local aman varieties achieved without the use of fertilizers are relatively high. Apparently, the low cropping intensity does not cause depletion of soil nutrients, while the long fallow (although there is intensive grazing) allows for restoration of soil fertility. Acidity problems due to the local presence of potential acid sulphate conditions have not been reported, but they could occur if the land were levelled. The potentially acid layers generally occur too deep (below 18 inches) to interfere with crop cultivation.

4.6.5 Shrimp cultivation in the Tidal Floodplain[28]

Parts of the Ganges Tidal Floodplain were traditionally used for shrimp cultivation. Ponds were constructed on tidally-flooded land in the dry season so that they could be filled with saline water at high tide and drained, if necessary, at low tide. In March-April, the ponds were stocked with shrimps caught in the rivers. Pond water was refreshed regularly, and the shrimps were harvested in July-August. That still allowed the farmer sufficient time to prepare the land (flushing of salts, ploughing, puddling) for the cultivation of t. aman.

The CEP polders have proved attractive to shrimp cultivators. In one kind of development, polders (or large parts of polders) are being inundated (mainly by breaching the embankment; sometimes by opening sluice-gates) and used for shrimp cultivation. In another, more-sophisticated, kind of development, large, well-laid-out, shrimp ponds up to 1-2 ac in size are constructed within and close to polder embankments, preferably on the more elevated ridges where they are safe from seasonal flooding but can still be filled with saline water and drained whenever necessary.

Under good management, shrimp farming can be highly profitable, especially if the ponds are well constructed, including inlet and drainage facilities. However, it is not clear at present to what extent shrimp farming interferes with crop cultivation. In cases where complete polders are inundated with saline water, cultivation of t. aman might become impossible unless the shrimps are harvested in time for the land to be drained so as to flush the salts from the soils before t. aman in planted. However, the saline conditions remaining after drainage will certainly affect crop yields and production. Also, the ponding of water on the land near the end of the dry season prevents cattle from grazing the area at the time

[27] *Sluice-gates I and II were constructed in an early phase of the CEP, before the implementation of the (Dutch-assisted) improvement programme.*

[28] *Shrimp cultivation was not practised in Polder 22 (at the time of the Consultant's visit). Some traditional ponds had been constructed by farmers on char land outside the polder embankment. The examples described in the text were observed in Polders 18/19, 20 and 32. A tentative estimate of the total area then used for shrimp cultivation in Paikgacha and Dumuria Thanas of Khulna District was about 10,000 ac, or 5 percent of the total land area (DDP, 1982b). A brief description and an identification of the problems related to shrimp cultivation in polders is considered to be relevant for this study, especially in relation to the problems which the DDP was having in Polder 22 in determining viable land use alternatives to the existing t. aman-fallow cropping system.*

when cattle-feed is most scarce. In polders where more sophisticated ponds are used, drainage and seepage water from the ponds was observed to spill into low areas, creating local drainage and salinity problems. Technical studies are needed to determine if shrimp farming and crop cultivation are compatible in the polders. Also, since the construction of ponds requires large financial outputs — provided by outside businessmen — socio-economic surveys are required to determine the social and economic benefits and costs of such enterprises (e.g., employment; land tenure; effect on land rents; etc.).

4.7 SPECIFIC PROBLEMS RELATED TO CONTINUOUS SUBMERGENCE OF SOILS

4.7.1 Zinc and sulphur deficiency

Due to the increased cropping intensity and higher yields that generally result from the introduction of flood control, drainage and irrigation, larger amounts of plant nutrients are removed from the soil than under pre-project conditions. In order to prevent depletion of the soils' natural fertility, nutrients that are being removed need to be replaced by the application of manure or chemical fertilizers.

In Bangladesh, where rice is the main crop, modest amounts of urea, TSP and MP fertilizers are usually applied to HYV paddy. These fertilizers provide the major nutrients N, P and K. As a result, fairly high and sustained yields have been obtained in wetland paddy cultivation: HYV boro 50-60 md/ac (paddy); HYV aus 30-35 md/ac; and HYV aman 40-45 md/ac.

However, in the late 1970s — in Bangladesh as well as in many other rice-producing countries (e.g., The Philippines, India, Pakistan, Japan) — deficiencies of zinc and sulphur developed in rice and affected yields under intensive agricultural management. These deficiencies became a particular problem in double and triple cropping systems under irrigated conditions. General aspects of zinc and sulphur deficiencies are discussed in separate sections below, dealing with specific aspects related to the occurrence of these deficiencies in major irrigation and drainage project areas in Bangladesh.

Zinc deficiency. Zinc is a micronutrient. Although it is essential for plant growth, only very small amounts are needed. Tissue of healthy plants may contain 20-35 parts per million (ppm) of zinc. The total amount of zinc removed by a rice crop producing 50 md/ac (paddy) is only about 80 g.

Zinc deficiency in rice generally shows as a patchy occurrence of stunted plants with rusty brown spots developing on the lower leaves, usually with a slightly chlorotic mid-vein. Severely-affected plants have entirely brown leaves; eventually, the plant dies. Zinc deficiency symptoms differ between varieties; so do critical zinc levels in the plants. Zinc deficiency symptoms usually develop 2-4 weeks after transplantation of the seedlings.

The availability of zinc in the soil depends on a number of factors, including the following.

a. Total zinc content in the soil. Normal ranges of total zinc are from 20-200 ppm, while available (soluble) zinc contents may vary from less than 1 up to 15 ppm. Zinc sources in the soil include ZnS, $ZnCO_3$, Zn_2SiO_4, $ZnSiO_3$, $Zn_3(PO_4)_4.4H_2O$, $ZnNH_4PO_4$ and $Zn(OH)_2$ (Randhawa *et al*, 1978). Coarse-textured soils commonly contain less zinc than fine-textured soils.

b. Reduced soil conditions decrease the concentration of zinc in the soil solution. Under submerged (reduced) conditions, zinc becomes immobilized in the form of ZnS, $ZnNH_4PO_4$ and $ZnSiO_3$, or other forms.

c. A high soil *p*H reduces the availability of zinc. The solubility of zinc in water decreases by a factor of 100 per unit of *p*H increase. The decrease in zinc concentration in the soil solution of acid soils upon submergence is partly due to the increase in *p*H which occurs under reduced conditions. Zinc deficiency is generally only observed in soils with a *p*H above 6.5-7.

d. A high organic matter content in the soil generally causes low availability of zinc. This effect is probably related to the accumulation of HCO_3 and organic acids in submerged and reduced soils due to decomposition of organic matter. Bicarbonate and organic acids appear to have a negative effect on zinc uptake by rice roots and on the transport of zinc ions in the plant.

There are several relatively easy ways to correct zinc deficiency in rice cultivation, viz.

- Drainage and drying of continuously flooded (irrigated) fields in the dry season: for example, by using a dry fallow or cultivating a dryland rabi crop.
- Application of zinc sulphate to the soil, either as a basal dressing at the time of transplantation or as a top-dressing when the deficiency symptoms develop.
- Dipping seedlings in a 2 percent zinc oxide suspension at time of transplantation.
- Giving a foliar spray with 0.5 percent zinc sulphate in solution.
- Planting tolerant varieties.

Zinc deficiency in rice was observed and studied in Bangladesh by many institutions from the mid-1970s. Among the research institutes involved were BRRI, BARI, INA and BAU. Agencies and organizations carrying out demonstrations and extension work were DAE, BADC, Soil Fertility Institute and several voluntary agencies. Up to 1982, little had been done to coordinate, integrate and standardize the work of these organizations. At a Workshop on Zinc Deficiency Problems of Irrigated Rice organized by BRRI in 1980, proposals were made for a national programme for the identification of zinc-deficient soils in Bangladesh, to be coordinated by BRRI: methods of sampling soils and plants, field registration, plot choice, and layout of trial and demonstration fields (BRRI, 1980b). However, with the departure of the proposed BRRI head of the programme, the effort was discontinued.[29]

Most of the results of trials and demonstrations that were carried out lacked information on the soils on which they were sited. Partial information was sometimes provided (topsoil *p*H, organic matter content, texture) but a comprehensive soil description and classification of the soils usually were lacking. Therefore, on the basis of the available data, it is impossible to make an assessment of the distribution and extent of the country's zinc deficiency problem. In general, the available data seem to confirm the general concept of the conditions under which zinc deficiency is likely to occur: i.e., calcareous deposits (Ganges alluvial soils); light-textured soils (silts, sandy loams and sands); and soils with a high organic matter content (peat soils, and floodplain basin soils). These soils are most extensive in the west and north-west of Bangladesh. Deficiency symptoms are particularly likely to occur in such soils under continuously wet conditions: e.g., in irrigation projects, and in low-lying sites.

In a nation-wide Fertilizer Demonstration and Distribution Project, the DAE with FAO/UNDP assistance established over 800 demonstration sites in farmers' fields during

---

[29]*A coordinated programme was later organized by BARC.*

the 1981 aman season. In addition to demonstrating the effects of N, P and K fertilizers, the programme also included zinc and sulphur treatments. In general, these demonstrations showed positive and economic responses to applications of N, NP and NPK fertilizers, with average yield increases over control of 31, 47 and 56 percent respectively at application rates of approximately 1 md/ac N, 0.75 md/ac P_2O_5 and 0.5 md/ac K_2O. Zinc sulphate, applied at a rate of 18 lb/ac (20 kg/ha), increased yields of t. aman (BR-4) over NPK by more than 3.5 md/ac on more than 85 percent of the demonstration plots. The average yield increase over NPK due to the zinc application was 18 percent, and the economic return increased by an average of 45 percent: (Khan & Valera, 1982).

However, again, little was done to identify the soils and soil conditions on the demonstration plots. That was due to a manpower problem. It was hoped that, with the appointment of an FAO Associate Expert in soils and fertilizers in 1982, soil identification would be made a regular part of the programme. Also, it was planned to supplement the on-going FAO/UNDP project with a project under the FAO Technical Cooperation Programme, to start in 1982, which would make available a Bangladeshi Agronomist/Soil Scientist for 18 months and an FAO consultant specializing in secondary and micro-nutrients for 9 months.

During the present study, an attempt was made to find a relationship between soil conditions and the occurrence of zinc (and sulphur) deficiency in rice cultivation. In the five drainage and irrigation projects which were visited (reported in earlier sections), and also in the Barura and Burichang deep tube-well irrigation areas in Comilla District and the Gaurnadi low-lift pump irrigation area of Barisal District, soil and land use observations were made and soil and plant samples were taken on sites that were reported to have zinc and sulphur deficiency problems. As a control, areas not reported to be affected by these problems were also investigated and sampled.

While carrying out these observations, it was found to be difficult to identify clear examples of zinc deficiency in some of the areas (DND, CIP) which had suffered from zinc deficiency in previous seasons. The explanation for this seemed to be that the autumn and winter of 1981-82 had been very dry, and soils that normally would have remained moist during those seasons had dried out, thus allowing the natural regeneration of available zinc levels through oxidation processes. Another, and probably more important, reason was that farmers in those areas had quickly adopted the practice of applying zinc sulphate to their paddy crops. Zinc sulphate had become available to farmers from 1981 in standard 5 kg bags; (BRRI's recommended dose is 5 kg per acre). The low, subsidized price (Tk30 per bag), the ease of handling the small bags and the dramatic effect observed on rice yields all contributed to the successful introduction of the practice.

The results of field observations and of soil and plant analyses are shown in Table 4.4 at the end of this chapter. It can be concluded from the number of randomly-observed sites and their confirmation by the results of plant analyses that zinc deficiency is a common disorder in areas of intensive paddy cultivation in Bangladesh. In the field, 28 cases of zinc deficiency were observed out of a total of 45 sites visited. Laboratory analyses of plant samples indicated zinc contents below critical values in 23 out of 57 samples. Zinc contents were below critical levels in 23 soil samples out of 31. Critical zinc levels were set at 20 ppm for plant tissue and 1 ppm for 0.05 NHO_3-soluble zinc in soil samples (Yoshida, 1981).

It should be noted that field observations and analytical results did not match each other in all cases. High zinc contents were determined in plants growing on some zinc-deficient soils (observation Nos DND 1-4; CIP 2; BIP 4-7; Gaurnadi 3-5), whereas applications of zinc sulphate reported by farmers were not always reflected in high zinc contents in soils and/or plants (DND 2; BIP 7 and 7; Gaurnadi 1 5). Also, zinc deficiency symptoms were observed on sites where the samples indicated high zinc contents (DND 3 and 4; CIP 2; BIP 4 and 5; G-K 2 and 8; Gaurnadi 3-5). The reverse was also observed, where plants without zinc deficiency symptoms were found to have low zinc contents (CIP 6b).

These discrepancies leave a number of questions to be answered. The most important appears to be the determination of the critical zinc content in the rice plant. Critical zinc content in the soil is generally accepted as 1 ppm (Yoshida, 1981; Sakai, 1979; BRRI, 1980b), although some scientists question the reliability of analysis of micronutrients in soils in general and of zinc in particular (Sakai, 1982, personal communication). Less agreement exists on critical levels of zinc in plants. Yoshida (1981) characterizes zinc contents below 10 ppm as 'definitely zinc deficient' and zinc levels below 20 ppm as 'likely zinc deficient'. Sakai (1979) and BRRI (1980b) use 27 ppm as the critical zinc level in plant tissue. In the ratings given in this study, Yoshida's 'likely critical value' of 20 ppm has been used as it gave the best correlation between laboratory data and field observations.

Another matter which needs further research is the rate of immobilization of zinc when zinc sulphate is applied to the soil. At several observation sites, plant zinc contents were above critical levels where zinc sulphate had been applied to the soil, yet zinc levels in the soil were below 1 ppm (DND 2; BIP 6; Gaurnadi 3-5). This suggests a very rapid immobilization of zinc. Since alkaline soil conditions did not prevail in any of these observation sites, the immobilization might be explained by the occurrence of strongly reduced soil conditions. Unfortunately, redox potentials could not be measured during this study, and time constraints prevented organic matter contents from being determined. Brief descriptions of the soils at the observation sites are given in Table 4.5 at the end of this chapter.

Sakai (1979) suggested that there might be an antagonistic effect of manganese and possibly of magnesium on zinc uptake by rice plants. This is not confirmed by the data in Table 4.4. Relatively high manganese contents in plants (over 900 ppm) do occur (CIP 7; G-K 1, 4, 9; Burichang 1), but corresponding zinc contents were found both below and above critical values.

On the basis of the limited data available, no clear relationship could be established between soil pH and the occurrence of zinc deficiency. The pH of the soil samples as determined in the laboratory ranged from 5.9 to 8.0, but high as well as low zinc contents were found within these samples.

Sulphur deficiency. Sulphur is considered a minor plant nutrient. It is needed by the rice plant in considerable amounts but, unlike the major nutrients N, P and K, it usually is not specifically applied as a fertilizer. Tissue of healthy rice plants contains at least 0.16 percent sulphur at the tillering stage, which is approximately equal to the phosphorus content in rice plants. The sulphur content decreases during plant development, and the critical sulphur content at plant maturity (ripening) is 0.06 percent (Yoshida, 1981). A rice crop producing 50 md/ac paddy extracts about 3.5 kg of sulphur from the soil.

Because sulphur, like nitrogen, is essential in the synthesis of amino acids (thiamine, cystine, methionine, etc.), enzymes and proteins in plants, the deficiency symptoms of both these nutrients are similar: rice plants are stunted; the leaves are narrow, short and erect; and they have a yellowish appearance.

Sulphur in the soil occurs mainly in organic forms and it becomes available for uptake by plants as sulphate ions by means of a mineralization process. Sulphur in the soil occurs to a limited extent in inorganic forms, mostly as metal sulphides (FeS, ZnS, CuS). Sulphur mineralization is optimal at relatively high temperature (40^0C) and at a relatively low soil moisture content (60 percent of field capacity). The rate of mineralization also depends on the presence of living plant material and on the sulphur content of the organic matter (Blair *et al.*, 1978). Total sulphur content in soils normally ranges between 20 and over 500 ppm S. Extremely high sulphur contents occur in acid sulphate soils, which may contain up to 10,000 ppm S. Under normal conditions, available sulphur (SO_4-S) varies from less than 1 ppm to 50 ppm or more, depending mainly on the redox potential of the soil. Under reduced conditions, such as prevail when soils are flooded, sulphate is transformed into sulphide and may precipitate as metal sulphides or form H_2S which, if present in high concentrations, is toxic to plants. The critical sulphate value in rice soils is generally considered to be 10 ppm SO_4-S.

In irrigated paddy cultivation, sulphur may be supplied to the crop in the irrigation water. In industrial areas, sulphur may also be supplied in polluted rainwater. On the other hand, leaching of sulphur (and other nutrients) may be considerable under continuously flooded conditions or under high rainfall.

The emergence of sulphur deficiency in wetland rice cultivation has resulted from three causes.

a. The increased extraction of sulphur from the soil due to higher crop productivity that is obtained in intensive cultivation systems including double and triple cropping of rice HYVs.

b. The more reduced soil conditions that occur in intensive irrigated cultivation systems compared with previous systems consisting of one wetland crop and a dryland crop or fallow.

c. The replacement of sulphur-containing N, P and K fertilizers by so-called high-analysis fertilizers that do not contain sulphur. Sulphate of ammonia was replaced by urea as the main N fertilizer in the early-1960s (BRRI, 1980a). Sulphate of ammonia contains 24 percent S (as well as 21 percent N), but urea does not contain any sulphur. Similarly, single superphosphate, which contains 12 percent S, was replaced by TSP which contains less than 1 percent S. Muriate of potash (KCl), the main K fertilizer used in Bangladesh, contains no sulphur. However, another K fertilizer, potassium sulphate, contains approximately 20 percent S, but this fertilizer is used only for tobacco cultivation.

Corrective measures to ameliorate sulphur deficiency in intensive rice cultivation systems include the following.

a. Use of a dry-season fallow or the cultivation of a dryland crop in the dry season instead of a flooded rice crop (boro).

b. Application of gypsum ($CaSO_4$) to the soil as a basal dressing at time of transplanting. Current (1982) application rates recommended are 65-80 kg/ha (BRRI) or 100kg/ha (DAE).

c. Application of elemental sulphur (S). No research data on this practice in Bangladesh are available. The practice might be promising in view of the acidifying effect of elemental sulphur, which could have a beneficial effect on nutrient availability (particularly of zinc) in calcareous soils on the Ganges Meander Floodplains.

d. Use of sulphur-containing N, P and K fertilizers: sulphate of ammonia, single super-phosphate, and/or potassium sulphate. Although this might appear to be a simple solution, the (re)introduction of these fertilizers could have serious implications for the country's high-analysis fertilizer industry. Storage and distribution costs would also be higher.[30] Balanced applications of individual nutrients are more difficult to achieve when compound fertilizers are used than when single-nutrient fertilizers are used.

e. Introduction of sulphur-coated urea granules. Sulphur coatings on urea granules reduce nitrogen losses that are caused by volatilization of ammonia, but they supply a small quantity of sulphur at the same time. Although only limited investigations have been carried out (up to 1982), this method appears to be promising (de Datta, 1978).

f. Application of farmyard manure and/or tank silt. These practices supply sulphur (and nitrogen) to soils and crops, but they negatively affect the availability of zinc.

g. Mulching and deep cultivation.

Sulphur deficiency in rice was observed in Bangladesh from 1976 when rice yields were reported to be declining in some irrigation project areas (DND, CIP, BIP). Crops showing nitrogen-like deficiency symptoms failed to recover from applications of nitrogen (or phosphatic or potash) fertilizers. The disorder was then diagnosed as due to sulphur deficiency and dramatic yield increases were obtained from applications of sulphur: see Table 4.2. After that, a number of government, international and private organizations became involved in research, demonstration and extension activities to ameliorate sulphur deficiency. However, a similar situation arose to that reported above for zinc deficiency and amelioration, with most agencies carrying out independent activities. This consultant believes that this situation resulted in an under-estimation of the extent of the sulphur problem and, consequently, a lack of clear recommendations regarding appropriate corrective measures, including appropriate application rates for sulphur fertilizers. At a Workshop on Sulphur Nutrition in Rice held at BRRI in 1978, proposals were made to organize an integrated approach to sulphur research and demonstration, including a survey of the sulphur status of the country's soils (BRRI, 1980a). The proposal was for BRRI to coordinate the programme, but a practical programme did not materialize.

Several authors have shown the negative effect of flooding on sulphur availability, and other authors have shown the better response of sulphur-containing fertilizers on rice performance in comparison with fertilizers not containing sulphur (BRRI, 1980a). However, as in the case of zinc deficiency, research results on sulphur lack comprehensive information on the soils on which the research was conducted. Therefore, it is impossible to assess the extent and distribution of the sulphur deficiency problem.

Results obtained from the FAO/UNDP-assisted DEA fertilizer demonstration programme clearly demonstrate that sulphur deficiency is widespread in Bangladesh. Application of gypsum at a rate of 1 md/ac (ca 100 kg/ha) on more than 800 demonstration plots on farmers' fields all over the country increased the yield of t. aman (BR-4) over the NPK control by more than 2.5 md/ac on more than 85 percent of the plots. The average yield increase over NPK due to the application of sulphur was 22 percent, and the economic return increased by an average of 44 percent (Khan & Valera, 1982). Most of the plots with

---

[30]*Also to be considered is the greater cost to the farmer in carrying low-analysis fertilizers from the place of purchase to his homestead and from the latter to his fields. In the case of N fertilizers, the farmer would need to carry two bags of sulphate of ammonia in order to supply the equivalent amount of nitrogen in 1 bag of urea.*

a low response to gypsum were located in Chittagong District, so it is concluded that industrial air and water pollution in this area provides considerable amounts of sulphur to the crop; surface and subsurface seepage of water from rocks in adjoining hill areas which contain sulphur (pyrite) may also contribute sulphur to the piedmont soils.

The installation of a TSP production plant at Chittagong led to a paradoxical situation. On the one hand, partly as a result of the import of this high-analysis phosphatic fertilizer (which does not contain sulphur), sulphur deficiency emerged in intensive rice cultivation. On the other hand, the manufacture of TSP produces gypsum as a non-commercial by-product which is stored in the open air on the factory premises. In 1982, it was reportedly available free of cost to anyone collecting it with their own transport. In 1981, BADC, Comilla, arranged for some truck-loads of gypsum to be applied to aus and aman crops in tube-well irrigation areas in Comilla District, but distribution at farm level apparently created problems with local fertilizer dealers, and the initiative was discontinued. In view of the widespread occurrence of sulphur deficiency, the absence of any other economic source of sulphur in the country and the availability of large quantities of gypsum at Chittagong at nominal (transportation) cost, the consultant recommended that BADC should initiate a nation-wide distribution system. In view of the prevailing uncertainty about the location and extent of sulphur deficiency, capacity would need to be built up gradually, year by year, as more details of the quantities of sulphur needed became available.[31]

A popular misconception needs to be cleared up regarding the effectiveness of zinc sulphate to ameliorate sulphur deficiency. Zinc sulphate contains only 11 percent elemental sulphur. Therefore, a standard application of zinc sulphate (the standard recommendation to correct zinc deficiency) only adds 1.2 lb of sulphur to the soil. That amount is negligible compared with the application rate of 19 lb/ac of sulphur recommended by DAE (Khan and Valera, 1982).

4.7.2 Nematode diseases in wetland rice cultivation

Continuous submergence of soils, such as occurs in intensively-cultivated, irrigated, rice cropping systems, has locally caused the spread of the soil-borne nematode diseases *ufra* and root-knot. Both diseases used to affect only deepwater aman, but they have now been observed in transplanted aman and boro paddy crops as well.

Ufra (*Ditylenchus angustus*, Butler) affects the stems of rice plants and causes stunted growth with twisted leaves and culms. Root-knot (*Meliodogyne incognita*, Chitwood) affects the roots of rice plants, where it forms nodules that limit nutrient transport, resulting in stunted plant development.

The consultant did not, in fact, observe a high incidence of these diseases in the project areas visited. Root-knot disease was observed locally in the G-K project area, and both root-knot and *ufra* diseases were observed in the Gaurnadi area of Barisal District. In the latter area, *ufra* disease in particular was causing damage to boro paddy and it was observed to

---

[31] *BADC did start gypsum distribution in the 1980s. A total of 12,880 tons was distributed in 1989-90 (mainly in the Districts of Rajshahi Division plus Jamalpur District), but the quantities moved varied considerably from year to year. One problem identified in the mid-1980s was the high acid content of the gypsum, which caused serious corrosion of trucks and rail wagons transporting the fertilizer. From about 1990, the TSP plant at Chittagong started to produce single-superphosphate (SSP), which contains sulphur: 108,000 tons were produced in 1992-93 (and 86,000 tons were also imported in that year). In the following year, only 82,000 tons of SSP were produced, and none was imported.*

affect newly-planted aus plots. However, the fact that both diseases are reported to be affecting boro and aus paddy as well as deepwater aman is a matter for concern.

Economic corrective measures are not available. The nematicide FURADAN 3G is effective but expensive (approximately Tk 200 per acre per application, and generally more than one application is required). Complete drying out of the soil, so as to dry out and kill the nematodes, is impractical as it would have to last for periods over six months, as otherwise at least the *ufra* nematode can still survive. Removal of all organic matter so as to deprive the nematodes of a food source is impractical, too. The diseases can be limited by burning plant residues and stubble, and by avoiding infestation of irrigation water with affected plant material. Also, the practice of selling seedlings, which is common in the Gaurnadi area, should be discouraged as infestations also occur in seedlings (Ou, 1975). Alternatively, seedlings should be brought from upland sites where the nematodes do not occur.

TABLE 4.4

Selected soil and plant analytical data for samples taken from water development project areas

Obs No[2]	Soil analytical data[1] pH	Zn ppm	SO₄-S ppm	N %	rice variety	growth stage[3]	NPK applied[4]	Zn	crop performance	deficiency observed[5] Zn	S	plant part sampled[6]	Plant analytical data[1] Zn %	S %	Mn ppm	Mg %	N %	N/S
Dhaka-Narayanganj-Demra Project																		
1	7.7	0.59+	13.8	0.09	IR8	till	+	-	mod	-	+	wp	32.8	0.11[0]	139	0.34	1.01	9.2
2	6.4	0.82+	14.2	0.16	IR8	till	+	+	mod	-	+	wp	28.4	0.13[0]	340	0.32	1.27	10.0
3	6.5	0.64+	17.7	0.19	IR8	till	+	-	poor	+	-	wp	23.9	0.16	239	0.44	1.85	11.4
4 tops	7.4	0.39+	18.4	0.09	IR8	till	+	-	v.poor	+	-	wp	39.0	0.24	843	0.51	3.29	13.9
subs	7.2	0.34	34.6	tr														
Chandpur Irrigation Project																		
1	7.4	5.96	2.53[0]		BR3	till	+	+	good	-	-	wp	25.6	0.14[0]	252	0.23		
2	7.2	0.84+	6.14[0]		BR3	till	+	-	poor	+	+	wp	21.3	0.15[0]	348	0.18		
4	7.9	0.87+	0.38[0]		4A BR3	till	+	-	v.poor	+	+	wp	12.4+	0.15[0]	216	0.83		
					4B BR3	till	+	-	mod	+	+	wp	15.1+	0.12[0]	178	0.54		
6	7.6	0.98+	1.53[0]		6A IR8	till	-	-	poor	+	+	6A.1 wp	19.5+	0.13[0]	229	0.67		
												6A.2 wp	14.2+	0.13[0]	312	1.30		
												ol	17.7+	0.10[0]	265	0.19		
					6B IR8	till	+	-	mod	-	+	wp	23.0	0.09[0]	996	0.19		
7	6.4	1.19	4.22[0]		IR8	head	+	+	good	-	-	wp						
8	5.9	1.25	4.29[0]		LV	ripe	+	-	good	-	-	wp	23.0	0.08[0]	635	0.11		
Barisal Irrigation Project																		
1	7.3	4.88	0.78[0]		BR3	till	+	+	poor (wet)	-	-	1A ol	34.9	0.12[0]	370		0.44	
												1B yl	42.5	0.17	150		0.28	
2	7.2	0.34+	0.38[0]		BR3	till	+	-	mod	+	-	wp	19.1+	0.14[0]	569		0.47	
3	7.4	0.53+	1.54[0]		BR3	till	+	-	mod	+	+	wp	19.7+	0.10[0]	356		0.28	
4	7.9	0.09+	1.92[0]		BR3	till	+	-	poor	+	+	4A ol	37.0	0.13[0]	505		0.50	
												4B yl	28.8	0.14[0]	255		0.22	
5	6.5	0.69+	2.30[0]		IR8	till	±	-	mod	+	+	wp	22.4	0.10[0]	241		0.40	
6	6.5	0.38	3.07[0]		6A BR3	till	±	-	mod	-	+	wp	30.1+	0.11[0]	481		0.39	
					6B BR3	till	+	+	mod	-	+	wp	34.9	0.14[0]	468		0.35	
					6C BR3	till	+	+	good	-	-	wp	36.3	0.16[0]	488		0.29	

(Contd.)

(Continued)

	Soil analytical data[1]				Field information							Plant analytical data[1]						
Obs No[2]	pH	Zn ppm	SO$_4$-S ppm	N %	rice variety	growth stage[3]	NPK applied	Zn[4]	crop performance	def. Zn[5]	def. S[5]	plant part sampled[6]	Zn %	S %	Mn ppm	Mg %	N %	N/S
7	6.2	0.57+	3.84[0]		IR8	till	+	–	mod	–	+	wp	22.4	0.10[0]	315		0.37	
8 tops	7.7	0.25+	3.84[0]		BR7	till	+	+	poor	+	–	8A ol	19.1+	0.16[0]	572		0.71	
subs	8.0	0.15+	4.22[0]									8B ml	15.6+	0.16[0]	474		0.76	
												8C yl	16.4+	0.13[0]	303		0.42	
9	8.0	0.06+	1.54[0]		IR8	till	+	–	mod	+	–	wp	15.1+	0.17	583		0.53	
10	7.1	0.57+	8.06[0]		IR8	till	+	–	mod	+	–	wp	17.1+	0.16	405		0.52	
11					BR9	till	+	–	mod	+	+	wp	18.4+	0.13[0]	394		0.46	
12					IR8	till	+	–	mod	+	+	wp	19.7+	0.13[0]	352		0.43	
Ganges-Kobadak Project																		
1	(7.5)[7]				BR3	till	+	–	mod	+	–	1A wp	27.9	0.16	617	0.66		
												1B ol	14.0[0]	0.14[0]	937+	0.62		
												1C yl	19.1+	0.16	423	0.45		
2	(7.5)				BR3	till	+	+	mod	+	–	wp	25.0	0.15[0]	332	0.41		
3	(8.0)				BR3	till	+	+	mod	+	+	3A wp	21.3	0.14[0]	384	0.42		
												3B ol	17.6+	0.13[0]	988	0.63		
5	(8.0)				BR3	ripe	+	–	mod	–	+	g	22.8	0.08	69	0.20	1.20	20.7
6	(7.5)				BR3	ripe	+	–	good	–	–	g	22.1	0.06	92	0.19	1.01	17.9
7	(7.5)				BR3	till	+	–	poor	–	+	wp	23.5	0.14[0]	541	0.40		
8	(7.5)				BR3	till	+	–	mod	+	+	wp	22.1	0.11[0]	638	0.31		
9	(7.5)				BR3	till	+	–	poor	+	–	9A wp	18.4+	0.18	724	0.57		
												9B ol	15.4+	0.20	1480	0.83		
13	(7.0)				LV	till	+	–	poor	+	–	wp	18.4+	0.21	500	0.63		
Barura[8]																		
1	7.5	0.89+	3.46[0]		BR3	till	+	–	v.poor	+	+	1A wp	15.5+	0.15[0]	247	0.49		
												1B ol	11.5+	0.14[0]	248	1.32		
2	8.0	2.25	1.15[0]		2A BR3	till	+	+	mod	–	+	wp	23.0	0.13[0]	398	0.48		
					2B BR3	till	–	–	poor	+	+	wp	10.0+	0.08[0]	292	1.54		

(Contd.)

(Continued)

	Soil analytical data[1]				Field information							Plant analytical data[1]						
Obs No[2]	pH	Zn ppm	SO_4-S ppm	N %	rice variety	growth stage[3]	NPK applied[4]	Zn	crop performance	def[5] Zn	def[5] S	plant part sampled[6]	Zn %	S %	Mn ppm	Mg %	N %	N/S
Burichang[8]																		
1	6.9	2.88	1.54[0]		1 BR3	till	+	+	mod	-	+	wp	25.7	0.06[0]	1398	0.48	1.15	19.6
2	6.5	1.46	1.92[0]		2 BR3	ripe	+	+	good	-	-	g	26.6	0.06				
3					3 BR3	till	+	+	mod	-	+	wp	26.6	0.09[0]	363	0.36		
Gaurnadi[8]																		
1	6.1	0.46[+]	56.4		1 grass fallow					(+)[10]								
										(+)[10]								
2	6.4	0.43[+]	39.2		2 ploughed													
3	7.3	0.57[+]	15.4[0]		3 IR8	ripe	+	+	poor[9]			3A wp	35.6	0.12[0]	410			
												3B wp	23.0	0.12[0]	975			
4	6.8	0.41[+]	40.7		4 BR3	till	+	+	mod	-	-	4 wp	24.3	0.22	65			
5	6.9	0.35[+]	18.8		5A BR3	till	+	+	poor[9]	+	-	5A wp	20.4	0.16[0]	60			
					5B BR3	till	+	+	poor[9]	+	+	5B wp	25.0	0.15[0]	71			
					5C BR3	till	-	+	poor[9]	+	+	5C wp	2.7	0.11[0]	118			

Critical levels for zinc and sulphur deficiency in soil and rice plants

Soil	1.0	10.0	Plant	tillering	wp	20	0.16
					wp	20	0.10
					wp	20	0.06
					gr	15	0.06
							17

Notes to Table 4.4:
1. Methods of analysis are described in Annexe 1.
2. The numbers of the observation sites correspond to those indicated on Figures 4.2, 4.4, 4.6, 4.8 and 4.10. Suffixes A, B, etc., are explained in Table 4.5. Brief descriptions of the soils and land use are given in Table 4.5.
3. Growth stage: till = tillering; head = heading; ripe = ripening.
4. The symbols +, ± and - indicate that moderate, small or no applications of NPK fertilizers had been made by the farmer.
5. The symbols + and - indicate that zinc or sulphur deficiency symptoms were/were not observed in the rice plants in the field.
6. Wp = whole plant; ol = old leaves; yl = young leaves; g = grain.
7. Figures in brackets refer to field measurement of pH.
8. Barura and Burichang are deep tube-well irrigated areas in Comilla District. Gaurnadi is a low-lift pump irrigated area in Barisal District.
9. Poor crop performance was due to *ufra* disease.
10. (+) = zinc deficiency was observed in the previous aman crop.

TABLE 4.5
Brief descriptions of observation sites

Obs No[1]	Physiography	Soil series[2]	Depth (cm)	Colour[3]	Texture[4]	Mottle colour[5]	pH[6]	Free CaCO3	Samples taken
Dhaka-Narayanganj-Demra Project									
1	Nearly level ridges	Jalkundi	0-15	vdg 5Y3/1	SiCL	lyb	7.0		Soil: 0-15 cm Plant: whole plant
			15-35	dg 5Y4/1	SiCL	sb+b; dg coatings	8.0		
			35-90	lob 2.5Y5/4	SiL/SiCL	sb	8.0		
			90-100+	og 5Y5/2	SiC	sb	8.0		
2	Lower slope of ridges	Naraibag	0-15	g N6/	SiCL	ob	7.5		Ditto
			15-100	og 5Y5/2	SiCL	sb+yb; dg coatings	8.0		
			100-120+	g 5Y5/1	SiCL	sb+b+py	8.0		
3	Basin margin	Naraibag	0-15	vdg 5Y3/1	SiCL	oy	8.0		Ditto
			15-80	o 5Y5/4	SiCL	ob; dg coatings	8.0		
			80-120	dg 5Y4/1	SiCL	sb+db+py	8.0		
4	(Not recorded)	Jalkundi over weathered Madhupur Clay	0-15	dg 5Y4/1	SiCL	oy	8.0		Soil: 0-15; 70-80 cm Plant: whole plant
			15-60	m: o, ob, yb, g 5Y5/3, 2.5Y4/4, 10YR5/4, N5/	SiCL/C		8.0		
			60-120+	m: yb, ry, g 5YR4/4, 5YR6/6, 2.5Y5/1	C		7.0		
Chandpur Irrigation Project									
1	Upper slope of slight ridge	Chandpur	0-15	o 5Y5/3	SiL	yb	7.0		Soil: 0-15 cm Plant: whole plant
			15-100	o 5Y4/3	SiL	yb; g coatings	7.5		
			100-120+	og 5Y4/2	vfSL		8.0		
2	Middle slope of slight ridge	Chandpur	0-15	og 5Y4/2	SiCL	yb	7.5		Ditto
			15-120+	o 5Y4/3	SiL	yb; g coatings	7.5		
3	Lower slope of slight ridge	Chandpur (?)	0-15	og 5Y4/2	SiCL	yb	7.5		None
			15-90	o 5Y4/3	SiL	yb; g coatings	8.0		
			90-120+	og 5Y5/2	L		8.0		
4	Border of shallow basin	Paikpara	0-10	dg 5Y4/1	SiCL	yb	7.5		Soil: 0-10 cm Plant: 4A- severely Zn+S deficient 4B- moderately Zn+S deficient
			10-60	o 5Y5/3	SiC	yb; dg coatings	8.0		
			60-120+	lob 2.5Y5/4	SiL		8.0		

(Contd.)

(Continued)

Obs No[1]	Physiography	Soil series[2]	Depth (cm)	Colour[3]	Texture[4]	Mottle colour[5]	pH[6]	Free CaCO$_3$	Samples taken
5	Upper slope of slight ridge	Chandpur	0-15 15-120+	o 10YR4/3 o 10YR4/3	SiL SiL	yb yb; g coatings	7.0 8.0		None
6	Top of slight ridge	Chandpur	0-15 15-60 60-90 90-120+	og 5Y4/2 o 5Y4/3 og 5Y4/2 m: og, yb 5Y4/2, 10YR5/4	SiL SiL SiCL SiL	b yb; g coatings yb; g coatings	8.0 8.0 8.0 7.5		Soil: 0-15 cm Plant: 6A.1 - whole plant severely Zn+S deficient 6A.2 - two old leaves of same 6B - non-deficient plant on adjoining plot
7	Top of slight ridge	Chandpur	0-15 15-80 80-120+	og 5Y4/2 o 5Y4/3 og 5Y4/2	SiL SiL SiL	yb yb; g coatings yb; g coatings	7.0 8.0 7.5		Soil: 0-15 cm Plant: whole plant
8	Basin bottom	Paikpara	0-15 15-75 75-120+	dg 5Y4/1 g 5Y5/3 o 5Y4/4	SiL SiCL SiL	yb dg coatings g	7.0 7.5 7.0		Soil: 0-15 cm Plant: whole plant
Barisal Irrigation Project									
1	Basin	Barisal, poorly drained phase	0-15 15-80 80-120+	g 5Y5/1 dg 5Y4/1 dg 5Y4/1	SiC C C	yb	8.0 8.0 8.0		Soil: 0-15 cm Plant: 1A - old leaves 1B - young leaves
2	Basin	Barisal, poorly drained phase	0-10 10-40 40-100 100-120+	g 5Y5/1 dg 5Y4/1 vdg 5Y3/1 dg 5Y4/1	C C C C	yb yb yb	8.0 8.0 8.0 8.0		Soil: 0-10 cm Plant: whole plant
3	Basin	Barisal, poorly drained phase	0-20 20-70 70-120+	g 5Y5/1 g 5Y5/1 dg 5Y4/1	SiC C C	b yb	8.5 8.0 8.0		Soil: 0-10 cm Plant: whole plant
4	Basin	Barisal, poorly drained phase	0-10 10-70 70-120+	g Y5/1 g 5Y5/1 dg 5Y4/1	SiC C C	yb yb	7.5 8.0 8.0		Soil: 0-10 cm Plant: 4A - old leaves 4B - young leaves
5	Basin	Barisal, poorly drained phase	0-10 10-60 60-80 80-120+	g N5/ dg N4/ dg N4/ dg N4/	SiC C SiC C	lob yb	7.5 8.0 8.0 8.0		Soil: 0-10 cm Plant: whole plant

(Contd.)

(Continued)

Obs No[1]	Physiography	Soil series[2]	Depth (cm)	Colour[3]	Texture[4]	Mottle colour[5]	pH[6]	Free CaCO3	Samples taken
6	Border of basin	Nalchiti	0-10	dg N4/	SiC		8.0		Soil: 0-10 cm
			10-45	dg N4/	SiC		8.0		Plant: whole plant on three, adjacent, increasingly S-deficient plots
			45-90	dgb 2.5Y4/2	SiCL	lob	8.5		
			90-120+	lob 2.5Y5/4	SiCL	dgb	8.5		
7	Border of basin	Nalchiti	0-15	dg N4/	SiCL		8.0		Soil: 0-15 cm
			15-80	dgb 2.5Y4/2	SiCL	lob	8.0		Plant: whole plant
			80-120+	m: dgb, lob 2.5Y4/2+5/4	SiCL		8.0		
8	Level basin	Mehendiganj	0-15	gb 2.5Y5/2	SiC		8.0		Soil: 0-15, 80-90 cm
			15-60	gb 2.5Y5/2	SiC		8.0		Plant: 8A - old leaves
			60-120+	g 5Y5/1	SiC		7.5		8B - medium leaves
									8C - young leaves
9	Level basin	Mehendiganj	0-15	ob 2.5Y5/2	SiC		8.0		Soil: 0-15 cm
			15-30	dgb 2.5Y4/2	SiC		8.0		Plant: whole plant
			30-65	dgb 2.5Y4/2	C	yb	8.0		
			65-120+	dg N4/	SiC	dgb	8.0		
10	Border of basin	Muladi	0-10	g 5Y5/1	SiC		7.5		Soil: 0-10 cm
			10-25	dg 5Y4/4	SiC		7.5		Plant: 10, 11, 12, whole plant on adjoining plots
			25-80	yb 10YR5/6	SiCL		8.0		
			80-120+	dg 5Y4/1	SiCL		8.0		
Ganges-Kobadak Project									
1	Lower slope of ridge	Pakuria	0-15	ob-dgb 2.5Y4/2	C		7.5	+	1A: whole plant
			15-80	b-db 10YR4/3	SiC/C		8.0	+	1B: old leaves
			80-120+	vdb 10YR2/2	C		8.0	+	1C: young leaves
2	Lower slope of ridge	Pakuria	0-15	dgb 2.5Y4/2	SiC		7.5	-	Whole plant
			15-45	b-db 10YR4/3	SiC		8.0	+	
			45-100	b 10YR5/3	C		8.0	+	
			100-120+	vdgb 10YR3/2	C		8.0	+	
3	Lower slope of ridge	Pakuria	0-15	dgb 2.5Y4/2	SiC		7.5	+	3A: whole plant
			15-100	b 10YR5/3	SiC		8.0	+	3B: old leaves
			100-130+	db 10YR3/3	C		8.0	+	

(Contd.)

(Continued)

Obs No[1]	Physiography	Soil series[2]	Depth (cm)	Colour[3]	Texture[4]	Mottle colour[5]	pH[6]	Free CaCo$_3$	Samples taken
4	High ridge	Sara (?)	0-25	ob-dgb 2.5Y4/3	SiCL		8.0	+	None
			25-40	ob 2.5Y4/4	SiL		8.0	+	
			40-120+	ob 2.5Y4/4	vfSL/LS		8.0	+	
5	Lower slope of ridge	Pakuria	0-15	dgb 2.5Y4/2	SiC		8.0	+	Grains
			15-50	b 10YR5/3	SiC	vdgb	8.0	+	
			50-120+	vdgb 10YR3/2	SiC	dyb	8.0	+	
6	Lower slope of ridge	Gangni	0-10	dgb 2.5Y4/2	C		7.5	-	Grains
			10-80	ob-dgb 2.5Y4/2	C		7.5	-	
			80-120+	lob 2.5Y5/4	C		7.5	-	
7	Ridge	(?)	0-25	dgb 2.5Y4/2	C		8.0	+	Whole plant
			25-50	ob-dgb 2.5Y4/3	C		8.0	+	
			50-80	ob 2.5Y4/4	vfS		8.0	+	
			80-120+	lob 2.5Y5/4	LS		8.0	+	
8	Ridge	(?)	0-15	dgb 2.5Y4/2	C		8.0	+	Whole plant
			15-60	ob 2.5Y4/4	SiC		8.0	+	
			60-100	ob 2.5Y4/4	LvfS		8.0	+	
			100-120+	lob 2.5Y5/4	LS		8.0	+	
9	Lower slope of ridge	(?)	0-15	dgb 2.5Y4/2	SiC		8.0	+	9A: whole plant
			15-40	lob 2.5Y5/4	SiC		8.0	+	9B: old leaves
			40-100	lob 2.5Y5/4	LvfS		8.0	+	
			100-120+	lob 2.5Y5/4	SL		8.0	+	
10	Lower slope of ridge	(?)	0-10	dgb 2.5Y4/2	Si		8.0	+	None
			10-50	ob 2.5Y4/4	vfSL		8.0	+	
			50-120+	ob 2.5Y4/4	SL		8.0	+	
11	Middle slope of ridge	Gopalpur	0-15	ob 2.5Y4/4	SiCL		8.0	+	None
			15-60	lob 2.5Y5/4	SiC		8.0	+	
			60-120	o 5Y5/3	SiL		8.0	+	
12	Basin	Batra	0-10	g N5/	C		8.0	+	None
			10-80	m: dgb, ob 2.5Y4/2-4/4	C		8.0	+	
			80-120+	o 5Y5/2	SiL		8.0	+	

(Contd.)

(Continued)

Obs No[1]	Physiography	Soil series[2]	Depth (cm)	Colour[3]	Texture[4]	Mottle colour[5]	pH[6]	Free CaCO₃	Samples taken
13	Basin	Mehendiganj	0-10	o 5Y5/3	SiC		7.0	-	Whole plant
			10-50	ob 2.5Y4/4	SiCL		8.0	+	
			50-120	lob 2.5Y5/4	SiCL		8.0	+	

Coastal Embankment Project, Polder 22[7]

Obs No[1]	Physiography	Soil series[2]	Depth (cm)	Colour[3]	Texture[4]	Mottle colour[5]	pH[6]	Free CaCO₃	Samples taken
1	Lower part of basin	(?)	0-10	dgb 2.5Y4/2	SiC		6.5	-	0-10 cm
			10-50	ob-dgb 2.5Y4/3	SiC	b, sb	7.0	-	
			50-100	dg N4/	SiC		8.0	+	
2	Lower part of basin	(?)	0-10	dgb 2.5Y4/2	SiCL		6.5	-	0-10; 30-80 cm
			10-80	dgb 2.5Y4/2	SiC	b, sb	7.0	-	
			80-120+	og 5Y4/2	SiC	dgb	8.0	+	
3	Ridge	(?)	0-10	dgb 2.5Y4/2	SiCL		4.5	-	0-10 cm
			10-35	dgb 2.5Y4/2	SiL	gb	5.0	-	
			35-80	vdgb 2.5Y3/2	vfSL	b	6.5	-	
			80-120+	dgrg 5GY4/1	vfSL		8.0	-	
4	Elevated part in basin	(?)	0-40	dgb 2.5Y4/2	SiCL		7.5	-	0-10; 40-50 cm
			40-60	vdg N3/	SiCL + organic matter		5.5	+	
			60-120+	dgrg 5GY4/1	LfS		8.0	+	
5	Elevated part in basin	(?)	0-50	dgb 2.5Y4/2	SiCL	b, sb	6.0	-	0-10; 50-60; 90-110 cm
			50-80	dgb 2.5Y4/2	SiL	b	4.5	-	
			80-120+	dg N4/	vfSL		8.0	-	
6	Ridge	(?)	0-20	gb 2.5Y5/2	SiCL	b, sb	7.5	+	0-10 cm
			20-60	lob 2.5Y5/4	SiL	b, sb	6.0	+	
			60-120+	dgb 2.5Y4/2	LS		8.0	+	
7	Basin	(?)	0-10	vdg 5Y3/1	SiL		8.0	-	0-10; 90-100
			10-70	vdg 5Y3/1	SiCL	dg, sb	8.0	-	
			70-120	vdgb 10YR3/2	peaty SiC		7.5	-	
8	Basin	(?)	0-15	dgb 2.5Y4/2	SiC		6.5	-	0-10; 80-90 cm
			15-60	vdgb 2.5Y3/2	SiCL	dg+org. matter	8.0	+	
			60-120+	bl N2/	peat		8.0	+	

(Contd.)

(Continued)

Obs No[1]	Physiography	Soil series[2]	Depth (cm)	Colour[3]	Texture[4]	Mottle colour[5]	pH[6]	Free CaCo3	Samples taken
9	Basin	(?)	0-20	vdgb 2.5Y3/2	SiC		6.5	-	80-90 cm
			20-40	dgb 2.5Y4/2	SiC		7.5	-	
			40-80	dgb 2.5Y4/2	peaty SiC	dg+org. matter	8.0	-	
			80-120+	bl N2/	peat		8.0	-	
Barura Deep Tubewell Irrigation Scheme, Comilla District									
1	Level ridge	Tippera	0-10	og 5Y5/2	SiL		7.0		Soil: 0-10 cm
			10-100	o 5Y5/3	SiCL		7.5		Plant: 1A - whole plant
			100-120+	o 5Y5/3	Si		8.0		1B - old leaves
2	Level ridge	Tippera	0-15	og 5Y4/2	SiL		7.5		Soil: 0-15 cm
			15-40	og 5Y5/2	SiCL		8.0		Plant: 2A - whole plant on S-deficient plot
			40-80	o 5Y5/3	SiL		8.0		2B - whole plant on adjoining Zn and
			80-120	o 5Y5/4	SiL		8.0		S-deficient plot
Burichang Deep Tubewell Irrigation Scheme, Comilla District									
1	Ridge	Jalkundi	0-15	dg 5Y4/1	SiCL		6.0		Soil: 0-15 cm
			15-100	log 5Y2	SiL	b+sb; dg coatings	7.5		Plant: whole plant
			100-120+	og 5Y5/2	SiCL		7.5		
2	Bottom of basin	Burichang	0-15	dg 5Y4/1	SiCL		8.0		Soil: 0-15 cm
			15-50	dgb 2.5Y4/2	siCL		7.5		Plant: 2 - grains
			50-100	g 5Y5/1	SiCL	yb	8.0		3 - whole plant on adjoining plot
			100-120+	ob 2.5Y4/4	SiL	yb	8.0		
Gaurnadi (Low-lift Pump Irrigation Scheme), Barisal District									
1	Basin margin	Muladi	0-10	gb 2.5Y5/2	SiCL		6.5		Soil: 0-10
			10-60	dgb 2.5Y4/2	SiCL		7.0		No plant sample
			60-120+	yb 10YR5/6	SiL		8.0		
2	Basin margin	Muladi	0-10	dgb 2.5Y4/2	SiC		7.0		Soil: 0-10 cm
			10-100	dgb 2.5Y4/2	SiCL		7.0		No plant sample
			100-120+	m: yb+dg 10YR5/6+N4/	SiL		8.0		
3	Basin	Nazirpur	0-10	dg 5Y4/1	SiCL		8.0		Soil: 0-10 cm
			10-25	m: yb+lob 10YR5/6+2.5Y5/6	SiC		8.0		Plant: whole plant (2X)
			25-120+	m: yb+g 10YR5/6+N5/	SiCL		8.0		

(Contd.)

(Continued)

Obs No[1]	Physiography	Soil series[2]	Depth (cm)	Colour[3]	Texture[4]	Mottle colour[5]	pH[6]	Free CaCO₃	Samples taken
4	Basin	Nazirpur	0-10	dg 5Y4/1	SiCL		8.0		Soil: 0-10 cm
			10-40	yb 10YR5/6	SiCL		8.0		Plant: whole plant
			40-120+	m: g+lob N5/ + 2.5Y5/6	SiCL		8.0		
5	Basin	(?)	0-10	dg 5Y4/1	SiCL		7.5		Soil: 0-10 cm
			10-50	dg 5Y4/1	SiC	ob	8.0		Plant: whole plant on three, adjoining, increasingly S-deficient plots
			50-120	g N5/	SiC		8.0		

Notes to Table 4.5:

1. The observation site numbers correspond to those shown on Figures 4.2, 4.4, 4.6, 4.8, and 4.10, and in Table 4.4.

2. Where correlation of the brief soil descriptions with known soil series was not possible, this has been indicated with a question mark (?).

3. Soil matrix colour has been indicated according to the names given in the Munsell colour chart. Abbreviated colour names are:

b	= brown	dyb	= dark yellowish brown	ob	= olive-brown	vdb	= very dark brown
bl	= black	g	= grey	og	= olive-grey	vdg	= very dark grey
db	= dark brown	gb	= greyish brown	oy	= olive-yellow	vdgb	= very dark greyish brown
dg	= dark grey	lob	= light olive-brown	py	= pale yellow	yb	= yellowish brown
dgb	= dark greyish brown	lyb	= light yellowish brown	ry	= reddish yellow	m	= prominently mottled
dgrg	= dark greenish grey	o	= olive	sb	= strong brown		

4. Abbreviated texture names used are:

C	= clay	LS	= loamy sand	SiC	= silty clay	SL	= sandy loam
L	= loam	LvfS	= loamy very fine sand	SiCL	= silty clay loam	vfSL	= very fine sandy loam
LfS	= loamy fine sand	Si	= silt	SiL	= silt loam		

5. See note 3 for abbreviated colour names. Grey and dark grey streaks that occur in some soil profiles were assumed to be disturbed subsoil coatings (gleyans).

6. The pH was measured in the field with a Hellige-Truog test kit.[1]

7. No plant samples were taken because there was no rice crop in the field at the time of sampling.

[1] Field test kit readings may be unreliable in wet soils.

Annexe 1

LABORATORY METHODS

Soil analysis

*p*H	*p*H-H_2O measured in air-dried 1:1 soil:water (wt/wt) suspension, 30 minutes after hand shaking.
EC	Electrical conductivity of soil samples measured in air-dried 1:2 soil:water (wt/wt) suspension after 60 minutes mechanical shaking and overnight settling of soil particles.
Zinc	Extraction with 0.05 HCl in air-dried 1:2 soil:HCl (wt/wt) suspension. Zinc measured in filtrate by spectrophotometer.
SO_4-S	Extraction with calcium dihydrogen-phosphate in air-dried 1:5 soil:extracting solution suspension. SO_4 measured in filtrate to which 6N HCl, gum acacia and barium chloride crystals are added, with turbidity meter. (Details in BRRI, 1980a.)
Nitrogen	Total nitrogen in the soil sample was determined by the Kjeldahl method.

Plant analysis

Zinc, sulphur, magnesium and nitrogen were all determined in a digest of 0.29 ground plant material with 5 ml of nitric acid (reagent grade) and 3 ml of perchloric acid (reagent grade) on a hot plate. (Details in BRRI, 1980a, b.)

Chapter 5

CHANGES IN SETTLEMENT AND RELATED NON-AGRICULTURAL LAND USE 1952-74[1]

Airphotos taken in 1952 and 1974 were compared in order to assess the extent to which settlements, roads, etc., had encroached onto agricultural land in seven selected Thanas. The study showed that remarkably little loss of agricultural land had taken place, despite a 58 percent increase in population during that period. The area 'not available for cultivation' in 1974 (13.3 percent) was found to be much lower than the figure of 26.5 percent given in the official agricultural statistics.

5.1 INTRODUCTION

5.1.1 Objective

The purpose of the study was to assess the regional and national changes which had taken place in the areas occupied by settlement and associated non-agricultural land use (roads, canals, brickyards, tanks, etc.) based on comparison of aerial photographs taken in 1952 and 1974.

5.1.2 Physical background

Extensive parts of Bangladesh are subject to flooding in the monsoon season. In the floodplain areas, which cover about 80 percent of the country, this seasonal flooding restricts the areas suitable for human habitation to the relatively higher parts of the landscape along the rivers or along abandoned river channels: i.e, river levees and former levees. These ridges of slightly higher land vary in size and shape with the size and nature of the rivers which formed them.

---

[1] *The author's experience in monitoring intensive crop production programmes in the 1970s had raised doubts about the reliability of the areas reported in the Thana agricultural statistics to be 'not available for cultivation'. Investigations during his field trips indicated that Thana officials were assuming an annual loss of land to settlement of 0.5 percent of the total area. That meant that, by 1980, nearly 40 years since the plot-by-plot survey in 1943 which served as the base, roughly 30 percent of the land was reported to be not available for cultivation in several Thanas that were checked, compared with proportions of 15-20 percent assessed during reconnaissance soil surveys carried out between 1963 and 1975. Accordingly, a consultant was engaged to investigate this discrepancy. This chapter is an edited version of the report on the study carried out by G. Serno, Airphoto Interpretation Consultant, under the FAO/UNDP Land Use Policy Project (Serno, 1981). Except where stated otherwise, the information relates to the time of the study, April-June 1981. In order to make that clear, statements originally made in the present tense have been converted to the past tense. Footnotes which appeared in the original document are given in normal font. Footnotes that have been added are given in italics.*

Where such ridges are absent, low or far apart — such as in floodplain basins or on estuarine floodplains — artificial platforms have been constructed on which to build settlements. These platforms are made by digging tanks (ponds) and using the excavated material to construct a mound whose surface is above normal flood-level. The height of the platforms varies from 3 to 12 feet above that of the surrounding land, according to local depths of seasonal flooding.

Because of the importance of seasonal flooding in determining settlement patterns, it was decided to use the physiography as the basis for this study, as the extent and depth of flooding depend on the physiography of the area. Reconnaissance soil survey maps on a scale of 1:125,000 were available for all the agricultural areas of the country, which provided the required information on the location and extent of the major physiographic units.

5.2 METHODOLOGY

5.2.1 General

In order to be able to correlate the information on settlements, etc., with local agricultural statistics, it was decided to conduct the study on a Thana basis.[2] Seven Thanas were selected for the study, representing some of the country's most extensive physiographic units. The location of these Thanas is shown on Figure 5.1.[3]

1. *Bahubal Thana*, Sylhet District: Eastern Surma-Kusiyara Floodplain, and Northern and Eastern Piedmont Plains.
2. *Chandina Thana*, Comilla District: Old Meghna Estuarine Floodplain.
3. *Baidya Bazar Thana*, Dhaka District: Old Brahmaputra Floodplain and Old Meghna Estuarine Floodplain
4. *Ghior Thana*, Dhaka District: Low Ganges River Floodplain and Young Brahmaputra (Jamuna) Floodplain.
5. *Mirpur Thana*, Kushtia District: High Ganges River Floodplain.
6. *Kishoreganj Thana*, Rangpur District: Active Teesta Floodplain and Teesta Meander Floodplain.
7. *Dupchanchia Thana*, Bogra District: Level Barind Tract.

Line transects were drawn at regular intervals in the same relative positions on the 1952 and 1974 airphotos. This was found to be the most suitable method for estimating the area occupied by settlements and associated non-agricultural land use (such as tanks), as well as to assess the changes which took place between 1952 and 1974. The 1952 airphotos were on 1:40,000 scale. Those of 1974 were on 1: 30,000 scale. Those for 1963 used in Chandina Thana were on approximately 1:50,000 scale.

In each physiographic unit within a particular Thana, the total number of millimetres where each line-transect crossed or touched a settlement, tank, road, etc., was measured

---

[2] *Thana: administrative unit with approximately 50,000-200,000 inhabitants and usually 50-150 sq. miles in extent.*

[3] *The Districts referred to in the list of Thanas and throughout this chapter are the old (pre-1982) Districts shown on Figure 1.1. The names of the physiographic units indicated in the list have been changed from those used in the original report so as to conform with the names of the agroecological regions shown on Figure 1.2.*

FIGURE 5.1
Location of study Thanas

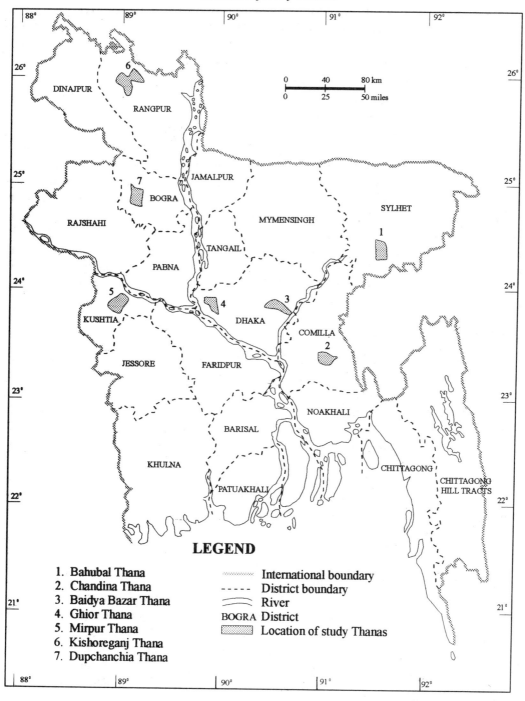

LEGEND

1. Bahubal Thana
2. Chandina Thana
3. Baidya Bazar Thana
4. Ghior Thana
5. Mirpur Thana
6. Kishoreganj Thana
7. Dupchanchia Thana

:::::::::::: International boundary
- - - - - District boundary
≡ River
BOGRA District
▓▓▓ Location of study Thanas

stereoscopically on the airphotos of the study years. For each physiographic unit, the percentage of the area occupied by settlements, tanks, etc., was then calculated for each study year as an average of all the transect lines within that unit. An average spacing between successive transect lines of 1,200-1,800 feet (depending on the size of the physiographic unit) was found to provide an acceptable compromise between the accuracy required and what could be accomplished during the limited time available for the interpretation. Due to the nature of the method used for the study, a number of possible errors exist in the figures calculated for the homestead area and percentages. These possibilities are discussed in Section 5.3

The term 'settlement' or 'homestead' refers to the area occupied by houses, threshing floors, etc., as well as the trees surrounding the houses, interspersed small vegetable plots and small patches of shrubs or grassland. Although the trees and vegetable plots are not really 'non-agricultural', it was not possible to differentiate them separately on the airphotos due to their small size. Also, houses built under trees are often hidden from stereoscopic view by overhanging branches, thus making it necessary to include the trees in the homestead area. Usually, agricultural fields more than 100-125 feet wide (i.e., more than about 25 decimals in area) occurring within a homestead area were not counted as belonging to the homestead area, but fields smaller than this could not be differentiated reliably.

The area of roads, railways, canals and brickyards was computed directly by measuring from airphotos. Village-to-village footpaths were not measured.

5.2.2 Detailed methodology

The boundaries of the selected Thanas and of the included physiographic units were drawn from the relevant 1:125,000 soil associations map onto both sets of airphotos. All soil associations within a physiographic unit or subunit in the map legend were grouped together. Thereafter, transect lines were drawn on the airphotos, starting with the 1974 set and beginning from the northern-most point of the Thana. Each transect line was given an identification number. The lines were then carefully transferred to the corresponding 1952 (or 1963) photos.

For Thanas with predominantly small physiographic units, transect lines were spaced 1,200 feet apart. For larger units, lines were spaced 1,800 feet apart. Usually, the density of sample lines for a Thana was kept constant, but for some small physiographic units a closer spacing of about 600 feet was used.

On each transect line, the number of millimetres where the line crossed or touched the area of a homestead, tank, etc., was counted, and the percentage of contacts was calculated for the whole of the lines crossing a particular physiographic unit. For Mirpur and Kishoreganj Thanas, a separate calculation was made of the decrease and/or increase in the area of homesteads and tanks which had occurred between 1952 and 1974.

When counts had been made for each physiographic unit, the average figure for the whole of the Thana was calculated. However, in several cases, units had to be left out from the calculation of the Thana average due to incomplete photographic coverage in one or both of the reference years.[4] Wherever possible in such cases, extrapolations were made from the area covered by photography of both years.

---

[4] *Full airphoto coverage was not available for Chandina and Mirpur Thanas, and for the Dhaka-Narayanganj-Demra project area which was also studied. Airphotos covering strategic infrastructure (cantonments, major*

5.2.3 Field checking

In order to find out the relative proportions of the land occupied by houses, trees and gardens within the homestead areas and to gain an impression of the space left for further expansion of houses within the homestead area as a whole, line transects were sampled in a small number of villages in each of the study Thanas. For this purpose, the terms 'productive' and 'non-productive' land were introduced. The latter term indicates the area occupied by houses, threshing floors, storage huts, etc., and the term 'productive' indicates those areas with trees of any kind, vegetable plots, shrubs, bushes, grassland, etc., within the homestead area.[5]

In a small number of villages selected from the airphotos on the basis of accessibility, representativeness and changes that had taken place between 1952 and 1974, transects were made by walking through the village on as straight a line as possible and counting the number of feet of 'productive' and 'non-productive' land encountered on the line. These counts were converted to a percentage figure. Such lines were taken 150 or 300 feet apart, depending on the size and shape of the village, and they were usually taken perpendicular to the main axis of the village. Due to the small size of the sample, the figures obtained should be considered as giving only an impression rather than an accurate percentage.

Usually, 3-5 villages in one Thana were studied in this way, but only one village was taken in Dupchanchia and Kishoreganj Thanas. The sampling method used yielded some additional information, especially in those villages with a dense tree cover where the houses were completely or partially hidden from photographic view. The technique was less useful in villages where the houses were grouped closely together with only a few trees planted beside them. That was because the houses in such villages were easily seen on the airphotos and thus an impression could easily be gained of the ratio of 'productive' to 'non-productive' land. This was the case in Dupchanchia Thana and to a lesser extent in Kishoreganj Thana.

In addition to this sampling method, informal interviews were held with villagers regarding items such as population increase between 1952 and 1974, increase in the number of houses, what areas were used for expansion of homesteads and any other subjects relevant for the particular Thana being studied. However, these interviews provided only an incomplete impression due to the limited number which could be undertaken within the limited time available.

5.3 RELIABILITY OF THE DATA

5.3.1 Interpretation differences

The first possible source of error is differences resulting from interpretation of airphotos. Airphoto interpretation is a subjective exercise, and differences can arise when the same photos are interpreted by different persons. Although the main features will be identified

---

bridges, major water-control project headworks, etc.) were classified as 'secret' by the Ministry of Defence and were not made available (or had the strategic areas blanked out).

[5] *Trees that do not bear fruit are considered productive because they generally are lopped for fuelwood or fodder. Similarly, shrubs and grassland provide rough grazing for domestic livestock, medicinal products, thatching material, etc.*

similarly, doubtful or transitional cases may give rise to a slight variability between persons in the estimated figures: e.g., whether an isolated large tree is counted or not, or a small, shallow tank is observed or not. The accuracy depends, *inter alia*, upon experience and the local reference level of the area studied. However, these interpretation judgements are likely to be constant for any one person. Therefore, each of the three photo-interpreters who contributed to this study worked on a set of 1952 and 1974 photos covering the same area. Cross-checks were made to minimize this source of error.

5.3.2 Small scale of photography

The relatively small scale of the airphotos sometimes made identification of homestead areas difficult, especially in the case of settlements with only a few houses without surrounding trees. This proved to be the case more particularly with the 1952 airphotos on the scale of 1:40,000. However, after identifying difficultly-visible tanks or homesteads on the 1:30,000 1974 airphotos, the 1952 photos were re-checked for their presence on them.

Apart from this, the measuring was done using millimetres as the basic unit. However, some homesteads or tanks were less than 1 mm wide on the photos (1 mm on the 1974 photos was equivalent to 90 feet on the ground; on the 1952 photos, 1 mm = 120 feet). This necessitated the use of fractions of millimetres to minimize the measuring error. Especially in Kishoreganj, Dupchanchia and Chandina Thanas, the many small tanks and/or homesteads complicated the counting process. If such a study is carried out in future, it is recommended that airphotos on 1:10,000 or 1:20,000 scale should be used in order to reduce measuring errors due to scale.

5.3.3 Quality of airphotos

Generally, the quality of the airphotos used was found to be satisfactory. An exception was the 1974 set covering Bahubal Thana, where the darkness of the photo-tone made it difficult to distinguish tanks occurring within the homestead area.

5.3.4 Overhang of trees

Trees growing on homestead land where the branches spread over adjoining agricultural land may have caused some slight exaggeration of the measured homestead figure. However, this factor would be constant for the 1952 and 1974 photos, since large trees are not cut frequently.

The exaggeration is likely to be largest for areas where many bamboo clumps occur, because large bamboo stems tend to spread out 15-20 feet from their base. This factor particularly affected Kishoreganj Thana, where bamboos were most common. Using an average branch-spread of 10 feet on each side of a transect line crossing a homestead area and an average of 25 mm of homestead area representing 10 separate villages on a transect line of 250 mm, that means $10 \times 2 = 20 \times 10$ feet = 200 feet (= 2 mm) of over-estimation, or an error of $2/25 \times 100\%$ = about 8 percent. However, branching out does not occur everywhere, so the exaggeration due to this factor is expected to be less than that. A reduction of 5 percent in the homestead area calculated in Kishoreganj Thana was applied, therefore, bringing the percentage homestead area down from 8.5 to 8.1 percent (in 1952).

Where homesteads are built on man-made platforms, the tree-overhang is less important than it is in more level areas, because the trees usually are growing from the top of the raised land. Thus, due to the outward slope of the platforms, the projection of the branches coincides approximately with the boundary between the foot of the platforms and the surrounding fields.

5.3.5 Tanks obscured by trees

Where the homestead area includes many trees, the branches may obscure the visibility of small tanks on the airphotos. This source of error does not arise for large tanks and for isolated tanks located outside homestead areas. Dense tree cover in villages was particularly observed in Bahubal and Dupchanchia Thanas. After field checking in Bahubal Thana, it was decided to apply a correction of 20 percent-decrease in the homestead area and a corresponding increase in the area occupied by tanks.

5.3.6 Incorrect transfer of transect lines

The incorrect transfer of transect lines from the 1974 airphotos to the 1952 photos proved not to be a significant source of error. However, in Mirpur Thana, it was not always easy to transfer the lines from the 1974 photos to the 1952 set due to the many changes that had taken place, related to the construction of the Ganges-Kobadak project irrigation system between 1952 and 1974.

5.3.7 Sampling error

The spacing of the line-transects determines to a large extent the sampling error which can be expected in measuring the area occupied by homesteads and tanks. Generally, the wider the spacing between transects, the larger the error is likely to be. Although the objective of the study was to detect changes in area rather than determine the precise area of homesteads and tanks, this source of error was never-the-less studied in more detail.

For every Thana studied, approximately 10 percent of the total area was selected for checking within one physiographic unit on the 1974 airphotos. Transects were drawn at a spacing of 300 to 450 feet apart (different in different Thanas). Thereafter, for every line, the total length of the line crossing homestead areas was measured in millimetres. First, the average (and presumably the most reliable) figure was obtained by considering all the lines. Thereafter, averages were calculated for spacings of 600, 900, 1,200 feet, etc., by eliminating intermediate lines from the calculations. For the 600 feet count, two figures were obtained by counting alternate lines; for the 900 feet spacing, three figures were taken; and so on. With a decreasing number of transect lines, the deviation from the average for the 300 feet spacing usually increased, because the number of lines showing 'extremes' in homestead area (far below or far above average) became relatively more important for determining the average for that spacing density.

For Kishoreganj and Dupchanchia Thanas, a 10 percent sample of the Thana area was found to be too small to provide a reliable check. That was because a single physiographic unit occupies most of these Thanas. Therefore, alternate transect lines were counted for the whole of these Thanas.

The results of this check obtained for the seven Thanas studied are shown in Table 5.1.

TABLE 5.1
Sample error for different line transect spacings

Thana	Soil association(s)	Spacing (feet)	Average homestead area (%)	Spacing selected (feet)
Bahubal	29, 30	600	13.23	2400
		1200	13.23 ± 0.5	
		2400	13.23 +1.7 to -2.8	
		4800	13.23 +2.6 to -3.2	
Baidya Bazar	42	300	8.76	1200
		600	8.76 ± 0.8	
		1200	8.76 +1.4 to -1.2	
		2400	8.76 +4.8 to -3.3	
		4800	8.76 +5.6 to -4.1	
Ghior	69	450	14.0	1350
		900	14.0 ± 1.9	
		1350	14.0 +1.9 to -2.5	
		1800	14.0 +1.5 to -1.9	
		2700	14.0 +80 to -4.1	
Mirpur	19	450	9.87	1800
		900	9.87 ± 0.5	
		1350	9.87 +2.2 to -1.5	
		1800	9.87 ±2.2	
		2150	9.87 +1.2 to -1.5	
		2400	9.87 +7.0 to -3.6	
Kishoreganj	2, 6a, 6b, 11b, 13, 14	450	8.78	1350
		900	8.78 ± 0.5	
		1350	8.78 +1.6 to -1.3	
		(1350)[1]	7.8	
		(2700)[1]	7.8 ± 0.2	
Dupchanchia	33, 34, 40	300	8.47	1350
		600	8.47 ± 0.6	
		900	8.47 +2.6 to -1.1	
		1200	8.47 +1.2 to -0.6	
		(1350)[1]	6.3	
		(2700)[1]	6.3 ± 1.9	

Note: 1. Alternate counting of all lines on 1952 airphotos.

5.4 DISCUSSION OF FINDINGS AND CONCLUSIONS[6]

1. There was remarkably little expansion of settlements and related non-agricultural land use between 1952 and 1974 in the seven study Thanas. Whereas the population of those Thanas increased by an average of 58 percent between 1951 and 1974, the area occupied by homesteads, roads, canals, etc., increased by only 0.8 percent.

---

[6] *In the original report, this section and the following one were presented after the discussion of the results for the individual Thanas. In this chapter, the detailed Thana results are presented in Annexe 1.*

2. It appears that the population increase between 1951 and 1974 was absorbed almost entirely within the existing settlement area, by building additional houses at the expense of trees, vegetable gardens, grassland, etc. The field observations supported this conclusion.

3. The population density and corresponding housing density became very high in some areas, notably in Baidya Bazar and Chandina Thanas, as well as in some basin areas of other Thanas: (see Table 5.2). In such areas, little space was left within the existing settlements for adding new buildings. Therefore, any further increase in population in those areas must lead to an expansion of existing settlements or the creation of new settlements, both at the cost of valuable agricultural land, unless multi-storeyed buildings replace the existing predominantly single-storeyed buildings or there is a significant rate of emigration from the Thanas.[7]

TABLE 5.2
Changes in population density within Thanas and within homestead areas

| Thana | Population density per sq. mile | | | | | |
| | Thana | | | Homestead area | | |
	1951	1974	Increase (%)	1952	1974	Increase (%)
Chandina	1694[1]	2324	37	25,633[1]	34,696	35
Baidya Bazar	1651	2632	59	18,346	29,250	59
Dupchanchia	902	1533	70	13,066	20,722	59
Kishoreganj	1040	1669	60	13,000	18,753	44
Bahubal	832	1121	35	12,234	16,489	35
Ghior	1134	1702	50	9,535	13,958	46
Mirpur	670	1380	106	5,634	12,006	113
Total[2]	**1079**	**1708**	**58**	**13,004**	**20,102**	**55**
Bangladesh	**761**	**1297**	**70**			

Notes: 1. 1961.
 2. Weighted average.

4. The proportion of the area occupied by settlements, tanks, roads, canals, brickyards and rivers in the seven Thanas in 1974 was 13.3 percent. The Agricultural Statistics for the seven Thanas showed 26.5 percent of the area 'not available for cultivation' in 1974-75. The big difference between these proportions appears to be due to an over-estimation by the Bureau of Agricultural Statistics of the annual rate of loss of agricultural land to settlements, roads, etc., since they started to collect such data (in 1943). This finding could imply that the area of land actually available (and used) for cultivation is under-estimated in the official statistics.[8]

[7] *The impression of the author (HB) during field travels in the 1980s and 1990s was that the trend was for a considerable expansion of rural towns, including District and Thana towns, and the development of former village markets (hats) into permanent bazars. This was in addition, of course, to the very considerable expansion of cities such as Dhaka, Chittagong and Khulna. These trends deserve to be examined in a new study.*

[8] *Applied to the whole country, the difference between these proportions could mean that more than 1 million acres more land was under cultivation than was reported in the official statistics. Dividing this increased area under cultivation by total crop production could also mean that figures for individual crop yields were*

5. Roads and adjoining borrow pits occupied about 0.3 to 1.1 percent of the total area (in different Thanas). Overall, their area almost doubled between 1952 and 1974, from 0.5 to 0.9 percent of the total area: (see Table 5.3).

TABLE 5.3

Percentage of Thana area occupied by roads, canals, brickyards and factories

Thana	1952	1974	Increase
Bahubal	0.1	0.2	0.1
Chandina	0.4	0.5	0.1
Baidya Bazar	0.1	0.8	0.7
Ghior	0.3	0.5	0.2
Mirpur	1.2	3.0	1.8
Kishoreganj	0.1	0.2	0.1
Dupchanchia	1.1	1.1	0.0
Average	**0.5**	**0.9**	**0.4**

6. The construction of irrigation canals in big irrigation project areas tends to consume a relatively large proportion of agricultural land (1.6 percent of the total area in Mirpur Thana in 1974).

7. The proportion of the area occupied by settlements and tanks is strongly influenced by the physiography, as is shown in Table 5.4 and discussed below.

   a. The active river floodplains, with their hazards of severe floods and river-bank erosion, show a very low homestead area or none at all (0 to 5.1 percent).

   b. The young meander floodplains have a high proportion of homestead area (16.9 to 19.4 percent). The Middle Meghna meander floodplain in Baidya Bazar Thana is a very young floodplain compared with those in Mirpur and Ghior Thanas, and hence has a lower percentage of homestead land.[9]

   c. The higher parts of old meander floodplains and the deeply flooded parts of the estuarine floodplain generally have a low to moderate proportion of homestead land (0.1 to 10.9 percent). The man-made land in Baidya Bazar Thana, with 22.3 percent, provides an exception.[10]

   d. The physiographic units with good agricultural land tend to have a relatively higher proportion of homestead land than those with poor agricultural land.

   e. Most (12 out of 15) physiographic units where settlements have to be made on high platforms because of deep seasonal flooding showed no significant increase in the homestead area between 1952 and 1974 (or between 1963 and 1974 in Chandina Thana).

---

lower than reported; alternatively, if the crop yields based on crop sampling were correct, then the country's total crop production was significantly higher than reported.

[9] *The Middle Meghna River Floodplain occupies the former active floodplain of the Brahmaputra river which was abandoned when the latter changed into its present Jamuna course about two centuries ago. The river flow and sediment load of the Meghna river have been insufficient to make more than minor changes in the physiography of the former active Brahmaputra Floodplain.*

[10] *Baidya Bazar Thana includes the site of Sonargaon, an old capital of Bengal. This site includes many cultivation platforms (together with adjoining tanks) which probably were settlement mounds in the ancient city.*

TABLE 5.4

Proportion of physiographic units occupied by homesteads and tanks in 1952 and 1974

Physiography	Thana	Homestead area (%)		Tanks (%)		Homestead area on flood-affected area (+ = Yes; - = No)	Increase in homestead area 1952-74 (+ = Yes; - = No)
		1952	1974	1952	1974		
Active floodplains							
Young Brahmaputra Floodplain	Baidya Bazar	2.5	2.5	0	0	+	-
Young Brahmaputra Floodplain	Ghior	5.1	4.9	0	0	+	-
Ganges River Floodplain	Mirpur	0	0	0	0	+	-
Teesta Floodplain	Kishoreganj	0	0.3	0	0	+	+
Young meander floodplains							
Middle Meghna Floodplain	Baidya Bazar	1.7	2.8	0	0	+	+
Young Brahmaputra Floodplain	Ghior	15.8	16.9	0.3	0.4	+	+
Young Ganges River Floodplain	Mirpur	18.1	19.4	0.2	0.7	-	+
Old meander floodplains (higher parts)							
Old Ganges River Floodplain	Ghior	13.7	13.9	0.7	1.3	+	+
Old Ganges River Floodplain	Mirpur	17.0	15.9	1.2	1.2	-	+
Mixed Old+Young Ganges River Floodplains	Mirpur	12.2	11.4	1.3	1.5	-	+
Little Jamuna Floodplain	Dupchanchia	19.7	21.3	4.1	4.8	-	+
Older Teesta Floodplain	Kishoreganj	8.1	9.0	0.3	0.5	-	+
Old meander floodplains (lower parts)							
Eastern Surma-Kusiyara Floodplain							
- basins	Bahubal	2.4	2.4	0.2	0.2	+	-
- ridges + basins	Bahubal	0.1	0.1	0.1	0.1	+	-
Ganges River Floodplain basins	Mirpur	0.3	8.1	0.6	1.0	-	+

(Contd.)

(Continued)

Physiography	Thana	Homestead area (%)		Tanks (%)		Homestead area on flood-affected area (+ = Yes; - = No)	Increase in homestead area 1952-74 (+ = Yes; - = No)
		1952	1974	1952	1974		
Old Meghna Estuarine Floodplain							
Levees	Baidya Bazar	7.0	7.0	1.1	1.1	+	-
Associated levees and basins	Baidya Bazar	10.9	10.9	1.3	1.4	+	-
Associated levees and basins	Baidya Bazar	5.0	5.0	0.1	0.1	+	-
Basins	Baidya Bazar	4.5	4.5	1.0	1.0	+	-
Man-made land	Baidya Bazar	22.3	22.3	7.5	7.5	+	-
Old Meghna Estuarine Floodplain	Chandina	6.6	6.6	6.2	6.3	+	-
Others							
Low hills	Bahubal	0	0	0	0	-	-
Piedmont plain	Bahubal	11.4	11.4	4.5	5.0	(Slight)	+
Level Barind Tract	Dupchanchia	6.3	6.7	4.0	4.1	-	+
DND project area	(Dhaka District)	6.7[1]	13.9[2]				
Total (excluding DND project area)		**8.3**	**8.5**	**1.4**	**1.6**		

Notes: 1. In 1968.
       2. In 1977.

f. Of the seven physiographic units which are not flood-affected or where the floodplain ridges are above flood-level, six showed an increase in the homestead area. The old piedmont plain in Bahubal Thana was the only physiographic unit where the highest parts are flood-free but there was no increase in the homestead area. There, the population increase was by far the lowest of all the Thanas studied.

g. Apparently, a significant increase in homestead area tends to take place only where the land suitable for human habitation is not affected by floods. That is most dramatically illustrated by the explosion of settlement which followed the provision of flood protection to part of the Dhaka-Narayanganj-Demra (DND) project area.

h. Land for making new homesteads, tanks, brickyards and factories generally comes from the relatively higher areas which, because of no or shallow flooding, generally have the highest agricultural value.

8. Considering the rapidly increasing population of Bangladesh and the goal of achieving self-sufficiency in foodgrain production, the conflict between the need for increased agricultural production and the need for ever more land for settlement and other non-agricultural purposes will become increasingly serious.

5.5 RECOMMENDATIONS

1. Because of Bangladesh's high population density and its predominantly agriculture-based economy, the minimum possible amount of land should be taken out of productive agricultural use for conversion to urban or industrial use. This could be achieved by one or more of the following methods.

    a. Designing zoning regulations to protect the best agricultural land for agriculture and to restrict the spread of settlement and industry to land of lower agricultural value. Zoning regulations are particularly needed for areas where flood-protection projects are planned, so that the provision of flood protection does not lead to a rapid expansion of settlement onto valuable agricultural land, as has happened in the DND project area.[11]

    b. Restricting land acquired for public and private buildings to the smallest area actually needed for the purpose. Preference should be given to vertical rather than horizontal construction (as is practised, for example, in Egypt, where pressure on agricultural land has also become very high). This restriction could be made easier by way of zoning regulations or by imposing severe acquisition taxes in the case of good agricultural land.

    c. Planning for the productive use of the land between or around buildings: for example, by cultivating fruit, vegetables, fodder, fuel or field crops, or by intensifying grazing and fish production.

    d. Designing road-side borrow pits in such a way that, wherever possible, they can be used as irrigation canals or reservoirs, for navigation and/or for fish culture.

    e. Restoring brickyards to an appropriate, specified, productive use immediately after the brick-making operations cease. That would involve the removal of all unused bricks and materials from the site, levelling of the land remaining above

[11]*See Chapter 24 for a more detailed discussion of land use zoning.*

the dry-season surface-water level, and cleaning up any remaining excavations so that they could be used for water storage, fish culture, cultivation of aquatic crops or other appropriate economic purposes.[12]

    f. Organizing brick-making in such a way that the minimum amount of land is made permanently unproductive. This might be accomplished in various ways, viz.

- Along stable river channels which carry silty material during the flood season, permanent brickyards could be developed by excavating sedimentation tanks alongside the rivers. Silt deposited during the flood season could be excavated during the following dry season (or after two or more years if it took more than one flood season to provide a satisfactory thickness of sediment in the tank).

- In deep silty or clay soils, farmers could sell only the top 12-18 inches of the soil in their fields for brick-making, and retain the use of their land for crop production.[13]

- Alternatively, in deep silty or clay deposits, deep excavations could be made so that the resulting tank could be developed for fish culture and/or for storing water for dry-season irrigation.[14]

2. As this study was conducted over a relatively short period, only seven Thanas could be covered. Although these Thanas were chosen to represent some of the country's most extensive physiographic units, the sample was too small to extend the conclusions nation-wide. It is recommended, therefore, that the assessment should be continued by the Consultant's counterparts in the Soil Survey Directorate (now SRDI) who assisted in this study. In addition to sampling other physiographic units, more samples should be studied within the extensive physiographic units examined on this study in order to check whether the conclusions drawn from this study hold good or not.

3. In continuing the programme, funds should be allocated for enlarging some of the airphotos. Depending on the time available, the area to be studied and the size of the settlements, the 1952 and 1974 airphotos could be enlarged to 1:10,000 scale. That would greatly facilitate sampling and the accuracy of measurements made. The enlargements should not be on too large a scale (e.g., 1:5,000) because of the resulting limited coverage and corresponding increased time needed for conducting the study.[15]

4. All the seven Thanas studied were predominantly rural. Given the marked population increase in and around urban areas, it is recommended that some Thanas with urban development should be included in future studies.

---

[12]*See Chapter 7 for a detailed discussion of brickyard reclamation.*

[13]*This practice, in fact, became widespread in the 1980s and 1990s. Very few new brickyards were seen after the late-1970s.*

[14]*See Chapter 17 for a description of the use of such excavations as irrigation reservoirs or fish tanks.*

[15]*It should be noted that satellite imagery is less suitable than conventional aerial photography for this kind of study. That is because the resolution (i.e., degree of detail) is much greater on airphotos than it is on satellite imagery on the same scale.*

Annexe 1

THANA-WISE DISCUSSION OF THE RESULTS

INTRODUCTION

In the following sections, a short description is given of the location, predominant soil textures, flooding depths, land use, population and population density for each of the study Thanas. Thereafter, settlement and other non-agricultural land use are described, and explanations are given of changes which took place between 1952 and 1974. The location of the Thanas is shown on Figure 5.1. It should be noted that all the Thanas studied were predominantly rural. None of them contained any important urban area.[16]

Land use within the homestead areas is not mentioned separately. It generally consists of fruit trees (such as mango, coconut, betelnut, jackfruit), other trees, bamboo, small vegetable plots, bushes and some grassland.

The soil association numbers shown in the tables and text refer to those described in the reconnaissance soil survey reports of the Districts in which the relevant Thanas are located. Land use and land capability ratings described are those described in the soil survey reports, except where more recent information is indicated.[17]

A1 BAHUBAL THANA

A1.1 General

Bahubal Thana is located about 40 miles south-west of Sylhet in Sylhet District. It occupies 56,960 acres (89 square miles). The main road and railway from Dhaka to Sylhet pass through the southern part of the Thana. There are no major rivers in or close to the Thana.

This Thana was covered by the reconnaissance soil survey report on Sunamganj and Habiganj subdivisions (SRDI, 1976). For the purposes of this study, three main physiographic units were recognized:

a. the low hills in the east of the Thana, occupying 28.5 percent of the Thana (soil associations 33 and 34);

b. the piedmont plains adjoining the hills in the southern part of the Thana, occupying 37.2 percent (soil associations 29 and 30); and

c. the Surma-Kusiyara Floodplain occupying 33.3 percent: this floodplain was subdivided into areas consisting of ridges and basins (soil association 7) and areas mainly comprising basins (soil association 8).

---

[16]*Throughout this Annexe, it should be kept in view that there have been considerable changes in land use in parts of some of the Thanas since the time of the study, especially in areas where tube-well irrigation has been provided.*

[17]*The physiographic units referred to in this Annexe are those referred to in the relevant reconnaissance soil survey reports.*

The low hills are strongly dissected and have short, steep slopes, with some areas of rolling to nearly-level relief. The summits are generally below 500 feet above mean sea-level (MSL). The piedmont plain generally has a gentle slope outward from the foot of the hills towards the Surma-Kusiyara Floodplain. The landscape of the Surma-Kusiyara Floodplain consists of nearly level ridges and extensive basins.

Medium-textured soils predominate in the hills. The piedmont plains have medium to heavy-textured soils. The soils on the floodplain are mainly clayey.

The hills lie above flood-level. Flooding is mainly moderately deep (3-6 feet) on the piedmont plains and on the Surma-Kusiyara Floodplain, but the upper parts of some ridges lie above normal flood-level. Deep flooding (6-12 feet) occurs in the floodplain basins.

Tea plantations occur in some parts of the hills, but most of the hill area is covered with forest, bamboo or scrub, with local patches of pineapple cultivation. Elsewhere, land use (as described in the soil survey report) ranged from broadcast deepwater aman paddy in floodplain basins to aus followed by transplanted aman paddy on the piedmont plains and on some floodplain ridges.[18] The piedmont plains were double-cropped, but single cropping prevailed over most of the floodplain. The land capability classification rating of the floodplain land was given as mainly moderate with some good and poor agricultural land.

Population data for Bahubal Thana are shown in Table 5.5. The figures show that Bahubal Thana had a higher population density than Sylhet District as a whole but that the growth rate was below the District average. Compared with Bangladesh as a whole, the population density in Bahubal Thana in 1951 was above the national average, in 1961 it was about equal and in 1974 it was below the average. Bahubal Thana had the lowest rate of population increase between 1951 and 1974 of the seven Thanas studied.

A1.2 Settlement and associated non-agricultural land use

The settlement pattern is clearly different in each of the three main physiographic units present in Bahubal Thana.

On the Surma-Kusiyara Floodplain, settlements are located on narrow, steep-sided, man-made ridges 6-12 feet high built on the natural river levees (floodplain ridges) or on other slightly higher land. The settlements are small and far apart: see Figure 5.2. They occupy about 2 percent of the floodplain area. In contrast with the sparsely-populated floodplain is the piedmont plain where settlements occupy about 11.4 percent of the land. There, the settlements generally are located on the broad flood-free ridges (see Figure 5.3) and, because of the absence of flooding, the houses are not built on artificial platforms or ridges. Settlements occupy only a minor part of the hill area.

It is interesting to observe that the Surma-Kusiyara Floodplain has such a low settlement density and the land is classified mainly as moderate, single-cropped, agricultural land,

---

[18]Sowing/transplanting and harvesting dates in this Thana are as follows.

Paddy type		Seeding/planting period	Harvesting period
Aus:	broadcast	15 March-15 May	July-August
	transplanted	15 March-31 May	July-August
Aman:	broadcast (deepwater)	15 March-30 April	November-December
	transplanted	15 July-15 September	November-December

FIGURE 5.2

Bahubal Thana: settlement pattern, basin area, Surma-Kusiyara Floodplain, 1974

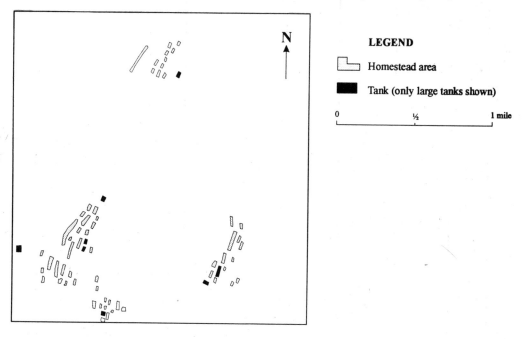

LEGEND

☐ Homestead area

■ Tank (only large tanks shown)

0   ½   1 mile

FIGURE 5.3

Bahubal Thana: settlement pattern, old piedmont plain, 1974

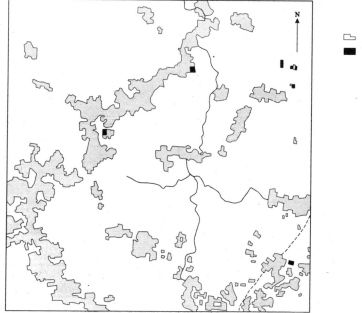

LEGEND

☐ Homestead area   - - - - Road

■ Tank (only large tanks shown)   ～ River

0   ½   1 mile

TABLE 5.5
Population data for Bahubal Thana

Area	Population			Population density per sq. mile			Population increase (%)	
	1951	1961	1974	1951	1961	1974	1951-1961	1951-1974
Bahubal Thana	74,043	83,021	99,784	832	933	1,121	12.1	34.7
Sylhet District				639	729	995	14.1	55.6
Bangladesh				761	922	1,297	21.2	70.4

TABLE 5.6
Bahubal Thana: changes in homestead and non-agricultural land use 1952-1974

Main physiographic units: Surma-Kusiyara Floodplain; piedmont plain; low hills

Physiographic units Description	Soil assoc.	Area (acres)	Roads, canals, railways (%)		Homesteads (%)		Tanks (%)		Others (%)	
			1952	1974	1952	1974	1952	1974	1952	1974
Surma-Kusiyara Floodplain										
ridges and basins	7	6,144	0.0	0.0	0.1	0.1	0.1	0.1	0	0.0
mainly basins	8	13,376	0.1	0.1	2.4	2.4	0.2	0.2	0	0.0
Piedmont plain: old piedmont plain	29, 30	21,184	0.2	0.2	11.4	11.4	4.5	5.0	0	0.1¹
Low hills	33, 34	16,256	0.1	0.1	Minor	Minor	0.0	0.0	0	0.0
Total		**56,960**	**0.1**	**0.1**	**6.8**	**6.8**	**1.7**	**1.9**	**0**	**0.1**

Note:　1.　Brickyard.

whereas the generally good, mainly double-cropped, agricultural land on the piedmont plain has a much higher settlement density. The reasons for the differences in the proportions occupied by homesteads are undoubtedly related to the difference in flooding depth and the corresponding differences in the effort and cost of building housing platforms above flood-level and in the quality of land for agriculture. The origin of the difference in settlement pattern probably goes far back in history, when the population was lower than at present, the demand for agricultural land was low and relatively large areas could be occupied by homesteads.[19]

Apart from a slight increase in the homestead area from 0.1 to 0.12 percent in soil unit 7 (ridges and basins on the Surma-Kusiyara Floodplain), the homestead area in this Thana remained virtually constant between 1952 and 1974: (see Table 5.6). This is not surprising in view of the relatively low population increase in this Thana between 1951 and 1974, and the low housing density in the homesteads on the piedmont plain where most of the settlements are concentrated.[20] Additional dwellings needed for the growing population were constructed within existing homestead areas, at the expense of trees, vegetable plots, shrubs, etc.

On the other hand, the housing density is very high in most of the settlements located on the narrow ridges in the deeply-flooded basin areas. A ratio of 'productive' to 'non-productive' land of about 5:95 percent was measured in one village, which leaves virtually no space for building additional houses. The alternatives for accommodating the expected population increase in these basin areas consist of constructing new platforms for habitation at the cost of agricultural land, building multi-storeyed houses within the existing homestead area, or migration of new families to other areas, which may not necessarily be within the same Thana.

Tanks occupy a minor area on the Surma-Kusiyara Floodplain, but they occupy about 5 percent on the piedmont plain. About three-quarters of the tanks are located near the homesteads, the remainder in the middle of the agricultural area. Several new tanks were dug between 1952 and 1974, part in the fields, part close to the homesteads.

The area occupied by roads, railways and adjoining borrow-pits remained constant at 0.1 percent. The construction of some short new roads in the tea plantations affected a minor area, but not sufficient to increase the percentage figures significantly. On the piedmont plains, a brickyard alongside the Dhaka-Sylhet road occupied about 30 acres, or 0.07 percent of the Thana.

A2 CHANDINA THANA

A2.1 General

This Thana is located about 10-15 miles west of Comilla town in Comilla District. It occupies an area of 49,920 acres (78 square miles). The main road from Dhaka to Comilla traverses the northern part of the Thana. There is no river of importance within the Thana.

---

[19] *A follow-up study could usefully investigate two other possible reasons for the differences in settlement and population density between the floodplain and piedmont plain areas: some of the population living on the piedmont plains but farming floodplain land; and a higher proportion of floodplain land owned by big, absentee, land-owners farming their land with the help of seasonal (possibly migrant) labour.*

[20] The ratio of 'productive' to 'non-productive' land was estimated at about 75:25 percent.

Chandina Thana was covered by the reconnaissance soil survey of Comilla District (SRDI, 1966). The Thana is situated on the Old Meghna Estuarine Floodplain. This consists of an almost-level plain of low relief with broad ridges and extensive shallow basins: (soil associations 11, 16, 21, 23, 26). The soils are mainly medium-textured on the higher parts and medium to fine-textured in the depressions. The area is mainly moderately deeply to deeply flooded (3-12 feet) in the monsoon season. The deepest flooding occurs in the western part of the Thana.

At the time of the soil survey, the land use consisted mainly of deepwater aman paddy, mixed with aus paddy or jute on the higher areas and usually followed by dry-season crops. The land capability classification rating was given as mainly good and moderate agricultural land, with moderate and deep flooding as the main limitation.

Population data for Chandina Thana are shown in Table 5.7. This Thana was the second-most densely populated Thana (after Baidya Bazar) of the seven Thanas studied. Compared with Comilla District as a whole, Chandina Thana showed an above-average increase in population. In 1951, the population density within this Thana was below the District average, while in 1974 it was above the average. The rapid growth may be due to the Thana's close proximity to Comilla town and to the Dhaka-Comilla highway. Chandina Thana is much more densely populated than Bangladesh as a whole. However, the increase in population was very close to the national average: 23.1 *versus* 21.2 percent between 1951 and 1961, and 68.9 *versus* 70.4 percent between 1951 and 1974.

A2.2 Settlement and associated non-agricultural land use

The settlement pattern in Chandina Thana is distinctly different from the patterns observed in the other six Thanas studied. The settlements are small and very scattered over the floodplain area, especially in areas where seasonal flooding is only moderately deep: see Figure 5.4. Many settlements consist of a small platform 4-6 feet high and about 150×150 feet in dimension. They include 5-50 houses and a tank from which the earth for the platform was excavated. The separate settlements are about 180 feet to 500 feet or more apart. In basin areas, where flooding is deeper, the settlements tend to be more concentrated, with many man-made ridges and platforms made close together.

Beside the platforms, there is invariably a tank, usually more or less equivalent in size to the area of the adjoining platform. The tanks most commonly are 60×60 feet to 120×120 feet in size, but a few are as large as 450×900 feet. Many are oriented with their long axis aligned approximately North-South.

The 1952 aerial photography was not available for use in this Thana. Therefore, the 1963 airphotos were compared with those of 1974. The study was made mainly in the central and western parts of the Thana, because the photo coverage was incomplete in the east.[21]

On the 1:50,000 scale of the 1963 photography, the transect sampling technique could not be used because of the small size of the homesteads on these photos. Instead, all new homesteads identified on the 1974 airphotos were counted and their area was measured. That was possible in this Thana because the scattered nature of the homesteads facilitated the detection of new sites. The area occupied by homesteads and tanks was measured using the line-transect sampling technique.

---

[21] *See footnote 4 above.*

TABLE 5.7
Population data for Chandina Thana

Area	Population			Population density per sq. mile			Population increase (%)	
	1951	1961	1974	1951	1961	1974	1951-1961	1951-1974
Chandina Thana	107,327	132,112	181,321	1,376	1,694	2,324	23.1	68.9
Comilla District				1,462	1,693	2,243	15.7	53.4
Bangladesh				761	922	1,297	21.2	70.4

TABLE 5.8
Chandina Thana: changes in homestead and non-agricultural land use 1963-1974

Physiographic unit: Old Meghna Estuarine Floodplain

Physiographic unit Description	Soil association	Area (acres)	Roads, canals (%)		Homesteads (%)		Tanks (%)		Others (%)	
			1963	1974	1963	1974	1963	1974	1963	1974
Old Meghna Estuarine Floodplain	11, 16, 21, 23, 26	49,920	0.4	0.4	6.6	6.6	6.2	6.3	0	0.1[1]

Note: 1. Industrial area.

FIGURE 5.4

Chandina Thana: settlement pattern, Old Meghna Estuarine Floodplain, 1974

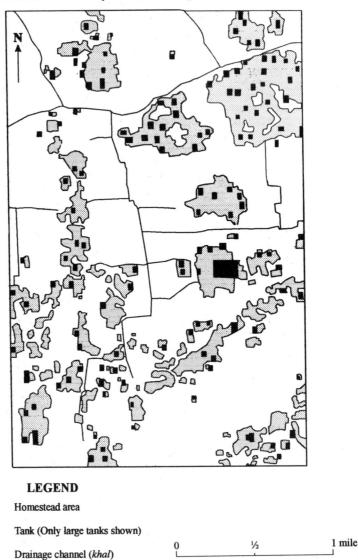

LEGEND

Homestead area

Tank (Only large tanks shown)

Drainage channel (*khal*)

0   ½   1 mile

The area occupied by homesteads was about 6.6 percent in 1974, and that of tanks was 6.3 percent. The increase in the area of homesteads and tanks since 1963 was less than 0.1 percent, about equally divided between the two. Several small new settlements were observed, all with a new tank alongside. However, their combined area was insignificant relative to the total area of the Thana. The new settlements were found in different parts of the Thana. Several were relatively close to Chandina town and to the main road. Others were far away from those areas, often alongside khals. The majority were separate from existing settlements.

The housing density was quite high. Ratios of 'productive' to 'non-productive' land of about 20:80 percent were measured, reflecting the high population density. The population density calculated for the homestead area increased from 25,663 per square mile in 1963 to 34,696 per square mile in 1974. Thus, it is apparent that, in Chandina Thana as elsewhere, the population increase was accommodated mainly within the existing homestead area. The expansion of settlements and the establishment of new settlements were limited due to the moderate or deep flooding, which necessitates the construction of man-made platforms, and by the very high density of population in relation to the available agricultural land, implying very high land values.

Drainage of the area is mainly by man-made canals (*khals*), which occupy about 0.3 percent of the area. No new khals were observed to have been dug between 1963 and 1974. Roads (mainly the Dhaka-Comilla highway) occupied about 0.1 percent of the total area.[22] Close to Chandina town, about 36 acres (0.07 percent of the total area) were converted to industrial use between 1963 and 1974. Details of the changes in settlement and non-agricultural land use in the Thana are given in Table 5.8.

A3 BAIDYA BAZAR THANA

A3.1 General

This Thana occupies an area of 42,240 acres (66 square miles) located about 10-15 miles south-east of Dhaka city in Dhaka District. It borders the Meghna river on its eastern side, and its southern-most point includes the confluence of the Meghna and Dhaleswari rivers. Several smaller rivers traverse the Thana. The main road from Dhaka to Comilla and Chittagong passes through the centre of the Thana.

Baidya Bazar Thana was covered by the reconnaissance soil survey of Dhaka District (SRDI, 1981). The physiography consists mainly of an alternation of gently undulating ridges and basins of the Old Brahmaputra Floodplain (soil associations 42, 47, 49) and the Old Meghna Estuarine Floodplain (associations 50, 52). Small areas of recent sediments of the Middle Meghna Floodplain occur along the Meghna river (associations 72, 73). In the extreme south, there is a minor area of the active floodplain of the Young Brahmaputra (Jamuna) Floodplain (association 54).

In the north-west, there are two soil units belonging to the Madhupur Tract (associations 8 and 19). These units were excluded from the study due to the scattered nature of the individual settlements, which were difficult to identify on the airphotos.

The floodplain soils in Baidya Bazar Thana mainly consist of silts and loams on the ridges, and clays and heavy clays in the basins. The seasonal depth of flooding ranges from about 3 feet on the higher parts to 10-15 feet in the depressions. Some man-made land near the centre of the Thana (soil association 52) is flood-free.

At the time of the soil survey in 1963-64, the basins were mainly double-cropped with mixed aus + aman paddy. Single, double and triple cropping patterns were practised on the ridges. Crops grown on these higher sites were mainly aus (or jute) followed by transplanted aman paddy, together with some vegetables. The land capability rating varied from unit to unit. Generally, the higher parts were rated as mainly good agricultural land and the basins as moderate agricultural land.

---

[22]*Subsequent to the study, the Dhaka-Comilla highway was up-graded, with a straightened and broadened road-bed and embankment, extensive borrow pits and a by-pass around Chandina town. Together, the new road and borrow pits consumed a seemingly extravagant amount of valuable agricultural land.*

Population data for Baidya Bazar Thana are shown in Table 5.9. The figures show that the population density in this Thana was higher than the average for Dhaka District in 1951 and 1961, but was virtually equal to the District level in 1974 (due to a relatively slower growth-rate in the Thana). The population density in the Thana remained more than twice the national figure between 1951 and 1974, although the growth-rate in the Thana was slightly below the national average. Presumably, the relatively greater increase in the District's population during the period was caused by the high rate of immigration into Dhaka city.

Baidya Bazar had the highest population density among the seven Thanas studied. The high population density may be partly explained by its relative proximity to the Dhaka-Narayanganj-Demra conurbation, providing employment and marketing opportunities. The relatively good communications within the Thana, both by road and along the many large and small rivers, may also have contributed, although it should be noted that the Dhaka-Comilla highway which passes through the Thana was opened only in 1965. The fact that the ancient capital, Sonargaon, lies within the Thana suggests that this area was also settled at an earlier period than most low-lying floodplain areas.[23]

A3.2 Settlement and related non-agricultural land use

The settlements in Baidya Bazar Thana are located on man-made ridges or platforms. These usually are 120-150 feet wide, or sometimes more. They are rather variable in length, ranging between about 300 feet and 1 mile: see Figure 5.5. They are constructed on the highest parts of the landscape formed by river-banks or the banks of former rivers. Their height depends on the normal depth of flooding in the area. It may reach 10 feet or more in those physiographic units subject to deep flooding.

With the exception of the relatively small soil unit 72, no changes were recorded in the amount of land occupied by homesteads between 1952 and 1974. The figure remained constant at 9.0 percent of the area. Considering the high population density in this Thana, as well as the 59.4 percent increase in population between 1951 and 1974, the absence of a change in homestead area may seem surprising.

However, most of this Thana is subject to moderately deep or deep flooding. The formation of a new settlement requires the construction of ridges or platforms 120-150 feet wide and several feet high, which is a considerable task. Moreover, the new platform, and the associated tank from which the material is excavated, consume valuable agricultural land. Instead of constructing additional platforms, new families build additional houses within existing homestead areas. The new houses occupy the space that was formerly used for vegetable plots, fruit trees, shrubs and grassland, all on top of the homestead platform. In this way, the housing density on the raised platforms gradually increases until most of the 'productive' land on the platforms is occupied by buildings. As an illustration, the population density in the homestead areas in this Thana in 1951 was 18,346 per square mile (108,977 persons on 9.0 percent of 66 sq. miles), while in 1974 it had increased to 29,250 per sq. mile.

---

[23]*Also probably relevant is the fact that, until about two centuries ago, the main Brahmaputra river channel passed through the Thana, implying that river traffic from Calcutta and the coast to north-east India followed this route instead of the Jamuna route further west that was followed subsequently. The small river alongside Sonargaon is still marked as the Brahmaputra river on the topographical maps.*

TABLE 5.9
Population data for Baidya Bazar Thana

Area	Population			Population density per sq. mile			Population increase (%)	
	1951	1961	1974	1951	1961	1974	1951-1961	1951-1974
Baidya Bazar Thana	108,977	134,252	173,748	1,651	2,034	2,632	23.2	59.4
Dhaka District				1,413	1,768	2,641	25.1	86.9
Bangladesh				761	922	1,297	21.2	70.4

TABLE 5.10

Baidya Bazar Thana: changes in homestead and non-agricultural land use 1952-1974

Main physiographic units: Old Meghna Estuarine Floodplain; Middle Meghna Floodplain; Madhupur Tract; Young Brahmaputra Floodplain

Physiographic units Description	Soil assoc.	Area (acres)	Roads, canals, railways (%)		Homesteads (%)		Tanks (%)		Others (%)	
			1952	1974	1952	1974	1952	1974	1952	1974
Madhupur Tract										
Mixed dissected terrace with valleys	8, 9	6,016	0	1.4	—[1]	—[1]	—[1]	—[1]	0	0
Old Brahmaputra Floodplain levees	42	5,800	0	0.2	7.0	7.0	1.1	1.1	0	0
Old Meghna Estuarine Floodplain: basins	43	1,216	0	0	4.5	4.5	1.0	1.0	0	0
associated levees and basins	50	8,896	0	0	9.0	9.0	0.5	0.7	0	0
Mixed Old Meghna and Old Brahmaputra Floodplains										
associated levees and basins	47	4,480	0	0	20.6	20.7	0.5	0.5	0	0
associated levees and basins	49	5,056	0	—[2]	5.0	5.0[3]	0.1	0.1[3]	0	0
man-made land	52	2,432	0.4	0.4	22.3	22.3	7.5	7.5	0	0
Young Brahmaputra Floodplain active floodplain	54	1,216	0	0[3]	2.5	2.5[3]	0	0[3]	0	0
Middle Meghna Floodplain: young meander floodplain	72, 73	1,536·	0	0[3]	1.7	2.8[3]	0	0	0	0
Total		36,736[4]	0.1	0.8	9.0	9.0	1.5	1.5	0	0.1

Notes: 1. Not studied.
2. Not available.
3. Estimated.
4. Excluding water bodies (5,504 acres).

FIGURE 5.5

Baidya Bazar Thana: settlement pattern, Old Meghna Estuarine and Old Brahmaputra Floodplains, 1952

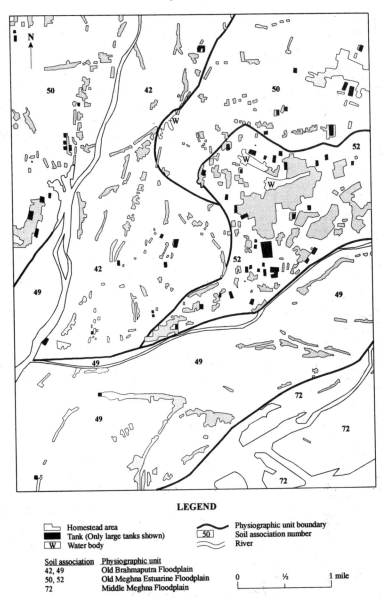

LEGEND

	Homestead area		Physiographic unit boundary
	Tank (Only large tanks shown)	50	Soil association number
W	Water body		River

Soil association	Physiographic unit
42, 49	Old Brahmaputra Floodplain
50, 52	Old Meghna Estuarine Floodplain
72	Middle Meghna Floodplain

0   ½   1 mile

In Baidya Bazar, the ratio of 'productive' to 'non-productive' land within the homestead areas is estimated at around 35:65 percent for most physiographic units. The ratio varies slightly from one unit to another (also from one village to another), with the higher 'non-productive' figures in depressions and lower figures in units with less-deep flooding.

The proportion occupied by homesteads is highest on the Old Brahmaputra Floodplain ridges: (see Table 5.10). Soil association 52 on this floodplain has 22.3 percent of the area occupied by homesteads. The Thana headquarters is located in this unit. More than

60 percent of this unit consists of small (less the 1 acre) man-made platforms and associated tanks.[24]

In the soil associations belonging to the Middle Meghna and the Young Brahmaputra Floodplains, the settlement percentage is much lower. That may be due to the greater risks of flood damage to crops and of erosion of settlements and agricultural land by the rivers, and the generally lower quality of the land for agriculture. The increase in homestead area in soil association 72 on the Middle Meghna Floodplain represents the establishment of a few new settlements associated with the formation of new land adjoining this unit.

The area occupied by tanks remained constant, despite a slight increase in soil units 47 and 50 on the Old Meghna Estuarine Floodplain. The tanks were mainly located close to the homestead areas.

The area occupied by roads and associated borrow-pits increased markedly between 1952 and 1974. That was mainly due to the construction of the Dhaka-Comilla road through the Thana, but there was also some loss of agricultural land to new village roads.

A4 GHIOR THANA

A4.1 General

This Thana is located in Dhaka District, approximately 40 miles west of Dhaka. It occupies 35,480 acres (56 sq. miles). The Kaliganga river crosses the eastern part of the Thana.[25] The Thana's western side lies about 5-10 miles east of the Jamuna river. The main road from Dhaka to Aricha passes through the southern part of the Thana.

Ghior Thana was covered by the reconnaissance soil survey of Dhaka District (SRDI, 1981). The Ganges Meander Floodplain occupies 58.4 percent of the Thana (soil association 69): (see Figure 5.6). The remainder is occupied by the Jamuna (Young Brahmaputra) Floodplain (soil associations 54, 55, 56, 57, 58, 63). The landscape consists of very gently undulating floodplain ridges and basins, with some abandoned river channels. The soils are mainly medium-textured (silts) on the ridges, and medium to heavy-textured (loams and clays) in the depressions. Ridge soils on the Ganges floodplain are calcareous. Seasonal flooding depths range from 2-8 feet on the ridges and 6-15 feet in the depressions.

The land use (at the time of the soil survey in 1963-64) consisted mainly of mixed aus + deepwater aman paddy followed by dry-season crops. The land was mainly triple-cropped, with some double-cropped land. Land capability ratings indicated that moderate and good agricultural land occupied most of the Thana, with limitations provided mainly by seasonal flooding and locally by droughtiness in the dry season or irregular relief. In soil association 54, there were severe risks of damage by floods, burial by new alluvium and river-bank erosion.

Population data for Ghior Thana are shown in Table 5.11. The figures show that population density in this Thana is lower than the average for Dhaka District but higher than the average for Bangladesh, and that the rate of population growth is significantly lower than in Dhaka District and in Bangladesh as a whole. The reasons for the relatively slow growth-rate — despite the Thana's relatively good communications since the opening

---

[24] Soil association 52 probably represents the area occupied by the ancient capital, Sonargaon.

[25] *The Dhaleswari river broke into the Kaliganga river in 1941.*

FIGURE 5.6

Ghior Thana: settlement pattern, Old Ganges and Young Brahmaputra Floodplains, 1952

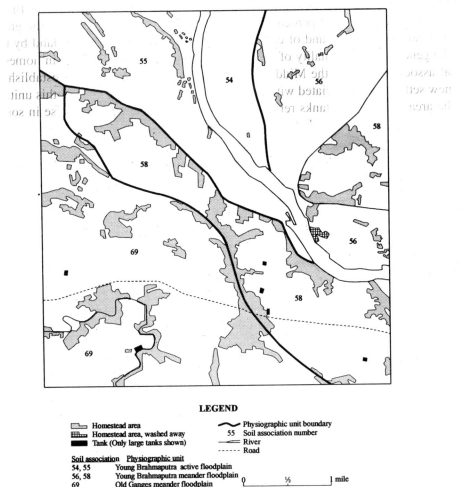

LEGEND

⬜ Homestead area		∿ Physiographic unit boundary
⬛ Homestead area, washed away		55 Soil association number
⬛ Tank (Only large tanks shown)		═ River
		----- Road

Soil association   Physiographic unit
54, 55   Young Brahmaputra active floodplain
56, 58   Young Brahmaputra meander floodplain
69   Old Ganges meander floodplain

0 _____ ½ _____ 1 mile

of the Dhaka-Aricha highway in the early-1960s — may be the restrictions on agricultural development imposed by deep flooding, the risk of flood damage to crops and the slow rate of irrigation development in the Thana up to 1974.

A4.2 Settlement and associated non-agricultural land use

The settlements in Ghior Thana are located on man-made ridges and platforms which are raised 2-8 feet above the surrounding land. The height of the raised land depends on the depth of seasonal flooding and varies with the physiography. Generally, the settlement pattern consists of elevated narrow ridges on the Young Brahmaputra Floodplain, while elongated bands of settlements are common on the Ganges Floodplain (and also in soil unit 58 of the Young Brahmaputra Floodplain). These settlements curve along the river levees and former river levees on which they are built. The width of the settlement bands is rather variable: the broad bands range from 300 feet to about 900 feet, and the narrow ridges from 150 to 300 feet.

TABLE 5.11
Population data for Ghior Thana

Area	Population			Population density per sq. mile			Population increase (%)	
	1951	1961	1974	1951	1961	1974	1951-1961	1951-1974
Ghior Thana	65,539	74,334	95,364	1,134	1,327	1,702	17	50.0
Dhaka District				1,413	1,768	2,641	25.1	86.9
Bangladesh				761	922	1,297	21.2	70.4

TABLE 5.12
Ghior Thana: changes in homestead and non-agricultural land use 1952-1974

Main physiographic units: Ganges River Floodplain; Young Brahmaputra Floodplain

Physiographic units Description	Soil assoc.	Area (acres)	Roads, canals, railways (%)		Homesteads (%)		Tanks (%)		Others (%)	
			1952	1974	1952	1974	1952	1974	1952	1974
Young Brahmaputra Floodplain										
active floodplain	54, 55	6,592	0[1]	0	5.1	4.9[2]	0[1]	0	0	0
young meander floodplain	56, 58	3,586	0.4	1.2	15.8	16.9	0.3	0.4	0	0
Ganges Floodplain										
old meander floodplain	69	20,928	0.4	0.5	13.7	13.9	0.7	1.3	0	0
Total[3]		**35,456**	**0.3**	**0.5**	**11.9**	**12.2**	**0.4**	**0.9**	**0**	**0.1**

Note: 1. 1952 airphotos not available. Partly estimated from unit 54.
      2. Village washed away.
      3. Excluding units 57 and 63; also water bodies (384 acres).

A slight increase in the homestead area in Ghior Thana between 1952 and 1974 was measured, from an average of 11.9 percent in 1952 to 12.2 percent in 1974. This increase was mainly due to the increase which took place on the Young Brahmaputra Floodplain: from 15.8 percent in 1952 to 16.9 percent in 1974. The increase on the Ganges Floodplain was small: from 13.7 to 13.9 percent. The increase represented an expansion of some existing settlements as well as the establishment of some new, usually small, settlements, probably related to the erosion of part or all of some villages along the Kaliganga river. The new settlements were all located on the ridges.

The average population density calculated for the homestead areas was 9,535 per sq. mile in 1951 (63,539 persons on 11.9 percent of the Thana area, or 6.664 sq. miles). It amounted to 13,958 per sq. mile in 1974 (95,364 persons on 12.2 percent, or 6.832 sq. miles). Thus, despite a slight increase in the homestead area, the bulk of the population increase was absorbed within the existing settlements by building additional houses at the cost of vegetable plots, trees, shrubs, etc.

A decrease in the homestead area was recorded in soil association 55 (active floodplain) and in associations 56 and 58 (Young Brahmaputra Floodplain). This was partly due to some villages being partly washed away between 1952 and 1974. In unit 55, this affected a total area of about 11 acres of homestead land, or 0.2 percent of the total area of the unit. In units 56 and 58, it involved about 12 acres, or about 0.4 percent of the unit area. The eroded villages were located close to the Kaliganga river: see Figure 5.6. The disappearance of part of these villages may explain at least a part of the increase in homestead area recorded elsewhere in the Thana.

The housing density within settlements is lower in Ghior Thana than in Baidya Bazar Thana, corresponding with the lower population density. In soil unit 58, the ratio of 'productive' to 'non-productive' land within settlements was estimated at 65:35 percent. In unit 69, the ratio was 70:30 percent. This low ratio indicates that there is still some land available for the expansion of housing within the existing settlements. The low ratio is related to the relatively lower flooding depth on the floodplain ridges in these units as compared with most of Baidya Bazar Thana, which facilitates the construction of ridges and platforms for homesteads. However, the housing density is considerably higher in units 54 and 55 where the flooding is deeper, the ridges suitable for settlement are narrower, and the erosion of older villages by the river has probably pressed the displaced persons to settle within neighbouring villages.

The area occupied by tanks increased from 0.6 percent to 1.0 percent: see Table 5.12. Although part of this increase may be due to better visibility of small ponds on the 1974 airphotos than on the 1952 airphotos, most of the increase represented newly-dug tanks near homesteads as well as in the fields. The increase was most noticeable on the Ganges Floodplain. At one site, a group of several new tanks was observed in the fields, which appeared to have been dug for catching fish as the seasonal floodwater recedes. The area occupied by roads and adjoining borrow pits increased from 0.3 percent to 0.5 percent.

A5 MIRPUR THANA

A5.1 General

Mirpur Thana lies approximately 5 miles west of Kushtia town in Kushtia District and about 100 miles west of Dhaka. It occupies 80,640 acres (126 sq. miles). The railways from

Kushtia towards Calcutta and from Khulna to northern Bangladesh traverse the Thana, as well as the road from Kushtia to Meherpur. The Ganges river forms the northern border of the Thana.

This Thana is located entirely on the Ganges River Floodplain. This comprises a typical meander floodplain landscape of ridges, basins and old channels. In general, the relief is smooth. Clay soils predominate in the basins and on the greater part of most ridges, but medium-textured soils (silts and occasionally sands) occupy the highest ridge crests. The higher and middle parts of the ridges are above normal flood-level, but the lower parts of the ridges and the inter-ridge areas are subject to shallow flooding (1-3 feet), or to moderately deep flooding (3-6 feet) in some soil units. The basins are moderately deeply to deeply flooded (6-12 feet). Flooding is mainly by rainwater, except near to the Ganges and its distributary channels.

At the time of the reconnaissance soil survey in 1969-70, land use on the higher ridges consisted mainly of aus paddy or jute followed by dry-season crops, together with some sugarcane. Broadcast or transplanted aman paddy followed by dry-season crops or fallow occurs on the lower parts of the landscape. The area was classified as mainly good agricultural land on the higher areas and mainly moderately good agricultural land in the depressions. The basins are partly slow-draining in the dry season.

In Mirpur, several physiographic subdivisions of the Ganges River Floodplain occur, viz.

    a. Adjoining the Ganges river, there is the Active Ganges Floodplain (soil association 1), occupying about 3.3 percent of the Thana.

    b. The Very Young Ganges Meander Floodplain (soil units 2, 3), occupies 0.6 percent of the Thana.

    c. Further inland, the Young Ganges Meander Floodplain occupies about 11.3 percent (soil units 4, 5, 6).

    d. The largest proportion belongs to the Old Ganges Meander Floodplain (soil units 9 and 15, occupying respectively 17.4 and 35 percent) and the mixed Old and Young Ganges Meander Floodplains (soil unit 19, occupying 32 percent).

Complete photo-coverage for both 1952 and 1974 was not available for the whole of soil units 1, 2, 3, 4 and 6. Units 2 and 3 were not covered at all. Where possible, estimations and extrapolations were made for the areas not covered by airphotos.

Mirpur Thana lies almost entirely within the Ganges-Kobadak irrigation project area. This project, the first large-scale project of its kind in East Pakistan/Bangladesh, was begun in 1954 and construction within Mirpur Thana had virtually been completed by 1974. Only soil unit 1 (the active floodplain) lies outside the project area.

The settlement pattern varies slightly between physiographic units, but the settlements are always concentrated on the levees along the present or former river courses. They usually form bands of varying length and width. The bands are narrower in the basin areas, where they may be 300-1,000 feet wide. They are wider (up to about 1,500 feet) in those units where floodplain ridges are prominent. Also, the length of the settlements is variable, and may reach up to 2½ miles. There are virtually no settlements on the active floodplain.

Population data for Mirpur Thana are shown in Table 5.13. The population of this Thana more than doubled between 1951 and 1974, giving it the highest growth rate among the seven Thanas studied. Despite this, Mirpur (with 1,380 persons per sq. mile) still ranked sixth in population density in 1974; only Bahubal Thana had a lower population density

TABLE 5.13
Population data for Mirpur Thana

Area	Population			Population density per sq. mile			Population increase (%)	
	1951	1961	1974	1951	1961	1974	1951-1961	1951-1974
Mirpur Thana	84,480	108,418	173,967	670	860	1,380	28.3	105.9
Kushtia District				645	841	1,374	31.9	113.0
Bangladesh				761	922	1,297	21.2	70.4

TABLE 5.14

Mirpur Thana: changes in homestead and non-agricultural land use 1952-1974

Main physiographic units: Ganges River Floodplain

Physiographic units Description	Soil assoc.	Area (acres)	Roads, railways (%)		Irrigation, drainage canals (%)		Homesteads (%)		Tanks (%)		Others (%)	
			1952	1974	1952	1974	1952	1974	1952	1974	1952	1974
Active Ganges Floodplain ridges	1	2,688	0	0[1]	0	0[1]	0	0[1]	0	0[1]	0	0[1]
Active Ganges Meander Floodplain: ridges	4, 5, 6	9,088	1.3	1.3	0	0.4	18.1	19.4	0.2	0.7	0	0
Old Ganges Meander Floodplain: ridges	9	14,016	1.6	1.7	0	2.4	17.0	15.9	1.2	1.2	0	0.1[2]
basins and associated ridges	15	28,224	1.4	1.4	0	1.9	8.3	8.1	0.6	1.0	0	0.2[2]
Mixed Old and Young Ganges floodplains: ridges and associated basins	19	25,920	0.8	0.8	0	1.5	12.2	11.4	1.3	1.5	0	0.1[3]
Total[4]		**79,936**	**1.2**	**1.3**	**0**	**1.6**	**11.9**	**11.5**	**0.9**	**1.1**	**0**	**0.1**

Note: 1. Estimated.
      2. Brickyard.
      3. Factory.
      4. Excluding units 2 and 3; also water bodies (256 acres).

then (1,171 per sq. mile). The population density and population increase for Mirpur Thana were similar to those for Kushtia District as a whole. The population density was about 11.9 percent below the national average in 1951 and 6.4 percent above the average in 1974. Presumably, the relatively large population increase was due not only to normal population growth but also to an influx of immigrants from other Districts (and possibly from India, which is only 20 miles away to the west).

A5.2 Settlement and associated non-agricultural land use

The population increase in Mirpur Thana is to some extent reflected in the percentage of the land occupied by homesteads. Many new settlements were established between 1951 and 1974, and there was also an expansion of some existing homestead areas. The overall increase in the homestead area amounted to about 1 percent, or 8.4 percent of the 1951 homestead area. The increase varied between physiographic units as follows:

a. approximately 1.3 percent on the ridges of the Young Ganges Meander Floodplain (soil units 4, 5, 6); the increase was as high as 1.9 percent in unit 5;

b. 0.9 percent on the ridges of the Old Ganges Meander Floodplain (soil unit 9);

c. about 1 percent in the basins of the Old Ganges Meander Floodplain (soil unit 15); and

d. 0.9 percent in the unit consisting of ridges and basins of the mixed Old and Young Ganges Meander Floodplain (soil unit 19).

The population density in the homestead areas increased from 5,634 persons per sq. mile in 1951 (84,480 persons on 11.9 percent of the Thana area) to 12,006 per sq. mile in 1974 (173,967 persons on 11.5 percent of the Thana area). The housing density was relatively low. In soil units 9 and 19, the 'productive' to 'non-productive' ratio was estimated to be about 70:30 percent.

The new settlements were mainly located on floodplain ridges, especially alongside roads, near road junctions and near the off-take of major irrigation canals. The largest new settlements were about 900 × 900 feet, but the majority were much smaller, often less than 300 × 300 feet and containing only a few houses. Sometimes, gaps existing between homestead areas in 1952 had been filled up by new settlements by 1974.

Several new settlements were recorded inside one basin area. These settlements were very small and consisted of only a very few houses. None-the-less, the fact that new settlements were being established in basin areas indicates that, with the improved drainage resulting from completion of the G-K project (which includes flood-protection works), the population was apparently taking advantage of the reduced flooding depths and constructing houses on land which formerly was considered unsuitable for habitation due to deep flooding.

The new settlements on the higher parts of the landscape could be related to the influence of the G-K project, but the higher parts were always above flood-level, so the influence of the project on the change in homestead area is not certain. In any case, the increase in homestead area due to new settlement is not reflected in the figures given in Table 5.14. In most units, there was, in fact, a net decrease in the homestead area between 1952 and 1974 (see Figure 5.7). Mirpur was the only one of the seven Thanas studied where this phenomenon was observed. The decrease in homestead area reflected the emigration of some Hindu families to India, particularly during the 1971 Liberation War.

FIGURE 5.7

Mirpur Thana: settlement pattern, Ganges Floodplain, 1974

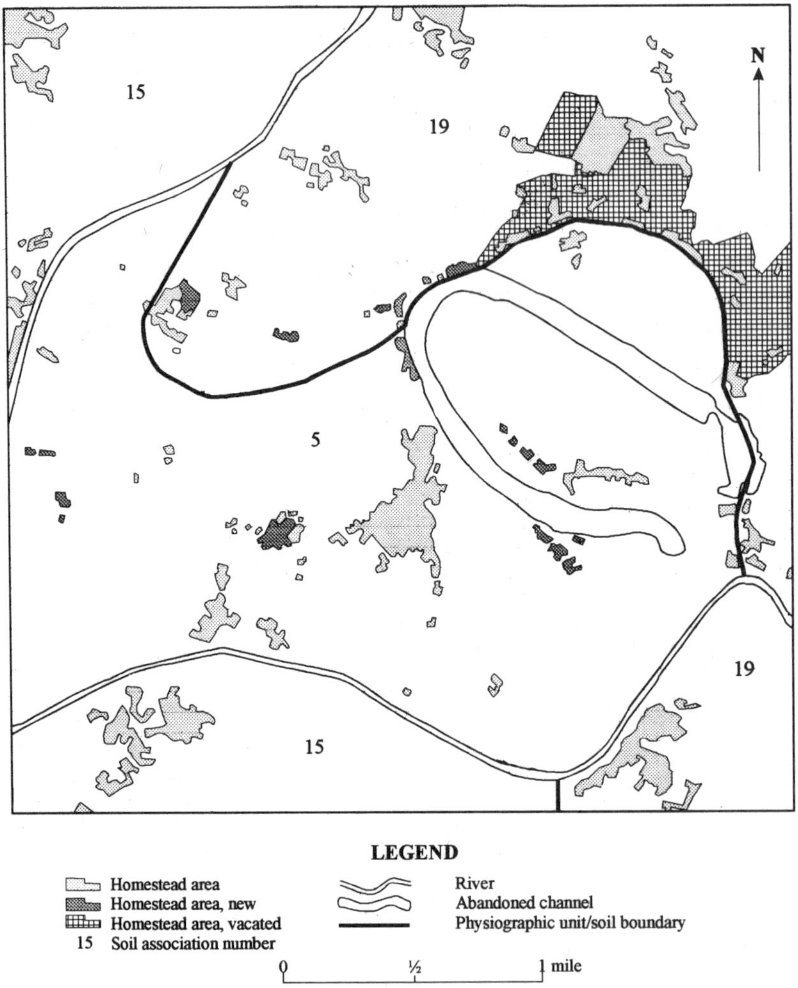

The emigrants either sold their property, when they were able to do so, or merely vacated it. The abandoned homestead sites were bought or taken over by neighbouring Muslim villagers, who usually cut down the trees, demolished the houses, and converted the sites to agricultural use, mainly for growing upland crops such as tobacco, vegetables and cotton.

It is difficult to estimate how many families actually left, as the houses seem to have been rather widely spaced in 1952. The decrease in homestead area amounted to approximately 2 percent in soil unit 9, about 1.2 percent in unit 15 (both part of the Old Ganges Meander Floodplain), and about 1.7 percent in unit 19 (mixed old and young floodplain). It was negligible in units 4, 5 and 6 (young floodplain).

The area gained for agricultural production by the decrease in homestead area was off-set by an increase in the area occupied by irrigation canals, drainage canals and embankments. The main canals in particular — which, together with the adjoining embankments, are over 450 feet wide — occupy a considerable area of land. The average area occupied by canals and embankments in the Thana as a whole is about 1.6 percent, but it is as much as 2.4 percent in soil unit 9.

The area occupied by tanks increased from 0.9 percent in 1951 to 1.1 percent in 1974. New tanks occur beside new settlements as well as near to existing ones. The area occupied by roads, railways and adjoining borrow pits remained almost constant (1.3 percent *versus* 1.2 percent). A few new roads were constructed between 1952 and 1974. Two brickyards were observed on the 1974 airphotos. They occupied about 0.1 percent of soil units 9 and 15 (about 16 and 45 acres respectively). A factory occupying about 33 acres was located in unit 19. All were located on land classified as good agricultural land.

A5.3 Comparison of conditions inside and outside the Ganges-Kobadak project area

In order to assess the influence of the G-K project on settlement and non-agricultural land use — specifically the homestead area — some areas in Gangni and Alamdanga Thanas outside the project area were also studied. These Thanas, which lie directly west and south-west of Mirpur, experienced a comparable population increase to Mirpur Thana between 1951 and 1974.

The units studied were part of the ridges of the Young Ganges Meander Floodplain (soil unit 5), basins and associated ridges of the Old Ganges Meander Floodplain (unit 15), and ridges and associated basins of the mixed Young and Old Ganges Floodplain (unit 19): see Figure 5.8. The findings are shown in Table 5.15. The figures show that an increase as well as a decrease took place. The increase was due to the establishment of many new settlements, mainly on the ridges, and along rivers and roads, in a similar way to what had occurred in Mirpur Thana. It appeared that either the flood protection provided by the G-K project also benefits areas not directly served by the project irrigation facilities, thus explaining the spread of the homestead area, or that new settlements had been built on the ridges because they are flood-free anyway. No new settlements were observed in basin areas.

The decrease in homestead area can be explained in a similar way to that reported in Mirpur Thana: namely, conversion of some former settlement sites to agricultural land following the emigration of former Hindu occupants.

It appears that there was a definite effect of the G-K project on the settlement pattern in Mirpur Thana in that new settlements were established on land where that would not have been possible previously due to flooding. It is interesting to observe that an increase in homestead area took place in this Thana despite the fact that it had the lowest density of housing within settlements of all the seven Thanas studied. That seems to support the hypothesis that the increased homestead area was linked to the flood protection provided by the G-K project.

However, the situation is complicated by the fact that most of the ridges were above flood-level even before project implementation. In addition, there seems also to have been a sizeable influx of immigrants. Whether this was related to the G-K project and the resulting increase in employment opportunities is not certain: more field checking would be required to determine that. In any case, the population density in Mirpur Thana was very low in 1951. Even without the establishment of the irrigation project, the population might

.

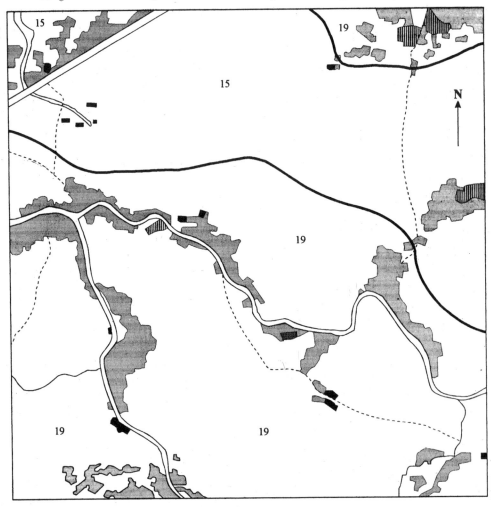

FIGURE 5.8

Gangni and Alamdanga Thanas: settlement pattern, Ganges Floodplain, 1974

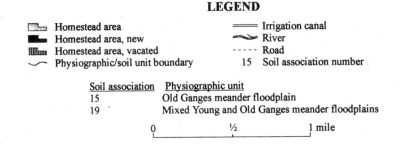

well have expanded rapidly by immigration, given the high population density in other parts of Bangladesh.[26]

[26]*Immigrant farmers from Noakhali and Comilla Districts were observed during soil surveys in the 1960s in Dinajpur, Kushtia and Jessore Districts.*

TABLE 5.15

Changes in homestead area in parts of Gangni and Alamdanga Thanas 1951-1974

Physiographic unit	Homesteads 1951 %	Homesteads 1974 %	Increase %	Decrease %	Net gain/loss %
Young Ganges meander floodplain (Soil assoc. 5)	9.2	10.9	2.3	0.6	+1.7
Old Ganges meander floodplain (Soil assoc. 15)	7.5	7.3	1.0	1.2	-0.2
Mixed Old and Young Ganges floodplains (Soil assoc. 19) ridges and associated basins	12.0	13.3	1.6	0.3	+1.3

A6   KISHOREGANJ THANA

A6.1 General

Kishoreganj Thana is located approximately 15 miles north-west of Rangpur town in Rangpur District. It occupies 65,280 acres (102 sq. miles). The River Teesta forms the eastern boundary. No major road or railway traverses the Thana.

The Thana is located on the Teesta River Floodplain. The landscape consists of low, nearly-level to very gently undulating ridges, scattered basins and some abandoned river channels. For the purpose of this study, two physiographic units were recognized:

a. the Active Teesta Floodplain, also indicated as the Teesta alluvial complex (soil unit 1 on Figure 5.10), which occupies 1,177 acres (1.8 percent of the Thana); and

b. the Teesta Meander Floodplain, comprising nearly-level to very gently undulating floodplain ridges (soil units 2, 6a, 6b, 11a, 13, 14), and occupying 61,639 acres (94.5 percent of the Thana).

Water bodies (mainly the Teesta river) occupy 2,464 acres (3.7 percent of the Thana).

The soils mainly have medium to light texture. Sandy to silt loam soils predominate in soil association 1, and sandy loams, silt loams and silty clay loams prevail in the remaining soil units.

About one-third of this Thana is not affected by floods in normal years (mainly units 2, 6a, 6b). Elsewhere, in units 11a, 13, 14, there is seasonal flooding 1-2 feet deep, except on the highest ridges, which remain above normal flood-levels. The active floodplain experiences shallow flooding and is subject to river-bank erosion and/or burial by new alluvium.

At the time of the reconnaissance soil survey in 1965-66, land use consisted mainly of aus paddy followed by dry-season crops on the ridges, and mainly aus paddy or jute followed by transplanted aman paddy on lower areas. Tobacco was an important rabi crop on the ridges. The land was mainly double-cropped, with some single-cropped land. The active floodplain was mainly barren or grassland, with some aus paddy or millet (*kaon*).

The land capability classes were indicated as mainly good agricultural land, with limitations due to droughtiness on ridge soils in the dry season, shallow flooding in the wet season on lower land, and some irregular relief. Locally, on some ridges, there was some moderate agricultural land subject to droughtiness early in the dry season. The active floodplain had mainly poor or very poor agricultural land, with severe risks of river-bank erosion, deep flooding, rapid flood-flow and poor physical soil conditions.

Population data for Kishoreganj Thana are shown in Table 5.16. Compared with Rangpur District as a whole, this Thana showed a higher population density, but the population increase in the Thana between 1951 and 1974 was below the District average. The more rapid population growth in the District may have been related to the growth of Rangpur town as a major urban centre.

The population density in Kishoreganj Thana was 36.7 percent higher than the national average in 1951 and 28.7 percent higher in 1974. Population growth was slightly below the national average of 21.2 percent between 1951 and 1961 and of 70.4 percent between 1951 and 1974. The cause of the lower population growth rate is not known, but it might have been related to the fact that the density was already high in 1951, and possibly also to the limitations imposed by severe flooding, river-bank erosion and alluvial sedimentation in areas close to the Teesta river.

TABLE 5.16
Population data for Kishoreganj Thana

Area	Population			Population density per sq. mile			Population increase (%)	
	1951	1961	1974	1951	1961	1974	1951-1961	1951-1974
Kishoreganj Thana	106,084	126,349	170,241	1,040	1,239	1,669	19.1	60.5
Rangpur District				787	1,025	1,470	30.2	86.8
Bangladesh				761	922	1,297	21.2	70.4

TABLE 5.17
Kishoreganj Thana: changes in homestead and non-agricultural land use 1952-1974

Physiographic unit: Teesta Floodplain

Physiographic units Description	Soil association	Area (acres)	Roads, canals (%)		Homesteads (%)		Tanks (%)		Others (%)	
			1952	1974	1952	1974	1952	1974	1952	1974
Teesta Floodplain active floodplain	1	1,177	0	0	0	0.3	0	0	0	0
older meander floodplain	2, 6a, 6b, 11a, 13, 14	61,639	0.1	0.2	8.1	9.0	0.3	0.5	0	0
Total[1]		**62,816**	**0.1**	**0.2**	**8.0**	**8.9**	**0.3**	**0.5**	**0**	**0**

Note: 1. Excluding water bodies (2,464 acres).

A6.2 Settlement and associated non-agricultural land use

The settlement pattern on the older Teesta Floodplain is quite different from that observed on the other major river floodplains. Due to the fact that considerable areas of the Teesta Floodplain are not subject to flooding in normal years, there is less restriction on the siting of settlements than occurs on most floodplains. Therefore, new settlements are rather scattered and not very large. They were found on the relatively higher areas which are not subject to regular flooding. No settlements were found in flood-affected basins.

The settlements usually are small. Only a few villages reach a size of 1,000 × 1,000 feet: (see Figure 5.9). The distance between settlements varies from 150-190 feet on the higher area to 0.5-1.5 miles across basins. Settlements are scarce on the active floodplain, but a few new settlements were recorded on the 1974 airphotos, located on the floodplain ridges.

In 1952, about 8.0 percent of the Thana was occupied by homesteads (Table 5.17). In 1974, the area had increased to 8.9 percent, representing an increase of 11.2 percent of the homestead area alone. Small new settlements were established, while the expansion of some existing settlements had also taken place. Part of the increased homestead area was caused by planting additional bamboo clumps around homesteads. Bamboo is widely grown as a cash crop on the Teesta Floodplain, and sold for construction purposes.[27] The new settlements were invariably found on the higher floodplain ridges.

The average population density within homestead areas was 13,000 persons per sq. mile in 1951 (108,084 on 8.0 percent of 102 sq. miles, or 8.16 sq. miles) and 18,753 per sq. mile in 1974 (170,241 on 8.9 percent of 102 sq. miles, or 9.08 sq. miles). Thus, despite the increase in the homestead area — part of which was caused by the additional area under bamboo and not related to new housing — a significant increase in population density occurred, indicating the absorption of most of the population increase within the existing homestead areas.

Whether new settlements were populated by immigrants from neighbouring villages or from India is not known for certain. Limited field checking indicated that both of these sources could have contributed.

In addition, settlements established by villagers whose homestead land near the Teesta river had been washed away made up part of the increased homestead area. In fact, close to the river in the eastern part of the Thana, the increase in homestead area was about 1.4 percent, compared with 0.6 percent in the western part. That suggests that people whose villages were washed away preferred to settle close to their original homes where their agricultural land or employment still existed. Study of the airphotos showed that about 30 acres of homestead land had been washed away on the older meander floodplain between 1952 and 1974. Given the average population density within settlements (i.e., 13,000 + 18,752 divided by 2), the loss of 30 acres of homestead land would displace 744 persons, or about 124 families at the average family size of six.

The percentage of tanks is low, but it increased from 0.3 percent in 1952 to 0.5 percent in 1974. The new tanks were mainly dug beside existing or new settlements. Tanks occur more frequently in the western part of the Thana than in the relatively higher eastern part. Since the settlements are built on flood-free sites, there is no need to excavate tanks in order to provide earth for homestead platforms. In addition, groundwater usually is present

---

[27]Bamboo matting is often used for making house walls as clay is not easily available on the Teesta Floodplain.

FIGURE 5.9

Kishoreganj Thana: settlement pattern, Teesta Floodplain, 1974

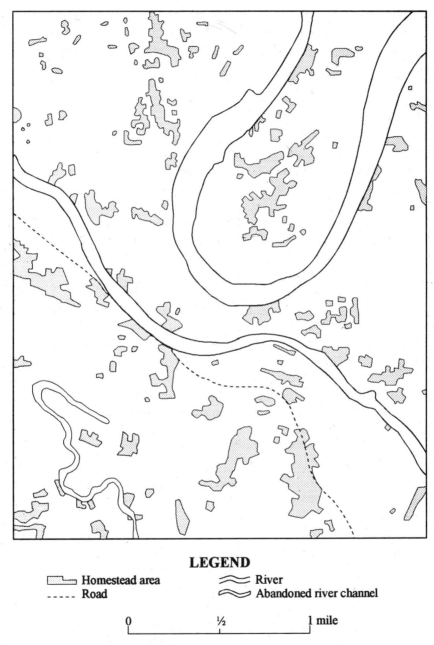

LEGEND

Homestead area	River
----- Road	Abandoned river channel

0   ½   1 mile

at a shallow depth, so water for domestic use can easily be obtained year-round from wells about 10-15 feet deep.

The area occupied by roads is small. It increased from 0.1 percent in 1952 to 0.2 percent in 1974. There are neither roads nor tanks on the Active Teesta Floodplain.

A7 DUPCHANCHIA THANA

A7.1 General

This Thana is located approximately 20 miles west of Bogra town in Bogra District. It occupies 40,320 acres (63 sq. miles). The main road from Bogra to Naogaon passes through the Thana.

The Level Barind Tract occupies 95.3 percent of the Thana (38,400 acres) in soil associations 33, 34 and 40. The remaining 4.7 percent of the Thana (1,920 acres) lies on the Little Jamuna Floodplain (soil unit 22).

The Level Barind Tract consists of an extensive area of nearly-level land underlain by the Madhupur Clay. This material gives rise (in this Thana) to mainly grey and yellowish-brown clay loam soils overlying a redder clay at depths of 1-2 feet on the higher parts and nearly-level areas. In the shallow depressions, mainly clayey soils are found. The flooding depth ranges between 1-3 feet on the relatively higher areas comprising about 95 percent of the landscape, and 3-6 feet in the shallow depressions.[28]

In 1970 when the reconnaissance soil survey of Bogra District was carried out, land use on the Barind Tract consisted mainly of transplanted aman followed by fallow in the dry season, but double-cropping of boro or aus paddy followed by transplanted aman had become common in recently-developed tube-well irrigation areas. The land capability classification was given as moderate agricultural land, subject to shallow seasonal flooding, with severe droughtiness in the dry season, and with moderately deep flooding in some shallow valleys.

The Little Jamuna Floodplain occupies a narrow strip (less the 1 mile wide) alongside the Nagar river on the eastern margin of the Thana. It comprises very gently undulating ridges and some basins, with only slight differences in elevation, but the unit also includes some man-made land. The soils are mainly medium-textured (silt loams). Flooding depths vary: 1-3 feet is common on the lower parts, while the man-made platforms and the higher parts of the floodplain ridges lie above normal flood-level.

Land use on the Little Jamuna Floodplain consisted of aus paddy or jute followed by dry-season crops; some sugarcane is also grown. The land was mainly double-cropped. The land capability classification is given as good and moderate agricultural land, subject to droughtiness in the dry season, some with shallow flooding and with irregular relief in places.

Population data for Dupchanchia Thana in 1951, 1961 and 1974 are shown in Table 5.18. The figures show that the population density was slightly higher than the average for Bogra District and much above the average for Bangladesh as a whole. The population growth rate was approximately similar to the average rate in Bogra District and in Bangladesh.

A7.2 Settlements and associated non-agricultural land use

The settlements in Dupchanchia Thana have a distinctive pattern, quite different from that found in meander floodplain areas. The villages are seen on the aerial photographs as irregular-shaped blocks, with dimensions between approximately 300×300 feet and $3,000 \times 3,000$ feet. These blocks are quite irregularly spaced, with distances of about 900 feet to 1½ miles between individual villages: see Figure 5.10. No relationship was observed

---

[28]*Flooding on the Level Barind Tract is by rainwater (or the raised groundwater-table).*

TABLE 5.18
Population data for Dupchanchia Thana

Area	Population			Population density per sq. mile			Population increase (%)	
	1951	1961	1974	1951	1961	1974	1951-1961	1951-1974
Dupchanchia Thana	56,799	67,358	96,607	902	1,069	1,533	18.6	70.0
Bogra District				851	1,048	1,485	23.2	74.5
Bangladesh				761	922	1,297	21.2	70.4

TABLE 5.19
Dupchanchia Thana: changes in homestead and non-agricultural land use 1952-1974

Main physiographic unit: Barind Tract

Physiographic units Description	Soil association	Area (acres)	Roads, canals (%)		Homesteads (%)		Tanks (%)		Others (%)	
			1952	1974	1952	1974	1952	1974	1952	1974
Little Jamuna meander floodplain	22	1,920	0.6	0.6[1]	19.7	21.3[1]	4.1	4.8[1]	0	0
Barind Tract	33, 34, 40	38,400	1.1	1.1	6.3	6.7	4.0	4.1	0	0
Total[1]		**40,320**	**1.1**	**1.1**	**6.9**	**7.4**	**4.0**	**4.1**	**0**	**0**

Note: 1. Partly extrapolated.

FIGURE 5.10

Dupchanchia Thana: settlement pattern, Level Barind Tract, 1974

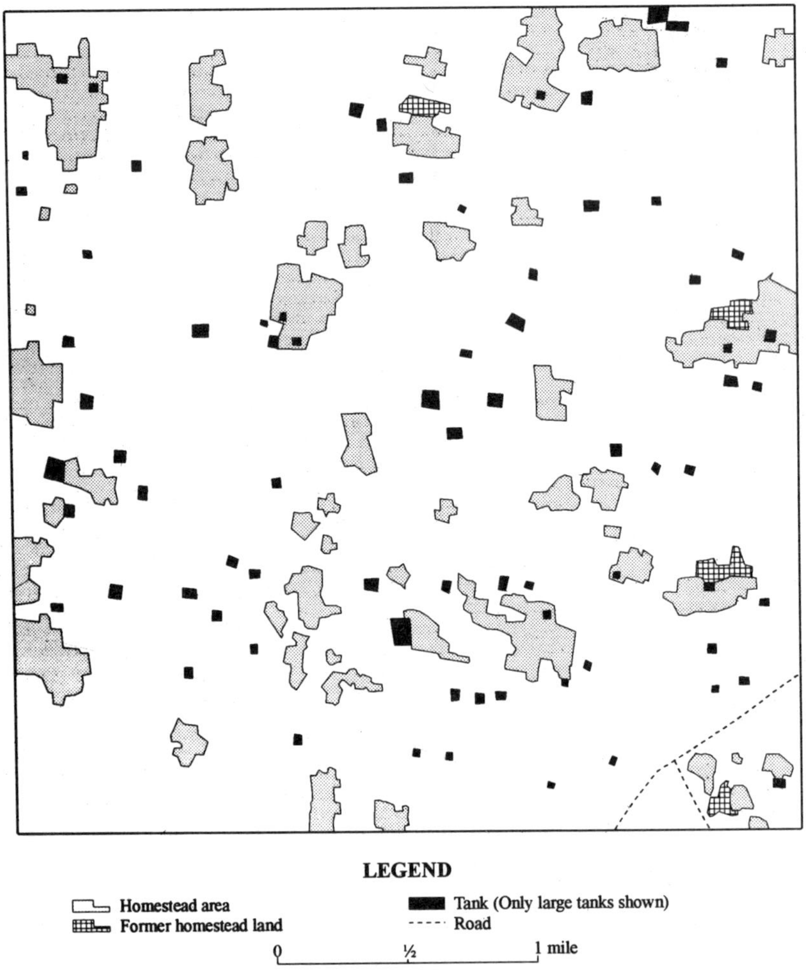

LEGEND

☐ Homestead area   ■ Tank (Only large tanks shown)
▦ Former homestead land   ---- Road

0   ½   1 mile

between the relative size of villages and their distance apart: two large villages may occur close together, or they may be several miles apart.

The different pattern on the Barind Tract is related to the uniform topography and the relatively shallow flooding. There was thus no need to locate villages closely together on flood-free sites, as in the country's floodplain areas. The houses are built on slightly elevated platforms about 1-1½ feet high.

On the Nagar river floodplain, settlements are built closely together. They are irregular in shape and occupy a major part of the floodplain.

A slight increase in the area occupied by settlements was recorded in this Thana, from 6.9 percent in 1951 to 7.4 percent in 1974 (Table 5.19). The increase took place on the Barind Tract as well as on the Nagar floodplain. The highest relative increase occurred on the floodplain, from 19.7 percent in 1951 to 21.3 percent in 1974, apparently due to the fact that the Thana centre is located on the floodplain and also because the highest parts of this floodplain are not affected by flooding.

On the Barind Tract, the increase in homestead area consisted of small expansions of some existing settlements. In the majority of villages, no increase in homestead area was observed. Considering the shallow flooding, and the sizeable increase in population, that is somewhat surprising. However, the traditional way of building houses closely together in a fortress-like compound with only a few houses outside the compound may provide an explanation.[29] It is apparent that the population increase was absorbed, as in the other Thanas studied, by building new houses close to those already existing within the homestead area, at the cost of vegetable plots, bushes and trees (and possibly also of tanks). The population density calculated for the homestead area went up from 13,066 persons per sq. mile (56,799 persons on 4.347 sq. miles) in 1951 to 20,722 per sq. mile (96,607 persons on 4.662 sq. miles) in 1974.

On the Barind Tract, many tanks occur close to the homesteads, often surrounded by trees. The percentage of the area occupied by tanks was the second highest (after Chandina) of all the seven Thanas studied. Some of the smaller tanks may have been obscured from detection on the airphotos by projecting tree branches. However, as the 1974 photography was of good quality, this would not affect the total figure significantly.

Tanks of all sizes occur, from as small as 15×15 feet to as large as 600×600 feet, with the most common being about 100×100 feet. About 10-20 percent of the area occupied by tanks occurs outside the homestead area. As in other Thanas, the tanks were used for domestic purposes as well as for irrigation of small plots. The tanks were about 3-6 feet deep and contained water throughout the year.

The area occupied by tanks increased slightly on the Barind Tract and more markedly on the Nagar floodplain. The area occupied by roads and adjoining borrow pits remained constant.

As is shown on Figure 5.10, small areas near some of the villages are indicated as former homestead land. These areas consist of slightly raised (1-1½ feet) platforms, now used for paddy seedbeds and vegetable cultivation. The average plot size within the former homestead land is considerably smaller than the average size of paddy fields (about 10×15 feet on the former homestead land *versus* about 100×100 feet or more for paddy fields). The small plots stand out clearly on the airphotos. Local information suggested that, more than 100 years ago, these areas were used as homestead sites and that they were vacated for a variety of reasons, such as cholera (or other epidemics), superstitious beliefs necessitating the abandonment of the site, and an increasing need for agricultural land due to increasing population pressure.[30] Pottery fragments were commonly found on such sites.

A8 THE DHAKA-NARAYANGANJ-DEMRA PROJECT AREA

A8.1 General

In order to assess the changes in non-agricultural land use taking place in a flood-protected area close to a major urban centre, the DND irrigation and drainage project area was selected for study. Unfortunately, aerial photography of this area was not available.[31] Therefore, some data on the project area supplied by BWDB were used.

---

[29]*Local information suggested that this type of settlement was designed as a means of protection against dacoits (bands of robbers).*

[30]*A possible additional reason might have been emigration of Hindu families after the partition of India in 1947 and again during the Liberation War in 1971.*

[31]*See footnote 4 above.*

The DND project area is located directly south-east of Dhaka city, between the Buriganga and Sitalakhya rivers. The Dhaka-Demra road passes through the area, dividing the flood-protected and irrigated part (Phase I) in the south from the northern part (Phase II) which is not flood-protected but has irrigation. The project area lies mainly on the Old Meghna Estuarine Floodplain in the east (soil association 50) and on a down-warped level part of the Madhupur Tract in the west (soil association 21). The whole area was seasonally flooded to depths of 6-12 feet before project implementation.[32]

Following the start of the project in 1968, there was a marked increase in the area occupied by homesteads in the flood-protected area. According to data provided by BWDB, based on surveys carried out in 1968 and 1977, there were 900 acres of homestead land in 1968 and 1,785 acres in 1977. That represents an increase from 6.9 percent of the area in 1968 to 13.7 percent in 1977, a relative increase of about 90 percent.

The new homesteads are clearly visible from the Dhaka-Comilla road. They are especially numerous in the area closest to Dhaka. There is a striking contrast between the area to the north of the road, which is irrigated but not flood-protected, and the area to the south which is irrigated and flood-protected. To the north, except for a few new homesteads adjoining the main road, virtually no new settlements are visible and the area is entirely cultivated with boro paddy except for the pre-project settlements on high, man-made platforms. To the south, the area between the pre-project settlements on high raised mounds is occupied by many, scattered, new, small settlements built on platforms only 1-2 feet high, with paddy fields between the individual homesteads.

Assuming that the spread of settlement began mainly after Independence in 1971, this means that the homestead area almost doubled in about 5-6 years. It is foreseen that, at this rate of expansion, the flood-protected part of the project area could be fully converted to an urbanized suburb of Dhaka by the year 2000.[33]

The strong influx of people, establishing new houses in an area which was formerly deeply flooded, clearly shows the effect that the removal of the flooding restriction can have on the settlement pattern. Formerly confined to the high, narrow, man-made platforms and ridges, settlements have spread out widely across the agricultural land. The proximity of the DND project area to the Dhaka-Narayanganj-Demra conurbation has undoubtedly aggravated the spread of settlement onto good agricultural land, but there seems little reason to doubt that an appreciable expansion would have taken place anyway with the provision of flood protection and drainage. The DND project, therefore, provides a useful indication of what might be expected to happen in other flood-protection project areas. The purpose of such agricultural development projects could be nullified unless a way is found to control the spread of settlement onto valuable agricultural land after flood protection and drainage had been provided.

---

[32]*A map of the DND project area is given in Figure 4.2.*

[33]*See Chapter 4, Section 4.2.3, footnote 6.*

Chapter 6

CHANGES IN FLOOD LEVELS[1]

Significant reductions in flood levels occurred in some parts of Bangladesh after soil surveys had been carried out in the 1960s. Those changes affected land use and agricultural potential. The extent and causes of the changes are described and appropriate recommendations are made.

6.1 BACKGROUND

The reconnaissance soil survey of Bangladesh was undertaken between 1964 and 1975. Particular attention was paid to recording information on the depth and duration of seasonal flooding and the risk of crop damage by flooding. That was because of the influence which those factors have on actual and potential land use.

During the 1970s, it became apparent that flood levels had changed in some floodplain areas since the time that they had been surveyed. Extensive areas that were formerly used for deepwater aman paddy were found to be growing transplanted aman paddy. It appeared that flood levels in the Brahmaputra-Jamuna river had been exceptionally high in the 1950s and 1960s following the 1950 Assam earthquake, but that river levels had returned to 'normal' in the 1970s after the sediments which choked the river channel following the earthquake had passed through Bangladesh.

In 1980, work had commenced on computerizing the data in the District/Subdivision reconnaissance soil survey reports. The purpose was to build up a natural resources data bank as the basis for making a comprehensive appraisal of the agricultural potential of the country's land and water resources (FAO, 1988). During the course of data compilation for that appraisal, it was decided to up-date the information on flood levels given in the original soil survey reports, because of the importance of flooding characteristics in determining land use and potential. The Consultant was appointed to assist the Soil Resources Development Institute (SRDI) in making those studies. The findings are reported below.

---

[1] *During field trips in the 1970s, the author (HB) observed that significant changes in cropping patterns had occurred in some parts of the country since the time that soil surveys of those areas had been carried out in the 1960s, suggesting that flood levels had changed in the intervening period. Accordingly, it was decided to study those changes as part of the on-going FAO Agroecological Zones (AEZ) Study. This chapter presents an edited and abbreviated version of the report on the study carried out by A.M. Ibrahim, Soil Survey Consultant, under the FAO/UNDP Agricultural Development Adviser Project (Ibrahim, 1984). Except where stated otherwise, the information relates to the time of the field study, February-June 1983. Statements originally made in the present tense have been converted to the past tense to make that clear. Footnotes which appeared in the original document are given in normal font. Footnotes that have been added are given in italics.*

6.2 THE STUDY

6.2.1 Objective and scope

The main purpose of the study was to up-date the soil survey information so that the land use potential could be correctly assessed for the on-going agroecological zones study.

In the reconnaissance soil survey reports, the main soil unit recognized was the *soil series*. This term covers a range of soils derived from similar parent materials under similar conditions of development and resembling each other closely in their major physical and chemical properties. Important subdivisions of individual soil series were made, where necessary, as *soil phases*. Phases were required mainly to differentiate soils flooded to different depths or for different durations, or with different degrees of risk to cultivation by floods, river-bank erosion or burial by new sediments.

The observed changes in flooding characteristics altered the soil survey information only at the soil phase level. Major changes in soil physical, morphological and chemical properties do not occur within a short period which would necessitate changes in the identification of soil series or in the grouping of soil series in soil associations.[2]

The division of soil series into soil phases is mainly made for agricultural purposes. Often, the difference between soil phases of a particular soil series is more important than the difference between two adjoining soil series. As an example, Silmandi series, Medium Lowland phase, cannot be used in the same way as Silmandi series, Medium Highland phase. Transplanted aman paddy can be grown on the Medium Highland phase of Silmandi series, but not on the Medium Lowland phase. On the other hand, transplanted aman can be grown on the Medium Highland phases of both Silmandi and the neighbouring Sonatala series, but with differences in yield potential because of differences in the physical and chemical properties of those two soil series.

The major factors determining the kinds of crop grown, cropping systems and intensity of land use are land levels in relation to depth of flooding in the rainy season, the time when floodwater drains from the land and soil moisture-holding capacity in the dry season. The five main depth-of-flooding land types recognized in the reconnaissance soil survey reports are defined in Table 1.2.

6.2.2 Methodology

The following steps were taken in carrying out the study.

a. The extent and effect of changes in flooding characteristics were examined in the field: i.e., the soil phases relating to depth of flooding, flood hazard and time of flood-drainage were re-assessed.

b. The extent of each revised soil phase was calculated and the phases were re-arranged in the soil association descriptions.

---

[2] *Two exceptions to this statement may be noted. One is where rivers erode former soil areas or deposit significant depths of new alluvium on older alluvium, thus changing the extent and/or the properties of soil series and soil associations formerly described and mapped. The other is where rapid soil development changes former raw alluvium into a developed soil within a period of 20-30 years: e.g., the break-up of alluvial stratification and the development of soil structure and mottle colours as a result of biological mixing, seasonal wetting and drying, and seasonal oxidation-reduction changes; and leaching of lime from topsoils on Ganges river alluvium and acidification of topsoils on other floodplains: (see Brammer, 1996, Chapter 8).*

c. Present land use was recorded for each soil phase.

d. Studies were also made to examine the effect of other environmental and land management factors on cropping patterns, including irrigation and flood protection.

The surveyed area comprised the floodplains of the Brahmaputra, Jamuna, Ganges, Meghna, Surma and Kusiyara rivers in the following (old) Districts.[3]

Jamalpur	Faridpur	Pabna	Comilla
Tangail	Kushtia	Bogra	Sylhet
Mymensingh	Rajshahi	Rangpur	

The study used the maps and technical information given in SRDI reconnaissance soil survey reports as a base. Soil associations with similar soils and environmental conditions were grouped together into broad mapping units. Traverse lines were selected to cross each of the broad units. Areas adjoining each traverse line were first examined on the airphotos. After carefully examining the physiographic pattern, the planned traverses were drawn on the airphotos.

Field studies were carried out along each traverse line. Soils, land use, flooding depth and flood hazard were examined and recorded. Information about land use and flooding depth was collected from local cultivators.

After completion of the fieldwork, the data collected in the field were analysed in the office, and the overall flooding pattern (depth, duration, etc.) was determined. The identification and extent of the soil phases in each soil association was then re-assessed.

6.2.3 Programme of work

The consultant was originally given three months for carrying out the study. The time was later extended to more than eleven months so as to cover all the areas where up-dating was needed and to revise the soil survey reports.

The consultant assumed duty on 24 January 1983. About two weeks were spent on an initial study of the soil survey reports, maps and airphotos, and in discussions with senior officials of SRDI about the work programme.

Fieldwork was undertaken between 9 February and 25 June 1983, with intermittent periods spent in SRDI headquarters to collect base material for successive field trips. The remaining period was spent in the compilation and analysis of the field data. During this period, all the soil associations for each soil survey report were up-dated in respect of land types, land use and land capability, and revised soil association map legends were prepared where necessary. The revised information was later transferred to the format used for entering the soil survey data into the AEZ project's computer data base.

6.3 FINDINGS

6.3.1 Flooding depth

The field studies showed that flooding depths had fallen significantly during the previous 10-15 years. The changes mainly affected the Brahmaputra-Jamuna Floodplain and adjoining

---

[3] The consultant did not survey Dhaka District. The re-survey of that District was carried out by a SRDI field party led by Mr Mahbubur Rahman, Deputy Director.

parts of the Ganges and Meghna Floodplains. The maximum change observed was about 2-4 feet on the Jamuna and Ganges rivers in Dhaka and northern Faridpur Districts. Upstream of the Jamuna-Ganges confluence, the change diminished to 1-2 feet in Jamalpur District. Downstream along the Ganges and Lower Meghna rivers, the change decreased to nil in the tidal zone of Barisal District. Upstream along the Ganges and Meghna rivers, the decrease fell to less than 1 foot above Hardinge Bridge and Bhairab Bazar respectively. In general, the decrease in flooding depth was more noticeable in floodplain basins than on the ridges.

6.3.2 External drainage

The fall in flood levels significantly improved the external drainage of floodplain basin soils. The period of monsoon-season flooding was less than had been recorded in the 1960s, and the extent of soils in the early-draining phase had increased at the expense of soils in the slow-draining phase. The effect of these changes was to increase the area of soils suitable for dryland rabi crops. The areas where the most significant improvements in drainage were observed are indicated in Table 6.1.

TABLE 6.1
Main areas where improvements in drainage were observed

District/Subdivision	Area benefited
Netrakona Subdivision	20-30 percent of some basins; no change in many basins
Jamalpur Subdivision	erratic
Faridpur District	5-10 percent of the area; locally 20 percent
Pabna District	generally 10-30 percent, but some basins showed little change
Bogra District	15-30 percent

6.3.3 Flood hazard

Sudden rise of floodwater often damages standing crops in basin areas. In the past, many areas suffered this hazard. The situation was found to have greatly improved in this respect. Major reductions in the area subject to flood hazard were observed in the areas shown in Table 6.2.

TABLE 6.2
Main areas where reduced flood hazard was observed

District/Subdivision	Area benefited
Netrakona Subdivision	10-25 percent
Faridpur District	more than 15 percent in soil unit 20; no significant changes in other basins
Kushtia District	about 10 percent
Pabna District	about 50 percent in some basins
Bogra District	2-10 percent

6.3.4 Land type

The decrease in flooding depth converted parts of former Lowland into Medium Lowland, Medium Lowland into Medium Highland, and Medium Highland into Highland in a more or less systematic way. In general, about 10-30 percent of the area was found to have changed land type in this way.

Besides the effect of the changed river regimes, embankments raised for flood control were also found to have caused appreciable changes in land types. Such changes were observed in all the surveyed areas except Gaibandha and Kurigram Subdivisions of Rangpur District and in Sylhet District. In those Districts, the slight variation of flooding depth had little effect on the land types recorded earlier.

In Tangail and Mymensingh Districts, some soil associations were subdivided at the phase level on the basis of the changes observed in land types. Soil association legends for the relevant soil survey reports in the year of survey and in 1983 are shown in Table 6.3. Table 6.4 summarizes the changes in land types in individual soil associations in each of the soil survey report areas studied. Only the soil mapping units examined in the field during the study have been included in the table. A detailed summary of the changes in land types by physiographic units within survey area reports is given in Table 6.5 at the end of this chapter.

TABLE 6.3
Changes in soil association names

Soil survey report	In the year of survey	In 1983
Tangail District	9. Ghatail association	9. Ghatail association
		a. Medium Highland phase
		b. Medium Lowland phase
	10. Ghatail-Balina association	10. Ghatail-Balina association
		a. Medium Highland phase
		b. Medium Lowland phase
Kishoreganj and Sadar Subdivisions of Mymensingh District	34. Lokdeo-Ghatail association	34. Lokdeo-Ghatail association
	a. Smooth relief phase	a. Medium Highland phase
	b. Irregular relief phase	b. Irregular relief phase
		c. Medium Lowland phase
	35. Ghatail-Lokdeo association	35. Ghatail-Lokdeo association
		a. Medium Highland phase
		b. Medium Lowland phase
	36. Ghatail association	36. Ghatail association
		a. Medium Highland phase
		b. Medium Lowland phase
	37. Ghatail-Balina association	37. Ghatail-Balina association
		a. Medium Highland phase
		b. Medium Lowland and Lowland phases

6.3.5 Land use

The main changes in cropping patterns observed in each District studied are listed in Table 6.5. The following observations were made in the field regarding changes in the major cropping patterns that had taken place since the time of the original soil surveys.

  a. Transplanted aus was being grown increasingly on floodplain ridges, especially in Sylhet and Mymensingh Districts.

TABLE 6.4
Changes in land types between soil survey report and 1983 study[4]

Soil map unit	Highland %	Med. Highland %	Med. Lowland %	Lowland %	Very Lowland %
Jamalpur District					
1	+20	+40	-60	-	-
2	+5	+34	-29	-10	-
4	+17	- 2	-10	- 5	-
5a	-	+15	+ 5	-20	-
5b	-	-	+30	-30	-
12	-	+30	-50	+20	-
Tangail District					
3	+20	-20	Same	-	-
5	+30	-30	Same	-	-
6	-	+35	- 5	-30	-
Netrakona and Mymensingh Sadar North Subdivisions					
14	+ 5	- 2	- 3	-	-
16	+11	- 3	- 8	-	-
18	+ 5	+10	- 5	-10	-
19	+10	Same	- 5	- 5	-
20	+ 5	+ 5	+10	-20	-
27	-	+10	- 5	- 5	-
Faridpur Sadar and Goalundo Subdivisions					
1	+20	-10	-10	-	-
2	+20	-10	-10	-	-
5	+15	- 5	- 5	- 5	-
10	+ 5	-35	-30	-10	-
11	+10	+20	-10	-20	-
Madaripur and Gopalganj Subdivisions of Faridpur District					
2	+15	+20	-37	+ 2	-
6b	+14	+11	-25	Same	-
7	+ 5	+25	-30	Same	-
9	+15	+20	-15	-20	-
10	-	+10	+30	-40	-
14	+18	+50	- 5	-63	-
17	-	Same	+10	-10	-
20	-	-	+14	-14	-
Kushtia District					
1	+ 5	+10	- 5	-10	-
2	+35	-20	-15	-	-
6	+35	-30	- 5	-	-
14	+20	+15	+30	- 5	-

(Contd.)

---

[4] No changes were recorded in the following survey areas: Kishoreganj and Mymensingh Sadar South Subdivisions; Kurigram and Gaibandha Subdivisions of Rangpur District; and Sylhet District (all Subdivisions).

(Continued)

Soil map unit	Highland %	Med. Highland %	Med. Lowland %	Lowland %	Very Lowland %
Rajshahi District					
11b	+30	- 5	-35	+10	-
16	+15	+ 7	-20	- 2	-
17	+30	+ 1	-31	Same	-
36	+ 8	+18	+59	-85	-
37a	-	+ 5	+70	-75	-
37b	-	-	+75	-75	-
Pabna District					
Ganges Floodplain					
1	+20	-10	-10	-	-
6	+10	+10	-10	-10	-
8	+15	-20	+10	·+ 5	-10
16	+ 5	+35	-10	- 5	-25
20	-	-	-	+50	-50
Jamuna Floodplain					
28a	+25	Same	-25	-	-
28b	-	+10	+30	-40	-
36a	+20	- 5	-15	-	-
Bogra District					
4a	+15	- 15	Same	-	-
11	+20	+ 5	-25	-	-
12	+10	+15	-25	-	-
13	+ 6	+ 9	-15	-	-
16	+10	+15	-25	-	-15
Brahmanbaria Subdivision of Comilla District					
1	-	-	+35	-35	-
11	-	-	+15	-15	-
14	-	Same	Same	Same	-
19	-	-	+20	- 5	-15

b. Jute cultivation had declined on floodplain ridges in Faridpur Sadar Subdivision. Sugarcane had replaced jute as an alternative cash crop.

c. The change from Medium Lowland to Medium Highland had allowed the introduction of transplanted aman in place of broadcast (deepwater) aman paddy. Also, the conversion of shallowly-flooded Medium Highland into very-shallowly-flooded Medium Highland had allowed the introduction of HYV aman.

d. Very-deeply-flooded basins of the Sylhet Basin in Kishoreganj Subdivision were being used only for boro paddy. In the deeper parts (about 20 percent), local boro varieties were being grown; HYVs of boro were being grown in the remaining area. In the past, boro paddy was grown only in the basin depressions with the help of residual surface water, and the remaining area was used either for deepwater aman paddy or for grazing. The situation had changed with the introduction of low-lift pump irrigation in the 1960s.

e. Cultivators reported that deepwater aman cultivation in the south of the Sylhet Basin used to be safe, but that, following the construction of the Bhairab Bazar railway bridge across the Meghna river, drainage became congested and the deepwater aman paddy crop was regularly damaged by sudden rise of floodwater. As a result, the cultivation of aman had been abandoned in many areas and the land used for dry-season cattle grazing.[5]

f. The major cropping patterns in the two eastern Subdivisions of Sylhet District remained the same as when originally surveyed, both on the ridges and in the basins, but the proportions had changed. In rapidly-flooded basins, the cultivators had brought more areas of grassland under local boro paddy cultivation, mainly with manual irrigation. Before the end of the rainy season, the cultivators start to retain water on their fields by erecting bunds. Also, they use surface water from khals, beels, etc. for irrigation. Because of the severe risk of early flash floods in April-May, early-maturing varieties of boro paddy are grown, namely Koia, Bogra, Gorsi. On the ridges, Chengri and Murali were common local aus paddy varieties. Chengri was grown on the higher parts of ridges than Murali, and gave better yields.

g. In the mid-1960s, about 70 percent of the land in Hakaluki haor remained fallow. Local boro paddy was cultivated on about 25 percent of the area, and dryland crops such as mustard, sesamum and potato were grown on the remaining 5 percent of the area. Intensive cultivation started from 1969, and about 80 percent of the area had been converted to local boro paddy cultivation. Cultivators complained about drainage congestion caused by the construction of embankments along the rivers.

h. HYV boro paddy cultivation had been introduced in piedmont basins in Netrakona Subdivision in the late-1960s, replacing the former deepwater aman paddy. On the associated ridges, HYV boro paddy was being grown in rotation with transplanted aman paddy (which was sometimes damaged by flash floods from the adjoining hills).

i. HYV boro paddy in Tangail District included IR-8 in the south and Purbachi in the north. Among transplanted deepwater aman paddy varieties, Chamara was grown in the south and Haloi in the north.

j. Purbachi had become one of the main boro paddy HYVs in Jamalpur District. Haloi and Morian were the main transplanted deepwater aman varieties. Haloi was reported to grow well on fine-textured soils.

---

[5] *The Bhairab Bazar railway bridge was built in the 1930s. Drainage congestion upstream probably was caused not only by constriction of the river by the bridge, but also by the high railway embankments built across the adjoining floodplains.*

TABLE 6.5

Land types and major cropping patterns by survey area and physiographic unit

District (Year of survey)	Physiographic unit	Land type			Major cropping pattern[1]		Remarks
		Name	% in year of survey	% in 1983	In year of survey	In 1983	
Jamalpur (1966)	Active and Young Jamuna Floodplains	Highland	nil	5-20	-	U/j-Rc; M/u-TA-F/Rc	Unit 10 is shown; other units on ridges have the same land types and land use, except for 10-30% increase in the boro area
		Medium Highland	0-75	40-60	U/j-Rc; UBA-Rc/F; Rc-F	U/j-Rc; M/u-TA-F/Rc; UBA-Rc; M+BA-Rc	
		Medium Lowland	65-95	35	Barren; U/BA-Rc	UBA/j-Rc	
	Ridges of Old Brahmaputra and Jamuna Floodplains	Highland	30	50	Sugarcane; U/j-TA-F/Rc	Sugarcane; U/j-TA-F/Rc	
		Medium Highland	55	55	U/j-TA-Rc	U/j-TA-Rc/F	
	Basins of Old Brahmaputra and Jamuna Floodplains	Highland	nil	0-15	-	J/u-TA-Rc; HYV boro-TA-Rc/F	
		Medium Highland	5-65	7-75	U/j-TA-F	HYV boro-TA-Rc/F; HYV boro-DTA	
		Medium Lowland	20-45	10-75	UBA-F; BA-F	Boro-DTA/F	
		Lowland	5-40	0-10	Boro-F	Boro-F	
Tangail (1966)	Active Jamuna Floodplain	Highland	nil	10	-	U/j-Rc; UBA-Rc	In the original report, the percentages of land types were not shown separately
		Medium Highland	-	55	UBA-Rc	UBA-Rc; U/j-TA-Rc	
		Medium Lowland	-	28	UBA-Rc	UBA-Rc; BA-Rc	
		Lowland	-	2	-	BA-F	
	Ridges of Jamuna meander Floodplain	Highland	nil	15-35	-	U/j-Rc; U/j-TA-Rc/F	
		Medium Highland	25-80	45-65	UBA-Rc; U/j-TA-Rc	U/j-TA-Rc/F; HYV boro-TA/DTA-F/Rc	
		Medium Lowland	10-65	6-10	UBA-Rc	HYV boro-F; HYV boro-DTA; UBA-Rc	
	Basins of Jamuna meander Floodplain	Highland	nil	<1	-	J/U-Rc	
		Medium Highland	nil	35	UBA-Rc	HYV boro-TA/DTA; U/j-TA-Rc/F; UBA-Rc	
		Medium Lowland	40-45	40-50	UBA/BA-Rc/F	HYV boro-DTA/F; UBA-Rc	
		Lowland	40-50	10	UBA/BA-Rc/F	HYV boro-F; UBA-F/Rc	

(Contd.)

(Continued)

District (Year of survey)	Physiographic unit	Land type			Major cropping pattern[1]		Remarks
		Name	% in year of survey	% in 1983	In year of survey	In 1983	
Netrakona and Sadar Sub-divisions of Mymensingh (1968)	Ridges of Old Brahmaputra Floodplain	Highland	45	50	U/j-TA-F/Rc	U/j-TA-Rc/F	
		Medium Highland	35	33	U/j-TA-F/Rc	U/j-TA-Rc/F; HYV boro-TA	
		Medium Lowland	5	2	BA-F	HYV boro-TA/TDA	
	Ridges with associated basins of Old Brahmaputra Floodplain	Highland	10-30	30-46	U/j-TA-F/Rc	U/j-TA-Rc/F	
		Medium Highland	5-60	15-30	U/j-TA-F; U/F-TA-F	HYV boro-TA-F; U-TA-F	
		Medium Lowland	20-45	14-40	BA-F	HYV boro-F; BA-F	
		Lowland	5-10	0-5	Boro-F	Boro-F	
	Basins of Old Brahmaputra Floodplain	Highland	0-5	0-10	U/j-TA-F/Rc	J/u-TA-Rc	
		Medium Highland	10-15	20-35	U/j-TA-F	U/j-TA-F/Rc; HYV boro-TA	
		Medium Lowland	15-30	10-50	BA-F	Boro-F/TA; BA-F	
		Lowland	40-70	10-60	Boro-F; grassland	Boro-F	
Sadar and Goalundo Subdivisions of Faridpur (1969)	Active and Very Young Ganges River Floodplains	Highland	nil	20	-	U/j-Rc	
		Medium Highland	70-75	60-65	J/U-Rc; UBA-Rc	UBA-Rc; U/j-Rc	
		Medium Lowland	20-25	10-15	UBA-Rc	UBA-Rc	
	Mixed Young and Older Ganges meander Floodplain	Highland	0-15	10-30	U/j-Rc	U/j-Rc; sugarcane	
		Medium Highland	25-50	35-45	UBA-Rc; U/j-Rc	BA-Rc; UBA-Rc; U-TA-F/Rc	
		Medium Lowland	15-50	10-38	UBA-Rc	UBA-Rc; BA-Rc	
		Lowland	5-25	0-15	BA-F	BA-F	
	Older Ganges meander Floodplain	Highland	0-10	0-15	U/j-Rc	U/j-Rc; sugarcane	
		Medium Highland	10-20	30-50	UBA-Rc	UBA-Rc; BA-Rc	
		Medium Lowland	50-55	20-45	UBA-Rc	BA-Rc; UBA-Rc; HYV boro-F	
		Lowland	15-30	5-15	BA-F; UBA-F	BA-F; HYV boro-F	

(Contd.)

(Continued)

District (Year of survey)	Physiographic unit	Land type			Major cropping pattern[1]		Remarks
		Name	% in year of survey	% in 1983	In year of survey	In 1983	
Madaripur and Gopalganj Subdivisions of Faridpur (1970)	Active and Very Young Ganges River Floodplains	Highland	nil	0-15	U/j-Rc	U/j-Rc	
		Medium Highland	20-25	25-40	U/j-Rc; UBA-Rc	UBA-Rc	
		Medium Lowland	70	33-50	UBA-Rc	UBA-Rc	
		Lowland	0-5	7-15	UBA-F	UBA/F-Rc; HYV boro-F	
	Young Ganges meander Floodplain	Highland	0-10	14-15	J/u-Rc	J/u-Rc; UBA-Rc	
		Medium Highland	30-60	35-41	J/u-Rc; UBA-Rc	UBA-Rc; j/u-Rc	
		Medium Lowland	25-65	38-39	UBA-Rc; BA-Rc	UBA-Rc; BA-Rc	
		Lowland	0-5	1-2	UBA-F	UBA-F	
	Old Ganges meander Floodplain	Highland	nil	0-15	-	J/u-Rc	
		Medium Highland	10-15	20-35	UBA-Rc; BA-Rc	UBA-Rc; BA-Rc; j/u-Rc	
		Medium Lowland	15-45	30-45	UBA-Rc	UBA-Rc; BA-Rc; HYV boro-F/BA	
		Lowland	30-65	5-25	UBA-Rc; BA-F	BA-F/Rc; HYV boro-F/BA	
	Lower Meghna estuarine Floodplain	Highland	nil	18-20	-	U/j-Rc	
		Medium Highland	5-10	8-55	U/j-Rc; UBA-Rc	UBA-Rc; HYV boro-DTA/BA-F	
		Medium Lowland	10-55	10-55	UBA-Rc	BA-Rc; UBA-F	
		Lowland	30-80	30-80	UBA/F-Rc	Boro-F; BA-Rc/F	
	Mixed Lower Meghna estuarine Floodplain and peat basins	Highland	nil	nil	-	-	
		Medium Highland	nil	nil	-	-	
		Medium Lowland	nil	14	-	UBA-Rc/F	
		Lowland	100	85	UBA-F; BA-F	UBA-F; boro-F	
Kushtia (1970)	Active Ganges River Floodplain	Highland	nil	5	U-Rc	U-Rc	Area outside Ganges-Kobadak Project
		Medium Highland	20	28	U/j/M-Rc/F; barren	U/j-Rc	
		Medium Lowland	50	45	ditto	U/UBA-Rc	
		Lowland	30	20	Barren	U/UBA-Rc; barren	
	Young Ganges meander Floodplain	Highland	10	45	J/u-Rc; sugarcane	Sugarcane; u/j-Rc	
		Medium Highland	65	35	UBA/j-Rc; sugarcane	UBA-Rc; U/j-Rc	
		Medium Lowland	10	5	UBA-Rc/F	UBA-Rc	

(Contd.)

(Continued)

District (Year of survey)	Physiographic unit	Land type			Major cropping pattern[1]		Remarks
		Name	% in year of survey	% in 1983	In year of survey	In 1983	
	Old Ganges meander Floodplain	Highland	5	25	J/u-Rc; sugarcane	Sugarcane; U/j-Rc	
		Medium Highland	20	35	UBA-Rc; u/j-Rc; sugarcane	UBA-Rc/F; U/j-Rc	
		Medium Lowland	55	25	UBA-Rc/F; BA-Rc/F	UBA-Rc/F	
		Lowland	15	10	UBA-F; BA-F	HYV boro-F; U-F	
Rajshahi (1966)	Old Ganges meander Floodplain	Highland	0-5	35-60	U/j-Rc	U/j-Rc; UBA-Rc	
		Medium Highland	40-55	30-55	UBA-Rc; U/j-Rc	UBA-Rc; BA-Rc	
		Medium Lowland	30-50	0-15	BA-F/Rc; UBA-F/Rc	BA-Rc; HYV boro-DTA	
		Lowland	nil	0-10	-	HYV boro-DTA/F	
	Mixed younger and older Ganges meander Floodplains	Highland	10-20	20-50	U-Rc	U/j-Rc; sugarcane	
		Medium Highland	10-30	31-34	UBA-Rc	UBA-Rc; BA-Rc; HYV boro-TA/DTA	
		Medium Lowland	25-40	14-25	UBA-Rc; BA-F/Rc	BA-F; HYV boro-F/DTA	
		Lowland	0-45	0-20	BA-F	BA-F	
	Old Little Jamuna meander Floodplain	Highland	nil	0-8	-	U/j-Rc	
		Medium Highland	nil	5-21	-	HYV boro-BA/F	
		Medium Lowland	0-20	70	BA-F	BA-F; HYV boro-BA/F	
		Lowland	75-95	0-20	BA-F	BA-F	
Pabna (Revised 1972)	Active and Very Young Ganges River Floodplain	Highland	nil	20-35	-	U/j-Rc	Land use in 1983 as recorded for soil association 2
		Medium Highland	5-70	50-60	U/j-Rc;UBA-Rc	U/j-Rc; HYV boro-F	
		Medium Lowland	25-75	5-15	UBA-Rc; BA-Rc/F; U/j-Rc	HYV boro-F; UBA-Rc	
		Lowland	5-60	0-5	BA-F/Rc	HYV boro-F	
	Young Ganges meander Floodplain	Highland	10-40	25-40	U/j-Rc	U/j-Rc; HYV boro-TA; sugarcane	
		Medium Highland	20-40	20-30	U/j-TA-Rc; UBA-Rc/F	HYV boro-TA; BA-Rc; U-TA-F/Rc	
		Medium Lowland	10-15	5-20	UBA-Rc/F	BA-Rc; UBA-Rc	
		Lowland	5-10	0-15	BA-F/Rc	BA-F	
		Very Lowland	0-15	nil	BA-F	-	

(Contd.)

(Continued)

District (Year of survey)	Physiographic unit	Land type			Major cropping pattern[1]		Remarks
		Name	% in year of survey	% in 1983	In year of survey	In 1983	
	Older Ganges meander Floodplain	Highland	5-10	5-10	U/j-Rc; sugarcane	U/J-Rc; HYV boro-TA; U/j-TA-F	
		Medium Highland	35-75	30-43	U/j-Rc; UBA-Rc; U/j-TA-Rc	HYV boro-TA; U/j-TA-F/Rc	
		Medium Lowland	5-50	10-15	UBA-Rc; BA-Rc/F	HYV boro-TA/DTA; UBA-Rc; BA-F	
		Lowland	minor-15	2-5	BA-F	BA-F	
	Oldest Ganges meander Floodplain	Highland	nil	8-15	-	UBA-Rc; U/j-Rc	
		Medium Highland	5-20	5-40	U/j-Rc; UBA-Rc; U/j-TA-Rc	UBA/-Rc; BA-Rc; HYV boro-TA	
		Medium Lowland	10-20	10-30	BA-Rc; UBA-Rc	UBA-Rc; HYV boro-F; BA-F/Rc	
		Lowland	15-35	15-50	UBA-Rc; BA-Rc/F	BA-Rc; HYV boro-F	
		Very Lowland	10-100	10-50	UBA-Rc; BA-F/Rc; grassland	BA-F/Rc	
	Jamuna and Karatoya meander Floodplains						
	a. Protected phase	Highland	10-15	25-40	U/j-Rc; U/j-TA-Rc/F	U/j-Rc; UBA-Rc	
		Medium Highland	45-70	4-65	U/j-Rc; UBA-Rc; U/j-TA-F/Rc	UBA-Rc; HYV boro-TA; U-TA-F/Rc	
		Medium Lowland	25-40	5-20	UBA-Rc/F	UBA-Rc; HYV boro-TA/DTA/BA	
	b. Unprotected phase	Highland	nil	0-5	-	-	Land use in 1983 as recorded for soil association 28b
		Medium Highland	0-5	25-28	UBA-Rc	UBA/J-Rc	
		Medium Lowland	40-55	45-50	U/j/M/F-Rc/F; UBA-Rc	UBA-Rc; HYV boro-F	
		Lowland	30-60	15-20	U/Til+BA-Rc; UBA-Rc	UBA-Rc	
Bogra (1970)	Karatoya-Bangali meander Floodplain	Highland	0-15	11-33	U/j-Rc	U/j-Rc; U/j-TA-Rc	
		Medium Highland	40-65	55-60	U/j-TA-F/Rc	U/j-TA-Rc/F; HYV boro-TA	
		Medium Lowland	30-45	2-20	UBA-F; BA-F	HYV boro-F; BA-F	

(Contd.)

(Continued)

District (Year of survey)	Physiographic unit	Land type			Major cropping pattern [1]		Remarks
		Name	% in year of survey	% in 1983	In year of survey	In 1983	
Brahmanbaria Subdivision of Comilla (1973)	Sandy and silty alluvium of Meghna Floodplain	Highland	nil	nil	-	-	
		Medium Highland	nil	nil	-	-	
		Medium Lowland	15	50	UBA-Rc; BA-Rc	BA-Rc; HYV boro-F	
		Lowland	55	20	BA-Rc;UBA-Rc	BA-Rc	
	Old Meghna Estuarine Floodplain	Highland	nil	nil	-	-	
		Medium Highland	0-40	0-40	U/j-TA-Rc/F	HYV boro-TA/DTA-Rc/F; U/j-TA-Rc	
		Medium Lowland	15-55	30-60	UBA-Rc; BA-Rc; U/j-TA-Rc/F	HYV boro-BA/TA/DTA; UBA-Rc; BA-Rc	
		Lowland	0-60	0-45	BA-F; UBA-Rc/F	HYV boro-F/Rc; BA-F/Rc	
		Very Lowland	0-45	0-30	BA-F	Boro-F	
	Tista Floodplain [2]	Highland	nil	nil	-	-	
		Medium Highland	0-minor	0-2	J-TA-F	J-TA-F	
		Medium Lowland	nil	0-5	-	HYV boro-F	
		Lowland	5-20	38-58	Boro-F; grassland	Boro (HYV & local)-F	
		Very Lowland	75-85	30-40	Boro-F	Boro (local)-F	

Notes: 1. The symbols used for crops/cropping patterns:

U	=	Broadcast aus	UBA	=	Mixed aus and aman
TU	=	Transplanted aus	TA	=	Transplanted aman
BA	=	Broadcast aman	DTA	=	Deepwater transplanted aman
J	=	Jute			

M	=	Millet
Rc	=	Rabi crops
F	=	Fallow
HYV	=	High-yielding variety

2. This is a local floodplain, not the Teesta Floodplain (Region 3).

Chapter 7

LAND MADE DERELICT BY NON-AGRICULTURAL ACTIVITIES[1]

This chapter is complementary to Chapter 5. It focuses on the extent of land occupied by brickyards and derelict tanks, and on possible ways to restore such sites to productive use. Some further information on rural settlements and urban land use is also provided.

7.1 INTRODUCTION

7.1.1 Objectives

The objective of the Consultant's mission was to assess, in selected areas of Bangladesh, the extent of village land made derelict by use for brick-making and other non-agricultural uses, and to recommend practical means for restoring derelict land to productive use.

7.1.2 Background

The study by Serno (1981) — see Chapter 5 — was undertaken to assess the rate of expansion of homestead land, based on a comparison of aerial photographs taken in 1952 and 1974. The conclusion was reached that, in the seven rural Thanas studied, the homestead area had increased from 8.3 to 8.5 percent and the area of tanks had increased from 1.4 to 1.6 percent, representing a net expansion of 0.4 percent during the 22 years.

The Agricultural Census of Bangladesh in 1977 (BBS, 1981) gave a figure of 11.3 percent for the uncultivated area as a proportion of the total farm area. Compared with the 1960 Census, the uncultivated area had decreased by 100,000 acres. A study by Aliff International (1981) calculated the homestead complex to be 11 percent of the total farm area. From the three sources referred to, it appeared that the figure for the 'uncultivated' area was about 11 percent.

Data presented at a Seminar on Integrated Rural Development (Islam, 1975) showed that settlement and associated non-agricultural land use amounted to 14.8 percent, while

---

[1] *During field trips in the 1970s, the author (HB) observed that new brickyards were taking significant amounts of land out of cultivation. Accordingly, it was decided to engage a consultant to study the extent of the problem and investigate possible ways to restore damaged land to productive use under a proposed Thana Land Use Development Programme. This chapter presents the findings and recommendations of the study carried out by T. Jager, Land Use Consultant, under the FAO/UNDP Agricultural Development Adviser Project (Jager, 1982). Except where stated otherwise, the information relates to the time of the field study, January-March 1982. Statements originally made in the present tense have been converted to the past tense to make that clear.*

permanent water bodies occupied 9 percent (total 23.8 percent). The view of the Department of Architecture of the Bangladesh University of Engineering and Technology (BUET) was that settlement would soon reach the 20 percent mark and that measures must be taken to limit further expansion.

The Consultant felt that adequate data were provided by the studies referred to above to ensure a reasonable estimate for the homestead area. How the homestead area was used is discussed in a later section. Apart from the expansion of human settlement, farmland was being encroached on for brick-making and the expansion of urban centres. Especially from 1970 onwards, the number of brickyards increased rapidly, occupying and consuming more land due to increased building activities: (see Table 7.1).

TABLE 7.1
Annual compound growth rate in the construction sector

Period	Annual growth rate %
1973-75	(−)2.3
1975-78	7.8
1978-80	17.8
1980-85 (projected)	14.4

Source: Bangladesh Draft Second Five-Year Plan, 1980-1985.

In 1981, the total number of brick-burning units in the private sector was estimated to be 2,102 (Aliff International, 1981), producing 1,200 million bricks annually. In addition, some 400 million bricks were being produced annually by private contractors for public sector agencies such as the Roads & Highways Department, Public Works Department and Bangladesh Water Development Board.[2] That probably brought the number of brickyards operating in 1981 to about 2,500, consuming about 145 million cubic feet of soil each year. Obviously, bricks are needed, and the demand will grow in the future, but use of the land should be such that the long-term land productivity is least affected. Abandoned brickyards should therefore be restored as economically productive sites.

Village tanks and ponds under good management can easily produce 12-18 maunds of fish annually: (see Chapter 17). Many of the tanks observed during fieldwork appeared to be derelict. Since derelict tanks could also be improved and then contribute to the country's need for protein, they were also included in the assessment of derelict village land.

Another menace to farm land is the expansion of urban centres. Of course, expansion of such population centres cannot be halted, but the quality of the farmland could be taken into account in planning urban expansion: (see Chapter 24). Also, the pressure on farmland could be reduced by using the land in such a way that the most economic use of it is made. That this is not always the case was frequently observed, especially around Government buildings. This aspect was also examined, therefore.

---

[2] *Bricks are needed not only for buildings and works structures. They are also needed for use in road foundations (both as whole bricks and crushed aggregate) because of the lack of suitable rock material for this purpose in Bangladesh.*

7.2 PROGRAMME OF WORK

The Consultant arrived in Bangladesh on 21 January 1982 and departed on 12 March 1982. As a start, a literature survey was carried out. Especially on brickyards, a number of relevant reports had recently been published (referred to in relevant sections below). Not much information was given, however, on the methods of excavation which determine, to a large extent, the possibilities of restoring the land to productive use. Neither were data available on the presence of abandoned brickyards. For this reason, field trips were made to Comilla, Sylhet, Kushtia, Rajshahi, Bogra and Mymensingh Districts. Apart from interviewing brickyard operators and farmers, estimates were made of the area under abandoned brickyards and the area of derelict tanks. In order to recommend on methods of restoring derelict brickyards to productive use, one abandoned brickyard was measured and a calculation was made of the number of man-months of labour that might be required for reclamation.

In addition, five of the seven Thanas studied by Serno were visited in order to estimate the area of fallow land and to gain an impression of the productivity of homestead land. In Rajshahi, some time was spent to find out whether land acquired by the Government for construction of buildings was properly used. In order to study waste of land in part of the Dhaka town area, an analysis was carried out with help of aerial photographs to determine the area not being used for construction purposes.

Originally, it had been intended to use airphotos for assessing the area occupied by brickyards. However, the most recent airphotos available were for 1974, while the majority of brickyards were of more recent dates. For that reason, it was decided not to make a detailed photo-analysis of selected areas. Fortunately, the study of brickyards made by Aliff International (1981) had become available, which provided valuable up-to-date information on the number and area of brickyards.

Results of discussions with many persons from different Government Departments and projects also contributed greatly to the final results of the mission.

The Consultant's findings and conclusions are reported in Sections 7.3-7.7 below.

7.3 BRICKYARDS

7.3.1 Introduction

A detailed study of brickyards in Dhaka District was conducted by Aziz (1979). Aliff International (1981) and Hussain (1982) also collected data regarding the number and size of brickyards. According to Aziz, half of the brickyards in Dhaka District were within urban areas. He estimated that, each year, about six acres of land were deeply excavated (average 25 feet) within urban and potential urban areas, and that about 70 percent of the brickyards procured their soil material through limited excavations (1-7 feet). The latter was considered more beneficial to farmers because, in that way, land formerly used for cultivating aman paddy could be then used for boro paddy. For that reason, one of his main recommendations was that brickyard operators should be stopped from making deep excavations and should be encouraged to use limited-depth excavations. Aziz gave an average quarry size as 1 acre.[3]

---

[3] *Further information on brickyards around Dhaka is given in Chapter 10, Section 10.3.1.*

7.3.2 Optimum depth of excavation

From the perspective of sustained land use, the optimum depth of brickyard excavation should be defined as the depth of excavation that least affects the potential for long-term food production. Frequently, because of the removal of a somewhat coarser-textured upper soil layer (usually silt loam or silty clay loam), boro paddy production can be increased as a result of shallow excavation. However, other crops (especially dryland rabi crops) will generally show a negative response to loss of surface soil material.

Since farmers consider paddy to be by far the most important crop, they will prefer shallow excavation so long as they expect a higher crop yield. However, since rabi crops are becoming more and more important, one questions whether excavation of the upper soil is wise in the long term.

On the other hand, despite the loss of farmland which it entails, deep excavation is not always harmful for food production. In urban and potential urban areas, deep excavation should be strongly discouraged. However, in rural areas, it can be argued that many bricks can be produced from a small area if deep excavations are made, provided that the sediments are suitable for brick-making, and the borrow-pit can later be transformed into a productive fish pond. Often, however, the deposits of suitable sediments are too shallow for deep excavations to be made.

A moderately deep excavation can be harmful for food production since the borrow-pit may contain some water during the dry season, which prevents its use for dryland rabi crops, but may not allow for a productive fish pond unless it is re-excavated. It was estimated during the study that excavation below 5 feet usually made crop production impossible, excavation between 3-5 feet could be harmful, while excavation to shallower depths was considered to be least harmful to crop production.

7.3.3 Area, depth and size of excavations

From data provided by Aziz (1979) and from road counts, an estimate is given in Table 7.2 of the area excavated in different depth classes in 1981. Given the assumptions made in Section 7.3.2, about 225 (45 + 100 + 160/2) acres of agricultural land were made unsuitable for agricultural use in 1981. If one further considers that deep and very shallow excavations were less common in previous years, the maximum area of land made unsuitable for agriculture during the previous ten years reached about 2,500 acres. That is a very rough

TABLE 7.2
Area occupied by brickyards by depth-of-excavation class

Depth of excavation (feet)	% of total	Area occupied (acres)
1.5-3	40	660
3-5	20	165
5-8	20	100
> 8	20	45

Source: Aziz (1979).

estimate, of course, but it nevertheless indicates that the area is relatively small. Much larger is the area occupied by the storage and furnace areas of brickyards. Aziz gave an average size of brickyards, excluding the quarry area, of 4.1 acres. Hussain (1982) gave a figure of 3.3 acres. The Consultant's findings indicated a slightly higher figure (4.5 acres). These figures suggest that the total area occupied by brickyards in 1981 was about 11,250 acres.

7.3.4 Methods of excavation

The methods of excavation observed on the field trips to Comilla-Srimangal, Kushtia-Rajshahi-Bogra and Mymensingh are discussed separately below.

Dhaka. Immediately around Dhaka city, brickyards were concentrated in areas with very deep silt loam and silty clay loam floodplain sediments. During the monsoon season, these areas are deeply flooded. Very deep excavations prevailed in these areas: borrow-pits up to 50 feet deep were observed. Usually, fish were found in such borrow-pits after the flood season, but proper fish culture was not practised.

The total number of private brickyards in Dhaka District was estimated at 424 (Aliff International, 1981). There were also four automatic brickyards. One such brickyard in Sabhar Thana was visited. There, the local Madhupur Clay was mixed with sandy loam (25 percent). To-date, about 7 acres had been deeply excavated (ca 20 feet). Since that area was of low agricultural potential, the operation was not considered to be a menace to valuable farmland. Apart from the excavation, the brickyard occupied about 8 acres. Another 700 acres, it was said, belonged to the brickyard and was being cultivated by share-croppers.

Comilla-Srimangal. In the Comilla area, shallow excavations prevailed. The reason was two-fold. Firstly, the farmers preferred to sell the upper part of the soil, either so as to dispose of loamy material in order to make the soil more suitable for boro paddy cultivation (on land where the upper part of the soil was underlain by clay), or so as to lower the land surface to flood-level so that moisture was more easily available to crops. Secondly, it was often found that the substratum proved too sandy or clayey to be suitable for brick-making. Where that material proved to be too sandy, usually 1½ feet of (silty) clay loam was left to maintain soil productivity. However, even where the loamy material was thick, the farmer was not willing to sell more soil than he considered was sensible.

Only twice was a moderately-deep excavation encountered in Comilla District. Field checking indicated that the operators appeared to be contractors to the Government Roads & Highways Department (RHD). At one site, three brickyards were observed close together, one being run by a contractor, the other two privately owned. The difference was striking. According to our informant, the land of the RHD site had been acquired 16 years previously, but operation of the brickyard had not started until 1981. Usually, private brickyard operators could not afford to buy land from farmers because of the high price (in return for the relatively shallow suitable silt loam deposits). Close to Comilla, the price of farmland (in 1981) was close to Tk.150,000 per acre.

The Deodar Cooperative in Comilla, located in the Chakla-Bharella soil association where the subsoil is clayey, paid farmers Tk.2,500 per acre for 1½ feet depth of surface soil material. Commonly, farmers who had sold soil material said that they spent Tk.1,500 per acre on fertilizer and manure, after which they said they obtained a higher paddy harvest than before.

One brickyard owner said that he paid Tk.2,000 per acre for 1 foot of upper soil material; another said that he paid Tk.5,000 per acre for 2 feet of material. The average was close to

Tk.2,000 per acre-foot. In the Comilla area, the brickyards were located on the country's most productive soils. Farmers were getting high yields due to good management and irrigation. Usually, three (sometimes four) crops were being grown in a year.

Comilla District had 130 brickyards (Aliff International, 1981). The size was smaller than in the rest of the country. It was estimated that about 500 acres of high-potential farmland was occupied by brickyards.

In the Srimangal area of Sylhet District, as in Comilla District, shallow excavations prevailed. Brickyard owners bought surface soil material from farmers, who were eager to preserve the agricultural potential of their land. Often, the subsurface material in this area proved to be too clayey for brick-making. The few brickyards observed occupied double-cropped land (aus-transplanted aman).

One brickyard practising deep excavation was observed near Srimangal town. The owner said that he had applied for a loan to enable him to stock the deeply-excavated area (ca 2 acres) with fish after completion of excavation work.

Dhaka-Kushtia. Out of a total of 32 brickyards observed, only at two sites was the shallow excavation method observed. Especially around Faridpur town, deep to very deep excavations (20 feet) prevailed. In Faridpur, one brickyard owner said that, due to the sandy texture of the upper soil layer (0-3 feet), he was requested by a farmer to transform part of his land into a fish pond, because he expected to obtain higher returns from fish-farming than from arable cropping.

Again, there was a significant difference in excavation depth between brickyards that were operated on Government contracts (*inter alia*, for BWDB) and those that were privately owned. Usually, excavations by private owners were deeper and more neatly excavated because they were planning to transform the sites into productive fish ponds. Apart from being shallower (12-14 feet), the Government-contract excavations were made more haphazardly, making possible future re-excavation for fish farming very expensive. The area around Faridpur occupied by brickyards operated by contractors was said to be about 90 acres.

Between Magura and Kushtia, only a few brickyards were observed, because building activities were almost nil in that area. The main crops grown on the land surrounding the brickyards were transplanted aman and wheat.

Kushtia-Rajshahi. Along the Kushtia-Rajshahi road, brickyards with deep borrow-pits containing water throughout the year were common. Usually, sandy loam was mixed with the clay loam or silty clay soil material to prevent the bricks from cracking after they were moulded. That is understandable because the lime-rich Ganges sediments contain montmorillonite (a cracking clay). The main crops in the area were sugarcane and transplanted aman paddy, the latter possibly followed by a rabi crop (tobacco). Shallow excavations were observed, due either to the presence of a sandy substratum or shallow groundwater. One such example was a 10-acre RHD brickyard where, although the shallowly-excavated land appeared to be suitable for boro paddy cultivation, that was not being practised.

Rajshahi. Around Rajshahi town, many firewood-operated brickyards were observed. The kiln usually had the shape of a house or tower (*bangla bhata*), as opposed to the big kilns with transportable chimneys observed elsewhere. It was said that, if only firewood was available, the *bangla bhata* gave better bricks. Usually, excavations in this area were very deep. That contractors can also do a good job was observed in Balia village where a well-excavated pond was found, suitable for re-excavation for fish farming. In most cases, the local soil material was mixed with 25 percent of sandy loam or silt loam material.

Bogra. Between Nator and Bogra, no operating brickyards were encountered. On the Barind Tract around Bogra town, Madhupur Clay material was used for brick-making. In order to prevent cracking of the moulded bricks, 50 percent sandy loam material (recent floodplain alluvium) was added. Only the coarser-textured, weathered Madhupur Clay was used. The unweathered subsurface clay was not considered suitable for brick-making at all. Nor was such material suitable for agriculture. Excavations were usually shallow and were hardly detrimental for agricultural potential considering the existing land use. Removal of the upper soil material would certainly affect the yields of rabi crops, but on the Barind Tract around Bogra town only a single crop of transplanted aman paddy was normally grown. With irrigation, two transplanted paddy crops could be grown (and should be encouraged).[4]

Mymensingh. Along the Dhaka-Tangail-Mymensingh road, the majority of brickyards procured their soil material from shallow excavations. They were especially concentrated in the area west of Joydebpur (Kunabari). North of Tangail, a few brickyards with moderately deep to deep borrow-pits were encountered. Brickyards in that area usually occupied very productive, silt loam, floodplain soils.

7.3.5 Discussion

Many deep excavations around Dhaka are located in potential urban areas. Reclamation in terms of filling up tanks would be very costly and possibly not feasible. Aziz (1979) calculated a figure of Tk.180,000 for filling a borrow-pit 28 feet deep occupying 1 acre. Using the tanks for intensive fish farming would seem to be the only economic possibility. In flooded areas, an embankment is needed to prevent the stocked fish from escaping from the pond during high floods. The investment can also be high, but Aziz considered that the returns to fish farming could be profitable under good management.

Deep borrow-pits in rural areas should also be stocked with fish. However, the Consultant was told that a deep tank belonging to the large automatic brick factory at Sabhar and excavated in the Madhupur Clay was not good for fish farming. Further research is needed to find out why that should be so. Possible reasons are low pH and related deficiency in calcium, and the high iron content.

Part of the moderately deep excavations should also be re-excavated to make them suitable for intensive fish farming. The excavated soil could be used for the embankment. The reclamation of abandoned brickyards is discussed in the next section.

In the case of Government-owned brickyards, it should be explicitly stated in future contracts that deep and moderately deep excavations should be made suitable for fish farming before the contractor leaves the site. The concerned Government Departments should examine the brickyard and specify how the contractor should carry out the required work. Why that is necessary is shown in the next section. The fish ponds could be rented to interested parties, based on long-term renewable leases.

---

[4] *Subsequent to the time of the study, tube-well irrigation spread extensively on the Barind Tract west of Bogra, converting much former single-cropped land growing local varieties of transplanted aman paddy into double-cropped HYV boro-HYV aman land.*

7.4 ABANDONED BRICKYARDS

7.4.1 Introduction

Brickyards operated by contractors to public sector agencies are abandoned when the required number of bricks has been made. Along the routes travelled by the Consultant, some 280 acres of abandoned and uncultivated brickyards were observed. Most of the land could easily have been reclaimed. Only one small abandoned brickyard was observed that was owned by a private person. Obviously, private owners seldom abandon their brickyards. If suitable soil is no longer available on the site, they buy material from neighbouring farmers and, if necessary, transport it by lorry to their site.

7.4.2 Findings

Abandoned brickyards were encountered throughout the country, even on the country's most productive soils. Not far from Comilla (at Kurpai), a recently-abandoned brickyard of 16 acres was observed, surrounded by irrigated land. A tube-well was present near the edge of the abandoned land. The newly-derelict land could easily have been cleaned and reclaimed, and transposed into high-potential agricultural land.

Between Srimangal and Comilla, an estimated 54 acres of abandoned brickyards were observed, all owned by RHD and abandoned between 1977 and 1981. Usually, the land had been acquired many years before the operators had started work. Of one RHD brickyard, which had become operative only recently, it was said that the land had been acquired 15 years earlier.

Many abandoned brickyards were counted along the Dhaka-Kushtia-Rajshahi road. The total estimate amounted to 153 acres, of which 3 acres had been occupied by a privately-owned brickyard and the rest by contractors to public-sector agencies.

One site about seven miles north of the Ganges river, along the road to Nator, had been abandoned in 1964. Part of the abandoned brick stock had the mark C and B which was used prior to 1963. The area, comprising about 25 acres of formerly double-cropped land (transplanted aman followed by a rabi crop, often tobacco), could easily have been reclaimed. Another 75 acres of abandoned brickyards were observed along the Nator-Bogra and Bogra-Nagarbari roads.

Just north of Jhenaida in Jessore District, a large abandoned RHD brickyard was observed, estimated at 30 acres. Part had been abandoned in 1965 and the rest in 1980. The area had been unevenly excavated.

Between Kaliakair and Mymensingh, the area of abandoned brickyards was estimated at about 30 acres. Just east of Tangail (Nagarjalpai), a large (15 acres) abandoned brickyard was observed which is described in detail in Annexe 2 to this chapter. Along this road, too, some reclaimed brickyards were present. South of Mymensingh, on the road to Bhaluka, many reclaimed brickyards were observed on highly productive farmland. According to the farmers, the time needed for restoration of the land used for brick storage amounted to two man-months per acre. Reclamation of the kiln area took more time and was often not yet complete.

An abandoned brickyard taken on lease by the Government was also visited. The farmers had cultivated their land again, apart from the kiln site which had not yet been returned to them. This example showed clearly that, if Government needed land for the establishment of brickyards, food production would best be served by temporary requisitioning of land in the form of a lease.

Table 7.3 gives information on the year of abandonment and the area made derelict for brickyards encountered on field trips to Comilla-Srimangal, Rajshahi-Bogra and Mymensingh. Obviously, there exist many more abandoned brickyards, but a reliable estimate for the whole country is not available.

TABLE 7.3
Year of abandoning brickyard and area made derelict

Year of abandoning	Area made derelict (acres)
1964	25
1965	15
1974	54
1975	27
1977	23
1978	26
1979	5
1980	58
1981	44
1982	2

Source: Consultant's counts along Comilla-Srimangal, Rajshahi-Bogra and Dhaka-Tangail-Mymensingh roads.

7.4.3 Discussion

The Consultant was disturbed by the amount of agricultural land that could be damaged by a relatively few contractors. Contractors to Government agencies were not bound by specifications regarding how to excavate the land or on how to restore the site after excavation ended. Private owners could not afford to handle their land in the same way.

Government generally acquired the land many years before brick-making started, obviously because of the rising land prices. However, that practice should be abandoned, because the farmers cultivating the land would keep their investments low because they did not know when the land would be taken over by the contractors, resulting in low crop returns.

Apparently, the former owners could buy back the land from Government for a nominal price when it was no longer required: see Annexe 1. Probably, the farmers were not properly informed, and procedures for recovering the land were too complicated. Therefore, Government should lease rather than acquire land. After brick production ceases, the land should be levelled and the farmers compensated for the losses of harvests and soil. RHD officials stated that they had abandoned such a system because it proved too costly as a result of unfounded claims by farmers (Annexe 1).

Reclaiming land occupied by abandoned brickyards is technically feasible. The problem is to determine who should do it and what happens to the reclaimed land. It was the Consultant's opinion that the best way to restore land would be to return it to the farmers for a nominal price. As mentioned earlier, there are legal provisions to do so. The farmers would then clean and level the land themselves before returning it to cultivation.

However, in the original land acquisition, as many as 40-50 farmers (possibly more) may have been involved. Also, because much of the land was acquired a long time before brick-making started, some of the former owners may have died in the meantime, which could give rise to ownership disputes.

If the farmers are not interested in recovering the land, or if there are ownership disputes that cannot be resolved, then the land could be reclaimed by the local government under the Rural Works Programme or the Food-for-Work Programme. A calculation of the cost of reclamation of an abandoned brickyard in terms of man-months of labour required is given in Annexe 2. After reclamation, the land could be rented to landless families.

In some places, contractors and private owners were observed to be operating within a close distance of each other. Government should preferably commission brick manufacture by private brickyard operators. However, where that might not be possible, the land should be obtained on a temporary lease starting just before brick-making actually starts.

7.5 Derelict Tanks

7.5.1 Introduction

During the Consultant's field trips, many derelict tanks were observed to be either dry or completely covered with water hyacinth. Road counts were made, and the ratios of clean tanks to derelict tanks were calculated. However, the Consultant's results are not reported here because it was found that a statistical analysis of data collected on tanks in 176 villages throughout Bangladesh had recently been made by the FAO Fisheries Advisory Project (BGD/72/016) (Hoq and Grant, 1979). The Consultant's observations were similar to the data provided by that survey. The latter survey also indicated whether or not the tanks were stocked with fish.

7.5.2 Findings and discussion

The Hoq and Grant survey findings are shown in Table 7.4. Those observers concluded that the total area occupied by tanks in Bangladesh was 359,000 acres, of which 115,000 acres (32 percent) were derelict. A total of 150,000 acres was used for fish culture, while they considered that an additional 94,000 acres could have been used for that purpose without re-excavation. When compared with the area occupied and consumed by brickyards (ca 13,750 acres), it seemed that more attention should be focused on the improvement of village tanks. However, ownership disputes created serious problems in that respect.

Especially in Dhaka District, the condition of village tanks was very poor. Almost 65 percent of the tanks were derelict. In Tangail District, as many as 80 percent were derelict, and in Bogra District 50 percent.

The Consultant observed that road-side ditches consumed much land, especially in deeply-flooded areas. Rather than one continuous ditch, a string of discontinuous borrow-pits was found on both sides of road embankments. The area affected was sometimes as much as 10 metres on each side. Many of the ditches were not used productively.

An attempt was made to carry out counts of derelict road-side ditches, but that proved difficult because, at the time of the field visits (February), farmers were still in the process of removing water hyacinth and planting boro paddy in some ditches. Shallow ditches were often being used for boro paddy seed-beds; moderately deep ditches were being used for

TABLE 7.4
Number and area of ponds and tanks in Bangladesh

Division District	Reporting Thanas	Area and number of village ponds and tanks (000)							
		Total		Used for fish culture		Ready to be used		Derelict	
		Acres	No	Acres	No	Acres	No	Acres	No
Chittagong	9/15	**129**	**562**	**56**	**229**	**41**	**171**	**32**	**162**
Chittagong	2/3	18	96	9	42	5	33	4	21
Chit'g H. T.	0/3	–	–	–	–	–	–	–	–
Comilla	2/3	36	213	18	96	9	52	9	65
Noakhali	3/3	34	129	16	49	9	36	9	44
Sylhet	2/3	41	124	13	42	18	50	10	32
Dhaka	10/11	**57**	**255**	**9**	**40**	**11**	**42**	**37**	**173**
Dhaka	3/3	15	63	3	11	2	6	10	46
Faridpur	3/3	15	107	3	17	4	25	8	65
Mymensingh	2/3	22	60	3	11	4	9	15	40
Tangail	2/2	5	25	<1	1	1	2	4	22
Khulna	12/13	**84**	**644**	**36**	**229**	**26**	**155**	**22**	**260**
Bakerganj	3/3	40	307	10	35	19	110	11	162
Jessore	3/3	14	80	8	48	1	6	5	26
Khulna	3/3	14	152	12	122	<1	7	2	23
Kushtia	3/3	6	29	4	15	1	5	1	9
Patuakhali	0/1	(10)	(76)	(2)	(9)	(5)	(27)	(3)	(40)
Rajshahi	13/14	**89**	**303**	**49**	**147**	**16**	**71**	**24**	**85**
Bogra	2/3	10	38	3	9	2	8	5	21
Dinajpur	3/3	20	67	11	45	3	11	6	11
Pabna	2/2	7	15	1	1	1	1	5	13
Rajshahi	3/3	31	65	20	42	5	12	6	11
Rangpur	3/3	21	118	14	50	5	39	2	29
Bangladesh	44/53	359	1764	150	645	94	439	115	680
Percent		100		42		26		32	
			100		36		25		39

Notes: 1. Source: Hoq and Grant (1979). Estimates were based on measurement of ponds and tanks in a sample of 176 villages in 44 Thanas of the 53 Thanas selected for survey in December 1978 and January 1979.

2. There was no information for Patuakhali District. Estimates were made on the basis of results from Bakerganj (Barisal) District.

growing boro paddy; and deep ditches were being used for fish culture. However, it was clear that the sites were not being used optimally. Between Comilla and Dhaka, the area of derelict road-side ditches was estimated to be at least 180 acres.

Obviously, as little productive land as possible should be used in road construction: (see Section 7.7.3). Where possible, deep, narrow borrow-pits should be excavated, so that less land will be lost to agriculture and better use could be made of the water body created, for example as an irrigation reservoir or channel. Also, evaporation losses would be reduced and more water preserved for irrigation from the same storage capacity.

7.6 LAND USE IN HOMESTEAD AREAS

7.6.1 Introduction

The 1977 Agricultural Census Report (BBS, 1981) gave the 'uncultivated' area — including cultivable waste, homesteads, ponds, ditches, roads, forests — as 2.48 million acres. Of this, 10.8 percent (269,000 acres) was considered to be cultivable waste, while the balance was occupied by homesteads, ponds, etc.

Serno (1981) provided an estimate of the productive to non-productive land ratios within homesteads. From his data, it was calculated that about 50 percent (weighted average) of the homestead area in the seven Thanas studied could be classified as unproductive, indicating the area occupied by houses, threshing floors, storage huts and fallow land. If extrapolated over the total 'uncultivated' area of 2.48 million acres reported in the Agricultural Census, the unproductive land would amount to 1.24 million acres.

Aliff International (1981) gave a total of 664,560 acres for the area covered by tree crowns in the homestead complex.

7.6.2 Findings and discussion

The Consultant made counts of homestead land use in eight villages (mainly in the Thanas studied by Serno). The data are presented in Table 7.5. The data seem to agree fairly well with data from other sources quoted above.

TABLE 7.5
Land use of homestead areas

Thana/Village	Land Use Proportions	(%)	Main Trees	Main Fuel Source
Bahubal Thana				
Subhatru village	Houses	25	1. Mango	Mango
	Trees, bamboo, banana	40	2. Bamboo	Cow dung
	Arable (+ tanks)	35	3. Banana	
	Fallow	5		
Jangalia village	Houses	25	1. Bamboo	Mango
	Trees, bamboo, banana	45	2. Mango	Cow dung
	Arable (+ tanks)	30	3. Jackfruit	
Comilla Thana				
Jaypur village	Houses	40	1. Mango	Mango
	Trees, bamboo, banana	20	2. Banana	Cow dung
	Arable (+ tanks)	20	3. Date palm	
	Fallow (+ derelict tanks)	20		
Chandina Thana				
Belaso village	Houses	65	1. Mango	Rice straw
	Trees, bamboo, banana	20	2. Jackfruit	Mango
	Arable (+ tanks)	10	3. Bamboo	Cow dung
	Fallow	5		

(Contd.)

(Continued)

Thana/Village	Land Use Proportions	(%)	Main Trees	Main Fuel Source
Baidya Bazar Thana				
Chotokrishnadi village	Houses	70	1. Mango	Rice + wheat straw
	Trees, bamboo, banana	10	2. Coconut	Jute sticks
	Arable	15	3. Betelnut	Korai (*Albizzia*)
	Fallow	5		
Mirpur Thana (Kushtia)				
Noapara-Boalbari village	Houses	15	1. Bamboo	Rice straw
	Trees, bamboo, banana	20	2. Banana	Mango
	Arable (+ tanks)	55	3. Mango	
	Fallow	10		
Kotubaria village	Houses	25	1. Bamboo	Jute sticks
	Trees, bamboo, banana	30	2. Coconut	Mango
	Arable (+ tanks)	35	3. Banana + Mango	Cow dung
	Fallow	10		
Dupchanchia Thana				
? village	Houses	40	1. Bamboo	Mango
	Trees, bamboo, banana	45	2. Korai (*Albizzia*)	Rice straw +
	Tanks	15	3. Mango	bamboo leaves
				Korai
	Fallow	<5		

Notes: 1. Source. Consultant's estimates made by walking through villages.
  2. The name of the village in Dupchanchia Thana is not given in the Consultant's report.

The area of fallow land varied greatly from one village to another. The highest value (20 percent) was recorded in Jaypur, but there seemed to be no obvious reason for such a high level in a densely-populated area close to Comilla town.

In the homestead area of the villages visited in Bahubal Thana, fallow land was negligible, just as it was in Dupchanchia Thana. In Mirpur Thana, the area of fallow land in Noapara-Boalbari village was relatively large, because the land had not been optimally used since the departure of several Hindu families. In Kotubaria village, most of the fallow land consisted of graveyards.

Generally, the area of fallow land was between 0 and 10 percent, with the average considerably below 10 percent. Those findings do not confirm the figure of 10.8 percent given in the Agricultural Census Report.

The mango tree was the main supplier of firewood in the villages studied. In many areas, cow dung was the second-most important source of fuel. Usually, only old mango trees were found to be being gradually converted to fuel. It was often observed that the farmers had planted new trees, but they never planted trees that could be used only for firewood.

Because of the increasing demand for firewood, experiments should be carried out with fast-growing species that occupy little space (such as Eucalyptus spp.). Farmers usually are very eager to carry out experiments, and if the seedlings could be supplied free of charge, the production of firewood could increase. At the same time, cow dung could be made available for use on the fields that are commonly in need of more organic matter.

In planting fast-growing tree species, it should be kept in mind that they should not be planted as pure stands because of the vulnerability of pure stands to strong winds and disease.

7.7 LAND USE IN URBAN AREAS

7.7.1 Introduction

The Consultant spent some time in trying to find out how land in urban areas was being used. Attention was focused on Rajshahi, Bogra and Dhaka. In Rajshahi, land use of the University and adjacent college campuses was studied. In Bogra, the Rural Development Academy, Government College and Cantonment areas were visited. For Dhaka, the Consultant's counterpart separately made an analysis of two sample areas.

7.7.2 Findings and conclusions

The campus of Rajshahi University occupies 740 acres of land. The land was formerly double-cropped with mixed aus+aman followed by rabi crops or was used for sugarcane. At the time of the study, the campus area was used as is shown in Table 7.6. Of the 286 acres of roads, buildings and playing fields, about 20 acres were found to be occupied by buildings and roads, leaving about 230 acres for playing fields.

TABLE 7.6
Land use in Rajshahi University campus in 1982

Land use	Area (acres)
Roads, buildings and playing fields	286
Botanical garden and research fields	29
Railway station and graveyard	17
Garden and kitchen garden	94
Unused lowlands and abandoned brickyards	35
Agricultural project	284 (of which 244 cultivated and 40 ponds)

The Agricultural Project, initiated in 1975, occupied 284 acres. The main crops grown were mixed aus + aman followed by sugarcane. Rabi crops were not grown. Farmers cultivating the surrounding farmland usually grew rabi crops as well. According to one employee who also owned farmland outside the project area, the yields on the Agricultural Project site were about half what the farmers obtained. That was confirmed by project officials. The profits were about Tk.700 per acre. An average labour force of 125 daily labourers was employed, paid Tk.10 per day. In addition, it was said that about 120 acres of abandoned brickyards had been reclaimed with tractors and levelling equipment, at a total cost of about Tk.100,000.

According to the Chief Engineer, the land had been purchased for the construction of buildings. Indeed, the master plan showed the area concerned as scheduled for occupation by buildings. However, it seemed improbable that that would ever occur. The procedure of obtaining land at a date when funds for building construction have not actually been secured seems highly questionable. If the Government requires land, it can be requisitioned at any time. As was shown in the Rajshahi University case, the purchase of land prior to the time of construction resulted in a very substantial loss (more than 50 percent) in agricultural production and many angry farmers who had been deprived of their land.

At the Engineering College in Rajshahi, teachers could obtain a lease from the college on land owned by the college. It seems questionable whether it is appropriate to supplement teachers' salaries in that way at the expense of the farmers. Generally, the land was found to be used well. At the Medical College and Hospital, crops were being grown even in backyards. On the other hand, an excessive area of playing fields (ca 13 acres) was observed.

In Habinagar village, Rajshahi, BWDB had destroyed the agricultural potential of 25 acres of double-cropped land for the construction of a groyne in the river Ganges. The area had been unevenly excavated, making it difficult to use the site for any useful purpose in the future.

The Bogra cantonment area (1,160 acres) was formerly mainly single-cropped with transplanted aman paddy, with some double-cropped aus-t.aman land. At the time of the study, 30 percent of the land was said to be under cultivation, for which farmers could take one-year leases. It appeared that the figure of 30 percent was too high: probably it was nearer to 20 percent. An estimated 15 percent of the acquired area was occupied by buildings. If agricultural production is to be maximized, the one-year leases should be replaced by renewable five-year leases: no farmer will invest in the land if someone else will reap the residual benefits.

The same comment applies to the Bogra Government College where the land not used by the college was rented to farmers on a yearly basis. The question remains: why was it necessary to acquire that land at all? In this case, the land had been acquired 20 years earlier.

The Bogra Academy for Rural Development occupies 42 acres of land which formerly was single-cropped transplanted aman land. Apart from the agricultural fields (18 acres), the site had not yet been put to optimum use. Most of the buildings area consisted of lawns.

7.7.3 Discussion

Land should not be taken from farmers many years before building activities start. Taking land from farmers and then hiring labour to cultivate it (as at Rajshahi University) seems to be an unacceptable practice. Also, renting out land to farmers on an annual basis undoubtedly leads to suboptimum crop production. In this case, renewable long-term (e.g., 5-year) leases should be considered.

District Land Allocation Committees chaired by the Deputy Commissioner should be properly informed about agricultural land values to ensure that the minimum amount of land is acquired and, if alternatives exist, then to take land of low agricultural value. SRDI and the Directorate of Agriculture (Extension & Management) have particular responsibilities in this respect.

Hussain (1982) stated: "The planning process is one of dialogue: not planning 'for', but 'with' the people. Local bodies have the local knowledge of the requirements of the land for various purposes, and their recommendations have to be given full weight before a local official gives a final verdict." That principle needs to be followed in all cases where it is proposed to acquire private land for public purposes, so that the public interest is genuinely taken into account.

Annexe 1

REPORT ON A DISCUSSION AT THE ROADS AND HIGHWAYS DEPARTMENT, DHAKA

[At the time of the study], there were just over 100 brickyards in operation owned by RHD, especially in rural areas where only a few private brickyards existed. Formerly, most of the bricks were manufactured in RHD-owned brickyards. By 1981, about 90 percent of the bricks were being produced by local brickyards. For instance, in Narsingdi, 24 private brickyards were working on Government contracts.

Previously, the majority of bricks were made for RHD in permanent or temporary brickyards. The land needed for the permanent brickyards was bought from the farmers at current prices, as stated in the transfer documents. However, that system put the farmer at a disadvantage because, when selling to private persons, extra cash was paid in order to avoid taxation. If the Government required the land, the farmer was forced to sell.

For temporary brickyards, the farmer received a certain amount of money for the soil used and a compensation sum for the loss of income from the fields. However, farmers were said to claim more harvests than they actually grew, so RHD had abandoned that system because it proved too costly.

In the case of permanently-acquired brickyards, the former owners were entitled to buy the land back after the brickyard had become redundant, at the same prices as they received initially. However, that procedure was said to be lengthy, and it involved much expenditure as well. In that respect, the farmers could obtain, against payment, the service of certain persons to accelerate the procedure. Former owners, for only Tk.20 per acre, could also take out leases on the land they had previously owned, once brick-making had ceased. Because, originally, the leases were for only one year, the farmers had shown little interest. More interest arose when renewable five-year leases were also made possible. In that case, it was more profitable for the farmers to clean and level the land. If the former owners were not interested, other farmers could apply for leases. However, the Consultant considered that the presence of many abandoned and unused brickyards showed that the leasing procedure was also complicated.

On temporarily-leased land, excavations usually did not exceed 5 feet in depth because RHD had to level the land before returning it to the farmers. On permanently-acquired land, there were no restrictions for the contractor in that respect, nor did he have to clean and level the land before abandoning it. Usually, the stacks of old bricks found in abandoned brickyards were those that did not meet the specifications set by RHD. In that case, the contractor could be sued to remove them. Alternatively, if Government was the owner, the bricks could be moved and used for road construction elsewhere.

Annexe 2

ESTIMATED LABOUR REQUIREMENT FOR RECLAIMING AN ABANDONED BRICKYARD

The accompanying sketch map (Figure 7.1) shows the land use in an abandoned brickyard just east of Tangail town. Table 7.7 shows the area occupied by each unit on the map.

TABLE 7.7
Land use in an abandoned brickyard

Land use	Area (acres)
Moderately-deeply excavated (ca 5 feet)	3.75
Irregularly excavated (0-5 feet)	0.70
Fallow with some bricks	2.90
Fallow with stacks of bricks	1.90
Kiln	1.75
Kiln surroundings	1.15
Brick storage	1.45
Arable land	0.90
Total	**14.50**

This Government-owned brickyard was abandoned in 1976. Bricks were imprinted WDC and MBC. An estimated 800,000 bricks were still present on the site. During the monsoon season, the area is deeply flooded. On the higher parts of the adjoining land, mixed aus + aman followed by a rabi crop (often wheat) was grown. On the lower parts, boro paddy was grown where irrigation water was available.

It was proposed to reclaim the affected area in such a way that boro paddy could be grown on the lower parts. That would involve the re-excavation of an irrigation tank of about 1 acre in part of the excavated area to a depth of about 12 feet. With the excavated material, part of the borrow-pit would be infilled by about 1-2 feet and an embankment about 3-8 feet high would be constructed, as shown in Figure 7.1. The soil material around the kiln site could be used for levelling the irregularly-excavated area. Due to deep flooding, the tank would not be suitable for intensive fish farming, unless an embankment about 10 feet high was constructed.

A calculation of the labour required to restore this site to productive use is given below.

Reclamation of two kiln sites: 2×40 man-months	= 80 man-months
Excavation of borrow-pit: 1 acre $\times$ 7 feet	= 100 man-months
Cleaning fallow land and brick-storage sites: 6.25 acres $\times$ 2 man-months/acre	= 12.5 man-months
Cleaning kiln surroundings	= 5 man-months
Total labour required	**= 197.5 (say 200) man-months**

FIGURE 7.1

Sketch map of abandoned brickyard, Nagarjalpai, Tangail

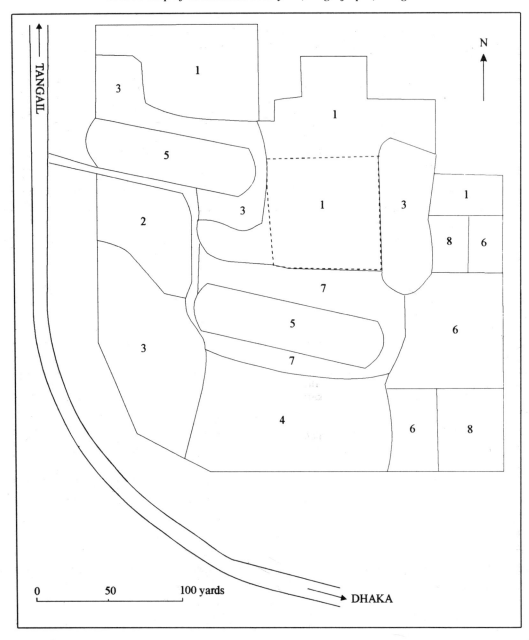

LEGEND

1	Moderately deeply excavated (5feet)	5	Kiln
2	Irregularly excavated (0-5 feet)	6	Brick storage
3	Fallow with some bricks	7	Kiln surroundings with many bricks
4	Fallow with some stocks of bricks	8	Arable (boro paddy)
- - - -	Boundary of proposed tank	====	Main supply route of brickyard

The calculation of the labour required to reclaim the kiln sites, fallow land and brick-storage area was based on data supplied by farmers in the Mymensingh area who had had experience in reclaiming abandoned brickyards. For the excavation, the labour requirement was based on an average productivity of 100 cubic feet of earth moved per labourer per day, as deduced from data supplied by brickyard operators.

The Consultant considered that the majority of abandoned brickyards encountered would need far less effort to reclaim than the example given here.

Chapter 8

SOIL CONSERVATION NEEDS[1]

The findings and conclusions of a 'task force' which toured the country's hill areas in 1982 to assess the state of soil degradation are reported. Recommendations are given for appropriate technical and institutional measures to combat soil erosion.

8.1 INTRODUCTION

With the exception of a few isolated areas, food production and other agricultural activities in Bangladesh are mainly confined to the generally flat floodplain and terrace areas. Since the 1950s, with an expanding population, increasing numbers of farmers have moved into the country's hill areas from the plains. Those farmers, with no previous experience of cultivating hill slopes, use practices which cause massive erosion of hill-sides, resulting in land degradation also in the lower catchment areas.

The 5,000 square miles of the Chittagong Hill Tracts is an area which has always been populated with hill farmers. With the exception of scattered areas of flat land in the valley bottoms, the traditional method of farming practised by the hill people was that of shifting cultivation on the hill slopes. As a result of natural population increase and the construction of the Kaptai Dam in the 1960s, whose reservoir flooded the better quality land, increasing numbers of farmers took up shifting cultivation of hill slopes, which resulted in a drastic reduction in the number of years when the land was under fallow. That, in turn, resulted in a deterioration of the soil structure and an increase in erosion, with consequent silting of the rivers and of the dam reservoir.

The Ministry of Agriculture and Forests in 1981 formed a 'Task Force', of which the Consultant was a member. The Consultant's terms of reference — which were essentially the same as those of the task force — were to:

a. make a preliminary assessment of the state of soil degradation and erosion in selected hill areas;

---

[1] *The author repeatedly drew Government's attention to the urgent need to address the problem of soil erosion in the country's hill areas, including those outside the Chittagong Hill Tracts. In 1982, a consultant was engaged to assess the extent of the problem and recommend suitable technical and institutional measures to address the situation. This chapter is an abbreviated and edited version of the report prepared by D. Layzell, Soil Conservation Consultant, under the FAO/UNDP Land Use Policy Project (Layzell, 1982), presenting mainly the findings and conclusions of the study. Except where stated otherwise, the information relates to the time of the field study, January-February 1982. Statements originally made in the present tense have been converted to the past tense to make that clear. Footnotes which appeared in the original document are given in normal font. Footnotes that have been added are given in italics.*

b. advise Government on the country's probable soil conservation needs during the next 5, 10 and 20-year plan periods, including a preliminary indication of manpower and institutional requirements;

c. assist Government to identify one or more sites suitable for a pilot conservation project; and

d. assist Government to prepare a project document for donor funding, specifying the institutional, manpower and fund requirements for a pilot soil conservation project.

The Consultant's findings and conclusions are reported in the following sections.

8.2 BACKGROUND INFORMATION

Low hills are found within several Districts of the country. The greatest concentration of these, and the highest to be found in Bangladesh, is in Chittagong Division: see Figure 1.2.[2] Geologically, this area consists of a series of parallel ranges of steeply-folded, consolidated and semi-consolidated, Tertiary sandstones and shales. The orientation of the ridges is generally NNW to SSE, with some transverse faults. Three series of rocks have been identified in the area, of which the two oldest series (Surma and Tipam) are exposed in the higher elevations of the anticlines, and the third (Dupi Tila series) has been eroded at higher elevations and now underlies low hills in the synclines. The flanks of the ridges are deeply dissected by geological erosion in a generally East-West direction and form lines of steep-sided, round-topped hills, locally termed the 'high bumpy hills'. Towards the centre of the valleys between the ranges, the hills become lower, more gently sloping and rather flatter on top ('low bumpy hills'). Some of the longer rivers have formed alluvial terraces, although this type of land is not very extensive.

The Brown Hill Soils of the hill areas have developed from the sedimentary rocks. They are extremely variable in texture, ranging from silty clay to loamy sand. Their suitability for agricultural use ranges from totally unsuitable, because of shallow depth to bedrock or droughtiness, to well suited on deep, fairly fertile soils. However, because of the topography and intense rainfall, all of the soils require intensive conservation practices, plus the application of manure and fertilizers to provide and maintain fertility under continuous cultivation.

The hill areas of Chittagong and CHT Districts extend northward through Tripura State of India into the southern part of Sylhet District where they eventually disappear below the Surma-Kusiyara Floodplain. On the northern boundaries of Sylhet and Mymensingh Districts, smaller areas of hills occur, running in an East-West direction at the base of the escarpment of the Shillong Plateau of the Indian State of Meghalaya. Further small areas of hills also occur along the eastern borders of Comilla and Noakhali Districts. In all, the hills account for about 12 percent of the total land surface of Bangladesh (Table 8.1).

8.3 STATE OF DEGRADATION AND EROSION

8.3.1 The erosion process

Erosion has two distinct forms. Firstly, natural or 'geological' erosion is the process by which the hills, mountains and valleys which make up the earth's surface have been

---

[2] *Chittagong Division included the old Sylhet, Comilla, Noakhali, Chittagong and Chittagong Hill Tracts (CHT) Districts.*

TABLE 8.1
Area and proportion of hill areas by District

District	Area (acres)	% of Bangladesh
Chittagong Hill Tracts[1]	3,183,520	9.02
Chittagong	687,360	1.95
Sylhet	359,400	1.02
Comilla	19,710	0.06
Noakhali	3,030	0.01
Jamalpur	24,520	0.07
Mymensingh	5,890	0.02
Total	**4,283,430**	**12.15**

Note: 1. Includes Bandarban District.

weathered and shaped by the action of wind, rain, snow, ice and floods in a process that has taken millions of years. The second form, namely 'accelerated erosion', is mainly attributable to man's interference with the natural environment, and is caused by the action of wind or water on a soil surface that has been cleared of its natural vegetation.

Wind erosion is generally found in the plains of the arid or semi-arid zones of the world. It generally is a result of overgrazing or cultivating grassland areas, which thus leaves dry soil exposed to high-velocity winds which detach and move the soil particles. The two major characteristics of wind erosion are heavy dust storms and dune formation, which are frequently associated with the process of desertification. Because of the humid climate and the rapidity with which weeds and crops grow, wind erosion is not a problem in Bangladesh.[3]

Conversely, in the steep hill areas of Bangladesh, the combination of cultivation and high-intensity rains form the ideal conditions for erosion by water. This type of erosion causes soil degradation in two distinct areas of a watershed: i.e., in the upper and lower parts of the catchment area.

In the upper catchment area, four erosion processes take place. In increasing degrees of severity, these are as follows.

a. *Raindrop erosion*. This is the loosening and movement of soil particles by the splash of raindrops. On any slope, there is always a net movement of particles in a downhill direction, no matter how gentle the rainfall.

b. *Sheet erosion*. When rainfall intensity exceeds the permeability or infiltration rate of the topsoil, run-off of water occurs. The movement of this water detaches soil particles and transports them downslope. This is the most insidious type of erosion. Annually, it removes thin layers or sheets of topsoil. It is not easily detectable by eye, but it can be confirmed by the silt load being carried by streams at the bottom of eroding hill-sides.

c. *Rill erosion*. When run-off water accumulates in slight depressions on a slope, the velocity increases, causing incisions (rills) 2-3 inches deep down the slope, thereby increasing the rate of soil removal.

d. *Gulley erosion*. This occurs when all the run-off water concentrates in natural valleys or drainage-ways where the highly-erosive water velocities cause deep gulleys to

---

[3] *See Brammer (1997), Chapter 8, for further comments on wind erosion and desertification in Bangladesh.*

form. These increase in size with each successive rainfall event through further erosion of the gulley bed and the undercutting of the sides and the head of the gulley, which cause soil material in the gulley walls to collapse and be washed away.

In the lower catchment area, the rapid run-off from bare hill-sides causes flash floods on land where river gradients flatten out. The silts and sands eroded from the hill-sides are first deposited in the river beds, causing the bed-level to rise to bank level. Thereafter, the sediments spread over the flat lands adjoining the river. Sediments are also deposited in reservoirs, thereby reducing the life-span of valuable hydro-electric or irrigation schemes.

Active soil erosion and land degradation are taking place in Bangladesh at an alarming rate. The extent of the area involved is not known, and it would require a major survey to quantify the problem. However, the Soil Conservation Task Force toured through two Districts, and their findings given in the following two sections confirm that the problem is widespread in the areas visited.

8.3.2 Sylhet District

The most destructive form of agriculture found in this District was pineapple growing, which causes massive erosion. The pineapple plants are planted in rows 3-4 feet apart which are oriented vertically down the slope. The inter-row spaces are clean-tilled by hoeing, thus leaving the already loosened soil highly vulnerable to sheet and rill erosion. It was estimated that the annual soil loss under pineapples was in excess of 100 tons per acre. With 12,000 acres under pineapple cultivation in 1981-82, this represents a major loss of the District's soil resources. The farmers freely admitted that, after five years, it became uneconomic to carry on cultivation because of reduced output. The land was then abandoned and new areas were cleared for the next year's planting. The silt from this area was being deposited in the Borak/Kusiyara river basin. Also under threat was the Monu River Irrigation Scheme, the upper catchment of which is in the hill areas where pineapples were being grown.

Thirty years previously, research on deepwater paddy in the Khowai/Balikhal river basins at Habiganj revealed that silt and plant nutrients were being deposited on paddy land at the rates shown in Table 8.2. In the thirty years that elapsed between that research and the present study, an expanding population probably had forced more people to move to the hill areas to live and farm, causing increasing siltation problems on the lowlands.

TABLE 8.2
Silt and nutrients deposited on Habiganj Deepwater Rice Research Station 1948-53

Land type	lbs/acre per annum[1]			
	Silt	N	P_2O_5	K_2O
High land	1963	18.92	5.61	27.64
Medium land	3585	40.40	10.04	52.88
Low land	5826	66.71	16.37	84.42
Very low land	9064	101.52	25.02	153.54

Note: 1. Average of four sites over five years (1948-1953).

The following example of lower catchment degradation, although not directly attributable to cultivation, illustrates the problem. At Shahzi Bazar, sunngrass was harvested annually on a 5,000-6,000 acre section of the Ragunandan Hills. At the end of the dry season, the whole area was burned to stimulate regrowth during the next rainy season. As a consequence of this practice, heavy run-off occurs on the denuded hills during the monsoon season, causing flash floods and the deposition of sand on the lowlands. River-bank erosion from the flash floods threatened a natural gas installation, and a retaining wall had to be built as a protective measure. Further downstream, sediment accumulated and was level with the top of the railway embankment at the time of the study team's visit, whilst the clearance under a nearby railway bridge had been reduced to 3-4 feet. During 1981, two road bridges were washed out due to the high river-bed levels and flash floods. A characteristic feature of the area was the piles of sand that farmers had removed annually from the paddy fields.

The tea plantations that were visited were, on the whole, well maintained and the ground cover provided by the tea bushes had reduced erosion to a minimum. The only isolated places where erosion was seen to be active were where planting had been carried out on very steep slopes. A typical example was where tea had been planted on an 85 percent slope of loamy sand, which had caused a landslide.

It was gratifying to see that the Bangladesh Air Force was using excess land within a semi-abandoned airfield for fruit production. On the advice of the Horticultural Board extension staff, pineapples had been planted on the contour, and even on bench terraces on steeper slopes. That showed that it can be done!

8.3.3 Chittagong District and Chittagong Hill Tracts

This large region contains the greatest concentration of hills in the country. It is subdivided administratively into the coastal areas of Chittagong and Cox's Bazar in the west and the Chittagong Hill Tracts in the interior.

At Raozan and Ramu near Cox's Bazar was seen the worst erosion of the field visits. That was taking place on the government-managed rubber plantations. It was found that the entire area was being completely cleared of ground vegetation twice a year, once just before the monsoon season and again during the rains. The topsoil in places had been completely removed by sheet erosion, exposing a poor subsoil. The bench terraces on which the trees had originally been planted had been eroded down to half of their original width of 8 feet due to lack of maintenance, thus exposing the roots of the rubber trees. Furthermore, where trees had been planted in lines down the slope, gulleys were forming. The management explained that the ground vegetation was cleared to facilitate the movement of rubber tappers.[4]

The Chittagong Hill Tracts cover an area of 5,093 sq. miles and account for 9 percent of the total land area of Bangladesh. In 1981, they were inhabited by 500,000 people of tribal origins, giving a population density of 100 per sq. mile (compared with the national average of 1,500 per sq. mile). With the exception of a few scattered areas of paddy land, the traditional method of farming was that of *jhum* (shifting) cultivation.

Under optimum conditions, the practice of shifting cultivation, although undesirable, is not highly destructive of the soil resources. In the context of the Hill Tracts, a piece of

---

[4] Whilst visiting the experimental oil palm plantations at Cox's Bazar, it was found that a leguminous plant (*Pueraria cintocina*) was being used to build up soil fertility and as a ground cover. The Task Force was informed that the legume had been imported by the rubber plantations!

hill-side is cleared of natural vegetation, burnt over and planted up with a wide variety of crops. No cultivation as such is carried out: the seeds are planted by dibbling or scratching the soil surface. The various crops are harvested progressively through the monsoon season and the dry season. When the area shows signs of declining productivity, the area is allowed to revert to forest for 8-10 years and thus rebuild its natural fertility and soil structure.[5]

However, two phenomena considerably altered this situation: firstly, the natural increase in population; and secondly, the construction of the Kaptai hydro-electric scheme, which inundated 300 sq. miles of the Karnafuli river basin which contained the majority of the arable land in the District, on the floodplain, terraces and low hills. Twenty-five thousand families were displaced, causing increased pressure on the land suitable for jhuming. The end-result was a decrease in the ratio between the time the land was under cultivation and under fallow, with a consequent decline in soil structure and increased erosion.

The rivers which drain into the reservoir showed signs of heavy siltation. Whereas, previously, the Forest Department could raft logs and bamboo down these rivers for six months of the year, by 1982 they could operate for only two-and-a-half months, and one 20-mile section of the river which formerly was navigable by heavy launches was inaccessible even by speedboats. Heavy siltation at this rate could jeopardize the life of the hydroelectric scheme which, in 1981, produced 625 million kilowatt hours of electricity, thus saving scarce foreign exchange on imports of fuel for generating power. It should be emphasized that 2.4 million acres of the Hill Tracts are Unclassed State Forest and are thus open to uncontrolled shifting cultivation.

The multi-sectoral Chittagong Hill Tracts Development Project (funded by the Asian Development Bank and UNDP) was taking steps to settle the tribal people on 5-6 acre plots in three catchment areas (Myani, Changi and Kasalong). One-third of the population of these valleys was from the 25,000 families which had been displaced by Kaptai Lake. The people were being settled in villages of 50-100 families, with rural development facilities such as schools, access roads and health services. The Bangladesh Agricultural Development Corporation (BADC) was making inputs such as seed and fertilizers available to the settlers.[6]

The Horticultural Development Board and the Forest Department were also settling 'jhumias'. The HDB was doing so on an individual basis, giving families credit for clearing, cultivating and preparing tree holes, repayable over 10 years, with a 3-year moratorium. The planting material was given free. It consisted of jackfruit, guava, custard apple, lemon, coconut, litchi, jujube, mango and cashew nut seedlings. The mixed orchards took about 8-10 years to reach maturity. The Forest Department also worked with groups of families, combining reafforestation with settlement. The plantations were of both hardwoods and pulpwood. Plans had been approved to plant 100,000 acres of forest during the current 5-Year Plan period.

The Forest Department formed a Jhum Control Division in 1962 with a mandate to bring back into production by afforestation land which had been destroyed and eroded by shifting cultivation. Under the scheme, 35,000 acres had been identified and brought under control, and was reclassified as Protected Forest.

---

[5] *Probably at least equally important is the role of fallow vegetation in shading out the weeds of cultivation.*

[6] *This project was subsequently closed and foreign assistance withdrawn because of political unrest in the Hill Tracts.*

A visit was made to the Forest Development and Training Centre at Kaptai where experiments in harvesting and logging techniques were being carried out for eventual use by contractors. The centre was also responsible for the introduction of new tools and the training of Forest Department personnel. The team was advised that the Extension Section covered soil conservation in the training given to forest field workers and farmers. The Training Centre staff pointed out that, when new plantations were being established, agri-silviculture was an accepted practice, whereby the forest labourers were allowed to grow crops between the trees for 1-2 years after planting in a system of 'controlled jhuming'.

The team met representatives of 27 families settled by the Hill Tracts Development Board under an integrated development programme. Each family had 5 acres on which fruit trees had been planted, whilst the steep areas were planted with teak. A major complaint of the families was that they had no food except during the main fruit-harvesting season. Family members either had to leave the area to work as labourers or cut timber to sell so that they could feed their families between the harvesting seasons. Another point of discontent was the lack of water and firewood near the village.

A day was spent at the Hill Tracts Agricultural Research Station (formerly known as the Soil Conservation Research Station) at Ramgarh. Considerable effort had been put into the development of this station since its opening in 1964. Much of the area had been bench-terraced and experiments had been carried out on growing all the major fruit trees, plus a variety of other crops such as maize, hill rice, hill cotton, etc., with varying degrees of success. Soil loss experiments had been carried out, but no basic data such as rainfall intensities or infiltration rates for the various soil types in the area were available. It would appear that little of the information that was available had been passed on to the Extension service and other interested parties. The visiting task force suggested that field days and lectures should be given to the local farmers so that they could apply some of the proven conservation practices on their own farms.

8.3.4 Conclusions

As a result of its field visits, the task force came to the following conclusions.

1. There was no overall plan to tackle the problems of erosion on a national basis. Even had there been such a plan, there was no department within government with the manpower or required expertise to carry it out. Various departments working within the hill areas were recommending practices allied to their own fields of expertise: the two obvious examples were HDB and the Forest Department who, not unnaturally, promoted the planting of fruit trees or commercial timber respectively. Other departments were advising farmers to practise contour cultivation and planting, but did not have the staff to demonstrate how to do it. Fortunately, the farmers had been told not to build terraces, as the installation of conservation works followed by lack of maintenance could have had disastrous effects, as was seen on the rubber plantations.

2. In the Chittagong Hill Tracts, various groups were involved in the settlement of displaced families and others. There did not, however, appear to be an integrated watershed management plan for the whole District detailing the different areas of land use. Examples were seen of settlement taking place on very steep slopes and teak forests being established on land suitable for agriculture. Villages were placed in areas with no provision for the supply of water and distant from a firewood source.

3. A greater effort should be made to settle people in areas where fuel and water are available or, alternatively, make provisions for a 'village woodlot' and the construction of a multi-purpose dam for minor irrigation and water supply. Due recognition should also be taken of the fact that people need to eat during the nine months of the year when fruit is not available. Of the five acres allocated to each family, at least one (and preferably two) acres should be suitable for growing crops other than fruit trees. Assuming that there are approximately 100,000 families in the Hill Tracts, 200,000 acres of suitable land would be required for growing food crops. The Forestal soil and land use survey report (Forestal, 1966) stated that the following areas of potentially suitable land capability classes exist:

Class A land (Good)	76,466 acres
Class B land (Moderate)	67,871 acres
Class C land (Poor)	366,622 acres
Total	**510,959 acres**

4. Various types of conservation practices are required according to the degree of slope. Table 8.3 gives a general outline of the practices and crops that might be applicable to the Hill Tracts. It needs to be pointed out, however, that a considerable amount of

TABLE 8.3
Conservation and cropping practices by slope class

Slope class	Conservation needs	Cropping practice
Flat	None	Rice production
1-10%	Contour cultivation and planting; possibly some terracing on upper slopes	Cereals and vegetables
10-30%	Intensive conservation works, mainly bench terraces	Cereals, vegetables, cash crops
30-50%	Bench terraces	Preferably fruit trees, but other crops if sufficient flatter land is not available
50-70%	Hill-side ditches to catch run-off water	Fruit trees, with heavy ground cover of lemon grass or a legume (*Pueraria cintocina*)
>70 %	Permanent forest	None

research is still required to find the correct combination of soils, conservation and cropping practices, crop variety and fertilizer application rates for optimum production on a long-term basis whilst at the same time keeping soil losses to within reasonable limits. The following food and cash crops have been suggested as possibly suitable under hill farming conditions.

Food crops	Hill rice, maize, sorghum, millet (*kaon*), pumpkins, sweet gourd, sweet potato, cassava/yams, beans (green and dried varieties), pigeon pea, chilli, sugarcane
Cash crops	Hill cotton, fruit trees (all varieties), banana, pineapple, groundnut, ginger, turmeric, black pepper, other spices, sesamum, mustard, lemon grass, coffee. If near factory facilities, tea and rubber might be grown on an out-grower basis

5. Due recognition needs to be given to the fact that, with the present rate of population increase, the country's population may have risen to 180 million by the year 2000 (UNFPA estimate).[7] To feed the extra people will require a drastic increase in production from the land presently under cultivation or an increase in the area under cultivation. The existing cropland is already being intensively farmed, and the only large areas available for expansion are within the country's hill areas. Currently, with the exception of the short fruit-harvesting season, the hill areas — despite the low population density — are net importers of cereals, vegetables and other foodstuffs. That is a situation that should be changed as soon as possible by the formulation and implementation of intensive hill farming practices to make the hill areas self-sufficient and, eventually, net exporters of food and other crop products.

8.4 Soil Conservation Needs

8.4.1 Institutional and manpower requirements

The Consultant's terms of reference required him to identify one or more sites for a pilot conservation project. However, as reported above, the task force found that farming of differing degrees of intensity was being practised on 4,283,430 acres of steep to very steep hill land with virtually no soil protection measures being applied, and that no Government department had the capability to formulate integrated watershed management plans, nor the personnel to implement them. Accordingly, the task force felt that the selection of pilot project sites would serve no useful long-term purpose, and that what was required was a project to train staff and thereby form the nucleus of a Watershed Management and Soil Conservation Division. The project should also develop a research and extension capability through which new techniques and practices could be demonstrated to other interested departments and farmers.

The basic terms of reference of the proposed new Division should be to formulate and implement methods of conservation farming for the long-term intensive use of Bangladesh's hill areas. The organization chart shown in Figure 8.1 gives the initial manpower requirements. The proposed 78-man unit would have 14 officers, 42 technicians, 5 administration and 17 supernumerary staff, of which 38 would be headquarters staff and the remaining 40 would be divided between four field units. The training of this nucleus staff, with the assistance of an international financing agency, would take five years. The Consultant recommended that the new Division should come under SRDI.[8]

During the following five-year period, the Division would be fully operational in the field. The headquarters unit would require strengthening of its planning capacity by the addition of a further two planning assistants and two planning officers, who would require overseas training. The field units would be increased from four to eight, so as to give full cover of the hill areas of the country. The four new units would be of the same size as the Srimangal unit, and based on Cox's Bazar, Chittagong, Sylhet and Durgapur.

The following ten-year period would be one of maximum activity. The new Division should by then have developed a sense of maturity and purpose, and should have formulated watershed management plans for the major problem areas. The field units would then

---

[7] *In fact, the country's population is estimated to be around 130 million in 1999.*

[8] *In the event, the proposed new Division was not formed, largely because of the intense rivalry between several agencies of the Ministry of Agriculture and Forests regarding who should operate the new organization.*

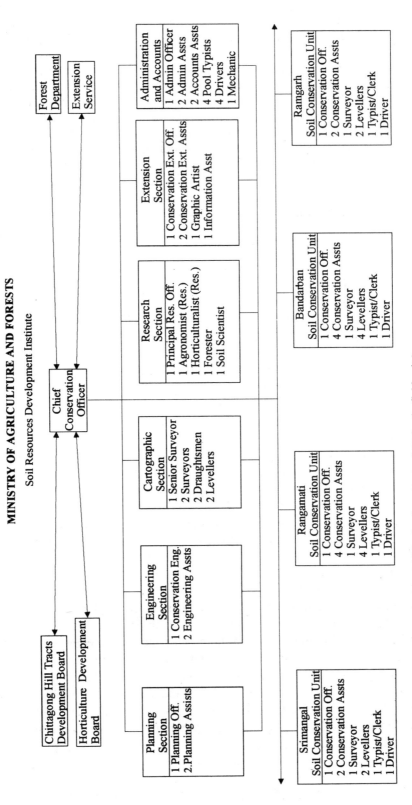

FIGURE 8.1

Organogram of proposed Watershed Management and Soil Conservation Division

MINISTRY OF AGRICULTURE AND FORESTS

Soil Resources Development Institute

Note. Provision will also include 26 labourers (10 for headquarters, and 16 for the field units).

be busy with implementation and training field workers from other departments in simple conservation techniques.

8.4.2 Recommendations

1. In the absence of any personnel within Bangladesh trained in the techniques of soil and water management, the Government should form a new Division of Watershed Management and Soil Conservation. The Division should initially be formed under the auspices of SRDI.[9]

2. In order to assist with formation of the new Division and staff training, the Government should approach an international financing agency for a technical assistance project.[10]

3. Soil conservation legislation is required on two major issues:

   a. to give Government the power, through the Ministry of Agriculture and Forests or the District Administration, to close an area to cultivation or any other land use, temporarily or permanently, where it is considered that the present land use practice is detrimental to the soil resources of the country or it is causing damage to land or property downstream; and

   b. to define the soil conservation practices that are required on various degrees of slope before cultivation is carried out; on land that is already in use, time limits should be set for the installation of such conservation works.

4. Immediate action is required to control the serious erosion threatening the future of the Government rubber estates. It is suggested that the Chairman of the Forest Industries Development Corporation should obtain the services of the staff of the Hill Tracts Agricultural Research Station at Ramgarh, through the Director of BARI, to advise on suitable remedial measures. One of those measures should be the planting of the legume *Pueraria cintocina* which was imported by the rubber plantations for use as a cover crop but never used. Private individuals who are developing rubber plantations should also be given technical advice on proper planting methods.

5. The task force should remain operational until such time as the new Watershed Management and Soil Conservation Division has been formed and is able to take over the duties of the task force.

---

[9] *In fact, two Agricultural Extension Officers had received training in soil conservation in the 1960s — one of whom had subsequently set up and managed the Soil Conservation Research Station at Ramgarh with commendable success — but that training had been in Iran on practices appropriate for arid and semi-arid environments. No-one had been trained in practices suitable for the steep, wet and poor soil environment of Bangladesh's hill areas. Subsequent to the Consultant's study, an SRDI officer from the Hill Tracts was given a six-months' scholarship under the author's project to receive training and experience in northern Thailand.*

[10] *The Consultant's report included a draft project document for a five-year FAO/UNDP technical assistance project (which did not materialize, inter alia, because of the lack of agreement on which agency should operate the project: see footnote 8 above). The draft project document is not reproduced in this chapter.*

Chapter 9

MANGO ORCHARD REHABILITATION[1]

The findings of a survey of mango orchards carried out in 1981-82 are described and recommendations are given for rehabilitating old orchards. Proposals are outlined for a technical assistance project to support mango orchard rehabilitation.

9.1 INTRODUCTION

9.1.1 Background

Mango production in Bangladesh decreased considerably in the 1970s. With the area under mango trees remaining approximately the same (100,000 acres), total annual production declined from 400,000 tons to 200,000 tons over a period of ten years. At first, heavy attacks by a psyllid bug (*Apsylla cistellata*) and by hoppers in mango-growing areas were considered to be the main cause of the yield decline. In 1979, the Ministry of Agriculture and Forests set up a task force for controlling these pests. With the assistance of a FAO consultant in mango pest control, an *Apsylla* and hopper control programme was set up. In 1981, it was realized that the decline in mango orchards was of a more general nature, and the assistance of a mango production consultant was requested from FAO. On the arrival of this consultant in December 1981, a new task force was set up for studying the needs for rehabilitation and development of mango orchards.

This consultant's terms of reference were, in consultation with the Project Manager (of the FAO Land Use Policy Project), to assist a Task Force on Mango Orchard Rehabilitation set up by the Ministry of Agriculture and Forests to:

a. organize and conduct a sample survey of the mango orchards in the west of Rajshahi District to assess their age, condition and productivity;

b. assess the needs for rehabilitation of old orchards to make them suitable for the introduction of modern management techniques;

c. recommend suitable rehabilitation methods, including institutional, manpower and credit requirements; and

---

[1] *A serious decline in mango production in the 1970s was initially attributed to severe pest attacks, but it was then recognized that there were more serious underlying problems of orchard management. Accordingly, it was decided to appoint a mango specialist to assess the status of orchards in the main mango production areas and recommend appropriate rehabilitation measures. This chapter presents an abbreviated and edited version of the consultancy report prepared by J.M Philippe, FAO Senior Horticulturist, (Philippe, 1982), under the FAO Land Use Policy Project (but funded by FAO Regional project, RAS/79/123). Except where stated otherwise, the information relates to the time of the consultancy, December 1981 to January 1982. Statements originally made in the present tense have been converted to the past tense to make that clear. Footnotes have been added by the author (HB).*

d. if considered appropriate, design a pilot rehabilitation project in one or more selected areas and prepare a project document for UNDP funding, specifying the institutional, manpower and fund requirements for such a project.

9.1.2 Ecological requirements of the mango tree

The mango tree originated in the Indian subcontinent. Therefore, it is at home in Bangladesh. It is classified as a subtropical to tropical tree, and has been grown in the Asian monsoon regions for several thousand years. However, although mango is grown extensively above the Tropic of Cancer, especially in India, it is more tropical in its temperature requirements than subtropical as it does not stand temperatures close to 0^0C. A young mango tree may be killed by a temperature of 0.6^0C (33^0F) for a short period.

Rainfall distribution is the most important single climatic factor for economic mango production. Without a dry period extending from two to three months prior to blooming, the mango produces vegetative growth but few or no flowers. In this regard, the climatic conditions in Bangladesh are adequate: the dry season in November-December makes the soil dry around the root system, and induces tree dormancy and flowering in January-February. Rains in November and December may have a negative effect on the number of inflorescences produced, although an occasional shower at that time is harmless. Annual effective rainfall and irrigation together must total at least 750 mm (about 30 ins). The whole country of Bangladesh is above this limit. However, one flood irrigation per month after flowering time (end-January) would be beneficial until the monsoon rains start.

Regarding soils, the mango tree is adaptable to many soil types, provided that a drained depth of at least 1.8 m (6 feet) is ensured throughout the year. In light and deep soils, the mango tree may develop its root system down to 8 m (24 feet). That is the reason why this fruit tree is highly resistant to a long drought. The optimal *pH* range for the mango tree is from 6.0 to 7.5. The soils in the main mango-growing areas in western Bangladesh come close to these requirements. In general, they are deep and sandy, with a water-table below 6 feet except possibly in the middle of the rainy season. On the Ganges River Floodplain in Rajshahi and Kushtia Districts, the soils are mainly calcareous in the topsoil and subsoil, with a *pH* around 7.8 to 8.4. On Teesta sediments in Dinajpur and Rangpur Districts, the topsoil often is more acid than *pH* 6.0, but the lower layers generally are in the range *pH* 6.0-7.0.

Mango flowers are very sensitive to humidity. Rains and even heavy dew during the blooming stage may considerably decrease or totally impede fruit setting. This is mainly due to the rapid development of the powdery mildew fungus (*Oidium mangiferae*) on the flowers under humid conditions. In Bangladesh, rains occasionally — and heavy dew more often — may hamper or impede mango fruit setting.

9.1.3 Mango production statistics

As is illustrated in Table 9.1, mango was the most important fruit crop in Bangladesh in 1978-79 in terms of area and the second one in terms of production. Total mango production in that (agricultural) year was estimated at 210,718 tons. The average yield of 4,932 kg/ha (53.7 maunds/acre) must be considered very low.[2]

---

[2] *Mango production in 1996-97 was 186,625 tons.*

Area, production and yield of fruit in Bangladesh 1978-79

Fruit	Area (acres)	Production (tons)	Yield (md/ac)	Yield (kg/ac)	Yield (kg.ha)
Mango	106,780	210,718	53.72	1,973	4,932
Banana	94,420	586,972	169.32	6,217	15,543
Jackfruit	47,110	190,411	110.02	4,042	10,105
Pineapple	36,155	137,421	103.46	3,800	9,500
Water melon	20,060	109,338	148.36	5,451	13,626
Litchi	6,980	10,749	41.92	1,540	3,850
Papaya	6,675	20,149	82.17	3,019	7,546
Guava	5,455	8,383	41.83	1,537	3,842
Jujube (*qul*)	3,625	4,168	31.30	1,150	2,874
Lime + lemon	3,750	3,474	25.22	926	2,316
Pomelo	2,565	4,015	42.61	1,565	2,913
Mandarin	1,930	2,384	33.62	1,235	3,088
Other citrus	6,010	8,470	38.36	–	–
Other fruits	10,430	21,428	55.92	–	–
Total	**351,945**	**1,328,080**	**101.94**	–	–

Source: Bangladesh Bureau of Statistics.

On the basis of 90 million inhabitants in 1981, the per capita consumption of mangoes was only 2.6 kilogrammes per year, or 13 medium-sized mangoes in a year. The total fruit production per capita was estimated at 16.5 kg/year or 45 gm/day. In order to give the people an adequate fruit diet, this quantity needed to be increased at least four-fold. An enormous effort would need to be made to increase fruit production and, in particular, mango production. Compared with other food commodity prices, fruit prices in Dhaka were very high, indicating a higher demand than supply.

Table 9.2 shows that, in less than ten years, mango production had decreased by 50 percent. During that period, the mango area remained approximately the same. The reasons for the decline are given in Section 9.2. Subsequent data from the Ministry of Agriculture and Forests (MAF) indicated that, in Rajshahi District, the main mango-growing area, yields had decreased from 13.3 tons/ha (5.32 tons/acre) in 1970-71 to 4 tons/ha (1.6 tons/acre) in 1979-80.

Table 9.3 shows mango area and production by District from 1976 to 1979. Out of the country's 23 agricultural Districts, only four — Rajshahi, Dinajpur, Rangpur, Kushtia — were important mango areas where grafted trees, called quality mangoes, were planted. Those four Districts in the west and north-west of the country constitute the mango belt of Bangladesh. In India, on the other side of the border, the same type of mango orchards occur. Partition of the subcontinent in 1947 divided this long-established mango production area in two. The remaining 19 Districts of Bangladesh produced less than 60 percent of the mangoes. In those Districts, mango trees were mainly scattered around homesteads and were generally grown from seedlings (locally called *guti*).

Regarding new plantings, each Government nursery (60 in total) was producing grafted mango seedlings each year. However, according to Horticultural Development Board (HDB)

TABLE 9.2
Mango production in Bangladesh 1970-1979

Year	Production (000 tons)
1969-70	393
1970-71	415
1971-72	360
1972-73	360
1973-74	296
1974-75	279
1975-76	267
1976-77	264
1977-78	251
1978-79	211

Source: Bangladesh Bureau of Statistics.

TABLE 9.3
Area and production of mango by District 1976-77 to 1978-79

District	1976-77		1977-78		1978-79	
	Acres	Tons	Acres	Tons	Acres	Tons
Rajshahi	24,085	62,919	23,350	55,146	23,220	38,370
Dinajpur	9,535	19,265	9,385	16,448	9,320	13,734
Rangpur	8,025	30,754	8,005	30,446	8,050	24,326
Kushtia	3,855	6,797	3,895	6,232	3,950	5,694
Other Districts	60,960	144,266	61,840	142,538	62,240	128,394
Total Bangladesh	**106,360**	**264,100**	**106,975**	**250,810**	**106,700**	**210,718**

Source: Horticultural Development Board, Dhaka.

data, the total number of grafted mango trees sold was not more than 40,000 per year for the whole country, and the majority of those were planted in home gardens. In 1981, only about 15,000 saplings were sold in the main mango Districts. Therefore, it appeared that very few new mango orchards were being planted in Bangladesh. At the current rate of nursery tree supply, it was estimated that it would take 150 years to renew all the existing plantations.

9.2   SURVEY OF MANGO ORCHARDS

Age of mango trees and size of orchards. Field trips were made to the four main mango-growing Districts. All four Districts were areas where traditional grafted mango trees were grown. The oldest orchards appeared to be more than 100 years old. The general impression was that most of the trees were more than 50-70 years old. According to data collected by MAF in Chapai Nawabganj Subdivision of Rajshahi District in 1981, 4 percent of the orchards were from 1 to 5 years old, 7 percent from 6 to 10 years, 21 percent from 11 to 20 years, 7 percent from 21 to 40 years, 26 percent from 41 to 60 years, and 5 percent above 60 years old. The census was carried out on a total of 50,000 trees. The Consultant was inclined to think that the age of the older trees had been underestimated and that at least

50 percent were over 60 years old. The percentages given above illustrate that the average age of the mango tree population was getting older each year.

In the same census by MAF, the size classification of orchards in five Thanas of Chapai Nawabganj Subdivision showed that 1,279 orchards (94 percent) were up to 5 acres (2 ha), 49 (4 percent) were between 5 and 10 acres (2-4 ha), and 17 (2 percent) were above 10 acres (4 ha).

An accurate census of the total number of farmers involved in mango production had not been taken.[3] However, the majority of families owned no more than 1-3 trees, and it was assumed that about one million families obtained part of their livelihood from mango production. Proper mango orchards were found only in Rajshahi, Dinajpur, Rangpur and Kushtia Districts.

Varieties. In the main mango-growing Districts, apart from isolated trees planted in villages, the vast majority of the trees were grafted. The main varieties were Langra, Gopalbhog, Kirshapati, Fazli, Mohanbhog and Aswina. The Langra and Fazli varieties were both very popular. Fazli has a large fruit weighing up to one pound. Aswina is a late variety. With this assortment of six cultivars (varieties), plus the early-ripening seedling fruits, the market was supplied with mangoes during three-and-a-half months (mid-May to end-August).

Yield. All mango growers who were questioned complained about the very low yield or the complete absence of fruit-set during the previous four years. The data in Table 9.2 show that low yields were already conspicuous in 1974. In Shibganj Thana of Rajshahi District, one farmer told the Consultant that, from his orchard of 250 trees (6 acres) which was probably more than 70 years old, he got only Tk.30,000 in 1980 and Tk.20,000 in 1981 from mango sales at auction. The average yield of 1.97 tons/acre (4 tons/ha) estimated by MAF for the whole country in 1978-79 probably was an over-estimation, at least for grafted trees.

Cultural practices. Before Partition in 1947, grafted mango trees were planted in orchards mainly as a status symbol. After planting, the tradition was that the trees never received any care. Until the time of the study, no tilling, no weeding, no fertilizing, no disease and pest control, and no flowering control were practised. As the trees were planted at wide spacing — generally 12 × 12 metres (36 × 36 feet), on the square — the orchards were intercropped with annual crops during the first 30 years. After 30 years, and up to 100 years or more, as their leaf canopies started to join and give heavy shade which impeded the growth of annual crops, the mango trees were left as a thick forest. The only orchard management practised was fruit harvesting.

Pests and diseases. Because the mango tree is native to the Indian subcontinent, all pests and diseases specifically parasitic on mango trees should be present in Bangladesh. Without artificial control, it should be expected that a natural biological balance would be established between tree growth plus fruiting and pest/disease populations. The more isolated the tree, the less it should suffer from pests/diseases, and the better its growth and fruiting.

Untreated mango orchards more than 40 years old which are kept as thick forests provide ideal centres for the breeding of pests and for insect population outbursts. Under

---

[3] *Surveys of land-holdings in Bangladesh are made difficult by the amount of concealed ownership by 'big' families, often absentee. Hearsay evidence at the time of the study suggested that a few families actually owned — and benefitted from — mango orchards covering several hundred acres, some extending over the border into West Bengal.*

such conditions, the biological balance reached is strongly disadvantageous for the mango tree, which very soon shows poor growth and scanty or no fruiting. This situation probably existed in Bangladesh for many decades or centuries, but the damage to mango trees appeared to have become more significant in recent years because very few new orchards had been planted in the past 20 years.

Two pests were mainly responsible for the decline in mango yields in the main production areas:

- a psyllid (*Apsylla cistellata*) inducing galls on axillary buds and thereby impeding growth of vegetative and flowering buds; and
- hoppers, which feed on leaves and inflorescences.

Both *Apsylla* and hoppers were described, their damage evaluated, and control measures recommended by a FAO Consultant (Singh,1979). Other insects, as well as several fungus and bacterial diseases, were also damaging the vegetative and fruiting growth of mango trees, but their influence on the yield decline was not evaluated. Each of these pests and diseases was considered to need careful study with a view to determining the most appropriate control measures.

Reasons for mango decline. In the 1970s, it was considered that the decline in mango yields in Bangladesh was primarily due to attacks by *Apsylla* and hoppers. However, the Consultant emphasized that infestations by these insect pests, although extremely important, was not the primary problem of the mango crop. The main problem was that mango trees in Bangladesh had never been treated as an agricultural crop. As referred to above, no cultural methods were practised. The result was that the soil, after a few harvests, had been depleted of nutrients and, year by year, the damaging insect, fungus and bacteria populations had built up until the growth and fruiting of the trees had been impeded.

Furthermore, annual crops had always been grown between the young and adult mango trees without taking into account the nutrient requirements of the latter. The consequence was that the intercrops were feeding on the nutrients needed by the mango trees. Sometimes, the intercrops were irrigated during the first two-and-a-half months of the dry season, which may have impeded mango flowering (referred to in Section 9.1.2 above).

The last major cause for declining yields of Bangladesh's mango orchards was the too-old age of the trees.

9.3   REHABILITATION AND IMPROVEMENT METHODS

9.3.1 Orchards older than 40 years

Experience acquired in several countries indicates that the useful life of mango trees is around 40 years. Thereafter, their yields start to decrease and they bear fruit in only one out of two to four years. Furthermore, economical pest and disease control on old trees becomes difficult (because of the height of the trees and the dense foliage); and, as was explained above, old trees become centres particularly suitable for insect breeding and infestation. Therefore, old mango trees planted in orchards older than 40-45 years should be systematically felled and the wood used for timber and firewood: (see Section 9.5). Trees in orchards less than about 40 years old could be rehabilitated, as is described in the next section.

9.3.2 Orchards less than 40 years old

Pest and disease control. Control of *Apsylla cistellata* should be carefully practised on all trees. Singh (*op. cit.*) recommended both injection and spraying methods, starting from 15 August, with dimethoate, monocrotophos or dicrotophos. He gave details in his report on insecticide concentrations and on applications. Singh stated that the injection method gave better results, but had the disadvantages of making deep wounds on branches that were difficult to cure, and of being more expensive. He did not mention that, for effective control, wounds had also to be made on scaffold branches every year, with the result that the tree would eventually be destroyed. For that reason, this study consultant did not recommend the injection method. The life-cycle of *Apsylla cistellata* should be studied each year in the main mango-growing Districts in order to determine with more precision the optimum starting dates for pesticide applications.

Mango hoppers must also be controlled every year. They probably cause as much damage to mango yields as *Apsylla*, by sucking sap from leaves and from inflorescences. Chemical control recommended by Singh should be followed: 0.16% carbaryl sprayed twice, at emergence of inflorescence and after fruit setting. Details are given in Singh's report (*op.cit.*).

Several diseases — in particular, powdery mildew (*Oidium mangiferae*) and anthracnose (*Colletotrichum gleosporiodes*) — need to be controlled. Powdery mildew may lead to crop failure when rain showers or heavy dew occur during blooming. Mildew can be controlled by adding Karathan, Maneb, Zineb or Dithane to carbaryl for spraying at emergence of inflorescences. The next application should be given at the peak of the flowering period in the form of dusting with a mixture of one part of copper dust (16%) and two parts of sulphur dust, for both mildew and anthracnose control (van der Meulen, 1971). Three months after the end of flowering, spraying should be continued three times at three-week intervals using copper oxychloride (containing 50% of copper) at a rate of 3 lbs/100 gallons (1.4 kg/454 litres). The addition of a spreader and sticker to the spray is essential.

Manuring. Rehabilitation of adult mango trees (above 10 years old) which have never received any care should include heavy applications of fertilizers. The type of fertilizers and their quantity will vary according to soil *p*H and soil chemical content. However, for trees that have been bearing fruit for several years without receiving any fertilizers, the types and yearly quantities given per tree should be, on average:

Urea	:	1.5 kg (3.3 lbs)
Triple superphosphate (46%)	:	1 kg (2.2 lbs)
Muriate of potash (KCl)	:	1.75 kg (3.85 lbs)
Magnesium sulphate (MgSO$_4$)	:	1.5 kg (3.3 lbs)

The amounts shown above should be divided into two applications. Half should be applied as soon as the flower panicles become visible and this should be followed by a heavy flood irrigation. The other half should be applied as soon as the crop has been harvested, in August. Fertilizers should be spread under and around the trees on an area at least one-and-a-half times as wide as the diameter of the tree canopy, and they should be worked into the soil.

Flower induction. Dormancy and flower initiation in mango trees are induced by dry soil conditions around the roots during approximately two-and-a-half months. Therefore, lack of flowers on a mango tree at blooming time may be caused not only by bud galls of *Apsylla* but also by rainfall, irrigation or a high water-table during the first two months of the dry season. Several farmers were seen to be growing irrigated annual intercrops in mango orchards during this period. That practice should be abandoned, as it drastically reduces the mango yields.

Irrigation. Adult mango trees do not need irrigation in a tropical climate where the rains during the monsoon season are 750 mm or more, which is the case in all parts of Bangladesh. However, adult orchards would yield better if a heavy flood irrigation of at least 10 cm (4 ins) was applied just after the appearance of flower panicles (in January) and thereafter at monthly intervals until the monsoon season starts.

Improvement of nursery methods. The main mango varieties grown at the time of the study were propagated by veneer-grafting in government nurseries located at the various HDB horticultural bases in the mango-growing Districts. Seedlings from mixed seeds were grown in rows and grafted when about one year old. The graftwood was collected from any grafted tree of a known variety, mostly from old trees. The grafted saplings were sold to farmers one year after grafting. They were transplanted with a ball of earth around the roots or with bare roots. As the mango root system is very sensitive, the latter method of transplanting leads to a high percentage of dead plants, up to 50 percent.

Nursery methods should be improved by following the practices described below.

  a. Seeds for rootstock should be collected from one polyembryonic variety that gives genetically homogeneous and strong seedlings.

  b. Budwood or graftwood should be taken from mother trees known to be true-to-type to the variety and high yielding.

  c. After germination in a seedbed, seedlings should be transplanted in containers made either of plastic or of metal, then grown, grafted and sold in these containers.

  d. Throughout their stay in the nursery, the seedlings and grafted trees should receive fertilizers and should be treated against pests and diseases.

At the time of the study, none of these practices was being used. They should be included in the activities of the proposed technical assistance project: (see Section 9.5).

9.3.3 Planting and managing new orchards

Planting. A mango orchard may be planted either on land where mangoes have not been grown in the past or on land from which old mango trees have just been pulled out. In the latter case, prior to planting, the soil must be treated with a pesticide (such as Furadan) that will kill the nematodes and other root pests of mango trees. The soil should be tilled several times. The mango trees should be planted three months after the soil pesticide application. The best planting time in Bangladesh is July.

Plant spacing should be 10×10 m (30×30 feet) or 10×5 m (30×15 feet). In the latter case, after 10-12 years, the intermediate trees should be pulled out so as to leave a general spacing of 10×10 m at the adult stage. When replanting an old orchard, the new tree rows should be placed between the old rows.

Pest and disease control. The programme and methods for pest and disease control should be the same as those described for adult trees: see Section 9.3.2.

Manuring. The saplings should be grown into healthy, strong, well-formed trees, especially during their first four years. Grafted trees bloom early, often from the third year. Fruits should not be left to develop to maturity during these first four years, so as to avoid weakening the trees. Prevention of flowering and promotion of growth are best achieved by liberal nitrogen feeding. Hence, during their first three years, the young trees should receive more nitrogen in proportion to their size than bearing trees. Types and amounts recommended by van der Meulen (*op. cit.*) according to tree age are given in Table 9.4. These doses should be applied in two doses, as recommended in Section 9.3.2.

TABLE 9.4
Types and amounts of fertilizers to be applied per mango tree per year

Age of tree (years)	Urea		TSP		MP		MgSO$_4$	
	kg	(lb)	kg	(lb)	kg	(lb)	kg	(lb)
1	0.15	(0.3)	0.20	(0.4)	–	–	–	–
2	0.30	(0.66)	0.4	(0.85)	–	–	–	–
3	0.40	(0.9)	0.6	(1.3)	–	–	–	–
4	0.55	(1.25	0.8	(1.7)	–	–	–	–
5	0.70	(1.5)	1.0	(2.2)	0.5	(1.0)	–	–
6	0.85	(1.85)	1.0	(2.2)	0.75	(1.5)	–	–
7	1.00	(2.2)	1.0	(2.2)	1.0	(2.0)	0.5	(1.0)
8	1.15	(2.5)	1.0	(2.2)	1.25	(2.5)	1.0	(2.0)
9	1.40	(3.1)	1.0	(2.2)	1.5	(3.0)	1.5	(3.0)

Source: van der Meulen (1971).

Irrigation and intercropping. The climate of Bangladesh is adequate for mango-growing without irrigation. However, periodic irrigations are beneficial to tree growth and yields. During their first three years in the orchard, the young trees should receive abundant irrigation, at least 5 cm (2 ins) every two weeks during the dry season to favour vegetative growth and prevent flowering. From the fifth year, irrigation should be dropped during the first part of the dry season, until the flower panicles have appeared: (see Section 9.3.2).

Intercropping with annuals may be practised. During the first four years, irrigated intercrops (especially legumes), grown at the beginning of the dry season with adequate fertilization, may be beneficial to the mango trees. From the fifth year, irrigated intercrops should not be grown during the first two-and-a-half months of the dry season. When intercropping, especially from the fifth year of mango trees, it would be wise to leave a circle of land free from crops under each mango tree on an area one-and-a-half times as wide as the diameter of the tree canopy, so as to avoid competition for water — and especially for nutrients — between the mango trees and the annual crop. Intercropping should be stopped when the mango trees start to cast shade on two-thirds of the orchard area.

9.4 COSTS OF ESTABLISHMENT AND MAINTENANCE

9.4.1 Establishment

Detailed costs of establishing one hectare (2.5 acres) of mango orchard are shown in Table 9.5. The assumptions made regarding inputs are as follows:

- Tools comprise one spade, one hoe, one pair of pruning shears and one saw.

TABLE 9.5
Costs of establishing one hectare of mango orchard in Takas[1]

Item	Unit	Quantity	Unit cost	Year 1	Year 2	Year 3	Year 4	Total
Equipment & supplies								
Sprayer	1	1	1500	1500	–	–	–	1500
Duster	1	1	1500	–	–	–	1500	1500
Tools	–	–	–	1000	–	–	–	1000
Fertilizers	Kg	775	4	300	600	900	1300	3100
Pesticides	Kg	10	160	200	300	500	600	1600
Fungicides & bactericides	Kg	10	80	100	150	250	300	800
Planting								
Grafted mango trees	One	100	15	1500	75[2]	–	–	1575
Ploughing and tilling[3]	–	–	–	500	–	–	–	500
Hole-digging & planting	m/d	10	25	250	–	–	–	250
Fencing each tree	One	100	10	1000	–	–	–	1000
Maintenance								
Weeding	m/d	10	25	25	50	75	100	250
Pruning & flower-removal	m/d	4	25	25	25	25	25	100
Fertilizing	m/d	10	25	25	50	75	100	250
Pest control (8 applications)	m/d	32	25	100	150	250	300	800
Irrigation	m/d	18	25	150	150	150	100	550
Total less contingencies				6675	1550	2145	4325	**14,675**
Contingencies @ 10%				668	155	213	432	1,468
Total for new planting				**7343**	**1705**	**2338**	**4757**	**16,143**
Soil treatment with pesticides				4000				
Total for replanting				**11,343**	**1705**	**2338**	**4757**	**20,143**

Notes: 1. Tk.19.3 = US $1 (in 1982). ·
      2. Replacement of dead trees (5%).
      3. Ploughing and tilling with oxen.

- Total quantity of fertilizers is as recommended in Table 9.4.
- Spraying costs are based on three applications of pesticides, three of fungicides/ bactericides and two of pesticides and fungicides mixed in the same solution, giving a total of eight applications per year, as recommended in Section 9.3.2.
- Number of irrigations is six per year during the first three years, and three per year during the fourth year.

The total cost of establishing one hectare of mango trees, including the first four years of maintenance prior to the first commercial fruit set, is Tk.16,143 (at 1982 prices). For replanting an old orchard, the costs would be Tk.20,143 because they include soil treatment with a pesticide before replanting: see Section 9.3.3.

In the case of replanting, the farmer receives an income of approximately Tk.200,000 per hectare from the sale of old trees felled for timber and firewood. This high figure was obtained by multiplying the sale prices of timber and firewood from one tree (Tk.2,000) by 100 (number of trees per hectare). The current rate of bank interest (15 percent) from Tk.200,000 would be Tk.30,000 per year, which is more than the total investment needed for planting and maintaining one hectare of new orchard for four years. The high income from mango timber should be the main incentive for farmers to cut down their orchards when they reach forty years of age and then replant them. Another incentive for replanting is that the farmer would be able to grow intercrops for a few years after replanting. The campaign for pulling out old trees should be publicized through radio broadcasts and television.

9.4.2 Operation and maintenance

The costs of operating and maintaining one hectare (2.5 acres) of mango orchard are detailed in Table 9.6. The figures show that, if modern techniques of management are used, the net return is very high, reaching Tk.95,020 per hectare (Tk.38,000 per acre) from the tenth year after planting. They also show that, from the second year of fruiting (corresponding to the sixth year after planting), all expenses incurred during the investment period (first four years) are covered. The very high returns indicated are partly due to the current high price of mangoes in local markets.

TABLE 9.6

Costs of operating and maintaining one hectare of mango orchard and returns in Takas[1]

Item	Year 5	Year 6	Year 7	Year 8	Year 9	Year 10
Yield (Kg/ha)	(2000)	(5000)	(6000)	(8000)	(10,000)	(12,000)
Marketable: 90%	1800	4500	5400	7200	9000	10,000
Discarded: 10%	200	500	600	800	1000	1200
Gross Return @ Tk.10/kg	18,000	45,000	54,000	72,000	90,000	100,000
Equipment & supplies						
Equipment[2]	1000	1000	1000	1000	1000	1000
Fertilizers[3]	1700	1900	2300	2700	3200	3200
Pesticides & fungicides	1600	2300	3000	3800	4800	4800
Labour[4]						
Weeding	200	300	400	500	600	600
Pruning	25	25	50	50	50	50
Fertilizing	125	125	150	200	250	250
Pest control[5]	400	600	850	1000	1200	1200
Irrigation	100	100	100	100	100	100
Harvesting	100	250	300	400	500	600
Total costs	**5150**	**8150**	**8150**	**9750**	**11,700**	**11,800**
Contingencies (10%)	515	815	815	975	1170	1,100
Total Recurrent Costs	**5665**	**7260**	**8965**	**10,725**	**12,870**	**12,980**
Net Return (Tk./ha)	**12,335**	**37,740**	**45,035**	**61,275**	**77,130**	**95,020**

Notes: 1. Tk.19.3 = US $1.

2. Depreciation of sprayers, duster and tools in four years.

3. Fertilizers (kg/ha): 425 in year 5; 475 in year 6; 575 in year 7; 675 in year 8; 800 in following years.

4. Tk.25/man/day.

5. Eight applications per year: ± 0.1% pesticides and ± 0.1% fungicides; 2500 litres/ha at 10 years old; average price of pesticides/fungicides = Tk.120/kg.

9.4.3 Credit requirements

In the case of replanting, the farmer does not need any loan. That is because, from the sale of old trees for timber, he will get an income that is approximately ten times greater than the investment during the first four years after replanting. He will start to get a profit from mango production in the fifth year after replanting.

Loans will be required in the case of new plantings. Very small and poor farmers should get a loan without fee at the rate of Tk.160 per mango sapling up to a maximum of 50 trees (enough for half a hectare). For larger farmers, and for orchards larger than half-a-hectare, it is suggested that the loans should be at low interest, around 5 percent. In both cases, there should be a five-year grace period, and reimbursement should be made over five years, from the sixth to the tenth year. After three years of technical assistance, as recommended in Section 9.5, a mango orchard planting project should be prepared, based on loans to small farmers.

9.5 CONCLUSIONS AND RECOMMENDATIONS

Felling mango orchards more than 40-45 years old was considered to be a prerequisite for the improvement and development of mango production in Bangladesh. These orchards, concentrated in Rajshahi, Dinajpur, and Kushtia Districts, consisted of approximately 700,000 trees covering about 8,000 ha (20,000 acres). That was 50 percent of the orchards of those Districts. A farm-to-farm census would be needed to obtain more accurate figures.

It was recommended that the Government should make plans to have these 700,000 old mango trees cut down and replaced over a period of five years (i.e., 140,000 trees per year). It was thought that it would not be too difficult to motivate the farmers to fell their old trees as they would receive an income of about Tk.2,000 from the timber of each tree, about 20 times higher than the income per year they were currently receiving from the fruit of the same declining tree.

During the five-year felling and replanting programme, the adjoining orchards less than 35-40 years old would be rehabilitated, as described in Section 9.3.2. The higher yields obtained from rehabilitated trees should normally more than compensate the loss of production due to pulling out old trees.

It was recommended that, at the same time, pilot modern mango orchards of 0.5 to 2 ha each should be established in the main mango-growing Districts of Rajshahi, Dinajpur and Kushtia. In each District, one pilot orchard (new planting) should be established at one HDB base and two orchards (one new planting and one replanting) on private farms of which the owners were willing to accept HDB supervision. This design would give a total of nine pilot orchards.

Given the continuous decline in mango production in the past ten years, the urgent need to increase mango production, the lack of national personnel fully specialized in modern methods of mango production research and extension, and the limited availability of government funds, it was recommended that Government should seek technical assistance for mango orchard rehabilitation, improvement and development.[4]

---

[4] *The Consultant's report included a draft project document for UNDP technical assistance to support a three-year project whose objectives were to create a mango production experiment station, establish pilot mango nurseries in three Districts, improve farmers' mango growing and management techniques, and train research and extension workers in modern methods of mango production. The project document is not reproduced in this chapter. To the best of the author's recollection, the proposed project did not materialize.*

Chapter 10

LAND USE REGULATION[1]

Factual information is provided from small-scale surveys showing the extent of loss of agricultural land to brickyards, industry and housing; also on the use of hill land for pineapple gardens. Existing laws and ordinances relating to land transfer and land use planning are reviewed, and recommendations are made to strengthen and supplement them in order to protect agricultural land against unplanned urban/industrial sprawl and unsound farming practices.

10.1 INTRODUCTION

Various attempts were made during the 1960s and 1970s to draw up Thana and village land use plans: see Chapters 19-22. With the country's increasing population, there was growing conflict between the need to increase agricultural production and the demands for land for urbanization, industrial growth, expansion of roads and highways, and other developments. At the same time, it was recognized that land was being badly used in some parts of the country. The need for central or local governments to be able to regulate land use for sound land-use planning seemed to be imperative.

The Consultant's terms of reference were as follows.

1. Study and report on existing Bangladeshi laws and ordinances relating to regulation of land use with a view to recommending practical measures to amend the laws/ordinances or introduce new regulations which would enable (central) Government or local government authorities to regulate land use, especially agricultural land, in the long-term national interest.

2. In consultation with the Project Manager of the FAO/UNDP Land Use Policy Project, carry out field investigations in at least three different areas of Bangladesh in order to provide quantified data on:

   a. the rate of loss of agricultural land to industrial/urban use, brickyards and destructive pineapple cultivation on hill land;

   b. the processes by which land is acquired or leased for such purposes; and

---

[1] *While assisting with various Thana and village-level food production programmes in the 1970s, the author realized that there were no effective ways for local governments to prevent avoidable losses of valuable agricultural land by bad land management practices and encroachment of settlement and industry. Accordingly, a consultant was engaged to examine legal aspects of land use planning in the country. This chapter presents an abbreviated and edited version of the report prepared by T. Hussain, Land Administration Consultant, (Hussain, 1982). The study was carried out under the auspices of the FAO/UNDP Land Use Policy Project, but was funded by the Ford Foundation. Except where stated otherwise, the information relates to the time of the field study, January-February 1982. Statements originally made in the present tense have been converted to the past tense to make that clear. Footnotes in italics have been added by the author (H.B.).*

c. what happens to such land after brick-making or cultivation ceases.

3. Present his findings and recommendations in the form of a report to the Ministry of Agriculture and Forests.

A total of 103 brickyards, 102 industrial units, 69 suburban housing projects and 60 pineapple gardens were surveyed, and a thorough survey was made of one *mouza* (revenue unit) in the Dhaka-Narayanganj-Demra Irrigation Project area. The fieldwork was carried out by investigators completing a set of pre-tested questionnaires and was supervised by the Consultant and a Survey Superintendent. The findings, conclusions and recommendations are reported in the following sections.[2]

10.2 REVIEW OF PREVIOUS STUDIES

10.2.1 Literature review

No comprehensive investigation of land use problems in Bangladesh had previously been attempted. A limited study of land use zoning in Dhaka District had been made by the Soil Survey Directorate (now SRDI) in 1975 which drew attention to the need for introducing measures to regulate the acquisition and use of agricultural land for non-agricultural purposes (Brammer, 1975; see Chapter 24).

Nuruzzaman (1979) undertook a study of physical planning legislation as part of his Master's degree thesis. He mainly described the needs for proper and adequate policy-making and planning regarding the use and development of land in urban areas. He pointed out, *inter alia*, conflicts of interest in the use of land and the haphazard construction of buildings in suburban areas which produced unplanned urban sprawl. He suggested enforcement of legal action by a duly empowered authority.

A reconnaissance study of changes in settlement and related non-agricultural land use was made under the FAO/UNDP Land Use Policy Project in 1981 (Serno, 1981; see Chapter 5). The objective was to assess regional and national changes which had taken place in recent years in the areas occupied by settlements, roads, canals, brickyards, tanks, etc., based on a comparison of aerial photographs taken in 1952, 1963 and 1974. The report recommended that, in view of the conflicting demands for increased agricultural production and for land on which to house and service the increasing population, ways must be found to minimize the loss of agricultural land to non-agricultural uses.

10.2.2 Steps taken within Bangladesh

No concrete and effective steps had been taken in the country towards restricting or regulating the conversion of agricultural land to non-agricultural uses. The only existing control mechanism relating to the use of land for development purposes was the District Land Allocation Committee of which the Deputy Commissioner was the Chairman. All cases for acquisition of land for housing, roads, canals, industry, embankments, etc., were referred to this committee for clearance.

---

[2] *A separate report prepared by the Survey Superintendent appeared as an annexe in the original report. Much of the material was similar to that in the body of the Consultant's report, so the annexe is not reproduced in this chapter. Such additional information as it contained has been incorporated in relevant sections of the chapter.*

10.2.3 Experience in other countries

Review of papers published on other countries, especially in Europe, indicated that a number of different measures had been taken to tackle land use issues. It had been widely recognized that the loss of agricultural land to urban, industrial and other uses posed a serious problem to the agro-economy of countries all over the world. The following quotation comes from the Report of the Expert Consultation on the methodology for planning rural areas held in Geneva, Switzerland, in July 1975.[3]

> "The loss of prime agricultural land to other uses and the resultant tendency for farming to be forced onto more marginal land, has begun to pre-occupy policy-makers in certain countries. It is now recognized that, though the expansion of urban activities and the accompanying transformation of rural areas close to cities is an inherent part of the development process, it is exactly because of this phenomenon that land use planning becomes essential. Some 'guiding hand' is needed to help ensure that the development process goes on in the 'right place', in the 'right form' and at the 'right scale and/or intensity' in order to contribute to the achievement of overall development goals and objectives. The main concern here is to protect land resources from some of the undesirable effects of the urban process."

In most European countries where the problem is of a similar nature, protection of agricultural land is provided by 'zoning' regulations. The implication of zoning is that a central or local government authority is vested with appropriate powers and makes a plan indicating desirable land use, and that anyone desiring to change the use of his land from one category to another must seek permission to do so and may be refused permission if the proposed use is not compatible with the plan. However, circumvention of existing zoning regulations is very frequent and easy, so the concerned authorities are tending to resort to stricter controls and to impose more rigorous legal measures to make protection absolute. In England, farmers have urged that derelict land should be used for non-agricultural projects, sparing agricultural land. Planners in Denmark are using marginal land for construction purposes to spare agricultural land, even at higher cost. The ceiling of the amount of agricultural land transferable is also fixed in some countries. Generally speaking, in European countries, formulation of land use policy and the planning and transfer of agricultural land to non-agricultural use is strictly monitored by the government or through some statutory agency.

Professor Kastrowicki of the Committee for Space (?) Economy of Sciences has observed that the first step in planning rural areas is to guarantee adequate protection of the areas of special value for rural functions against unnecessary encroachment of much more aggressive exogenous functions (industry, urban construction, highways, etc.), the development of which should be directed to areas having little suitability for rural functions. Where a definite land use policy is required but is lacking, rational land utilization and conservation may be retarded or misdirected (FAO, 1971c).

Measures to protect agricultural land in other countries consist of:

a. stemming the growth of townships at the cost of agricultural land;

b. keeping a close watch on the movement of prices of agricultural land so that alluring prices do not tempt agriculturalists to sell their land for non-agricultural uses and to check land speculation;

---

[3] *The original report does not give a full reference to this report. The Expert Consultation may have been organized by FAO.*

    c. total banning of the sale of agricultural land to any party other than an agriculturalist, except with the permission of the prescribed authority;

    d. prohibiting uneconomic fragmentation of land by law; and

    e. conferring on farmers the statutory right to pre-empt agricultural land.

10.3 SURVEY FINDINGS

10.3.1 Brickyards

The locations of the brickyards surveyed are shown in Table 10.1. Of the total of 103, the vast majority were established after 1975 (Table 10.2). At the time of establishment, the brickyards used, on average, 3.62 acres of land, falling to 3.33 acres by the end of the period. The excavations used, on average, 0.32 acres of land and the average depth was 4.15 feet. When asked about the cost of recovery of such land for agricultural use, only 48 of the units gave a direct answer; they indicated that the average recovery cost would be about Tk.10,000 per acre.

    Table 10.3 shows the quantity of land used by brickyards in three villages in Fatullah Thana (south-east of Dhaka). While there was only one brickyard in 1960-65 occupying 0.42 percent of the total area of the three villages, there were 50 brickyards in 1981 occupying 12.94 percent of the total area. This area is flooded 6-15 feet deep for five months during the rainy season.

    Table 10.4 shows the nature of the land use on the present brickyard sites when the last Survey and Settlement operation concluded in 1918. Only 2.66 percent was then used for agriculture, 26 percent was under brickyards and 69 percent was fallow (but considered cultivable). Immediately before the sites were acquired for brickyards, 93 percent of the land was classified as agricultural (Table 10.5).

    Regarding the mode of acquisition, about half the land was purchased, 15 percent was inherited, and the remainder acquired on temporary, renewable lease (Table 10.6). Such leases are held under legally valid instruments, often duly registered. During the period of lease, which normally is renewed, the land can be used for making, drying, burning and selling bricks, according to the stated terms and conditions. Such leases never lead to *de facto* ownership of the land. At the same time, they do not bind the lessees to restore the land to any prescribed use.

    Table 10.7 shows that the majority of brickyards are used for brick-making for only 2-4 months of the year. For the remainder of the year, most are used for storing or selling bricks or are left unused, either under fallow vegetation or under water (Table 10.8).

    All the respondents interviewed said that brickyards could be used indefinitely, although not for excavation. Most of the manufacturers brought soil material from other places to make bricks. When asked about the kind of land from which such material was brought, 10 percent said that it came from agricultural land and 5 percent that it came from non-agricultural land. Import of soil from rural areas appeared to have been a recent development around Dhaka and other urban areas where suitable soil for brick-making was either not available or was very costly because of high land values.

    The survey did not cover areas in the countryside far from Dhaka. However, especially along trunk roads, many abandoned brickyards were seen, often with stacks of unused bricks and considerable areas of vacant land.[4] These brickyards related mainly to government

---

[4] *See also Chapter 7, Section 7.4.*

TABLE 10.1
Location of brickyards surveyed

Mouza	Thana	No of units
Dapa Indrakpur	Fatullah	15
Hariharpur	"	8
Pagla	"	12
Dhupatita	"	6
Kaliganj	"	8
Fatullah	"	3
Siarchar (Panchabati)	"	1
Hajaribam	Keraniganj	1
Kartadail	"	1
Jagira	"	2
Pangaon	"	13
Kandapara	"	8
Bill Akhalia	Sabhar	2
Jadurchar	"	4
Kadamtali	Demra	2
Kullarchar	Dhamrai	2
Baidal	Joydebpur	15
Total		**103**

TABLE 10.2
Amount of land used by brickyards in surveyed mouzas

Year started	No of brickyards	Total land used		Average land used		Average size	
		When started (acres)	In 1981 (acres)	When started (acres)	In 1981 (acres)	Land dug (acres)	Depth (feet)
1940-50	1	6.75	4.00	6.75	6.75	1.00	20.00
1950-60	2	7.83	7.83	3.92	3.92	–	–
1960-70	13	58.39	49.76	4.49	3.83	0.75	10.08
1970-75	15	71.26	59.65	4.75	3.98	0.46	2.78
1975-80	60	187.92	183.58	3.13	3.06	0.23	3.24
1981	12	40.41	37.74	3.37	3.15	0.13	3.33
Total	**103**	**372.56**	**342.56**	**3.62**	**3.33**	**0.43**	**6.57**

TABLE 10.3
Amount of land used by brickyards in selected villages

Year started	No	Land used (acres)	Total land in villages (acres)	Land used by brickyards (%)
1960-65	1	5.50	1316.40	0.42
1965-70	6	21.76	"	1.65
1970-75	9	40.06	"	3.04
1975-80	28	86.59	"	6.58
1981	6	16.50	"	1.25
Total	**50**	**170.41**	"	**12.94**

Note: Data from surveys in Dapa Indrakpur, Pagla, Hariharpur, Dhupatita and Kaliganj villages in Fatullah Thana.

TABLE 10.4
Classification of land presently used for brickyards in 1918 settlement operation

Classification	Area (acres)	Proportion (%)
Agricultural	9.92	2.66
Brickyard	98.51	26.44
Cultivable fallow	258.76	69.46
Tank/ditch	1.75	0.47
Alluvial land	3.33	0.89
Non-agricultural	0.25	0.08
Total	**372.52**	**100.00**

Note: Data relate to the mouzas listed in Table 10.1.

TABLE 10.5
Land use on brickyard sites at time of land acquisition

Land use	Area (acres)	Proportion (%)
Agricultural	340.58	93.05
Non-agricultural	8.76	2.39
Cultivable fallow	16.62	4.54
Miscellaneous	–	0.01
Total	**365.96**	**100.00**

Note: Data relate to the mouzas listed in Table 10.1.

TABLE 10.6
Mode of land acquisition of brickyard sites

Mode	Area (acres)	Proportion (%)
Inheritance	57.13	15.33
Long/short-term lease	189.01	50.73
Business partner	126.47	33.94
Others	–	–
Total	**372.61**	**100.00**

Note: Data relate to the mouzas listed in Table 10.1.

TABLE 10.7
Period of operation of brickyards

Months used per year	No of establishments	Proportion (%)
2	10	9.71
3	69	66.99
4	22	21.36
5	1	0.97
6	1	0.97
Total	**103**	**100.00**

TABLE 10.8
Off-time use of brickyards

Use	No of establishments
Fallow	35
Storage and sale of bricks	7
Fallow + storage and sale	33
Fishery	2
Horticulture	3
Agriculture	2
Flooded	21
Total	**103**

road-building contracts, not commercial brickyards. In the countryside, there was no need to bring material from distant places in areas where soil material was easily available and cheap. Also, in areas subject to alluvial accretion, no adverse effect was caused: the material excavated was more or less recouped by silt deposited from the floodwater. In other areas, soil fertility was impaired where the entire topsoil was removed. Despite this, the practice of buying topsoil from farmers seemed to be on the increase.

In the sample areas around Dhaka city, brickyards generally consisted of three divisions:

a. the part occupied by the kiln;

b. the area used for making, drying and storing burnt bricks before they were sold; and

c. the part used as a borrow-pit from which material was excavated for brick-making.

The part occupied by the kiln is very badly damaged, and its reclamation for agricultural use would be very expensive and possibly uneconomic. Moreover, a brick-kiln can be used for many years, using material imported from other areas when the local supply has been exhausted. Thus brick-kiln sites can be considered as permanently lost to agriculture.

The area used for making, drying and storing bricks does not depreciate much in quality. However, like the kiln site, it continues in use annually while the brickyard operates, even though it may actually be used for brick-making for only 2-4 months in a year.

Some deep pits created by the excavation of soil material for brick-making were observed in the surveyed areas. These pits gave the appearance of tanks, but most were lying useless, and covered by water hyacinth and other aquatic weeds. Although they could have been developed as a profitable fishery, these derelict pits were not being used by the brickyard owners, but they were still retained by them. Most of the owners held the land on temporary lease; only a few held them on a proprietary basis.

10.3.2 Industries

Table 10.9 shows the Thanas where the 102 industrial units surveyed were located. Among the units surveyed, none had been established before 1950, 12 had been established in 1950-60, 27 in 1960-70 and 59 in 1970-80, showing an accelerating trend with time (Table 10.10). The same table shows that the average area of land used per unit varied between decades, but had averaged 1.69 acres over the period 1950-81.

Table 10.11 shows the classification of the land used by these industries at the time of the last survey and settlement operation which concluded in 1918. Nearly all the land was cultivable fallow at that time. At the time of the study, the respondents said that more than 90 percent of the land had been agricultural land or cultivable land temporarily lying fallow (Table 10.12). Almost 90 percent of the land had been acquired by purchase (Table 10.13).

TABLE 10.9
Location of industrial units surveyed

Thana	No of units
Rupganj	24
Demra	33
Sabhar	14
Tongi	16
Baidya Bazar	6
Joydebpur	7
Dhamrai	1
Cantonment (Dhaka)	1
Total	**102**

TABLE 10.10
Amount of land used by industries in surveyed Thanas

Year of establishment	No of establishments		Total area of land used (acres)	Average area used (acres)
	No	%		
1940-50	–	–	–	–
1950-60	12	11.76	9.15	0.76
1960-70	27	26.47	68.76	2.55
1970-75	12	11.76	11.00	0.92
1975-80	47	46.08	76.08	1.62
1981	4	3.92	7.14	1.79
Total	**102**	**100.00**	**176.16**	**1.69**

TABLE 10.11
Classification of land presently used for industries in 1918 Settlement operation

Classification	Area (acres)	Proportion (%)	No of establishments
Agricultural	2.00	1.16	1
Cultivable fallow	164.01	95.26	57
Ditch	0.45	0.26	4
Highland suitable for homesteads	4.11	2.39	6
Homesteads	1.42	0.82	3
Not reported	0.17	0.11	1
Total	**172.16**	**100.00**	**102**

TABLE 10.12

Land use on industrial sites at time of land acquisition

Land use	Area (acres)	Proportion (%)	No of establishments
Agricultural	145.52	84.52	51
Fallow	15.69	9.11	34
Non-agricultural	10.96	6.37	17
Total	**172.16**	**100.00**	**102**

TABLE 10.13

Mode of land acquisition of industrial sites

Mode	Area (acres)	Proportion (%)	No of establishments
Inheritance	5.84	3.39	18
Purchase	154.72	89.87	73
Long/short-term lease	10.65	6.19	11
Business partner	0.11	0.06	2
Others	0.84	0.49	1
Total	**172.16**	**100.00**	**105**

Note: The discrepancy between the inclusion of 105 units in this table and 102 units in the other tables relating to industrial units is not explained in the original text.

Almost all the respondents interviewed said that they did not necessarily need agricultural land for setting up industries. Availability of raw materials, proximity to market, transport and other necessary facilities were the prime considerations in selecting sites. Other things being equal, they said that they would prefer to set up industries on high non-agricultural land which was less expensive to develop.

The installation of industries after 1960 was apparently linked with the establishment of the Industrial Development Corporation in erstwhile East Pakistan in the 1960-70 decade. The slow-down in expansion in 1970-75 probably was due to economic disruption caused during and immediately after the Liberation war in 1971, but there was a rapid expansion after 1975.

Fertile floodplain land along the Sitalakhya and Buriganga rivers was highly expensive to develop for urban use because it was low-lying. However, this area became attractive to entrepreneurs setting up new industries due to the transportation facilities provided by the rivers and by the Dhaka-Chittagong road, its proximity to the Dhaka-Narayanganj market for industrial products, and the availability of cheap labour. Thus most of the former cultivable land was lost to agriculture.

It was found that industries of different sorts were being installed haphazardly in the same area, without conforming to any predesigned development plan. The absence of a well-prepared plan resulted in avoidable waste of good quality agricultural land. Instances were not uncommon of industrial establishments being set up in residential areas.

The industries covered by the survey occupied land acquired by proprietary right through inheritance, by outright purchase or on long-term lease for periods exceeding ten years, without any restriction or pre-condition regarding the use of the land. No big nationalized or privately-owned industries were included in the survey, but it was recognized that many such industries had acquired land far in excess of their actual requirements, ostensibly for future expansion or simply to provide the luxury of privacy.

10.3.3 Human settlements

A housing society is a body corporate, constituted on a voluntary or cooperative basis under the laws of the land with the common objective of acquiring and developing land, providing other facilities and distributing the land among its members for building residential houses. A large number of such housing societies were functioning in and around Dhaka city and some other urban areas of the country.

An area of 1,213.50 acres of land in 50 mouzas of six Thanas in and around Dhaka city were surveyed during the study. Forty-nine housing societies were surveyed. They included 67 housing projects. Table 10.14 shows where they were located. Except for a few established in Mohammedpur, Mirpur and Joydebpur Thanas during the 1950s and 1960s, most societies had been established between 1975 and 1980 (Table 10.15). That table shows that the units varied greatly in size, between 3.3 acres and 100 acres.

Table 10.16 shows the classification of the land used by the housing projects at the time of the last survey and settlement operation which concluded in 1918. About one-third of the land was then agricultural, almost 20 percent cultivable fallow, and the rest non-agricultural. At the time of the study, the respondents said that about two-thirds of the land had been agricultural before acquisition, about 10 percent cultivable land temporarily lying fallow, and about one-quarter non-agricultural land (Table 10.17). Almost all the land had been acquired by purchase; less than 5 percent had been obtained on lease (Table 10.18).

The housing societies had distributed plots ranging between two and ten *kathas* (1 *katha* = 1/60th acre) in size. Almost all the land had been distributed, but houses had been built on only a small proportion of it. At the time of the study, land development was going on or the land was lying vacant.

In addition to the housing societies, 36 individual housing schemes were included in the survey, averaging 0.06 acres in extent. All the land had been acquired by purchase and all had been agricultural land, both at the time of the last settlement operation and immediately before the houses were built.

The results of the survey in Dania mouza in the Dhaka-Narayanganj-Demra (DND) Irrigation Project area were checked with comparable figures of the State Acquisition Settlement records of 1962. There was a sharp increase in the number of houses and in the area under housing in this supposedly agricultural project area between 1975 and 1981, as is shown in Table 10.19.[5] The DND project had been initiated in 1961 on 14,732 acres of agricultural land. By 1977, the cultivable area had decreased to 13,077 acres due to the spread of houses, brickyards and other non-agricultural developments. By 1981, the agricultural area was reduced to 11,341 acres. The reduction occurred in the part of the project area south of the Dhaka-Demra road which was flood-protected and drained. The Dania mouza which was surveyed lay in this part of the project area.

Many of the housing societies surveyed were functionally unsound, run purely as business enterprises by a group of rich people, including those earning foreign exchange abroad, attracted to invest in real estate by the rapid urbanization that took place after 1971

[5] *The DND project became operational in 1968. For additional information on settlement in the DND project area, see also Chapters 4 and 5.*

TABLE 10.14
Location of housing projects surveyed

Thana	No of units
Muhammadpur	11
Mirpur	10
Sabhar	34
Joydebpur	3
Gulshan	3
Tongi	1
Demra	1
Mohakhali	1
Tejturibazar	1
Others	2
Total	**67**

Note: Some of the Thanas listed are metropolitan police stations.

TABLE 10.15
Amount of land used by housing projects in surveyed Thanas

Year of establishment	No of projects	Total area (acres)	Average area (acres)
1940-50	–	–	–
1950-60	1	100.00	100.00
1960-70	5	55.78	11.16
1970-75	6	227.34	37.89
1975-80	54	787.85	14.59
1981	1	3.30	3.30
Total	**67**	**1174.27**	**17.53**

TABLE 10.16
Classification of land presently used for housing projects in 1918 Settlement operation

Classification	Area (acres)	Proportion (%)
Agricultural	410.89	34.99
Fallow	228.96	19.50
Non-agricultural	534.42	45.51
Total	**1174.27**	**100.00**

TABLE 10.17
Land use on housing project sites at time of land acquisition

Classification	Area (acres)	Proportion (%)
Agricultural	753.09	64.13
Fallow	109.00	9.28
Non-agricultural	309.87	26.39
Not reported	2.31	0.20
Total	**1174.27**	**100.00**

TABLE 10.18
Mode of land acquisition of housing project sites

Mode	Area (acres)	Proportion (%)
Purchase	1129.65	96.20
Long/short-term lease	44.62	3.80
Total	**1174.27**	**100.00**

TABLE 10.19
Number and extent of houses in Dania mouza 1962-1981

Year	Total area (acres)	Area under houses (acres)	No of houses	Proportion of land under houses (%)
1962	828.95	50.33	176	6.07
1975[1]	828.12	59.15	323	7.13
1981	829.12	102.23	1621	12.33

Note: 1. Revisional settlement operation, in progress.

and leading to the mushroom growth in cooperative housing societies. Almost all the societies expressed their willingness to take up more projects. Although these societies were avowedly organizations aimed at rehabilitating their members by providing residential accommodation through joint efforts, many were, in fact, instruments for land speculation. The initiators, often very few in number, invested in land merely to distribute it piecemeal to newly-enrolled members. However, the land appeared to be being distributed in economic units, with plot sizes seldom exceeding 0.16 acre.

10.3.4 Pineapple gardens

All the 60 pineapple gardens surveyed were in Maulvi Bazar and Srimangal Thanas of Sylhet District. None had been established before 1950, only one in 1950-60, 14 in 1960-70 and 45 in 1970-80, showing the increasing trend with time (Table 10.20). That table shows that they occupied an average of 7.92 acres of land, with a range between 6.43 and 8.96 acres.

The pineapple gardens were not previously part of tea gardens. The latter were settled in perpetuity, either by Government or by previous landlords. Nor do they come within the category of unclassified state forests. The survey did not reveal any case of squatters. At the time of the last Survey and Settlement operation in Sylhet District, carried out between 1950 and 1960, the land occupied by the pineapple gardens surveyed in this study was classified as *tila* (hillock), *began* (garden) or *chhan khola* (land used for cutting grass), indicating that some of the land was then classified as horticultural. At the time of acquisition, about one-third was classified as agricultural, about one-quarter fallow and the rest non-agricultural (Table 10.21). About one-fifth had been obtained by inheritance, almost half by purchase, and most of the rest on lease (Table 10.22).

Informants told the study team that pineapples could be grown for a few years without apparent damage to the soils. Possibly the garden owners had misgivings about the purpose of the study for, in fact, pineapple cultivation by the methods practised on the hill-slopes is

TABLE 10.20
Amount of land used by pineapple gardens in surveyed Thanas

Year started	No of gardens	Total land used		Average land used	
		When started (acres)	In 1981 (acres)	When started (acres)	In 1981 (acres)
1940-50	–	–	–	–	–
1950-60	1	5.00	8.00	5.00	8.00
1960-70	14	140.70	125.50	10.05	8.95
1970-75	32	273.10	257.90	8.53	8.06
1975-80	13	74.80	83.55	5.75	6.43
Total	**60**	**493.60**	**474.95**	**8.23**	**7.92**

TABLE 10.21
Land use on pineapple garden sites at time of land acquisition

Classification	Area (acres)	Proportion (%)
Agricultural	182.10	33.43
Fallow	131.55	24.16
Non-agricultural	231.00	42.41
Total	**544.65**	**100.00**

TABLE 10.22
Mode of land acquisition of pineapple garden sites

Mode	Area (acres)	Proportion (%)
Inheritance	116.25	21.56
Purchase	256.55	47.59
Long/short-term lease	164.35	30.48
Others	2.00	0.37
Total	**530.15**	**100.00**

highly destructive to the soil.[6] The heavy rains in this area wash away the topsoil through channels between the plant rows, rendering the soil unproductive within a very short time. However, no case of abandoned pineapple gardens came to notice during the survey.

10.4 EXISTING LAWS AND REGULATIONS

10.4.1 Existing situation

No statutory steps to regulate the use of agricultural land appear to have been taken before the enactment of the East Bengal State Acquisition and Tenancy Act, 1951, except in the Chittagong Hill Tracts. That act was the pioneer legislation, containing prohibitory measures

---

[6] *See also Chapter 8, Section 8.3.2.*

for protecting agricultural land from passing into non-agricultural use. Section 90 of the Act prohibits the transfer of the holding of a *raiyat* (tenant), or a share or portion thereof, except to a *bona fide* cultivator, without previous written permission from the competent Revenue authority on specific grounds. The penalty for contravening this provision amounts to forfeiture of the land so transferred. Section 76 of the Act also provides that no land shall be settled by the Government with a person unless that person is an agriculturalist. Section 96 confers the right of pre-emption to agricultural tenants holding land contiguous to land transferred. Unfortunately, all these regulatory provisions appear to have lain in the statute books without any effect, due to the absence of any rule framed thereunder prescribing the machinery to take cognizance of cases of contravention, impose penalties and take other measures to enforce them.

Section 18, subsection 2, clauses (d) and (h) of the Chittagong Hill Tracts Regulation, 1900, empowers the Government to make rules to regulate or restrict the transfer of land and to regulate the requisition by Government of land required for public purposes in the Hill Tracts. These rules are enforceable by the Deputy Commissioner of the District.

The East Bengal Transfer of Agricultural Lands Act, 1951, was enacted to prohibit the transfer of agricultural land exceeding a prescribed ceiling (10 standard *bighas* = 3.33 acres) to any person, agriculturalist or otherwise, on pain of fine and/or forfeiture of the land. One of the objectives underlying this enactment probably was to restrict the transfer of agricultural land in bulk for non-agricultural uses. This legislation saved big areas of agricultural land from falling freely into the hands of non-agriculturalists. However, for unknown reasons, this Act was repealed in 1968.

One of the existing land-taxation measures applicable to the transfer of immovable property (including land) is the capital gains tax payable under the Finance Act on the basis of the market value of such property. Additionally, the annual ground rent (later termed land development tax) is considerably higher for land used for commercial, industrial and residential purposes than is the rate payable for agricultural land.

10.4.2 Inadequacies of existing provisions

The existing provisions of the East Bengal State Acquisition and Tenancy Act, 1951, are not only ineffective, but they are also quite inadequate. In the first place, this Act does not provide for the prevention of agricultural land transfers as speculative transactions. Secondly, there is no bar to completely changing the character of agricultural land by way of excavations, as in the case of brickyards. The absolute right of a person to use his landed property in any way he likes so long as it does not transgress on the rights of others can retard the use of the full potential of agricultural land. The absence of any effective machinery to enforce the provisions of Sections 76, 90 and 96 of the Act, referred to above, is another retarding factor.

The biggest obstacle to the retention of agricultural land for purely agricultural use is the alluring prices offered by those wishing to convert such land to non-agricultural uses. The Consultant's survey showed instances of the best agricultural land having been purchased when land of lower quality could have been used. The speculative price of land in and around urban areas is a factor tempting poor agriculturalists to sell their land to industrialists and house-builders. Unfortunately, too, the properties which make soil material suitable for brick-making are similar to those which make a good agricultural soil.

10.4.3   Identification of areas of intervention

In Bangladesh, as in other developing countries, it is hardly possible to draw specific limits specifying the area of intervention in matters of land use. The rapid expansion of urbanization, industrialization, housing settlements, communications and other developments causes tremendous pressure on agricultural land. The use of land for brick-making, which is associated with major infrastructural developments, aggravates the situation. Green-belts around urban areas recede rapidly. Therefore, areas where townships are growing seem to be the first region that calls for intervention. Vast areas of the finest agricultural land are being usurped by the construction of buildings and roads. The scope of the existing District Land Allocation Committee is limited because the committee is guided by considerations of the suitability of a site for the purpose for which the applicant seeks to purchase it and of fairness to the existing land owners. The committee has no responsibility to preserve agricultural land nor to curb speculative land prices. This appears to be a field where intervention is needed.

The need for intervention is most acute in and around urban areas where haphazard, unplanned developments are proceeding. City master plans contemplate zoning land for different uses with a view to controlling private development throughout an urban area. Some land planners have thought of special area plans and controls embracing specific areas, such as infrastructure impact plans which provide a basic framework for assessing and restricting the secondary impacts of major infrastructure investments such as highways, water supply and sewerage systems, steel mills or petroleum refineries.

Planning and regulatory agencies are also concerned with layouts within the sites of proposed residential, commercial, industrial or mixed projects. The sites are referred to as 'subdivision plans' and the control system applicable to them as 'subdivision controls'. Such sites are called 'site development schemes' in the Paurashava Ordinance, 1977, Section 96, of the Town Planning Rules (Section 11) (Kaplan, 1980).

The scope of intervention can also extend to the purchase of development rights in urban areas: i.e., the public acquisition of development rights. The scheme assumes the creation of some form of an urban development land trust, the broad purpose of which would be the acquisition of interests in land in advance of the requirements of a specific urban improvement scheme. The initial activities of the trust would be limited to the acquisition of development rights only, the owners being left with their existing use rights until and unless the land is actually needed for construction purposes (Urban Development Directorate, 1979).

In rural areas, local bodies may need to have recourse to zoning regulations for development planning. Intervention in these areas is becoming increasingly important in order to protect valuable agricultural land. Similarly, in hill areas, steps need to be taken for the conservation of hill slopes and other land.

10.5 CONCLUSIONS AND RECOMMENDATIONS

10.5.1   General

Except for the pineapple-growing area in Sylhet District, the areas surveyed lay within a radius of about twenty miles from the outskirts of Dhaka city. It was assumed that the findings would not differ materially from conditions in other regions of the country where urban activities were expanding. Thus, the study findings were considered to be an adequate guide to the formulation of a land use policy and for framing an action programme for the country as a whole.

10.5.2 National policy

The big impact of fast-expanding development projects has started to be felt and thoughts on how to regulate land use are emerging, as was referred to in Section 10.2.1. Professor James has observed that legislative measures can help to frame policies for the best use of land and its control (James, 1973). Nuruzzaman (*op. cit.*) opined that a regulatory process cannot work unless the agencies entrusted with planning are provided with adequate enforcement powers under enabling laws: powers to regulate, to control, to adopt rules and to make bye-laws (rules framed by an implementing agency under the General Act). Such controls would have the effect of restricting individual property rights in the interest of the community as a whole. Gracknell in an article dealing with land use policy also commented as follows.

> "Legislation is, of course, a dynamic process. New legislation aims to adapt the law to the condition and concerns of the 1980s. Clearly the trend in land policy, in Europe at least, is somewhat more legislative intervention to ensure a fair deal to the farmers and society in general."[7]

The existing situation in Bangladesh with regard to land use regulation is rather dismal. The erratic sprawl of houses and industry, the imprudent alignment of roads and buildings, and the avoidable waste of good agricultural land for non-agricultural purposes where land of poor or moderate quality is available are some of the common features of the existing situation. In this small country with a teeming population, the rational and prudent use of land is imperative. The national economy being almost wholly agro-based, every inch of agricultural land needs to be protected from wastage. Therefore, a sound land use policy should be considered to be a national issue of paramount importance.

The national issue can be spelt out as follows. Any legislation in the field of planning has to offer the possibility of two types of plan: the municipal plan and the regional plan, all within the framework of national policy objectives (Corver, date?). In rural regions, what is needed is 'developmental' as much as 'protective' planning. These are areas where multi-sectoral development is required in order to improve rural employment and incomes. Here, land development planning has to deal with the optimum integration of land use covering agriculture, forestry, recreation, communications, nature conservation, rural industries, etc. Consequently, not only is an integrated approach essential to the development of rural areas, but land use planning is the vital component of this process.

A comprehensive national land use plan should take into account, *inter alia*, the following policy issues.

1. Unplanned use of land in 'growth centres' and human settlements is seriously straining the scarce land resources of Bangladesh, besides causing health, sanitation, environmental and socio-economic problems, which need control, regulation and guidance through legal and administrative interventions.

---

[7] *The original report gives the source as M.P. Gracknell in an article on land use policy in 'World Agriculture' without further details.*

2. Irrigation-based modern agriculture, especially through cooperatives, must have institutional support in relation to the layout of distribution channels, unrestricted access to water and non-conflicting cropping patterns.

3. Overall rural development by way of land reforms, tenurial changes, etc., which are needed for optimum land use has to be ensured through a legal framework.[8]

Two other matters which need to be reflected in national land use policy are the conservation of forest and soils in hill areas, and ensuring that land acquired for private or public purposes is fully used for its intended purpose.

10.5.3 Land reform

For optimum land use in Bangladesh, measures aiming at land reform are inescapable. This subject covers:

    a. fixing a ceiling on land holdings at a much lower level than the present;

    b. conferring tenurial rights on share-croppers, or otherwise protecting their interests; and

    c. consolidation of land holdings.

A pilot project on land consolidation taken up towards the end of 1960 ended in a fiasco. The project was in Debiganj and part of Boda Thanas in Dinajpur District, covering 175 square miles, and work was completed on 30 June 1962. Although the consolidation operation was duly completed and notified in the official Gazette, it had to be nullified by another notification because of the strong opposition which came from the small farmers and *bargardars* (tenants) in the area. The matter was studied by the Land Revenue Administrative Enquiry Committee, East Pakistan, 1963. The committee recommended that "no further scheme for compulsory consolidation of holdings be taken up in any area of East Pakistan."[9]

The fixing of a ceiling on land holdings has engaged the attention of land planners for a long time. The East Bengal Land Acquisition and Tenancy Act, 1951, fixed the ceiling at 100 *bighas* (33 acres), but this was raised to 375 *bighas* in 1961 under the Ayub regime. The ceiling was reduced again to 100 *bighas* by a notification issued under the Bangladesh President's Order No 98 of 1972.

However, the fate of share-croppers has remained unchanged. Although a law was contemplated at the time of Partition in 1947, no specific enactment followed. Additionally, the problem relating to fragmentation of holdings, due mainly to the Muslim laws of inheritance, presents a staggering problem in Bangladesh. The Land Revenue Commission in 1959 found that more than 50 percent of cultivators had less than 3 acres of land per

---

[8] Note reference No LGRDC/SECY/186/81 dated August 19, 1981, of the Secretary, Ministry of Local Government, Rural Development and Cooperatives, Dhaka.

[9] *Readers should note that the term 'land fragmentation' has two connotations: the division of land among family members on the death of the family head, leading to a decreasing size of family land owned in successive generations; and the distribution of family land in scattered plots in different parts of a village (or in neighbouring villages). Land consolidation legislation aimed to deal with the former situation, not the latter. The expansion of small-scale irrigation and use of power-tillers in recent years could lead to a spontaneous consolidation of scattered land holdings because of the greater convenience to farmers of managing contiguous fields with mechanized practices.*

family. The remainder were either landless or marginal farmers.[10] This matter needs to be tackled at the national level to ensure optimum land use.

10.5.4 Consultant's recommendations

It is now universally recognized that there must be a comprehensive land use policy for the nation as a whole. Such a policy would cater for the development needs of urban areas and also take care of the special requirements of rural areas covered by Thana and Union Parishads (Councils). However, the framing of a national land use policy is an innovatory undertaking, which needs to be backed by a strong political will. Given the political will, the determination of national land use policy would need to be followed by legislative enactments and administrative measures providing the manner and areas of intervention, as indicated below.

1. In the first place, a new law should be enacted to serve as an umbrella for city master plans, urban development plans and the proposed Thana Land Use Development Programme.[11] An enabling law of this kind should give the legal backing for implementing Government's national land use policy. The law should back special area plans, infrastructure impact plans, and subdivision plans and controls (discussed in Section 10.4.3). However, in the existing socio-economic context, it is open to serious doubt whether the law should also embrace any scheme for the purchase of development rights in urban areas. The law should also give institutional support to ensure proper layout of irrigation distribution channels, unrestricted access to water and non-conflicting cropping patterns, as indicated in Section 10.5.1.

2. In almost all countries abroad, zoning appears to have been accepted as one of the ways for achieving proper land use. However, this also has some inherent drawbacks. It has been observed that zoning causes inflation of land prices. It may also create conflicts of interest in matters such as irrigation, communications and sanitation. Besides, circumvention of zoning regulations has been found to be easy and frequent. In spite of all these constraints, zoning of land around cities (e.g., to provide for 'green-belts') and also in some rural areas (e.g., for the siting of industrial estates) may need to be planned and administered by Government agencies, city authorities and other local bodies with the backing of the enabling law referred to above.

3. The existing provisions of the East Bengal State Acquisition and Tenancy Act, 1951, should be strengthened and their scope expanded. In the first place, the relevant provisions regarding transfer of land and right of pre-emption should be made more comprehensive, with powers to frame necessary rules to empower agencies to function in an effective manner. Similarly, the Chittagong Hill Tracts regulation, 1900, should be amended to cover regulation of the use and transfer of land in more clear terms and language, and also to ensure proper soil conservation. As regards other laws pertaining to local bodies — such as the Paurashava Ordinance, 1977; Local Government Ordinance, 1976; and other laws governing the administration of Dhaka Municipal Corporation, Dhaka Improvement Trust, Khulna Improvement Trust and other such bodies — such bodies should be given powers to regulate and

---

[10]*The Report on the Agricultural Census of Agriculture, 1983-84, (BBS, 1984), found that 79.88 percent of the country's rural population owned less than 3 acres and 8.67 percent were totally landless. If those owning homestead land but no cultivable land were included, the landless figure was 19.6 percent.*

[11]*See Chapter 22.*

control land use within the areas of their jurisdiction and to frame rules and bye-laws for creating control mechanisms to enforce them effectively.

4. Effective land-taxation measures could also serve as a deterrent to the conversion of agricultural land to non-agricultural use. The existing taxation provisions in this respect are contained in the Land Development Tax Act, 1980, and the Finance Act, 1981. At present (1981), land development tax (originally known as 'ground rent') is Tk.3 per acre for agricultural land up to a total land holding per family of 8.25 acres, and Tk.15 per acre if the total land holding exceeds 8.25 acres. For non-agricultural land in Dhaka, Chittagong and Khulna cities, this tax is payable at Tk.2,250 per acre; for other municipal areas, the rate is Tk.750 per acre if the land is used for commercial or industrial purposes. However, if the land is used for residential purposes, the rate is Tk.600 per acre in Dhaka, Chittagong and Khulna city areas and Tk.300 in other District headquarters. In other parts of the country, the land development tax is Tk.500 per acre for land used for industry or commerce and Tk.250 per acre for residential and other purposes.

In effect, the tax measures described above have not proved effective because of the absence of day-to-day reporting of land use conversions to the local revenue authorities. Accordingly, Government should make it mandatory, by executive orders, for all such conversions to be reported to Thana revenue officials for the registration of transfer documents and mutation of transferees' names in the Collector's records. This could easily be done, as in the case of the capital gains tax payable to the income tax authorities, who insist that land registration officers will not register any transfer deed until the gains tax is paid. As for the capital gains tax itself, payable under the current Finance Act, the existing rates appear to be reasonable.

5. As described earlier, the District Land Allocation Committees presently have only limited scope in the matter of land acquisition. Through executive directives, these committees need to be made more effective instruments to control abuse and wastage of agricultural land, and also to ensure intensive use of land acquired for non-agricultural purposes (both by private and public bodies).

6. Thana planning also embraces Union and village-level planning. Any action programme to enforce legal and administrative measures for regulating the use and transfer of rural land should involve Thana and Union Parishads and Gram Sarkars.[12] These bodies have full knowledge of the requirements of land for various local purposes and their recommendations need to be given full weight before a local official entrusted with the enforcement of legal or administrative measures gives a final verdict. The role of these local bodies is so vital that legal or other administrative restrictions on the free transfer of agricultural land by sale or by other means for any purpose other than agricultural use ought not to proceed without their direct participation.

---

[12]*Gram Sarkars (village governments) were subsequently abolished and the development functions of Union Councils reduced: see Chapter 22.*

PART III

LAND USE POLICY AND PRINCIPLES

The three chapters in this part describe the policies and principles underlying the contents of the chapters on national and local-level planning which are included in Parts IV and V. Chapter 11 on national land use policy sets out the basic principles of rational land use and the responsibilities of national and local-level governments for implementing them. These principles are amplified in Chapter 12 in describing a strategy for plant production to meet national and local fuel, fodder and construction needs. Chapter 13 deals specifically with the principles of land management in Bangladesh's hill areas.

Chapter 11

NATIONAL LAND USE POLICY[1]

*Nine principles of rational land use for sustainable development are proposed, and their rationale
and implications are explained. The responsibilities of government officials and local government
councils for land use planning and development are indicated.*

11.1 INTRODUCTION

Land, water, the monsoon climate, and the inherited experience and skills of its people are
Bangladesh's most important natural resources. Until recently, these resources were sufficient to
support the country's population at a modest standard of living, except in years with
catastrophic floods, cyclones or drought. However, the rapid rise in population in the past
few decades has surpassed the capacity of these resources to support all the country's population
at a satisfactory level using traditional production techniques within the traditional social
system.

   Fortunately, Bangladesh's wealth of natural resources is such that production can be
greatly increased by the use of appropriate modern technology such as irrigation, drainage,
improved crop varieties and fertilizers.[2] Accordingly, the national land use policy must be
to develop and use the full potential of every available piece of land, source of water, and
able-bodied man and woman for producing food and industrial crops, livestock, fish and
forest products so as to support all the country's population at a satisfactory standard of
living.

11.2 PRINCIPLES

In order to achieve the above objectives, the following principles must be followed.

   1. **All land will be used in such a way that it will be handed on to future generations in
      an improved condition for productive use.**

---

[1] *This chapter is based on a draft discussion paper which the author prepared for the Ministry of Agriculture and
Forests in December 1979 at a time when the Government of Bangladesh was seeking to achieve foodgrains
self-sufficiency and decentralize rural and agricultural development planning to Thana, Union and village levels.
At that time, the author was involved in the training course for a pilot Thana land use development planning
programme at the Bangladesh Academy for Rural Development, Comilla: see Chapter 22. The names of local-level
institutions have been retained as they were in 1979. The development functions of Thana and Union Councils were
subsequently reduced and village committees were abolished.*

[2] *The opportunities for accelerating the pace of agricultural development are reviewed in Brammer (1997).*

This means that land must be managed so as to maintain (and, if possible, improve) soil fertility and to prevent erosion.

2. **The full production potential of all land will be developed, using appropriate modern technology and management techniques.**

This means that:

   a. existing knowledge — including traditional knowledge — of the country's land and water resources and of modern production technology must be used and increased for planning improved land use throughout the country;

   b. existing systems of land ownership and tenancy which prevent land and water resources from being used to their full potential must be replaced by equitable systems which encourage increased production;[3]

   c. small farmers and fishermen must be provided with production credit and insurance at reasonable interest rates;

   d. producers must be assured of essential input supplies and a fair market price for their increased crop, livestock, fisheries and forestry production.

   In addition, cooperative or group farming must be strongly encouraged so as to overcome the constraints on increased cropping intensity and production which fragmented land holdings and small plot sizes provide.

3. **Within available resources, priority will be given to investments in land and water development which will provide the maximum sustained production increases consistent with acceptable standards of social security.**

This means that:

   a. in each area — village, Union, Thana, District, Division (or hydrological region) — the physical constraints which prevent sustainable, high-yielding, production of crops, livestock, fish and/or forest products must be identified, and plans should be made for removing these constraints to the extent possible within existing or foreseeable fund allocations from local and national sources;

   b. at national, regional and local levels, plans must be made for the rational development of water resources for irrigation and other essential uses, viz.–

      i. wherever feasible, surface water supplies must be conserved by the building of cross-dams, the excavation of new channels and the desilting of existing tanks and channels;

      ii. priority in the allocation of surface-water supplies for irrigation must be given to areas where groundwater supplies are insufficient for irrigation requirements;

      iii. priority in groundwater development must be given to the use of dug wells, hand pumps and shallow tube-wells, except where the use of deep tube-wells is

---

[3] *Reviews of Thana data for HYV rice area and fertilizer off-take made in 1974 and 1985 respectively showed that the spread of modern technology was most rapid in areas of predominantly small land holdings and slowest in known areas of big land holdings (Khulna, Barisal, Patuakhali, Noakhali Districts, western and northern border Districts, and Sylhet District): see Brammer (1985); Brammer (1997), Chapter 10. These areas of big land-holdings and low-input farming are also the traditional areas of surplus rice production. That apparent anomaly is explained by the fact that, under traditional share-cropping terms, land-owners receive 50 percent (or more) of production, generally without providing any production inputs or management support. Even with low production levels of, say, half-a-ton of rice per acre (1.25 t/ha), a land-owner with 10 acres (4 ha) could therefore receive 2.5 tons of rice per year as his 'share'. That is more than twice the amount he might need annually to feed his family, leaving a large surplus which he could sell to meet his other needs.*

the only practical means for providing water to the whole of an area needing irrigation;[4]

    iv. within any particular area, priority must be given to providing irrigation for land where this will produce the greatest net increase in annual crop production;

c. irrigation water must be used economically, so that the benefits of irrigation can be provided to the maximum possible area of land, viz.–

    i. on permeable soils, irrigation should be used for cultivating water-economical crops such as wheat, vegetables, pulses or oilseeds, followed by appropriate broadcast (or line-sown) kharif crops such as aus, deepwater aman, jute, etc.

    ii. transplanted rice (boro, aus or aman) should be grown with irrigation on impermeable soils;

    iii. a rotational, round-the-clock system of water distribution must be organized in order to reduce distribution losses;

    iv. irrigation channels must be lined along sections where seepage losses during continuous operation exceed about 10 percent of flow;

d. increased production must not be obtained at the expense of cultivators on other land — for example, by depriving them of existing water supplies or by causing increased waterlogging — nor must it reduce employment opportunities for existing tenants and agricultural labourers.

4. **Priority will be given to production methods which will increase total rural employment.**

This means that:

a. labour-intensive techniques must be used for constructing embankments, roads, canals, soil conservation works, etc.;

b. cropping intensity must be maximized on all kinds of land;

c. service and processing facilities should be provided as close as possible to the crop, livestock, fishery or forestry production areas; and

d. agricultural production and processing equipment should be priced at such a level that its use will not encourage a net displacement of labour.[5]

5. **All land and water will be used in such a way that it does not harm the legitimate interests of other individuals, groups or communities.**

This means that:

a. sloping land in hill and terrace areas which is unsuitable for cultivation must be planted to tree crops or forest so as to reduce run-off of water which might damage land, crops, property or water supplies in lower areas by flash floods or sedimentation;

---

[4] *The discouragement of deep tube-wells apparently conflicts with the advocacy of cooperative or group farming in Principle 2. The explanation is that, despite their greater efficiency in theory, deep tube-wells provided problems in practice because of their greater unit cost and the difficulty of organizing irrigation groups where as many as one hundred cultivators, with diverse social and farming interests, might be involved in a command area.*

[5] *Disincentives to purchase and/or use labour-displacing equipment could also be effected through the imposition of national or local sales taxes and annual licences.*

   b. for the same reason, and so as to prevent erosion of their own soils, farmers using cultivable land in hill and terrace areas must use appropriate soil conservation techniques;

   c. the customary rights of existing water users for irrigation, navigation, fishing, etc., must be respected; changes in water-flow, such as might be caused by digging a drainage channel, making a cross-dam or constructing an embankment, should be made only with the agreement of those who might suffer economic loss because of the change;

   d. no-one (be it farmers, factory-operators, or others) should use fertilizers, pesticides or other materials in such a way that these could, directly or indirectly, damage crops, livestock, fisheries or any other economic interest of users or occupants of land, water or property onto or into which the chemicals or effluents might be carried by air or water;

   e. farmers must cooperate with their neighbours in growing crops, using irrigation water, draining their land, or raising or lowering the level of their land in such a way that does not endanger cultivation or other land use in adjoining fields, tanks or channels; also, farmers must cooperate with their neighbours in controlling weeds, pests and diseases so that these do not spread onto adjoining fields;

   f. where compensation needs to be paid for loss of water rights or for damage to land or crops, this should be provided promptly, in cash or in kind, on a scale commensurate with the actual deprivation of incomes or livelihoods involved, taking into account reasonable alternative opportunities which are available for employment and income during the period of loss.

6. The minimum possible amount of land will be taken out of productive agricultural use for conversion to urban and industrial use.

This means that:

   a. Municipal, Thana and Union Councils must make regulations to control the transfer of land within their borders so that, to the maximum extent feasible, good quality agricultural land is preserved for productive agricultural use; this implies that, where a choice exists, new housing, offices, factories, roads, brickyards, refuse dumps, etc., should be sited on land of the lowest agricultural quality which is conveniently available;

   b. the Bangladesh Public Works Department and Municipal, Thana and Union Councils must make regulations to control building standards so that wastage of land is avoided; these authorities should only approve compact lay-outs, and they should give preference to multi-storey designs where these would be appropriate;[6]

   c. Municipal, Thana and Union Councils should grant permission for siting new brickyards and borrow areas only on the condition that the operators will, within a specified time-limit, restore the land to a specified, appropriate, productive use (such as for crop production, fish culture, irrigation use, etc.);[7]

---

[6] *The background to this proposed regulation was that experience showed that government agencies often acquired extravagant amounts of land for new buildings: see Chapter 7, Section 7.7.*

[7] *Land formerly was acquired to extract soil material for making bricks on the site and the site generally was used for only one or two years, then abandoned leaving a deep excavation, a derelict kiln and piles of unused bricks. In 1979, the author first observed a different practice being used near Comilla, where farmers merely sold the uppermost 1-1½ feet (30-45 cm) of soil to brickyard operators and then continued cultivating the*

d. Municipal, Thana and Union Councils must seek to persuade owners — including Government owners — of derelict brickyards, borrow sites, tanks and other waste land to restore such land to an appropriate productive use. If persuasion fails, these authorities must use powers of compulsory acquisition to take over such land themselves and, either directly or by auction of the site, restore the land to productive use for agriculture or for fish culture.[8]

7. **Irrigation, drainage, embankment, road and railway development will be planned and executed in such a way that minimizes the loss of land from productive agricultural use.**

This means that:

a. structures should be rigorously designed so as to minimize the amount of land acquired;

b. where a choice exists, structures should be sited on land of the lowest agricultural potential available so as to minimize the loss of agricultural production;

c. where feasible, borrow areas should be left in a condition suitable for productive use, either as irrigation canals, for fish production or for cultivation;

d. embankments must not cause increased flooding or waterlogging of adjoining land which might damage crops directly or indirectly;

e. cross-dams should be built only where they will not reduce the flow of water to down-stream areas below the quantity required for legitimate established or foreseen uses (for example, for irrigation, navigation, fisheries or domestic use);

f. drainage of haors, beels and khals for catching fish should not be carried out in such a way as will waste water which could otherwise be used for irrigation.[9]

8. **Wherever feasible, measures will be undertaken to minimize the impact of natural disasters on agricultural production and other economic activities.**

This means that, in disaster-prone areas, priority must be given to:

a. providing soil conservation, flood-protection, drainage and/or irrigation so as to eliminate or reduce the incidence of damage by floods, storm surge or drought and to intensify cultivation in the relatively safe dry season; and

b. making contingency plans so that appropriate agricultural rehabilitation measures can be introduced with the minimum delay following disastrous losses of crops, livestock, structures or means of production.[10]

Also, within Government-operated flood protection, drainage and other land development project areas, the project authority must frame and administer land

---

remaining soil. That practice quickly spread to other floodplain areas of the country. Borrow areas are sites where soil material is excavated for constructing a road, railway or flood embankment on adjoining land. The site is acquired as part of the land acquired for building the embankment and is administered by the acquiring authority (usually a Government agency). Usually, old brickyards and borrow pits contain water for part or all of the year.

[8] An assessment was made of the area of land occupied by derelict brickyards and possible ways of reclaiming them for productive use: see Chapters 7 and 10.

[9] An important principle not referred to in the original text was the need to provide adequate and timely compensation to people whose interests might be adversely affected by development activities on neighbouring land.

[10]Disaster mitigation measures are described in detail in Brammer (1999).

use regulations which will prevent the spread of settlement and industry onto land where people and property would be seriously endangered in case of a breach in an embankment, failure of pumps, etc. Project authorities must have contingency plans available for retiring or strengthening embankments, replacing pumps, etc., in time to prevent catastrophic damage, and for evacuating endangered people and livestock to specified safe areas in case a disaster cannot be avoided.

9. **Central and local government authorities will provide the appropriate infrastructure so that land and water development facilities, input supplies and technical advice are readily available to producers and so that the latter can market their produce at a fair price.**

This means that the established procedures of the Union and Thana Works Programme and Irrigation Programme must be supported and strengthened for the purpose of:

a. identifying local development needs and opportunities;

b. providing technical advice;

c. approving the use of development funds;

d. implementing approved schemes;

e. maintaining and repairing structures and equipment in a timely manner;

f. motivating individuals and groups to adopt improved agricultural, livestock, fisheries and forestry practices;

g. improving communications to facilitate the movement of input supplies, provision of services and marketing of produce;

h. providing improved storage and distribution facilities for input supplies;

i. providing procurement, processing or marketing facilities; and

j. improving farmers' crop drying, processing and storage facilities.

In the case of large-scale projects for flood protection, irrigation or soil conservation, the relevant project authority must provide this infrastructure, but it will do so in full consultation with Union and Thana Councils so as to ensure that local information and needs are adequately taken into account.

11.3 IMPLEMENTATION

In order to implement this national land use policy, the following responsibilities will be allocated.

1. The Agricultural and Rural Development Council[11] will be the supreme body responsible for directing and reviewing the implementation of national land use policy.

2. The Divisional Development Boards and District Development Committees will direct and implement national land use policy within their respective areas of responsibility. They will initiate or review proposed land use development schemes, and will recommend or approve the allocation of funds for implementing such schemes within the limits of their financial authority. These boards and committees will comprise the respective Divisional/District heads of the relevant development Ministries, Directorates, Corporations and Commodity Boards, together with an appropriate number of Members of Parliament from the area.

[11]*This was a council of Ministers.*

3. Thana and Union Development Committees, with the help of appropriate Thana and Union officials, will continue to be responsible for identifying, planning and implementing small-scale land use development schemes according to the established procedures of the Thana and Union Works Programme and Irrigation Programme.[12]

4. Thana and Union Councils will also be responsible for making and enforcing appropriate regulations (bye-laws) governing land use within their boundaries. This responsibility will include the zoning of land to ensure that, to the maximum possible extent, good quality agricultural land is preserved for productive use, that the minimum amount of land is sacrificed for housing, offices, roads and industrial use, and that land used for brickyards is restored to specified productive use within a specified time-limit.

5. Village Land Use Development Committees will be set up to supersede the existing Village Food Production Committees. Their functions will be to assist the Thana and Union Councils in increasing production and employment by:

   a. identifying the needs and opportunities for improved land use (including agricultural, livestock, fisheries and forestry production);

   b. motivating cultivators to form production, credit and marketing cooperatives;

   c. persuading and motivating land-owners and cultivators to adopt improved practices which will maximize production;

   d. persuading and motivating land-owners and cultivators to consolidate their land holdings or to form cooperative farming blocks in areas where it is considered that land fragmentation or small plot sizes are obstacles to increasing production;

   e. if necessary, imposing social sanctions on land-owners or cultivators who are unwilling to adopt improved land use practices, or who plan or attempt to use practices which the Committee considers will be harmful to the cultivators' own land or to their neighbours' land or crops;

   f. organizing the monitoring and treatment of harmful pests and diseases affecting crops and livestock;

   g. organizing the monitoring and amendment of land quality so as to ensure that embankments, drainage, irrigation, land levelling, tillage practices and cropping practices do not adversely affect production in the short term or the longer term.

6. Village Land Use Development Committees will also be responsible for reconciling disputes involving land or water use within their village or with neighbouring villages. Any disputes which a Village Committee is unable to settle will be referred to the Union Council for reconciliation. The Union Council will refer any disputes which it is unable to settle to the Thana Council for reconciliation.

7. The Thana Council will be responsible for negotiating agreements with neighbouring Thanas regarding surface-water rights: that is, the minimum quantity of water which it will receive from or pass on to neighbouring Thanas during the low-flow season. Any disputes in this respect will be referred to the District Development Committee for arbitration.

8. The Ministry of Agriculture and the Bangladesh Water Development Board (BWDB) will make available existing technical information on climate, soils, topography,

---

[12]*At the time that this policy statement was drafted, it was intended to add, also, a Thana and Union Land Use Development Programme: see Chapter 22.*

surface-water and groundwater hydrology, present land use and land use potential in a readily usable format for use by officials and the people's elected representatives at national, Divisional, District, Thana, Union, and village levels.[13] These organizations will arrange for the training of officials and elected representatives in the use of this information for planning improved land use. They will also arrange for additional regional and local surveys and studies to be carried out so as to improve existing knowledge of land and water resources, land use practices and socio-economic factors influencing production.[14]

---

[13]*This statement reflected the fact that most of such technical data was classified as 'restricted' and as such was not readily available to potential users (including users in other Government agencies).*

[14]*The memo to the Ministry of Agriculture and Forests which accompanied the draft policy document included two further points, viz.*

  i. *The scope of the existing Village Food Production Committees needed to be changed so as to indicate a broader responsibility for intensive land use development. These committees needed to be reactivated. One of the reasons why, in general, those committees had failed to operate was that the 'village' on which they were based was a social non-entity. Such committees needed to be based on natural social units if they were to come and stay alive. In some cases, the appropriate unit might be the para (a small kinship group living together in part of a village); or, at least, each para should be represented on the village committee, so that everyone felt involved.*

  ii. *The implementation of a land use policy would need education. The philosophy needed to be introduced into bureaucratic thinking and planning, into Agricultural Extension training, into school, college, training institute and university education, and into newspaper, radio and TV publicity.*

Arrangements for launching a Thana Land Use Development Programme on a national scale were under preparation when the Zia Government fell in 1981 and were never reactivated.

Chapter 12

LAND USE POLICY AND BIOMASS PRODUCTION[1]

A strategy for plant production to meet national fuel, fodder and construction needs has to be considered in the context of overall land use policy. This chapter briefly reviews environmental, social, economic and institutional factors which provide the development context within which biomass production should be planned.

12.1 INTRODUCTION

Biomass production — the production of plant material, for whatever purposes — has to be considered in the context of existing land use and future land use policy. Land is required for many purposes, including the production of agricultural crops and livestock, forestry, housing, industry, roads, etc. Because of the high population pressure on land, there is acute competition between these alternative kinds of land use. Land-owners use their land in ways which they consider will give them the best advantage, according to the characteristics of the land and their individual resources and needs. That land use may not always be the best from the point of view of the community in which they live or of the nation.

The production of plants to supply fuel, fodder or construction materials can take place, therefore, only where it has a comparative advantage over alternative forms of land use or it is a by-product of some alternative form of land use. Examples are the production of forest trees on hill slopes which are not suitable for agriculture, and the use of jute sticks for fuel, fencing, etc., after the fibre has been extracted for use or sale. Comparative advantage is determined by the interaction of several factors, including:

a. environmental conditions (soils, climate) which determine what it is possible to produce;

b. market demand, which determines the specific kinds and quantities of products which various kinds of consumers need;

c. market prices, which reflect the balance between supply and demand; the availability of acceptable substitutes; costs of production, transportation and storage; and the consumers' purchasing capacity after meeting their other consumption needs; and

d. the technology available, both for the producer and the consumer.

---

[1] *This chapter is based on a paper prepared for a Training Workshop on Rural Energy organized by the Bangladesh Planning Commission in October 1984 and intended to be included in a Workshop Training Manual. Footnotes which appeared in the original paper are given in normal font. Footnotes that have been added are given in italics.*

Biomass production cannot be considered in isolation. It must be considered within the overall context of biological production, including physical, social and economic aspects. The following sections give a brief review of the main factors influencing land use policy in order to provide the development context within which biomasss production must be considered.

12.2 ENVIRONMENTAL FACTORS

Land use policy in Bangladesh is strongly determined by:
- land and soils;
- climate;
- cultural traditions; and
- the high and increasing population pressure on the land.

Land and soils. Bangladesh's land and soils are suitable for growing a wide range of plants and crops, especially in the dry season. In the rainy season, heavy rainfall and widespread flooding make conditions better suited for wetland crops, especially paddy, than for dryland crops.
- Eighty percent of the country is occupied by floodplain land. Most of this land is flooded or wet for 3-5 months in the rainy season. Some low-lying land stays wet all through the dry season as well.
- Eight percent of the country is occupied by terrace land (the Madhupur and Barind Tracts). Part of this is well-drained Highland; part lies wet in the rainy season. The soils generally do not store moisture for dry-season plant growth as well as floodplain soils do.
- Twelve percent of the country is occupied by hills. These mainly have very steep slopes which are susceptible to erosion if they are not kept covered by vegetation.

Many floodplain soils hold moisture well after the end of the rainy season. Such soils can produce dryland rabi crops (e.g. pulses, oilseeds, wheat) without irrigation. Irrigation is needed mainly for growing boro paddy, which requires more water than most soils can provide naturally. Irrigation is also needed for growing dryland rabi crops on soils which do not store sufficient moisture to satisfy full plant requirements.

Flooded soils receive nutrients from biological activity in the floodwater (not from silt, which most soils do not receive regularly). However, for intensive cropping using modern technology, natural fertility must be supplemented by the use of fertilizers, both on floodplain soils and on terrace and hill soils.

Climate. The monsoon climate provides 5-8 wet months (when rainfall exceeds potential evapotranspiration rates) and 4-7 dry months (when potential evapotranspiration exceeds precipitation). The rainy season is longer and wetter in the East (average rainfall more than 100 inches) than it is in the West (average rainfall less than 60-70 inches). Variations in rainfall from year to year cause relatively frequent floods and droughts. The first half of the dry season is cool; the second half is hot.

The climate is suitable for plant growth throughout the year (where soil moisture supply is sufficient or irrigation can be provided). Tropical crops such as sugarcane and banana can be grown all through the year, and temperate crops such as wheat and potato can be grown in the cool winter months.

Cultural traditions. Rice is the preferred cereal food in Bangladesh. Even though people recognize that wheat is a more sustaining food, they are prepared to pay 50 percent or more higher prices in the market for rice than for wheat. This makes it more profitable for farmers to grow boro paddy than wheat with irrigation, except on permeable soils which are not suitable for growing transplanted paddy.

For this reason, about 80 percent of the country's 5 million acres of irrigated land is used for paddy.[2] The same amount of irrigation water could irrigate 13 million acres of wheat. Of course, not all the soils in irrigated areas may be suitable for wheat cultivation; but if only half the water was used on paddy and half on wheat, that could produce 10 million tons of foodgrain (2.5 million rice; 7.5 million wheat) compared with approximately 4.2 million tons at present (3.6 million rice; 0.8 million wheat).

These figures are theoretical, of course. Because of the strong consumer preference for rice, farmers could not find a market for 7.5 million tons of wheat in the near future. The market price for wheat would then crash, making it unprofitable for farmers to grow wheat. A similar situation exists for potato: 1.2 million tons seems to be about as much as Bangladeshi consumers wish to eat at present; industrial uses have scarcely developed yet.

Population. The high and rapidly-increasing population density is an important factor to be considered in present and future land use policy. The present area of agricultural land is about 22 million acres (ca 9 million ha), and there is little possibility to expand this area. Indeed, the growing population pressure will tend to reduce the cultivable area as new houses, factories, offices and roads are built.[3]

Assuming no change in the available land area, the cultivable area per head and the national foodgrain requirement to feed the population up to the year 2000 A.D. are as shown in Table 12.1. Present foodgrain production is around 15-16 million tons, depending on the vagaries of rainfall and flood. Thus, foodgrain imports of 1-2 million tons are needed each year to bridge the gap.[4]

12.3 POTENTIAL AND CONSTRAINTS

Present crop yields are low, as is shown in Table 12.2.

Potential yields of modern rice and wheat varieties are at least 4 tons per acre. Sugarcane yields in some countries average over 100 tons per acre. The best farmers in Bangladesh produce rice yields of 2-2.5 tons per acre (= 80-100 maunds of unhusked paddy) and 2,000 maunds per acre of sugarcane. Thus, there is considerable scope to increase yields and production.

Constraints which prevent most farmers from reaching the high yields which the best farmers obtain are numerous. They include the following.

    a. *Land tenure*. About 50 percent of the land is owned by land-owners with 5 acres or more. Such farmers generally are not interested in using intensive cultivation methods.

---

[2] *The irrigated area in 1983-84. By 1996-97, the irrigated area had increased to 9.12 million acres. The proportion of the irrigated area used for paddy cultivation apparently remained around 80 percent.*

[3] A seven-Thana study showed less than 1 percent loss of land to settlements, etc., between 1952-74 when population increased by 58 percent in those Thanas: (see Chapter 5). The rate of loss is higher, of course, in peri-urban areas.

[4] *By 1997-98, the population was estimated to be 125 million and foodgrain production 20.66 million tons. Average annual cereal imports over the five years 1993-94 to 1997-98 were 1.87 million tons.*

TABLE 12.1
National foodgrain requirement

Year	Population (millions)	Agricultural land per head (acres)	Annual foodgrain requirement (million tons)
1984	96	0.23	17
1990	113	0.195	20
2000	147	0.15	26

TABLE 12.2
Average national crop yields[5]

Crop	Yield
Aus	0.35 tons/acre (= 9.5 maunds)
B. aman	0.41 tons/acre (= 11.2 maunds)
T. aman	0.57 tons/acre (= 15.5 maunds)
Boro	0.90 tons/acre (= 24.5 maunds)
Wheat	0.75 tons/acre (= 20.4 maunds)
Jute (fibre)	3.2 bales/acre (= 15.5 maunds)
Sugarcane	18 tons/acre (= 490 maunds)

Many are absentee owners who prefer to rent out their land to share-croppers on terms which give the tenant no incentive to invest in modern technology.

b. *Poverty*. Many small farmers are too poor to invest in the recommended doses of fertilizers, pesticides, etc., which are needed to obtain high yields. Those who do not own bullocks must wait until other farmers' bullocks are available for hire, which may delay the sowing of their crops until after the optimum time.

c. *Natural disasters*. Frequent floods and drought reduce average crop yields on much of the land. Frequent crop losses also impoverish farmers. The risk of natural disasters, and the consequent risk of economic losses, discourage farmers in disaster-prone areas from investing heavily in fertilizers, etc.

d. *Purchasing power*. There has been a rapid growth in the proportion of landless families in rural areas in the past few years. By now, about half the rural population is landless and dependent for its livelihood on trade, rural industry or agricultural labouring. With landlessness expected to increase still further, and with the labour force predicted to grow at over 1 million per year in future, it will be increasingly difficult for landless families to find adequate employment in rural areas. This will depress average incomes and purchasing capacity, which in turn will depress the price of rice and wheat, and so make it less profitable for farmers to grow these crops.

Therefore, even if Bangladesh were to produce all the foodgrain which it needs to eat — which is technically feasible — there is a danger that the poorest people may not have enough money to buy all the food they need. That would limit the market demand and prices, and so reduce farmers' economic incentives to produce the surpluses needed to feed other people.

The same argument applies to biomass production for energy or other uses. Poor people spend 60-80 percent of their available income on buying food, so they have little to spare for buying fuel or construction materials.

---

[5] *1 (long) ton = 27.22 maunds/acre = 2.51 tonnes/ha.*

e. *Institutions.* Although it is recognized that present land tenure systems provide a serious constraint on rapid agricultural development, it is also recognized that it will be difficult to change these systems in the short term because there is no effective institutional arrangement for bringing about desirable changes.[6] Other examples of institutional constraints on development are outlined below.

   i. The lack of an appropriate institution to promote, install and maintain equipment such as biogas plants, grain driers, etc. The Department of Agricultural Extension field staff could not handle this specialist and full-time task. Soon after small-scale irrigation equipment was introduced in the 1960s, BADC was created to provide the required services to install and maintain the equipment. A similar arrangement may be needed for other kinds of equipment, until such time as there is sufficient business for the private sector to take over.

   ii. There is no institution which can provide the integrated services required for hill land development: i.e., land use planning; forestry; soil conservation engineering; research; extension; storage and marketing; communications; etc. No single one of the existing government institutions can handle, provide or coordinate all these specialist services.[7]

12.4 AGRICULTURAL POLICY

Government's policy is to ensure the basic needs of the population for food, shelter, health, education and security. Agricultural objectives are to achieve nutritional self-sufficiency and to produce crops and crop-products to expand industry, exports and employment opportunities. Measures used to stimulate increased agricultural production include:

- provision of irrigation, drainage and flood protection in order to increase cropping intensity, crop yields and security of production;
- provision of credit to enable farmers to purchase production inputs; and
- foodgrain procurement to guarantee farmers a reasonable market price for their surplus rice and wheat production.

12.5 LAND USE POLICY

Land use regulation. Government has no effective means to regulate land use, except in urban areas and in some forest areas. Even in so-called reserve forest areas, abuse by *jhum* cultivation and illicit timber extraction is common. Elsewhere, land-owners are free to do what they want with their land. They grow whatever crops they wish to grow for their own subsistence or which they think will be profitable to sell. They can leave their land fallow if they wish. They can also sell their land for non-agricultural use — e.g., housing, factories, brick-making — if they so wish.[8]

---

[6] *Two additional points need to be made.*

  1. *Areas of big land-ownership mainly coincide with disaster-prone or difficult environments, particularly in the north and west of the country, on river char land, near the coast and in hill areas. Periodic crop losses and/or low crop yields make it difficult for small farmers to survive in these areas.*

  2. *Lack of political will is also an important factor which subdues pressure for change: political leaders often are big land-owners themselves; and small farmers and landless agricultural labourers are constrained by traditional patron-client relationships (as observed in the regions referred to above).*

[7] *Also see Chapter 8, Section 8.4.1, footnote 8.*

[8] *See Chapter 10 for details.*

Pricing policy. Government can influence farmers to grow crops which it considers nationally important by offering support prices or incentive prices. This is done by the Food Department offering a fixed procurement price for rice and wheat, which means that farmers do not run the risk of losing money if market prices fall too low after a good harvest (if the Food Department can support the offered price). Sugar mills offer guaranteed prices to cane-growers in the mill zones, and the Cotton Development Board arranges fixed prices for cotton growers. Private tobacco firms also offer fixed prices for tobacco.

On the other hand, Government has not been successful in providing farmers with a guaranteed price for jute, and sugarcane, cotton and tobacco farmers are not always able to obtain the 'guaranteed' price. Problems exist with determining quality, selling/buying small amounts, farmers' indebtedness, and cheating of illiterate farmers by officials or purchase agents. Probably no significant improvement can be expected without stronger organizations to protect farmers' interests (such as marketing cooperatives) and more widespread education.

An additional way in which Government can influence farmers' cropping decisions is by manipulating input prices. Subsidies on fertilizers and irrigation equipment in the 1960s and 1970s encouraged widespread adoption of modern technology to increase yields and production. However, cheap prices discourage efficient use, both of fertilizers and of irrigation water. If the full economic cost of irrigation water was charged, this might encourage more farmers to grow wheat instead of boro paddy, and so enable a bigger area to be irrigated with the same amount of water (and also enable a greater amount of foodgrains to be produced).

Social control. Within irrigation command areas, farmers' choice of crops is partly determined by what their neighbours want to grow and by irrigation schedules. Thus, before an irrigation season begins, farmers must jointly decide whether to grow wheat *or* boro paddy, since the two crops cannot be irrigated side-by-side without the wheat being damaged (by seepage from neighbouring flood-irrigated boro paddy fields). Similarly, they must jointly decide when to start irrigating. Those decisions may also determine which crop or crops they grow on the same land in the preceding or following seasons, as well as the crops they grow on non-irrigated land.

Similar forms of social control are needed for 'social forestry'. They would also be needed for soil conservation farming in hill areas. Social controls are also needed — but are still very weak — for controlling certain plant pests and diseases.

Local government. Although Thana and Union Councils have no powers to regulate land use, they are in a position to influence land use by identifying and implementing schemes under the Thana Works Programme which they consider are in the public interest: e.g., minor drainage and flood protection works; rural roads; small-scale irrigation. A system of Thana Development Planning was set up by the Rural Development Academy at Comilla (now BARD) during the 1960s, but it largely fell into abeyance after 1970. A Thana Land Use Development Planning Programme was tested at Comilla in 1979-80, but did not progress beyond the pilot stage.[9] With the recent (1982) creation of Upazilas (Sub-Districts) and decentralization of planning to the Upazila and Union Parishads (Councils), there is the opportunity — and the need — to revitalize the local government planning system tested and proved in previous decades.[10]

---

[9] *See Chapter 22.*

[10] *Decentralization of powers to Upazila and Union Parishads was short-lived. Subsequent militaro-bureaucratic and political governments restored Upazilas to their former name of Thanas, and withdrew the independent financial powers they had been given.*

Consideration deserves to be given to empowering local governments to regulate land use so as to minimize the loss of valuable productive land to urban development. Local governments would be in a much better position than central government to enforce such regulations, being more knowledgeable about local land qualities and more sensitive to local needs.[11]

Hill land use. The traditional form of *jhum* cultivation was not highly destructive of hill land resources. However, increased population pressure on the land — especially since the filling of Kaptai Lake drowned most of the valuable valley land — has reduced the fallow vegetation period between cycles of cultivation to less than five years. In many areas, forest no longer regenerates between cultivation periods but is replaced by grass or bamboo; destructive fires annually burn the grass and scrub vegetation; and the hill slopes are thus much more exposed than they formerly were to heavy rainfall and consequent soil erosion. The spread of commercialized pineapple cultivation in accessible areas, with the crop planted in rows up and down the slopes, has further aggravated the situation regarding soil erosion and flash floods.

Appropriate methods of using hill land without causing soil erosion and destruction are well known internationally. They are not being adopted in Bangladesh because there is no appropriate institution to organize the multi-disciplinary activities involved — forestry, agriculture, engineering, marketing — and there are few or no officials specifically trained in the techniques of hill agriculture, soil conservation and integrated land use planning. Also, hill land development has received a low priority in relation to agricultural development in floodplain areas where more rapid development is possible.[12]

Four strong arguments exist for paying more attention to hill land development than in the past, viz.

a. In its tight demographic and economic situation, Bangladesh can ill afford to waste or squander any of its environmental resources;

b. the hill areas provide the greatest remaining potential in the country for producing woody vegetation for timber, poles, pulp, fuel, etc.;

c. soil conservation on hill land is urgently needed to reverse the increasing risk of flash-flood damage on adjoining plain land (both agricultural and urban); and

d. the economic livelihood of the hill people needs to be improved and stabilized.

12.6 BIOMASS PRODUCTION

The preceding review leads to the following conclusions in relation to biomass production for energy and other uses.

1. Bangladesh's tropical environment is highly suitable for biomass production virtually throughout the year.

2. Wet or flooded conditions during the rainy season on most kinds of floodplain and terrace land limit the area suitable for growing trees to land lying above normal flood-level.[13] Most agricultural land is used for short-term annual crops: mainly rice

[11] *See Chapter 24 for a more detailed discussion of the need to preserve good agricultural land against indiscriminate urban and industrial development.*

[12] *See Chapter 8 for a detailed discussion of soil conservation needs in Bangladesh's hill areas.*

[13] *The main exception is mangrove forest in the Khulna and Chakaria Sunderbans.*

and jute in the rainy season, and a wide range of dryland crops and irrigated boro paddy in the dry season.

3. The high and growing population density and the predominance of small farmers mean that there is acute pressure to produce food crops and cash crops.

4. Bangladeshis have a strong preference to grow and eat rice as their staple food, even where other crops would produce equal (wheat) or higher (maize, potato) yields.

5. Frequent natural disasters (floods, drought, cyclones, hail) make agricultural production risky: more in some areas than others.

6. Government's agricultural development policy is to expand irrigation, flood protection and drainage so as to provide farmers with a more secure environment for crop production.

7. Where irrigation (and drainage) is provided, farmers generally give priority to increasing rice production; acreages under jute, sugarcane, wheat, oilseeds and pulses generally decrease in such areas.

8. Farmers are highly independent in spirit. Cooperatives generally have not been successful. 'Community forests' would therefore be difficult to organize and manage. Homestead forestry and the cultivation of trees as multi-use cash crops on individual holdings are likely to be more successful techniques, except possibly in traditional forest areas.

9. Farmers are highly responsive to market prices. Therefore, if scarcity of fuelwood forces the price of fuelwood up, farmers with land suitable for fuelwood production will start to grow suitable fuelwood plants when it becomes more profitable for them to do so than to grow alternative food or cash crops.[14] The value of quick-growing trees as cash crops needs to be demonstrated. Fertilizers probably will need to be used to maintain continuous high yields.

10. Unfortunately, as fuelwood prices rise, poor households may be unable to purchase all the fuel they need. Alternative sources of energy — e.g., solar — may be needed for the poor and the landless.

11. Government presently has no effective means to regulate agricultural land use in the public interest. Therefore, it has to use input-output pricing policies to influence farmers' cropping decisions. To-date, it has proved difficult for Government to maintain output-support prices on all occasions.

12. The power to regulate land use so as to minimize the loss of agricultural land to urban/industrial use needs to be delegated to local governments.

13. Soil and land use maps and data need to be provided to Thana and Union Councils and officials as the basis for planning improved land use (including increased bio-mass production where there is a locally-felt need for this). Education and training of both the public and officials in the use of such information offers the best means to increase awareness of the need for balanced land use in the community interest.

14. Although Bangladesh's soils — especially floodplain soils — are fertile, their fertility needs to be supplemented with fertilizers and/or manure for high-yielding crop

---

[14]*About the time that the author left Bangladesh (1986), farmers interviewed in several areas said that they were growing jute as much for the value of the sticks for domestic fuelwood as for the cash return from the fibre. Also, farmers in several areas were observed to be growing fields of Sesbania (dainchya) to produce fuelwood. These crops are of particular interest in Bangladesh because they are annual crops that can be grown on seasonally-flooded land.*

production. More Research and Extension efforts are needed to improve the efficiency of fertilizer use.

15. More Extension effort is also needed to motivate farmers to make and use farmyard manure more efficiently. However, it would be impractical to maintain soil fertility solely by the use of organic manure. The nutrient concentration in the fertilizers used in Bangladesh is about 100 times higher than in manure. Therefore, 1,000 maunds (ca 27 tons) or more of manure per acre per year might be needed for intensive crop production. Apart from the difficulty in supplying such amounts, it would be impractical for farmers to carry such quantities to their fields (mainly by head-load).

16. Similarly, it would be impractical for small farmers to grow green-manure crops to maintain soil fertility. Small farmers need to maximize production of subsistence and cash crops from their small holdings. However, pulses on dryland sites and *dainchya* (like a deepwater *ipil-ipil*) on wetland sites provide soil fertility benefits in addition to their primary functions of providing food and biomass.

17. Urea/ammonia treatment offers promise as a means to increase the feeding value of rice and wheat straw (including HYV straw which is not relished) for cattle.

12.7 CONCLUSION

Since environmental conditions are highly suitable for plant production for the various purposes for which biomass is required, and since farmers are highly responsive to economic factors, the greatest needs for developing more rational land use which will provide balanced production of food, industrial crops, export crops and biomass are:

a. Research and Extension programmes to find out and demonstrate optimum biological production patterns and techniques under different agroecological and socio-economic conditions;

b. education of officials, local government leaders and farmers about local land, soil and water resources in relation to land use development possibilities and needs;

c. generation of more on-farm and off-farm employment so as to maintain or increase consumers' purchasing capacity and so maintain commodity prices at levels which are attractive to producers; and

d. Government policies — including research, land development and input-output pricing policies — which will encourage and enable land-owners to produce crops and commodities to the greatest national advantage.

Chapter 13

PRINCIPLES OF LAND USE DEVELOPMENT IN HILL AREAS[1]

Simple, practical measures are outlined for planning sustainable land use in hill areas using established soil conservation practices.

13.1 LAND USE ZONING

1. **Divide the area around each village into three zones:**
   - *Close*: where intensive management can be provided.
   - *Intermediate*: where only semi-intensive management can be provided.
   - *Distant*: where only protective management can be provided.

   Get each village to decide which of its lands to allocate to each of these zones. The radius of these zones will depend on the size and needs of the village, and the availability of land suitable for intensive and semi-intensive management.

2. **In the close zone:**
   i. concentrate use of manure, compost, fertilizers, on this land;
   ii. plant all crops on contour rows;[2]
   iii. mulch all arable crops with cut grass and weeds;
   iv. weed intensively;
   v. repair damage to crop rows, bunds, drains, etc., after each heavy rainfall.

3. **In the intermediate zone:**
   i. grow mainly tree crops;
   ii. plant trees on step terraces;

---

[1] *This chapter has been adapted from a briefing paper prepared for the Secretary for Agriculture in December 1975. That paper assumed that Agricultural Extension staff would work with village food production committees then in vogue to implement the principles. That assumption proved too optimistic: Extension staff had little training in soil conservation techniques; and very few were recruited from hill people with experience of hill farming conditions. A more detailed description of the principles of hill land development is given in Brammer (1997), Chapters 6 and 16. Soil conservation needs are also reviewed in Chapter 8 of this volume.*

[2] *Dibble-sowing of mixed crops, as in traditional jhum cultivation, is, in fact, as good a soil conservation measure as planting crops in rows, especially where the crop mix includes a scrambling pulse or gourd crop whose foliage quickly covers the ground surface. Planting in rows on the contour is needed if crops (e.g., maize) are grown in single stands. Even with crops grown in rows, it is preferable to interplant them with a cover crop (such as beans) which will protect the soil surface between the rows.*

iii. plant cover crops to protect the soil surface, at least until the trees provide adequate cover;

iv. use fertilizers, sprays, etc., and weed as recommended for individual crops;

v. inspect fields after periods of heavy rainfall and repair any erosion damage.

4. **In the distant zone:**

i. maintain existing protective forest cover and ban *jhum* cultivation; or

ii. plant forest, either for wood production or for land protection.

13.2 PRINCIPLES OF LAND MANAGEMENT IN THE CLOSE ZONE

1. **On slopes less than 5 percent** (i.e., less than 5 feet rise in 100 feet horizontal distance):

i. make horizontal fields along the contour;

ii. between cultivated fields, either:

   • make a contour bund to intercept run-off and lead it safely to a soak-away drain; or

   • leave an uncultivated strip (or a semi-intensive cultivation strip) at least as wide as the intensively cultivated strip;

iii. plant all crops in horizontal rows; (see footnote 2 above);

iv. grow suitable crops, as indicated in Section 13.5 below.

2. **On slopes of 5-15 percent:**

i. make narrow horizontal fields along the contour;

ii. make a large contour bund and a drain at the bottom of each field;

iii. lead water from the drain safely to a soak-away drain;

iv. plant cover crops on the bund;

v. preferably, leave an uncultivated strip or a semi-intensively cultivated strip between every two or three fields;

vi. plant all crops in horizontal rows (on ridges or beds, if necessary); (see footnote 2 above);

vii. grow suitable crops, as indicated in Section 13.5 below.

3. **On slopes of 15-35 percent:**

i. make level terraces;

ii. make a strong retaining wall to prevent the terrace collapsing; this wall should be of hard rock, but can also be of brick, wood or bamboo where suitable rock is not available locally;

iii. lead water away from each terrace safely to a soak-away drain or a protected vertical drain;

iv. make a large horizontal bund and a drain above the terrace wall;

v. plant cover crops to protect the bund and terrace wall;

vi. plant all crops on horizontal rows (on ridges or beds, if necessary); (see footnote 2 above);

vii. grow suitable crops, as indicated in Section 13.5 below.

4. **On slopes steeper than 35 percent:**

   i. grow only tree crops; preferably, grow close-growing trees for fuelwood;

   ii. if fruit trees are grown, plant these on step terraces;

   iii. between the trees, grow cover crops (or natural grasses which are regularly slashed) to ensure that the soil surface is covered with vegetation or a mulch in both the rainy season and the dry season.

13.3 PRINCIPLES OF LAND MANAGEMENT IN THE INTERMEDIATE ZONE

1. **On slopes less than 5 percent:**

   i. use methods and crops similar to those described for similar land in the close zone, but choose crops which need less intensive management; or

   ii. grow tree crops, provide occasional contour bunds to lead storm-water safely away to soak-away drains, and either grow a cover crop or allow weeds to grow between the trees which are periodically slashed to provide a mulch covering the soil surface.

2. **On slopes of 5-15 percent:**

   i. grow tree crops;

   ii. plant in contour rows;

   iii. make occasional contour bunds to lead storm-water safely away to a soak-away drain;

   iv. grow a cover crop between the trees, or allow weeds to grow which are periodically slashed to provide a mulch covering the soil.

3. **On slopes of 15-35 percent:**

   i. grow tree crops;

   ii. plant in contour rows on step terraces;

   iii. make occasional contour bunds to lead storm-water safely away to a soak-away drain;

   iv. grow a cover crop between the trees and on bunds, or allow weeds to grow which are periodically slashed to provide a mulch covering the soil.

4. **On slopes steeper than 35 percent:**

   i. wherever possible, leave under protective forest;

   ii. alternatively, plant forest or fuelwood blocks; plant trees on step terraces.

13.4 PRINCIPLES OF LAND MANAGEMENT IN THE DISTANT ZONE

1. **On slopes less than 5 percent:**

   i. use crops and conservation methods similar to those described for the close zone, but choose crops which need less intensive management;

   ii. alternatively, use for growing fodder grasses or legumes, or for grazing; or

   iii. plant to forest.

2. **On slopes steeper than 5 percent:**

   i. leave under protective forest, or make timber or fuelwood plantations;

ii. plantations should be in belts along the contour; trees should be planted on step terraces;

iii. leave fire-breaks between plantations; a continuous fire-watch should be maintained during the dry season, and villages should be prepared to control any fires which threaten protective forest, plantations, cultivated areas or settlements.

13.5 CROP SUITABILITY

1. **Suitable arable crops for the close zone:**
   i. *Perennial:* pineapple, ginger, turmeric, banana (preferably on moist sites or with some irrigation).
   ii. *Annuals with long growing period:* hill cotton, pigeon pea, sugarcane (for chewing or *gur*), cassava, yams, arum (*kochu*).
   iii. *Quick-maturing kharif crops:* summer vegetables, groundnut, sorghum, millet (*kaon*), maize, sesamum, cowpea, maskalai. Aus paddy can be inter-sown between beds of perennial crops, or between every two or three rows of long-growing crops.
   iv. *Early rabi crops:* mustard, maskalai, sesamum; winter vegetables (with irrigation).

2. **Suitable arable crops for the intermediate zone:**
   i. *Perennial*: ginger, turmeric.
   ii. *Annuals*: hill cotton, pigeon pea, cassava, yams, arum, sesamum, cowpea, maskalai, groundnut, mustard.

3. **Suitable tree crops for the close zone:**
   Close-growing trees which need close management or attention: e.g., tea, coffee, rubber, citrus, guava.

4. **Suitable trees for the intermediate zone:**
   Bigger trees with more open spacing, or trees which require less intensive management: e.g., rubber, jackfruit, mango, cashew.

5. **Suitable trees for the distant zone:**
   Species suitable for timber, pulp-wood or fuel-wood, on the recommendation of the Forest Department.

6. **Suitable cover crops:**
   Grasses, legumes or other broad-leaved plants, alone or in mixed stands, whose foliage (alive or dead) covers the soil surface, preferably throughout the year. In the close zone, crops such as maskalai and gourds can be used.

13.6 LAND CLASSIFICATION

If villagers wish to make a Village Development Plan based on land classification, they can use the following classes.

- **Slopes**

  A – less than 5 percent
  B – 5-15 percent
  C – 15-35 percent
  D – 35-60 percent
  E – More than 60 percent.

- **Soils**

    VS – very sandy (deep sands)

    S – sandy

    L – loamy

    C – clayey

    d – deep (more than 2 feet to hard rock)

    s – shallow (less than 2 feet to hard rock).

- **Remarks**

    1. If possible, avoid cultivating shallow soils, very sandy soils and clay soils on slopes. Put such soils under protective forest.
    2. Do not build bench terraces on slopes steeper than about 15 percent on clay soils or over shaley rock. That is liable to cause landslides during heavy monsoon rainfall.
    3. Villagers will need to be trained in slope measurement, which is not difficult.
    4. Cultivators may have their own system for classifying soils which could be used so long as it differentiates satisfactorily between sandy and clayey soils, and between deep and shallow soils.

13.7 DAMS

1. Small dams can be constructed across small active gulleys, using stone (where available) or fences of wood or bamboo. Priority should be given to making dams near the heads of gulleys, then later down-stream. Such dams may need repair or replacement every dry season.
2. Bigger dams across small valleys or large gulleys should be provided with a spillway big enough and strong enough to allow the safe overflow of the maximum expected storm flow, taking into account the additional flow expected from drain outlets on adjoining cultivated land. Again, such dams should be built in sequence from the top of a valley to the bottom of the valley. Big dams need to be designed by skilled engineers.

13.8 ADDITIONAL REMARKS

1. Make annual targets for bringing land under soil conservation or afforestation.
2. Organize emergency village groups to inspect and repair damaged conservation bunds, etc., after every heavy rainfall event. Conservation works must be regarded as communal rather than individual property, but the individual can be made responsible for maintaining his section of the communal structure.
3. Organize fire-watching and fire-control in the dry season.
4. Soil conservation demands skill and constant vigilance. It is perhaps better not done at all than done badly or not maintained satisfactorily.

13.9 POSTSCRIPT

The following quotations from Henle (1974) following a mission to China are relevant when considering soil conservation measures for Bangladesh's hill areas.

1. "All slopes with an inclination more than 25^0 [= 45%] have been barred from tilling and reserved for protective plantation." (p.149).

2. "The cost of terracing is high; in Shanxi, it was given as being from 800 to 12,500 man-days per hectare [= 320 to 5,000 man-days per acre] of newly-terraced field. This is all done by the farmers themselves, almost always without mechanical aid and with no special remuneration (i.e., only against work-points which are counted toward the overall revenue of the collective)." (p.148).

3. "The counter-action [against erosion] has been carried out entirely by the communes which, each winter, build millions of small dams in erosion gulleys to catch topsoil. One or twice a year, the holes created by the damming of torrents are emptied out and the soil is carried back, usually by shoulder-pole, to the hill-sides being terraced." (p.148).

4. "The present level of planting protective tree stands has been estimated by Chinese officials as 20-25 million trees per year." (p.148-9).

5. "In spite of all efforts, the survival [of trees in afforestation schemes] is often low, sometimes only around 10 percent of the trees planted. This explains why, in spite of extensive works, the forest area has not grown faster. Some areas had to be re-worked more than five times." (p.123).

PART IV
TECHNICAL INFORMATION TO SUPPORT PLANNING

The five chapters in this part provide information and ideas for use in planning more intensive land use as a means to increase food production and rural employment. Chapter 14 describes the kinds of information contained in soil survey reports. Chapters 15 to 17 provide guidelines for selecting sites for small-scale land and water development schemes which could be implemented by local-government councils, and Chapter 18 describes techniques that could be used to bring various kinds of waste land and fallow land into productive use.

Chapter 14

SOIL SURVEY AND LAND USE PLANNING[1]

The physical information used for agricultural land use planning in Bangladesh was derived from reconnaissance soil surveys. This chapter briefly describes the kinds of information provided in soil survey reports which can be used for planning rational land use for sustained agricultural development in Bangladesh.

14.1 INTRODUCTION

The objectives of the Soil Survey Project, which was set up in 1961 with assistance from FAO and the UN Special Fund,[2] were:

'To survey and appraise the soil resources of the country. ... This survey will furnish the Government with an inventory of the major soil resources of the whole country and will assist in planning land development projects especially for land settlement, irrigation and drainage, soil conservation and afforestation, and the overall economic development of the country.'

Two important points should be noted about these terms of reference.

1. The project was not set up to survey the fertility status of the country's soils with a view to providing fertilizer recommendations to farmers. The latter service is properly the function of the Soil Fertility Institute.

2. In order to complete the evaluation of the country's soil resources within a reasonable period — 6-8 years was initially envisaged — the soil survey was necessarily planned on a reconnaissance scale. It would have taken more than 60 years to make a detailed survey of the present Bangladesh with the financial and man-power resources available. None-the-less, the survey that was carried out was more detailed in character than the term 'reconnaissance' sometimes connotes. That was because of the more detailed requirements of agricultural planning in the intensively-farmed conditions of this country.

The reconnaissance soil survey of Bangladesh was carried out between 1964 and 1975. Annexe 1 to this chapter lists the names and dates of the reports on individual

---

[1] *This chapter draws on information originally presented in Brammer, 1974a, c, 1975a and 1984a.*

[2] *The Soil Survey Project was an all-Pakistan project. After Bangladesh became independent in 1971, the former East Pakistan Directorate of Soil Survey eventually became the Soil Survey Department, then later the Soil Resources Development Institute (SRDI). The UN Special Fund later became the United Nations Development Programme (UNDP).*

Districts/Subdivisions published by the Soil Survey Project/Department.[3] Those reports represent a body of information which few countries in the world possess.[4]

14.2 INFORMATION COLLECTED

The survey carried out was essentially a field survey. Particular attention was paid to describing the physical environmental conditions which affect plant growth, especially the growth of crops suitable for the climate. These physical conditions are of two kinds.

First, there are the inherent physical properties of the soils themselves: properties such as texture, structure, consistence, porosity, etc, both in the surface and the subsurface layers. Those properties are important for plant growth because they affect the ability of a soil to absorb and store moisture for use by plants.[5]

Secondly, there are the external physical properties of soils. Most important amongst these in Bangladesh are hydrological conditions. Particular attention was paid on the soil survey to recording the depth and duration of seasonal flooding, as well as the degree of hazard to crop production by flash floods, rapid rise or flow of floodwater, burial by new alluvium, river-bank erosion and storm surge. These hydrological properties are important because they largely determine whether wetland or dryland crops can be grown in the monsoon season; also whether crop sequences such as aus/jute-rabi crops, aus-transplanted aman or mixed aus+deepwater aman are practised, a single crop of deepwater aman is grown or the land is left fallow in the monsoon season.

The duration of seasonal flooding also helps to determine which crops can be grown in the dry season. For instance, because long-staple cotton and cigarette tobacco should be sown by the end of September if good yields are to be obtained, those crops can only be grown on soils that normally are not flooded or wet after about mid-September. Similarly, mustard and most winter vegetables should be sown in October, wheat in the second half of November, and most other rabi crops not later than end-December. Obviously, such crops can only be grown satisfactorily on soils that are free from floodwater by those dates. In addition, the soils must either store sufficient moisture to support the crops to maturity in the dry season or they must be suitable for irrigation.

In addition to recording the internal and external physical characteristics of the soils, the existing land use was also recorded at each sampling point. That enabled land use practices to be correlated with soil and hydrological conditions. That, in turn, provided a valuable guide for evaluating land capability within each survey area.

The information recorded in the field on soil physical properties was supported, to a considerable extent, by questioning farmers on their own fields about flooding conditions, cropping practices and crop yields. In addition, soil samples were collected for laboratory analysis, partly in order to confirm determinations of soil texture and soil reaction (pH) made in the field, partly to provide information on the chemical properties of individual

---

[3] *The report on the reconnaissance soil survey of the Chittagong Hill Tracts summarizes a 9-volume report on a survey carried out by a Canadian team (Forestal, 1966).*

[4] *Subsequent to the completion of the reconnaissance soil survey, SRDI undertook a programme of semi-detailed soil surveys of individual Thanas. The reports on those surveys were published in Bengali.*

[5] *Subsequent to the completion of the reconnaissance soil surveys, detailed soil moisture studies were made in various parts of the country (Joshua & Rahman, 1983a, b). The findings of these and an earlier exploratory study (Huizing, 1970) were summarized in Brammer, 1996, Chapter 14.*

soils, such as cation exchange capacity (an indicator of a soil's capacity to hold plant nutrients) and the contents of organic matter, nitrogen, calcium, potash, etc. It is important to realize that, while information on such chemical properties can provide a broad indication of soil fertility, such data cannot be used to indicate fertilizer requirements for specific crops. Those requirements need to be determined by field trials carried out on the individual kinds of soils identified by soil survey.

14.3 METHOD OF SOIL SURVEY

The kind of soil survey carried out was termed 'reconnaissance'. In fact, because of the amount of information collected, the survey was more detailed than the term 'reconnaissance' sometimes indicates. None-the-less, it is important to realize that the survey *was* of a reconnaissance nature. The soil maps do not show individual soils. As is explained below, they show what are termed 'soil associations'.

The information was collected in the field along traverses varying between about one and six miles (roughly 1.5-10 km) apart, depending on the complexity of the soil patterns found. Traverses were selected to cross the landscape at right angles so as to pick up differences in soil properties and characteristics related to differences in relief and drainage. Holes were dug by spade and auger to a depth of 90 cm or more at purposively selected intervals along traverses in order to examine soil changes occurring along the line of traverse. Individual soils were identified and the boundaries between them were determined in relation to relief and drainage characteristics. At each inspection point, details of the properties of individual soil layers were recorded: thickness; colour, including colour patterns (mottles); texture; consistence; structure; porosity; inclusions such as iron or lime concretions, roots and coatings on the faces of cracks and pores; etc. Periodically, deep pits were dug so as to examine soil profiles in greater detail and to collect samples to send for laboratory analysis.

Information for the areas lying between traverses was extrapolated by interpretation of air photos. The air photos were particularly helpful because the patterns they show closely reflect the relief of the ground, and soil differences within a particular area usually are related to differences in relief and drainage.

Individual soil series and soil phases were identified in the field.[6] However, because of the reconnaissance nature of the survey, it was not possible to map the extent of individual soil series and phases.[7] Instead, the soils were mapped as what are termed 'soil associations'. These are groups of related soils which occur in sequence between the highest and lowest parts of the landscape in a particular area. For instance, in most floodplain regions, there is a sequence of sandy or silt loam soils on ridge crests, followed downslope by silty clay loam soils on the middle parts of ridges and then by clay soils in the depressions. This pattern of lighter-textured, permeable, non-flooded or shallowly-flooded soils on ridges and heavier-

[6] *A soil series is a group of soils formed from the same parent material under similar conditions of climate, drainage, vegetation and time, and having the same kind and sequence of horizons which have similar properties. Soil series are given locality names (e.g., Sonatala series) for ease of reference. A soil phase is a subdivision of a soil series (or other soil unit) differentiated because of different management requirements: e.g, Highland and Medium Highland depth-of-flooding phases; level and sloping phases; flash-flood hazard phase.*

[7] *Because of the intricate patterns in which soils often occur on Bangladesh's floodplains, very detailed surveys would be required in order to map individual soil series and phases. The semi-detailed surveys carried out by SRDI, like the reconnaissance surveys, mapped soil associations.*

textured, less permeable, more deeply flooded soils in depressions may repeat itself over large areas of a particular floodplain region, so that the pattern can be mapped as a single unit: a soil association.

An estimate was made in the field of the proportions in which individual soil series and soil phases occurred on each traverse. Therefore, although the actual boundaries of individual soils may not be shown on reconnaissance soil survey maps, the overall proportions which the individual soils occupy within a particular association were indicated in the soil survey report and these proportions can be converted into areas (acres/hectares). The proportions between the component soils may vary from place to place within the area mapped as an association, so the proportions given represent an average for the association as a whole. If the proportions between the soils varied significantly in different parts of a region, separate associations were mapped in order to indicate, for instance, differences between areas where loamy soils predominate and others where clay soils are more important. Similarly, separate associations were mapped to indicate differences between areas that are more deeply flooded than other parts or are more exposed to particular hazards such as flash floods, storm surges, river-bank erosion, etc.

The field survey information was collected, correlated with information for other areas and evaluated, then a report and maps were prepared. The soil survey report provides a comprehensive account of the soils, existing land use and land capability of the survey area. In the report, each soil series and soil association is described in detail and a crop suitability table is presented showing, on a scale of four, the relative suitability of individual soil series and phases for a range of climatically-adapted crops under irrigated and non-irrigated conditions. The reconnaissance soil survey report thus provides a first estimate of the kinds of soils occurring in a particular area, their approximate extent, their physical and chemical properties, their existing land use, their suitability for growing particular crops, and their overall capability for improved use.[8]

14.4 SOIL SURVEY INTERPRETATION

The soil survey was designed in such a way that agricultural research, extension and planning staff could readily obtain information from soil survey reports on the location and extent of soils suitable for particular crops or other uses. However, it was soon realized that the intended users were not able to use the reports, perhaps because they were discouraged by the formidable amount of information which they contained.[9] Therefore, various attempts

---

[8] *The reconnaissance soil survey reports published in the 1960s and 1970s are still useful for regional land use planning. However, it is important to realize that environmental conditions and land use may have changed in some areas subsequent to the completion of the surveys: see Section 14.7 below. More up-to-date information on soils and land use is available for many areas in Thana semi-detailed soil survey reports published by SRDI (in Bengali).*

[9] *In Brammer (1974a), it was stated that, even after the change in report format described in footnote 11 below, soil survey reports remained unused by all except foreign consultants employed by the then EPWAPDA (now BWDB). That situation was attributed to the fact that students of Agriculture and Soil Science were not taught about soils as a field subject but as a subject for academic and laboratory study. Virtually nothing was taught about the soils of Bangladesh, about soils in relation to landscape features or about soil properties in relation to land capability and crop suitability. No matter how simple the presentation, therefore, the soil survey reports appeared to be in a foreign language, as it were, because the user had little or no understanding of the basic concepts involved: i.e., how soils occur in Nature; how their properties vary from place to place as well as in time; and how their properties affect crop suitability and land management. Such information cannot be*

were made in the 1960s to interpret the information for direct use by planners, research and extension staff, resulting in the publication of a number of separate, simplified or summarized reports and guidelines: see the list given in Annexe 2 to this chapter. Eventually, the Soil Survey Department set up a Soil Survey Interpretation Division in the early-1970s. Amongst the early interpretations made were the estimates of the areas suitable for HYV rice and wheat production (Brammer, 1974b, 1975b: see Brammer, 1997, chapters 10, 11). The reconnaissance soil survey data eventually provided the basis for the Agroecological Zones Project study (FAO, 1988).

For agricultural research and extension staff, the most important use of the soil survey information is to assist them in locating suitable sites for agronomic and fertilizer trials and demonstrations on suitable soils. Each soil survey report contains information on the location of the major soils, their drainage and moisture characteristics, their existing land use and their suitability for a wide range of crops. For trials and demonstrations that are to provide the basis for recommendations or advice to farmers on agronomic or fertilizer practices, the trials/demonstrations should obviously be located on soils that have a wide extent in a particular area so that the results can be applied as widely as possible on similar soils.

So far as agricultural planning is concerned — whether by central planners or by District/Thana Extension officials — the most important use of the soil survey information is for identifying the location and extent of areas suitable for particular crops which Government might wish to introduce or expand within the country or within a particular area: e.g., groundnut, sunflower, HYV aman. Similarly, the location and extent of soils suitable for particular crop rotations can be determined. Methods for using soil survey report information for these various purposes are described below in Chapters 21-23.

The reconnaissance soil survey information should not be extended below the level required for Thana planning. For village-scale planning, detailed soil surveys will be required.[10] It must be accepted that such detailed surveys will be slow. It is estimated that, under Bangladesh's environmental and agricultural conditions, detailed surveys could not be carried out at a rate of more than about 16,000 acres (6,400 ha) per professional man-year. In some complex floodplain areas, the rate might be even slower. Thus it might take at least 1,375 man-years to cover the 22 million acres (8.8 million ha) of agricultural land in Bangladesh. That is apart from the professional man-power needed for laboratory, cartographic and editorial support, and for the technical and administrative manpower needed to service the survey organization. The choice lies between employing a relatively small number of soil surveyors for 50-100 years or a larger number to complete the task in, say, 10-20 years.

14.5 SOIL ASSOCIATION DESCRIPTION

Each soil association shown on the reconnaissance soil survey map is described in the report text in the form of a table.[11] Table 14.1 shows an example of a soil association table.

---

obtained from the laboratory determination of soil nutrient status, which was the general understanding of the purpose of soil surveys at that time.

[10] *A method for making village agricultural development plans is described in Chapter 20.*

[11] *In the earliest reports published, the soil mapping units were described in narrative style, but experience showed that intended users had difficulty in extracting relevant information in that form. Therefore, from 1968, the information on soil associations (as well as on land use and land capability) was presented in the*

Figure 14.1 illustrates how the soils of this association, their properties and land use are related to the relief within the association. Selected laboratory data for important soils in this association are given in Table 14.2. This example is from the Old Brahmaputra Floodplain in the east of Dhaka District, but it illustrates features which are found in soil associations occurring in most of the country's floodplain regions.

Each soil association description includes the following information.

- In the central column, the name of each soil series (plus soil phase) in the association.
- To the left of that column, the position in the relief which each soil occupies, the approximate percentage of the relief which each soil occupies, and a simple description of each soil (sufficient to distinguish it from its neighbours: a detailed description of each soil series is given in an appendix section of the soil survey report).
- To the right of the central column, brief statements about present land use, factors which may limit the use of each soil, and possible improvements in land use which could be made.
- At the foot of the table, more information about land use, land capability and development possibilities for the association as a whole.

In Figure 14.1 and Table 14.2, note how the selected soil properties change between the higher and lower members of the association, viz.-

- an *increase* in clay and organic matter contents as one moves down-slope, together with an increase in the related cation exchange capacity; and
- a *decrease* in topsoil *p*H down-slope, indicating a change from mildly alkaline to very strongly acidic;[12] note that the subsoil is near-neutral in reaction in all the soils.

14.6 CROP SUITABILITY

Each soil survey report includes a crop suitability table which shows the relative suitability of each soil series and phase in the survey area for a wide range of crops under irrigated and non-irrigated conditions. Four classes are used, ranging from 1 for well suited to 4 for not suited. Table 14.3 gives an example of the suitability of the soils of the soil association illustrated in Table 14.1 for a range of crops under irrigated conditions.

14.7 LIMITATIONS

The reconnaissance survey information has a number of limitations which planners and other report users should be aware of, viz.

    a. The map and report text do not provide information about specific sites. They describe the general pattern in which individual soils occur in the relief within areas mapped as soil associations, and the relationship between the soils, cropping patterns and potential crop suitability. For detailed information about specific sites, a site inspection must be made.

---

form of tables, and second editions of all but two of the earlier reports (Sylhet Sadar and Maulvi Bazar; Tangail) were subsequently re-issued in that format: see Annexe 1.

[12] *This refers to dry-season conditions. All topsoils become near-neutral (pH around 7.0) when they become continuously submerged during the rainy season. The pH of the subsoil and lower layers generally does not change between seasons.*

b. The position of soil boundaries on the map is often approximate. There are three main reasons for this:

   i. precise boundaries may not exist in the field: changes in soils often occur gradually across an area, so differences between one side of an area and another have to be shown by drawing a boundary at a convenient intermediate place;

   ii. boundaries are not mapped in the field but are interpolated from scattered sampling points and by interpretation of air photos; and

   iii. intricate boundaries are smoothed out in order to represent them on a map where 1 inch equals 2 miles (i.e., 1:125,000 scale).

c. The proportions for individual soils shown in the soil association tables are estimates for the association as a whole. However, these proportions are not uniform throughout an association. In any particular area, somewhat different proportions may occur; also, one or more of the minor soils may not be present, or there may be small areas of other soils not described in the table (although these often will be soils that are described for a neighbouring association).

d. Significant changes in soils and land use have taken place in some areas since the reconnaissance surveys were made in the 1960s and 1970s, viz.

   i. Normal flood-levels — i.e., those which farmers expect when they plant their crops — have fallen on the Brahmaputra-Jamuna Floodplain and adjoining parts of the Ganges, Atrai and Meghna Floodplains (Ibrahim, 1984; see Chapter 6). The change increases from 1-2 feet (60-90 cm) in Jamalpur District to 3-5 feet (90-150 cm) in Dhaka, Faridpur and Pabna Districts near the junction of the Jamuna and Ganges rivers, then decreases to nil in the tidal area in Barisal District. In areas where flood-levels have fallen since the 1960s, the areas suitable for transplanted aman and for rabi crops are greater than originally reported, and the area formerly used for deepwater aman (and for mixed aus+aman) has decreased.

   ii. Flood-levels have been reduced artificially in areas where flood protection and drainage projects have been implemented: e.g., in the Dhaka-Narayanganj-Demra (DND) project area and the Chandpur Irrigation Project area.

   iii. The area under irrigation has greatly expanded, with consequent changes in cropping patterns since the time of the survey.

   iv. Cropping patterns have been intensified in various other ways: e.g., transplanted aus has replaced broadcast aus in several areas, and HYVs of paddy have replaced local varieties in many areas since the time they were surveyed.

   v. Some areas alongside the main rivers and in the Meghna estuary have changed due to bank-erosion and new alluvial deposition. Elsewhere, parts of some soil associations have been lost due to the spread of towns and cities.

The limitations described above do not mean that the reconnaissance soil survey reports cannot be used for agricultural planning, research and extension. What they do mean is that the reports must be used intelligently, keeping in mind these limitations. Planners should use the report information as a guide for identifying soil conditions in an area, and then supplement this information by site inspections to confirm actual field conditions.[13]

---

[13] *The Soil Resources Development Institute (SRDI) can assist by providing information for Thanas that have been covered by semi-detailed soil surveys and by training agricultural planners, research and extension staff in how to use soil survey reports and information.*

TABLE 14.1[1]
Sonatala-Silmandi association

Position	Approx. percent of unit	Subsoil characteristics	Series, phase, land type	Present main land use	Limitations	Possible improvements
Highest part of ridges	Minor	Grey sand	Tengar Char, H	Aus-early rabi crops; mesta; fruit trees; aman seedbeds	Droughty. Low fertility. Sometimes has compact silty topsoil	Add tank silt or much manure. Provide hand irrigation. Grow high-value kharif and rabi fruit, vegetables, banana
Ditto	40	Grey-brown silt loam; often overlies sand at 1-2 feet	Sonatala, MH	Ditto; also, aus/jute-t.aman-rabi crops	Shallow flooding. Shallow soils similar to Tengar Char soils	Ditto, but less suitable for kharif dryland crops and banana
Middle part of ridges	15	Grey-brown silty clay loam; often overlies sand at 1-3 feet	Silmandi, MH	Ditto, but no fruit trees	Shallow flooding. Shallow soils droughty	Ditto. Improve crop and water management
Lower part of ridges	10	Ditto	Silmandi, ML	Mixed aus+aman/jute-rabi crops	Moderately deep flooding. Shallow soils droughty in dry season	Improve crop and water management
Basins	5	Grey/dark grey, mottled yellow-brown, silty clay	Naraibag, ML	Ditto	Moderately deep flooding. Topsoil dries hard; heavy and sticky when wet	Ditto. HYV boro with irrigation, possibly followed by transplanted deepwater aman
Ditto	10	Ditto	Naraibag, L	B.aman-khesari/fallow	Ditto, but deeper flooding	Ditto

(Contd.)

(Continued)

Position	Approx. percent of unit	Subsoil characteristics	Series, phase, land type	Present main land use	Limitations	Possible improvements
Basin centres	5	Dark grey heavy clay	Siddhirganj, L	B.aman-fallow	Deep flooding. Stays wet early in dry season. Heavy topsoil consistence.	Ditto. Use early-maturing boro varieties
	10		Homesteads, water			

Environmental characteristics. This unit extends in a long strip through parts of Shibpur, Kaliganj, Narsingdi and Araihazar Thanas. It comprises linear floodplain ridges with a few depressions and channels between them. The proportions between the soils vary considerably from place to place. Minor areas of sandy Barar Char and clayey Gorargaon soils occur in perennially wet channels and depressions. Seasonal flooding ranges from nil on the highest ridge crests to about 10 feet in the lowest depressions. Flooding is mainly by accumulated run-off from local rainfall.

Land use association 5a. Mainly triple with some double-cropped land: mainly aus or jute followed by transplanted aman followed by rabi crops.

Land capability association 1. Mainly good and very good agricultural land: seasonally-flooded ridges and basins.

Development possibilities. The floodplain ridge soils are well suited for intensive rabi crop cultivation, for which they need small-scale irrigation, the use of as much compost/manure as possible, balanced fertilizer use and v on Tengar Char and shallow Sonatala soils — the use of mulches. Kharif crops need improved crop and water management for increased production of banana, jute, HYV aus and HYV aman (on MH soils). Basin soils need irrigation so as to grow HYV boro, possibly followed by transplanted deepwater aman.

If part or all of this unit were to be included in a pump-drainage scheme, the ridge soils would become Highland and the basins become Medium Highland. The ridge soils would then become suitable for dryland crops throughout the year, Silmandi soils for irrigated HYV boro-HYV aman or for rainfed HYV aus followed by t.aman, possibly followed by irrigated wheat or rainfed other dryland crops; and basin soils mainly for irrigated HYV boro followed by HYV aman, or for rainfed HYV aus-t.aman.

Note: 1. Slightly modified from the description given in the Dhaka District reconnaissance soil survey report, revised edition, 1981.

FIGURE 14.1

Soil characteristics and land use in Sonatala-Silmandi association, Dhaka District

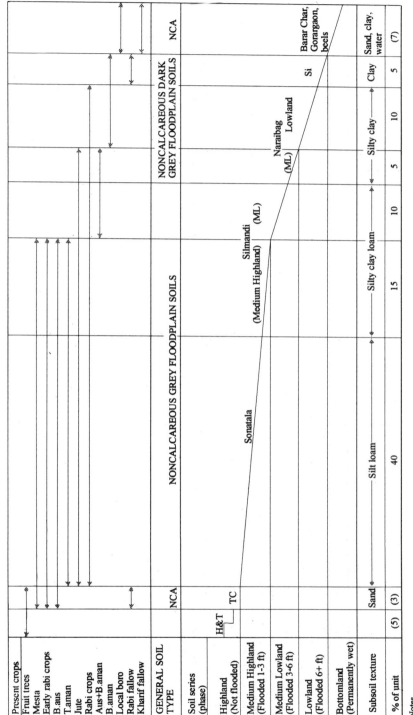

Notes
1. Adapted from Dhaka District reconnaissance soil survey report, revised edition (1981), soil association 41. Land use refers to 1964 conditions.
2. Fruit trees include mango, jackfruit, banana, betelnut, etc.
3. Early rabi crops include vegetables, mustard, mashkalai.
4. Rabi crops include wheat, mustard, pulses, etc.
5. Abbreviations mean: NCA = Noncalcareous Alluvium; H&T = Homesteads and tanks; TC = Tengar Char series; ML = Medium Lowland phase; Si = Siddhirganj series.
6. Numbers in brackets are arbitrary percentages to cater for soils indicated as 'Minor' in the report and for subdividing 'Homesteads and water' (given as 10 percent in the report) into 'Homesteads, tanks' on Highland and 'beels' on Bottomland.

TABLE 14.2

Selected laboratory data for the soils of Sonatala-Silmandi association, Dhaka District

Soil series, phase	Layer	Clay (%)	CEC m.e.%	Organic matter[1] %	Nitrogen %	pH
Sonatala, MH[2]	Topsoil	10	13	0.90	0.08	7.5
	Subsoil	10	14	0.43	0.05	6.9
Silmandi, ML	Topsoil	40	15	1.70	0.11	5.1
	Subsoil	30	15	0.78	0.04	7.0
Naraibag, L	Topsoil	47	19	2.57	0.11	5.3
	Subsoil	47	21	1.34	0.06	7.3
Siddhirganj, L	Topsoil	45	22	4.81	0.24	4.6
	Subsoil	62	26	1.93	0.11	6.8

Notes: 1. Divide by 1.724 to obtain organic carbon percentage.
2. This example was taken from the Report on the Reconnaissance Soil Survey of Kishoreganj and Sadar South Subdivisions, Mymensingh, 1977.

TABLE 14.3

Suitability of the soils of Sonatala-Silmandi association for crop cultivation, with irrigation[1]

Series, phase, land type[2]	Paddy								Kharif dryland				Rabi dryland								Perennial			
	B.aus	B.aman	T.aus (local)	T.aus (HYV)	T.aman (local)	T.aman (HYV)	Boro (local)	Boro (HYV)	Jute	Maize	Pulses, oilseeds	vegetables, chilli	Wheat, barley	Maize	Sorghum, kaon	Cotton	Potato, tobacco	Groundnut	Pulses, oilseeds	Vegetables, chilli	Sugarcane	Pineapple	Banana, pan	Mango, litchi
Tengar Char, H	2	4	3	4	3	3	4	4	3	4	3	4	2	3	2	4	3	2	2	2	4	4	4	4
Sonatala, MH	2	1	2	3	1	3	3	3	2	4	4	4	1	2	2	4	2	2	2	1	4	4	4	4
Silmandi, MH	2	1	2	2	1	1	3	3	2	4	4	4	1	2	2	4	2	2	1	1	4	4	4	4
A , ML	2	1	4	4	4	4	3	3	2	4	4	4	1	1	1	4	2	2	2	1	4	4	4	4
Naraibag, ML	3	2	4	4	4	4	1	1	3	4	4	4	4	4	4	4	4	4	2	4	4	4	4	4
A , L	4	3	4	4	4	4	2	2	4	4	4	4	4	4	4	4	4	4	4	4	4	4	4	4
Siddhirganj	4	4	4	4	4	4	2	2	4	4	4	4	4	4	4	4	4	4	4	4	4	4	4	4
Barar Char	4	4	4	4	4	4	3	4	4	4	4	4	4	4	4	4	4	4	4	4	4	4	4	4
Gorargaon	4	4	4	4	4	4	3	3	4	4	4	4	4	4	4	4	4	4	4	4	4	4	4	4

Notes: 1. 1 = well suited. 2 = moderately well suited. 3 = poorly suited. 4 = not suited.

2. H = Highland. MH = Medium Highland. ML = Medium Lowland. L = Lowland.

Annexe 1

RECONNAISSANCE SOIL SURVEY REPORTS PUBLISHED BY THE SOIL RESOURCES DEVELOPMENT INSTITUTE[1]

Title[2]	Year of publication
1. Sadar and Maulvi Bazar Subdivisions, Sylhet District	1965
2. Pabna District (First edition)[3]	1966
3. Comilla Sadar North and South Subdivisions (First edition)	1966
4. Dhaka District (First edition)	1967
5. Tangail District	1967
6. Jamalpur Subdivision (First edition)	1967
7. Sadar Subdivision, Rangpur District (First edition)	1967
8. Nilphamari Subdivision, Rangpur District (First edition)	1967
9. Noakhali District and Chandpur Subdivision of Comilla District (First edition)	1967
10. Barisal District and part of Bagerhat Subdivision	1968
11. Rajshahi District (2 volumes)	1968
12. Netrakona and Sadar North Subdivisions, Mymensingh District	1969
13. Nilphamari and Sadar Subdivisions, Rangpur District (Revised edition)	1969
14. Thakurgaon Subdivision, Dinajpur District	1970
15. Kurigram and Gaibanda Subdivisions, Rangpur District (2 volumes)	1970
16. Goalundo and Faridpur Sadar Subdivisions	1971
17. Noakhali District and Sadar North, Sadar South and Chandpur Subdivisions of Comilla District (Revised edition)	1971
18. Gopalganj and Madaripur Subdivisions, Faridpur District	1972
19. Bogra District and part of Dinajpur Sadar Subdivision	1972
20. Kushtia District	1973
21. Satkhira Subdivision, Khulna District	1973
22. Sadar North Subdivision, Chittagong District	1976
23. Sunamganj and Habiganj Subdivisions, Sylhet District	1976
24. Dinajpur Sadar Subdivision	1976
25. Sadar South and Cox's Bazar Subdivisions, Chittagong District	1976
26. Jessore District	1977
27. Pabna District (Revised edition)	1976
28. Khulna Sadar and Bagerhat Subdivisions, Khulna District	1977
29. Jamalpur Subdivision (Revised edition)	1977
30. Brahmanbaria Subdivision, Comilla District	1977
31. Kishoreganj and Sadar South Subdivisions, Mymensingh District	1977
32. Dhaka District (Revised edition)	1981
33. Chittagong Hill Tracts	1986
34. Chhagalnaiya and Parshuram Thanas, Feni Subdivision (Unpublished draft)	1986

Notes: 1. From 1961 until 1971, reports were published by the FAO/UNSF Soil Survey Project of Pakistan (PAK-6). Thereafter, reports were published by the Soil Survey Directorate (later Department), which eventually became SRDI.

2. The original report title is given. Former Subdivisions of Districts were subsequently made Districts and the old Districts abolished. The old Districts are shown on Figure 1.1.

3. Where a first edition is indicated, this has been superseded by a revised edition, indicated further down the list.

Annexe 2

LIST OF SOIL SURVEY INTERPRETATION REPORTS AND TECHNICAL GUIDES PUBLISHED BY THE SOIL SURVEY PROJECT 1961-1975[14]

1. Summaries of Agricultural Development Possibilities

Dacca District	1967
Jamalpur and Tangail Subdivisions	1967
Sylhet Sadar and Moulvi Bazar Subdivisions	1967
Rangpur Sadar and Nilphamari Subdivisions	1967
Noakhali District and Chandpur, Sadar North and Sadar South Subdivisions of Comilla District	1967
Barisal District	1968
Pabna and Rajshahi Districts	1968

2. Guides for Agricultural Research and Extension Staff

Suggestions for use of reconnaissance soil survey maps and reports in selecting soil fertility trials sites	1965
How to identify the General Soil Types of East Pakistan	1969
How to use the soil survey report for agricultural development planning at the Thana and Union levels	1969
Preliminary guide to the selection of land and crops for irrigation in East Pakistan	1970

Simplified guides for Thana agricultural development planning:
    Sabhar, Natore, Gaibandha, Iswarganj, Laksham, Comilla Kotwali, Sherpur,
    Sylhet Sadar Kotwali, Mymensingh Kotwali, Rangpur Kotwali, Putia
	1970

Zoning of land for cotton cultivation in Bangladesh	1972
Report on tobacco soils of Bangladesh	1972
Rajshahi District: land resources and cropping potentiality	1973

3. Special Interpretation Reports

Dacca District: zoning of land for agriculture and urban use	1970
Comparison of expected benefits from irrigation and pump drainage on six East Pakistan landscapes	1970
Soil and physiographic conditions affecting rehabilitation of the cyclone devastated areas in East Pakistan, November 1970	1970
Ditto for 19 individual Thanas in the devastated area	1971
Report on salinity survey of the cyclone-devastated areas of East Pakistan	1971
The potential for rainfed HYV rice cultivation in Bangladesh	1974
The contribution of soil survey to agricultural research	1974
Disaster preparedness planning: precautionary and rehabilitation measures	1975
Method for determining recommended land use in an area from reconnaissance soil survey reports	1975
Land suitability for HYV rice and wheat cultivation in Bangladesh	1975
The potential for HYV wheat cultivation in Bangladesh (preliminary edition, without maps and tables)	1975
Future expansion of wheat cultivation in Bangladesh beyond 1975-76	1975

---

[14]*See Note 1 to Annexe 1.*

4. Project Technical Guides[1]

1. General levels and rates of survey coverage	1964
2. Methods of soil analysis	1964[2]
3. Soil sample tags and field sample numbering system	1964
4. Mapping units	1964
5. Use of the portable Wheatstone (conductivity) bridge in soil survey field operations	1964
6. A land capability classification for use in East Pakistan	1965[3]
7. Crop suitability classification	1965
8. Notes on soil and environmental conditions required by the major crops of East Pakistan	1965
9. Form for the completion of soil association data in East Pakistan	1966
10. Principles of agricultural development in East Pakistan	1967
12. Interpretation of soil analytical data	1967
15. Flow sheet for production of reconnaissance soil survey reports and maps	1969
18. Cutting and weighing soil maps and calculating area and percentages of mapping units	1968
18. (lab) Laboratory methods of soil moisture analysis	1970
19. S.I. units and physico-chemical nomenclature in soil science	1970
20. Soil moisture analysis (methods of interpretation)	1970

Notes: 1. These guides were published on an all-Pakistan basis. Only those relevant for East Pakistan (Bangladesh) are listed.
   2. Revised edition 1968.
   3. Revised edition 1971.

5. FAO Publications

Pak-6 Technical Report 2: Agricultural development possibilities in Bangladesh	1971
Pak-6 Technical Report 3: The soil resources of Bangladesh	1971

In addition to the reports listed above, numerous journal articles were published (especially in the Pakistan Journal of Soil Science) in order to inform teachers and students about soil survey findings and techniques.

Chapter 15

SELECTING SITES FOR FOOD-FOR-WORK SCHEMES[1]

Guidelines are given to assist Agricultural Extension staff in identifying sites suitable for small-scale irrigation, drainage and soil conservation schemes which could be implemented under the Food-for-Work Programme. More detailed information on individual types of scheme is given in Chapter 16.

15.1 TYPES OF SCHEME

Agricultural schemes supported by the Food-for-Work Programme must meet the following basic requirements.

a. They must be designed to increase agricultural production (e.g., by means of irrigation or drainage).

b. The work must be suitable for carrying out predominantly by hand labour.

c. The schemes must be confirmed as technically feasible by competent specialists and authorities: the World Food Programme (WFP) requires a satisfactory feasibility report on proposed projects before they can be considered for assistance.

15.2 ROLE OF AGRICULTURAL EXTENSION STAFF

Agricultural Extension staff have three main responsibilities in connection with the identification and implementation of agricultural schemes supported by the Food-for-Work Programme.

a. *Identification* of schemes, including site selection and determination of the area to be benefitted.

b. *Advice* to other officials regarding agricultural aspects of proposed schemes. This might involve preparing those parts of a technical feasibility report which deal with agricultural matters: e.g., number of farmers to be compensated for loss of land for embankment schemes; number of farmers benefitting from a scheme; acreage benefitting; crops to be grown; net increase in crop production expected; net benefit in employment expected.

---

[1] *This chapter is based on a manual prepared to guide Agricultural Extension staff to identify sites suitable for small irrigation, drainage and flood-embankment schemes which could be taken up under the Food-for-Work Programme (Brammer, 1975d). The Food-for-Work Programme was supported by the UN World Food Programme and USAID's CARE programme. This chapter is concerned only with support for small schemes suitable for implementation under the Thana Works Programme and the Thana Irrigation Programme. The instructions could be adapted for use by NGOs involved in rural development.*

c. *Organization* of farmers. This includes Extension work to inform farmers of the objectives of proposed schemes and the expected changes in cropping patterns and practices that will be required. Assistance must be given, where relevant, in organizing cooperative groups, providing seed of new crops or varieties, providing demonstrations, arranging for the supply of fertilizers, plant protection materials, pumps, etc., and organizing the construction of field bunds, irrigation channels, drains, etc.

It is *not* the role of Agricultural Extension staff to execute or supervise earth-moving work. That is an engineering responsibility. The role of Agricultural Extension staff during the construction phase of schemes is to act on the farmers' behalf: e.g., to maintain liaison with the supervising engineer so as to advise him on agricultural aspects of schemes; to ensure that the minimum damage is done to agricultural land; and to keep farmers well informed about the agricultural benefits to be provided by schemes.

15.3 RELATION TO THE THANA IRRIGATION PROGRAMME

The fact that schemes are being considered for food-for-work programme assistance does not mean that the procedures of the Thana Irrigation Programme (TIP) should be or can be by-passed. Small-scale agricultural schemes involving irrigation or drainage development *must* be considered part of the TIP. Food-for work programme assistance merely provides the means to execute schemes when funds from Government or local government sources are not available.

Accordingly, the selection and approval of schemes must follow TIP procedures laid down in the TIP Manual. In brief, the procedures require the following.

a. Local involvement in the selection of schemes.

b. Survey of proposed sites by the Thana Irrigation Team comprising technical staff of Agricultural Extension, IRDP (now BRDB) and, where necessary, BWDB.[2]

c. Preparation of a feasibility report and plan.

d. Approval of the plan by Thana and District Agricultural Development Committees, after clearance by BWDB in the case of water development schemes.[3]

In submitting schemes for food-for-work programme assistance, District Agricultural Extension Officers (DEOs) must indicate what stage of the TIP clearance procedure each scheme has passed. Only schemes which have been approved by the District Agricultural Development Committee can be accepted in the final list to be included in the annual food-for-work programme. DEOs must take whatever steps they consider necessary to ensure that suitable schemes are processed and approved without undue delay.

15.4 RESPONSIBILITY FOR SELECTION OF SCHEMES

It is important that schemes be well selected and planned. That is partly to ensure that the optimum production benefits are obtained. It is also because, once earth-works have been undertaken, it may not be possible to remedy mistakes.

---

[2] *In 1975, when the original manual was published, the Thana Irrigation Team also included the Thana Irrigation Officer of BADC.*

[3] *Thana Irrigation Programme procedures are summarized in Chapter 16, Annexe 1.*

Accordingly, DEOs must take personal responsibility for ensuring that schemes are properly selected and planned. Thana and Union Extension staff can assist in pre-selection and survey work, but they are not technically qualified to design and plan such schemes; also, such staff may be subject to pressure by interested parties in their work area. Wherever possible, therefore, DEOs should visit the site of each proposed scheme, preferably as part of a team also comprising BWDB and BRDB officers. During this visit, the team should discuss the purpose of the scheme, the suitability of the site, the layout of the development area and the preparation of the development/production plan with the Thana Irrigation Team, the Circle Officer (Development), local leaders and farmers.

The final scheme proposal must be signed by the officer responsible for inspecting the site and preparing the plan. It must be countersigned by the DEO if he has delegated a subordinate officer to visit the site.[4]

15.5 GUIDELINES FOR SELECTION OF SCHEMES

15.5.1 Scope

Schemes suitable for execution under the Food-for-Work Programme include irrigation and drainage schemes requiring excavation or desilting of khals and tanks, building of cross-dams and construction of local flood-embankments. Construction of terraces could be undertaken in suitable hill and terrace areas. Although not providing direct production benefits, schemes involving construction of roads or deepening of navigation channels could be included in proposals if it is considered that improvement of communications to and from local markets would lead to a significant increase in agricultural production.

Site selection in river floodplain, tidal floodplain and Highland areas is considered under separate headings below.

15.5.2 River floodplain

This includes all floodplain land except that which is affected by tidal conditions in the dry season (whether saline or not) and areas of floodplain that stand above normal flood-levels (i.e., Highland). Those areas are discussed, respectively, in Sections 15.5.3 and 15.5.4.

Excavation or desilting of khals and old river channels. Most floodplain areas are criss-crossed by numerous old channels or khals, some of them more-or-less silted up. Deepening or enlargement of such channels would often provide the simplest means of providing irrigation or drainage in an area. Where such channels do not exist, or where they are too far apart for all the intervening land to be irrigated from them or drained by them, consideration can be given to excavating new khals. Also, in many places, borrow-pits alongside roads or paths can be enlarged or extended so that they provide a continuous khal. Wherever possible, all new or desilted khals should be linked up to a perennial river,

---

[4] *When the original manual was published, DEOs were able to delegate such visits to Subdivisional Agricultural Officers (SDAOs). With the administrative reorganization of Districts in 1982, Subdivisions were made into Districts, and the former SDAOs became Deputy Directors of Agriculture (DDA). In the meantime, a cadre of Subject Matter Specialists (SMSs) had been created in the Department of Agricultural Extension at (new) District and Thana levels. It would be appropriate for DDAs to delegate responsibilities to a relevant SMS to inspect proposed schemes.*

possibly using multiple-pump installations or double-lifting. Where such connections can be made, the excavated channel can be used as a storage tank.

Some old channels are marked on topographical maps. They are much more easily identified on airphotos, and DEOs should obtain sets of airphotos for their District.[5] When topographical maps and airphotos are not available, a simple map will need to be made by following channels on the ground in the dry season. This map should also show possible routes by which channels (old or new) can be linked with a perennial river, beel, etc. With the help of an engineer or surveyor, a line of levels should be taken along each channel or proposed new khal so that estimates can be made of the depth to which the khal must be excavated in order for water to flow along it from a perennial source (or in order for it to provide drainage). Sections of khals where de-watering might be needed before excavation work can begin should be marked on the map.

Drainage khals should follow the lowest land to the nearest point where they can conveniently be connected with a drainage outlet. This connection may have to be provided by cutting through a high river-bank or silted-up mouth of a khal at a conveniently low or narrow point.

Irrigation khals should be sited high enough on the relief that the water can conveniently be distributed from them by pump or traditional devices. They should not be sited so high that they follow sandy ridges or that their intake is too high to connect with a perennial river at its low-flow stage (unless double-lifting will be used).

Road-side khals can be used to provide irrigation or drainage, so long as the approval of road engineers is obtained. Such khals are most suitable in areas of deep silty or clay soils on almost-level floodplain land. They are less suitable in areas where the floodplain land is undulating and where the underlying layers are sandy along part or all of the road alignment.

The advice of engineers must be sought where khals are to be excavated or deepened. The slope of the khal sides will vary according to the type of alluvial material and the depth to which the excavation will penetrate below the depth of permanent saturation. Engineering advice should be sought, too, regarding the width of land to be left between the foot of the road embankment and the edge of the borrow-pit khal. This shoulder of land (called the berm) is necessary to prevent water in the khal from affecting the road foundations. In general, the width of the berm should not be less than one-and-a-half times the height of the embankment or than the depth to which the khal will be excavated. For example, if the road embankment is 4 feet high and the khal is to be excavated 6 feet deep, the berm should be at least $1\frac{1}{2} \times 6 = 9$ feet wide. Alternatively, if the road embankment is 4 feet high and there already is a berm 6 feet wide, the khal should not be excavated deeper than $6 \times 6/9 = 4$ feet.

In all cases, it must be made certain that a proposed irrigation or drainage scheme will not adversely affect other water users. It must also be made certain that the perennial river with which a khal will be connected can, in fact, supply the amount of irrigation water envisaged. The number of pumps must be limited to the flow of water available. If khals cross the land of more than one village, Union or Thana, agreements must be made between

---

[5] *Satellite imagery can also be useful, but small khals may not be readily visible on the 1:50,000 scale generally available. Those using satellite imagery (as well as airphotos) should take into account physical changes that may have taken place in the landscape since the date when the imagery/photos were taken: e.g., changes in river course; blocking of channels by new sediment deposition.*

leaders of these areas before excavation work starts, so that each community takes only its agreed share of the water (and pays for it accordingly). These matters must be cleared with BWDB and local government councils before schemes are approved.

In the case of khals used as storage tanks after monsoon-season floodwater recedes, the volume of water must be measured (in acre-feet). The number of pumps or other irrigation devices must then be limited to the amount of water available. The method of calculating the amount of available water is described in Chapter 17, Annexe 1. In the case of long khals crossing the land of more than one village, Union or Thana, it may be necessary to build cross-dams so that each community can store its own share of the water retained in the khal at the end of the rainy season. These cross-dams may need to be provided with sluice-gates to regulate water-flow along khals in the rainy season.

Desilting of cut-off channels. Cut-off channels or beels can often be identified on maps and (more easily) on airphotos. However, local information is usually an adequate guide for identifying such sites that are suitable for deepening or enlargement in order to increase the amount of water available for irrigation. Wherever it is feasible, such sites should also be linked with a perennial river by means of a khal so as to further increase the amount of water available for irrigation.

Surveys of cut-off channels and beels which it is proposed to extend should include test-pits dug in the dry season, either within the channel or in the land across which it might be extended. The rate of flow of groundwater through the underlying sediments can be measured by hand-baling or pumping. Where the sediments are sandy, rapid inflow of water may make it impractical to de-water the site for excavation by hand labour.

Surveys should also be made to indicate the amount of earth to be moved and the volume of water that can be stored or provided after excavation. The method of calculating the amount of available water is described in Chapter 17, Annexe 1. The number of pumps or other irrigation devices must be limited to the volume or flow of water available after completion of the excavation work.

Excavation or desilting of tanks. There are many *khas* (government-owned) tanks that would be suitable for desilting by food-for-work schemes. In parts of the country where there are no alternative irrigation (or domestic) water supplies from rivers or wells, excavation of communally-owned tanks might be possible as part of a Union or Thana food-for-work programme. The demand for such tanks or tank improvements should be ascertained from the community or communities before a programme is prepared.

The depth to which new tanks should be excavated or to which old tanks can be re-excavated depends partly on the nature of the underlying material and partly on the depth of the water-table during the dry season. This information must be obtained by test-pitting during the dry season. In sandy materials, tanks will only hold water to the level of the water-table, so tanks may only be practical in sites where the water-table stays high during the dry season. If only irrigation or domestic water supply has to be considered, it may be less costly to provide open wells or tube-wells than to excavate tanks. However, tanks may be preferred where fish-farming is also being considered or in the case where an old tank exists which only requires desilting. In silty and clay materials, tanks may be expected to hold water well, at least from 1-2 years after excavation/re-excavation when the bottom has been puddled or silted over. An entrance may need to be left at a suitable place in the spoil embankment to allow floodwater (or surface run-off) to enter the tank to fill the tank during the rainy season.

Agreements regarding water use and water rights should be drawn up by Revenue officials in the case of *khas* tanks and between land-owners in the case of other tanks. In general, privately-owned tanks should not be regarded as eligible for assistance from the food-for-work programme unless either the land-owners provide the required amount of food (or cash equivalent) to the programme for undertaking the excavation work or they enter into a formal agreement to allow cooperative use of the water.

The use of tanks for both irrigation and fish farming is described in Chapter 17. The methods of calculating the amount of available water in a tank and how much land can be irrigated from the stored water are described in Chapter 17, Annexe 1.

Flood embankments. Proposals for major flood embankments along rivers can only be dealt with by BWDB. Proposals for small or local embankments along minor rivers or small sections of major rivers can be made by local people through Thana Irrigation Programme procedures. District and Thana Agricultural Extension staff can help local communities to identify needs and opportunities, and to formulate proposals for funding and execution under the food-for-work programme.

In selecting flood embankment schemes, particular care needs to be taken that construction of an embankment will not adversely affect other areas. For example, construction of embankments along water courses in hill-foot and haor areas may protect the adjoining area from floods, but at the expense of areas downstream which receive the additional flood discharge (and its sediment load). This applies both to submersible and to major embankments. Also, embankments along hill-foot streams may actually *increase* the risk of flood damage, because deposition of sediment within the embankments after a flood may eventually raise the level of the river-bed until it is higher than that of the surrounding land, thus eventually leading to breaching of the embankment and catastrophic flooding of adjoining land. Therefore, proposals for embankment schemes must always be carefully checked with BWDB to ascertain whether or not they can be undertaken without danger of causing damage to cropped areas elsewhere.[6]

River loop cutting. Cutting across loops in river channels is sometimes feasible. It can be undertaken with two objectives. One is to increase the rate of river flow and thus remove floodwater from an area more quickly. The other is to save land from being eroded on the outer bank of a meander.

Loop cutting is most likely to be successful in areas of decayed or dying river channels such as occur in parts of the Ganges, Teesta and Old Brahmaputra floodplains and along rivers crossing the Barind and Madhupur Tracts. In areas of active river channels, such as occur particularly near major rivers and in high-rainfall areas of Sylhet, loop cutting may give temporary relief from flooding and erosion, but the increased rate of flow of floodwater is likely to increase flooding and losses of land by erosion downstream. Therefore, the net result could be counter-productive. Accordingly, all proposals for loop-cutting schemes must be referred to BWDB for a technical opinion on possible consequences before they are finalized and approved.

---

[6] *The Thana Irrigation Team reviewing an embankment proposal should also ascertain whether the embankment would interfere with the rights of local water users such as for fishing and navigation. Where possible, sluices or regulators should be provided and formal arrangements should be made for their operation so as to satisfy the needs of such users as well as farmers who want flood protection. Agreement should be reached between all interested parties before a scheme is finalized and forwarded for approval.*

15.5.3 Tidal floodplain

This includes areas where the rivers are tidal in the dry season: i.e., most of Chittagong, Noakhali, Patuakhali, Barisal and Khulna Districts, and parts of Jessore, Faridpur, Dhaka and Comilla Districts. Both freshwater and saline water areas are included. Some of the development techniques used in river floodplain areas are also suitable for implementation in tidal floodplain areas: e.g., excavation and desilting of khals, cut-off channels and tanks; provision of flood embankments; and loop-cutting. In addition, two other types of schemes can be considered in tidal areas: cross-dams on tidal creeks; and embankments to provide flood protection against tidal flooding. The two latter possibilities are discussed under separate headings below.

Cross-dams on tidal creeks. It is an established practice in parts of Patuakhali and Khulna Districts to build cross-dams across tidal creeks to store water after the end of the rainy season. It is mainly done to store fresh water in areas where tidal water would otherwise become saline in the dry season. It can also be done in some non-saline areas to store water at high tide level so that irrigation can be practised for a longer period of the day. In this case, it is necessary to provide a simple sluice-gate in the cross-dam to allow water to enter the creek at high tide and to prevent it from flowing out again as the tide ebbs.

There are almost innumerable sites where such cross-dams can be built in Khulna, Patuakhali and Barisal Districts. Sites are fewer in Noakhali and Chittagong Districts. Dams are simplest to construct on small creeks. Their precise location will depend on local requirements. It must be ascertained from local leaders whether a permanent cross-dam (with sluice) is required or merely a temporary one which will be built each year when water needs to be stored and then breached to allow boats and fish to enter in the rainy season.

In saline areas, cross-dams should be built near to the junction with a major channel so as to maximize the amount of fresh water that can be stored. Construction must be organized early enough so that the dam can be completed before the water starts to become saline. A spillway or *outlet* sluice-gate should be provided which will allow excess water to drain out without damaging the dam if there is heavy rainfall after the dam has been completed. These structures can be simple: matting for a spillway; and one or more pipes with hinged flaps for a sluice-gate.

In fresh-water areas, the location of dams and timing of construction are less critical. However, both intake and outlet sluice-gates should be provided: an intake sluice below normal high-tide level; and an outlet sluice or spillway above high tide level so as to drain out excess water without damaging the dam if there is heavy rainfall after the dam has been built. Both sluice-gates and spillways can be simple structures, as indicated in the paragraph immediately above.

In all cases, the DEO should seek the advice of a BWDB engineer regarding the design of the dam: i.e., the design, capacity and siting of sluice-gates and spillways; protecting the dam face and foot against erosion; and arrangements to be made for breaching the dam, if required, at the end of the dry season. Engineers should also assist in estimating the amount of water available for irrigation and the number of pumps or other irrigation devices that can be installed. In saline areas, local information should be collected on the date when water normally starts to become saline in the area, so that construction work can be scheduled for completion before that date.

Flood-protection embankments. Building of flood-protection embankments in tidal areas can be considered under three circumstances:

a. to protect transplanted aman paddy from freshwater river flooding in August-September;

b. to protect aus, aman or boro paddy against flooding by saline water during normal or exceptional high tides; and

c. to protect crops (mainly aman) against moderate and low storm surges in areas outside the Coastal Embankments, including new *char* land in the Meghna estuary.

In general, such embankments need not be high: usually no more than 3-4 feet in the case of a and b above, but perhaps 5-10 feet in the case of c. In all cases, DEOs must consult an engineer regarding the feasibility, siting and design of such embankments.

In the case of embankments against river flooding, it has to be determined whether embankments alone will provide protection or whether pump drainage will also be needed to drain water from inside the empoldered area. In saline areas, tidal sluices may be sufficient to provide drainage.

Construction of embankments outside the Coastal Embankments can be considered, provided that:

a. they will protect several hundred acres of land against normal tidal flooding and low or moderate storm surges;

b. they are sited so that they are not likely to be breached by river-bank erosion within about five years; and

c. the land protected is suitable for cultivation either in the rainy season or the dry season (or both).

Sluice-gates will usually have to be provided to allow drainage of rainwater during the rainy season. Wherever possible, areas outside the Coastal Embankment or on large *chars* should be made into a series of medium-sized polders — say 300-600 acres in extent — so that breaching of one part of the outer embankment would not damage crops throughout the whole of the embanked area. Internal embankments should be linked with the main Coastal Embankment or with a road or 'cluster village' so as to provide a safe evacuation route to a cyclone shelter when cyclone warnings are given. Although DEOs can recommend embankments of this kind, such embankment works should be considered as major projects, especially where they would protect areas greater than 300-600 acres. Major embankments must be considered to be the responsibility of BWDB.

15.5.4 Highland

Under Highland are included hill areas, the Madhupur and Barind Tracts, and high floodplain ridges standing above normal high flood levels. Provision of cross-dams and excavation or desilting of tanks provide the main opportunities. In some places, minor rivers and channels could be improved for irrigation or drainage purposes by desilting or loop-cutting. Terracing could be undertaken with food-for-work assistance in parts of the Northern and Eastern Hills, and the Madhupur and Barind Tracts. Excavation or desilting of tanks is described in Section 15.5.2. The two other main possibilities are described below under separate headings.

Cross-dams. Construction of cross-dams is a familiar technique for providing an irrigation source in parts of the eastern hill areas. Cross-dams might also be feasible in parts of the Madhupur and Barind Tracts.

In hill and hill-foot areas, sites to look for are those where the stream has a perennial flow; where the valley is relatively flat (so that as large a reservoir as possible can be provided); where the soils are not too sandy; and, if possible, where a spillway can be provided separate from the main cross-dam.

On the Madhupur and Barind Tracts, valleys with perennial streams are few. However, it might be practical to build dams where local experience indicates that valleys remain wet or stream-flow continues during at least the first half of the dry season. Sites to look for are those with clay soils, at a relatively narrow point of a valley and with a large area suitable for irrigation downstream.

It may be practical to build permanent dam structures in some places on the Madhupur and Barind Tracts. Such dams must be provided with adequate spillways to allow the safe discharge of rainy-season flow. It is usually not practical to build permanent small dams in hill and hill-foot areas where the alluvial materials often include permeable sand layers and the underlying rock may also be sandy and pervious. Also, in the latter areas, there is a considerable flow of water in streams during flash floods, which would require costly spillways to be provided.

For all cross-dams, the DEO should consult a BWDB engineer regarding the siting and the design of the dam and the layout of the irrigation distribution system; how much water can be made available for irrigation; and the possible impacts building a cross-dam might have on the established rights of other water users. Water rights agreements need to be made between communities along the stream or valley in order to regulate the amount of water that can be taken out at any particular point.

Construction of terraces. Schemes for construction of terraces can be considered in two areas.

   a. In eastern hill areas, for soil conservation purposes, especially within the catchment area of Kaptai Lake and the catchment areas of hill streams subject to flash floods which damage crops in adjoining hill-foot areas.

   b. On rolling or undulating land in parts of the Madhupur and Barind Tracts, mainly to allow paddy to be grown on land that is presently uncultivated. .

In hill areas, terracing can only be safely recommended on slopes of less than about 35 percent (about 1 in 3) and on soils deeper than about 3 feet. Advice regarding design, method of construction and crops that could be grown should be sought from the Soil Conservation Research Station at Ramgarh.

There is insufficient experience with terracing on the heavy clay soils usually underlying uncultivated parts of the Madhupur and Barind Tracts for a large-scale scheme to be recommended at present. However, food-for-work assistance could perhaps be used for establishing terraces on one or more pilot areas of, say, 5-10 acres where the physical and economic feasibility of this form of development could be studied. The main problem in designing such terraces is to provide a safe means of draining storm water during heavy rainfall so that drains do not become gullies.[7]

---

[7] *The problems of building terraces in hill areas are described in Brammer (1997), Chapters 6 and 16. See also Chapters 8 and 13 in this book. Problems of water harvesting and terracing on the Barind Tract and the Madhupur Tract are described respectively in Chapters 8 and 9 of Brammer (1997).*

15.6 PRECAUTIONS

In proposing schemes, DEOs should give careful fore-thought to possible adverse consequences that might occur. Some examples of questions that need to be answered are listed below.

    a. Will building a cross-dam deprive downstream communities or farmers of water they need for established domestic, fishing or irrigation uses?

    b. Will excavation of a khal lower the water-table and thereby seriously reduce water-levels in neighbouring wells and tanks?

    c. Will building a flood embankment (or road embankment) cause floodwater to be ponded on neighbouring agricultural land during the rainy season?

    d. Will loop-cutting or desilting of old channels lead to increased flood damage downstream or increased bank-erosion because of the increased rate of water-flow during the rainy season?

    e. Will run-off from terraces increase the risk of gulley erosion or landslides on hill slopes or increase the risk of flash floods in adjoining valleys?

    f. Does the scheme design provide an adequate safety margin to prevent loss of, or serious damage to, structures (e.g., a dam) in the case of exceptionally heavy rainfall or early floods?

Answers to these and similar questions need to be provided before schemes are submitted for approval. This will usually involve consulting a BWDB engineer. The possibility of adverse consequences needs to be avoided by designing structures that take such points into consideration or by limiting development to correspond with the amount of irrigation water available. For irrigation schemes in particular, an estimate must be made of the amount of water to be made available so that proper estimates can be made of the area that can be irrigated, the number of pumps (or other irrigation devices) that can be used and the size of distribution channels to be provided. Water rights agreements must be made between established and proposed water users before schemes are finally approved so as to avoid the risk of conflicts arising later.

Chapter 16

SELECTING SITES FOR SMALL WATER DEVELOPMENT SCHEMES[1]

This chapter is complementary to Chapter 15. It provides specific instructions to Agricultural Extension staff to help them identify and assess simple kinds of water development schemes whose implementation could increase agricultural production, incomes and employment in rural areas of Bangladesh. These instructions are also suitable for use by NGOs involved in rural development.

16.1 PREFACE

This guide gives simple instructions for identifying sites suitable for small irrigation, drainage and flood protection schemes. It is intended for use by District and Thana Agricultural Extension staff for training Union-level Extension staff and Village Food Production Committees. It is more comprehensive and detailed than the earlier manual on selecting sites for Food-for-Work schemes (Brammer, 1975d; see Chapter 15).

This guide should be used together with the Manual on the Thana Irrigation Programme (published by the Ministry of Local Government, Rural Development and Cooperatives). That manual gives details of the procedures to be followed in identifying sites for small irrigation schemes, for checking their technical feasibility and for requesting funds for implementation from Union, Thana and District Development Committees. Similar procedures can be used for identifying, checking and requesting funds for small drainage and embankment schemes to be carried out under the Thana and Union Works Programmes. A summary of the Thana Irrigation Programme procedures is given in Annexe 1 to this chapter.

16.2 INTRODUCTION

16.2.1 Types of water resource

1. Do any parts of the village lands need irrigation, drainage or flood protection? If so:
   a. what are the water resources that could be used for irrigation?
   b. how could drainage be provided?
   c. are there any places where an embankment could provide flood protection?

---

[1] *This chapter is based on a manual prepared to guide Agricultural Extension staff in identifying suitable sites for small irrigation, drainage and flood-embankment schemes which could be taken up by Village Food Production Committees with funds provided by Union, Thana and District Development Committees (Brammer, 1977).*

2. Possible surface-water irrigation sources include:

    a. rivers or khals which have flowing water throughout the year;

    b. rivers or khals which become dry in the dry season;

    c. road-side borrow pits;

    d. cross-dams on hill streams and tidal creeks;

    e. haors, beels and cut-off channels;

    f. tanks.

3. Where land cannot be irrigated from surface-water sources, examine the possibility of using underground water. Knowledge about existing open wells, hand pumps and tube-wells can provide information on:

    a. the depth to water at different times of the year;

    b. the amount of water possibly available; and

    c. the quality of the water.

4. If groundwater of good quality is available, the type of irrigation that could be provided is determined by the depth to the water-table during the growing season when it will be used, the surface relief and the kind of soil. That is:

    a. *artesian wells* can be used where groundwater flows to the surface under its own pressure;

    b. *open wells* and *hand pumps* can be used where the groundwater is near the surface or where the area that can be irrigated from one point is small because of sandy soil or irregular relief;

    c. *shallow tube-wells* can be used where the groundwater is moderately deep (less than about 25 feet) or the area that can be irrigated from one point is less than about 20 acres;

    d. *deep tube-wells* can be used where the groundwater is deeper than about 25 feet and where the relief and soils are suitable for distributing water over 50-100 acres from one point.

5. Where neither surface water nor groundwater exists which can be used for irrigation, cultivate the soils so as to make the maximum use of rainfall: see Section 16.6.2.

6. Where land needs drainage or protection from flash floods, high floods or salt-water flooding, try to locate sites where:

    a. existing channels could be deepened or widened;

    b. new channels could be cut, if necessary;

    c. earth platforms could be made to raise fields above flood-level;

    d. flood-protection embankments could be constructed; or

    e. simple structures such as sluice-gates or culverts could be provided.

7. Most kinds of irrigation, drainage or embankment need technical knowledge for planning, design and implementation. Therefore, after you have identified possible sites for small water development schemes, seek advice from an engineer of BWDB or the Local Government Engineering Department (LGED):

    a. to find out whether or not the proposed scheme is technically feasible; and

b. if it is considered feasible, to design the scheme so as to give maximum benefits.[2]

16.2.2 Principles of water development and use

1. In choosing areas for irrigation, give priority to:

   a. land which cannot produce a good dry-season crop without irrigation; and/or

   b. land which can be irrigated by simple equipment such as *dons*, swing baskets, open wells, hand pumps or bamboo tube-wells.

2. Where a choice of irrigation techniques exists, give preference to the least expensive and the simplest to organize. For example:

   a. artesian wells in preference to other types of irrigation;

   b. irrigation from a surface-water source in preference to irrigation from shallow or deep tube-wells;

   c. shallow tube-wells in preference to deep tube-wells.

3. Site irrigation pumps and tube-wells so that they can irrigate the maximum possible area. This usually will mean siting them on the highest land which will allow water to be distributed to the suitable land. For irrigation from groundwater, give preference to sites which will allow water to be distributed in more than one direction.

   However, where the highest land is too sandy to be suitable for irrigation, site the pump or tube-well at some distance from the highest point where more loamy or clayey soils occur which are more suitable for irrigation. This will reduce wastage of water in sandy fields and channels, and allow water to reach a bigger area of land suitable for irrigation.[3]

4. Where possible, site road embankments or flood embankments so that the adjoining excavation (borrow pit) can also be used as an irrigation or drainage canal, or as a water reservoir for irrigation or fish production.

5. Consider other people's water requirements. For example:

   a. do not site tube-wells near to river channels or khals if use of the tube-wells will lower the water-table so that the river or khal would become dry at a time when it is normally used for irrigation or fishing by other people;

   b. do not site tube-wells (deep or shallow) in areas where that might make existing open wells, hand tube-wells or artesian supplies go dry, *unless* the new tube-well(s) would also be used to supply drinking water or irrigation water to a bigger area than that covered by the existing supply;

   c. do not construct a cross-dam or make a canal which would prevent water from reaching communities downstream which are already using the water for irrigation, domestic supplies, fishing, etc.;

---

[2] *Design should include estimates of construction costs and of annual operation and maintenance (O&M) costs. It should also include an indication of potential knock-on impacts of scheme implementation which might adversely affect the lives or livelihoods of other people: e.g., flood protection or drainage of one area increasing the flood vulnerability of a downstream area. Means of mitigating such adverse impacts should be included in the scheme design. If that is not considered feasible, the potential impacts should be identified in the scheme plans so that the Thana or District approving authority could negotiate mitigation measures (including compensation) between the scheme beneficiaries and potential losers before approving the scheme for implementation.*

[3] *In the case of LLPs which need to be sited on a river-bank, a lined channel may need to be provided to carry water across the permeable, sandy, river-bank soils so as to minimize seepage losses. Channels could be either pucca or lined with plastic, metal sheets or other suitable material.*

    d. do not build embankments or leave spoil heaps alongside canals which might prevent water draining off the land after heavy rainfall or at the end of the rainy season.

6. If proposed water development schemes will or might affect other users, either within the village (Union or Thana) or elsewhere:

    a. make agreements with the other users on the amount of water that can be taken and when it can be taken; and/or

    b. compensate people who will lose land or water rights which they have previously enjoyed.

7. Grow boro paddy where:

    a. the soils are better suited for transplanted paddy than they are for dryland crops: that is, they can be puddled to hold water on the surface for at least one week after irrigation;

    b. *and* the water supply is sufficient to provide sweet-water irrigation up to at least mid-April (and preferably up to at least end-April);

    c. *and* the area is not subject to early floods in most years.

8. Grow dryland rabi crops (such as wheat, tobacco, vegetables) where the soils are not too saline for these crops before about mid-February *and*

    a. the soils are not suitable for boro paddy: that is, it is difficult to make water stay on the soil surface after irrigation;

    b. *or* the groundwater-level falls below about 10 feet before about mid-February in areas irrigated by hand pumps or from open wells;

    c. *or*, on sites where the soils are suitable for both boro paddy and dryland crops, the irrigation of dryland crops would allow a bigger area to be irrigated and more farmers to grow high-yielding irrigated crops.

16.3 SURFACE-WATER IRRIGATION

16.3.1 Rivers and khals

1. Rivers or khals usually pass through more than one village, Union or Thana, Some pass through more than one District. Therefore, consider the needs of all users of the water in preparing plans for using a river or khal for irrigation.

2. If the river or khal flows all through the dry season, the amount of water that can be used for irrigation is determined by:

    a. the lowest flow expected during the irrigation period; and

    b. the minimum amount of water required to meet the needs of other users such as existing irrigation groups, fishermen or boatmen.

3. If the river or khal normally becomes dry before the end of the dry season, the amount of water that can be used for irrigation depends on:

    a. the amount of flow during the cold season when dryland crops such as wheat or early vegetables could be grown with irrigation on suitable soils;

    b. the amount of water that could be stored behind cross-dams: see paragraph 6 below; and

    c. the minimum amount of water required to meet the needs of other people using the channel as a water source.

4. Do not make plans to use more water for irrigation than is actually possible, taking into account the factors described in paragraphs 1-3 above.[4]

5. If there is not sufficient water flow in the river or khal to satisfy the needs of all possible users, the approving authority (at village, Union, Thana or District level) must limit the quantity of water which each community can take during particular months.

6. In order to increase the area that can be irrigated, examine the following possibilities.

   a. Make more efficient use of existing irrigation equipment by, for example:

      i. making lined channels (*pucca* or with metal or plastic sheets) so as to distribute water more efficiently;

      ii. growing dryland crops such as wheat or vegetables on permeable soils and boro paddy on heavy soils;

      iii. growing wheat or other dryland crops on the maximum suitable area in the first part of the dry season, before the period of lowest flow;

      iv. irrigating crops only when necessary.

   b. Increase the flow of water in the river or khal by, for example:

      i. desilting or widening the channel;

      ii. excavating a canal to join the channel with a bigger river, if possible;

      iii. pumping water into the channel from a bigger river.

   c. Build one or more cross-dams on the channel (or provide sluice-gates) so as to increase the depth of water in the channel. If a cross-dam is built, provide a spill-way so as to:

      i. allow regulated amounts of water to pass downstream for other water users; and

      ii. prevent the dam from being washed out by an early flash flood before the end of the irrigation season.

   d. Build cross-dams (or provide sluice-gates) at the bottom ends of cut-off loops, where such loops exist. Water stored in the loop at flood-level can then be released gradually (or pumped) into the main channel to increase the available flow in the low-flow period.

7. For precautions to be considered when planning cross-dams, see Sections 16.3.3 and 16.3.4 below.

8. For suitable crops to grow with irrigation, see Section 16.6.1.

16.3.2 Road-side borrow pits

1. Examine the possibility of using road-side borrow pits as a source of irrigation water.

2. Road-side borrow pits which are continuous — or which can be made continuous by additional excavation — can be used in the same way as khals: see Section 16.3.1.

---

[4] *The background to this instruction was experience such as the following example witnessed by the author in Bogra District. A small river in that District had a low flow (recorded in a publication of BWDB's Hydrology Directorate) of about 20 cusecs: i.e., sufficient to supply ten 2-cusec low-lift pumps used to irrigate boro paddy. The following exchange took place between the author and a group of local farmers and officials: Qu. 'How many pumps were fielded on this river last year?' Ans. 'Fourteen.' Qu. 'Did the river become dry?' Ans. 'Yes.' Qu. 'How many pumps do you plan to field this year?' Ans. 'Twenty-one.'*

3. Road-side borrow pits which hold water for most or all of the dry season can be used and improved in the same way as tanks: see Section 16.3.6.

4. Conditions are very suitable for converting road-side borrow pits into irrigation channels where:

   a. the land is almost level; *and*

   b. there is deep silty or clay soil alongside; *and*

   c. there is a river or khal nearby from which water can be diverted or pumped into the road-side channel.

5. Conditions are less suitable for using road-side borrow pits as irrigation channels where:

   a. the land is uneven; *or*

   b. the adjoining soils include layers of sand.

6. Where conditions are suitable for using borrow pits as irrigation channels, make a plan to provide distribution channels leading off the main road-side channel to the areas of soils most suitable for irrigation. If possible, plan these secondary channels in such a way that the soil material excavated from them can be made into a road, path or flood embankment.

   Similarly, when new roads are planned, examine the possibility of aligning them so that the adjoining borrow pits can be used as irrigation channels.

7. Do not plan to use more water for irrigation than is available, keeping in view the needs of other users.: see Section 16.3.1, paragraph 4 above

8. In all cases where it is desired to use or extend a road-side borrow pit as an irrigation source, consult a highways engineer for advice on how to carry out the work without causing damage to the road. In general, the following precautions should be taken.

   a. A shelf of land (*berm*) should be left undisturbed between the bottom of a road embankment and the top of the borrow pit. The width of this berm will depend on the height of the embankment, the depth of the excavation to be made, and whether the soil material is sandy, silty or clayey. If engineering advice is not available, leave a berm which is at least 1½ times as wide as the embankment is high, or at least 1½ times as wide as the borrow pit is (or will be) deep, whichever is the greater.

   b. In thick silty or clayey material, the sides of the borrow pit can be vertical, but normally they should be made sloping to prevent them from collapsing. The precise slope required varies in different materials.

   c. Make arrangements to desilt the intake channel each year after the rainy season, if this is found to be necessary.

   d. Also, make arrangements, if necessary, to desilt the borrow pit periodically, and to remove weeds and debris which reduce the quantity or flow of irrigation water.

   e. Spoil removed from the borrow pit should not be left on the bank of the excavation where it can:

      i. wash back into the excavation; and/or

      ii. pond water on the adjoining land which could damage crops.

9. For suitable crops to grow with irrigation, see Section 16.6.1.

16.3.3 Cross-dams on hill streams

1. Select sites in or near hills where:

   a. there is a river or stream which flows for most or all of the dry season;

   b. the valley is fairly flat, so that a large amount of water can be stored behind a dam;

   c. the width of the valley or channel is fairly narrow, so as to minimize the amount of material that has to be excavated and moved in constructing a dam;

   d. the site is not far from the land to be irrigated, so as to reduce seepage losses in the irrigation channel or reduce the expenditure required to line the channel;

   e. the subsoil material is not too sandy; and

   f. if possible, a spill-way can be provided separate from the cross-dam (for example, into a cut-off channel which by-passes the dam).

2. Make the cross-dam high enough to divert water into off-take channels which will command the area selected for irrigation. If the cross-dam is built of sandy material and if the river-bed is sandy, make the cross-dam broad at its base and do not make the dam too high, otherwise water flowing through the sand may eventually wash out the dam.

3. Preferably, line the off-take channel close to the reservoir with mats or plastic sheets so that the flowing water does not erode the channel bed and sides. Alternatively, use pipes or *pucca* channels if the site is one which will be used for irrigation every year.

4. Provide a spill-way which will:

   a. allow enough water to pass through to meet the needs of down-stream users; and

   b. allow early flash floods to pass through without washing out the dam.

5. One way of providing a spill-way is to bury several 6-inch pipes in the cross-dam, leaving their entrances at different levels so that they can take off different amounts of flood-flow according to the water-level behind the dam.

6. The channel below the spill-way should be protected in some way so that water coming over or through the dam does not cause erosion downstream. Erosion can be prevented if the spill-way water:

   a. falls into deep water in the channel below the dam; *or*

   b. is led through pipes or over mats until it enters the channel below the dam; *or*

   c. falls on rocks or bricks which break the force of the falling water.

7. Wherever possible, seek technical advice from an engineer of BWDB or LGED for designing cross-dams, spill-ways and off-take channels.

8. Estimate the amount of water that can be used for irrigation, taking into account:

   a. the size of the area suitable for irrigation;

   b. the crops to be irrigated; and

   c. the amount of water that must be allowed to pass the dam and the irrigated area in order to meet the needs of downstream users.

9. For suitable crops to grow with irrigation, see Section 16.6.1.

16.3.4 Cross-dams on tidal creeks

1. In coastal areas where the water in tidal creeks becomes saline in the dry season, cross-dams built at the end of the rainy season can store sweet water for irrigation (and other uses).

2. In non-saline tidal areas, cross-dams can be used to store water in channels at high tide-level so that irrigation can be continued during the period of low tide when the level of water in the channel might otherwise be too low to supply water.

3. In saline areas, build the cross-dam in a creek near the junction with a major river channel so as to use the whole of the creek channel for storing fresh water.

    a. Build the dam before the water in the creek begins to become saline.

    b. In case there is heavy rainfall during the dry season, make a spill-way, or provide an *outlet* sluice, which will allow excess water to drain out of the creek without washing out the dam.

    c. Estimate the amount of water that can be stored in the creek which can be used for irrigation: see Chapter 17, Annexe 1.

4. In non-saline areas, build the cross-dam in a place where it will store enough water for irrigating the adjoining land.

    a. Make a spill-way, or provide an *outlet* sluice, which will allow excess water to drain out without washing out the dam in case there is heavy rainfall during the dry season. The outlets should be higher than the level of high tides.

    b. Provide an *intake* sluice which will let water pass above the dam at high tide, but which will close to prevent water escaping when the tide begins to fall.

    c. Estimate the amount of water that can be stored in the creek after high tide which can be used for irrigation: see Chapter 17, Annexe 1.

5. Wherever possible, seek technical advice from an engineer or BWDB or LGED for designing cross-dams, spill-ways and sluices.

6. Use *dons*, swing baskets or small pumps for irrigating from the stored water. Use the water economically, so as to obtain the maximum benefit from the water source.

7. For suitable crops to grow with irrigation, see Section 16.6.1.

16.3.5 Haors and beels

1. *Haors* and *beels* (*jheels, baors*) are depressions which stay wet through all or most of the dry season. Those that contain a large amount of water can be used to provide irrigation (if the surrounding land is suitable for irrigated crop production).

2. Water can be lifted to suitable land adjoining the haor or beel by *dons*, swing baskets or pumps.

3. Estimate the amount of water available for irrigation use in the haor or beel: see Chapter 17, Annexe 1. Take into account the amount of water which may not be usable for irrigation because it is:

    a. too low or too far from land where it could be used;

    b. needed for other purposes (e.g., fishing).

4. Do not make plans to use more water for irrigation than is actually available: see Section 16.3.1, paragraph 4 above.

5. Examine the possibility of expanding the area that can be irrigated by:

   a. making more efficient use of irrigation water: see Section 16.3.1, paragraph 6a;

   b. increasing the storage capacity of the haor or beel by such means as: desilting; building a cross-dam or embankment across drainage outlets; diverting water into the haor/beel from a nearby river; etc.

6. For suitable crops to grow with irrigation, see Section 16.6.1.

16.3.6 Tanks

1. Make a survey of all tanks (including road-side borrow pits) in the village.

2. Decide which tanks must be reserved for domestic water supply or for other non-agricultural uses.

3. Prepare plans for desilting old tanks which could be used for irrigation, for fish farming or both. Where necessary, plan to dig new tanks for these purposes.[5]

4. Where tanks will be used only for irrigation, make them as deep as is possible so that they will store the maximum amount of water. The depth to which tanks can be excavated depends partly on:

   a. whether the underlying material is permeable (allowing water to pass through easily) or impermeable (heavy clay); and

   b. partly on the depth of the soil water-table in the dry season.

   This information must be obtained by digging test pits during the dry season. If sandy material is encountered, the tank may only hold water to the level of the water-table. In silty or clayey material, tanks can hold water above the level of the dry-season water-table if the bottom and sides are puddled.

5. Where tanks will be used for both irrigation and fish farming, do not make them too deep: see Chapter 17. Seek advice from the Thana Fisheries Officer on the proper depth of water for maximum fish production.

6. Estimate the amount of water in the tank which can be used for irrigation: see Chapter 17, Annexe 1.

7. Decide how the available water can be used most efficiently and profitably for irrigation: see Section 16.3.1, paragraph 6a. See Section 16.6.1 for suitable crops.

8. Decide which method of irrigation will be used: *don*, swing basket, pump. Decide where the irrigation equipment should be sited. If necessary, limit the number of irrigation units or the number of hours per month when they can be operated, so as to prevent waste of water.

16.4 GROUNDWATER IRRIGATION

16.4.1 Artesian wells

1. Artesian water is groundwater that comes to the surface under its own pressure, without pumping. Areas with artesian water occur in a few places near the foot of the

---

[5] *New tanks are particularly needed in the western half of the Barind Tract where groundwater resources available for irrigation are limited. Possible social and technical problems that may be faced in 'water harvesting' in this region are discussed in Brammer (1997), Section 8.4.4.*

Northern and Eastern Hills in Sylhet, Comilla and Chittagong Districts, and locally on the Madhupur Tract in Mymensingh District.

2. Use the following methods to make the best use of artesian groundwater.

   a. Use pipes to control the outflow. Use either galvanized iron (GI) or plastic pipes, or hollow bamboos.

   b. Space the artesian wells so that all the suitable land can be irrigated. This may mean reducing the number of existing wells in some areas.

   c. Construct field channels to distribute water to as many fields as possible, without allowing water to run to waste. Line channels with plastic sheet, if necessary.

   d. Prevent the sinking of deep or shallow tube-wells in the neighbourhood which would reduce the flow of artesian water, *unless* this would lead to expansion of the total area irrigated. In the latter case, it might be possible to:

      i. use hand pumps or shallow tube-wells in the affected artesian area; or

      ii. limit the use of tube-wells until after farmers in the artesian areas have finished irrigating an early rabi crop (e.g. vegetables), then use the tube-wells for irrigating boro or early aus paddy .

3. For suitable crops to grow with irrigation from artesian water, see Section 16.6.1.

16.4.2 Open wells

1. Use open wells for irrigation where there is a plentiful groundwater supply within about 10 feet from the surface during the period when irrigation is needed:

   a. during the rainy season, if irrigation is needed for aman seed-beds, kharif vegetables, or the aus or aman crops in times of drought;

   b. during the cold weather (up to about mid-February) for early rabi vegetables, wheat, tobacco, cotton, etc.;

   c. during the hot season (April-May) for boro paddy, aus paddy (including seed-beds), deepwater aman (broadcast or transplanted), jute, and summer fruits and vegetables.

2. If there is no other possible irrigation source, open wells can be used for irrigation where the groundwater-table is deeper than 10 feet, but this requires more time and effort to lift the water.

3. If the groundwater supply is very plentiful within 10 feet from the surface, consider the possibility of providing a Persian wheel (an endless chain of buckets turned by a bullock). Seek advice from an agricultural engineer on how to make a Persian wheel.

4. In sandy soils, line the well with matting to prevent the sides from collapsing.

5. In all soils, make a fence or wall around the top of the well to prevent children or animals from falling into the well. This is especially important on soils which go under water during the rainy season or during heavy rainfall, when the well opening may not be seen.

6. For suitable crops to grow with irrigation, see Section 16.6.1.

16.4.3 Hand pumps

1. Hand pumps (including rower pumps) can be used for irrigation under similar conditions to open wells: that is, where there is a plentiful supply of groundwater within about

10 feet from the surface during the period when irrigation is needed: see Section 16.4.2, paragraph 1, for details.

2. Where the water-table falls below 10 feet, pumping becomes harder. That reduces the area that can be irrigated satisfactorily.

3. Consider the possibility of increasing the ease and efficiency of pumping by providing one of the following
   a. a longer handle;
   b. a double handle (see-saw) which can be operated by two people;
   c. a foot-operated pump;
   d. a heavy wheel;
   e. a small motor.[6]

4. Do not place hand-pumps within a radius of several hundred feet of a deep tube-well or shallow tube-well if the operation of the bigger tube-well will lower the water-table below the depth of operation of the hand pump during the period when it is needed for irrigation. It may still be possible to site hand-pumps in such areas if the hand-pump is used to irrigate early rabi crops before the bigger tube-well is used for boro paddy. Make agreements between tube-well groups and other farmers so that all may benefit.

5. For suitable crops to grow with irrigation, see Section 16.6.1. Because of the hard work needed for pumping, give preference to growing crops which:
   a. have a high value (e.g., tobacco, fruit, vegetables, spices);
   b. use less water than paddy (e.g., wheat);
   c. might otherwise die from a drought occurring during the rainy season (e.g., aus, aman, jute, kharif vegetables).

16.4.4 Shallow tube-wells

1. Shallow tube-wells (STWs) are really small tube-wells with a pipe less than 4 inches in diameter and a pump less than 1-cusec capacity. They do not necessarily pump water from a shallower depth than 'deep' tube-wells.[7]

2. STWs are suitable where:
   a. groundwater is available within about 20-25 feet below the ground-surface;
   b. the water is not too saline;
   c. the soils and relief are suitable for irrigation water to be distributed to 20-30 acres (depending on the size of the engine and the crops to be irrigated).

3. If the conditions in paragraph 2 are met, give preference to sites where:
   a. no other kind of irrigation is possible or convenient;

---

[6] *The area that can be irrigated by one hand pump can also be increased. The author recalls seeing a farmer in Kushtia District irrigating 2 ha of tobacco by moving his hand pump and two pipes between his scattered fields, irrigating them in rotation: (Brammer, 2000), Chapter 7, Section 7.2.3.*

[7] *Ordinary shallow tube-wells (usually referred to as STWs) use a centrifugal pump which can pump water from about 20-25 feet. Deep tube-wells (DTWs) generally use a force-mode pump which can pump water from greater depths. Deep-set shallow tube-wells (DSTWs) are STWs with a force-mode pump which can pump from greater depths than ordinary DTWs. During droughts, farmers in some areas have been observed to dig pits and place their STW pumps up to about six feet below the ground surface so as to pump water from as deep as 30 feet.*

b. farmers cannot grow a reliable crop or high-value crop without irrigation: for example, on light-textured Highland soils or on basin clays;

c. there are no land disputes or personal conflicts which might prevent the formation of an efficient irrigation group.

4. Do not site STWs:

a. where there are DTWs which lower the water-table below the depth from which the STW can pump water efficiently, *unless* the DTW will not be operated until after an early rabi crop has been grown around the STW;

b. near rivers or khals if operation of the STW will lower the level of water in the channel and deprive other people of their established water rights;

c. where operation of the STW will lower the water-table to the extent that open wells or hand-pumps nearby are put out of action.

5. Site STWs on a relatively high place where water can be distributed in more than one direction. This will reduce the amount of water lost in distribution channels (if these are not lined).

6. On permeable soils, consider the possibility of lining distribution channels. *Pucca* channels are expensive. Therefore, consider using cheaper alternatives, such as:

a. on loamy or clay soils, puddle the channel bed by hand or foot; if possible, keep the channel continuously wet so that it does not crack; also, remove weeds regularly;

b. alternatively, use mats or plastic sheets: these will need to be tied down so that they are not easily disturbed by wind, animals or children.

7. Operate STWs for as many hours per day as possible. Electric and slow-speed diesel engines can be operated round-the-clock. Kerosene and high-speed diesel engines may need to be stopped every few hours to allow cooling. None-the-less, no engine need be operated for less than 12 hours per day (unless water supplies are not sufficient for continuous pumping). Therefore:

a. provide 2 or 3 well-qualified drivers who will operate the engine on a shift system;

b. organize distribution of water on a fixed rota, preferably employing 1 or 2 channel-men (at least for night operations) to distribute water according to requirements;

c. keep channels and field bunds continuously repaired so as to reduce wastage of water.

8. For suitable crops to grow with irrigation, see Section 16.6.1.

16.4.5 Deep tube-wells

1. Deep tube-well (DTW) is the term generally used for a tube-well with a pipe more than 4 inches in diameter and a pump with a capacity of 2 cusecs or more. DTWs are not necessarily deeper than so-called 'shallow' tube-wells: see Section 16.4.4, paragraph 1.

2. DTWs are suitable where:

a. groundwater is plentifully available, preferably within 20-30 feet from the surface when pumping starts and not deeper than about 50 feet during pumping;

b. the water is not saline;

c. the soils and relief are suitable for irrigation water to be distributed over at least 20 acres for each 1 cusec of pump capacity;

d. it is possible to organize a large number of farmers into a cooperative irrigation group.

3. If the conditions in paragraph 2 are met, give preference to sites where:

    a. no other kind of irrigation is possible or convenient; (DTWs are very expensive);

    b. farmers cannot grow a reliable crop or a high-value crop without irrigation: for example, on basin clays presently used only for deepwater aman where irrigation would make it possible to grow much-higher-yielding HYV boro paddy instead;

    c. there are no land disputes or personal conflicts which might interfere with the organization of an efficient irrigation group.

4. Do not site DTWs:

    a. where operation of a DTW would put existing STWs, hand-pumps or open wells out of action by lowering the water-table, *unless* satisfactory agreements can be made to operate the DTW at a time when it would not interfere with irrigation from the other sources: e.g., by using the smaller wells until end-February for irrigating early rabi crops, then using the DTW after end-February to irrigate boro paddy;

    b. near rivers or khals if operation of the DTW will lower the level of water in the channel and thus deprive existing users of the channel of their established water rights.

5. Site DTWs on relatively high places where water can be distributed in more than one direction (preferably in more than two directions). This will reduce the amount of water lost by seepage in the distribution channels. However, if the highest land has very permeable soils, site the wells lower down the slope on more loamy or clayey soils.

6. On permeable soils, consider the possibility of lining distribution channels. *Pucca* channels are expensive, so consider whether cheaper alternative types of lining can be used: see Section 16.4.4, paragraph 6.

7. DTWs with electric or slow-speed diesel engines should be operated for 23-24 hours a day for maximum efficiency. It is inefficient and unnecessarily expensive to operate such engines for only a few hours a day, especially to switch them on and off several times a day. Therefore, unless water supplies are not sufficient to allow continuous pumping:

    a. provide 2 or 3 well-qualified drivers who will operate the engine round-the-clock on a shift system;

    b. organize distribution of water on a fixed rota, preferably employing 1 or 2 channel-men (at least for night operations) to distribute water according to requirements;

    c. keep channels and field bunds continuously repaired so as to reduce wastage of water.

8. For suitable crops to grow with irrigation, see Section 16.6.1.

16.5 DRAINAGE AND EMBANKMENT

16.5.1 Introduction

1. Examine whether drainage of part or all of the village land is needed to increase total crop production in the village.

2. Examine the drainage possibilities that exist. These might include one or more of the following:

    a. desilting of existing rivers or khals;

    b. excavating new khals;

    c. loop-cutting on rivers or khals passing through the village;

    d. digging field ditches;

    e. providing bridges or culverts in road or other embankments;

    f. providing sluice-gates;

    g. providing pump drainage;

    h. making flood embankments;

    i. making cultivation platforms.

    Details regarding each of these techniques are given below in Sections 16.5.2 to 16.5.10.

3. For drainage to be effective:

    a. there must be a lower place for the water to drain into (usually a river or beel);

    b. the drainage channels must be big enough to carry the required amount of water;

    c. embankments may be needed to keep out water coming from adjoining higher areas, for example if flash floods are liable to occur.

4. If an area is drained, it may also be necessary to provide irrigation to part or all of the land to allow crop production at another time of the year.

5. Drainage works should only be undertaken if this will not remove water from the land where it is needed for other purposes (for example, as a source of irrigation water or for fish production) *unless*:

    a. the total benefits to the village from the scheme are significantly higher than the losses; and

    b. people who would suffer a loss are properly compensated.

6. Also, drainage works should not be undertaken if drainage of water will harm the interests of other farmers or villages upstream or downstream, for example by:

    a. draining off water needed for aman or boro paddy cultivation in area upstream;

    b. causing floods downstream, due to more rapid drainage;

    c. preventing movement of fish for spawning.

7. Therefore, before planning or undertaking any drainage works:

    a. take into account the needs of other water users;

    b. make definite agreements with them regarding the changes to be made in water-level or water-flow; and

    c. pay proper compensation, if necessary, to those who will suffer loss of production or livelihood as a result of implementation of the scheme.

8. Drainage is a matter which needs expert technical advice. Therefore, consult an engineer of BWDB or LGED before starting any major drainage or flood-protection scheme.

9. For details of crops that can be grown on drained land, see Section 16.6.1.

16.5.2 Desilting of rivers or khals

1. Identify channels which can be desilted to provide improved drainage.
2. If the channel needs to cross more than one village, make agreements with the other villages for the whole channel to be excavated to a suitable outlet.
3. Get a surveyor to measure land levels along the channel in order to calculate how deep the channel needs to be excavated in different places in order to provide the required drainage.
4. With the help of an engineer, estimate the width of the channel needed to provide the required drainage.
5. Get an engineer to design the desilted channel, taking into account:
   a. the desired water level on the land or in the channel after drainage;
   b. the permeability or impermeability of the river-bed material;
   c. the slope of the channel sides which is needed to prevent them from slumping;
   d. the maximum flow of water expected in the channel;
   e. the need for cross-dams or sluice-gates to regulate flow;
   f. other possible uses of the desilted channel, such as fishing, navigation, irrigation.
6. Get an engineer to calculate the amount of earth to be excavated for desilting the channel.
7. Plan where to place material removed from the channel so that it will not cause water to be ponded on the adjoining land. Where practical, use the material to make a road or footpath, and make bridges or culverts in this to provide through drainage. Alternatively, use the material to make raised cultivation platforms: see Section 16.5.10.

16.5.3 Excavation of new khals

1. Identify sites where new khals could help to improve drainage. Generally speaking, these sites should be:
   a. across the lowest area, except where it might be practical to cut across a low or narrow ridge of higher ground;
   b. suitable for linking with a bigger channel.
2. Follow the same procedures as are described for desilting rivers and khals in Section 16.5.2. In brief:
   a. get a surveyor to measure land levels along the proposed line of the khal;
   b. get an engineer to design the depth and width of the khal so as to provide the amount of drainage required and to suit the soil materials along the line of the khal (to be found out by making test pits in the dry season);
   c. calculate the amount of earth to be removed and plan where to place it;
   d. take into account other possible uses of the khal, and of the excavated material.
3. Before making detailed plans or commencing excavation, make agreements with other villages for carrying out the work along the whole length of the khal, taking into account the needs of all those who will use the khal.
4. Also, make arrangements to compensate farmers and other people who will lose land or benefits they have previously enjoyed.

16.5.4 Loop cutting

1. Examine the possibility of cutting through the narrow neck of any river loops which occur in the village (Union or Thana). Straightening the course of river channels in this way can help to drain floodwater more quickly. On the other hand, the increased speed of river flow following loop-cutting can:

    a. increase flooding in downstream areas;

    b. increase the rate of river-bank erosion downstream.[8]

2. Therefore, before starting any loop cutting scheme:

    a. seek technical advice from an engineer of BWDB;

    b. make agreements with any villages downstream which might be adversely affected by the scheme;

    c. make arrangements to pay proper compensation to any farmers who lose land where the loop is cut.

3. Examine the possibility of using the proposed cut-off loop as a reservoir for irrigation water or for fish production.

16.5.5 Field ditches

1. Field ditches can be dug to remove surplus water from fields. They are mainly needed on:

    a. level Highland or Medium Highland to remove water after heavy monsoon rainfall which might damage aus, aman or other kharif crops, especially at the seedling stage;

    b. on all types of land in the dry season or the pre-monsoon season where either irrigation water or heavy rainfall might damage rabi crops (especially early rabi crops, wheat, maize, and summer fruits and vegetables) and young kharif crops (especially aus, jute, broadcast aman).

2. Make a plan which will provide drainage for a whole block of land. Field ditches are only effective if they can be linked with bigger ditches, khals or rivers to lead away the surplus water. This usually requires cooperation between several farmers.

3. Take care that ditches do not cause erosion. Special care is needed:

    a. on sloping land (even where the slope is very small);

    b. on heavy silty and clay soils;

    c. near the place where the field ditch joins a bigger ditch or channel;

    d. in the valley or channel below the outlet of the ditch.

4. If there is a danger that ditches will erode and form gulleys:

    a. control the outlets from fields by using pipes, bricks or pieces of wood in the field bunds for the water to flow through or over without touching the soil;

    b. make the ditches wide enough to carry the expected flow of water: broad shallow ditches are less likely to erode than deep narrow ditches;

---

[8] *Loop cutting on some rivers in eastern Sylhet had the unforeseen consequence of enabling the rivers to carry more sediment downstream, which caused silting up of some haor areas formerly used for boro paddy cultivation.*

    c. make control structures at intervals along the ditch to reduce the speed of water flow; in effect, this means making steps in the ditch, to let the water fall safely from one level to the next:

        i. use bricks, boards or other strong material to make the steps in small ditches;

        ii. in bigger ditches, it may be necessary to make *pucca* structures, especially where they join khals or rivers.

5. Inspect ditches regularly, especially following heavy rainfall, to remove blockages and repair any damage that may have been caused.

6. Provision of field ditches to drain water rapidly off one area of land could increase the risk of flood damage in lower areas, including areas far away from the drained land. This danger should be kept in view in planning to provide field drains. Therefore, the plans should first be inspected and approved by the local BWDB or LGED engineer.

16.5.6 Provision of culverts in embankments

1. If road embankments block drainage of water from adjoining fields:

    a. provide culverts or bridges in the low spots if the embankment is locally constructed; or

    b. request the Union/Thana Council or District Development Committee to arrange for a culvert or bridge to be provided if the embankment is under the control of a higher authority such as BWDB or the Roads & Highways Department.[9]

2. If culverts or bridges are to be made locally, make sure that they are:

    a. wide enough to drain water during periods of heavy rainfall or floods without causing wash-out of the embankment;

    b. strong enough to support the kinds of vehicles and loads expected to pass over them.

3. If flood embankments block drainage of water from adjoining fields, request the Union/Thana Council, District Development Committee or BWDB to provide a sluice-gate (see Section 16.5.7 below) or a pump of suitable capacity to drain the ponded water quickly when needed (see Section 16.5.8 below).

16.5.7 Sluice-gates

1. Sluice-gates are structures made to control the level or flow of water in channels. They are of two main kinds:

    a. automatic;

    b. hand (or motor) operated.

2. Automatic sluice-gates can be used in tidal areas (as described in Section 16.3.4):

    a. to allow *outflow* of water at low tide and prevent *inflow* of salt water at high tide;

    b. to allow *inflow* of fresh water at high tide and retain this water on the upstream side when the tide falls in the channel outside the sluice-gate.

---

[9] *If it is not practical to provide a drainage outlet for water ponded behind an embankment, compensation should be provided to farmers whose incomes have been adversely affected by the ponded water.*

These sluice-gates consist of a hinged flap (of wood or concrete) which swings open with flow in one direction and closes tight under the force of water-flow in the other direction.

3. Hand (or motor) operated sluice-gates can be used to control water levels and flow in both tidal and non-tidal channels. The gates are opened or closed according to the requirements for irrigation, drainage, flood control or other purposes. Alternatively, they can be set to allow a fixed quantity of water to pass through.

4. Seek advice from an engineer of BWDB or LGED regarding the siting, design and construction of sluice-gates before any are planned or installed. Take into account any possible adverse effects the installation or operation of the sluices might have on other land and water users in the area (such as fishermen, boatmen, shrimp farmers).

16.5.8 Pump drainage

1. Pumps can be used to drain low-lying land so that this land can be used for growing high-yielding crops in the kharif season (as well as in the rabi season, if irrigation is also provided).

2. For this kind of drainage, an embankment usually has to be constructed around an area (polder) or along a river or khal to keep river floodwater out of the area. One or more pumps are then sited on (or in) the embankment to lift rainwater ponded inside the polder into a channel outside the embankment; it may be possible to use the same pumps to lift irrigation water into the area from outside the embankment in the dry season.[10]

3. Areas possibly suitable for small polder schemes are:

   a. areas lying between existing road, railway or flood embankments;

   b. small areas lying between an embankment and a Highland area;

   c. valleys in hill and terrace areas.

4. Pump drainage schemes need to be designed by an engineer. Seek advice from the local BWDB engineer about the feasibility of constructing polders for pump drainage if you consider that suitable sites exist in the area. In general, schemes benefitting more than about 500 acres would need to be built and operated (at least initially) by BWDB. Smaller schemes could be built, operated and maintained by the Thana (or Union) Council under the Thana Works Programme.

5. In planning a scheme, take into account any possible adverse effects the proposed drainage works and pumping might have on other land and water users in and outside the area (such as fishermen, boatmen, other farmers).

16.5 9 Flood embankments

1. Embankments of three kinds can be considered for protecting land and crops against flood damage:

   a. submersible embankments, to protect land against early floods;

---

[10]*It should be kept in view that, under Bangladesh's environmental conditions, drainage requires about five times greater pumping capacity than is required for irrigation of the same area of land. Therefore, if reversible pumps are installed, either only one-fifth of the pumping capacity may be needed to provide irrigation to the drained area, or up to five times greater area could be irrigated than the pumps could drain effectively.*

b. high embankments, to protect land from high river floods;

c. embankments in tidal areas, to keep out salt water.

2. *Submersible embankments* are embankments built high enough to protect haor and beel areas against early flash floods, but which go under water during normal monsoon-season floods. They are mainly built to protect boro paddy against flood damage. They can also be useful, in suitable areas, to protect aus or deepwater aman against early floods at the seedling stage.

Submersible embankments can be built on river-banks surrounding haors or across piedmont plains (gently sloping floodplain land near the foot of hills). In the latter case, embankments should be built across the floodplain above the basin land where boro paddy is grown and, where possible, one or both ends of the embankment should be sited so as to divert the floodwater into a channel or depression where it will not damage crops. The height of the embankment should be determined by local experience of the maximum height reached by early floods in most years. Preferably, sluice-gates or regulators should be provided in suitable places to control the entry of floodwater into the basin land in the monsoon season so that water flowing over the embankment does not erode the embankment, thus requiring costly repairs to be made in the following dry season.

3. *River embankments* to protect land against high monsoon-season floods should be built on the highest land available, except where they have to cross another channel or avoid a village. However, they should not be built near to river-banks which are liable to be eroded by the river.

An embankment by itself may not be sufficient to protect crops from flood damage. Sluice-gates or pumps may also be needed to drain out rainwater accumulating in depressions within the protected area. In considering whether a flood embankment should be built or not, give careful thought to investigating whether an embankment would achieve the desired objective or not.

4. *Embankments in tidal areas* can be built to keep saline water off the land in areas not protected already by the Coastal Embankment.[11] These embankments may not need to be higher than about 3-4 feet if they are built on the river bank. Embankments crossing creeks need to be provided with sluice-gates to control drainage from adjoining land: see Sections 16.3.4 and 16.5.7.

It may not be practical to build embankments high enough to keep out storm surges in exposed coastal areas. However, smaller embankments built inside Coastal Embankment polders might be useful for reducing the flow of storm-surge floodwater; also to provide roads or paths for people to use for reaching cyclone shelters.

Where new land has formed outside the Coastal Embankment, it may be possible to create new polders by building new embankments nearer to the present coast-line. Sluices should be provided to drain out rainwater during the monsoon season.

5. Before planning or building any embankment:

a. seek advice from the local BWDB engineer regarding the feasibility of constructing the embankment for the purpose intended;

---

[11]*The so-called Coastal Embankment is a misnomer. The embankments (built and maintained by BWDB) occur not only along parts of the coast; they also occur along tidal rivers up to 150 km inland, enclosing large areas of land in what are termed 'polders'.*

b. make definite arrangements to maintain and repair the embankment, sluice-gates, etc., in future years so that the embankment scheme remains effective;

c. pay proper compensation to those who will lose land or other means of livelihood (such as fishing rights) if the embankment is built;

d. make agreements for building the embankment with neighbouring villages, Unions or Thanas which the embankment would have to cross.

16.5.10 Cultivation platforms

1. In low-lying areas which cannot easily be drained, consider the possibility of building soil platforms on which crops can be grown above flood-level. The excavation from which the soil material is taken for building a platform can be used as a tank or ditch to provide irrigation, for fish-farming, or for both: see Section 16.3.6.

2. Soil platforms can be of three kinds.

   a. Large platforms can be built above highest flood-levels. Such platforms can be used for growing fruit trees, kharif and rabi vegetables, betel vine (*pan*), aus paddy, aman seed-beds, or other kharif and rabi crops, with or without irrigation.

   b. Beds about 6-12 feet wide can be raised above highest flood-level for the cultivation of small fruit trees (such as guava), kharif and rabi vegetables, aus paddy, or other kharif and rabi crops, using hand irrigation from the ditches between the beds. This system is suitable in areas where the land stays wet all through the year but where flooding is not very deep, as in some fresh-water tidal areas. If the soil is peaty, the platforms can be made of silt carried from nearby river-banks or river-beds and mixed with the peat.

   c. In deep basin sites, platforms can be raised only a few feet above the dry-season water-level for the cultivation of rabi crops but not kharif crops (except, perhaps, early aus paddy or deepwater aman sown or transplanted after the rabi crop).

3. After construction, add new material from the tank or ditch every year to keep the surface of the platform above flood-level. Also, protect the sides of the platforms against soil erosion by covering them with vegetation (grasses or climbing beans or gourds). Make drains of pipe or wood (e.g., hollow palm trunks) to lead run-off water from the top of the platform safely into the tank or ditch.

4. For crops suitable for cultivation on raised platforms, see Section 16.6.1.

16.6 SOILS AND CROPS

16.6.1 Crop suitability

1. Table 16.1 (including the notes at the end of the table) shows the kinds of crops that can be grown with irrigation and without irrigation on different kinds of land and soil.

2. It must be recognized that this information is highly generalized. It should be used only as a guide, subject to modification by local experience on specific kinds of land and soils in different parts of the country.

3. The table refers to present flooding conditions. If any area will be drained, refer to the new drainage condition when using the table and notes. For example:

   a. if late-draining Medium Lowland is drained by field ditches, it may become suitable for crops shown for early-draining Medium Lowland;

b. if Medium Lowland or Lowland is embanked and pump-drained, it may become the same as Highland or Medium Highland;

c. if cultivation platforms are raised above flood-level, the soil on the platforms becomes the same as Highland.

16.6.2 Soil moisture conservation

1. On non-irrigated land, it is important to make efficient use of rainfall and to store as much moisture in the soil as possible for use by crops in dry periods: that is, in the dry season for rabi crops, and in the pre-monsoon and monsoon seasons for kharif crops.

2. On irrigated land, it is equally important to make efficient use of water, both irrigation water and rainwater, so as to irrigate the maximum possible area with the water available and to reduce the costs of irrigation.

3. For dryland crops (such as fruit, vegetables, oilseeds, pulses, wheat, broadcast paddy, jute, etc.), use one or more of the following practices to prevent unnecessary loss of soil moisture.

   a. Plough as deeply as possible to break up a ploughpan (if a ploughpan exists). However, this may not be desirable in soils where the ploughpan is needed to hold water on the surface for transplanted paddy.[12]

   b. If the field will remain fallow in the dry season, plough the soil while it is still moist after the previous kharif crop has been harvested (if this is possible). This will destroy weeds and keep the soil surface 'open' so that it can absorb the first rain showers that occur.

   c. Break up the soil surface by ploughing, hoeing or weeding so that it can easily absorb moisture from rainfall or irrigation.

   d. Mix as much manure or compost as possible into the soil.

   e. For dryland crops, cover the soil surface with a mulch of leaves, straw or cut weeds.

   f. Cultivate crops which cover the soil surface quickly; or grow a mixture of crops which together will quickly cover the soil surface.

   g. On irrigated land:
      i. irrigate only when necessary;
      ii. make fields level so that water spreads evenly to all parts of the field; and
      iii. either make small bunds to divide the field into smaller plots, or irrigate along furrows.

4. For wetland crops such as transplanted paddy, use the following practices to reduce water losses:

   a. make the field level;

   b. plough as deeply as possible (without breaking up the ploughpan);

   c. puddle the topsoil thoroughly;

---

[12]*In many soils used for transplanted paddy, it would be an advantage to have the ploughpan at a greater depth so as to increase the volume of soil in the cultivated layer available for moisture storage and root-development. This might require the use of strong bullocks or a tractor/power-tiller equipped with a rotary plough instead of a disk plough.*

d. make field bunds as high as is practical, especially on non-irrigated land;

e. inspect field bunds regularly, especially after heavy rainfall or irrigation, and keep the bunds repaired;

f. keep the field well weeded;

g. on irrigated land, do not allow the topsoil to become dry and cracked between irrigations.

TABLE 16.1

Land use in relation to seasonal flooding in Bangladesh[1]

Land type and normal maximum flooding depth	Permeable soils — Suitable crops or crop rotations		Impermeable soils — Suitable crops or crop rotations	
	Without irrigation	With irrigation	Without irrigation	With irrigation
Level Highland — not flooded (or only flooded within field bunds on impermeable soils)	1. Broadcast aus or mesta, followed by early rabi crops 2. Kharif vegetables and oilseeds, followed by early rabi crops 3. Fruit trees, banana	1. HYV aus (line-sown) or jute, followed by tobacco, rabi groundnut or mustard 2. Kharif vegetables, followed by rabi vegetables, tobacco, etc. 3. Sugarcane, pineapple, banana, fruit trees	1. (High rainfall areas) Broadcast, line-sown or transplanted aus, followed by transplanted aman 2. (Low rainfall areas) Transplanted aman	1. HYV boro (or transplanted HYV aus), followed by HYV aman
Medium Highland — shallowly flooded (6"–3 ft): (see Note 5)	1. (Early draining) As 1 above 2. (Late draining) Mixed aus+aman, followed by middle rabi crops	1. (Early draining) As 1 above 2. (Late draining) HYV aus (line-sown) or jute, followed by LV transplanted aman	1. (High rainfall areas) Broadcast, line-sown or transplanted HYV/LV aus, followed by LV transplanted aman 2. (Low rainfall areas) LV transplanted aman 3. (Ganges River Floodplain) Mixed aus+aman, followed by middle rabi crops (only on early-draining land)	1. HYV boro, followed by transplanted aman 2. (Ganges River Floodplain) Broadcast aman, followed by wheat (only on early-draining land)

(Contd.)

(Continued)

Land type and normal maximum flooding depth	Permeable soils		Impermeable soils	
	Suitable crops or crop rotations		Suitable crops or crop rotations	
	Without irrigation	With irrigation	Without irrigation	With irrigation
Medium Lowland (3-6 ft flooding) - without serious risk of flood damage	1. (Early draining) Mixed aus+aman, followed by middle rabi crops 2. (Late draining) Mixed aus+aman, possibly followed by pulses or *kaon*	1. (Early draining) Mixed aus+aman, followed by wheat, groundnut, some rabi vegetables, potato 2. (Late draining) Mixed aus+aman, possibly followed by pulses or *kaon* 3. (Permanently or nearly-permanently wet) LV or HYV boro	1. Mixed aus+aman, or broadcast aman alone	1. HYV boro
Lowland (>6 ft flooding) - without serious risk of flood damage	1. (Early draining) Broadcast aman, followed by wheat (part), pulses or oilseeds 2. (Late draining) Broadcast aman, possibly followed by pulses or *kaon* 3. (Permanently or nearly-permanently wet) LV boro	1. (Early draining) Broadcast aman, followed by wheat (part), pulses or oilseeds 2. (Late draining) Broadcast aman, possibly followed by pulses or *kaon* 3. (Permanently or nearly-permanently wet) LV or HYV boro	1. Broadcast aman 2. (Permanently wet) LV boro	1. HYV boro
Medium Lowland and Lowland (>3 ft flooding) - with serious risk of flood damage	1. As 1-3 above, but broadcast aman subject to damage or loss in some years, and boro may be unsuitable on sites liable to early floods	1. As 1-3 above, but broadcast aman subject to damage or loss in some years, and boro may be unsuitable on sites liable to early floods	1. As 1-2 above, but broadcast aman subject to damage or loss in some years	1. LV or HYV boro (except on sites liable to early flooding)

Notes: 1. *Permeable soils* allow rainwater and irrigation water to enter and drain through without causing waterlogging. They include sandy loams, most silt loams and some friable silty clay loams and clays which do not have a ploughpan. Many permeable soils also store water well for use by dryland rabi crops, unless they are underlain by sand within 2-3 feet.

2. *In impermeable soils*, rainwater and irrigation water enter and move through the soil only very slowly. When puddled, they hold water on the surface. They include some silt loams, silty clay loams and clays, especially where the soils have a ploughpan. Most impermeable or puddled soils do not store moisture satisfactorily for use by dryland rabi crops, and they are poorly suited for irrigation of such crops because water stands on the surface too long.

3. *HYV aus* (broadcast or line-sown) can be grown where there is adequate soil moisture (from natural storage, rainfall or irrigation) in April or May and where flooding is not deeper than 1-2 feet by the time of harvest (June-August), according to variety and time of planting). HYV aus can be transplanted on soils that can be puddled (after sufficient rainfall or irrigation). If HYV aus is to be followed by HYV aman, a quick-maturing variety must be grown, sown in early-April and harvested by mid-July.

4. *HYV aman* can be grown on soils that are not flooded deeper than about 6 inches at the time of transplanting (July or August, according to variety) and which hold water on the surface until at least the time of flowering (early-October).

5. *Local aman varieties* can be transplanted in water up to about 1 foot deep and in the month of September (although yields decrease progressively with time of transplantation after early-September). Some of this land on the Brahmaputra and Meghna floodplains may have been flooded up to 3 or more feet deep at flood peak in July or August, but transplanting is done as the floodwater recedes.

6. *HYV boro* can be grown on soils that are not flooded deeper than about 3-6 inches at the time of transplanting (January-February) or deeper than 1-2 feet at the time of harvesting (May-June, according to variety), and which hold water on the surface naturally or from irrigation through the dry season.

7. *Early-draining soils* are those which become free from floodwater or waterlogging in September, October or November.

8. *Late-draining soils* are those which remain flooded or waterlogged until December or later.

9. *On the Ganges River Floodplain*, broadcast aman is grown on Medium Highland as well as on more deeply flooded land. The peak of the Ganges floods is in late-August or September, which prevents transplanted aman from being grown except on Highland or very-shallowly-flooded Medium Highland (except in flood-protected areas).

10. *Dryland rabi crops*, as listed below, can be sown in the months indicated if the land is free from flooding or waterlogging by this time.

Some crops — such as cotton, tobacco, mustard, wheat, khesari, lentils and most rabi vegetables — are very susceptible to damage or destruction by waterlogging following late monsoon rains or heavy winter rains, especially if they are grown on puddled or relatively impermeable soils (such as after transplanted aman).

Crops sown later than the months indicated may give low yields or interfere with the timely sowing of a following aus, jute or broadcast aman crop.

Early rabi crops

September: tobacco, cotton, groundnut, sweet potato, brinjal, chilli, radish, winter vegetables, *kaon*, sorghum.

October: tobacco, groundnut, mustard, sweet potato, winter vegetables, chilli, radish.

Middle rabi crops

November: mustard, rapeseed, groundnut, potato, sweet potato, winter vegetables, chilli, gram, fodder legumes, wheat (HYV and local).

December (first half): as November, but less suitable than November for most crops.

Late rabi crops

December (second half): sweet potato, chilli; some pulses and late winter vegetables.

January: As December (second half); melon.

February: chilli, *kaon*, sorghum, sesamum, melon.

Annexe 1

THANA IRRIGATION PROGRAMME PROCEDURES

The procedures to be followed for identification, technical scrutiny and approval of small water development schemes laid down in the Thana Irrigation Manual are described in summary form below. Refer to the Thana Irrigation Manual for full details.

1. Village Committee (for example, Village Food Production Committee) identifies possible water development schemes with assistance of the *Gram Krishi Kurmi* (Village Extension Agent).

2. Chairman of Village Committee submits proposals for suitable schemes to the Union Council.

3. Union Council examines schemes submitted from Village Committees. Any schemes that are in conflict with others are eliminated. Union Council Chairman sends a list of recommended schemes to the Thana Council.

4. Thana Council requests the Thana Irrigation Team to survey the sites for technical feasibility. (The Thana Irrigation Team consists of the Thana Irrigation Officer and Thana Agricultural Extension Officer, plus any other Thana officers who may be co-opted to assist in the investigations.)

5. Thana Irrigation Team reports its technical findings to the Thana Council and prepares draft project plans for each selected site.

6. Thana Council scrutinizes draft project plans and forwards recommended schemes to the District Development Committee.

7. District Development Committee refers the draft Thana plans to District-level officers of BWDB, BADC, Agricultural Extension, Fisheries, Livestock, IRDP (now BRDB), Rural Development, Relief and Rehabilitation, etc., for technical scrutiny and recommendations.

8. Recommended Thana plans are considered by the District Development Committee. Approved schemes are recommended to relevant Ministries for implementation.

9 Approved schemes are implemented through relevant Government organizations in coordination with Thana and Union Councils, and Village Committees.

Chapter 17

USE OF TANKS FOR IRRIGATION AND FISH FARMING[1]

The factors to be considered in using village tanks for both irrigation and fish production are reviewed.. A method is described for calculating the amount of water available in a tank, taking into account evaporation, seepage and other losses.

17.1 INTRODUCTION

In many parts of Bangladesh, tanks provide the only available source of irrigation water. Often, they also provide the most convenient source of protein food, through the fish they supply. However, conflicts of interest sometimes arise between farmers and fishermen over the use of tanks (and beels) for their respective purposes. This conflict is unnecessary. If use of water is properly organized, the interests of both farmers and fishermen can be served, with advantages to both.

There are many thousands of derelict tanks in Bangladesh. They occur particularly on the Barind Tract, parts of the Madhupur Tract, the older floodplain areas and near the foot of the Northern and Eastern Hills. In 1975, Government launched a programme for desiltation of *khas* (Government-owned) tanks under the Rural Works Programme, primarily for fisheries development.[2] However, it is recommended that, wherever conditions are suitable, joint farmers' and fishermen's cooperatives should be organized to make full use of the production potential of tanks for both fish farming and irrigation. Similarly, it is recommended that joint farmer-fishermen's cooperatives be organized around non-*khas* tanks. Such cooperatives could obtain loans for tank desilting, either through IRDP (now BRDB) or the Agricultural Development Bank (BKB). Loans could also, perhaps, be given in the form of wheat to provide 'food-for-work' support for the execution of the work.[3]

---

[1] *This chapter is based on guidelines prepared for Agricultural Extension staff to assist them in helping Village Food Production Committees to maximize food production from local land and water resources (Brammer, 1975e). Footnotes in normal font were in the original document. Those given in italics have been added.*

[2] See 'Manual on Reclamation of Derelict Tanks under Rural Works Programme', first draft, February 1975, prepared for the Ministry of Local Government, Rural Development and Cooperatives in cooperation with the (then) Ministry of Forestry, Fisheries and Livestock and the Ministry of Land Administration and Land Reform.

[3] *Food-for-work programme assistance would be appropriate for desilting khas tanks but not non-khas tanks, which are privately owned. Experience in the 1970s and 1980s showed that it was very difficult to reclaim derelict tanks: khas tanks because of corrupt vested interests in tank management; privately-owned tanks,*

17.2 MANAGEMENT SYSTEMS

If the water is to be used for both irrigation and fish farming, a choice has to be made between two systems of tank management, viz.

System 1. All the water is used for irrigation, all the fish are caught and the tank is re-stocked with fish fry every year. Re-stocking can be either naturally during the flood season or artificially by introducing fish fry when the tank refills in May-June. Suitable fish species for introduction are the major carps: *catla, rui, mrigal*. Medium-sized fry should be used so that they reach an acceptable size within the 6-9 months growing period.

System 2. The tank is not completely drained for irrigation each year. Fish such as *Tilapia nilotica* are used which breed in the tank. Sufficient breeding population is preserved through the dry season to ensure rapid expansion and growth during the following rainy season.

In system 2, it is an advantage to deepen the centre or one end of the tank to, say, 3 feet below the remainder of the tank. This provides a sump in which the fish can concentrate when the water above this level is used for irrigation. In large tanks, this sump should not be less than 1 bigha (= ⅓-acre) in extent. In tanks smaller than 1 acre, the sump should be not less than one-third of the bottom area of the tank. Shade should be provided, either by locating the sump where it benefits from the shade of trees growing on the bank of the tank or by ensuring partial cover of water plants (e.g., lotus) or tall grasses (reeds). Irrigation should only be allowed from the higher part of the tank, so that water remains in the sump throughout the dry season to maintain adequate breeding stock. It may, in fact, be advantageous to drain the sump every second year or so, in order to control predator fish and re-stock with a balanced mixture of new fry.

There is little difference in yields of fish between the two management systems. Under good management, 1000-1500 pounds (12-18 maunds) of fish per acre can be obtained under both systems. The main difference between the systems is in the type of fish produced, and this will determine the system preferred by fishermen in individual cases.

For combined irrigation and fisheries use, two things are necessary:

1. knowledge of the amount of water available in the tank for irrigation (and the area of crops that this can properly irrigate); and

2. a cooperative agreement between farmers and fishermen regarding management and use of the water to serve both their interests satisfactorily.

These pre-requisites are described in the following sections.

17.3 CALCULATION OF IRRIGATION POTENTIAL

The volume of water in a tank that can be used for irrigation can be measured by multiplying the area of the tank by the depth of water available for irrigation (in feet), deducting losses due to evaporation, seepage and other uses, and then dividing the result by 43,560 to obtain the net amount of water available for irrigation in acre-feet (1 foot of water spread over 1 acre). Details of the methods of calculation are given in Annexes 1 and 2 of this chapter.

---

which are often under joint family ownership, because of the difficulty in getting agreement between family members, many of whom may no longer be resident in the village.

Tank irrigation can be used in one of two ways:

a. early in the dry season, for dryland rabi crops such as vegetables, tobacco and wheat; or

b. in the second half of the dry season, for boro paddy or for timely sowing of aus, jute or deepwater aman.

The first method is most suitable where the soils to be irrigated are moderately permeable: i.e., loams, clay loams and friable clays. With vegetables, tobacco and wheat, 1 acre-foot of water can irrigate about ¾-acre (= 75 decimals) of land, so long as it is applied in moderate doses (3-4 inches) so that there is no undue loss by percolation below the root-zone. On rapidly-permeable soils requiring frequent irrigation, the area that could be irrigated would be less.

The second method is most appropriate for irrigating boro paddy on heavy silty or clay soils that can be thoroughly puddled to hold water continuously on the surface between irrigations. Irrigation of boro paddy is most efficient if the crop is transplanted at the end of January or early in February.[4] Early-maturing varieties should be used. One acre-foot of water can irrigate about ¼-acre (=25 decimals) of land, if the topsoil is thoroughly puddled and irrigation is applied frequently enough to prevent the topsoil from drying and cracking.

If boro paddy is line-sown and grown on moderately-permeable soils under dryland conditions like broadcast aus, 1 acre-foot of water could probably irrigate about ¾ = acre (= 75 decimals) of land. On more permeable soils, a smaller area could be irrigated, and it might be preferable to use the water for wheat or other dryland rabi crops.

For broadcast (or line-sown) aus, deepwater aman and jute, 1 acre-foot could probably irrigate about 1.5 acres (= 150 decimals) if two irrigations were given, or 1 acre if three irrigations were given (assuming 4 inches irrigation for land preparation and sowing, and 4 inches for each subsequent irrigation). On rapidly-permeable soils, a smaller area could be irrigated.

The areas given above are indicative only. More land can be irrigated per acre-foot of tank water if the surrounding soils remain moist for part of the dry season and can thus supply part of the crop water requirement before irrigation is needed. Less land can be irrigated on sandy soils where part of the water is lost by seepage in distribution channels and by percolation below the root-zone in fields; also on land which is not well levelled and ploughed, so that water is not evenly distributed in fields.

Using the figures given above, a tank with 10 acre-feet of available water could irrigate 7.5 acres of rabi vegetables, tobacco, wheat or line-sown boro paddy on suitable soils, or 10-15 acres if used to ensure timely sowing of broadcast (or line-sown) aus, deepwater aman or jute. The same amount of water could irrigate 2.5 acres if applied to boro paddy transplanted end-January or early February on soils that could easily be puddled. In both cases, the acreage covered would be less on excessively permeable soils (and with inefficient water distribution).

---

[4] There is little advantage in transplanting earlier than end-January because, except near the coast, HYV boro seedlings make little growth until day temperatures begin to rise, after about mid-February. Transplanting end-January or early-February allows time for seedlings to become established, ready to commence rapid growth about two weeks later.

17.4 COOPERATIVE USE OF TANKS

Tanks can provide a multi-use asset if agreement is reached on irrigation and fishing schedules. Farmers' and fishermen's representatives must jointly agree on tank management policy:

a. whether to drain the tank fully or not each year; and.

b. whether to use the irrigation water early or late for dry season crops.

In addition, farmers must agree not to use the tank for jute retting and not to use plant protection chemicals during the rainy season within the area from which water drains into a tank.

There are advantages to both groups if fertilizers or manures are added to tanks. The recommended rates for fish farming are 1 maund of urea, 1½ maunds of TSP and 10 seers of MP per acre-foot of water retained in a tank at end-October (when the tank is full). The fertilizer should be added in ten equal monthly instalments, omitting December and January. Animal manure can be added where tanks are not used to supply domestic water. The cost of tank fertilization should be shared by both farmers and fishermen because both parties will benefit. Fishermen benefit by increased fish production. Farmers benefit by the use of water and tank-silt enriched by increased vegetation residues and fish excreta.[5]

Additional benefits can be derived from the tanks by using them for duck farming. This helps to control vegetation growth around the tank margins as well as to enrich the tank with their excreta.

In order that the productive potential of tanks might be fully utilized, joint farmer-fishermen's cooperatives need to be organized for each tank that is not individually owned and that is suitable for both irrigation and fish production. The interests of both parties need to be represented on the management committee. Where tanks have other uses — e.g., duck-farming, horticultural use on the banks, public water supply — those interests deserve to be represented on the management committee, also.

---

[5] Further details of tank management for fish culture can be obtained from staff of the Fisheries Department and from the Manual referred to in footnote 2.

Annexe 1

CALCULATION OF AVAILABLE WATER IN A TANK

In the following calculations, all measurements given are in feet and the volume of water available for irrigation is determined in acre-feet (= 1 foot of water covering 1 acre). For each of the steps described below, an example is worked out to illustrate the procedure.

The same procedure can be used for calculating the amount of water stored in a borrow pit, khal or reservoir, except that estimates may also need to be made about the length of khals or beels, their average depth or width, and of water flowing into such water bodies.

The method is not suitable for measuring the amount of water available in a channel with flowing water. That has to be measured in the channel itself. However, a flow of 1 cusec provides approximately 1 foot of water on 1 acre of land (i.e., 1 acre-foot) in 12 hours.

Step 1. Multiply the length times the width of the tank at the level of the water when irrigation is expected to begin.

E.g. (1): $300 \times 200 = \underline{60,000 \text{ sq. feet}}$.

Step 2. Multiply the length times the width at the bottom of the tank, or at the expected level of the water when irrigation will end.

E.g. (2): $270 \times 180 = \underline{48,600 \text{ sq. feet}}$.

Step 3. Add the figures obtained in Steps 1 and 2, then divide by 2. This gives the average area of the tank during the irrigation period, assuming that the sides of the tank have a regular slope.

E.g. (3): $60,000 + 48,600 = 108,600$, divided by $2 = \underline{54,300 \text{ sq. feet}}$.

If the tank has vertical sides, then Steps 2 and 3 are omitted.

Step 4. Multiply the figure obtained in Step 3 by the depth of water in the tank: either the average depth, or the difference in water-level between the beginning and end of the irrigation period. This gives the *gross volume of water available for irrigation*.

E.g. (4): $54,300 \times 6 \text{ (depth in feet)} = \underline{325,800 \text{ cubic feet}}$.

Step 5. To find out the *net amount of water available for irrigation*, subtract from the gross volume the sum of losses expected from evaporation, seepage, domestic use, etc., during the irrigation period: see Annexe 2. In most tanks, evaporation is the main source of loss. Seepage is generally small, especially after two-three years from excavation or desiltation. In some hill-foot sites, seepage *in* from a high water-table may counter-balance evaporation and other losses, especially at the beginning of the dry season.

Step 5a. Evaporation loss is calculated as shown below. The figures given are approximate monthly evaporation rates for Bangladesh. Rates may be slightly higher in the west and north-west of the country, and slightly lower in the east and in coastal areas. In the final fraction in each line, the first figure given represents inches of evaporation loss; the second figure converts this amount into feet. The first figure can be altered if experience shows that evaporation is more or less than the amount shown.

November   :   multiply area in Step 3 by 3/12
December   :   "   "   "   "   "   " 2/12
January   :   "   "   "   "   "   " 2/12
February   :   "   "   "   "   "   " 3/12
March   :   "   "   "   "   "   " 5/12
April   :   "   "   "   "   "   " 7/12
May   :   "   "   "   "   "   " 6/12

Sum the individual monthly losses from November up to the last month in which water is needed for irrigation, then deduct this total from the figure obtained in Step 4.

E.g. (5a): November : $54,300 \times 3/12$ = 13,575
            December : $54,300 \times 2/12$ = 9,050
            January   : $54,300 \times 2/12$ = 9,050
            February : $54,300 \times 3/12$ = 13,575
            ½ March   : $54,300/2 \times 5/12$ = 11,312
            Total evaporation loss   = 56,562

Therefore, 325,800 (gross volume) – 56,562 (evaporation loss) = <u>269, 238 cu. feet</u> (net)

Step 5b. If there is evidence of seepage loss, multiply the area given in Step 3 by the seepage loss (in feet), and subtract the result from the figure obtained in Step 5a. Assuming 1 foot loss by seepage:

E.g. (5b): $54,300 \times 1 = $ <u>54,300 cu. ft</u>

Therefore, 269,238 (net volume, 5a) – 54,300 (seepage loss) = <u>214,938 cu. ft</u> (net).

Step 5c. If there is evidence of any other significant loss of water, this should be calculated as for Step 5b: i.e., multiply the area given in Step 3 by the assumed loss (in feet), and subtract the result from the figure obtained in Step 5b. Assuming 9 inches taken for domestic use:

E.g. (5c): $54,300 \times 9/12 = $ <u>40,725 cu. ft</u>

Therefore, 214,938 (net volume, 5b) – 40,725 (other loss) = <u>174,213 cu. ft</u> (net).

Step 6. Divide the figure obtained in Step 5c (or in Step 5a if there are no seepage or other losses) by 43,560 to convert the volume of water available for irrigation to acre-feet.

E.g. (6): $174,213$ (net volume, 5c) $\div 43,560 = 3.99$ acre-feet

say <u>4 acre-feet</u>

Step 7. Calculate the area of crops that this amount of water can irrigate, assuming that 1 acre-foot of water can irrigate ¾-acre (75 decimals) of dryland rabi crops (wheat, potato, vegetables) or ¼-acre (25 decimals) of transplanted boro paddy. If used on line-sown aus, jute or deepwater aman, 1 acre-foot could irrigate 1.5 acres if two irrigations were given and 1 acre if three irrigations were given.

      E.g. (7): Dryland rabi crops   :   75 decimals × 4 acre-feet = <u>3 acres</u>

              or Transplanted boro   :   25 decimals × 4 acre-feet = <u>1 acre</u>

              or Aus, jute (2 irrigations) :   150 decimals × 4 (acre-feet) = <u>6 acres</u>.

Annexe 2

MEASUREMENT OF EVAPORATION, SEEPAGE AND OTHER LOSSES FROM TANKS

The measurement of gains and losses of water from tanks could provide an interesting and useful programme for students' participation. The method described below requires only simple equipment.

1. ***Direct measurement of water losses***. Obtain either a surveyor's measuring pole, or obtain a straight bamboo pole and mark this clearly in feet and inches. Place the pole firmly in the tank where it can easily be read from the bank. Make weekly readings of the water level indicated on the pole, measured to the nearest inch. Record the measurement in a note-book against the date of the observation. Keep the note-book in a safe place so that it can be referred to in future years, for comparison of readings on particular dates.[6]

2. ***Rainfall***. Measure rainfall and evaporation at a convenient site near the tank. The site should be about 20 × 20 feet square. It should not have any obstacles within about 30 feet from it on any side that would interfere with rainfall or air movement, so select a place that is well away from buildings or trees. Make a strong fence around the site to keep out animals, poultry and children. Place the rainfall jar and evaporation pan (described below) near the centre of the site.

   Measure rainfall in a can or jar with vertical sides. For direct measurement of rainfall, mark one side of this can or jar in tenths of an inch. Alternatively, use the can or jar to collect rainwater which will be poured into a graduated cylinder for measurement. (If a graduated cylinder is used, it may be necessary to make a conversion scale from metric units to 1/10th-inch units.) Place the measuring can or jar in a hole in the ground so that the rim stands 2 inches above the ground surface. Make rainfall readings weekly during the dry season (say, December to February) and daily during the remainder of the year. Record the readings in a note-book.

3. ***Evaporation***. Measure evaporation loss from a tank of water. The tank should be about 18 × 18 inches in dimension and 6-12 inches deep. If possible, a hole should be made in the ground and the tank placed in it so that the rim of the tank stands 2 inches above the ground surface. Make sure that the tank is level after it has been placed on or in the ground. The surrounding area should be under grass which is kept short; alternatively, if the ground is bare, it can be covered with straw or leaves, so that the ground surface does not become unduly hot when it is sunny, and so that rainfall does not splash from the ground surface into the tank. Place thin wire mesh or cotton threads over the tank to prevent birds from drinking the water.

   Before the evaporation tank is placed at the observation site, make measurements to determine the volume of water (in cubic inches) that is needed to fill 1-inch depth in the tank. Then make a table to show the volume of water represented by

---

[6] *If measurements of rainfall and evaporation will be made at the same place as tank water-levels are measured, make five columns side-by-side on the note-book pages with the following headings. Column 1: date of observation. Column 2: tank water-level. Column 3: rainfall. Column 4: evaporation measured. Column 5: total evaporation.*

1/100th-inch divisions. The volume of water added can then be converted directly into evaporation loss in 1/100ths of an inch.

At the observation site, fill the evaporation tank to a mark half-an-inch below the rim of the tank. Measure evaporation loss at weekly (or daily) intervals by recording the amount of water that needs to be added to the tank to bring the water-level back to the original mark. Record this figure in the column next to the rainfall figure measured on the same day. Make allowance for any rainfall received since the last observation by adding the rainfall amount to the evaporation figure measured. Record this figure as 'Total evaporation' in the last column.

Recordings of evaporation from a shallow tank surrounded by soil (especially from bare soil) are likely to be higher than from a large or deep tank, especially from a natural tank surrounded, as such tanks often are, by buildings and trees. Actual evaporation from a natural tank may be expected to be about two-thirds of the loss measured in an evaporation tank.

4. ***Domestic water consumption***. If desired, make estimates of the amount of water withdrawn from a tank for domestic use by carrying out a sample survey over a typical day or week. First make a pilot survey to measure the volume of water contained in the pitchers, buckets or other containers that are used. During the sample survey, count the number of containers of various sizes that are taken out during a day, then record the total volume of water taken out in gallons. One gallon equals 0.159 cubic foot (6.29 gallons = 1 cubic foot). Using this figure, calculate the number of cubic feet of water taken out during a day. Calculate the total estimated domestic water use during the irrigation period by multiplying the figure obtained for one day by the number of days during the irrigation period. Convert this total to a figure representing the equivalent reduction in water level in the tank by dividing the domestic use figure in cubic feet by the area of the tank (measured in Annexe 1, Step 3).

5. ***Seepage***. It is difficult to measure seepage loss directly. It is simplest to assume that loss by seepage is equivalent to the total loss of water as measured on the pole minus the losses due to evaporation and domestic use.

Keep in view that some tanks *receive* water by seepage during the rainy season and for some weeks at the beginning of the dry season. In such cases, seepage gains may compensate evaporation and other losses during the early part of the dry season. This can be calculated by subtracting the actual loss measured on the pole from the sum of the calculated losses from evaporation and other factors.

E.g.:   7 inches evaporation + 5 inches domestic use = 12 inches.

12 inches – 4 inches measured loss = 8 inches gain by seepage.

Chapter 18

USE OF WASTE LAND AND FALLOW LAND[1]

The terms waste land and fallow land are defined. The reasons why various kinds of land remain waste or fallow are explained, and techniques are described for bringing such land into productive use, especially for crop production.

18.1 INTRODUCTION

There is considerable interest in Bangladesh in bringing waste land and fallow land under cultivation. This is because of the urgent need to produce more food to feed the expanding population whilst at the same time reducing food imports to the lowest possible level so that scarce foreign exchange can be used to import raw materials and manufactured goods for a more rapid development of the country.

The density of rural population in Bangladesh now averages about 2,000 per square mile. Under these demographic conditions, there must usually be severe physical limitations on land which remains uncultivated or otherwise unproductive during part or all of the year. Techniques for overcoming such limitations are mainly known, but they are often costly to adopt and some may not be economic to provide under existing conditions.

In most areas of relatively lower population density, as in the north of Dinajpur District, some land is still single-cropped which could be used for an additional kharif or rabi crop. Such land is apparently mainly owned by relatively big land-owners. Economic incentives or social inducements may be needed to bring this land under more intensive cultivation.

It needs to be kept in view that bringing waste and fallow land under cultivation may not be the quickest or most economic method of increasing crop production in all parts of Bangladesh. Considerable production increases could be obtained in many areas by intensifying crop production on existing cultivated land by, for example:

　a. substituting high-yielding varieties (HYVs) for traditional crop varieties;

　b. using fertilizers, plant protection materials, irrigation, etc.;

---

[1] *This chapter is based on a paper prepared for the Ministry of Agriculture in January 1976 (Brammer, 1976). After reading this paper, the then Secretary for Agriculture commented that it was not useful to him because it did not tell him what to do. In fact, the paper was written as an information paper in an attempt to dispel somewhat gung-ho attitudes to land use development for a rapid increase in food production which were prevalent amongst administrators, engineers, agriculturalists and NGOs in the early years following Independence in 1971 and especially after the traumatic experience of the 1974 flood and famine.*

c. using better methods of crop husbandry, including deeper and more thorough ploughing, optimum seed rates or plant spacing, and better weeding; and

d. using better methods of harvesting, threshing, drying and storage.

A balanced view needs to be taken in crop production strategy so that each type and area of land is used and developed according to its properties and potential, as evaluated by experienced farmers, land classification specialists, agriculturalists and, sometimes, economists.

18.2 DEFINITIONS

Waste land (in Bangladesh) is land which remains permanently uncultivated. *Culturable waste* is waste land that is considered suitable for cultivation (at least in theory). Waste land includes seven main types of land, viz.

1. Land which is too deeply flooded in the rainy season for kharif crops to be grown reliably and which *either* is unsuitable for dryland rabi crops to be grown because it stays too wet during part or all of the dry season *or* is unsuitable for wetland rabi crops (mainly boro paddy) to be grown because it becomes too dry in the dry season (in the absence of irrigation) or because it is too deeply flooded early in the dry season and/or there is a high risk of damaging flash floods in the pre-monsoon season. Large areas of such land occur in many floodplain basin sites. They mainly have heavy clay soils.

2. *Char* land which is either too sandy, too wet or too exposed to the risk of bank erosion or damaging floods for crops to be grown at any time of the year.

3. Land which is too saline in both the rainy season and the dry season. (This includes some *kosh* soils which contain toxic chemical compounds.)

4. Peat soils which stay wet all through the year and which are too soft to support cultivators or plough-cattle for land preparation.

5. Hill land which is too steep, rocky or inaccessible for cultivation.

6. Shallow terrace soils on rolling relief.[2]

7. Uncultivated land in urban and industrial areas, including land that has been acquired for building but not used, derelict brickyards and abandoned factory sites.

Fallow land is cultivable land which is temporarily not under cultivation. It may lie fallow during one or more cropping season of the year (*current fallow*), or it may lie fallow for a whole year or more between periods of cultivation (as in *jhum cultivation*, where the fallow period may last for several years). Land may remain fallow for a variety of reason, viz.

1. In hill areas under *jhum* cultivation, land is left fallow for several years between periods of cultivation so that sufficient soil fertility can be built up under natural vegetation to support another one or two years of crop production.[3]

2. In floodplain and terrace areas, land may remain fallow in the rabi season because:

a. it stays too wet in November-December when most rabi dryland crops should be planted: this is mainly transplanted aman land where the puddled topsoil stays too

---

[2] *The terrace referred to here is a physiographic unit elevated above floodplain level, which in Bangladesh comprises the Madhupur and Barind Tracts. The terraces referred to in Section 18.4 are artificially-levelled areas made on hill slopes to make fields suitable for cultivating arable crops.*

[3] *Another important reason for leaving hill land fallow is to control the weeds of cultivation.*

wet after the aman is harvested; also, some basin land which drains slowly in the dry season; or

b. it quickly becomes dry after the end of the rainy season: this includes some heavy basin clays, some sandy soils and many transplanted aman soils which have a puddled topsoil and a ploughpan; or

c. it becomes too saline in the dry season, often in combination with a or b; or

d. rabi crops have been lost after sowing, due to flooding of fields by late rains (e.g., accompanying a cyclone) or heavy winter rains.

3. In floodplain and terrace areas, land may remain fallow in the kharif season because:

a. it is too deeply flooded for kharif crops to be grown safely; or

b. it is exposed to serious loss of crops by early floods (including flash floods), or by rapid rise or rapid flow of floodwater (as on some *char* land and basin land); or

c. there is not enough time for planting kharif crops after harvesting boro paddy and before the land becomes flooded in the monsoon season; or

d. the rainy season is too short for both an early kharif crop (aus or jute) and a late kharif crop (transplanted aman) to be grown under rainfed conditions; or

e. the land is too deeply flooded for aman paddy to be transplanted after an aus or jute crop is harvested; or

f. kharif crops have been lost (or not sown) due to early floods, heavy rainfall, a cyclone (± a storm surge), hail or exceptional drought or salinity.

18.3 RECLAMATION OF WASTE LAND

18.3.1 Deeply-flooded waste land

Such land occurs mainly in the Sylhet-Mymensingh haor areas, parts of Chalan Beel (the Lower Atrai Basin) and locally elsewhere in deep basin sites. Reclamation of such land would require:

a. flood protection and drainage if it is to be used for kharif crops; and/or

b. irrigation if it is to be used for rabi crops (mainly boro paddy).

Flood protection and drainage are expensive to provide and maintain. They may not be feasible in all deeply-flooded areas, either because of the very large volumes of rainwater to be pumped out against high heads, or because of the difficulty of maintaining embankments and intake/outlet channels along unstable river banks. Irrigation usually has to be provided at the same time as flood protection and drainage.

Where adequate surface water is not available for irrigation, the feasibility of providing tube-well irrigation needs to be examined; (shallow tube-wells are more convenient to provide than deep tube-wells in most basin areas). Failing this, the possibility of excavating large tanks should be examined. Basin sites usually are suitable for the excavation of deep tanks. Spoil from new or desilted tanks could be used to make a high embankment around them which would prevent rapid siltation of the tanks by floodwater and help to store additional water (from rainfall) above ground-level.

Some irrigated basin land might benefit from the construction of submersible embankments to protect boro paddy against early river floods. Such embankments would not provide protection for kharif crops against flooding caused by heavy local rainfall; indeed, embankments might increase crop damage to kharif crops by preventing rainwater from draining off the land.

Not all waste land in basins is suitable for reclamation. Some is on irregular relief, the higher parts of which cannot be reached by irrigation or which it would be costly to level for irrigation. Some haor areas, too — especially near to the northern hills — provide natural spill areas for absorbing flash floods entering the Sylhet Basin from the Shillong Hills. Embankment of such haors, with a view to bringing the land under boro paddy cultivation, might have adverse effects downstream in areas of established boro paddy cultivation. Not only might embankment of the rivers pass on the floods downstream, together with the hazards of increased channel siltation and bank erosion, but the abstraction of surface water to irrigate boro paddy on the reclaimed land would reduce the amount of irrigation water available in downstream areas. The result might be a net *decrease* in the area of boro paddy that could be cultivated.

Therefore, hydrological (and geomorphological) studies are needed in haor and other basin areas to determine the optimum methods of regulating flood-flow and distributing scarce irrigation water. Improvement of traditional grazing lands to support more cattle in the dry season might provide longer-term benefits on 'waste' land than uncontrolled embankment of rivers to open up such areas for boro paddy cultivation in ignorance of the hazard of reducing crop production in areas of established boro paddy cultivation.[4]

18.3.2   Char waste land

Chars occur in and alongside river and estuarine channels. Large areas of such land lie waste in the Teesta, Brahmaputra, Jamuna, Ganges and lower Meghna channels. Permanent reclamation of such land would generally not be feasible. That usually is because such land is exposed every year to the risk that it will be washed away by bank erosion or will be buried by new alluvial deposits. Some land also is unsuitable for cultivation because it consists of deep sand or it is saline.

New *char* alluvium generally is unsuitable for cultivation at first because it has poor physical properties. Silty and clay deposits stay wet and non-porous (like raw meat) for 1-2 years after deposition. That makes them unsuitable for dryland rabi crops and for satisfactory root development in wetland crops (boro, aus, aman paddy). Sandy deposits are too droughty and infertile for satisfactory crop growth, except where they are underlain by silty material at a shallow depth.

Temporary reclamation of waste *char* land might possibly be feasible where the risk of erosion or burial by new alluvium during the following crop season is not considered too great *and*:

a. the soils are suitable for the cultivation of a kharif or rabi crop; or

b. special techniques can be used to make the land suitable for crop production; or

c. special techniques or crops can be used under emergency conditions (e.g., after a major flood or storm-surge disaster) which might not be economic but which might be used to prevent famine.

---

[4] *This recommendation went unheeded. Hill-foot haors were reclaimed for boro paddy cultivation on a piece-meal basis — and haors downstream suffered increased flood damage and siltation.*

Most suitable land under a is quickly brought under cultivation by settlers on *char* land. Techniques and crops suitable for conditions b and c still need to be tested by research institutes. Possibilities include the following.

i. Where sand overlies wet silt (or where raw silt overlies sand) at 6-18 inches:
   - make planting holes or trenches;
   - mix the sand and silt in the holes or trenches by hand cultivation;
   - preferably, also mix in organic matter or fertilizers;
   - sow suitable dryland rabi crops: on land that can be prepared before mid-December, vegetables, sweet potato, potato, groundnut, mustard, pulses, barley, possibly wheat; on land available in December-January, sesamum, melon, *khira*, *kusum phul*; on land not available before February, sorghum, *kaon*, sesamum;
   - alternatively, on land where the risks of early floods, bank erosion and/or new deposition are not considered too high, sow aus, deepwater aman, jute.

ii. On thick, wet, silty or clay alluvium where irrigation can be provided by low-lift pump, hand pump or traditional devices and where the risk of early flooding is not too great:
   - level the land, if necessary, and make field bunds;
   - plough or hand-cultivate the land;
   - transplant early-maturing boro paddy;
   - use fertilizers (especially N and P);
   - irrigate as necessary.

iii. On thick, wet, silty or clay alluvium where irrigation cannot be provided (or where boro paddy cannot be grown because of the risk of early flooding):
   - make planting holes or trenches;
   - allow the excavated soil to become moist (but not dry);
   - mix the excavated soil with available organic matter (e.g., partially-decayed water hyacinth plants) and replace in the holes or trenches;
   - if sand is available within a short distance, carry this to the site and mix with the excavated soil and organic matter;
   - preferably, add some fertilizer (especially N);
   - sow crops as in (i);
   - apply cut grass and weeds as a mulch between the crop rows.

iv. On deep sands:
   - make planting holes or trenches while the sand is still wet or moist;
   - mix the excavated soil with available organic matter and replace in the holes or trenches;
   - if wet silt or clay is available within a short distance, carry this to the site and immediately place it at the bottom of the holes or trenches before replacing the excavated soil plus organic matter;
   - preferably, add fertilizers (especially N);
   - sow crops as in (i);
   - irrigate if possible (preferably by hand methods);
   - if unable to irrigate, apply cut grass and weeds as a mulch between the crop rows.

18.3.3 Saline waste land

Such land occurs in:

    a. the Khulna and Chakaria Sunderbans;

    b. small areas of similar land under mangrove vegetation near the mouths of rivers in the south of Chittagong District;

    c. land near the Khulna and Chakaria Sunderbans which has been cleared from former mangrove forest;

    d. tidal land outside the Coastal Embankment;

    e. some basin centres subject to tidal flooding with saline water in both the rainy season and the dry season.

Reclamation of soils under mangrove (Sunderbans) vegetation is difficult and expensive. It usually takes several years before satisfactory crop yields can be obtained. Reclamation may not be feasible or economic in all areas. Soils under mangrove vegetation — Acid Sulphate Soils (*kosh*) — contain sulphur compounds which release sulphuric acid if they are exposed to the air. The resulting extremely acid soil conditions are toxic to plants. Reclamation of such soils would involve:

- embanking the land to protect it from tidal flooding;
- excavating a network of drainage channels;
- providing one or more tidal sluices (and possibly pumps);
- during the first one or two years after embankment, flushing the toxic compounds from the soils by periodically allowing saline water through the sluice-gates to flood the land and then be drained off;
- then, if practical, adding heavy doses of lime to the soils to reduce the extreme acidity; (around the Khulna Sunderbans, flooding with river water which contains slightly-calcareous sediment might reduce the need to add lime);
- finally, growing transplanted paddy, with or without irrigation.

Reclamation of other tidal saline soils would involve embanking the land to prevent flooding with salt water. This may not be feasible on land outside existing embankments, except where extensive areas of new *char* land have formed since the existing embankments were built. New embankments would require sluices-gates to be provided to allow rainwater to drain from the area during the rainy season.

18.3.4 Peat soils

Peat soils occur mainly in the Gopalganj-Khulna Beel areas of Faridpur, Barisal and Khulna Districts. Smaller areas occur in some Sylhet and Mymensingh haors, some beel areas elsewhere and some valleys in the Northern and Eastern Hills (mainly in the south of Sylhet and the north of Comilla Districts).

Reclamation of peat soils is expensive. Large-scale reclamation by drainage is not recommended. Drainage allows peat to dry out and shrink. Semi-decomposed peat crumbles to a powder when dry and rapidly disappears by oxidation. Well-decomposed peat (muck) hardens irreversibly if is allowed to become dry, forming lumps like coal. In both cases, the ground surface falls to the level of the new water-table within a few years. This might be below sea-level in the case of the Gopalganj-Khulna peat basins. Renewed expenditure would then be required for additional drainage, probably by pumps. Some peat soils near Khulna would also become extremely acid and toxic to plants if they were drained, like the Acid Sulphate Soils described under Saline waste land above.

Farmers near Swarupkati and Bisarkandi in Barisal District have reclaimed peat areas by importing alluvium from nearby river banks or channels, mixing the alluvium with the peat and forming raised beds about 150 feet long and 12 feet wide. These beds are raised just above normal flood-level. Ditches between the beds contain fresh water throughout the year which can be used to irrigate crops by hand, if needed. Guava, kharif and rabi vegetables, sugarcane (for chewing) and aus paddy are the main crops grown on the beds. Arum (*pani kochu*) is grown on the edges of the ditches.

Elsewhere in parts of the Gopalganj-Khulna Beels, farmers carry alluvium from river banks or river beds to spread over the peat to form a silty topsoil thick enough to support them and their draught animals. Such land is mainly used to grow boro paddy. Both there and in areas where raised beds are made, it is fortunate that the Ganges river alluvium is calcareous and rich in weatherable minerals. This helps to neutralize the acidity of the peat and compensate for its low nutrient content.

18.3.5 Waste hill land

This land is mainly too steep and rocky for cultivation. There probably is very little such land: most uncultivated hill land either is in a fallow phase of a *jhum* cultivation cycle or is under reserve forest. Any remaining waste hill land should be placed or kept under protective forest to minimize run-off and reduce the hazard of flash floods in valleys and on neighbouring plain land. Methods of cultivating hill soils are discussed in greater detail below in Section 18.4.

18.3.6 Waste terrace land

Such land includes areas of undulating or rolling relief on the Madhupur and Barind Tracts where heavy impervious clay occurs at less than about 3 feet below the ground surface. Soils with heavy clay at less than 1 foot below the surface usually are left under poor grassland or scrub. Where the clay substratum occurs at 1-3 feet, the soils usually are under poor *sal* forest.

In their present state, these soils are unsuitable for cultivation of either dryland or wetland crops. They are waterlogged following heavy monsoon rainfall, but they dry out quickly between rainy periods and after the end of the rainy season. Under grassland, or where forest on the Madhupur Tract has been cleared for cultivation, the soils shed water by surface run-off, leading to the risk of gulley erosion (and to flash floods in the numerous valleys which cross these areas).

Reclamation of this land for cultivation would require the construction of terraces (as are found on similar soils and relief in the High Barind in western Rajshahi District).[5] This would be expensive on such heavy clays and on such irregular relief. Terraced soils

---

[5] *The terraces on valley sides in the High Barind apparently were built by big land-owners about two centuries ago.*

would only be suitable for transplanted paddy cultivation. If it is planned to make such terraces on the Madhupur Tract, preferably:

a. the heavy, cracking clay exposed on levelled terraces should be buried by 6-12 inches of silty material from adjoining valleys (or a neighbouring floodplain area) so as to provide a topsoil that is easier to plough and puddle than the clay;

b. drainage outlets between terraces should be made *pucca* (or pipes should be used) so that run-off from terraces would not cause gulleys to form; and

c. irrigation should be provided (where feasible); because of the small area that could be commanded from individual irrigation points and the depth to ground-water in many areas of rolling relief, deep-set shallow tube-wells may need to be used rather than the usual deep tube-wells.[6]

18.3.7 Waste urban and industrial land

Such land includes undisturbed land taken up in excess of building requirements, school grounds, land disturbed by brickyard excavations, refuse dumps, old buildings, tanks, and etc. Similar kinds of waste land also occur in some villages. Some of this land is suitable for cultivation, if required. Crop suitability depends on the nature of the land, viz.

a. soil texture, which affects moisture-holding capacity and ease of root development;

b. land level in relation to depth and duration of seasonal flooding;

c. availability of irrigation;

d. amount of levelling, clearing of debris and vegetation, etc. required; and

e. soil fertility, partly depending on the degree of topsoil disturbance (as by excavation, levelling, dumping) and partly on availability of fertilizers or manure.

In general terms, suitable crops for this kind of waste land are:

i. rice on level land with relatively impermeable soils: aus, deepwater aman, transplanted aman, boro according to depth of flooding and availability of irrigation;

ii. arum (*pani kochu*) on wetland that is not more than shallowly flooded;

iii. kharif vegetables on permeable Highland soils;

iv. rabi vegetables on permeable Highland and Medium Highland soils which drain early enough in the dry season, preferably with irrigation;

v. a wide range of other crops on poor soils, so long as they are not flooded or waterlogged during the growing season (and provided that they can be protected from grazing animals):

- root crops such as ginger, turmeric, arum (*mukhi koshu*), yams (*pesta*), sweet potato (both kharif and rabi);

- oilseeds such as mustard, kharif and rabi groundnut and sesamum, safflower (*kusum phul*);

---

[6] *In the High Barind, groundwater is mainly too deep for tube-well irrigation to be practical and the rainy season is only sufficiently long for a single paddy crop (transplanted aman) to be grown. On the lower relief of the Madhupur Tract, tube-well irrigation appears to be feasible; also, the rainy season is sufficiently long for two transplanted paddy crops (aus and aman) to be grown without irrigation if quick-maturing varieties are used. Boro paddy could be grown with irrigation, but water losses in distribution channels on these cracking clays might be too high to make this economical (unless a pipe distribution system were to be used).*

- legumes such as maskalai, pigeon pea, lentil, *sim* beans;
- fruits such as pineapple, melon, pumpkin and various fruit trees;
- fibre crops such as *mesta* and sunnhemp;
- thatching grasses.

Crop growth is liable to be irregular on land that has been greatly disturbed, and nutrient deficiency or toxicity symptoms may appear, especially on land that has previously been used for dumping of urban or industrial waste. Crops showing serious symptoms need to be examined by agricultural research specialists.

18.4 RECLAMATION OF FALLOW LAND

18.4.1 Fallow hill land

Fallow land in hill areas is normally recovering from *jhum* cultivation. In earlier times, the fallow period was probably 10-15 years or more, followed by 1-2 years of cultivation. Today, with increased population pressure, the fallow period is sometimes not more than 2-3 years and the period of cultivation may extend beyond 2 years. Under these circumstances, reclamation of fallow hill land implies reclamation of the land for permanent cultivation or controlled use. The measures to be used depend mainly on soil slope and depth, viz.

a. On slopes less than about 5 percent
   - cultivate all crops in fields aligned along the contour;
   - use manure, compost and/or fertilizers to maintain soil fertility;
   - mulch all crops grown in rows;
   - preferably, leave strips of tree crops or forest vegetation between cultivated strips, or make contour bunds between fields to lead run-off safely into adjoining uncultivated land; and
   - inspect fields regularly following periods of heavy rainfall and repair crop ridges, bunds, etc.

b. On slopes between about 5-15 percent:
   - preferably, grow tree crops; plant trees on step terraces;
   - if arable crops are to be grown, make fields on broad-based terraces;[7]
   - use manure, compost and/or fertilizers to maintain soil fertility;
   - mulch arable crops grown in rows;
   - grow cover crops between tree rows, or maintain a cover of weeds which are slashed regularly and left on the ground surface;
   - make contour bunds at the bottom of all fields, or cultivate crops on broad-based terraces, with drains to carry away run-off water safely into adjoining uncultivated land;
   - preferably, leave strips of forest or tree crops between fields used for arable crops;
   - inspect fields regularly following periods of heavy rainfall and repair any damage done to crop ridges, contour bunds, drains, terraces, etc., so that gulleys do not form.

---

[7] *Bangladesh's hill soils are generally poorly suited for terracing because of the very heavy rainfall experienced, the relatively incoherent nature of the soils, the general lack of suitable rock for making retaining walls and, in areas where rock occurs, the susceptibility of the soils to landslide erosion.*

c. On slopes between about 15-35 percent:
- use practices recommended in b above;
- avoid growing field crops if at all possible; however, it might be possible to grow field crops between newly-planted tree crops;
- if field crops are grown, give preference to those which quickly cover the whole ground surface to protect the soil against run-off and erosion.

d. On slopes steeper than about 35 percent:
- preferably, keep the land under protective forest, or plant trees which can eventually be used for timber, fuelwood or pulpwood; (all land steeper than 60 percent should be kept under protective forest);
- if tree crops are grown, plant them on step terraces, protect the soil surface with a cover crop or slashed weeds, and use fertilizers to maintain soil fertility.

Since most land in Bangladesh's hill areas has slopes steeper than 60 percent, the implications are that:

i. considerable areas that are now under *jhum* cultivation must be retired from cultivation and reafforested with trees of economic value suitable for timber, fuelwood, pulp, matchwood, medicinal products, etc.; and

ii. cultivation of arable field crops and fruit trees must be intensified in areas with deep soils on slopes less than 35 percent using appropriate soil conservation practices listed under a-d above.

Tree crops suitable for cultivable hill areas are: tea, coffee, rubber, jackfruit, citrus, guava; also cashew and possibly avocado in areas south of the Karnafuli river.

Arable crops suitable for cultivable hill areas are: aus paddy, maize, millets, kharif vegetables, groundnut, kharif and rabi legumes, *mesta*, hill cotton, kharif and rabi sesamum, mustard, sweet potato, potato, ginger, turmeric, arum, yams, cassava and pineapple.

In general, hill soils are low in fertility. They need heavier use of fertilizers than most floodplain soils if satisfactory crop yields are to be obtained. Frequent top-dressings of urea (and other soluble fertilizers) are needed to replace nutrients lost by rapid leaching of the soils under the heavy rainfall conditions of the hill areas.

18.4.2 Rabi fallow land

Floodplain and terrace land which stays fallow in the dry season is mainly unsuitable for the cultivation of rabi crops unless drainage and/or irrigation can be provided. Special cultivation techniques might be used to make cropping possible on some soils, mainly under emergency conditions. Greatly increased production could be obtained on some soils presently producing low-yielding rabi crops by introducing new crops and by using better management techniques, including use of fertilizers.

a. On land affected by a high water-table during the early part of the dry season, drainage could be provided by making surface drains on terrace upland and floodplain ridge soils, or by making raised beds on lower land. Such works would only be worth-while:

i. where early drainage would not interfere with production of a preceding aman crop;

ii. where cultivation of a rabi crop would not interfere with the timely sowing of a following aus or jute crop (especially important on parts of the Teesta floodplain where the soils presently stay moist enough for aus and jute to be sown in February-March, without waiting for pre-monsoon rainfall); or

iii. under emergency conditions, following the loss of a preceding aman crop due to flood, cyclone, pest/disease attack, etc.

> Drained land might be suitable for non-irrigated rabi dryland crops on soils which retain moisture well or where there is a high water-table in the dry season. With irrigation, dryland crops could be grown on permeable soils and boro paddy on impermeable soils.

b. Irrigation would enable rabi crops to be grown on many soils which presently remain fallow in the dry season. In saline areas, cross-dams could be built to store fresh water in creeks after the end of the rainy season. In other areas where surface-water or groundwater supplies are not available for irrigation use, cross-dams could be built in valleys in hill and terrace areas, and tanks could be excavated on floodplain and terrace land: see Chapter 16. Wherever possible, dammed creeks and tanks should also be used for fish farming: see Chapter 17.

i. On impermeable soils, boro paddy could be grown with irrigation on land which is not subject to the hazard of early floods.

ii. On moderately permeable soils, and in areas where irrigation water is scarce, a quick-maturing boro paddy variety could be direct-seeded (line-sown or dibble-sown) in order to economize in water use. Alternatively, quick-maturing dryland crops such as vegetables, potato, sorghum, millet, oilseeds, possibly wheat and barley, might be grown if their cultivation would fit in between the harvesting of aman and the sowing of a following kharif crop. Cultivation of the rabi crops on raised beds might be necessary to provide a better seed-bed and sufficient aeration of the topsoil. Irrigation would be applied along furrows between the beds. In saline areas, a mulch should be applied between crop rows on the beds so as to reduce the concentration of salt at the soil surface during the dry season.

iii. On permeable soils which drain before mid-December (either naturally or after provision of artificial drainage), dryland crops could be grown so long as this would not interfere with cultivation of a more important kharif crop (e.g., aman before the rabi season and/or aus or jute after the rabi season). Choice of a dryland rabi crop to be grown would be determined by earliness of drainage, soil permeability, market opportunities, and availability and cost of irrigation.

c. Various practices might be adopted under emergency conditions following disastrous crop losses in the preceding kharif season, viz.

i. Raised beds could be made for cultivation of early rabi vegetables, wheat, barley, sweet potato, potato, mustard, groundnut, etc. On soils that dry out quickly, the soil surface should be covered with a mulch. On some land, it might be possible to provide irrigation from hand pumps or shallow dug wells.

ii. On transplanted aman land and on heavy clays, holes or trenches could be dug by hand to penetrate through the puddled topsoil and ploughpan. Then early or late rabi crops could be sown, according to the time of drainage. Such land normally dries out quickly, so quick-maturing crops should be grown or irrigation provided (from hand pumps, shallow dug wells or traditional devices, where feasible).

18.4.3 Kharif fallow land

Floodplain and terrace land which stays fallow in the rainy season is mainly unsuitable for the cultivation of kharif crops unless large-scale pump drainage is provided, which is expensive. Drainage of this kind of land would need a detailed feasibility study and is beyond the scope of this chapter.

It generally is impractical to sow broadcast deepwater aman after boro paddy. However, on land which does not flood too early, it might be possible to transplant suitable deepwater aman varieties. In general, deepwater aman varieties give low yields when transplanted (often because they are transplanted too deep in the soil). They could only be transplanted successfully where floodwater does not begin to rise within about four weeks after transplanting, to allow the seedlings to recover from transplanting shock.[8]

On land not flooded more than 1-2 feet deep, long seedlings of suitable transplanted aman varieties could be planted following the harvesting of jute, so long as this could be completed not later than mid-September and cultivation of aman would not delay the sowing of a more important rabi crop.

In areas where floodwater does not flow too rapidly and where winds do not cause large waves to form on expanses of floodwater, 'floating gardens' might be built of banana stems, water hyacinth, straw, etc., with a layer of soil on top. This technique is used in some flooded areas for cultivating *kadu* (*lau*). There would seem to be no reason why other rabi vegetables should not be grown in the same way in suitable areas. In shallow water, the beds could be heaped directly on the soil.[9] In deeper water, floating beds would need to be held in place with stakes.

---

[8] *During the late-1970s and the 1980s, there was a considerable expansion of the practice of transplanting deepwater aman following the harvesting of boro paddy. Experience showed that the land most suitable for this practice was basin-margin land on Medium Lowland where the risk of early flooding was relatively low. It is an advantage to grow an early-maturing HYV boro so that aman seedlings can be transplanted by end-May. The deepwater aman benefits from the residues of fertilizers applied to the previous boro crop and from a relatively weed-free environment; (weeding of broadcast-sown aman generally requires considerable effort during the 4-6 weeks that it is grown as a dryland crop before fields become flooded). Seedlings of deepwater aman up to about 2 feet in length are often used.*

[9] *This practice was later observed in Arial Beel: see Brammer (1997), page 29.*

PART V
LOCAL-LEVEL PLANNING

The six chapters in this part describe various methods which were tried between 1970 and the early-1980s for bringing reconnaissance soil survey information into use for improved land use planning at regional and local levels. Chapter 19 reviews points relevant for countries such as Bangladesh which were made at an international workshop on land use planning. Chapter 20 describes a method for making village agricultural development plans, while Chapters 21 and 23 describe two methods for making Thana land use plans. Chapter 22 explains the rationale behind an attempt made to set up a Thana Land Use Planning Programme in the early-1980s. In all these chapters, emphasis is given to participatory methods which could not only enable Agricultural Extension staff to build on farmers' local knowledge and experience but also harness farmers' interest in identifying and adopting methods which would increase local and national food production. The final chapter, Chapter 24, shows how soil survey information can be used in regional planning to protect valuable agricultural land against undue encroachment by settlement and industry.

Chapter 19

LAND USE PLANNING IN THE TROPICS[1]

This summary of issues raised at a Land Use Planning Workshop emphasizes the need for greater official and public awareness of the need for sustainable land use, greater public participation in land use planning, the creation of central, regional and local land use planning authorities, and the provision of measures that would enable plans to be implemented.

19.1 INTRODUCTION

The Commonwealth Secretariat, jointly with the Bangladesh Ministry of Agriculture, organized a Training Workshop in Land Use Planning in the Tropics at the Bangladesh Agricultural Research Institute (BARI), Joydebpur, 21-26 January 1984. This constituted the first part of a two-part Workshop, the second half of which was held the following week at Ahmedabad, India.

Two participants came from each of four Asian and five African Commonwealth countries. At Joydebpur, resource persons were drawn from several Bangladeshi institutions, as well as from FAO and the British and Australian aid agencies.

The resource persons introduced topics covering widely ranging aspects of land use planning:

- concepts;
- role in national economic development;
- methods of resource survey, evaluation and planning;
- environmental issues;
- local-level planning;
- agrarian reform; and
- land use regulation.

Participation in all the discussions was vigorous, serious and practically oriented. This reflected the good choice of participants who were actively involved in land use planning, in one way or another, in their own countries; also, the increasing concern being felt — at least among professionals — about issues related to land degradation in most of the countries.

---

[1] *This chapter is based on an article which the author wrote for ADAB News (Brammer, 1984b) to inform NGOs and agricultural extension workers about the discussions and recommendations made at an international workshop on land use planning.*

19.2 COMMON EXPERIENCE

Country papers read by participants indicated a considerable commonality of experience, viz.

- a generally low level of political, bureaucratic and public awareness of the serious issues raised by the growing over-exploitation of land and other natural resources;
- inadequate means to regulate abuse of natural resources;
- allocations of funds and manpower far below the requirements to prevent further degradation of natural resources; and
- weak coordination of policies and programmes between a multitude of agencies involved in the use or development of natural resources.

Bangladesh, of course, provided no exception to this general situation. Only Malaysia seemed to have achieved a well-coordinated and successfully-implemented national land use policy. That reflected the existence of a strong central planning authority directly under the Prime Minister, the priority given to plantation agriculture, and the existence of an environment where the man-land ratio was still low relative to that in many developing countries. Elsewhere, where population pressure on resources was high, the natural tendency was for exploitation to meet today's needs to take priority over conservation to meet the needs of tomorrow.

The Workshop offered no panacea solutions. The two greatest needs identified for arresting and reversing current deteriorating trends were:

- the introduction of vigorous educational programmes to increase public awareness of the serious issues involved (and it was felt that awareness needed building up as much amongst politicians and officials as it did amongst the general public); and
- the establishment of a high-level National Land Use (or Natural Resources) Planning Authority to coordinate development planning and implementation, together with the formation of similar planning bodies at District and local levels.

19.3 PARTICIPATORY PLANNING

There was general agreement that planning and regulation were insufficient by themselves to achieve rational land use. Plans and laws have to be respected if they are to be effective. Therefore, it was strongly felt that the public must be involved in plan preparation and implementation. In that way, people would come to know and appreciate the basic issues involved in the rational management of the resources on which their livelihoods depended. Thereby, they would more likely accept greater personal and community responsibility for preventing abuse of their resources. This objective — participatory planning — provided the rationale behind the Thana Development Planning model developed at BARD, Comilla, in the 1960s.

Above and beyond local planning needs, however, there was felt to be a need for each country to develop a guiding philosophy for the use, development and control of its natural resources. Such a philosophy should not be limited to surveying and evaluating the physical resources alone. Planning and development concern people. Therefore, there was considered to be a need to pay more attention than in the past to assessing economic, social and cultural factors, taking into account also regional diversity and the need for employment generation.

The development of this national planning philosophy should be the responsibility of the central planning authority. However, this central body should not comprise only administrators and technocrats. In order to keep it sensitive to public opinion — and, equally important, in order itself to sensitize public opinion — the central planning authority should include representatives of the public, preferably elected ones. The same need was felt for there to be public representation in regional and local planning bodies.

Public representation was not regarded as providing a panacea, of course. Several participants related horror stories about forest reserves or soil conservation works being destroyed as a result of political intervention. None-the-less, it was generally felt that public involvement in planning was essential for educating the public about the need to regulate the use of their natural resources. In the long term, self-regulation was held more likely to succeed than top-down regulation, with its 'us-against-them' implications.

19.4 OTHER POINTS

Amongst the many other useful points which emerged from the papers and discussions were the following.

    a. Zoning regulations may be needed to prevent undue amounts of valuable agricultural land from being lost to urban or industrial use. Such regulations may be more easily enforceable if they are made by elected local governments than if they are made by a central government. None-the-less, central government guidance or incentives to local governments might be needed in this respect.

    b. Reports on soil and other natural resources surveys should be presented in terms which non-specialists can understand. To help in developing such an understanding, specialists should assist in training planners and implementers how to use such information. Additionally, education courses at primary to university levels should pay more attention to developing a greater awareness among students of the basic factors involved in the rational use of natural resources.

    c. A distinction should be made between land capability and land evaluation. Land capability implies mainly physical suitability, whereas land evaluation also takes into account economic suitability. For example, a soil and land capability survey might rate a large tract of land as suitable for growing potatoes: i.e., the soils and climate could produce high yields of potatoes under normal good management. However, potato cultivation might be profitable only in areas of suitable soils which are close to markets or cold stores. A land evaluation assessment would take this economic factor into account and rate only those areas of the physically suitable soils within an economic radius of markets as actually suitable for potato production; other areas would be rated unsuitable. However, that assessment might change if a new road or cold store were provided which made it economic for farmers to grow potatoes in an area of physically suitable soils. Land capability, therefore, indicates a long-term assessment of suitability, valid as long as the physical conditions remain constant, whereas a land evaluation provides a short-term assessment related to specific economic conditions.[2]

---

[2] *Land capability is also based on current environmental conditions and technical knowledge. Capability could change in the future with a change in the environment (e.g., due to artificial drainage of wet land) or the introduction of new technology (e.g., the development by research of new crop varieties better adapted for the environmental conditions than those currently known).*

d. Planners should try to provide their clients with a range of development options, not a single 'this is it' plan based solely on the planners' judgement of what is the optimum technical solution. Clients may give more weight to political, social or economic considerations than would a bureaucratic or technical planner. However, in that case, planners should provide their clients with an assessment of the relative costs and benefits of the alternative options, including the cost of benefits foregone by not taking the technically optimum solution. Those costs might include, for instance, the costs of providing alternative means of sustenance for future populations deprived of resources which are depleted by the present generation as a result of an expedient decision being taken regarding current land use practices.

e. In addition to formulating physical plans, planners should plan the actions needed to ensure that plans can be implemented. Those actions might include legal, administrative and educational measures, as well as the provision of incentives for people to substitute conservation-oriented practices for their out-moded traditional practices.

f. More research is needed to support land use planning. Particular areas needing attention are:

- techniques to speed up resource surveys and evaluations so as to produce interim results which planners can use until the results of more comprehensive surveys and evaluations become available; and

- land use or farming systems studies to test and develop practical and economic land management systems in environments where soil conservation or agro-forestry practices are needed to sustain productive use of the land.

19.5 FOLLOW-UP

Participation in the organization of this Workshop forcibly drew the attention of the Agriculture and Forest Division of the Ministry of Agriculture to the neglect of land use planning issues in Bangladesh. In their opening addresses to the Workshop, both the Minister for Agriculture and the Secretary of the Agriculture and Forest Division referred to unsatisfactory, laissez-faire attitudes to land and water resources and called for corrective actions to be taken.

An immediate benefit of this Workshop, therefore, was a decision of the Agriculture and Forest Division to organize a national symposium on land use policy and planning which would draw together senior members of relevant agencies to review the current situation and to discuss actions needed to develop the country's land and water resources in a rational, ecologically sound manner. It was hoped that the national symposium would be followed by regional, District and local-level meetings at which issues of local importance could be raised and discussed. The proposed opening up of issues concerning natural resources exploitation and conservation was timely in view of (the then current) Government's decision to decentralize a large share of development planning authority to Thana Councils.[3]

---

[3] *The author does not recall whether the proposed national symposium actually materialized. Probably it did not. The policy of decentralized planning was reversed by a subsequent government.*

Chapter 20

VILLAGE AGRICULTURAL DEVELOPMENT PLANS[1]

This chapter shows how to help village people to make a plan to increase agricultural production in their village. The procedure is interactive, following a series of ten questions which lead to decisions about crop production targets and a programme of activities and inputs for achieving the targets.

20.1 INTRODUCTION

20.1.1 Preamble[2]

The questionnaire which follows has been prepared to assist in drawing up Village Agricultural Development Plans. It is designed for use — after translation into simple Bengali — by Union Agricultural Assistants, Rural Academy lecturers, college students, NGOs, etc. The questions are designed to:

1. create an awareness amongst farmers of the opportunities for increased crop production and income which exist in their village;
2. lead farmers to take decisions which will increase their production and incomes;
3. persuade farmers to commit themselves to targets for increased production;
4. lead farmers to set up an organization, such as a Chashi (Farmers') Club, which will help to sustain interest in planned development and which will provide a specific forum for discussions with the Union Agricultural Assistant (UAA) on his regular visits to the village; and
5. lead farmers to set up their own small trial and demonstration plots on which they can test and assess new crops, varieties and techniques under their own conditions.

Users should perhaps not be unduly concerned about the realism and practicality of the plans which might be produced in answer to the questions. That is because the most

---

[1] *The author prepared two models for making village agricultural development plans in November 1975. These models did not involve the use of soil survey maps and reports. The objectives and principles of the two models were similar, but Model 1 was designed for use by Village Agricultural Development Committees and Model 2 was designed for use by Union-level Agricultural Extension staff. This chapter is mainly based on Model 2, but material from Model 1 has been incorporated where relevant. In the covering letter to Model 1, it was suggested that the models be distributed to a number of government and non-government agencies for their comments before final editions were prepared. The author did not receive any comments and, to the best of his knowledge, the models were never tested or used.*

[2] *This section is based on the covering letters sent to the Secretary for Agriculture when forwarding the drafts of Models 1 and 2.*

important objective at this stage is to create an awareness amongst farmers of the oppor-tunities which exist for increasing their agricultural production and incomes. If targets are not met, farmers will soon learn how to make their plans more realistic in future years.

Farmers will learn to make realistic plans all the sooner if they are encouraged to feel that the plans are *their* plans; that they are not made merely to satisfy Government or political objectives, or to make shopping lists for Government hand-outs. UAAs and other outsiders who assist farmers in preparing plans are there mainly as catalysts and accelerators. To the maximum extent possible, therefore, these outside workers must draw the information and decisions from the farmers in such a way that the farmers feel involved in preparing their own development plan and responsible for executing it.

The questions are not intended to produce answers for academic research. The information is meant to be used in the village. If the questionnaire succeeds in arousing farmers' interest in adopting improved cropping practices, then Thana and Union Agricultural Extension staff will have to be prepared to answer a lot of questions. In order to meet this demand, two major steps will need to be taken, viz.

1. Preparation of Extension kits so that Thana and Union Extension staff can assist in preparing and following up village agricultural development plans. Simple pamphlets, flip charts and posters dealing with improved crop varieties and cultivation techniques are needed.

2. Preparation of regular schedules by Thana and Union Agricultural Extension staff for their visits to villages participating in village development planning. UAAs should visit each village in their Union on a particular day of the week at fortnightly intervals and with specific objectives in view. UAAs assisting in preparing a village development plan should be prepared to camp in a village for several days to help sustain interest in completing the plan.

20.1.2   Objectives

The aim of the following questionnaire is to draw up a village plan for agricultural development. The questionnaire is designed to be completed by a UAA, Rural Academy lecturer, college student, or NGO worker, in consultation with leading farmers and young farmers. It is important that the farmers be fully involved in preparing the plan. It is *their* plan.

The completion of the questionnaire will involve a lot of discussions with and amongst farmers. It may take many hours — spread over several days — to complete in detail. The questioner will need to camp in the village or visit it daily until the plan is completed.

It might be better, in fact, to divide the village lands into a number of blocks of about 100 acres and make separate plans for each block in turn. It is not only easier to make plans for blocks of this size, but it is also easier to manage blocks of this size than it would be to manage the whole of the lands in a village within one plan. However, the plans of individual blocks will need to be integrated into a comprehensive village plan to ensure that there are no conflicts between blocks (e.g., in irrigation or drainage plans).[3]

---

[3] *Not referred to in the original models, but also needing to be considered is the mechanism for avoiding or resolving possible conflicts between the development plans of neighbouring villages. The UAA and/or the local Union Council member could undertake this responsibility in the first instance, using traditional methods of conflict resolution (salish) where appropriate. More difficult cases could be referred to the Union or Thana Council for resolution.*

The end-result of the questioning should be a map showing the areas of land in the village (or block) which are suitable for various crops and crop rotations, especially for HYV paddy and wheat and for high-value cash crops. Copies of the map should be made for the UAA, Thana Agricultural Extension Officer (TEO), Circle Officer (Development), Union Council and village school. Most important, however, copies of the map must stay in the village for the villagers to see and to use. One way to make this effective would be to paint the main features of the map on a board which could be placed at a prominent place in the village. Maps of different blocks could be placed alongside each other for comparison (and competition).

This map, together with tables made as a part of the plan, should be used as Extension tools. They can serve as a focus for discussions with farmers on improved cropping practices, soil management practices, agricultural problems, etc. They can also serve as a basis for preparing production plans for on-coming cropping seasons. The map and tables may need to be brought up-to-date annually or seasonally. This will help to sustain interest in the village development plan.

Alongside the map in the village, another board (or boards) could be fixed to show plot numbers in a left-side column and, in following columns, the names of the crops which each farmer intends to grow in each of the following aus, aman and rabi seasons. Farmers should be encouraged to record the crops which they intend to grow on each plot or (subplot). HYVs of boro, aus, aman and wheat should be recorded separately from local varieties. HYVs can be specified by name (e.g., Chandina, BR3, Sonalika).

If the area in decimals of each plot (and subplot) is recorded on each board, the total area under each crop can be calculated. These areas could then be compared with the potential acreages for each crop — particularly HYVs — estimated during the completion of the questionnaire. The actual and potential acreages of HYV paddy and wheat crops can then be written on a separate board, together with the actual and potential acreages of high-value cash crops. The effect of this might be to bring social pressure to bear on farmers to grow HYVs and cash crops on land that is suitable for such crops.

20.1.3 Comprehensive village plans

The questionnaire given in the following sections is incomplete. It deals only with crop production. Similar questionnaires are needed to assist in planning other aspects of village development such as:

a. livestock and fisheries development;

b. industrial development: e.g., processing of agricultural products (rice mills, oil mills, grain drying); workshops for making and repairing farm implements; brick-making; weaving; etc.;

c. Works Programme development: e.g., road-making; road maintenance; drainage; land levelling; building construction; raising platforms above high flood-level; making cyclone shelters; etc.;

d. development of services: e.g., sanitation; health care; family planning; adult education; grain storage; dealerships for agricultural commodities; cooperatives; etc.;

e. women's programme development: e.g., child care; preparation of food from new crops (e.g., soyabean, sorghum); sewing and handicrafts; literacy; etc.

So as not to over-burden the village community with too much questioning, it might be best to take these questionnaires in stages. The crop production plan could be taken first, as a model. The village leaders could then be asked which aspects of village development they considered next most important. The appropriate questionnaire could then be taken to the village for discussion on a suitable future date, by mutual consent.[4]

Alternatively, in an advanced village, the village participants could be asked to form groups to consider each of the questionnaires. In effect, this could be a 'village workshop'. The end-result would be a series of development plans. These would need to be integrated into a comprehensive village development plan. Representatives of each of the workshop groups should sit on the elected Village Development Committee to try to ensure implementation of their share of the plan.

On the whole, the step-by-step approach seems more likely to produce lasting results. The results of hurried 'workshops' tend to be superficial 'nine-day wonders': the whole community is not — and does not feel — involved in the preparation of the whole plan. It is better to take time over the preparation of a plan in which the whole community believes and feels involved. A step-by-step approach helps to sustain interest in planning, so that planning itself comes to be accepted as a normal part of community life. For similar reasons, the completion of questionnaires and preparation of plans should not be unduly rushed.

The basic objective of this type of village development planning is 'self-help'. (This does not need to be shouted from the roof-tops: 'self-help' themes tend to discourage local interest and participation, except by touts.) The purpose of the questionnaires is to create an awareness of the opportunities for development which exist. The role of outside workers is to help villagers to identify these opportunities and to lead them to take decisions to use these opportunities.

The purpose of the village plan is to stimulate action for development. In-so-far as is possible, this action should be by members of the village: e.g., decisions by individual farmers to grow HYVs; to form an irrigation group; to improve poultry production; to cooperate in building a grain store; etc.

The plan should not be framed mainly in terms of dependence on Government (or NGO) assistance. Undoubtedly, however, a sound and active village development plan will attract Government inputs such as irrigation facilities, Works Programme funds, Extension advice, etc. This aspect could be stressed in introducing and preparing village development plans.

20.1.4 Other aspects

Two last aspects of village development planning deserve attention.

1. The plans must be technically sound. Enthusiasm by itself is not enough. For example, plans to cultivate waste land and fallow land are sometimes too ambitious, leading to failure and ultimate disappointment. This brings development planning into disrespect, and it may set back progress for many years.

   Before ambitious plans for new developments such as cultivation of waste or fallow land are set in motion, the technical reasons why this land has remained uncultivated in the past need to be sought and examined. The reasons are often known to experienced village farmers. The appropriate technical officials then

---

[4] *Separate questionnaires would need to be prepared by appropriate specialists from the Livestock, Fisheries, Rural Development, etc., agencies or by the Rural Development Academies.*

need to be consulted to find out how best the technical problems might be overcome and whether long-term benefits are likely to exceed short-term costs.[5]

2. The preparation of village development plans is essentially self-centred. But many villages (or blocks) cannot be developed by themselves in isolation from other communities or farmers. For example:

    a. village roads may need to be linked up with roads of other villages;

    b. a bridge may be needed to serve the roads of more than one community;

    c. a river or beel can be used by only a certain number of irrigation pumps;

    d. building a cross-dam may interfere with water supplies of downstream users;

    e. provision of DTWs may lower the water-table, and so deprive STWs, HTWs, open wells, artesian wells, even streams, of water presently used by other farmers.

    Therefore, Village (or Block) Development Committees may need to select leaders who can negotiate agreements with neighbouring communities or groups of farmers on matters of mutual interest such as improvement of roads and sharing of water. These external and internal affairs need to be considered realistically in preparing village (or block) development plans.

20.2 QUESTIONNAIRE

Question 1.   What kinds of land are there in the village (or block)?

First, find out from the farmers which land types exist. Definitions of land types are given in Table 20.1. The main land types which usually occur are indicated in the example shown in Table 20.2. The names of these land types show whether the land is above normal flood-level or not and how deeply it is flooded in normal years.

These land types may not all occur in every village. There may also be more subdivisions of these land types in some areas. Question the farmers to find out whether more subdivisions occur, and write the names of these under 'Others' in the list given in column 2 of Table 20.2.

Examples of some of the subdivisions which occur are shown in the table. The difference between these subdivisions are important for agriculture. They must be recognized and shown separately in the tables prepared later in this questionnaire.

Put a tick mark (√) in the 'Land' column against the name of each land type (or subdivision) which occurs in the village or block:

    a. put two ticks (√√) against important land types;

    b. put one tick (√) against land types which occupy only a small area.

The 'Soil' column of Table 20.2 will be completed later, in answering Question 2.

Question 2.   What kinds of soils are there on each of the land types?

Make a list of the soil types which occur in the village or block. Farmers usually recognize some or all of the soil types listed and defined in Table 20.1. Not all of those soil types may occur in every village, nor will all of them occur in every land type. Farmers in some areas may recognize more soil types. Ask questions to find out whether any other types occur. Write the names of these soil types in the list.

---

[5] *See Chapter 18 for a realistic assessment of possible ways to bring waste land and fallow land into productive use.*

TABLE 20.1
Definitions of land and soil types

Land types

Highland (H)	Land above normal flood-level.
Medium Highland (MH)	Land which is seasonally flooded up to about 1-3 feet deep. On suitable soils, it is suitable for transplanted aman.
Medium Lowland (ML)	Land which is seasonally flooded up to about 3-6 feet deep. It is usually suitable for mixed aus + aman to be grown, but flooding is too deep for normal varieties of transplanted aman to be grown.
Lowland (L)	Land which is seasonally flooded deeper than about 6 feet. It is too deeply flooded for aus to be grown, but it may be suitable for deepwater aman to be grown.
Bottomland (B)	Land in basin centres which stays wet for most or all of the year (regardless of how deep flooding is in the rainy season). It is often used for boro paddy (local varieties), but it is not suitable for broadcast aus and aman to be grown.
Terrace	Level or rolling Highland which stands above adjoining floodplain level, as on the Madhupur and Barind Tracts.

Note: Very Lowland (VL), seasonally flooded deeper than about 10 feet, is recognized in some areas.

Soil types

Very sandy (VS)	Deep sands or coarse sands which hold too little water for most crops to be grown satisfactorily
Sandy (S)	Fine sands, or loamy soils which overlie deep or coarse sand at a shallow depth (1-2 feet). They are often suitable for crops that need a light soil (such as vegetables), but they need a lot of water if irrigated.
Loamy (L)	Usually deep silt loams or sandy loams which are permeable in the subsoil. However, topsoils puddled for growing transplanted paddy are impermeable.
Clayey loam (CL)	Grey terrace and floodplain soils usually are impermeable. Red and brown terrace soils usually are permeable (except in the substratum of shallow soils).
Clay (C)	Includes impermeable grey terrace and floodplain soils, and permeable red-brown terrace soils
Peat (peaty) (P)	Soil formed mainly of organic matter, in permanently-wet depressions. Such soils may be too soft for cultivation, except where the peat is buried by a clayey topsoil.

Permeability types

Permeable	Lets water enter and pass through without causing waterlogging. Permeable soils usually are suitable for crops that need good drainage (such as tree crops, dryland crops and broadcast paddy crops).
Impermeable	Does not let water enter or pass through quickly. Impermeable soils usually are suitable for transplanted paddy, but not for dryland crops and most tree crops.

Question the farmers to find out which soil types occur in each of the land types marked with ticks in the table prepared in Question 1 (i.e., Table 20.2). Show the soil types by using the letter symbols given against the names of the soil types listed in Table 20.1. Give suitable letter symbols for any other soil types listed. For example, if sandy, loamy and clayey loam soils occur on level floodplain Highland, write 'S, L and CL' in the 'Soils' column against 'Highland - Level Highland on floodplain' in the table (Table 20.2). Underline the symbols used for the most important soil types.

TABLE 20.2
Village agricultural development plan: land and soil types

(1) Land type	(2) Subdivision	(3) Land	(4) Soil
Highland	Raised land (platforms or banks of tanks) Level land on floodplain Level land on hills or terrace (*khiar* or *lal mati*) Gently sloping hill or terrace Steeply sloping hill or terrace Others (describe)		
Medium Highland	Raised land (platforms) Level floodplain Level terrace (*khiar* or *lal mati*) Sloping terrace Others (describe)		
Medium Lowland	(Describe)		
Lowland	(Describe)		
Bottomland	(Describe)		

Question 3. What crops are grown at present on each land and soil type?

First, make a set of tables such as the example shown in Table 20.3. Make separate tables for each land type: that is, for Highland, Medium Highland, etc., or for subdivisions of them. In areas where there is irrigation, make separate tables for irrigated and non-irrigated land. Table 20.3 gives an example for Medium Highland, not irrigated.

In the left-side column of each table, write the names of the soil types which occur on that land type (or subdivision). Leave a space of several lines between each soil type so that information on crops can be written in the following columns.

At the top of the four other main columns, write 'Kharif-1', 'Kharif-2', 'Rabi-1' and 'Rabi-2' respectively.[6] Make two columns under each of these crop-season headings: the first for present crops; the other for potential crops (to be filled in when answering Question 4).

Ask when flooding normally starts and ends on each soil type. Write the names of these months under the name of the soil type in column 1. Preferably, use Bengali calendar months.

For each land and soil type in turn, ask what are the main crops grown in each season at present. Then ask what other crops are grown. Write the names of these crops in the 'Present' column for the appropriate crop-season, according to the season when they are grown. Show HYV aus, aman, boro and wheat as separate crops from local varieties. Underline the name or names of the most important crops.

---

[6] *Kharif-1 is the first part of the rainy season, corresponding with the period when broadcast aus and jute are normally grown. Kharif-2 is the second half of the rainy season, when transplanted aman is the main crop grown. Rabi-1 includes the first part of the dry season corresponding with the cool winter period when pulses, oilseeds, wheat and potato are grown. Rabi-2 comprises the second part of the dry season, corresponding with the hot pre-monsoon period when boro paddy and summer fruits and vegetables are grown. The beginning and end dates of all these seasons overlap. They also vary between different parts of the country, according to the dates when the rainy season normally begins and ends in different regions.*

TABLE 20.3

Present and potential land use

Medium Highland: level floodplain; shallowly flooded; not irrigated

| Land type | Kharif-1 (Aus) | | Kharif-2 (Aman) | | Rabi | | | |
| | | | | | Rabi-1 | | Rabi-2 | |
Soil type (period of flooding)	Present	Potential	Present	Potential	Present	Potential	Present	Potential
Sandy (June-Sept)	Aus	Aus	Fallow	Fallow	Maskalai	Sweet potato	Rabi-1 continues	Rabi-1 continues
	Mesta	Mesta	Fallow	Fallow	Fallow	Groundnut, sorghum	Fallow	Rabi-1 continues
Loamy (June-Oct)	Aus	HYV aus 12/16	Fallow	Fallow	Mustard	HYV wheat 16/16	Rabi-1 continues	Rabi-1 continues
	Jute	Jute	Fallow	Fallow	Radish, maskalai, wheat		Fallow/rabi-1 continues	
Clayey loam (June-Nov)	Aus	HYV aus 14/16	T.aman	T.aman	Fallow	Fallow	Fallow	Fallow
	Jute	Jute	Fallow	T.aman	Lentil, maskalai, wheat, mustard	Fallow	Fallow/rabi-1 continues	Fallow/rabi-1 continues

For each soil type, first record the names of the crops grown in the kharif-1 season at present. Next, for the same soil type, record the names of the crops grown in the kharif-2 season. Then do the same for the rabi season. In-so-far as is possible, write the names of crops opposite the names of the crops which they normally follow, so as to show the main crop rotations. If land is left fallow in any season, write 'Fallow' in the appropriate column.

For crops which grow during more than one season, write the name of the crop in all the columns during which it grows. For example, deepwater aman would be named in the kharif-1 and the kharif-2 columns, and perennial crops (such as tree crops) would be named in all the columns.

Table 20.3 gives an example of a table completed for questions about present land use.

Question 4. What crops can be grown in future on each soil type in order to increase production?

Record the answers to this question in the 'Potential' columns of the table prepared for Question 3 (i.e., Table 20.3). Write the names in such a way as to form crop rotations which include HYV paddy, HYV wheat and high-value cash crops to the maximum extent feasible. Work out these crop rotations in full consultation with the farmers.

Question farmers thoroughly to make sure that the improved crops and rotations are practical for the land and soil types against which they are shown, and for the flooding characteristics and for irrigation supplies likely to be available within the next five years. Check that the replies are satisfactory by referring to the flooding period recorded for each soil type and to the information given in Annexe 1 to this chapter.

a. First ask the farmers on which land and soil types they consider that they could grow HYV aus:

   i. without irrigation;

   ii. only with irrigation.

   Land and soil conditions required for cultivation of HYV aus are described in Annexe 1 of this chapter. If the farmers do not know what conditions are needed for growing HYV aus, these conditions should be explained to them before they state how much land is suitable for HYV aus. On the land and soil types considered suitable for HYV aus, ask: can HYV aus be grown on all the land? If not, on how much? The answer probably will be given in annas (1/16th of a rupee): write the answer as a fraction (e.g., 12/16).

b. Next, ask the farmers on which land and soil types they consider that they could grow HYV aman:

   i. without irrigation;

   ii. only with irrigation.

   The land and soil conditions required for cultivation of HYV aman are described in Annexe 1. Ask: can HYV aman be grown on all of the land and soil type? If not, on what proportion of it? Record the answer in annas, as suggested for HYV aus above.

c. Next, ask on which land and soil types HYV boro could be grown:

   i. without irrigation;

   ii. only with irrigation.

The land and soil conditions required for HYV boro are described in Annexe 1. Ask: can all the suitable land be irrigated? If not, how much could be irrigated within the next three years? Record the answer in annas, as suggested for HYV aus above. (Alternatively, for irrigated boro, the answer could be recorded in acres.)

d. Ask on which land and soil types HYV wheat could be grown:

i. without irrigation;

ii. with irrigation (if available).

The land and soil conditions required for HYV wheat are described in Annexe 1. Ask: can wheat be grown on all the suitable land and soils? If not, on what proportion of it could it be grown? Record the answer in annas, as suggested for HYV aus above.

e. After obtaining the information about the potential for growing HYV paddy and wheat, ask which other high-value crops could be grown in the kharif and/or rabi seasons:

i. without irrigation;

ii. with irrigation (if available).

Write the answers in the relevant seasonal column, as illustrated in Table 20.3. For these cash crops, start with the kharif-1 season. Ask which land and soil types are suitable for the following crops. Use the list given in Annexe 3 of this chapter as a guide.

i. Fruit trees, banana, pineapple, sugarcane, ginger, turmeric.

ii. Kharif vegetables, maize, sorghum, millets, pulses, fodder legumes, oilseeds.

iii. Any other high-value crops suitable for the kharif season.

For the kharif-2 season, ask which land and soil types are suitable for the following cash crops. Use the list given in Annexe 3 as a guide.

i. Perennial and annual crops continued from the kharif-1 season.

ii. Kharif groundnut, sweet potato, maize, sorghum, millet, pulses, cotton.

iii. Any other high-value crops suitable for the kharif season.

For the rabi-1 season, ask which land and soil types are suitable for the following crops. Use the list given in Annexe 3 as a guide.

i. Perennial crops continued from the kharif season.

ii. Early rabi crops: tobacco, cotton, chilli, early winter vegetables, potato, oilseeds, maize.

iii. Middle rabi crops: chilli, onion, garlic, groundnut.

For the rabi-2 season, ask which land and soil types are suitable for the following cash crops. Use the list given in Annexe 3 as a guide.

i. Late rabi (or summer) crops: melon, chilli, maize, sorghum, millet.

ii. Any other high-value cash crops suitable for the season.

Question 5.   *How much land and soil of each type is there in the village (or block)?*

The tables completed in answer to questions 3 and 4 provide a statement of present and potential land use. The next step is to find out how much land and soil of each type there is, and to measure the area under each kind of crop and crop rotation. Questioning of farmers probably will not give reliable figures of acreages (although farmers' estimates can be used for broad planning purposes and for discussions of future cropping policy). The most reliable way to record land, soil and crop acreages is to make maps, as is described below.

First, make two tracings of the *mouza* map of the village (or block) showing plot boundaries.[7] On both copies of these maps, draw the boundaries between the different land and soil types. Find out these boundaries by questioning farmers about where these boundaries lie in relation to field plots shown on the mouza map. Walk out in different directions over the village lands so as to fix these boundaries by discussion with farmers in the field.

Show land type boundaries with thick lines. Show soil type boundaries with thin lines. (Alternatively, show land type boundaries in red pencil and soil type boundaries in orange or brown pencil.) Show, also, the boundaries of homestead land, waste land, tanks, rivers, khals, etc. Areas of permanent water in rivers and beels should be shown in blue pencil.

Also show the sites of existing tube-wells, LLPs, open wells and sites where traditional irrigation devices are used.

Ask how deep the water-table is:

i. at the end of the rainy season;

ii. at the end of the dry season.

Write this information for each unit on the map (if the information is known, or if groundwater exists). Show the depth in feet as a fraction: depth at end of rainy season over depth at end of dry season (e.g., 3/25).

On Map 1, show the main crops and crop rotations for each land and soil type. This can be done either by colouring the map units or by using capital letter symbols for each type of rotation. Use the capital letter symbols shown in Annexe 2 of this chapter to represent each type of crop rotation or land use.

Make a table at a convenient place on Map 1 to show the land and soil types in the left-side column. Then, in the next four columns, show the proportions of HYV boro, aus, aman and wheat grown in each unit at present. This proportion will be recorded as estimated by the farmers. It can be recorded in annas (i.e., fractions of 16). See the example given in Table 20. 4.

On Map 2, show the main potential crops and crop rotations for each land and soil type, as recorded for Question 4. Use the symbols listed in Table 20.5 for individual crops, and show rotations by linking the symbols with hyphens: e.g., U-TA-F; B-TA.[8] For mixed crops, use the plus (+) sign: e.g., U + BA = mixed broadcast aus and aman. For crops that are interchangeable in rotations (mainly where jute is substituted for broadcast aus once every three or four years), use the oblique (/) sign: e.g., U/J.

It usually will not be possible to show all the potential crops and crop rotations without making a plot-by-plot survey. Only the main crops and rotations need be shown. The main aim of making Map 2 is to draw the farmers' attention to the potential for growing high-yielding or high-value crops on particular land and soil types which they can recognize.

---

[7] *Mouza maps are cadastral maps on a scale of 16 inches to 1 mile (1:3,960).*

[8] *Note that the symbols used in the table are different from those used in the map units. The symbols used in the table are abbreviations for individual crops whereas those used on the map are symbols for crop rotations.*

TABLE 20.4
Present land use: proportion of land under HYVs

Land/soil type	HYV boro (annas)	HYV aus (annas)	HYV aman (annas)	HYV wheat (annas)
Highland				
Level Highland				
Sandy	0	0	0	0
Loamy	0	0	0	0
Man-made platforms	0	0	0	0
Medium Highland - very shallowly flooded				
Loamy	0	1/16	0	0
Clayey	1/16	1/16	4/16	1/16
Medium Highland - shallowly flooded				
Loamy	0	1/16	0	1/16
Clayey loam	1/16	2/16	0	2/16
Medium Lowland				
Clay	2/16	0	0	0

TABLE 20.5
Crop symbols

Symbol	Crop
U	Local aus
<u>U</u>	HYV aus
TA	Local transplanted aman
<u>TA</u>	HYV transplanted aman
TDWA	Transplanted deepwater aman
BA	Local broadcast aman
<u>BA</u>	Improved broadcast aman (in areas where improved Habiganj varieties are already known by farmers)
B	Local boro
<u>B</u>	HYV boro
<u>W</u>	HYV wheat
T	Low-value tree crops (not in orchards)
<u>T</u>	High-value fruit crops (e.g., mango orchards, pineapple, banana)
<u>P</u>	Other high-value perennial crops (e.g., sugarcane, ginger, turmeric)
K	Low-value kharif dryland crops
<u>K</u>	High-value kharif crops (e.g., vegetables)
R	Low-value rabi dryland crops (e.g., pulses, fodder legumes, *tishi, til, kusum phul, gurjan*)
<u>R</u>	High-value rabi dryland crops (e.g., vegetables, potato, tobacco, groundnut, improved oilseeds, soya bean)
F	Fallow

Next, make a table at a convenient place on Map 2. The table should be similar to that illustrated in Table 20.4, but 'potential' should be substituted for 'present' in the title. Show the land and soil types in the left-side column. Then, in the next four columns, show the proportions of each unit which the farmers estimate are potentially suitable for HYV boro, aus, aman and wheat. These proportions can be recorded in annas, as in the table on Map 1.

When both maps have been completed, the areas of each of the land and soil types can be measured. This can be done in various ways. The best way probably is to use squared paper, or tracing paper on which ¼-inch squares have been drawn. On the scale of the mouza map (16 inches = 1 mile), 1 inch = 330 feet and a ¼-inch square = 82.5 × 82.5 feet = about 15 decimals. On a map on a scale of 8 inches to 1 mile, then a ¼-inch square = 60 decimals.

By using the tables of proportions on Maps 1 and 2, the actual and potential acreages of HYV paddy and wheat crops can be calculated (approximately).

Question 6.   *How much of the village land can be irrigated?*

The aim of this question is to obtain information for making a village irrigation plan. The same methods will be used as are described in the Thana Irrigation Manual.[9]

First, ask farmers which areas are suitable for the kinds of irrigation listed below. Make a table showing the list of land and soil types prepared in answer to Questions 1 and 2. For each unit, put two ticks (√√) in a column on the right-side for the methods which the farmers consider most important. Put one tick (√) for less important methods. For methods which are not considered practical, leave the space blank.

a. Traditional methods (*don*, swing basket, open well, etc.).

b. Low-lift pump.

c. Hand tube-well.

d. Shallow tube-well.

e. Deep tube-well.

f. Cross-dam.

g. Canal (by BWDB).

Prepare the base map for Map 3. This will be the Village Irrigation Map. Show the same basic information as is given on Maps 1 and 2: i.e., boundaries of field plots; rivers, khals, beels, tanks, roads, etc.; and land and soil type boundaries.

Form a Village Irrigation Survey Team. This should consist of two or three farmers' representatives and an *amin* (surveyor). With this team, visit the different areas which are considered suitable for irrigation. Discuss on the spot whether the water supply and soils are suitable for irrigation (as described below). After discussion, mark on Map 3 the areas accepted as suitable for irrigation. Use the symbols given in the Thana Irrigation Manual, Appendix D.

Surface-water sources. For irrigation by traditional lift methods or LLPs from surface-water sources, ask the following questions.

a. Is there sufficient surface water to last through the dry season for the number of irrigation units suggested?

b. If the answer is 'yes', how much land can be irrigated from each site? Obtain estimates for two kinds of crops: transplanted paddy (boro or aus) and dryland crops (wheat, vegetables). Give numbers to the sites, and make a list giving the farmers' estimates of how many acres (or decimals) could be irrigated at each site: first for paddy; then for other crops.

---

[9] *The method is outlined in Chapter 16, Section 16.2 and Annexe 2, of this volume.*

c. If the answer is 'no', which of the units numbered in paragraph b above should be given preference? Draw a circle around those numbers in the list of sites.

d. Are the land and soil types at the suggested sites suitable for irrigation? Refer to the tables of land and soil types given in Annexe 3. Take into account the fact that more than one land and soil type may occur within the command area of an irrigation site.

e. If the answers to the questions in paragraphs c and d above alter the estimates of irrigation sites or crop acreages made in paragraph b, make a new table showing the numbers of the sites recommended for irrigation from surface water sources, and the acreages of transplanted paddy (boro or aus) and of dryland crops that could be irrigated at each site.

Shallow groundwater. For irrigation by HTWs or STWs, ask similar questions to those asked about irrigation from surface-water sources. Ask the questions in the same order, and write the answers on separate sheets of paper.

Hand tube-wells are best suited for irrigation under the following conditions.

a. Water-table not more than 10 feet below the ground surface during the growing period of the crops to be grown; (check the depth to groundwater shown on Map 1).

b. For use by family labour.

c. For growing vegetables, fruit, spices, potato or wheat.

Shallow tube-wells are best suited under the following conditions.

a. Water-table 10-25 feet below the ground surface during the growing period; (check the information shown on Map 1).

b. Where farmers use hired labour (as well as family labour).

c. Where farmers wish to grow transplanted paddy (though other crops can be grown if the soils are better suited for dryland crops than for transplanted paddy).

If groundwater is considered to be available at a suitable depth, ask the following questions.

a. Which areas are suitable for HTWs and which for STWs? Show these areas separately on Map 3.

b. How many HTWs and STWs can be sited in each of these areas? On suitable soils, HTWs can irrigate about 30 decimals of transplanted paddy or 60-75 decimals of dryland crops. STWs can irrigate about 5 acres of transplanted paddy or 10-15 acres of dryland crops on suitable soils. Give numbers to the suitable areas on the map. Write these numbers in a table such as that described above for surface-water irrigation. For each numbered area, give the farmers' estimate of the acreage that could be irrigated for transplanted paddy and for dryland crops.

c. Are the land and soil types in each area suitable for irrigation of the crops suggested by the farmers? Refer to the tables of land and soil types given in Annexe 3. Take into account the fact that more than one land and soil type may occur within the command area of an irrigation site.

d. If the answers to questions in paragraph c alter the estimates of irrigation areas or crop acreages made in paragraph b, make a new table showing the recommended areas (by map number) and the acreages of transplanted paddy and/or of dryland crops that could be irrigated in each area.

Deep groundwater. For irrigation by DTWs, ask similar questions to those asked about irrigation by HTWs and STWs. Deep tube-wells are considered suitable under the following conditions.

    a. Where there is not enough surface water available for irrigation.

    b. Where groundwater exists, but is too deep for easy use by HTWs or STWs throughout the growing season of the crops farmers want to grow.

    c. Where there are large areas of almost-level land with loamy, clay loam or clay soils suitable for irrigation of crops such as transplanted paddy, wheat or sugarcane.

Deep tube-wells should not be sited within ¾-mile of rivers or khals that are used for irrigation, nor within areas that are already used satisfactorily for irrigation by HTWs or STWs.

Where conditions are considered suitable for irrigation by DTWs, ask the following questions.

    a. How many DTWs are needed to irrigate the area of suitable land and soil types? Give each site a number and make a table listing these numbers.

    b. How much land can be irrigated from each suggested DTW site? Obtain separate estimates for transplanted paddy and for dryland crops. Write these estimates against the DTW numbers in the table made in paragraph a.

    c. Are the land and soil types at each of the suggested sites suitable for irrigation? Refer to the tables of land and soil types given in Annexe 3. Take into account the fact that more than one land and soil type may occur within a DTW command area. Sites should not be considered suitable if less than 25 acres per cusec for transplanted paddy or less than 40 acres per cusec for dryland crops can be irrigated.

    d. If the answers to questions in paragraph c alter the estimates of irrigation sites or crop acreages made in paragraph b, make a new table showing the number of sites recommended for DTWs and the acreages of transplanted paddy and/or of dryland crops that could be irrigated at each site.

Canal irrigation. Where conditions are considered suitable for canal irrigation from a BWDB irrigation project or from a cross-dam, ask the following questions.

    a. Where can canals or field channels be sited so as to irrigate the most suitable land? Give each canal or field channel a number. Write these numbers in a table similar to that described for surface-water irrigation above.

    b. How much land can be irrigated from each canal or channel? Obtain estimates from farmers of the acreages of transplanted paddy and/or of dryland crops that could be irrigated from each of them. Write these estimates in the table against the number of the canal/channel.

    c. Are the land and soil types at each of the suggested sites suitable for irrigation? Refer to the tables of land and soil types given in Annexe 3. Take into account the fact that more than one land and soil type may occur within the command area of a canal or channel.

    d. If the answers to questions in paragraph c alter the estimates of irrigation sites or crop acreages made in paragraph b, make a new table showing the numbers of the canals or channels recommended for irrigation and the acreages of transplanted paddy and/or of dryland crops that could be irrigated from each of them.

Village Irrigation Development Plan. From the answers collected for the questions above, prepare a village irrigation development plan. Make a table such as that illustrated in Table 20.6 to show, first, the present acreages under irrigation. Then show the acreages which the village leaders consider they could bring under irrigation next year by each irrigation method (where these are suitable), then in the following years until all the area considered suitable is brought under irrigation.

Question 7.   How much HYV paddy and wheat can be grown next year, and how soon can all the potential area suitable for HYVs be put under these crops?

The aim of these questions is to get farmers in the village (or block) to fix targets for HYV cultivation in the next 1-3 years.

First make a table such as that illustrated in Table 20.7 to show the following information.

   a. The present acreages (or proportions) of HYV aus, aman, boro and wheat, irrigated and non-irrigated.
   b. The acreage which farmers consider should be their targets for each of these crops next year.
   c. Targets for the following year.
   d. Targets for subsequent years until all the potential area suitable for HYV cultivation is under HYVs.

Question 8.   What other inputs are needed in order to achieve the HYV cultivation targets?

Make a table such as that illustrated in Table 20.8. Complete the table by asking farmers the following questions.

   a. Is there enough seed of HYV boro, aus, aman and wheat of suitable varieties in the village for the planned increase in area?
   b. If not, how much new seed will need to be obtained from outside the village? Write in the table the names of the varieties requested and the amount of seed required (in maunds).
   c. Is there a dealer for fertilizers and pesticides in the village? (Yes/No).
   d. If not, how far away is the nearest dealer (in miles)?
   e. Is a dealer needed in the village? (Yes/No).
   f. Are other inputs or services needed for achieving the targets? If so, write the villagers' suggestions in the table, including their suggestions for obtaining each of them.

Question 9.   What sort of village organization is needed to make sure that the Village Development Plan is implemented and kept up-to-date?

Ask the questions given in the example shown in Table 20.9 and make a list of the answers in the adjoining column. Cross out items that are not accepted.

Question 10. Do farmers want to have their own crop demonstration plots in the village?

The purpose of this question is to get farmers to select plots in each important land and soil type where they themselves can try new crops or HYVs, different fertilizer doses, different methods of cultivation, etc.

TABLE 20.6
Targets for irrigation coverage

Irrigation method	Present		Year 1		Year 2		Year 3		Year 4	
	No	Acres	No	Acres	No	Acres	No	Acres	No	Acres
Indigenous methods	27	10	27	15	27	15	27	15	27	15
Low-lift pumps	2	60	3	150	5	250	5	250	5	250
Hand tube-wells	0	0	5	3	20	15	40	30	60	45
Shallow tube-wells	0	0	1	5	3	15	6	30	10	50
Deep tube-wells	0	0	0	0	0	0	0	0	0	0
Canals/cross-dams	0	0	0	0	0	0	0	0	0	0

TABLE 20.7
Targets for HYV paddy and wheat cultivation

HYV crop	Potential acreage	Present		Year 1		Year 2		Year 3		Year 4	
		With irrigation	Without irrigation	With irrigation	Without irrigation	With irrigation	Without irrigation	With irrigation	Without irrigation	With irrigation	Without irrigation
Boro	300	60	0	155	0	265	0	280	0	300	0
Aus	200	0	30	0	60	0	100	0	150	0	200
Aman	300	0	50	0	100	0	200	0	300	0	300
Wheat	200	10	30	13	60	30	120	45	200	60	200

TABLE 20.8

Village agricultural development plan: inputs and services needed

Input/service needed	How/where to obtain	Quantity needed[1]
Seed		
HYV boro		
HYV aus		
HYV aman		
HYV wheat		
Other (describe)		
Fertilizers		
Urea		
TSP		
MP		
Other (describe)		
Pesticides		
(Describe)		
Irrigation equipment		
DTW		
STW		
HTW		
Other (describe)		
Credit		
(Describe)		
Other		
(Describe)		

Note: 1. Indicate whether needed for this year or for next year. The figures need only be rough estimates at this stage. More precise figures will be obtained when preparing targets in Table 20.12.

TABLE 20.9

Village agricultural development plan: village organization

Question	Answer
1. Should there be a village organization?	Yes/No
2. If so, what kind of organization?	Chashi Club
	Elected Committee
	Cooperative
	Other (Describe)
3. How should members be selected?	By size of land holding
	By para (or household)
	By cooperative society
	By land type
	Other (Describe)

(Contd.)

(Continued)

Question	Answer
4. How many members should there be?	3
	5
	More (give number)
5. For how long should the selected members stay as members?	2 years
	1 year
	Shorter (describe)
6. Should anyone from outside the village (or block) be selected as a member (or adviser)?	Union Council member.
	Union Agricultural Assistant.
	Other (Name)
7. a. Where will the organization meet?	(Describe)
b. Is it necessary to build a meeting hall?	Yes/No
c. If yes, where should the hall be built?	(Describe)
d. How will funds be provided?	(Describe)
8. How often should the organization meet to discuss business?	Every 2 weeks
	Every week
	More/less often (Describe)
9. a. Is any help needed from outside the village to set up the organization?	Yes/No
b. If yes, which organization or person can help?	(Describe)
10. Which person in the village (or block) should be made responsible for setting up the organization to implement the village agricultural development plan?	(Give name)

The demonstration plots need not be big. One decimal is enough for each crop, variety or method being tried. Seed of new crops or varieties can be supplied by the UAA, and he can give advice on recommended fertilizer doses and other cultivation requirements. The UAA should visit these plots for discussions with Demonstration Farmers and neighbouring farmers whenever he visits the village during a crop-growing season.

Ask the villagers to select farmers willing to provide demonstration plots and to serve as Demonstration Farmers. Explain that these farmers will not be Government farmers. However, they will be given priority in receiving seed of new crops or varieties, as well as advice about new cultivation techniques.

Ask for the name of one farmer on each important land and soil type shown on the maps. Where part of the land is irrigated, one Demonstration Farmer should be selected for the irrigated part and one for the non-irrigated part.

Prepare a table such as that illustrated in Table 20.10 to record the names of farmers proposed as Demonstration Farmers. A copy of this form must be kept by (or sent to) the UAA so that he can contact the Demonstration Farmers on his regular visits to the village.

20.3 THE PLAN

The village (or block) agricultural development plan consists of two parts:

  a. the targets shown in the tables prepared in response to questions 6 and 7 (illustrated in Tables 20.6 and 20.7); and

TABLE 20.10
Names of demonstration farmers

Land type	Soil type	Name	Plot No
Highland	Sandy	A.A. Aaaaa	111
	Loamy	B.B. Bbbbb	222
Medium Highland – very shallowly flooded	Loamy, irrigated	C.C. Ccccc	333
	Loamy, not irrigated	D.D. Ddddd	444
	Clayey loam, irrigated	E.E. Eeeee	555
	Clayey loam, not irrigated	F.F. Fffff	666
Medium Highland – shallowly flooded	Loamy	G.G. Ggggg	777
	Clayey loam	H.H. Hhhhh	888
Medium Lowland	Clay	I.I. Iiiii	999

b. a programme for achieving these targets, based on the answers to questions 4 and 10.

The targets as shown in the tables should be copied in large letters on a board in the Chashi Club or in a prominent place in the village. If the village has been divided into several blocks for planning purposes, each block should have its own board in the Chashi Club or in the village.

Ask the farmers if they could also have a board in the Chashi Club or in the village to show each farmer's own targets for crop production on his land. This would need a new table to be made with the headings shown in the example given in Table 20.11. The column headings and plot numbers could be painted on the board. The remaining information could be written in chalk (for boards protected from rain) so that it could easily be kept up-to-date.

The plan programme will consist of three main parts:

a. a list of the inputs needed;

b. a list of any excavation or building works needed in support of the plan; and

c. a schedule of dates on or by which action should be taken to provide inputs and commence or complete works.

For each crop season, prepare a table with the headings shown in the example given in Table 20.12. Under 'Name of input or works', write the names of the inputs or works to be provided. These might include some of the following:

a. Inputs

  i. Irrigation equipment as shown in the example given in Table 20.6.

  ii. Fuel and lubricants needed for irrigation equipment (by name).

  iii. New HYV seed needed: see Table 20.8.

  iv. Fertilizers needed: show individual fertilizers by name.

  v. Pesticides needed (by name).

  vi. Credit needed: give the name of the institutions from which credit will be obtained.

  vii. Others (describe).

TABLE 20.11

Farmers= targets for crop production

Land type: Soil type:

Plot number	Name of farmer	Area (decimals)	Crop to be grown		
			Kharif-1	Kharif-2	Rabi

Note: 1. HYV crops should be named: e.g., Chandina, BR3, Sonalika.
       2. Rabi can be divided into Rabi 1 and Rabi 2, if necessary.

TABLE 20.12

Village Agricultural Development Plan: inputs and works required

Village: Block:

Name of input or works	Amount	Date to start action	Date to complete action

b. Works

   i. Irrigation channel.

   ii. Drainage channel.

   iii. Field channels/ditches.

   iv. Levelling of fields.

   v. Excavating tanks.

   vi. Building roads, paths, bridges, culverts.

   vii. Repairing roads, paths, bridges, culverts.

   viii. Building a go-down (e.g., for grain storage).

   ix. Building a Chashi Club meeting hall.

   x. Making a notice board.

   xi. Others (describe).

In the 'Amount' column, write the quantities of the various inputs needed for the crop season: in numbers, gallons, maunds, etc. For Works, write the quantities of the various materials required (such as bricks, bamboo poles, etc.) and the number of man-days of labour required for each Works item.

In the last two columns, write the dates when the various stages of obtaining inputs and carrying out Works programme activities should begin and end. For example:

a. For obtaining fertilizers, action should start with the village or block committee preparing its list of fertilizers to be ordered by farmers from the dealer (or direct from the wholesale go-down). Action ends with the date by which the fertilizers must reach individual farmers. If individual farmers buy their own fertilizers, action starts and ends on the same date.

b. For digging an irrigation channel, action should start with the date on which the plan for digging the channel is discussed by the farmers involved; (alternatively, if the plan has already been agreed, give the date on which work should start). Action ends on the date by which the work must be completed.

Write the names and plot numbers of Demonstration Farmers for each crop season on the notice board: see the example given in Table 20.10. Send a copy of this list to the UAA.

If a Chashi Club is formed, place a list of names of the Chairman and members on the Chashi Club (or village) notice board. Send a copy of this list to the UAA.

Arrange dates when the Chashi Club (or other committee) will meet to discuss action and progress of the development plan. The plan must be kept up-to-date. Regular meetings are needed to discuss preparations for the next crop season.

If, during implementation, changes need to be made in the annual plan or in the 3-year (or 5-year) plan — e.g., because of a natural disaster — make appropriate alterations in the tables shown in Tables 20.6, 20.7 and 20.11.[10]

---

[10]*Not discussed in the original documents was the desirability of the Village Committee (together with the UAA) reviewing, at the end of a crop season and/or the crop year, what was actually achieved during the plan period in relation to targets. Such reviews can provide useful lessons for preparing more realistic plans in future and for identifying problems that need to be overcome.*

Annexe 1

LAND AND SOIL CONDITIONS SUITABLE FOR HYV PADDY AND WHEAT

A. HYV AUS

a. Transplanted aus

1. Level land, or artificially-levelled land.
2. Highland, or Medium Highland that normally is not flooded deeper than about 1 foot before the time of harvesting (in June, July or August, according to variety and time of transplanting).
3. Soils which can easily be puddled to hold water on the surface for 1-2 weeks after heavy rainfall or irrigation. These soils usually are clay loams or clays, or loamy soils with a strong ploughpan.
4. Soils and irrigation water not saline or only slightly saline during the growing period.
5. Land with low risk of damaging floods during the growing period (May to July-August).

b. Broadcast, line-sown or dibble-sown aus

1. Level or gently sloping land.
2. Highland, or Medium Highland that is not flooded deeper than about 1 foot by the time of harvesting (in June, July or August, according to variety and time of transplanting).
3. Loamy, clay loam or clay soils. Deep sandy loams are also suitable in high rainfall areas.
4. Land with low risk of damaging floods during the growing period (May to July-August).

B. HYV AMAN

1. Level land, or artificially-levelled land.
2. Highland, or very shallowly flooded Medium Highland which is not flooded deeper than:
   i. about 6 inches at the time of transplanting (in June, July or August, according to variety); and
   ii. about 1 foot after the plants have become established.
3. Soils of any texture (usually impermeable loam, clay loam or clay), so long as:
   i. they can be puddled to hold water on the surface for 1-2 weeks after heavy rainfall or irrigation; or
   ii. they have a naturally high water-table all through the growing period (July to October or early-November).
4. Soils or floodwater not more than slightly saline during the growing period.
5. Land with low risk of damaging floods during the growing period.

C. HYV BORO

1. Level land, or artificially-levelled land.
2. Highland, Medium Highland, Medium Lowland or Lowland which is not flooded deeper than:
   i. about 6 inches at the time of transplanting (in January to mid-March); and
   ii. about 1 foot before the time of harvesting (May-June).
3. Soils of any texture (usually clay loam or clay), so long as:
   i. they can be puddled to hold water on the surface for 1-2 weeks after irrigation; or
   ii. they stay wet naturally in the dry season until April or May.
4. Soils and irrigation water not saline, or only slightly saline, during the growing period.
5. Land with low risk of damaging floods (including flash floods) during the growing period.

D. HYV WHEAT

1. Level or very gently sloping land.
2. Highland, Medium Highland or Medium Lowland which normally is not flooded or wet later than end-November at the latest. Preferably, the land should not be wet after end-October so that the land can be prepared for sowing by mid-November.
3. Soils on which water does not stand on the surface for more than 24 hours after irrigation or heavy rainfall occurring in November-December. (That makes most soils used for transplanted aman unsuitable for wheat.)
4. Loamy, clay loam or clay soils, so long as:
   i. they are permeable; and
   ii. they do not overlie a layer of either sand or heavy clay at less than about 2 feet below the ground surface (and preferably not at less than 3-4 feet below the surface).
5. Soils and irrigation water not saline, or only becoming slightly saline near the end of the growing period (i.e., in March-April).
6. Land with low risk of damaging early floods (including flash floods) during the growing period.

Annexe 2

SYMBOLS FOR PRESENT LAND USE

Symbol	Crop or crop rotation
A	Dryland crops throughout the year
	1. *Perennial*: sugarcane, banana, pineapple
	2. *Kharif*: maize, sorghum, millet, groundnut, soyabean, sunflower, vegetables, beans, fodder legumes, sweet potato
	3. *Rabi*:
	a. *early*: cotton, tobacco, vegetables, potato, radish, mustard, maskalai
	b. *middle*: wheat, onion, garlic, potato, sweet potato, chilli, groundnut, soyabean, rapeseed, gram, lentil, maskalai, khesari
	c. *late*: melon, khira, sorghum, millet, soyabean, sunflower, sesamum
B	Fruit trees: mango, litchi, jackfruit, guava, citrus
C	Drought-resistant crops only: sorghum, millet (*bajra, kaon, cheena, bhurra, shama*), groundnut
D	Broadcast aus followed by early rabi crops (see A3a)
E	Broadcast aus or mesta followed by early rabi crops (see A3a)
F	Broadcast aus or jute followed by middle rabi crops (see A3b)
G	Broadcast aus or jute followed by late rabi crops (see A3c)
H	Broadcast aus or jute followed by transplanted aman followed by middle or late rabi crops (see A3b, A3c)
I	Broadcast aus or jute followed by transplanted aman followed by rabi fallow
J	Mixed broadcast aus (or jute) and deepwater aman followed by middle rabi crops (see A3b)
K	Mixed broadcast aus (or jute) and deepwater aman followed by late rabi crops (see A3c)
L	Mixed broadcast aus (or jute) and deepwater aman followed by rabi fallow
M	Broadcast aman followed by middle rabi crops (see A3b)
N	Broadcast aman followed by late rabi crops (see A3c)
O	Broadcast aman followed by rabi fallow
P	Transplanted aman followed by rabi fallow
Q	Local boro followed by kharif fallow
R	HYV boro (or aus) followed by local transplanted aman
S	HYV boro (or aus) followed by HYV aman
T	HYV boro followed by kharif fallow
U	Jhum cultivation (mixed aus, cotton, sesamum, beans, etc.)
V	Grassland cut for thatching material
W	Grassland used for grazing
X	Forest or bamboo
Y	Homestead land partly used for cultivation (e.g., fruit trees, vegetables, spices)
Z	Homestead or urban land not used for crops

Notes: 1. It is not necessary to record subdivisions of 'A' on the land use map. The numbers and letters are given for ease of reference for rabi crops included against other symbols.

2. Since this list was prepared in 1975, a number of new rotations have been identified which could be indicated as follows:

    Ia   Transplanted aus (local varieties) followed by transplanted aman (local varieties) followed by rabi fallow.

    Ib   Transplanted HYV aus followed by transplanted aman (local varieties) followed by rabi fallow.

    Ic   Transplanted HYV aus followed by transplanted HYV aman followed by rabi fallow.

    Ka   Mixed aus+aman followed by early rabi crop (maskalai, khesari, mustard) followed by late rabi crop (*kaon*, chilli, sesamum)

    Ra   HYV boro followed by transplanted deepwater aman followed by rabi fallow.

    Rb   HYV boro followed by transplanted deepwater aman followed by mustard/rapeseed.

3. For G, H, K and N: because the sowing season of aus and jute overlaps with the growing season of late rabi crops, this rotation is possible only where aus or jute are intersown through the standing late rabi crop.

Annexe 3

CROPS AND CROP ROTATIONS IN RELATION TO LAND AND SOIL TYPE

Tables 20.13 to 20.18 which follow provide a guide to the kinds of crops and crop rotations which are suitable for particular kinds of land and soils in Bangladesh. The information has been much simplified and generalized, so the information given should be checked against local information and experience wherever possible.

Separate tables are given for Highland, Medium Highland, Medium Lowland and Lowland. In each of these main land types, five main textural classes are recognized: very sandy, sandy, loamy, clay loam and clay; peaty is also recognized for Lowland. Crops suitable under non-irrigated and irrigated conditions are shown separately.

Permeable soils let rainwater enter and pass through without causing waterlogging. Many permeable soils also store moisture well for use by dryland rabi crops, unless they are sandy or are underlain by sand at less than 2-3 feet.

Impermeable soils do not let water enter or pass through easily. When puddled, the soil holds water on the surface for several days after heavy rainfall or irrigation. Impermeable soils include some silt loams, clay loams and clays, especially where the soils have a strong ploughpan. Most impermeable soils do not store moisture well for use by dryland rabi crops, and they are poorly suited for irrigation of such crops.

Early-draining soils are those which normally are not flooded or wet after end-November.

Late-draining soils are those which stay flooded or wet until December-January or later.

On the Ganges River Floodplain, broadcast aman is often sown on Medium Highland (as well as on more deeply flooded land). The peak of the Ganges river floods is in August-September, which prevents transplanted aman from being grown on shallowly-flooded land (except in flood-protected areas and in areas not connected with the main Ganges river channel).

Dryland rabi crops are listed below against the month or months in which they can be sown. The following points need to be taken into account in using this information.

  i. Land must be free from flooding or waterlogging by the month shown.

 ii. Crops sown later than the months shown may grow but would give reduced yields.

iii. Late sowing may delay the sowing of a following kharif crop.

 iv. Some crops — such as cotton, tobacco, mustard, wheat, khesari, lentil and most rabi vegetables — are easily damaged or killed by flooding or waterlogging, as may happen on impermeable soils, especially if they are over-irrigated or there is heavy rainfall after they have been planted.

Early rabi crops include those that can or should be sown in the following months.

September: tobacco, cotton, early rabi vegetables, early potato, sweet potato, radish, brinjal, chilli, maskalai.

October: tobacco, rabi vegetables, potato, sweet potato, radish, chilli, mustard, maskalai.

Middle rabi crops include those that can or should be sown in the following months.

November: wheat, barley, mustard, rapeseed, groundnut, potato, sweet potato, rabi vegetables, chilli, onion, garlic, lentil, gram, khesari, maskalai.

December (first half):   as November, but yields may be less than with November sowing.

Late rabi crops include those that can or should be sown in the following months.

December (second half):   potato, sweet potato, chilli, gram.

January: As December (second half).

February: chilli, sorghum, millet (*kaon*), sesamum.

TABLE 20.13

Crops suitable for Level Highland

Soil type	Permeable soils		Impermeable soils	
	Suitable crops and rotations		Suitable crops and rotations	
	Without irrigation	With irrigation	Without irrigation	With irrigation
Very sandy	1. Ginger, turmeric 2. Kharif groundnut, sweet potato	Not suitable	–	-
Sandy	1. Fruit trees, banana, ginger, turmeric, pineapple 2. Kharif vegetables, sorghum, millets, mesta, followed by early rabi crops	1. Usually unsuitable 2. Broadcast aus, kharif vegetables, followed by kharif groundnut, early rabi vegetables, potato, tobacco	–	-
Loamy	1. Fruit trees, banana, ginger, turmeric, pineapple 2. Broadcast HYV aus, kharif vegetables, groundnut, pulses, followed by early or middle rabi crops	1. Banana, pineapple, sugarcane 2. Broadcast HYV aus, jute, kharif vegetables, groundnut, followed by tobacco, rabi vegetables, wheat, potato	1. (High rainfall areas) HYV aus, followed by HYV aman 2. (Low rainfall areas) HYV aman 3. (Low rainfall areas) HYV aus, followed by local aman	1. HYV boro or aus, followed by HYV aman
Clayey loam	As for loamy soils above	As for loamy soils above	As for loamy soils above	As for loamy soils above
Clay	As for loamy soils above, but may be less suitable for middle rabi crops	As for loamy soils above	As for loamy soils above	As for loamy soils above

Notes: Permeable clayey loams and clays are mainly red and brown Madhupur and Barind Tract soils; also some hill soils.

TABLE 20.14

Crops suitable for Sloping Highland

Soil type	Permeable soils		Impermeable soils	
	Suitable crops and rotations		Suitable crops and rotations	
	Without irrigation	With irrigation	Without irrigation	With irrigation
Very sandy	1. Ginger, turmeric, pineapple 2. Groundnut, sweet potato	Not suitable	-	-
Sandy	1. Fruit trees, banana, pineapple, ginger, turmeric 2. Kharif vegetables, sorghum, millets, broadcast aus, followed by early rabi crops 3. Broadcast aus, followed by kharif groundnut, fodder legumes	1. Banana, pineapple, improved fruit trees, etc. 2. Kharif vegetables, broadcast aus, followed by kharif groundnut, early rabi vegetables, potato, tobacco	-	-
Loamy	As for sandy soils above	As for sandy soils above	Broadcast aus, sorghum, millets, followed by early rabi crops	As without irrigation
Clayey loam	As for sandy soils above	As for sandy soils above	As 1 above, (but often unsuitable for cultivation)	As without irrigation
Clay	-	-	Usually unsuitable	Usually unsuitable

Notes: 1. Sloping soils are only suitable for cultivation where soil conservation measures are used. That means that crops (except tree crops on gentle slopes) must be cultivated in rows or strips along the contour or on terraces. Wherever possible, the soil surface must be kept covered with vegetation or a mulch. Drains from terraces or contour bunds must be protected with a grass cover (or made *pucca*) so that they do not turn into gulleys. Slopes steeper than 60 percent are difficult to manage for tree crops and should be kept under (or planted to) forest.

2. Transplanted aman could be grown on impermeable soils if level terraces were made. Drainage outlets would need to be protected so that they would not turn into gulleys.

TABLE 20.15

Crops suitable for Medium Highland, very shallowly flooded

Soil type	Permeable soils Suitable crops and rotations		Impermeable soils Suitable crops and rotations	
	Without irrigation	With irrigation	Without irrigation	With irrigation
Very sandy	Kharif sorghum, millets, groundnut, sweet potato, (if flooding ends before end-August)	Not suitable	-	-
Sandy	1. As for very sandy soils above 2. (High rainfall areas) Broadcast aus, mesta, followed by early rabi crops 3. (Low rainfall areas) Sorghum, millets, followed by early rabi crops	1. Usually unsuitable 2. Broadcast aus, followed by kharif groundnut, early rabi vegetables, potato, tobacco	-	-
Loamy	Broadcast HYV aus, followed by early or middle rabi crops	Broadcast HYV aus, jute, followed by early or middle rabi crops	1. (High rainfall areas) HYV aus, followed by HYV aman 2. (Low rainfall areas) HYV aman 3. (Low rainfall areas) HYV aus, followed by local aman	HYV boro or aus, followed by HYV aman
Clayey loam	As for loamy soils above	As for loamy soils above	As for loamy soils above	As for loamy soils above
Clay	As for loamy soils, but may be less suitable for middle rabi crops	As for loamy soils above	As for loamy soils above	As for loamy soils above

Notes: 1. The crops listed above are suitable on soils that are not saline (or are only slightly saline) during the growing period. Soils which are saline for most of the dry season usually are unsuitable for rabi crops, aus and jute.

2. A quick-maturing HYV aus should be grown (preferably transplanted) if it is to be followed by transplanted aman on non-irrigated land.

TABLE 20.16

Crops suitable for Medium Highland, shallowly flooded

Soil type	Permeable soils — Suitable crops and rotations		Impermeable soils — Suitable crops and rotations	
	Without irrigation	With irrigation	Without irrigation	With irrigation
Very sandy	1. Kharif sorghum, millets, groundnut, sweet potato, (if flooding ends before end-August) 2. (High rainfall areas) Broadcast aus, followed by fodder legumes	Not suitable	–	–
Sandy	1. As 1 above 2. (High rainfall areas) Broadcast aus, mesta, followed by early rabi crops	1. Usually unsuitable 2. Broadcast aus, followed by early rabi vegetables, potato, tobacco	–	–
Loamy	Broadcast HYV aus, jute, followed by early or middle rabi crops	Broadcast HYV aus, jute, followed by early or middle rabi crops	1. (High rainfall areas) Transplanted HYV aus, followed by transplanted LV aman 2. (Low rainfall areas) HYV aus, followed by LV aman 3. (Low rainfall areas) Transplanted LV aman	HYV boro or aus, followed by transplanted LV aman
Clayey loam	As for loamy soils above	As for loamy soils above	As for loamy soils above	As for loamy soils above
Clay	As for loamy soils above, but may be less suitable for middle rabi crops	As for loamy soils above	As for loamy soils above	As for loamy soils above

Notes: 1. HYV aus is suitable on soils that are not subject to early flooding.

2. Soils which are saline for most of the dry season usually are unsuitable for rabi crops, aus or jute.

3. A quick-maturing HYV aus should be grown (preferably transplanted) if it is to be followed by transplanted aman on non-irrigated land.

TABLE 20.17

Crops suitable for Medium Lowland

Soil type	Permeable soils		Not suitable	Impermeable soils	
	Suitable crops and rotations			Suitable crops and rotations	
	Without irrigation	With irrigation		Without irrigation	With irrigation
Very sandy	Try rabi fodder legumes, sesamum		Not suitable	-	-
Sandy	1. Mixed aus+aman; possibly followed by early rabi crops 2. Melon, khira, sorghum, millets, sesamum, followed by fodder legumes	1. Usually unsuitable 2. Early aus or jute, followed by potato, rabi groundnut; rabi vegetables if flooding ends early enough; followed by melon and late rabi vegetables		-	-
Loamy	Mixed aus+aman, followed by early or middle rabi crops	1. As for 2 above 2. Mixed aus+aman, followed by wheat, potato, late rabi vegetables		Mixed aus+aman; possibly followed by early or middle rabi crops	HYV boro
Clayey loam	As for loamy soils above	As for loamy soils above		As for loamy soils above	HYV boro
Clay	As for loamy soils above, but may be less suitable for aus and rabi crops	As for loamy soils above		Broadcast aman; possibly followed by pulses or fodder legumes if floodwater leaves early enough	HYV boro

Notes:
1. Soils which are saline for most of the dry season usually are unsuitable for rabi crops, aus or jute.
2. On soils subject to serious risk of flood damage, grow high-value rabi crops as much as possible.
3. Use quick-maturing varieties of boro on land where there is a risk of early floods.

TABLE 20.18

Crops suitable for Lowland

Soil type	Permeable soils		Impermeable soils	
	Suitable crops and rotations		Suitable crops and rotations	
	Without irrigation	With irrigation	Without irrigation	With irrigation
Very sandy	Try fodder legumes, sesamum, melon, *khira*	Not suitable	–	–
Sandy	1. Broadcast aman, possibly followed by early or middle rabi crops 2. Melon, *khira*, sorghum, millets, sesamum, followed by fodder legumes	1. Usually unsuitable 2. Rabi vegetables, potato, groundnut, followed by melon, possibly followed by broadcast aman	–	–
Loamy	Broadcast aman, followed by early or middle rabi crops if flooding ends early enough	Wheat, rabi vegetables, groundnut, if flooding ends early enough, followed by broadcast aman	Broadcast aman; possibly followed by fodder legumes if flooding ends early enough	1. HYV boro 2. Local boro if water is too deep for HYV boro
Clayey loam	As for loamy soils above	As for loamy soils above	As for loamy soils above	As for loamy soils above
Clay	As for loamy soils above	As for loamy soils above	As for loamy soils above	As for loamy soils above
Peaty	Boro?	–	Boro?	–

Notes:
1. On soils subject to serious risk of flood damage, grow high-value rabi crops as much as possible.
2. Use quick-maturing varieties of boro where there is a risk of early floods.
3. On Bottomland where broadcast aman cannot be grown, provide irrigation wherever possible: grow boro on impermeable soils; make raised beds on permeable loams, clayey loams and clays for growing rabi vegetables, potato, *khira*, melon, or other high-value crops.
4. Peaty soils usually are unsuitable for cultivation, but some are used for boro, broadcast aus or broadcast aman. Where they have a topsoil of alluvium more than 6 inches thick, they are better suited for boro.

Chapter 21

SABHAR THANA SOIL GUIDE[1]

This chapter provides a specific example of how to use the information given in a reconnaissance soil survey report to make a Thana agricultural development plan.

21.1 INTRODUCTION

This chapter contains information on the soils of Sabhar Thana and how to use them. The information is taken from the report on the reconnaissance soil survey of Dhaka District (SRDI, 1981), but the language has been made as non-technical as possible.[2] The chapter contains six main sections:

21.2. How to identify the general soil types of Sabhar Thana.

21.3. Descriptions of each general soil type, together with tables showing crops suitable for each soil type.

21.4. Tables showing the proportions and acreage of each general soil type in the 16 units shown on the soil map of Sabhar Thana (Figure 21.1).

21.5. Suggested priorities for agricultural development.

21.6. Recommendations for soil fertility and agronomic trials.

21.7. A glossary of technical terms used.

The information in this chapter should be used with caution, for the reasons indicated below.

a. The information given in this soil guide has been simplified. More detailed technical information is given in the Report on the Reconnaissance Soil Survey of Dhaka District.

---

[1] *This chapter presents a model prepared by the author showing Soil Survey staff how to prepare simple guidelines for Agricultural Extension staff on how to use soil survey information for Thana agricultural development planning (SRDI, 1975). This edition replaced an earlier edition prepared in 1970 (SRDI, 1970a). That edition was used as a basis for a trial field training programme for Extension staff in Sabhar Thana in 1970-71. That trial was considered successful in terms of the acquired ability of the Extension staff to use the information, but it was not followed up by the Extension staff actually using the information for planning on their return to their work stations. Similar guides were prepared for another 11 Thanas in different parts of the country: see the list given in Chapter 14, Annexe 2, Section 2. Those guides were superseded by the Thana soil survey report extracts prepared for the Thana Agricultural Development Programme described in Chapter 23, Section 23.3.2.*

[2] *At the time that the original Thana guide was prepared, the reconnaissance soil survey report on Dhaka District was in narrative style (SRDI, 1967). A revised edition was issued in 1981 with the soil, land use and land capability information presented in tabulated format (SRDI, 1981).*

FIGURE 21.1
Sabhar Thana soil associations

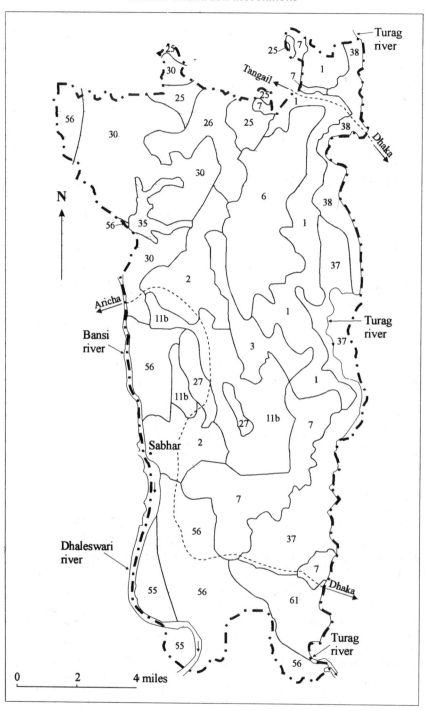

See legend on opposite page.

FIGURE 21.1 (CONTINUED)
SABHAR THANA SOIL ASSOCIATIONS (1965)

MAP LEGEND

MADHUPUR TRACT

DEEP UPLAND SOILS

LEVEL TERRACE
[1] Tejgaon series

[2] Tejgaon-Noadda association

[3] Tejgaon-Chandra association

[6] Chandra-Noadda association

DEEPLY DISSECTED TERRACE WITH LOCAL ALLUVIUM IN VALLEYS
[7] Tejgaon-Khilgaon association

[11b] Tejgaon-Kalma association, cultivated phase

SHALLOW UPLAND SOILS

DEEPLY DISSECTED TERRACE WITH LOCAL ALLUVIUM IN VALLEYS
[25] Gerua-Salna-Kalma association

[26] Gerua-Chhiata-Kalma association

[27] Bhatpara-Kalma-Gerua association

DEEP AND SHALLOW UPLAND SOILS

DISSECTED TERRACE WITH LOCAL ALLUVIUM IN VALLEYS
[30] Khilgaon-Tejgaon-Gerua complex

SOILS OF BROAD VALLEYS
[35] Karail-Kajla association

[37] Kajla-Jatrabari association

[38] Kajla-Turag association

YOUNG BRAHMAPUTRA FLOODPLAIN

ACTIVE FLOODPLAIN
[55] Sonatala-Dhamrai complex

YOUNG MEANDER FLOODPLAIN
[56] Dhamrai-Sabhar Bazar association

OLD MEANDER FLOODPLAIN
[61] Pagla-Kajla association

— · — Thana boundary
——— Soil association boundary
⌒⇌ River

b. The soil map (Figure 21.1) does not show the boundaries between individual soils. It shows boundaries between *soil associations*. Soil associations usually include more than one type of soil. This chapter shows how to identify each general soil type.

c. The information given about crops and crop rotations is based on the best information available at present (i.e., in 1975). It must be expected that agriculturalists working in the Thana will improve on this information as they gain experience with irrigation, new crop varieties and improved equipment. They should keep this guide up-to-date themselves regarding crop performance on different soils.

21.2 HOW TO IDENTIFY THE GENERAL SOIL TYPES OF SABHAR THANA

Seven main kinds of soil, called *general soil types*, have been recognized in Sabhar Thana. These are:

1. Deep Red-Brown Terrace Soils
2. Brown Mottled Terrace Soils
3. Shallow Red-Brown Terrace Soils
4. Grey Terrace and Valley Soils[3]
5. Acid Basin Clays
6. Grey Floodplain Soils
7. Noncalcareous Alluvium.

A brief description of each of these general soil types is given in Section 21.3. The general soil type can be identified by answering the following questions. (Refer to Section 21.7 for definitions of technical terms.)

A. Does the soil occur:

  a. on *Highland*? If so, go straight to question B;

  b. in a *byde*? If so, go straight to question E; or

  c. on *floodplain land*? If so, go straight to question F.

B. If the soil occurs on *Highland*, is the *substratum* (below about 2-3 feet):

  a. mainly *red* and rather *friable*? If so, go to question C; or

  b. mainly *grey* and *compact*? If so, go to question D.

  Note. Soils in (a) usually occur on level Highland or flat-topped uplands (*chalas*). Soils in (b) usually occur on small, rounded, *chalas*, but they sometimes occur on level Highland, also.

C. If the soil has a mainly *red substratum*, is the *subsoil*:

  a. mainly *red, brown or yellow-brown*? If so, the soil is a *Deep Red-Brown Terrace Soil*;

  b. mainly *pale brown* with reddish mottles? If so, the soil is a *Brown Mottled Terrace Soil*; or

  c. mainly *grey* with reddish mottles? If so, the soil is a *Grey Terrace Soil*.

---

[3] *These were later divided into Deep Grey Terrace Soils, Shallow Grey Terrace Soils and Grey Valley Soils. All three of these soil types occur in Sabhar Thana. Summary descriptions of all the general soil types occurring in Bangladesh are given in Table 1.4.*

D. If the soil is on *Highland* and has a mainly *grey compact clay substratum*, is the subsoil:

    a. mainly *red, brown or yellow-brown*? If so, the soil is a *Shallow Red-Brown Terrace Soil*; or

    b. mainly *grey*? If so, the soil is a *Grey Terrace Soil*.

    Note. The Grey Terrace Soils may have *either* a red friable clay substratum (as indicated in Cc) *or* a grey compact clay substratum (as indicated in Db).

E. If the soil is in a *byde*, is it:

    a. mainly *light grey* and *silty*? If so, the soil is a *Grey Valley Soil*; or

    b. a *grey or dark grey heavy clay*? If so, the soil is an *Acid Basin Clay.*

F. If the soil is on *floodplain land*, is it:

    a. *stratified* within 10 inches from the ground surface? If so, the soil is *Noncalcareous Alluvium*; or

    b. *not stratified* within 10 inches from the ground surface? If so, the soil is:

        i. an *Acid Basin Clay* if it has a *grey or dark grey heavy clay subsoil*; or

        ii. a *Grey Floodplain Soil* if it has a *grey or light grey, rather friable, loamy or silty clay subsoil.*

    Note. Acid Basin Clays occur both in *bydes* (as indicated in Eb) and on floodplain land (as indicated in Fb).

Now turn to Section 21.3 to check the description of the general soil type you have identified.

21.3 DESCRIPTIONS OF GENERAL SOIL TYPES AND THEIR AGRICULTURAL DEVELOPMENT POSSIBILITIES

This section gives a brief description of the main features of each of the general soil types occurring in Sabhar Thana and indicates what are the most suitable crops and crop rotations for each soil type, with and without irrigation.

For each soil type, three main layers are described: *topsoil*, *subsoil* and *substratum*. The precise definition of these terms, together with definitions of the drainage terms used, is given in the glossary in Section 21.7.

Each general soil type includes several different soils. These are called *soil series*. Soil series within a general soil type differ from each other mainly in the colour or texture of the subsoil. Soil series are named after the place where they were first identified, but they can occur in other places as well. The name is just a label, so that the same soil can be described by the same name wherever it occurs.

Following the description of the general soil type given below, the included soil series are listed and the main features which differentiate them from each other are indicated. Detailed technical descriptions of each soil series are given in the Dhaka District soil survey report.

Following each soil description, suitable crops and crop rotations are indicated for irrigated and non-irrigated conditions. Crops and crop rotations are indicated by the use of capital letters. These letters refer to the list of crops and crop rotations given in Table 21.1 e.g., 'B' refers to 'Fruit trees: mango, litchi, jackfruit, lemon, possibly other citrus'. The crop or

TABLE 21.1

Suggested crops and crop rotations[4]

A.	Dryland crops throughout the year.
	a. *Perennial*: sugarcane, banana, pineapple.
	b. *Kharif*: maize, sorghum, millet, soyabean, other oilseeds, vegetables, fodder legumes.
	c. *Rabi*: wheat, sorghum, millet, groundnut, mustard, soyabean, other oilseeds, tobacco, cotton, vegetables, potato.
B.	Fruit trees: mango, litchi, jackfruit, guava, lemon, possibly other citrus.
C.	Drought-resistant kharif and/or rabi crops: millet (*koan, cheena, bajra*), sorghum (*jowar*), groundnut.
D.	Broadcast aus followed by very early rabi crops: cotton, tobacco, vegetables, potato.
E.	Broadcast aus or mesta followed by early rabi crops: radish, mustard, pulses.
F.	Broadcast aus or jute followed by long-term rabi crops: wheat, barley, maize, groundnut, potato, chilli, vegetables, sunnhemp.
G.	Broadcast aus or jute followed by short-term rabi crops: mustard, legumes, sesamum (*til*), linseed (*tishi*), millet (*kaon, cheena, bajra*), sorghum.
H.	Broadcast aus or jute followed by transplanted aman followed by short-term rabi crops (see G).
I.	Broadcast aus or jute followed by transplanted aman followed by rabi fallow.
J.	Mixed aus + aman followed by long-term rabi crops (see F). Jute is locally substituted for aus in this rotation.
K.	Mixed aus + aman followed by short-term rabi crops (see G). Jute is locally substituted for aus in this rotation.
L.	Mixed aus+aman followed by rabi fallow. Jute is locally substituted for aus in this rotation.
M.	Broadcast deepwater aman followed by long-term rabi crops (see F).
N.	Broadcast deepwater aman followed by short-term rabi crops (see G).
O.	Broadcast deepwater aman followed by rabi fallow.
P.	Transplanted aman followed by rabi fallow.
Q.	Local boro followed by kharif fallow.
R.	HYV boro (or aus) followed by transplanted aman (local varieties).
S.	HYV boro (or aus) followed by HYV aman.
T.	HYV boro followed by kharif fallow.

crop rotation considered most suitable is underlined. Additional notes are given at the foot of each description.

It is assumed that good management practices will be used. Good management means that:

- the fertility status of the soil will be maintained by the use of manure or fertilizers;
- weeds will be removed and plant protection measures used where necessary; and
- sloping soils will be protected against erosion.

---

[4] *Since this list was prepared in 1975, a number of new rotations have been identified which could be indicated as follows:*

Ia. *Transplanted aus (local varieties) followed by transplanted aman (local varieties) followed by rabi fallow.*

Ib. *Transplanted HYV aus followed by transplanted aman (local varieties) followed by rabi fallow.*

Ic. *Transplanted HYV aus followed by transplanted HYV aman followed by rabi fallow.*

Ka. *Mixed aus+aman followed by early rabi crop (maskalai, khesari, mustard) followed by late rabi crop (kaon, chilli, sesamum).*

Ra. *HYV boro followed by transplanted deepwater aman.*

Rb. *HYV boro followed by transplanted deepwater aman followed by mustard/rapeseed.*

Detailed recommendations regarding the kinds and amounts of fertilizers to use on different crops and soils cannot be given in this chapter. That information needs to be obtained by carrying out trials on the soils themselves. See Section 21.6 for a discussion of the kinds of trials which need to be carried out on the soils of Sabhar Thana.

1. DEEP RED-BROWN TERRACE SOILS

General characteristics

Soils on level Highland. Well drained to moderately well drained.

Topsoil: Reddish brown, brown or greyish brown. Loamy.

Subsoil: Reddish brown, brown or yellow-brown, with little or no pale brown or grey colours (mottles). Clay loam or clay. Not compact, but may become hard when dry.

Substratum: Red mixed with pale brown or grey. Not compact. May continue to 20 feet or more.

Soil series

Kashimpur: dark red subsoil. More clayey than Tejgaon. Well drained.

Tejgaon: red or reddish brown subsoil. Well drained.

Belabo: yellow-brown subsoil, with red and brown mottles. Moderately well drained.

Tejkunipara: yellow-brown subsoil, with few or no reddish mottles. Moderately well drained.

Crop suitability

Differentiating characteristics of soil series	Crop suitability with irrigation	Crop suitability without irrigation
a. *Topsoils never or rarely under water* Kashimpur, Tejgaon	a. *Level sites*: <u>A</u>, <u>B</u>, D, <u>F</u>, G b. *Sloping sites*: not recommended	a. B, C, <u>E</u> b. <u>B</u>. Fuelwood, kharif fodder legumes
b. *Topsoils occasionally wet for several days after heavy monsoon rainfall* Belabo, Tejkunipara	a. *Level sites*: E, <u>H</u> b. *Level sites if provided with field drains*: <u>A</u>, B, D	a. E, <u>G</u> b. B, F, <u>G</u>

Notes: 1. The underlined crops and crop rotations will probably give the best results.

2. These deep red and brown soils are 'phosphate fixing'. Therefore, phosphatic fertilizers should be placed in bands along crop rows (or around trees), not broadcast on the soil surface.

3. The subsoil is infertile. It should not be brought to the surface by land levelling or deep ploughing.

4. Cultivation of kharif dryland crops on ridges or beds would be an advantage on all soils to prevent waterlogging during periods of heavy rainfall.

5. These soils are permeable, so irrigation channels should be lined to prevent seepage losses.

6. Mulching of perennial, rabi and kharif dryland crops would be an advantage to reduce moisture losses during dry periods and keep soil temperatures down during hot weather.

7. Drains near valley edges must be protected by *pucca* structures to prevent water flowing from them causing gulley erosion.

2. BROWN MOTTLED TERRACE SOILS

General characteristics

Soils on level Highland; also on flooded terrace land and the slopes of small *chalas*. Mainly somewhat poorly drained.

Topsoil: Brown, pale brown or grey. Loamy.

Subsoil: Pale brown, mixed with yellow-brown or reddish brown. Clay loam or clay. Not compact, but may become hard when dry.

Substratum: Red mixed with pale brown or grey. Clay. Not compact. May continue to 20 feet or more.

Soil series

Noadda: On level Highland. Subsoil pale brown mixed with yellow-brown or reddish brown. Somewhat poorly drained.

Sayek: On sloping sides of *chalas*. Subsoil mainly red, mixed with pale brown. Mainly moderately well drained.

Payati: On small *chalas*, or edges of *chalas*, below normal flood-level. Subsoil mainly red, mixed with pale brown. Seasonally flooded; poorly drained.

Rajasan: Similar to Payati, but topsoil is greyer and more silty due to mixture with floodplain alluvium (in which many mica flakes can be seen sparkling).

Crop suitability

Differentiating characteristics of soil series	Crop suitability with irrigation	Crop suitability without irrigation
a. *Level sites, occasionally wet for 1-2 weeks in monsoon season* Noadda	E, F, G, <u>H</u>	E, <u>I</u>
b. *Sloping sites, above normal flood-level* Sayek	Not recommended	Fuelwood, kharif fodder legumes
c. *Sloping sites, seasonally flooded* Payati, Rajasan	Not recommended	G

Notes: 1. The underlined crops and crop rotations will probably give the best results.

2. These soils will probably need more frequent irrigation than Deep Red-Brown Terrace Soils.

3. Irrigation channels should be lined to reduce seepage losses.

4. Phosphatic fertilizers should be placed in bands along crop rows, except for transplanted aman where the fertilizer can be broadcast and ploughed into the soil at the time of puddling.

5. If kharif dryland crops are grown on level land, they should be planted on ridges or beds to provide drainage.

6. Mulching of kharif and rabi dryland crops would be an advantage so as to reduce moisture losses and keep topsoil temperatures down.

7. Drains near valley edges must be protected by *pucca* structures to prevent water flowing from them causing gulley erosion.

3. SHALLOW RED-BROWN TERRACE SOILS

General characteristics

Mainly soils on low, rolling *chalas*. Occasionally on small, flat-topped, *chalas*. Moderately well to somewhat poorly drained due to heavy clay subsoil or substratum.

Topsoil:	a. Under grassland or cultivation: reddish brown, brown or brownish grey. Clay loam or clay.
	b. Under forest: about 1 inch of greyish silt.
Subsoil:	Reddish brown, brown or yellow-brown. Clay loam or clay. Hard or very hard when dry. Sticky and plastic when wet. Usually only 1-2 feet thick.
Substratum:	Grey, usually mixed with red or brown. Clay. Compact. Continues for 10 feet or more.

Soil series

Gerua:	Subsoil reddish brown. Clay.
Salna:	Subsoil yellow-brown. Loamy.
Bhatpara:	Grey heavy clay at less than 1 foot. Patches of hard lime concretions (*kankar*) occur at an irregular depth in some soils.

Crop suitability

Differentiating characteristics of soil series	Crop suitability with irrigation	Crop suitability without irrigation
a. *Level Highland, well drained* Gerua (deep phase)	A̲, D, E, F̲, G	C, E̲
b. *Level or gently rolling Highland, somewhat poorly drained* Gerua (shallow), Salna, Bhatpara	Not suitable	Not suitable for improved agriculture. Forestry on Gerua and Salna. Grazing on Bhatpara.

Notes[5]: 1. The underlined crops and crop rotations will probably give the best results.

2. Level upland sites usually are small (less than 2 acres) and may be difficult to irrigate economically.

3. The clay subsoil and substratum of these soils cracks when dry. Therefore, irrigation channels should be lined.

4. Phosphatic fertilizers should be placed in bands along crop rows (or around trees).

5. In the deep phase of Gerua series, the grey heavy clay substratum is deeper than 3 feet. In the shallow phase, the substratum is met at 1-3 feet.

6. The subsoil of Gerua and Bhatpara soils should not be exposed at the surface by land-levelling or deep ploughing.

7. Mulching of kharif and rabi dryland crops would be an advantage.

---

[5] *The measures described in this chapter are simple ones which Extension staff (and NGOs) could advise farmers to use. In principle, it would be possible to make bench terraces on sloping Gerua, Salna and Bhatpara soils for growing transplanted paddy (preferably with irrigation): see Section 21.6, paragraph 8 below.*

4. GREY TERRACE AND VALLEY SOILS

General characteristics

Soils on level Highland and Medium Highland, and in sloping *bydes*. Usually shallowly flooded by rainwater in the monsoon season.

Topsoil:	Grey. Silty.
Subsoil	Grey (almost white when dry), mixed with yellow, brown or red. Usually silt loam; sometimes silty clay loam or silty clay.
Substratum:	a. In valleys: similar to subsoil.
	b. On uplands: *either* red mixed with grey, rather friable clay; *or* grey mixed with red, compact clay.

Soil series[6]

Chandra:	On level Highland or Medium Highland. Substratum is mainly red, permeable, and friable (not compact).
Chhiata:	On level Highland or Medium Highland. Substratum is mainly grey, impervious, compact clay. Depth to substratum can vary between 1 and 3 feet within short distances (5-10 feet). Large lime nodules (*kankar*) sometimes occur in the substratum, at a variable depth.
Demra:	Heavy grey clay substratum occurs immediately below the topsoil, at 6-10 inches. Lime nodules occur at a variable depth, sometimes at the soil surface. In Sabhar Thana, Demra soils occur in small patches amongst Chhiata soils.
Kalma:	In *bydes*. Silt loam to silty clay loam subsoil.
Genda:	In *bydes*. Silty clay subsoil.

Crop suitability

Differentiating characteristics of soil series	Crop suitability with irrigation	Crop suitability without irrigation
a. *Highland and Medium Highland, with red-mottled substratum* Chandra	I, R, S	I, P
b. *Highland and Medium Highland, with grey compact clay substratum* Chhiata, Demra	I, R, S	I, P, R, S
c. *Byde, Medium Highland* Kalma	I, R, S	I, P, R, S
d. *Byde, Medium Lowland* Kalma, Genda	L, Q, T	L, O

Notes: 1. The underlined crops and crop rotations will probably give the best results.

   2. Irrigation channels on Chandra, Kalma and Genda soils should be lined to reduce seepage losses.

   3. All these soils depend on a strong ploughpan to hold water on the soil surface for transplanted paddy cultivation. If this ploughpan is broken up by deep ploughing, it must be reformed by puddling with a country plough if the soils

---

[6] *Chandra series was subsequently reclassified as a Deep Grey Terrace Soil, Chhiata and Demra series as Shallow Grey Terrace Soils, and Kalma and Genda series as Grey Valley Soils: see footnote 3 above.*

are to be used for transplanted paddy. (Without a ploughpan, these soils lose bearing capacity when wet, so would be unsuitable for cultivation of kharif crops in the rainy season.)

4. These soils are not well suited for cultivation of dryland crops, whether with irrigation or without irrigation. Dryland crops can be grown with careful management if ridges or beds are made, surface waterlogging is prevented and the soil surface is covered with a mulch.

5. HYV aman can be grown only where flooding is very shallow (less than about 6 inches) at the seedling stage in July-September.

6. HYV boro or aus can only be grown where flooding is less than about 1 foot deep at the time of harvesting (in May-June for boro; June-July for aus).

5. ACID BASIN CLAYS

General characteristics

Soils of deeply-flooded valleys and floodplain basins. Poorly or very poorly drained.

Topsoil: Grey or dark grey. Usually clay, sometimes loamy or peaty.

Subsoil: Grey or dark grey. Heavy clay.

Substratum: Variable, but grey clay usually continues to below 3 feet, and sometimes includes dark grey or black clay or peat layers.

Soil series

Kajla: Grey or dark grey subsoil. Mainly in floodplain basins. Poorly drained.

Khilgaon: Grey or dark grey subsoil, with dark grey, non-peaty layers. Mainly in deep *bydes*. Poorly drained.

Ghazipura: Similar to Khilgaon, but with paler grey layers below each dark grey layer. Mainly in broad *bydes*. Poorly drained.

Karail: Mainly dark grey subsoil, overlying one or more peat layers. Topsoil often peaty. Mainly in deep *bydes*. Very poorly drained.

Crop suitability

Differentiating characteristics of soil series	Crop suitability with irrigation	Crop suitability without irrigation
a. *Remaining wet throughout the dry season* Karail	Q, T	Q, T
b. *Not remaining wet throughout the dry season* Kajla, Khilgaon, Ghazipura	Q, T	a. *Medium Lowland*: L b. *Lowland*: O

Notes: 1. The underlined crops and crop rotations will probably give the best results.

2. HYV boro can only be grown on land where water-levels fall below about 6 inches in December-February and where flooding is not deeper than about 1 foot at the time of harvesting in May-June. In the lowest sites, local boro varieties or quick-maturing HYVs should be grown to avoid the risk of damage by early floods.

3. Irrigation may not be needed on Karail soils which normally remain wet throughout the dry season.

6. GREY FLOODPLAIN SOILS

General characteristics

Soils of the Dhaleswari and Bansi floodplains, and part of the Turag floodplain. Poorly drained. Seasonally flooded. These soils differ from Acid Basin Clays in being much less acid in the subsoil and from Noncalcareous Alluvium in not being stratified within 10 inches from the surface.

Topsoil: Grey (may appear dark grey when wet). Usually silty; sometimes sandy or clayey.

Subsoil: Grey, usually mixed with many small brown mottles. Shiny grey coatings on faces of cracks. Sandy loam, silt loam, clay loam or clay.

Substratum: Grey or dark grey. Stratified sand and silt (or sometimes clay).

Soil series

Turag: Subsoil sandy. Mainly on river banks. Browner than the other soils.

Sonatala: Subsoil grey or grey-brown. Silt loam (sometimes fine sandy loam). Very friable. Mainly on higher parts of floodplain ridges.

Dhamrai: Subsoil grey. Silty clay loam. Firmer than Sonatala. Mainly on higher parts of floodplain ridges.

Singair: Subsoil grey. Silty clay. More friable than Sabhar Bazar. Mainly in floodplain depressions.

Sabhar Bazar: Similar to Singair, but subsoil heavier and firmer.

Crop suitability

Differentiating characteristics of soil series	Crop suitability with irrigation	Crop suitability without irrigation
a. *Medium Highland, sandy subsoil* Turag	Not suitable	C̲, E, G
b. *Medium Highland, sandy loam or silt loam subsoil* Sonatala	F̲, G	E, F, G̲
c. *Medium Lowland, sandy subsoil* Turag	Not suitable	C, F, K̲
d. *Medium Lowland, sandy loam or silt loam subsoil* Sonatala	F, G, J̲, K	J, K̲
e. *Medium Lowland, clay loam or clay subsoil, topsoil not wet after end-November* Singair	F, J̲, K, T̲	F, G, J̲, M
f. *Medium Lowland, clay loam or clay subsoil, wet until December-January* Dhamrai, Singair, Sabhar Bazar	K, T̲	K̲, L, N, O
g. *Medium Lowland or Lowland, clay subsoil, topsoil wet after end-January* Sabhar Bazar	T̲	O (if soils become dry) Q̲, T̲, (if soils stay wet)

Notes: 1. The underlined crops and crop rotations will probably give the best results.

2. HYV boro can only be grown where flooding is less than about 6 inches deep at the time of transplanting in January-March and less than about 1 foot deep at the time of harvesting in May-June. In depression sites, only local boro varieties or quick-maturing HYVs should be grown so as to avoid the risk of damage by early floods.

3. Since the time of the soil survey (in 1964), parts of these soils in soil associations 38 and 56 have been deeply buried by new alluvium (described under Noncalcareous Alluvium).

4. Part of these soils has irregular relief with rapid changes in soil texture from place to place, making it difficult to distribute irrigation water satisfactorily. It might be easier to use STWs or HTWs in such areas than to use LLPs or DTWs.

5. Irrigation canals should be lined where they cross sandy and silt loam soils.

6. Canals near river channels and *khals* may need desilting after every flood season.

7. NONCALCAREOUS ALLUVIUM

General characteristics

Soils of very young alluvium on parts of the Dhaleswari, Bansi and Turag floodplains. Poorly or very poorly drained. Seasonally flooded. These soils differ from Grey Floodplain Soils and Acid Basin Clays in consisting of raw alluvium, either from the ground surface or within 10 inches below the surface. Near river channels, these soils are liable to be buried by new alluvium or to be washed away each flood season. If they are not buried by new alluvium or washed away for 10-15 years, they usually turn into Grey Floodplain Soils, except in sites where they remain wet throughout the year (as in channels and beels).

Topsoil: Grey sand, silt or clay.

Substratum: Grey, stratified, sand and/or silt and/or clay. Layers may be of different colours: grey, dark grey, pale brown.

Soil series

Sandy alluvium: Grey or brown sand on floodplain land. Usually mixed with some thin grey silty layers.

Silty alluvium: Grey (occasionally brown), silt loam to silty clay on floodplain land. Usually overlies sand within 2 feet.

Barar Char: Grey or dark grey, mainly sandy, in old river beds or beels. Usually remains wet throughout the dry season.

Khaler Char: Similar to Barar Char, but mainly silty material.

Gorargaon: Similar to Khaler Char, but mainly clayey material.

Crop suitability

Differentiating characteristics of soil series	Crop suitability with irrigation	Crop suitability without irrigation
a. *Medium Highland, sandy subsoil* Sandy alluvium	Not suitable	C
b. *Medium Highland, silty subsoil* Silty alluvium	T?	C, K
c. *Medium Lowland or Lowland, wet for most or all of dry season* Barar Char, Khaler Char, Gorargaon	Q, T	O (if seasonally dry) Q, T, (if perennially wet)

Notes: 1. The underlined crops and crop rotations will probably give the best results.

2. Relief often is irregular, making distribution of irrigation water difficult.

3. The characteristics of this land may change over time due to burial by new alluvium or river-bank erosion.

4. Where silty alluvium remains undisturbed by new depositions or by erosion for 10-15 years, the soils change to Grey Floodplain Soils (except in perennially wet sites) and may then become well suited for early jute and for rabi crops such as chilli, tomato, pulses, *cheena* and *kaon*.

21.4 CHARACTERISTICS OF INDIVIDUAL SOIL ASSOCIATIONS

Table 21.2 gives the approximate area of each of the general soil types present in the 16 soil associations shown on Figure 21.1. Table 21.3 shows the position in the landscape occupied by each of the 16 soil associations.

21.5 SUGGESTED PRIORITIES FOR AGRICULTURAL DEVELOPMENT[7]

1. Approximately 19,000 acres of well drained and moderately well drained land on level Highland occur, mainly in the east and south-central parts of the Thana: (soil associations 1, 2, 3, 7, 11b). This land is well suited for cultivation of dryland crops throughout the year if irrigated. Irrigation will have to come mainly from DTWs, but Highland adjoining the Turag, Bansi and Dhaleswari rivers could perhaps be irrigated by large LLPs, provided that this would not deprive floodplain land of water needed for irrigation.

2. Approximately 13,000 acres of poorly drained or somewhat poorly drained Highland and *bydes* occur, mainly in the central and western parts of the Thana: (soil associations 3, 6, 11b, 25, 26, 27). Without irrigation, this land is well suited for cultivation of aus and transplanted aman (including one HYV). With irrigation, an extra HYV aus or aman could be grown. This land would need more irrigation than the land included in paragraph 1 above. Irrigation will have to come mainly from DTWs. This land is poorly suited for growing dryland crops, with or without irrigation.

3. Approximately 12,000 acres of land in broad *bydes* and floodplain basins on the eastern and western margins of the Thana (soil associations 7, 30, 35, 37, 38, 56, 61) are well suited for cultivation of irrigated HYV boro. Irrigation could come mainly from LLPs, but tube-wells might be needed in some *bydes* within the Madhupur Tract.

4. Floodplain land along the Bansi and Dhaleswari rivers (soil association 55, 56) mainly grows crops satisfactorily without irrigation. Increased use of fertilizers is the main requirement. Where irrigation can be provided, HYV aus or boro could be grown in basins and rabi vegetables on ridges. High-cost permanent structures are not recommended because of the risk that these floodplain areas will be buried by new alluvium unsuitable for irrigation.

5. *Chalas* in soil associations 25, 26, 27 and 30 are mainly unsuitable for irrigation or for improved agriculture. They are better used for forestry, rough grazing or for settlement sites. The *bydes* in these associations are included in the recommendations made in paragraph 2 above.

21.6 RECOMMENDATIONS FOR SOIL FERTILITY AND AGRONOMIC TRIALS

1. *Crops*. Agronomic trials and demonstrations are needed with crops and crop varieties which are presently unknown or little known in the area. On Deep Red-Brown

---

[7] *The land areas referred to are those measured at the time of the soil survey (1964). Since that time, substantial areas of land in Sabhar Thana have been overwhelmed by urban and industrial development, so the areas available for agricultural development will now be less than indicated. Also, some floodplain land referred to in paragraph 3 has been buried by new alluvium, thus reducing the area reported suitable for intensive agricultural development. Extension staff should take these changes into account in using soil survey information for agricultural development planning.*

TABLE 21.2

Sabhar Thana: approximate area (acres) of General Soil Types in soil associations

Soil association (see map)	Deep Red-Brown Terrace Soils	Brown Mottled Terrace Soils	Shallow Red-Brown Terrace Soils	Grey Terrace and Valley Soils	Acid Basin Clays	Grey Floodplain Soils	Noncalcareous Alluvium	Homesteads and water	Total area
1	6,000	+	+	+	+	-	-	500	8,543
2	1,900	900	+	+	+	+	-	250	2,705
3	1,650	+	-	550	300	-	-	250	2,782
6	+	2,700	-	3,500	+	-	-	750	7,665
7	4,000	-	-	+	2,000	-	-	600	6,622
11b	4,000	-	-	2,000	+	-	-	650	6,656
25	+	-	1,500	600	+	-	-	+	2,353
26	-	-	1,300	1,450	+	-	-	150	3,214
27	-	-	3,000	1,500	+	-	-	+	4,909
30	1,500	+	2,700	+	1,900	+	+	750	7,731
35	-	-	-	-	750	-	-	+	780
37	-	-	-	-	4,300	2,600	+	1,000	8,530
38	-	-	-	-	1,000	1,900	+	300	3,205
55	-	-	-	-	-	-	1,600	+	1,670
56	-	+	-	-	+	12,800	+	1,400	14,240
61	-	-	-	-	900	1,800	+	-	2,933
River	-	-	-	-	-	-	-	-	587
Total									**85,125**

Notes: 1. Areas calculated by >counting squares= method, so are approximate. The total area of the Thana is as given in the 1961 Population Census Report.
2. + = soil occurs in small amounts. - = soil not recorded.

TABLE 21.3
Characteristics of individual soil associations

Soil association (See map)	Landscape	General Soil Types present	Position in landscape	Approximate proportion of association
1	Level Highland with only few broad *bydes*	Deep Red-Brown Terrace Soils	Higher parts of Highland	More than 70%
		Brown Mottled Terrace Soils	Lower parts of Highland	Minor
		Grey Terrace and Valley Soils	Depressions, *bydes*	Minor
		Acid Basin Clays	Lower *bydes*	Minor
2	Level Highland with a few broad *bydes*	Deep Red-Brown Terrace Soils	Higher parts of Highland	60%
		Brown Mottled Terrace Soils	Lower parts of Highland	30%
		Grey Terrace and Valley Soils	Depressions	Minor
		Acid Basin Clays	Broad *bydes*	Less than 10%
3	Gently sloping Highland and level depressions with few broad *bydes*	Deep Red-Brown Terrace Soils	Higher parts	More than 60%
		Grey Terrace and Valley Soils	Depressions	20%
		Acid Basin Clays	Broad *bydes*	Less than 15%
6	Nearly level Highland with broad low ridges and poorly drained depressions	Deep Red-Brown Terrace Soils	Highest parts on edge of *bydes*	Minor
		Brown Mottled Terrace Soils	Broad low ridges	35%
		Grey Terrace and Valley Soils	Broad depressions, few *bydes*	45%
		Acid Basin Clays	Lower *bydes*	Minor
7	Level Highland areas up to half-a-mile broad, separated by broad *bydes*	Deep Red-Brown Terrace Soils	Level Highland	60-80%
		Brown Mottled Terrace Soils	Seasonally-flooded edge of Madhupur Tract	Minor
		Grey Terrace and Valley Soils	Higher *bydes*	Minor
		Acid Basin Clays	Broad *bydes*	20-30%
11b	Ditto	Deep Red-Brown Terrace Soils	Level Highland	70%
		Shallow Red-Brown Terrace Soils	Tops of small *chalas*	Minor
		Grey Terrace and Valley Soils	Most *bydes*	30%
		Acid Basin Clays	Lowest *bydes*	Minor

(Contd.)

(Continued)

Soil association (See map)	Landscape	General Soil Types present	Position in landscape	Approximate proportion of association
25	Low rounded *chalas* and narrow *bydes*	Deep Red-Brown Terrace Soils	Highest level Highland areas	Minor
		Shallow Red-Brown Terrace Soils	Most *chalas*	65%
		Grey Terrace and Valley Soils	*Bydes*; few level tops of *chalas*	More than 20%
26	Ditto, but with some small level Highland areas	Shallow Red-Brown Terrace Soils	Sloping *chalas*	40%
		Grey Terrace and Valley Soils	Flat-topped *chalas*	20%
		Ditto	*Bydes*	About 30%
		Acid Basin Clays	Deep *bydes*	Minor
27	Rounded *chalas* and mainly narrow *bydes*	Shallow Red-Brown Terrace Soils	*Chalas*	60%
		Grey Terrace and Valley Soils	Narrow *bydes*	30%
		Acid Basin Clays	Broad *bydes*	Minor
30	Complex of flat-topped and rounded *chalas*, broad *bydes* and floodplain	Deep Red-Brown Terrace Soils	Level Highland	20%
		Brown Mottled Terrace Soils	Low rounded *chalas*	Minor
		Shallow Red-Brown Terrace Soils	Rounded *chalas*	More than 20%
		Acid Basin Clays	Broad *bydes* and *beels*	35%
		Grey Floodplain Soils	Floodplain in west	Minor
		Noncalcareous Alluvium	Ditto	Minor
35	Deep *bydes* and *beels*	Acid Basin Clays	*Bydes* and *beels*	100% (20% *beel*)
37	Turag floodplain	Acid Basin Clays	Floodplain basins	More than 45%
		Grey Floodplain Soils	Floodplain ridges	More than 25%
		Noncalcareous Alluvium	Floodplain ridges	Not known, but probably increasing
38	Turag floodplain	Acid Basin Clays	Floodplain basins	More than 30%
		Grey Floodplain Soils	Floodplain ridges and depressions	} 60%. Liable to change
		Noncalcareous Alluvium	Ditto	} each flood season }

(Contd.)

(Continued)

Soil association (See map)	Landscape	General Soil Types present	Position in landscape	Approximate proportion of association
55	Dhaleswari floodplain	Grey Floodplain Soils Noncalcareous Alluvium	Floodplain ridges and depressions	} 100%. Proportions } liable to change each } flood season
56	Dhaleswari and Bansi floodplains	Grey Floodplain Soils Noncalcareous Alluvium	Floodplain ridges and depressions	} 100%. Mainly Grey } Floodplain Soils, but } new alluvium has } covered part of the } area since 1964.
61	Lower Turag floodplaim	Acid Basin Clays Grey Floodplain Soils Noncalcareous Alluvium	Basins Floodplain ridges Ditto	30% } Figures for 1964. 60% } New alluvium has Minor} covered much of this area since 1964

Note: 1. Grey Terrace and Valley Soils include Deep Grey Terrace Soils, Shallow Grey Terrace Soils and Grey Valley Soils which were not recognized separately when the original guide was written.

Terrace Soils and Brown Mottled Terrace Soils, trials are needed with improved sugarcane varieties, HYV wheat, sorghum, millet (including *bajra*), maize, oilseeds (groundnut, mustard, soyabean), fodder grasses and legumes, as well as kharif vegetables. Trials are also needed with aus (line-sown), aman and boro on these and other soils, using irrigation for aus and boro.

2. *Soil fertility trials*. Routine trials are needed to find out fertilizer requirements of the important general soil types occurring in the Thana. Trials should be made on a soil series basis. Both irrigated and non-irrigated conditions should be tested.[8]

3. *Phosphate trials*. The Deep and Shallow Red-Brown Terrace Soils, and to a lesser degree the Brown Mottled Terrace Soils, are phosphate fixing. Trials are needed to compare banding versus broadcasting of fertilizers. Comparisons should also be made between various types of phosphatic fertilizers, in combination with and in the absence of organic manures.

4. *Irrigation*. Trials are needed to find out water requirements of the major crops on the important general soil types. Trials should be made on a soil series basis.

5. *Water management*. Trials are needed on the important general soil types to find out the most convenient and economical methods of lining irrigation channels to reduce seepage losses.

6. *Ploughing*. The country plough in general use forms a ploughpan in most terrace, *byde* and floodplain soils. This ploughpan is an advantage for transplanted paddy, but it is harmful for other crops because it prevents deep root penetration. It also prevents irrigation water from penetrating quickly into the subsoil for use by dryland crops. Trials are needed with the following techniques:

   a. to break up the pan and reform it at a greater depth in soils used for transplanted paddy, whether irrigated or not; and

   b. to break up the pan and prevent it from reforming in soils used for broadcast aus, jute, deepwater aman and especially dryland crops, both under irrigated and non-irrigated conditions.[9]

7. *Mulching*. The benefits of mulching for both kharif and rabi dryland crops need to be tested on the important general soil types used for these crops, especially on Deep Red-Brown Terrace Soils.

8. *Terracing*. The feasibility and economics of constructing terraces on Shallow Red-Brown Terrace Soils (especially Bhatpara and Gerua series) need to be tested. Terraced soils would best be used for transplanted paddy, preferably with irrigation. After levelling, silty topsoil material may have to be brought in from adjoining *bydes*

---

[8] *Also needed, but not referred to in the original document, are trials to determine the long-term fertilizer requirements for sustained agricultural production. Trials of the kind carried out in the 1970s and 1980s mainly indicated the fertilizer response on soils that had not previously received fertilizers, which could give a misleading picture of the annual or seasonal requirements with sustained use of fertilizers, especially for phosphatic and potash fertilizers. Trials should include some to determine whether or not zinc, sulphur and possibly other micronutrient deficiencies occur under intensive cropping.*

[9] *Techniques could include periodic knifing or deep ploughing, which would probably require the use of 4-wheel tractors; periodically making ridges or beds on which to grow dryland crops; or periodically growing deep-rooting crops (e.g., pigeon pea or Sesbania). In using the first two techniques, care should be taken not to bring subsoil material into the topsoil in Deep and Shallow Red-Brown Terrace Soils. Breaking up the ploughpan in Grey Terrace and Valley Soils is not recommended because that would turn the soils into an uncultivable quagmire in the following rainy season.*

or floodplain land. *Pucca* drainage outfalls might be needed to lead run-off safely from one terrace level to the next, and from the bottom terrace into the *byde*.

21.7 GLOSSARY[10]

Basin. The lowest part of a floodplain landscape, usually saucer-shaped.

  Byde. Valley.

  Chalas. Upland areas on the Madhupur Tract.

  Compact. Dense. Difficult to penetrate with a knife or spade when wet, moist or dry.

  Deep soil. a. In terrace soils, a soil in which there is no impedance to root or water penetration.

  b. In floodplain soils, a soil in which the substratum (defined below) is deeper than about 3 feet from the surface.

Drainage. The relative rapidity with which water is removed from the soil by surface run-off or by flow through the soil. The drainage classes used are:

- *Well drained*. Water moves from or through the soil sufficiently quickly that water does not stand on the soil surface for more than a few hours and the soil does not remain wet in the uppermost 2-3 feet for more than 2-3 days after heavy rainfall or irrigation.

- *Moderately well drained*. Water may stand on the soil surface for a few days following heavy monsoon rainfall and the soil may remain wet in the uppermost 2-3 feet for 1-2 weeks during the monsoon season.

- *Somewhat poorly drained*. The soil remains wet for several weeks during the monsoon season and water may stand on the surface for 1-2 weeks at a time following periods of heavy rainfall.

- *Poorly drained*. The soil remains wet for several weeks during the monsoon season and the surface is flooded for several weeks or months, but the soil surface does not stay wet throughout most of the dry season.

- *Very poorly drained*. The soil remains wet throughout most or all of the year.

- *Seasonally flooded*. The soil is submerged by rainwater or river-water for a period of a few weeks or months every monsoon season.

- *Impeded drainage*. Movement of water through the soil is slowed down or prevented by an impervious layer (such as the heavy clay substratum in Shallow Red-Brown Terrace Soils).

Field drains. Small ditches (or underground pipes) to carry away excess monsoon rainfall or irrigation water so that the soils in adjoining fields remain well drained.

Flood coatings. Shiny films of soil material (appearing like wet mud) occurring on the surfaces of cracks and pores in the subsoils of some floodplain soils.

Friable. Easily broken between the fingers or by ploughing when moist.

General soil type. A group of soils which have formed in the same way and which have broadly similar properties. Bangladesh has several hundred different soil series (defined below), but these have been grouped into 21 general soil types for the sake of simplicity.[11]

---

[10]*This glossary formed part of the original document and refers only to terms used in this chapter.*

[11]*When the original document was prepared in 1975, only 17 general soil types were recognized. Subsequently, the Grey Terrace and Valley Soils were divided into separate Deep, Shallow and Valley types, and Grey Floodplain Soils were divided into Calcareous and Noncalcareous types: see Table 1.4.*

Highland. See *Land levels in relation to flooding*.

Internal drainage. The relative rapidity with which water moves through the soil.

Land levels in relation to flooding.[12] The depth to which land normally is submerged in the middle of the monsoon season. Four *land types* are recognized in Sabhar Thana, viz.

- *Highland.* Land above normal flood level.
- *Medium Highland.* Land normally subject to shallow flooding (1-3 feet).
- *Medium Lowland.* Land normally flooded up to 3-6 feet.
- *Lowland.* Land normally flooded deeper than 6 feet.

Landscape. The overall surface relief of a tract of land. For example, floodplain landscapes normally include both ridges and basins; some parts of the Madhupur Tract comprise a succession of *chalas* and *bydes*; and other parts of the Madhupur Tract have level Highland without *bydes*.

Lowland. See *Land levels in relation to flooding* above.

Medium Highland. Ditto.

Medium Lowland. Ditto.

Moderately well drained. See *Drainage* above.

Mottled (mottles). With patches of different colours occurring side by side.

Noncalcareous. Not containing lime.

Peat (peaty). Consisting mainly of decomposed plant remains.

Phosphate fixing. A soil property which rapidly converts phosphatic fertilizer into a form which plants cannot use. The usual remedy is to concentrate phosphatic fertilizer applications in narrow bands along crop rows or around trees instead of broadcasting the fertilizer over the soil surface.

Ploughpan. The layer below the cultivated layer which has been made compact by repeated pressure during ploughing when the soil is wet or moist.

Poorly drained. See *Drainage* above.

Ridges. Two kinds of ridges are referred to in the text:

    a. the relatively higher parts of floodplain landscapes; and

    b. cultivation ridges made in fields on which to grow dryland crops which require good drainage.

Shallow soil. a. In terrace soils, a soil which overlies heavy clay at less than about 3 feet from the ground surface.

       b. In floodplain soils, a soil in which the substratum (defined below) occurs at less than about 3 feet below the surface.

Soil association. A group of soils occurring side-by-side in a regular pattern within a particular landscape. For example, soil association 3 on the soil associations map of Sabhar Thana is described as including Tejgaon series occupying about 60 percent of the area on gently sloping Highland, together with small areas of Kashimpur Series on high valley edges and Belabo and Tejkunipara series on lower slopes, and with Chandra series occupying about 20 percent in depressions. This pattern of soils, in approximately the same proportions, occurs on all Highland ridges and depressions within the boundaries of soil association 3.

---

[12]*See Table 1.2 for a more detailed classification of land types.*

Neighbouring soil associations may have similar soils, but in different proportions because of differences in the landscape.

Soil series. Soils closely similar in appearance and properties, especially in colour, and texture of the subsoil, and developed from the same kind of parent material under similar conditions of climate, vegetation and drainage operating over a similar period of time.

Stratified. In layers, like the pages of a book or like a pile of books. The layers are usually of different texture. In some raw silty alluvium, the material may be like jelly when it is wet, and the fine stratification may only be seen when the material becomes moist or dry.

Subsoil. The layer below the topsoil which generally has not been disturbed by cultivation. In floodplain soils, the stratification present in the original alluvium has been broken up by plant roots and soil animals. Strictly speaking, the layer changed by soil formation should extend to more than 10 inches below the ground surface before it is recognized as a true subsoil.

Substratum. The layer below the soil (topsoil or subsoil) which has not been altered by soil-forming processes. In floodplain soils, the substratum is stratified and may contain buried soil layers. The deeply-weathered, red-mottled substratum in Deep Red-Brown Terrace Soils, Brown Mottled Terrace Soils and some (i.e., Deep) Grey Terrace Soils is regarded as the parent material from which these soils have developed, even though this material is itself greatly altered from its original state as Madhupur Clay as a result of mainly geological weathering processes.

Terrace (1). A relatively level upland area. In the case of the Madhupur Tract, the land has been raised by earthquakes above the level of the surrounding floodplain land. Parts of the Madhupur Tract were formerly level but have been cut into by *bydes* and the upland areas between the *bydes* have been rounded by erosion. However, the summits of the *chalas* still rise to about the same level, showing that they once formed part of a continuous level landscape.

Terrace (2). Artificially levelled field made on sloping land.

Texture. The relative proportions of different particle sizes within the soil which determine whether it is sandy, silty, loamy or clayey.

Topsoil. The surface layer of the soil. Usually, this layer has been disturbed by cultivation, and includes the ***ploughpan*** (defined above). In uncultivated forest soils, the topsoil is the surface layer darkened by humus.

Well drained. See ***Drainage*** above.

Chapter 22

BACKGROUND TO THANA LAND USE PLANNING[1]

This chapter describes an attempt made to establish a programme for Thana land use planning in the early 1980s. It provides the background to understanding the methods described in Chapter 23.

22.1 INTRODUCTION

In 1979, the author was invited to prepare a manual on land use planning for use by local government administrations (Brammer, 1979). The purpose was to bring into use for local-level planning the wealth of information on the soils of Bangladesh collected during the reconnaissance soil survey of the country carried out between 1964 and 1975.

Instead of setting up an independent land use planning system, it was decided to add land use planning to the system of Thana development planning which had been introduced and tested at the Academy for Rural Development (now BARD) at Comilla during the 1960s. During that period, models were prepared for the creation of small-scale rural development infrastructure: first, Thana drainage and embankment plans; then Thana road plans; and later, Thana irrigation plans. Annual plans for each of these development programmes were assembled in the form of a Thana Plan Book covering a five-year planning period. The location of proposed schemes was shown on a series of Thana maps. One set of maps showed what the Thana Council proposed to do in each plan period. Another set showed what the District Approving Authority approved and allocated funds for. Later in the 1960s, Union Plan Books were also prepared.

Procedures were established for preparing, reviewing, revising, approving and implementing the plans through Thana and Union Councils. Thus, the system was a participatory planning system which combined the wealth of practical local experience of the people (through their elected local government representatives) with the administrative and technical knowledge of the available government officials.[2]

In the 1960s, little technical knowledge was available at local levels about land and water potentials. The Thana plans were prepared, therefore, mainly on the basis of local

---

[1] *This chapter is based partly on a paper prepared for a training course on the Training and Visits system of Agricultural Extension and Management held at the Graduate Training Institute, Bangladesh Agricultural University, Mymensingh, 11 November, 1984, (Brammer, 1984c), and partly on the Preface and Chapter 1 of Brammer (1983).*

[2] *The Thana planning system developed at the Comilla Academy is described and reviewed in the collected works of Akhter Hameed Khan, especially Volumes II and III (Khan, 1983a, b). The environmental and cultural background to the planning system is described in Volume I (Khan, 1981).*

knowledge of experienced farmers and political leaders: e.g., where drainage problems existed; where roads were needed; and where surface-water and groundwater supplies existed which could be used for irrigation. It was decided that development could not be delayed until technical officials carried out formal surveys to assess the resources.

By the late 1970s, however, the situation was different. A great deal of technical knowledge had been gained about the country's natural resources. Reconnaissance soil surveys carried out during the 1960s and 1970s provided valuable information on the country's soils and their cropping potentials. Surveys of both surface water and groundwater provided considerable practical information on usable water resources. Much experience was gained, too, with water distribution and management, and the use of modern technology such as HYV seeds and fertilizers.

In 1979, therefore, it was decided to re-vitalize the Thana planning system which had lost impetus during and after the Liberation period. The manual referred to above was prepared as a basis for training Thana-level officials in how to use the new technical information for local-level planning. Details of the training programme are given below. Subsequent developments are described in a final section.

It is important to understand that the system of planning developed by the Comilla Academy is not top-down: i.e., plans prepared by government officials for the benefit of the people. Nor is it bottom-up planning: i.e., plans prepared by people's committees or councils for their own implementation. It is 'up-and-down' planning: i.e., the identification of schemes by dialogue between local people and technical officials, and formal approval of the schemes by democratically-elected local governments with budgets provided by central government.

22.2 TRAINING PROGRAMME

The manual prepared in 1979 described a method for using soil survey reports to prepare Thana land use plans.[3] For each soil association in a Thana, tables and maps could be prepared showing the area and proportions of land suitable for particular crops: e.g., for rainfed HYV aman, irrigated wheat, etc. This information could help Agricultural Extension staff to:

    i. identify the total potential for growing particular crops in their work area;

    ii. identify specific areas where such crops could be grown; and

    iii. develop extension programmes jointly with local farmers and elected councillors in order to increase agricultural production according to soil-crop suitability.

Such information could also help Extension staff to discuss with local people the measures they considered necessary to remove or reduce constraints impeding an increase in agricultural production: e.g., flood protection, drainage or irrigation works; roads to improve input supply and 'marketing of produce; provision of credit for crops or cultivation methods needing greater financial resources than traditional practices; etc.

The first stage in developing the Thana land use planning programme in 1979 was to train Thana development officials in how to use the soil survey information. For this

---

[3] *The original paper included a section describing the information given in reconnaissance soil survey reports. That section has been omitted here because the information is given in greater detail in Chapter 14 of this volume.*

purpose, the Soils Institute (SRDI) prepared a soil survey report for each Thana which contained an extract of relevant soil association and crop suitability tables and a soil map from the District soil survey report. Then, groups of officials from selected Thanas were brought to BARD, Comilla, or the Graduate Training Institute, Mymensingh, for two weeks' training. Those officials included the senior administrative official (then called the Circle Officer, Development), the Agricultural Extension Officer, the Rural Development Projects Officer (or the Cooperatives Officer) and the Rural Works Programme Supervisor, together with the Chairman of the Thana Council.

The training given was entirely practical. It involved each group working through exercises on the soil survey report and map of their own Thana in order to determine the suitability for irrigated and non-irrigated crop production of the different soil associations occurring in their Thana. Two days were spent in fieldwork, mapping land use and discussing crop suitability with farmers in the area around the training venue at Comilla or Mymensingh.

22.3 VILLAGE LAND USE MAPS[4]

During the pilot testing phase of the programme at Comilla in 1979, it was recognized that land use in Bangladesh was so complex that the different kinds of land use occurring in a Thana could not be shown satisfactorily on the Thana maps, which are on a scale of 1 inch to 1 mile (1:63,360). Even on Union maps on 4 inches to 1 mile scale (1:15,840), it was difficult to show full details of land use. Therefore, in order to map land use, the cadastral (*mouza*) maps on 16 inches to 1 mile scale (1:3,960) had to be used.

The second stage in implementing the local-level planning programme, therefore, was to train local educated youths in how to map land types and different kinds of land use. They were given a standard legend of symbols to use on the mouza maps. Mapping was done with the help of the local Union Council member.

This system was found to be much better than that of using the Union Extension Agent to prepare such maps. In the first place, the Union Assistant was too busy on other scheduled activities under the T & V programme. Secondly, he was not always a local man, and so his mapping activities and questions about land use were liable to make local residents suspicious about possible land acquisition or taxation. On the other hand, local youths knew their village land well, and their mapping activities did not arouse the same suspicions. It was found that they needed only 2-3 days' training before taking up the work, and that they could complete the mapping of one-third of a Union in about two weeks.[5]

After the maps had been checked and compiled, the Thana Extension Officer had to reduce the information onto the Union maps on 4 inches to 1 mile scale, using the same standard symbols. It was found that the information could not be reduced further onto the Thana map scale (1 inch = 1 mile), so the Thana land use map comprises the collection of all the Union land use maps in the Thana.

---

[4] *Another system for village development planning is described in Chapter 20.*

[5] *Villages and Unions vary in size, but average about 1 and 10 square miles respectively (2.6 and 26 km². In the Union near Comilla where the system was tested during the pilot phase of the programme, the same youths were able to work over a number of villages. Where that might be unacceptable because of conflicts between villages, separate groups of youths would need to be trained for different villages, which would slow down progress and might lead to uneven quality of the information collected.*

22.4 PLAN PREPARATION

The mouza and Union maps provide the basis for preparing new land use plans. Those maps show the following kinds of information:[6]

- village sites;
- rivers, canals, lakes, etc., (classified according to their potential use as irrigation sources);
- ponds (classified according to their fisheries potential);
- land types (land levels in relation to flooding);
- level and sloping land;
- present cropping patterns and other land use;
- sites of different kinds of irrigation equipment or structure and the irrigation command area.
- flood protection embankments, roads, bridges, sluices, etc.

This information, combined with the crop suitability information derived from soil survey reports, provides the basis for dialogue between Extension staff, local farmers and elected councillors on what the opportunities are for increasing production from the land and water resources, what are the constraints to be overcome, and what schemes can be identified for improved land use. That land use might include forestry, fisheries and livestock development, where appropriate, just as much as schemes to increase crop production.

The result of the dialogue is a list of schemes identified for inclusion in the Union or Thana Development Plan, and a map indicating the location of all the schemes. It is then the responsibility of Extension staff to prepare formal scheme proposals to present to the Union/Thana Council, and to amend them as those Councils may require. Eventually, of course, Extension staff will be involved in implementing the schemes and in assisting farmers to adopt new crops, cropping patterns or techniques which implementation of approved schemes may involve.

It should be added that this planning activity is not antagonistic to the T & V Extension system. In a sense, it is basic to the success of the T & V Extension system. That is because, if it is to succeed, any Extension system must be based on a sound understanding of the physical environment and its agricultural potential, as well as on an understanding of the farmers' constraints and needs. The land use planning model described above has the capacity to strengthen the T & V (or any other) Extension system, therefore. It was not designed to undermine or supersede it.

22.5 PROGRAMME EXPERIENCE

Altogether, about 400 councillors and officials from a total of 94 Thanas were given training during 1980-82. However, the land use planning programme failed to take root. No Thana plans were actually made on the basis of the training given. The programme was suspended in June 1982.[7] There were three main reasons why the programme failed, viz.

a. Local governments were not strong. They were dominated by government officials.

---

[6] *This list was adopted from the existing Thana and Union Development Plan maps. The only additional information collected related to land characteristics and land use.*

[7] *The main reason for the suspension was lack of departmental interest in the programme, reflected in the fact that less than 50 percent of those nominated to attend the 15 training courses organized between February and June 1982 actually turned up.*

b. Government departments were strongly centralized. Each department had its own programme. Officials were responsible to their departmental supervisors, not to the Circle Officer who was supposed to coordinate local development activities; much less were they answerable to the Thana Council. This independent departmental approach made it difficult to proceed with coordinated planning activities.

c. Government officials were subject to frequent transfer. Within six months of training being completed, about half the officials trained under the programme had been transferred to other Thanas or promoted.

Subsequent to that experience, there was considerable decentralization of authority to Thana and Union Councils. Considerable amounts of development funds were allocated directly to those councils to spend on schemes, without reference to a District Approving Authority. The manual on Thana land use planning was revised accordingly, as described below, with a view to training in land use planning being resumed in the near future. However, re-introduction of the programme was delayed because of the serious floods which occurred in 1984, which meant that priority had to be given to relief and rehabilitation activities.[8]

22.6 REVISED MODEL

The revised manual described a method for preparing Thana (and Union) Agricultural Development Plans (Brammer, 1983).[9] It was intended to be used by Thana Agricultural Extension Officers. Agricultural Extension staff were given a stronger role to play, with responsibility to:

i. identify the potentials for development, including irrigation potential;

ii. organize discussions with farmers' groups and elected councillors, leading to the identification of suitable development schemes and extension programmes; and

iii. prepare annual and 5-year plans for presentation to Union and Thana Councils for their examination, discussion and approval.

The basis for planning was the Thana soil survey report (described in Section 22.2) and up-to-date information on surface-water and groundwater hydrology to be obtained from the Bangladesh Water Development Board (BWDB).[10]

Although the revised manual was primarily concerned with how to use technical information in preparing agricultural development plans, the method followed the participatory planning model developed at the Comilla Academy in the 1960s. That methodology recognized that the technical knowledge of officials, no matter how good, is an insufficient basis for planning and development unless it is supplemented by:

a. farmers' detailed knowledge of the local environment, based on years or generations of experience of soil and crop behaviour in good years and bad years; and

b. the farmers' acceptance that proposed changes will, in fact, satisfy their actual needs.

---

[8] *In the event, the proposed programme was not re-introduced after the change in government in 1985. Subsequent governments reduced the powers and functions of Thana and Union Councils.*

[9] *The revised model provides the basis for the methods described in Chapter 23.*

[10]*In the original manual, the Bangladesh Agricultural Development Corporation (BADC) was also referred to as a source of hydrological information because, at that time, BADC was responsible for providing and maintaining most deep and shallow tube-wells in the country.*

Participatory planning, therefore, requires that a dialogue be developed between technical officials and local residents as equal partners in the planning and development process. In that sense, it is neither top-down nor bottom-up. It is both.

Whereas the emphasis in the earlier programme described in Section 22.3 was on the preparation of village land use maps, the revised manual focused on specific activities which are the responsibility of the Thana Agricultural Extension Officer. Experience during the pilot testing phase of the programme and subsequent training courses indicated that this official had the primary role to play in Thana agricultural development planning and that he would need to take the lead in the technical aspects of plan preparation. The revised manual showed how to identify:

a. the crops, crop rotations or other kinds of land use which are suitable in the Thana, with irrigation and without irrigation;
b. where the areas occur which are suitable for those crops, rotations or other kinds of land use;
c. the approximate area which is suitable for each kind of crop or land use;
d. the potential for irrigation in different areas; and
e. the kinds of problems which exist, and possible ways to solve them.

Those activities are described in Chapter 23 and followed by a description of how to use the information, through participatory planning processes, for preparing 5-Year Agricultural Development Plans at Union and Thana levels.

Chapter 23

THANA AGRICULTURAL DEVELOPMENT PLANNING[1]

This chapter describes, step by step, the methods by which Agricultural Extension staff can help to prepare a Thana agricultural development plan based on available technical information and in consultation with informed people in the Thana. Successive sections describe the planning objectives, the responsibilities of officials and local government councillors, how to prepare crop suitability, irrigation and problem area maps, and how to prepare the plan. The chapter includes examples of the forms to be used, as well as annexes providing technical guidelines.

23.1 OBJECTIVES

The objectives of Thana agricultural development planning are to increase agricultural production, rural employment and rural incomes through the rational use of the country's land, water and human resources. The rational development of those resources involves:

a. making use of all available technical information;

b. making use of the experience of local farmers; and

c. involving Union, Thana and District Councils in the preparation, review, approval and implementation of agricultural development plans.

The purpose of the manual described in this chapter is to show Thana Agricultural Extension Officers and their staff how to use the available soil survey and hydrological information for preparing agricultural development plans. However, plans which consider only the physical factors (soils, water, climate) are unlikely to be realistic. Agricultural plans, in particular, involve people. Therefore, the Comilla model of participatory planning has been retained, combining the practical experience of local farmers, the technical knowledge of officials and a joint assessment of what changes it is feasible to make in the physical environment and in farming practices during the short period of a plan and within the financial resources likely to be available.

Agricultural Extension staff have a key role to play in Thana agricultural development planning. Because of their technical expertise, it is their responsibility to draft the plans for review and approval by Union and Thana Councils. As Extension specialists, they also have an important role to play in describing and demonstrating new techniques to farmers so that plan targets can be achieved.

---

[1] *This chapter is based on a draft manual on Thana land use planning prepared for the Ministry of Agriculture in 1983 (Brammer, 1983). Footnotes which appeared in the original document are given in normal font. Footnotes that have been added are given in italics.*

However, it must be realized that these plan targets do not comprise merely the achievement of increased crop yields and production. Increased yields and production are not enough if farmers cannot sell their surplus production at a profit, or if they leave a proportion of the population without employment and incomes with which to buy their basic needs. Extension staff, therefore, must also be aware of the need to create infrastructure and promote techniques which will generate increased employment, so that the benefits of development can be enjoyed by all the population of their Thana. As educated people and as Extension specialists, it is their duty to draw the attention of members of Union Councils, Thana Councils and cooperative societies to this important objective of agricultural development planning.

Increased agricultural production must not be obtained by over-exploiting soil or water resources, thereby depriving future generations of their means of livelihood. Nor must it be achieved by depriving inhabitants of other areas of their means of livelihood. Therefore, those responsible for preparing and implementing agricultural development plans must be aware of the basic principles of land use planning (described in Chapter 11).

23.2 RESPONSIBILITIES

23.2.1 Outline

The Thana planning system involves responsibilities of different kinds for institutions and officials at different levels. In brief:

a. Thana and Union Councils direct Thana and Union technical officials to prepare and revise plans; they review plans at their own levels; and they implement plans approved by the District Council.

b. Technical officials at Union and Thana levels draft Union and Thana plans, and assist the Union and Thana Councils to implement the plans.

c. Technical officials at District level provide technical support to Thana officials and, as members of the District Agricultural Development Committee, they review Thana agricultural development plans.

23.2.2 Local government councils[2]

The Thana Council has overall responsibility for preparing and implementing the Thana agricultural development plan. Specifically, the Thana Council:

a. directs the Thana Agricultural Extension Officer (TEO) to prepare or revise the Thana agricultural development plan;

b. reviews Union agricultural development plans, particularly to ensure that the proposals of the individual Unions do not conflict with the proposals of other Unions or with their established land and water rights, and to reconcile any conflicts which may arise in those respects;

c. incorporates approved portions of the Union plans into the Thana plan;

d. reviews the draft Thana agricultural development plan prepared by the TEO; if necessary, it requests the TEO to amend parts of the draft plan and resubmit the plan for review;

---

[2] *The development responsibilities of Thana and Union Councils were subsequently greatly reduced.*

e. forwards the approved draft Thana agricultural development plan to the District Council for review and approval;

f. implements the plan approved by the District Council;

g. informs Union Councils of the schemes approved within their respective agricultural development plans and transmits funds for their implementation;

h. ensures regular monitoring and review of the progress of implementation of the Thana plan and of the Union plans which form a part of it; and

i. makes any revisions in the plan made necessary by natural disasters and delays in implementation of the plan.

The Union Council has overall responsibility for preparing and implementing the Union agricultural development plan. Specifically, the Union Council:

a. directs the Agricultural Block Supervisor (BS) to prepare or revise the Union agricultural development plan;

b. reviews the draft Union agricultural development plan and reconciles any conflicts which may exist between schemes prepared for different areas or villages within the Union; if necessary, the Council directs the BS to amend portions of the draft plan and resubmit the plan for review and approval;

c. forwards the draft Union plan to the Thana Council for review and approval;

d. implements the plan approved by the Thana and District Councils;

e. ensures regular monitoring and review of the progress of implementation of the plan; and

f. makes any revisions in the plan made necessary by natural disasters and delays in implementation of the plan.

The District Council has three main responsibilities in agricultural development planning, viz.

a. through the District Agricultural Development Committee, it ensures that individual Thana plans do not conflict with the plans of other Thanas (including those in other Districts), particularly in respect of water use;

b. it reviews and approves Thana plans and sanctions the release of funds for approved schemes within Thana plans; and

c. it monitors and evaluates the progress of individual Thana plans through a system of regular monitoring, accounting and audit.

23.2.3 Government officials[3]

The Thana Agricultural Extension Officer is the technical officer responsible for drafting and, if necessary, revising the Thana agricultural development plan and for organizing the technical support needed to implement the plan. Specifically, the TEO;

a. compiles the technical information needed for preparing Union and Thana agricultural development plans;

---

[3] *Responsibilities allocated to BADC Thana Irrigation Officers and Executive Engineers in the original manual have been omitted in view of the subsequent handing over of small-scale irrigation to the private sector. Some of the responsibilities of these officials have been added to those of Thana and District Agricultural Extension officials, where relevant.*

b. assists his Block Supervisors to prepare their Union agricultural development plans;

c. coordinates the activities of those technical officers at Thana level who are involved in providing information for the preparation or revision of the Thana plan, or who are responsible for implementing one or more components of the plan;

d. submits the draft Thana agricultural development plan to the Thana Council;

e. assists the Thana Council in implementing the approved plan;

f. through a system of regular inspection and reporting by officials under his control, monitors and evaluates the progress of implementation of the plan, and reports his findings and recommendations to the Thana Council and to his Deputy Director of Agriculture;

g. recommends to the Thana Council any revisions of the plan made necessary by natural disasters and delays in implementation; and

h. in addition, reviews applications to the Thana Council for the siting of small-scale irrigation equipment to ensure that the equipment requested is suitable for the location, that an adequate supply of water is available to operate the equipment for the season and crops specified in the application, and that the relevant BS has certified that the proposed site is suitable for the declared purpose.[4]

The Block Supervisor is the technical official responsible for assisting the Union Council to prepare and implement the Union agricultural development plan. Specifically, the BS:

a. with the assistance of the TEO, prepares the draft Union agricultural development plan and submits this to the Union Council; if necessary, he also prepares revised drafts, as directed by the Union Council;

b. assists the Union Council to implement approved plans;

c. assists the Union Council to monitor and evaluate the progress of implementation of the plan, and to make any revisions made necessary by natural disasters or other factors which may delay implementation;

d. reports regularly to the Union Council and to his TEO on activities carried out in support of plan preparation and implementation; and

e. at the request of the Union Council, physically inspects sites for which applications have been made to the Council for placing irrigation equipment, and certifies on the application form whether or not the selected site has suitable relief and soils for the proposed kind of equipment to irrigate the minimum area of land specified for that kind of equipment.[5]

The Thana Subject Matter Specialist (SMS), under the direction of the TEO:

a. assists the TEO to prepare the draft Thana agricultural development plan;

---

[4] *Although not referred to specifically in the original document, the TEO is also responsible for preparing the Thana contingency plan against natural disasters. The TEO's responsibilities in this respect are described in Annexe 4 to this chapter.*

[5] *In 1983, low-lift pumps and tubewells for irrigation were still mainly provided by Government. Sales of irrigation equipment were subsequently privatized. Approval for siting irrigation equipment still deserves to be approved by local councils in order to avoid conflicts over water use and over-exploitation of water resources. Guidelines for the siting of irrigation equipment are given in Annexe 1.*

b. gives technical support to the work of BSs by directly solving technical problems which they report or by referring the problems to District SMSs for solution; and

c. organizes the training of BSs and farmers in subjects relating to plan implementation.

The District Deputy Director of Agriculture (DDA) is responsible for organizing, coordinating, monitoring and evaluating all Government agricultural services in the District. In relation to Thana agricultural development plans, he is responsible for:

a. giving necessary technical support to TEOs in the preparation and implementation of their Thana agricultural development plans;

b. as a member of the District Agricultural Development Committee, reviewing Thana agricultural development plans and recommending to the District Council whether individual Thana plans are technically sound and satisfy national agricultural development objectives or, if not, what amendments are needed to make them acceptable;

c. ensuring that a regular system of inspection, monitoring, evaluation and reporting of the activities of TEOs and their staff is followed;

d. obtaining information from BWDB on surface-water and groundwater supplies available for irrigation in the District and supplying relevant information to TEOs; and

e. recommending to the District Agricultural Development Committee how permits for the use of available water supplies should be allocated between Thanas.

23.3 CROP SUITABILITY MAPS[6]

23.3.1 Introduction

The preparation of crop suitability maps and tables is the responsibility of the TEO. This task is the essential first step required for drafting the Thana agricultural development plan.

As described step by step below, the method may appear long and tedious. In reality, the method is logical and simple. With a little practice, the TEO should be able to prepare all the required maps and tables within a few days.

23.3.2 Verification of soil survey report

First, the TEO requests his DDA to verify that the information on soils and crop suitability given in the Thana soil survey report is up-to-date.[7] The DDA will consult the nearest office of SRDI to obtain the required information. If the information is considered up-to-date, the DDA will inform the TEO accordingly.

If the soil survey information is not considered up-to-date — e.g., because of changes caused by river-bank erosion, formation of new char land, implementation of new flood

---

[6] *The original manual was prepared before computers came into widespread use. The crop suitability maps described in this section could more easily be made today using Geographical Information Systems (GIS) technology.*

[7] *The Thana soil survey reports referred to in this chapter are those prepared by SRDI in the early 1980s from District/Subdivision reconnaissance soil survey reports. Subsequently, SRDI carried out semi-detailed soil surveys of many Thanas. The method described in this chapter would need slight modification to suit the information given in the new Thana reports.*

protection or drainage projects, etc. — the DDA will request the SRDI office to provide up-dated maps and crop suitability tables as soon as possible. On receipt of these, the DDA will transmit the revised information to the TEO.

23.3.3 Preparation of base map

Simultaneously with Step 23.3.2, the TEO will up-date information given on the 1 inch = 1 mile Thana map. Many of these maps are quite old, and information on roads, rivers, Union boundaries, etc., is sometimes out-of-date. It is essential for development planning that this information be brought up-to-date.

The TEO will collect the following kinds of information by consulting his colleagues at Thana and Union level, as well as Thana and Union Council members:

a. new settlements, factories, etc.;

b. present position of rivers, khals, etc.;

c. flood-protection embankments, sluices, pump stations, etc.;

d. roads of various categories;

e. railways;

f. bridges, ferries, markets, etc.;

g. any other infrastructure considered relevant for development planning.

The TEO will make field visits, where necessary, to verify the information. He will record the new information on the Thana map by means of the conventional signs given in the relevant chapter of the Thana Plan Book. He should make a large number of copies of this map. Individual copies of the map will be needed for each major crop suitable for cultivation, for showing irrigation potential, and for showing 5-year and annual development plans.

In the same way, the TEO will also up-date the information shown on the Union maps and make copies on which to show information for Union development planning: see Sections 23.5 and 23.6.

23.3.4 Transfer of soil boundaries

Examine the soil associations map in the Thana soil survey report to find out whether the scale is 1 inch = 1 mile or 1:125,000 (= approximately 1 inch = 2 miles).

If the soil associations map is on the 1-inch scale, copy the soil association boundaries directly onto a copy of the Thana map (which is on the 1-inch scale).

If the soil associations map is on the 1:125,000 scale, the soil association boundaries must be enlarged to fit the scale of the Thana map. Use the following simple method to make this enlargement.

a. Draw a grid of ¼-inch squares in pencil on the soil associations map (or, preferably, on a tracing of that map). Strengthen the vertical and horizontal lines at 1-inch intervals.

b. Draw a grid of ½-inch squares on the Thana map. Make sure that the lines at the bottom and left sides represent the same position on the map as the bottom and left-side lines do on the soil associations map. Strengthen the vertical and horizontal lines at 2-inch intervals.

c. For the squares on the soil associations map through which soil boundaries pass, transfer details of those boundaries to the equivalent squares on the Thana map: i.e., keep the shape of the boundary and its relative position in the squares the same, but increase the size by two.[8]

d. Copy the soil association numbers into each unit on the new Thana map.

e. Use an orange pencil or ink to show the transferred soil boundaries and numbers clearly.

f. Erase the pencil grid lines on the Thana map (if the original map was used).

The transfer of soil boundaries must be done carefully. Errors made at this stage can lead to mistakes being made in the preparation of the agricultural development plan. Therefore, carefully check the work to ensure that the soil boundaries drawn on the Thana map truly represent the boundaries given on the original soil map.

23.3.5 Crop suitability tables

The crop suitability tables given in the Thana soil survey report give ratings for a wide range of crops for each soil series and phase occurring in the Thana. The rating numbers have the following meanings:

1 = the crop is well suited for cultivation on the soil.

2 = the crop is moderately well suited for cultivation on the soil.

3 = the crop is poorly suited (or marginal) for cultivation on the soil.

4 = the crop is unsuitable for cultivation on the soil.

The ratings given refer to 'normal' conditions of weather, flooding and cultivation. In exceptionally wet or dry years, or in years with exceptionally high floods, crops may be damaged or give low yields on soils that are rated 1 or 2. Similarly, soils rated 3 (or even 4) may be capable of producing satisfactory yields if intensive methods of cultivation are used: e.g., cultivating wheat on ridges and irrigating by hand, as is practised on impermeable Barind Tract soils near Bogra which are rated 3 for the usual methods of growing wheat.

It is also important to realize that the ratings given in the crop suitability tables refer to each crop considered independently of other crops. However, the cultivation of some crops would prevent some other crops from being grown on the same land. This is obvious in the case of, say, aus and jute: if aus is grown, jute cannot be grown on the same piece of land in the same year, but aus could be grown in one year and jute in another year if the farmer wished to grow both crops. A similar situation exists in the case of wheat and, say, rabi pulses. A choice has to be made between the seasonal crops which are suitable on the same kinds of land and soil.

A more difficult case to deal with is where the cultivation of one crop would compete with the cultivation of a crop grown in another season. For example, a soil may be rated as suitable for both HYV aus and HYV aman under rainfed conditions, but it may not be practical to grow HYV aman after HYV aus in western Districts where the

---

[8] *If a boundary is complex in any place, or if the TEO does not feel confident about using the method, the size of the grid can be reduced to 1/10-inch on the soil map and 1/5-inch on the Thana map.*

rainy season is too short for the HYV aus-HYV aman rotation. Therefore, a choice has to be made to grow *either* HYV aus *or* HYV aman. For the crop not selected, the crop suitability rating effectively becomes 4 (unsuitable) if the farmer wishes to grow the other crop.

Crop competition must be taken into account, therefore, when using crop suitability tables and maps for preparing agricultural development plans. For the major crops to be included in development plans, the plans must be made on the basis of rotations actually or likely to be used in the area. For example, if it is planned to expand the HYV aus area, then the area under local aus varieties and jute may need to be reduced; and if HYV aus and HYV aman cannot be grown in rotation in the Thana, then land should be allocated either to HYV aus or to HYV aman, but not counted twice, (though it should be kept in mind that it might be possible to grow a local aman variety after HYV aus). Close contact with progressive farmers will help to keep development plans realistic.

It must also be kept in mind that the release of new crop varieties may change the present suitability ratings. For example, the release of cold-tolerant paddy HYVs might make some soils in the Sylhet haors suitable for HYV boro which presently are rated 4 for this crop (but 1 or 2 for local boro varieties, which are cold-tolerant). Also, the release of a photoperiod-sensitive HYV aman in future might enable rainfed HYV aus and HYV aman to be grown in rotation on soils in western Districts where, with existing HYVs of aman, a choice has to be made between HYV aus and HYV aman. TEOs must keep themselves up-to-date with such changes through Subject Matter Specialists. Ideally, the latter should sit with the District officers of SRDI to prepare, jointly, a crop suitability table for the District for each new variety which is released, including ratings for crop rotations in which the new variety may fit.

The following sections describe how to prepare crop suitability tables from the information given in the Thana soil survey report, how to prepare crop suitability maps, and how to prepare crop rotation suitability tables and maps.

23.3.6 A. How to prepare crop suitability tables

Step A1. Prepare a table, using Table 23.1 as a model for the layout of columns and headings.[9]

Step A2. Write the title at the top of the table. Use separate tables for irrigated and non-irrigated conditions.

Step A3. In columns 1 and 2 of the table, make a list of the soil series, soil phases and land types in each soil association described in the Thana soil survey report. Write only the soil association numbers in column 1; do not write the names of the associations. Write the names of the soil series, soil phases and land types in column 2. Write 'Total' at the bottom of column 2 for each soil association before starting on the next soil association. See Table 23.1 for spacing.

Step A4. In column 3, write the proportion (%) of each soil association which the individual soils occupy, as given in the soil association tables.

[9] *The examples given in Tables 23.1 to 23.6, 23.10 and 23.11 were derived from the reconnaissance soil survey report on Comilla Kotwali Thana. Only five of the 11 soil associations occurring in that Thana have been included in the tables, as examples. The soil associations map of Comilla Kotwali Thana is reproduced (on a smaller scale) in Figure 23.1. This figure (and Figure 23.2) were not included in the original manual.*

Step A5. For each soil association, write the total area of the association at the bottom of column 4.[10] The area is given at the top of each soil association table in the soil survey report, either in acres or in square miles.

   a. If the figure is given in square miles, convert to acres by multiplying the figure by 640.

   b. If the figure is to be converted to hectares:

      i. multiply the figure for square miles by 256; or

      ii. divide the figure in acres by 2.5.

Step A6. Calculate the area which each soil series occupies in each soil association. To do this, multiply the total area of the soil association given in column 4 by the percentage of the association which each soil occupies. For example, in Table 23.1, the total area of soil association 1 is shown as 7,710 acres, and the proportion which Kotbari series occupies is given as 25 percent. Therefore, multiply 7,710 acres by 25 and divide by 100 to obtain the area of Kotbari soils in the association (1,928 acres). Make these calculations for all the soils in every association, and write the area against each soil name in column 4: see Table 23.1.

Step A7.

   a. Turn to the appropriate crop suitability table in the soil survey report: i.e, without irrigation, or with irrigation. See Table 23.2.[11]

   b. Select the crops of interest for inclusion in the Thana agricultural development plan.

   c. Write the names of the selected crops at the tops of the columns from 5 onward, as shown in Table 23.1. Make additional columns, if necessary, on a separate sheet. Remember to place crops under irrigated and non-irrigated conditions on separate tables.

Step A8. For each soil listed in column 2, find out the crop suitability rating of each crop shown at the tops of columns 5 onward. Write this rating number (or symbol) on the left side of the column, under 'Rating': see Table 23.1.

Step A9. Soils rated 1 or 2 can be considered suitable for the crop. Therefore:

   a. for each soil rated 1 or 2, write the area of the soil on the right side of the column; (take the area figure from column 4);

   b. for each soil rated 3 or 4 (or if some other symbol is used), write a dash (-) in the area column. See Table 23.1.

Step A10. For each soil association, add up the area figures given in each crop column. Write the total at the bottom of the column. The latter figure shows the gross area suitable for the crop in the soil association.

Step A11. For each crop, add up the total figures calculated in Step A10 to provide the grand total area suitable for the crop in the Thana. Write these figures at the bottom of the respective crop columns; (not shown in Table 23.1, which gives data for only a part of the Thana.

Step A12. For each crop, calculate the percentage of each soil association which is suitable for the crop. Do this by either:

   a. adding up the relevant percentage figures given in column 4 for the soils for which crops are rated 1 or 2; or

---

[10]*If hectares are used, be careful to be consistent in the use of hectares throughout the preparation of the development plan.*

[11]*Table 23.2 did not appear in the original manual. It has been added here for readers' convenience.*

TABLE 23.1

Gross area suitable for selected crops, without irrigation

(1) Soil assoc.	(2) Name	(3) %	(4) Acres	(5) B.aus (LV)		(6) T.aus (HYV)		(7) T.aman (LV)		(8) T.aman (HYV)		(9) HYV wheat		(10) Fruit trees	
	Series, phase, land type			Rating	Acres	Rating	Acres	Rating	Acres	Rating	Acres	Rating	Acres	Rating	Acres
1	Kamuri-L[1]	12.5	963	2	963	4	-	4	-	4	-	4	-	2	963
	A -R	13.5	964	4	-	4	-	4	-	4	-	4	-	3	-
	Lalmai	27	2,082	4	-	4	-	4	-	4	-	4	-	4	-
	Khadimnagar	18	1,388	4	-	4	-	4	-	4	-	4	-	4	-
	Salban	3	231	3	-	4	-	4	-	4	-	4	-	3	-
	Kotbari	25	1,928	2	1,928	3	-	2	1,928	3	-	3	-	4	-
	Settlement + water	2	154												
	Total		**7,710**	**(37.5%)**	**2,891**	**(0%)**	**-**	**(25%)**	**1,928**	**(0%)**	**-**	**(0%)**	**-**	**(12.5%)**	**963**
2	Sankochail	60	2,115	4	-	4	-	4	-	4	-	4	-	3	-
	Kharrera	15	529	4	-	4	-	4	-	4	-	4	-	3	-
	Pritimpasa[2]	3	106	2	106	2	106	1	106	2	106	3	-	4	-
	Rangari	5	176	2	176	1	176	1	176	2	176	3	-	4	-
	Tarapur	2	70	2	70	2	70	2	70	3	-	2	70	4	-
	Bharella-MH[2]	10	353	2	353	1	353	1	353	1	353	3	-	4	-
	Settlement + water	5	176												
	Total		**3,525**	**(20%)**	**705**	**(10%)**	**705**	**(20%)**	**705**	**(18%)**	**635**	**(2%)**	**70**	**(0%)**	**-**

(Contd.)

(Continued)

(1) Soil assoc.	(2) Name	(3) %	(4) Acres	(5) B.aus (LV) Rating	Acres	(6) T.aus (HYV) Rating	Acres	(7) T.aman (LV) Rating	Acres	(8) T.aman (HYV) Rating	Acres	(9) HYV wheat Rating	Acres	(10) Fruit trees Rating	Acres
3	Sankochail	2	148	4	–	4	–	4	–	4	–	4	–	3	–
	Bijipur	2	148	2	148	4	–	2	148	2	148	3	–	4	–
	Pritimpasa-H³	2	148	2	148	2	148	1	148	2	148	3	–	4	–
	Rangari	22	1,628	2	1,628	1	1,628	1	1,628	2	1,628	3	–	4	–
	Bharella-MH	28	2,072	2	2,072	1	2,072	1	2,072	1	2,072	3	–	4	–
	Chakla-MH⁴	11	814	3	–	3	–	2	814	4	–	4	–	4	–
	A -ML	11	814	3	–	3	–	4	–	4	–	4	–	4	–
	Settlement + water	22	1,628												
	Total		**7,400**	**(54%)**	**3,996**	**(52%)**	**3,848**	**(65%)**	**4,810**	**(54%)**	**3,996**	**(0%)**	**–**	**(0%)**	**–**
5	Rangari	10	903	2	903	1	903	1	903	2	903	3	–	4	–
	Tarapur	5	451	2	451	2	451	2	451	3	–	2	451	4	–
	Bharella-MH²	60	5,415	1	5,415	1	5,415	1	5,415	1	5,415	3	–	4	–
	Debidwar-MH⁴	5	451	2	451	1	451	2	451	3	–	2	451	4	–
	A -ML	5	451	2	451	4	–	4	–	4	–	2	451	4	–
	Settlement + water	15	1,354												
	Total		**9,025**	**(85%)**	**7,671**	**(80%)**	**7,220**	**(80%)**	**7,220**	**(70%)**	**6,318**	**(15%)**	**1,353**	**(0%)**	**–**

(Contd.)

438   *Land Use and Land Use Planning in Bangladesh*

(1) Soil assoc.	(2) Name	(3) %	(4) Acres	(5) B.aus (LV)		(6) T.aus (HYV)		(7) T.aman (LV)		(8) T.aman (HYV)		(9) HYV wheat		(10) Fruit trees	
				Rating	Acres	Rating	Acres	Rating	Acres	Rating	Acres	Rating	Acres	Rating	Acres
6	Lalmai	3	218	4	–	4	–	4	–	4	–	4	–	4	–
	Salban	3	218	3	–	4	–	4	–	4	–	4	–	3	–
	Bijipur	25	1,816	2	1,816	4	–	2	–	2	1,816	3	–	4	–
	Tarapur	5	363	2	363	2	363	2	363	3	–	2	363	4	–
	Bharella-MH[2]	40	2,906	2	2,906	1	2,906	1	2,906	1	2,906	3	–	4	–
	Olipur	7	509	4	–	2	509	1	509	3	–	4	–	4	–
	Settlement + water	17	1,235		–		–		–		–		–		–
	Total		7,265	(70%)	5,085	(52%)	3,778	(77%)	5,594	(65%)	4,722	(5%)	363	(0%)	–

Notes:
1. Level and rolling phases were differentiated in the Comilla District soil survey report, but the proportions were not given. Half the area has arbitrarily been allocated to each phase.
2. Medium Highland phase inferred from depth of flooding described in the report.
3. Highland phase inferred from relief position described in the report.
4. Chakla and Debidwar series are described in the Comilla District report as being flooded 2-4 feet deep: i.e., overlapping Medium Highland and Medium Lowland. Half the area has arbitrarily been allocated to each phase.

TABLE 23.2

Crop suitability ratings of soil series and phases in Comilla Kotwali Thana[1]

Soil series, phase	Crop suitability rating[2]																	
	Wetland crops					Annual dryland crops							Perennial dryland crops					
	Aus	Broadcast aman[3]	Transplanted aman	Boro	Jute	Wheat	Millet	Chilli	Pulses	Tobacco	Vegetables	Oilseeds	Sugarcane	Banana	Pineapple	Citrus	Betel nut	Coconut
Bharella, MH	2	*	2	1	3	1	2	2	2	2	2	2	3	4	4	4	4	4
Bijipur	2	*	2	3	2	2	1	1	1	1	1	1	3	4	4	4	4	4
Chakla, MH	3	*	2	1	3	4	4	3	3	4	4	3	4	4	4	4	4	4
, ML	3	2	4	1	3	4	4	4	4	4	4	4	4	4	4	4	4	4
Debidwar, MH	1	*	3	1	2	1	2	2	2	2	2	2	4	4	4	4	4	4
, ML	2	1	4	1	2	2	2	3	3	3	3	3	4	4	3	4	4	4
Kamuri	3	4	4	4	4	4	4	4	3	4	4	4	4	4	4	4	4	4
Khadimnagar	4	4	4	4	4	4	4	4	4	4	4	4	4	4	3	4	4	4
Kharerra	4	4	4	4	4	4	4	4	4	4	4	4	4	4	4	4	4	4
Kotbari	2	*	2	3	3	4	3	3	3	4	4	3	4	4	4	4	4	4
Lalmai	4	4	4	4	4	4	4	4	4	4	4	4	4	4	4	4	4	4
Olipur	1	*	1	1	4	4	4	4	4	4	4	4	4	4	4	4	4	4
Pritimpasa, H	2	*	1	3	3	3	3	3	3	4	4	3	4	4	4	4	4	4
, MH	2	*	2	3	3	3	3	3	3	3	3	2	4	4	4	4	4	4
Rangari	2	*	4	4	3	4	4	2	2	2	2	4	3	4	4	4	4	4
Salban	3	*	4	4	4	4	4	4	4	4	4	4	4	4	3	3	4	4
Sankochail	4	*	4	4	4	4	4	4	4	4	4	4	4	4	3	3	4	4
Tarapur	3	2	4	4	4	4	4	4	4	4	4	4	4	4	4	4	4	4

Notes: 1. Extracted from the Reconnaissance Soil Survey Report of Noakhali District and Sadar North and South Subdivisions of Comilla District (SRDI, 1970). The ratings were made before HYVs of paddy and wheat came into general use.

2. Dry-season irrigation is assumed for boro paddy, wheat and vegetables. Without irrigation, most soils rated 1 or 2 for those crops would be rated 3 or 4.

3. For broadcast aman, * = not rated for soils that are not deeply or moderately deeply flooded.

b. multiplying the area suitable for the crop in the association by 100, then dividing this figure by the total area of the soil association (given at the bottom of column 4).

Write this percentage figure in brackets at the bottom of the relevant crop column for each soil association. Double check these calculations. It is important that they be correct, because these figures will be used in making the crop suitability maps at a later stage.

Step A13. Make an abstract table showing the percentage and area in each soil association which are suitable for each of the selected crops: see the example given in Table 23.3. Take these figures from the bottom line of the relevant columns in each soil association. These figures will be used in preparing the gross crop suitability maps: see the example given in Table 23.3.

Step A14. Add up the column figures in the abstract table to give the gross area which is suitable for each of the selected crops in the Thana.

Step A15. After the table 'without irrigation' has been completed, prepare a similar table for crop suitability 'with irrigation'.

23.3.7   B. How to prepare crop suitability maps

For each crop included in the tables prepared in Section A above, make a map showing the proportion of each soil association which is considered suitable for the crop under the condition specified (i.e., either without irrigation or with irrigation). Each map will show two kinds of information:

a. the map itself, coloured to show the relative suitability of each soil association for the crop in broad percentage suitability classes; and

b. a table showing the actual area and percentage suitable for the crop in each soil association.

The method for making these maps is described step by step below.

Step B1. For each of the selected crops, take (or make) a copy of the Thana soil map referred to in Section 23.3.2 above. Leave sufficient space at the bottom or on one side of the map for placing a table showing the area suitable for the crop in each soil association (see Steps B3-4) and the legend (see Step B8).

Step B2. Write the title of the map in a suitable position at the top of the map: e.g.,

> **CROP SUITABILITY**
> **HYV Aman – with irrigation**

Step B3. For each crop suitability map, prepare a table listing:

a. the soil association numbers;

b. the percentage of each soil association suitable for the crop; and

c. the area suitable for the crop in each soil association.

Take these figures from the table prepared in Steps A13-15. See Table 23.4.

Step B4. Write this table in a convenient place at the bottom or on one side of the map.

Step B5. Decide on the number and range of the suitability percentage classes to be represented on the map. Usually, it will be best to show not more than five or six classes: see Table 23.5. In cases where it is considered that these classes do not show differences

TABLE 23.3

Gross area suitable for selected crops without irrigation (abstract)

Soil assoc.	Acres	B.aus (LV)		T.aus (HYV)		T.aman (LV)		T.aman (HYV)		Wheat		Fruit trees	
		%	Acres	%	Acres	%	Acres	%	Acres	%	Acres	%	Acres
1	7,710	37.5	2,891	0	-	25	1,928	0	-	0	-	12.5	963
2	3,525	20	705	10	352	20	705	18	635	2	70	0	-
4	7,400	54	3,996	52	3,848	65	4,810	54	3,996	0	-	0	-
5	9,025	85	7,671	80	7,220	80	7,220	70	6,318	15	1,353	0	-
6	7,265	70	5,085	52	3,778	77	5,594	65	4,722	5	363	0	-
etc.													
Grand total													

TABLE 23.4

*Comilla Kotwali Thana: area and proportion of soil associations suitable for HYV aman,
without irrigation*

Soil association	Suitable %	Gross area (Acres)
1	-	0
2	18	635
4	54	3,996
5	70	6,318
6	65	4,722
7	22	195
10	37	8,201
21	42	1,267
23	27	332
26	39	867
33	26	5
Total	**39**	**26,538**

TABLE 23.5

Examples of crop suitability percentage classes

4 classes	5 classes	6 classes
Less than 10%	Less than 5%	Less than 5%
10-24%	5-24%	5-19%
25-49%	25-49%	20-39%
50% or more	50-74%	40-59%
	75% or more	60-79%
		80% or more

between areas satisfactorily, other class ranges can be used. Preferably, however, the same class ranges should be used for all the crop suitability maps in the Thana, in order to avoid confusion.

Step B6. Decide on a suitable colour scheme for the crop suitability classes. Use the same colour scheme for all the crop suitability maps. A suitable colour scheme is to use the sequence of colours in the rainbow, using red for the lowest class, orange for the next lowest class, then yellow, followed by green, blue and, if necessary purple. In order to avoid possible confusion, do not colour rivers, beels, etc., blue; leave such areas without colour on the map.[12]

Step B7. On each crop suitability map, colour each soil association according to the classification scheme decided on in Steps B5 and B6. For example, if it is decided to use six classes, the soil associations listed in Table 23.4 would be coloured as is shown in Table 23.6 for non-irrigated HYV transplanted aman.

---

[12]*In the example given in Figure 23.2, a black-and-white shading system has been substituted for the colours suggested to indicate class differences.*

TABLE 23.6
Example of crop suitability class colour scheme

Soil association	% suitable for HYV t.aman	Class (%)	Colour
1	0	<5	Red
2	18	5-19	Orange
4	54	40-59	Green
5	70	60-79	Blue
6	65	60-79	Blue
7	22	20-39	Yellow
10	37	20-39	Yellow
21	42	40-59	Green
23	27	20-39	Yellow
26	39	20-39	Yellow
33	26	20-39	Yellow

Step B8. Write a legend at a convenient place on each map to explain what the colours mean: see the example given in Figure 23.2.

Step B9. Make as many copies of each map as may be needed for use in preparing the Thana agricultural development plan, for inclusion in the Thana Plan Book, for distribution to the Thana Council and other Thana offices, and for display in the Thana Extension Office.

Step B10. For display purposes, it can be useful to place a set of maps side by side so as to show the differences between soil associations in their suitability for selected crops. It may be particularly interesting to show differences between crop suitability under irrigated and non-irrigated conditions.

However, the Thana map scale may be too big for this purpose, except for large displays at an exhibition. Usually, it will be necessary to reduce the scale of the crop suitability maps prepared on the Thana map scale. If so, decide whether to reduce the Thana map to that of the 1:125,000 scale used in the Thana soil survey report or to 1:250,000 scale. If the soil survey map scale is to be used, make the required number of copies of this map. If necessary, draw two (or four) copies of the map on one piece of paper, so that one completed map can easily be compared with another: (e.g., suitability under irrigated and non-irrigated conditions). Leave enough space around each map for placing the map title, legend and crop suitability table.

Decide which maps should be shown side-by-side. Then copy the information from the relevant crop suitability maps prepared in previous steps. Use the same title, colour scheme, legend and crop suitability table as on the original crop suitability map. Alternatively, make a single colour legend for all the maps shown on a single sheet, together with a table combining the information given in the tables shown on the individual maps: i.e., showing the proportions and areas of the crops in separate columns, as shown in the example given in Table 23.7.

Step B11. In order to make a base map on a smaller scale, use the method of squares similar to that described in Section 23.3.4, viz.

   a. First, draw a grid of ½-inch squares on the soil associations map (1:125,000 scale). If the boundaries are complex, use a 2/10th-inch grid.

FIGURE 23.1

Comilla Kotwali Thana soil associations

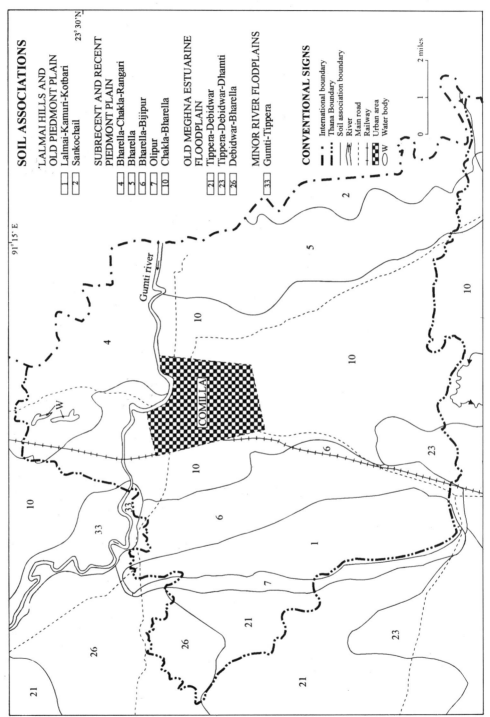

FIGURE 23.2

Comilla Kotwali Thana: suitability of soil associations for HYV aman

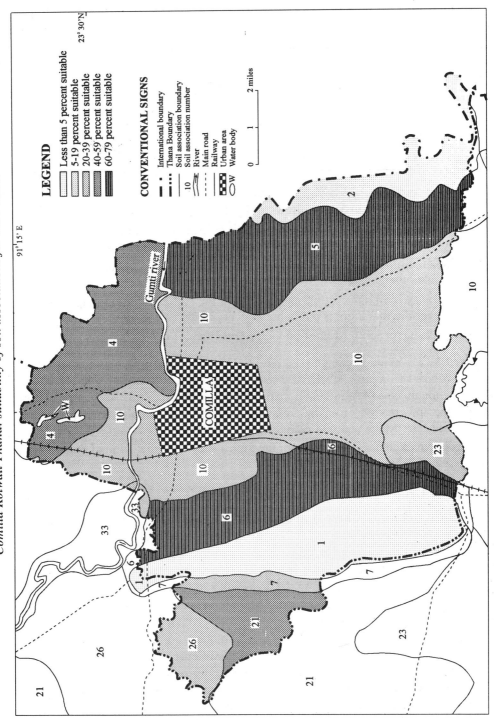

TABLE 23.7
Example of crop suitability map table

Soil association	Acres	Rainfed HYV aus		Rainfed HYV aman	
		% suitable	Acres	% suitable	Acres
1	7,710	0	0	0	0
2	3,525	10	352	18	635
4	7,400	52	3,848	54	3,996
5	9,025	80	7,220	70	6,318
6	7,265	52	3,778	65	4,722
etc.					
Grand total					

b. Next, draw a grid of ¼-inch squares on a suitable piece of paper. (If a 2/10th-inch grid was drawn in Step a, draw a grid of 1/10th-inch squares.)

c. Draw the Thana boundary and the soil association boundaries on the new small map by copying details from equivalent squares on the bigger map.

d. When all the boundaries have been transferred and checked, use orange pencil or ink to mark them clearly.

e. Copy the soil association numbers from the soil association map onto the new map. Make sure that there is a number in every unit.

f. Erase the pencil grid lines on the original map, if necessary.

Step B12. Decide which crop suitability maps should be placed together for comparison. Draw copies of the new small base map side-by-side on a piece of paper of suitable size. Leave enough space around each map for placing the map title and crop suitability tables. Copy the information from the relevant original crop suitability maps, using the same colour scheme. Make a single colour legend for all the maps, and a single table combining the crop percentages and areas from the tables shown on the original crop suitability maps, as described in Step B10 above.

23.3.8 C. Crop rotation suitability

The tables and maps prepared in Sections 23.3.6 and 23.3.7 show the suitability of crops considered independently of each other. However, in most parts of Bangladesh, crops normally form part of double-crop or triple-crop rotations, so each crop must be considered in relation to the crops which may precede or follow it in rotations. Therefore, it is desirable to make tables and maps showing the areas suitable for the most important rotations actually or likely to be practised in the Thana. The method is described below.

Step C1. Make a list of the main crop rotations which occur in the Thana, or which might be introduced if new crops, varieties or techniques (e.g., irrigation) are introduced. Make separate lists for irrigated and non-irrigated conditions.

For some crops, it may be necessary to consider rotations of crop varieties or groups of varieties. For example, the following rotations could be considered for non-irrigated conditions on soils that are not suitable for dryland rabi crops if transplanted aman is grown:

   local b. aus - local t.aman

   local b.aus - late HYV aman (e.g., BR10, BR11)

quick-maturing HYV aus - local t. aman

quick-maturing HYV t.aus - late HYV t. aman

long-maturing HYV aus - local t. aman.

It may also be useful to include some rotations which are not practical or suitable in the Thana, so as to make it clear to users that they have been considered: e.g.,

long-maturing HYV t.aus - long-maturing HYV t. aman.

Step C2. Make a list of all the crops, varieties and variety groups which occur in the rotations listed in Step C1: see Table 23.8.

TABLE 23.8

Selected list of important crop rotations in Comilla Kotwali Thana[1]

Kharif-1	Kharif-2	Rabi
Non-irrigated		
B.aus (LV)	T.aman (LV)	Fallow
"	" (Pajam)	"
"	Long-maturing HYV aman (BR3)	"
T.aus (LV)	Quick-maturing HYV aman (BR10,11)	"
Quick-maturing HYV t.aus	" " " " "	Wheat
" " " "	T.aman (LV)	"
Long-maturing HYV t.aus	"	"

Note: 1. This is only a partial list, selected for the purpose of demonstration only.

Step C3. Against each crop, variety or group, write the optimum and last recommended planting date and harvesting date for the Thana: see Table 23.9. It is useful for this information to be given in the form of a crop calendar: see Figure 23.3. The District Deputy Director of Agriculture (or the appropriate Subject Matter Specialist) should guide the TEO in preparing these tables and the crop calendar.

TABLE 23.9

Planting and harvesting dates of important crops in Comilla Kotwali Thana[1]

Crop	Planting date[2]		Harvesting date	
	Optimum	Latest	Optimum	Latest
Non-irrigated				
B.aus (LV)	15 April	15 May	15 July	15 August
T.aus (LV)	15 May	30 June	31 July	15 September
Quick-maturing HYV t.aus	25 May	30 June	10 August	15 September
Long-maturing HYV t.aus	25 May	15 June	25 August	15 September
T.aman (LV)	31 July	15 September	30 November	15 December
T.aman (Pajam)	31 July	31 August	30 November	15 December
Long-maturing HYV aman	15 July	15 August	1 November	30 November
Quick-maturing HYV aman	31 July	31 August	1 November	20 November
Wheat	15 November	31 December	1 March	10 April

Note: 1. These dates are not definitive. They are given for demonstration purposes only.

2. For broadcast aus, date of seeding. For transplanted aus and aman, date of transplanting.

FIGURE 23.3

Comilla Kotwali Thana: crop calendar for important crops

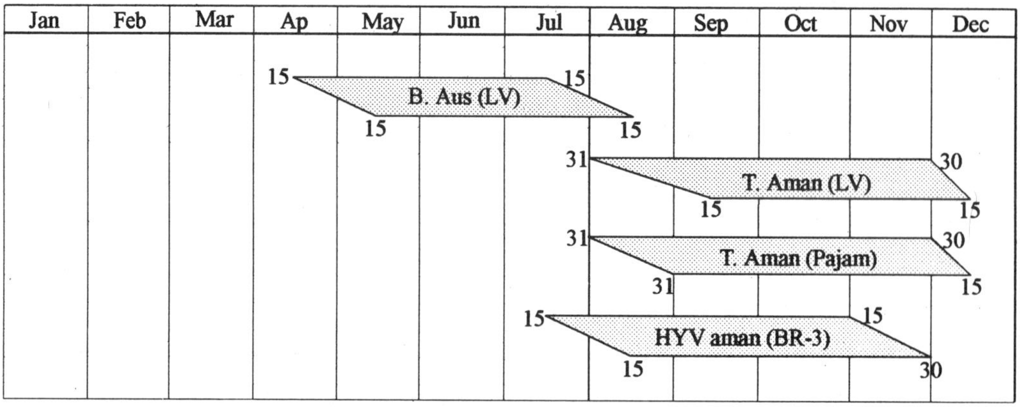

Jan	Feb	Mar	Ap	May	Jun	Jul	Aug	Sep	Oct	Nov	Dec

B. Aus (LV) — 15 (Ap) to 15 (Jul); 15 (May) to 15 (Aug)

T. Aman (LV) — 31 (Jul) to 30 (Dec); 15 (Sep) to 15 (Dec)

T. Aman (Pajam) — 31 (Jul) to 30 (Dec); 31 (Aug) to 15 (Dec)

HYV aman (BR-3) — 15 (Jul) to 15 (Nov); 15 (Aug) to 30 (Dec)

Notes
1. This is only a partial list, selected for the purpose of demonstration only.
2. These dates are not definitive. They are given for demonstration purposes only.
3. For broadcast aus, date of seeding. For transplanted aman, date of transplanting.

Step C4. Make a crop rotation suitability table. Use the lay-out shown in Table 23.10. If only a few crops are included, more than one crop rotation can be included on a single sheet, as is illustrated in Table 23.10. Separate tables must be used for irrigated and non-irrigated conditions.

Step C5. In column 1 of the suitability table, copy the names of the soil series, phases and land types given on the crop suitability tables in the Thana soil survey report.

Step C6. Count the number of individual crops included in the first rotation to be assessed, and allocate one column in the table to each crop. If another crop rotation can be accommodated on the same sheet, draw a thick double line between the last column of the first rotation and the beginning of the next rotation. Write the name of the crop rotation(s) over the respective columns. See the example given in Table 23.10.

Step C7. At the top of column 2, write 'Reference crop'. (Do the same at the top of the first column of any other rotation included on the same work sheet.) Under this heading, write the name of the first crop in the rotation and the season in which it is grown. Usually, as in the example shown in Table 23.10, this will be the first kharif crop. However, in some cases, it may be preferable to use some other main crop (e.g., t. aman or boro) as the reference crop against which to match planting and harvesting dates. If that is done, it is best to be consistent for all the crop rotation suitability tables so as to avoid confusion.

Step C8. At the tops of the following columns, write the names of the main crops (or varieties) which occur in rotation with the reference crop, together with the seasons in which they are grown. Use additional sheets, if necessary.

   a. In the case of double-crop rotations, give one column each to all the crops or varieties which occur in rotation with the reference crop: see Table 23.10, columns 3-5.

   b. For triple-crop rotations, only one of the second-season crops can be considered at a time, although more than one crop could be included in the third season, if desired: see Table 23.10, columns 7-8.

TABLE 23.10

Comilla Kotwali Thana: suitability of crop rotations, without irrigation. (Working table 1)[1]

Soil series, soil phase, land type (1)	B.aus (LV)- T.aman				Quick-maturing HYV t.aus-quick-maturing HYV aman-wheat		
	Reference crop	Other crops			Reference crop	Other crops	Rabi
	Kharif-1	Kharif-2			Kharif-1	Kharif-2	
	(2)	(3)	(4)	(5)	(6)	(7)	(8)
	B.aus (LV)	T.aman (LV)	T.aman (Pajam)	HYV aman (BR3)	Q-m HYV t.aus	Q-m HYV aman	Wheat
Hill soils							
Kamuri-L	2	4	4	4	4	4	4
" -R	4	4	4	4	4	4	4
Khadimnagar	4	4	4	4	4	4	4
Kharrera	4	4	4	4	4	4	4
Lalmai	4	4	4	4	4	4	4
Salban	3	4	4	4	4	4	4
Sankochail	4	4	4	4	4	4	4
Floodplain soils							
Bharella-MH	2	2	2	2	1	1	3
Bijipur	2	2	2	2	3	2	3
Chakla-MH	3	2	2	4	3	4	4
" -ML	3	4	4	4	3	4	4
Debidwar-MH	1	2	2	4	1	3	2
" -ML	2	4	4	4	4	4	2
Kotbari	2	2	2	2	3	3	3
Pritimpasa-H	2	1	1	2	2	2	3
" -MH	2	2	2	2	1	2	3
Olipur	4	4	4	3	2	3	4
Rangari	2	2	2	2	1	2	3
Tarapur	2	2	2	3	2	3	2

Note: 1. For demonstration purposes only. The selected soils occur in soil associations 1, 2, 4, 5 and 6 of the Comilla Kotwali Thana soil survey report.

Step C9. For the reference crop, write the crop suitability rating for each soil named in column 1. Copy this number from the crop suitability table in the Thana soil survey report.[13] Be careful to choose the proper table: 'with irrigation', or 'without irrigation'.

Step C10. For any soil rated 3 or 4 for the reference crop, immediately write the number 4 on the right side of all the other crop columns of the rotation. (If the reference crop is not suitable for the soil, then obviously the rotation is not suitable for the soil under the conditions specified.)

Step C11. Taking the second crop next, consider whether this crop (or variety) can conveniently be grown after the reference crop (or variety), taking into account:

a. the normal harvesting date of the reference crop;

b. the optimum and latest sowing or transplanting dates of the crop or variety named in the second season: use the crop calendar made in Step C3 (Figure 23.3) as a guide;

c. the need to leave two weeks' turn-around time between successive crops, unless the second crop will be relay-planted through the first crop or some other minimum-tillage practice will be used to reduce the turn-around time; and

d. whether or not the cultivation of one crop will adversely affect soil conditions for a following crop.[14]

Step C12. For those crops in column 3 which have not already been rated 4 in Step C10, copy from the crop suitability table the present suitability rating of the crop named in column 3. Write this rating on the left side of column 3.

Step C13. For those crops that have been rated 3 or 4 in Step C12, write the number 4 on the right side of column 4.

Step C14. For the remaining soils which have been rated 1 or 2 on the left side of column 3, decide whether or not this rating is still correct if the crop is grown in rotation with the reference crop, taking into account the following factors.

a. If the optimum harvesting date of the first crop leaves sufficient turn-around time for the second crop to be planted before its last planting date, copy the rating number given at the left side of column 3 on the right side of that column.

b. If the harvesting date of the first crop is too close to the last planting date of the second crop to leave a sufficient turn-around time between the crops, then write 3 or 4 on the right side of column 3:

i. write 3 if the harvesting period is within 14 days of the latest planting date for the second crop;

ii. write 4 if the harvesting date is after the latest planting date for the second crop.

c. If the first crop spoils soil conditions for sowing or planting the second crop, write 3 (or 4, if serious) on the right side of column 3.

---

[13]For any crop or variety not specifically included in the crop suitability tables in the Thana soil survey report, request the SMS to prepare new ratings in consultation with District staff of SRDI.

[14]The puddling of topsoils for transplanting paddy usually reduces the suitability of soils for a following dryland crop by at least one suitability class from the rating which the soil would have if transplanted rice were not grown. For soils traditionally used for transplanted aman, the degradation of the topsoil by puddling has usually been taken into account already by SRDI in preparing the crop suitability tables given in the Thana soil survey report.

Step C15. In double crop rotations, repeat Steps C12-C14 for each of the remaining crop columns of the rotation.

Step C16. For the third crop in triple-crop rotations, follow these steps:

a. For any soil rated 3 or 4 in the second column, write the number 4 on the right side of the third crop column. (The number 4 will already have been written for soils rated 3 or 4 for the reference crop: see Step C10.)

b. For the remaining soils, copy from the Thana crop suitability table the present suitability ratings of the third crop. Write these rating numbers on the left side of column 3.

c. Repeat Steps C12-C14 for the third crop in relation to the *second* crop (i.e., not in relation to the reference crop).

d. If there are other crops occupying third place in the rotation (e.g., rabi pulses, rabi oilseeds, etc.), repeat Steps C12-C14 for each of those crops in turn, matching each of them separately against the *second* crop (i.e., not the reference crop, and not the other crops in the third crop group).

Step C17. On completion of Steps C4-C16 for all the crop rotations — or on completion of those steps for the first one or two rotations if it is desired to see an example of the eventual end-product — make another working table (as illustrated in Table 23.11) to summarize the findings obtained so far, viz.

a. In column 1, write the names of all the soil series, phases and land types used on Table 23.10.

b. At the top of the remaining columns, write the names of all the main crop rotations. Use abbreviations instead of full names so as to save space.

In this table, the crops named in the second or the third group must be treated as separate rotations. For example, in Table 23.10, the B.aus-t.aman rotation taken together in columns 2-5 has been separated into its three component rotations in transferring the information to Table 23.11, viz.

B. aus (LV) - T. aman (LV)
     "   -   " (Pajam)
     "   -   " (BR3).

Step C18. In column 2, write the suitability rating number of the *last* crop in the rotation against each soil named in column 1, as was shown in the last column for that crop rotation in Table 23.10. In the case of double-crop or triple-crop rotations where more than one crop is included in the second or third group, write the suitability rating number given in the first column of the second (or third) group.

Step C19. Repeat Step C18 for the remaining columns of the working table until each individual crop rotation has been covered. Compare the examples given in Tables 23.10 and 23.11 to see which information is transferred from the first table to the second table.

Step C20. The table completed in Steps C18 and C19 provides a crop rotation suitability table similar to the crop suitability table given in the Thana soil survey report. It provides the basis for preparing crop rotation suitability tables for each soil association and, thereby, for making crop rotation suitability maps.

Step C21. Make crop rotation suitability tables. Use the same method as that described for making crop suitability tables in Section 23.3.6, Steps A1-A15.

TABLE 23.11

Comilla Kotwali Thana: suitability of crop rotations, without irrigation. (Working table 2)[1]

Soil series, soil phase, land type	Crop rotations			
	B.aus (LV) -TA (LV)	B.aus (LV) -TA (Pajam)	B.aus (LV) -TA (BR3)	Q-m HYV t.aus -q-m HYV aman -wheat[2]
(1)	(2)	(3)	(4)	(5)
Hill soils				
Kamuri-L	4	4	4	4
" -R	4	4	4	4
Khadimnagar	4	4	4	4
Kharrera	4	4	4	4
Lalmai	4	4	4	4
Salban	4	4	4	4
Sankochail	4	4	4	4
Floodplain soils				
Bharella-MH	2	2	2	4
Bijipur	2	2	2	4
Chakla-MH	4	4	4	4
" -ML	4	4	4	4
Debidwar-MH	2	2	4	4
" -ML	4	4	4	4
Kotbari	2	2	2	4
Pritimpasa-H	2	2	2	4
" -MH	2	2	2	4
Olipur	4	4	4	4
Rangari	2	2	2	4
Tarapur	2	2	4	4

Notes: 1. For demonstration purposes only. Information derived from Table 23.3.

2. Q-m = quick-maturing.

Step C22. Make crop rotation suitability maps. Use the same method as that described for making crop suitability maps in Section 23.3.7, Steps B1-B8.

23.4 IRRIGATION MAPS[15]

23.4.1 Introduction

The Thana irrigation maps included in the Thana Plan Book made in the 1960s show the following kinds of information:

a. the position of the surface-water which could be used for irrigation;

---

[15]*The method described below was designed for the administrative arrangements in force in 1983 when Thana Councils were responsible for approving small-scale irrigation schemes, and BADC and BKB were responsible for supplying irrigation equipment. The powers of local government were subsequently reduced, and the supply of irrigation equipment was transferred to the private sector. The method described would be suitable for use if, as seems desirable, local governments were empowered to license irrigation equipment as a means of regulating water use (and raising local taxes).*

b. the sites of existing irrigation schemes; and

c. the plans for expanding irrigation schemes during a 5-Year Plan period.[16]

In many parts of the country, sufficient information on groundwater is now available for such information to be added to Thana irrigation maps. The following sections describe the methods for making Thana irrigation maps showing both surface-water and groundwater resources available for development.[17]

Two methods are described below. Method 1 assumes that Thana and District Councils function as planning authorities. Method 2 is for conditions where local-level planning is the responsibility of central government officials.

23.4.2   Thana irrigation map 1

D. Method 1

Step D1. The Thana Agricultural Extension Officer (TEO) will prepare Irrigation Map 1 showing up-to-date information on the following items.[18]

   a. All rivers, khals, beels, etc., in the Thana, whether used for irrigation or not. Use the map symbols shown in Annexe 2 of this chapter.

   b. The position of all low-lift pumps (LLP). Use different symbols for pumps of different sizes (i.e., fractional-horsepower, 1-cusec, 2-cusec, 5-cusec, etc.).

   c. The position of all deep tube-wells (DTW). If there is more than one size of DTW, use different symbols to show the different types.

   d. The position of all shallow tube-wells (STW). If there is more than one size of STW, use different symbols to show the different types (including deep-set STWs).

   e. Any extensive areas where hand tube-wells (HTW) are used for irrigation.

   f. Any extensive areas where traditional irrigation devices (including dug-wells) are used for irrigation.

Step D2. The TEO will prepare a table for adding to Irrigation Map 1 showing the following information, as illustrated in Table 23.12.

   a. In the upper part of the table:

      i. in column 1, the name of each river, khal, beel, etc., actually used for irrigation.

      ii. in the next group of columns (2), the total cusecs of water estimated to be used on each river, khal, etc., by existing LLPs, gravity schemes and traditional irrigation devices; and

      iii. in the third group of columns (3), the estimated total area irrigated from each river, khal, etc.

---

[16]*At that time, virtually all small-scale irrigation was by low-lift pumps and deep tube-wells provided by BADC for officially-approved 'schemes' prepared by Thana Councils.*

[17]*Although not indicated in the original manual, the methods described are suitable for keeping irrigation maps up-to-date annually, taking into account irrigation development during the previous year. It has been assumed that farmers will prefer to grow boro paddy with irrigation where soils are suitable for that crop. If at some future time, farmers should change their preference to growing a dryland crop (such as wheat or vegetables) instead of boro, then appropriate changes should be made where relevant in the methods described.*

[18]*In the original document, responsibility for preparing this map and the table described in the following paragraph was allocated to the BADC Thana Irrigation Officer.*

TABLE 23.12

Availability of surface water and groundwater in XYZ Thana[1]

A. Surface water

(1) River, khal, beel	(2) Estimated cusecs used				(3) Area irrigated (acres)				(4) Total permissible cusecs	(5) Balance available cusecs
	LLP[2]	Cross-dam	Traditional	Total	LLP	Cross-dam	Traditional	Total		
1. ABC river	(20) 40	10	–	50	800	300	–	1100	100	50
2. DEF khal	(12) 20	–	5	25	400	–	80	480	50	-5[3]
3. GHI beel etc.	(8) 10	–	5	15	100	–	100	200	15	0
Total	**70**	**10**	**10**	**90**	**1300**	**300**	**180**	**1780**	**135**	**45**

B. Groundwater

Union	Existing DTWs			Existing STWs			Existing HTWs			Existing dug-wells			Total	
	No	cusecs	acres	No	cusecs	acres	No	cusecs	acres	No	cusecs	acres	cusecs	acres
1. abc	12	24	480	20	10	100	30	0.4	10	20	0.2	5	34.6	595
2. def	0	–	–	0	–	–	40	0.4	2.5	60	0.6	15	1.0	17.5
3. ghi etc.	8	16	320	50	25	250	60	0.6	15	20	0.2	6	41.8	591
Total	**20**	**40**	**800**	**70**	**35**	**350**	**130**	**1.4**	**17.5**	**100**	**1.0**	**26**	**77.4**	**1203.5**
Grand total (A + B)													**167.4**	**3023.5**

(Contd.)

Ground water (Continued)

Union	Total permissible cusecs			Balance available cusecs		
	Deep	Shallow	Total	Deep	Shallow[4]	Total
1. abc	50	100	150	26	89.4	115.4
2. def	40	20	60	40	19	59
3. ghi	60	140	200	44	114.2	158.2
etc.						
Total	**150**	**260**	**410**	**110**	**222.6**	**332.6**
Grand total (A + B)			**545**			**377.6**

Notes: 1. Hypothetical, for demonstration purposes only.

2. The number given in brackets is the number of LLPs (both 2-cusec and 1-cusec).

3. Implies that the water source is over-exploited and the number of LLPs/traditional devices should be reduced in the common interest. However, the existing equipment is still not using the full potential: 20 cusecs should irrigate at least 500 acres (of paddy), but only 480 acres are actually irrigated, indicating suboptimum efficiency of use.

4. Suitable for allocation between STWs, HTWs and dug wells.

b. In the lower part of the table, separately for each Union (1, 2, 3, etc.):

   i. the total number of DTWs installed at present, the total cusecs of water used by those DTWs and the total area actually irrigated by them;

   ii. similar information for STWs;

   iii. similar information for HTWs;

   iv. the number of dug wells used for irrigation at present and the estimated total area irrigated from them; and

   v. the total cusecs and area irrigated from all groundwater sources at present.

The two sets of columns at the right side of the table ('Total permissible' and 'Balance available') should be left empty at this stage. They will be filled in later by the Deputy Director of Agriculture (DDA).

Step D3. Put a title on the map and the year to which the water information refers. Make four copies of this map.

Step D4. The TEO will forward three copies of Irrigation Map 1 to the Thana Circle Officer for Development[19] with a request that two copies be forwarded to the District Council for completion.

Step D5. The District Council will request the District Agricultural Development Committee to give its recommendation on the amount of surface water and groundwater actually available for irrigation use in the Thana. In making its recommendation, the committee will take into account the following kinds of information.

a. The historical low flow in rivers, as recorded by the Hydrological Survey of BWDB.[20]

b. Information available from BWDB and the Department of Public Health Engineering on the availability of groundwater supplies.

c. The existing and anticipated future needs of water users in neighbouring Thanas, and any foreseen developments which could increase or decrease the availability of surface water or groundwater supplies in future years (e.g, barrages upstream; major irrigation canal projects upstream or downstream; urban and industrial expansion; etc.).

The DDA and the BWDB Executive Engineer will together review the available information on groundwater supplies and draw boundaries on Irrigation Map 1 indicating zones where, respectively, priority should be given to development by HTWs, STWs or DTWs (in that order of priority), or where supplies are not sufficient for tube-well development.[21]

The committee will give its recommendations to the District Council on the permissible use of irrigation water in the Thana by filling in the last two columns of the table on Irrigation Map 1: see the examples for surface water and groundwater given in Table 23.12.

Step D6. The District Council, after endorsing (or amending) the recommendations made by the District Agricultural Development Committee, will return the completed Irrigation

---

[19]*In the original document, called the Thana Nirbahi Officer.*

[20]It may be satisfactory to take the minimum flow in nine years out of ten as the acceptable limit.

[21]*The order of priority may change with time: e.g., if expansion of STW irrigation threatens to exhaust available irrigation supplies or if shallow groundwater resources are reduced for any reason, then DTWs may become the most appropriate means to make optimum use of the available groundwater.*

Map 1 to the Thana Council with a request for it to prepare Irrigation Map 2 (irrigation potential) and Irrigation Map 3 (draft 5-year irrigation development plan). The method for making those maps is described below in Sections 23.4.3 and 23.6.2 (footnote 38).

E. Method 2[22]

Step E1. Same as Step D1.

   Step E2. Same as Step D2.

   Step E3. Same as Step D3.

   Step E4. The TEO will forward three copies of Irrigation Map 1 to the DDA with a request that he obtain the information needed for completing the last two columns of the map table (Table 23.12).

   Step E5. The DDA will consult the BWDB Executive Engineer regarding the availability of surface water and groundwater for the Thana.

   a. In the case of surface water, the Executive Engineer will take into account:

      i. the historical low flow in each river, khal, etc., listed on Irrigation Map 1; and

      ii. the existing and foreseen needs for surface water from each river, khal. etc., by other users, both inside and outside the Thana, including non-agricultural users.

   On this basis, the Executive Engineer will recommend the number of cusecs of water which may safely be allocated for irrigation from each river, khal, etc., and will fill in the last two columns of the table on Irrigation Map 1 (see Table 23.12) for the sections relating to surface water.

   b. In the case of groundwater, the Executive Engineer will use all available technical information available to him to assess groundwater supplies in the Thana. He will then draw boundaries on Irrigation Map 1 to show areas where groundwater supplies are, respectively:

      i. suitable for HTWs or STWs to be used;

      ii. not suitable for development by HTWs or STWs, but where DTWs (or deep-set STWs) could be used; and

      iii. not suitable for development by tube-wells.

   c. The Executive Engineer will then fill in the last two columns of the table on Irrigation Map 1 for the sections relating to groundwater.

   Step E6. After the last two columns of the table on Irrigation Map 1 have been filled in, the DDA will return one copy of the map to the TEO with instructions for the TEO to proceed with making Irrigation Maps 2 and 3.

23.4.3 Thana irrigation map 2

The TEO will use the information on the completed Irrigation Map 1 for making Irrigation Map 2 showing the irrigation potential in the Thana, using the methods described below. Steps F1-F5 below describe the method for showing surface-water potential on the map. Steps G1-G4 describe the method for showing the groundwater potential.

---

[22]*The method described below was included in the original document 'as an interim measure, until such time as Thana and District Councils become fully functional as planning authorities'.*

If there is no potential for surface-water irrigation in the Thana:

a. carry out Steps F1 and F2 described below;

b. make a table with the headings given in Step F5d;

c. write 'Nil' under columns 3-7 in that table; and

d. proceed to Step G1.

F. Surface-water potential

Step F1. Make a new base map for Irrigation Map 2 by copying the map information from Irrigation Map 1. Do not copy the table on Map 1 (Table 23.12): a new table will be prepared for Irrigation Map 2.

Step F2. On the new map, copy the soil association boundaries from the Thana soil map. Show the soil boundaries in orange pencil or ink.

Step F3. Draw pencil lines at a distance of half-a-mile from each bank of each river. khal, beel, etc., which has a usable irrigation supply (as indicated in the table on Irrigation Map 1).[23] These lines show the maximum distance to which water can normally be distributed by a 2-cusec LLP.

Step F4. Determine the actual amount of land suitable and available for irrigation within the 1-mile wide strip alongside each water course. Within each such strip of land, draw a pencil line around areas that obviously are not available for irrigation because, for example:

a. they are occupied by villages, factories, roads, embankments, etc.;

b. they could not be reached by distribution channels because of higher land, khals, beels, etc.:

c. they are shown on the soil map as having sandy *char* land, irregular relief or other land poorly suited for irrigation.[24]

Draw a strong green line over the pencil lines surrounding the remaining areas which are considered to be suitable for LLP irrigation. In the following steps, this area is called 'the irrigable strip'.

Step F5. Find out how much land is suitable for irrigation within each soil association lying within the green lines drawn in Step F4. Calculate this area by the following method.

a. For each soil association, find out from the Gross Crop Suitability Table prepared in Section 23.3.6 (see Table 23.1) what are the proportions of each soil association occupied by soils rated as suitable under irrigated conditions for boro, wheat, potato, or other crops which might be grown with irrigation in the area.

b. Give separate unit numbers, if necessary, to different areas of a soil association lying within each irrigable strip. Separate unit numbers are needed where:

i. the association occurs on both sides of the river or khal; the two sides must be considered as separate irrigation units;

ii. the association occurs in different places along the river or khal; and

---

[23]Half-a-mile = ½-inch on the Thana map scale.

[24]Some of this land may be suitable for irrigation by traditional irrigation devices, dug wells, HTWs or small STWs. Site inspections may be needed to find out whether such small-scale methods could be used. Areas that are found suitable should be marked on Irrigation Map 2 with an appropriate symbol (see Annexe 2), and the areas should be included in the tables to be prepared in Steps F5 and G1-G5.

iii. khals, beels, or other barriers occur within the association which could not be crossed by an irrigation channel.

For each subunit of an association, use the association number and follow it with a capital letter (e.g., 1A, 1B, 1C, etc.).

c. Calculate the area of each soil association, or parts of an association, which lie within the irrigable strip. Do this by:

i. drawing a grid of 1/10th-inch squares over the area (or on transparent paper which can be laid over the map);

ii. counting the number of squares and part-squares lying within the boundaries of the area being measured; and

iii. multiplying that number by 6.4 to give the area in acres (or by 2.56 to give the area in hectares).

d. Make a table with the column headings shown in Table 23.13.

TABLE 23.13

Present and potential area irrigable from surface water

(1) River/khal	(2) Soil association	(3) Gross irrigable area (acres)	(4) Existing LLPs (cusecs)	(5) Present irrigated area (acres)	(6) Available irrigated area (acres)	(7) Additional LLPs possible (No)
Gumti	4					
	5					
	10A					
	10B					
	10C					
	33A					
	33B					
Grand total						

e. For each river, khal, etc., fill in columns 2 and 3 before adding the data for the remaining columns. In column 2, list each subdivision of a soil association separately, if necessary.

f. Add up the information in columns 3-7 to give the total area and numbers of pumps for each river, khal, etc., and the grand totals for the Thana.

g. Copy the completed table onto Irrigation Map 2. Leave sufficient space on the map to add the information on groundwater potential, to be provided in the next section.

G. Groundwater potential

Step G1. Prepare a table with the headings shown in the example given in Table 23.14. Fill in the columns as described below.

Col. 1 (Unions)

a. First, look at the completed Irrigation Map 1 to find out which Unions in the Thana are shown as having a potential for irrigation from groundwater.

b. Write the names of the Unions in column 1, leaving sufficient space between the names to add the relevant information for the Unions in column 2. (In other words, prepare columns 1 and 2 at the same time.)

TABLE 23.14

Groundwater irrigation potential in XYZ Thana[1]

| (1) Union | Soils | | | | Permissible irrigation | | | | | Allocation[2] | | | |
| | Soil association | | Irrigable | | DTWs | | STWs | | Total | DTWs | | STWs | |
	(2) No	(3) Acres	(4) %	(5) Acres	(6) Cusecs	(7) Acres	(8) Cusecs	(9) Acres	(10) Acres	(11) No	(12) Acres	(13) No	(14) Acres
1. abc	1	1,000	70	700						5	231	31	467
	2	2,000	40	800						5	264	36	533
	3	3,000	30	900						6	297	40	600
Total		6,000		2,400	50	1,250 (33%)	100	2,500 (67%)	3,750	16	800	107	1,600
2. def	2	3,000	30	900						7	360	12	180
	3	2,000	50	1,000						8	400	13	200
	4	1,000	60	600						5	240	8	120
Total		6,000		2,500	40	1,000 (67%)	20	500 (33%)	1,500	20	1,000	33	500
3. ghi	5	2,500	0	0									
	6	2,500	0										
Total		5,000		0	60	1,500 (30%)	140	3,500 (70%)	5,000	Nil	0	Nil	0
etc.													
Thana total		**17,000**		**4,900**	**150**	**3,750**	**260**	**6,500**	**10,250**	**36**	**1,800**	**140**	**2,000**

Notes: 1. Hypothetical example. Figures relate to Table 23.12.

2. This includes existing tube-wells; i.e., deduct existing tube-wells in order to find the balance remaining available for fielding.

3. The allocation of shallow groundwater is in terms of STWs. If HTWs or dug-wells exist or are planned, their water requirement must be deducted from that actually allocated for STWs:

   1 cusec = 2 STWs = 30 HTWs = 60 dug-wells.

4. The area figures given against the number of DTWs and STWs assume 25 acres per cusec. This is for transplanted paddy. If a dryland crop (e.g., wheat, potato) will be grown, assume 50 acres per cusec.

c. For any Union lying wholly within an area without irrigation potential, write the name of the Union in column 1 and write 'Nil' in the following columns.

Col. 2 (soil associations)

Against the name of each Union which has a potential for irrigation, list the soil associations occurring in the Union. Exclude soil associations which:

    a. lie wholly in parts of the Union shown on Irrigation Map 1 as having no groundwater potential; and

    b. lie wholly within areas shown on Irrigation Map 2 as suitable for LLP irrigation.

Col. 3 (Area)

Calculate the area of each soil association in each Union. Exclude those parts of associations which lie within areas shown as suitable for irrigation by surface water. Calculate the area by the method described above in Step F5c.

Col. 4 (% irrigable)

Calculate the percentage of the soil area which is suitable for irrigation in each soil association in each Union. In order to do this:

    a. refer to the crop suitability table prepared in Section 23.3.6, Steps A1-A15;

    b. decide whether wheat or boro will be the main crop grown in the area, or whether farmers are likely to grow both;

    c. if boro is likely to be the main crop irrigated, add up the percentage figures for the soils rated as suitable for irrigated boro — usually this will be HYV boro — in each soil association, and write the total in column 4;

    d. if wheat is considered likely to be the main crop grown with irrigation, add up the percentage figures for the soils rated as suitable for wheat with irrigation, and write the total in column 4;

    e. if both boro and wheat are likely to be grown with irrigation:

      i. add up the percentage figures for the soils rated as suitable for boro;

      ii. add to the figure the percentage figures for the soils rated as suitable for wheat but not suitable for boro; and

      iii. write the total percentage figure in column 4.

Col. 5 (area irrigable)

    a. Calculate the area of soils suitable for irrigation in each soil association in each Union. Do this by multiplying the area of the soil association given in column 3 by the percentage figure for the association in column 4.

    b. From these figures, calculate the total area suitable for irrigation in the Union and write this figure on the 'Total' line.

    c. Then add up all the Union totals to give the total area suitable for irrigation from groundwater in the Thana and write this figure in the appropriate space (Thana total) at the bottom of the column.

Cols 6 & 7 (DTWs permitted)

For each Union, write the figure for the total cusecs available for DTW irrigation in the 'Total' line of column 6. Take this figure from the column headed 'Deep' under 'Total permissible cusecs' in the table prepared in Step D5 above (illustrated in Table 23.12).

Multiply the number of cusecs by 25 to give the number of acres irrigable (or by 10 to give the number of hectares irrigable). Write this figure in column 7.[25]

Cols 8 & 9 (STWs permitted)

For each Union, write the permissible cusecs available for STWs in the total line of column 8. Take this figure from the column headed 'Shallow' under 'Total permissible cusecs' in the table prepared in Step D5 (illustrated in Table 23.12).[26]

Multiply the number of cusecs by 25 to give the number of acres irrigable (or by 10 to give the number of hectares irrigable). Write this figure in column 9.

Col. 10 (Total area)

For each Union, add up the area figures given in columns 7 and 9, and write the total in column 10. This figure gives the total area that could be irrigated by tubewells from the available groundwater.

Cols 11-14 (DTW, STW allocation)

For each Union, allocate the permissible number of DTWs and STWs as follows.

a. Compare the figures for the total irrigable area (column 5) and total permissible area (column 10).

  i. if the figure in column 5 is the same as or smaller than the figure in column 10, use the method described in paragraph b below;

  ii. if the figure in column 5 is bigger than the figure in column 10, use the method described in paragraph c below.

b. (Column 5 figure the same as or less than column 10 figure.)

  i. **DTWs**. Allocate DTWs between soil associations in proportion to their respective areas and the share of DTWs in the total permissible area (i.e., the figure in column 7 divided by the figure in column 10, as percent). For example, in the example given in Table 23.14, abc Union has 1,250 acres permissible DTW irrigation (column 7), to be divided by 3,750 acres total permissible area (column 10) = 33 percent.[27] Then:

$$\text{Association 1: 700 acres irrigable} \times 33\% = 231; \div 50 \text{ acres per DTW}$$
$$= 4.62 \ (= 5) \text{ DTWs.}[28]$$
$$\text{Association 2: 800 acres irrigable} \times 33\% = 264; \div 50 \text{ acres per DTW}$$
$$= 5.28 \ (= 5) \text{ DTWs.}$$
$$\text{Association 3: 900 acres irrigable} \times 33\% = 297; \div 50 \text{ acres per DTW}$$
$$= 5.94 \ (= 6) \text{ DTWs.}$$

[25]If it is expected that a dryland crop such as wheat will be grown, multiply the cusecs figure by 50 to give the irrigable acreage (or by 20 for the number of irrigable hectares).

[26]The allocation of shallow groundwater is in terms of STWs. If HTWs or dug wells exist or are planned, their water requirement must be deducted from that allocated for STWs, using the following rule of thumb: 1 cusec = 2 STWs = 30 HTWs = 60 dug wells.

[27]This figure can be written after the area figure in column 7. The balance (67%) can be written after the STW figure in column 9 for use in later calculations.

[28]Assuming 2-cusec delivery, a DTW should irrigate at least 50 acres of transplanted paddy. If a dryland crop such as wheat will be grown, divide by 100.

Total = 792 acres = 16 DTWs

Enter these figures in columns 11 and 12 respectively.

ii. **STWs**. Allocate STWs in the same way as described above for DTWs, but use the appropriate share of water (i.e., the figure in column 9 divided by the figure in column 10) and allow 15 acres per STW (for transplanted paddy) or 30 acres per STW if a dryland crop will be grown. For example in the example given in Table 23.14, 67 percent of the water is available for use by STWs (already calculated when allocating DTWs). Then:

Association 1: 700 acres irrigable × 67% = 469; ÷ 15 acres per STW
= 31.27 (= 31) STWs.

Association 2: 800 acres irrigable × 67% = 536; ÷ 15 acres per STW
= 35.73 (=36) STWs.

Association 3: 900 acres irrigable × 67% = 603; ÷ 15 acres per STW
= 40.20 (= 40) STWs.

Total = 1,608 acres = 107 STWs

Enter these figures in columns 13 and 14 respectively.

c. (Column 5 figure more than column 10 figure.)

i. **DTWs**. Allocate DTWs between soil associations in proportion to:

the proportion of the total permissible area (column 10) to the total irrigable area (column 5); and

the proportion of the permissible DTW area to the total permissible area, as calculated in b(i) above. For example, in the example given in Table 23.14, def Union:

1. 1,500 (column 10) ÷ 2,500 (column 5) = 60%; and
2. 1,000 (column 7) ÷ 1,500 (column 10) = 67%.

Multiply 60% by 67% = 40.2 (round to 40) percent.

Thereafter, proceed as in paragraph b above:

Association 2: 900 acres irrigable × 40% = 360; ÷ 50 acres per DTW
= 7.2 (= 7) DTWs.

Association 3: 1,000 acres irrigable × 40% = 400; ÷ 50 acres per DTW
= 8 DTWs

Association 4: 600 acres irrigable × 40% = 240; ÷ 50 acres per DTW
= 4.8 (= 5) DTWs

Total = 1,000 acres = 20 DTWs

Enter these figures in columns 11 and 12 respectively.

ii. **STWs**. Allocate STWs in the same way as is described for DTWs above, but use the appropriate share of the water (i.e., the figure in column 9 divided by the figure in column 10), and allow 15 acres per STW (for transplanted paddy) or 30 acres if a dryland crop will be grown. For example, in the example given in Table 23.14, def Union:

1. 1,500 (column 10) ÷ 2,500 (column 5) = 60%; and

2. 500 (column 9) ÷ 1,500 (column 10) = 33%.[29]

Multiply 60% by 33% = 20 percent.

Then:

Association 2: 900 × 20% = 180; ÷ 15 acres per STW = 12 STWs.

Association 3: 1,000 × 20% = 200; ÷ 15 acres per STW = 13.3 (= 13) STWs

Association 4: 600 × 20% = 120; ÷ 15 acres per STW = 8 STWs

Total = 500 acres   = 33 STWs

Enter these figures in columns 13 and 14.

Step G2. Add up the figures in the respective columns to give:

a. the totals for each Union; and

b. the grand totals for the Thana.

Step G3. Copy the total figure for each Union onto the table on Irrigation Map 2 in the space below the surface-water information. Use separate sections for DTWs, STWs and HTWs (if the latter are allocated separately). For each section, use the headings shown in Table 23.15.

Step G4. On Irrigation Map 2, mark (in green) the areas potentially suitable for irrigation by, respectively, HTWs, STWs and DTWs, using the symbols given in Annexe 2.

23.5 PROBLEM AREA MAPS

23.5.1 Introduction

The TEO will prepare one or more Thana Problem Area Maps, using the method described in Section 23.5.2 below. The purpose of these maps is to focus attention on problems which it might be possible to reduce, remove or by-pass through Thana Works Programme schemes, special Extension programmes, etc., carried out under the Thana Development Plan. A basic list of the main problems which may be encountered in different parts of the country is given in Table 23.16. Suggested ways of dealing with these problems are described in Annexe 3 to this chapter.

23.5.2 H. Problem area map

Step H1. Make a list of the problems which affect crop production and agricultural development in different areas of the Thana. Table 23.16 provides suggestions. The TEO should use this list only as a guide. He should make his own list of problems and number them consecutively. He should add any other problems which he considers important in any part of his Thana and which he considers could be reduced or removed by suitable development schemes.

Step H2. Transfer the soil association boundaries from the Thana soil map to the Union maps. The Union maps are on 4 inches = 1 mile scale (1:15,840). Therefore, the scale must be increased four times. Use the method described in Section 23.3.7, Step B11, but draw a grid of 1/10-th inch squares on the Thana map and a grid of 4/10-inch squares on the Union map. Be careful to make the grid lines fit the same relative positions on both maps.

---

[29]This figure has already been calculated, as the balance, when calculating (2) for DTWs above. See also footnote 27.

TABLE 23.15

Present and potential area irrigable from groundwater

(1) Union	(2) Soil associations	(3) Area not irrigable (acres)	(4) Existing tube-well irrigation (cusecs)			(5) Present irrigated area (acres)	(6) Available irrigated area (acres)	(7) Additional number of tube-wells permitted		
			DTW	STW	HTW			DTW	STW	HTW
Total Union abc										
Total Union def										
Total Union ghi										
etc.										
etc.										
etc.										
Total Thana										

TABLE 23.16

Guide list of possible problems affecting agricultural development

1. Water stands in fields after heavy rainfall or irrigation.[1]
2. Waterlogging.
3. Early flooding.
4. Flash floods.
5. Deep flooding (normal).
6. Risk of abnormally high floods.
7. River-bank erosion.
8. Risk of burial by new sediments.
9. Drought-prone soils.
10. Shortage of irrigation water.
11. Puddled soils with a strong ploughpan.
12. Heavy soils (difficult to cultivate with bullocks).
13. Shortage of draught animals.
14. Irregular relief (in floodplain and terrace regions).
15. Sloping soils (in hill and terrace regions).
16. Soil fertility problems; (these can be subdivided, if necessary, where specific nutrient problems have actually been identified, such as zinc deficiency).
17. Saline soils.
18. Saline flooding
19. Shrimp farming.
20. Poor communications.
21. Land ownership (e.g., big land-owners not interested in using improved methods of cultivation).

Note: 1. This is a problem for dryland crops and for young broadcast aus, broadcast aman and jute.

Step H3. Draw the soil boundaries boldly on the Union map. Use orange pencil or ink.

Step H4. Number the soil associations on the Union maps in orange pencil or ink. If there are no soil boundaries inside the Union, write only the soil association number.

Step H5. Hold one or more meetings in each Union to identify problems and the areas where they occur. Consult the Block Supervisor, Union/Thana Council members, cooperative group managers, Contact Farmers, etc. Make field visits to problem areas to verify the nature of the problem, to estimate the size of the area affected, and to observe and identify the kinds of land, soil and crops affected. Discuss with local farmers their ideas on how the problem could be reduced or removed. Record this information in the form of a table, as indicated in Table 23.17.

Step H6. Mark the problem areas on the Union map as follows.[30]

   a. For each problem area which is big enough to be shown separately on the Union map:

      i. draw a boundary around the affected area in red pencil or ink;

      ii. inside the boundary of each problem area, write (in red) the appropriate number for the problem as shown in the list of problems prepared in Step H1;

      iii. if any area has more than one problem, write all the relevant numbers alongside each other and draw a red rectangle around the numbers.

---

[30]If there are too many problems to show clearly on one map, make separate maps to show individual problems or groups of problems.

TABLE 23.17
Problem areas and suggested remedies

(1) Village(s)	(2) Problem	(3) Estimated area affected (acres)	(4) Land/soil/crop affected	(5) Farmers' suggested remedy	(6) Block Supervisor's comments
ABC	1. Water stands in fields after heavy rainfall	50	Aus, jute	Make culvert in road	TEO/DDA to contact R&H Engineer
etc.					

b. For problem areas that are too small to show separately on the Union map:

   i. where the problem area can be located precisely on the map, write the appropriate problem number in red as close to the actual place on the map as possible, and draw a red circle around the number; or

   ii. where the problem occurs at several places in a soil association because it is found on particular soils or positions in the relief — e.g., waterlogging — write the problem number in red alongside the soil association number and draw a red circle around both numbers; if more than one problem occurs in relation to soils and relief in any association, write all the numbers against the soil association number and draw a red line around all the numbers.

Step H7. Write a legend on the Union map to explain what each coloured boundary and problem number means. Use the layout suggested in the example given in Table 23.18.

TABLE 23.18
Problem areas in abc Union

Problem No Description	Area affected (acres)	Suggested solution
1.		
2.		
3.		

Step H8. Write a title on the map. If only one map is made, use the title 'Problem areas'. If more than one map is made, entitle the maps 'Problem areas — Map 1', 'Problem areas — Map 2', etc.

Step H9. Make additional copies of the Union Problem Areas Map(s) for use in the Union by the Block Supervisor, Union Council, managers of cooperative groups, school teachers, etc. Two copies of the map(s) should go to the TEO.

Step H10. Reduce the information shown on the Union Problem Areas Maps to the Thana Problem Areas Map (or Map). Use the method described in Step H6 for showing the problems on the Thana map scale.

Step H11. Write an appropriate legend and title on the Thana map, as described for the Union maps in Steps H7-10 above.

Step H12. Make additional copies of the Thana Problem Areas Map(s) for placing in the Thana Plan Book, for sending to the Thana Council, relevant Thana technical officers, the District Deputy Director of Agriculture, and for use in displays.

23.6 Development Plans

23.6.1 Introduction

The maps and tables showing crop suitability, irrigation potential and problem areas, taken together, provide a good basis for preparing realistic Thana and Union agricultural development plans. However, it may not be practical to do immediately everything which could be done or which needs to be done. For example, funds may not be available to do everything at once; not all farmers may be ready to make technological changes at once; or some investments may be possible only after other schemes have made conditions suitable for them. Therefore, priorities have to be decided upon.

The method described below is one of participatory planning. It requires that a dialogue be developed between technical officials and experienced community leaders and farmers to discuss the information given on the maps showing crop suitability, irrigation potential and problem areas. These discussions should be oriented towards:

a. identifying practical methods which could be taken to develop the land and water potential more fully and more rapidly in different parts of the Thana; and

b. establishing a tentative order of priorities for the suggested development schemes identified.

It is the responsibility of the TEO to lead this activity and provide the technical input.[31] Two methods are described: the detailed, formal method in Section 23.6.2; and a simpler method in Section 23.6.3 which the TEO could use until the detailed plan has been made.

23.6.2 I. How to prepare a five-year plan

The detailed formal method for preparing a 5-year plan is described in Steps I1-I44 below.

Step I1. Transfer the relevant information from the Thana Irrigation Map 2 onto a copy of each Union map. Use the method of enlargement described above in Step H2.

Step I2. For each Union, prepare a table with the headings shown in the example given in Table 23.19.

Step I3. In column 1 of the table, list the problems identified in the Union, as shown on the Union Problem Areas Map(s)

Step I4. In column 2, give the location of each problem: e.g., by village, khal or soil association.

Step I5. The TEO will visit each Union in turn to obtain the opinions of the Union Council (or Thana Council ward members), KSS managers, the Block Supervisor, etc., on how the problems listed in column 1 should be dealt with. The TEO will write their suggestions in column 3.

---

[31]*The TEO may, of course, delegate parts of plan preparation to appropriate Thana Subject Matter Specialists, and will involve Block Supervisors in the preparation of plans for their Unions, but he must take personal responsibility for the technical reliability of the plan document.*

TABLE 23.19

abc Union: problems and proposed solutions[1]

(1) Problem	(2) Location	(3) Local suggestions	(4) TEO=s recommendation	(5) Implementation by	(6) Priority
1. Waterlogging of fields after heavy rainfall	Highland and Medium Highland soils used for b.aus, jute	Gov=t to provide *pucca* drains	Farmers to make better field drains	Extension demonstration programme	M
2. Flash floods	Soil associations 2, 4; valleys in 1	Government to provide embankment	1. Take up soil conservation, horticultural and afforestation schemes on hills 2. Excavate more drains 3. Maintain existing drains	1. District Council; Horticultural Development Board; Forest Department 2. BWDB 3. Food-for-work programme	H
3. Not enough water to irrigate all land	Southern half of soil association 6	Government to build canal	1. Persuade farmers to grow wheat and potato on loamy Highland and Medium Highland soils; boro only on clay soils 2. Organize farmers to use rotational irrigation 3. Provide *pucca* channels on loamy soils near river-bank	1. Extension programme 2. Ditto 3. Thana Irrigation Programme scheme	H

Note: 1. Hypothetical example. For demonstration purposes only.

Step 16. In column 4, the TEO will give his own suggested solutions to the problems.

Step 17, In column 5, the TEO will write his own suggestions for carrying out the proposals made in columns 3 and 4: e.g., by the farmers; Food-for-Work Programme; Thana Works Programme; BWDB; Extension programme; etc.

Step 18. In column 6, the TEO will record the consensus of opinion in the Union about the order in which the suggested development schemes should be executed. Use the symbols H = high priority, M = medium priority, and L = low priority.

Step 19. For each Union, prepare a second table, using the model given in Table 23.20, to show irrigation targets for the Union.

Step 110. In columns 1, 2 and 3 respectively of Table 23.20, write the total permissible number of LLPs for the Union, the number of LLPs presently in use, and the balance remaining available for allocation. Take this information from the Thana Irrigation Map 2. Allocate pumps between Unions in proportion to the area of land irrigable by LLPs in each Union along rivers, khals, etc., passing through the Unions. Leave column 4 empty at this stage.

Step 111. In columns 5, 6 and 7 respectively, fill in the relevant details for HTWs, as described for LLPs in Step I10. Leave column 8 empty at this stage.

Step 112. In columns 9, 10 and 11 respectively, fill in the relevant details for STWs, as described for LLPs in Step I10. Leave column 12 empty at this stage.

Step 113. In columns 13, 14 and 15 respectively, fill in the relevant details for DTWs, as described for LLPs in Step I10. Leave column 16 empty at this stage.

Step 114. Preferably, the Union Council should fill in columns 4, 8, 12 and 16: i.e., the targets for fielding LLPs, HTWs, STWs and DTWs during the following five years. Alternatively, the TEO will complete these columns after consulting Union Council members, etc. The targets set for each year should be realistic.

Step 115. The Union Council (or the TEO) will forward the table showing irrigation targets to the Thana Council as a preliminary request for the allocation of LLPs and tube-wells for installation during the following 5-Year Plan. Schemes will be prepared later, after the plan has been approved.[32]

Step 116. On the basis of the information compiled in Tables 23.19 and 23.20, the TEO will assist Block Supervisors to draft a 5-Year Plan for agricultural development in each Union. This activity will be undertaken on behalf of the Union Council.

Step 117. First, the TEO will consider what it is feasible to include in the 5-Year Plan, taking into account:

a. the potential for increasing crop production under both non-irrigated and irrigated conditions, as recorded in the tables illustrated in Tables 23.1, 23.3, 23.12 and 23.14;

b. the problems identified, and the feasibility of removing them during the plan period, as recorded on the table illustrated in Table 23.19; (the TEO should also obtain information through his DDA regarding any proposed BWDB projects which might affect agricultural development in different Unions of the Thana);

c. the irrigation targets, as indicated in the table illustrated in Table 23.20; and

d. the capacity of local markets (including Government purchase centres) to absorb any increased agricultural production.

---

[32]*Despite the handing over of irrigation equipment supply to the private sector, the Thana Council could usefully retain authority to allocate licences for siting such equipment: see footnotes 5 and 15 above.*

TABLE 23.20
abc Union: irrigation targets for 5-Year Plan[1]

	No of LLPs[2]				No of HTWs				No of STWs				No of DTWs			
	(1) Permitted	(2) Used 1982	(3) Balance	(4) 5-Year Plan target	(5) Permitted	(6) Used 1982	(7) Balance	(8) 5-year Plan target	(9) Permitted	(10) Used 1982	(11) Balance	(12) 5-Year Plan target	(13) Permitted	(14) Used 1982	(15) Balance	(16) 5-Year Plan target
	20	5	15	20	1,000	30	970	500	145	20	125	100	25	12	13	25
				1. 8				1. 50				1. 30				1. 14
				2. 10				2. 100				2. 50				2. 17
				3. 15				3. 200				3. 75				3. 20
				4. 20				4. 350				4. 100				4. 23
				5. 20				5. 500				5. 125				5. 25

Notes: 1. Hypothetical example. Based on figures given in Table 23.12.
2. Given in terms of 2-cusec pumps.

Step I18. For each Union, prepare a separate table such as the example given in Table 23.21 for each crop season. This step should be carried out at the same time as Step I22 (identification of development schemes): the crop area and production targets calculated in Step I18 must reflect the targets predicted in Step I22. Fill in the respective columns of the table as follows.

Column 1: For each soil association in turn, list the main crops grown at present or which it is planned to introduce during the 5-Year Plan period. List HYVs separately. Use variety names, if desired, for new HYVs for which there are special Extension programmes.

Columns 2-4: Estimate the area occupied by those crops under non-irrigated and irrigated conditions. Since crop statistics are not kept separately for individual soil associations, the TEO and the Block Supervisor must use their best judgement for estimating the area of the different crops (including HYVs) grown in each soil association.[33] This may be a difficult task, but no-one is in a better position to make these estimates than the Thana and Union Extension officials. They should, of course, consult Union Council members, KSS managers and experienced farmers during the preparation of the tables in order to benefit from their detailed local knowledge.[34]

Columns 5-7: Make realistic area and production targets for year 1 of the plan period for each crop listed in column 1. Take into account:

a. the planned expansion of irrigation in each soil association, as shown in the tables prepared in Steps I10-14;

b. the planned execution of schemes designed to reduce or remove the problems identified;[35]

c. a realistic estimate of the rate at which farmers will adopt new crops, varieties and technology;

d. the incompatibility of some crops in rotations: i.e., use the crop rotation suitability tables prepared in Section 23.3.6, Steps A1-A15;

e. the need to leave adequate turn-around time between crops grown in rotation;

f. the size of the probable market available for cash crops; and

g. the reduction in area of some subsistence crops which may occur as irrigation, drainage and HYV crops expand.

Columns 8-11: Make realistic targets for years 2-5 of the plan period.

Step I19. Combine the information given in the separate soil association tables to make a single table of targets for each crop season for the whole Union. Calculate production from the average yields expected, and add up cereal production figures separately. See the example given in Table 23.22.

---

[33]Either individual HYVs can be named, or they can be grouped in maturity periods: e.g., short duration, medium duration, long duration.

[34]*This task would be made easier if village land and soil type maps were available: see Chapter 20, Section 20.2, Question 5.*

[35]The execution of some development schemes (e.g., flood protection, drainage) will have the effect of creating new soil phases (e.g., flood-protected phase). Such new phases may need new crop suitability ratings from those provided in the Thana soil survey report. The TEO should request his DDA to obtain revised crop suitability ratings for the new conditions from the District (or Divisional) SRDI office.

TABLE 23.21

abc Union: 5-Year Agricultural Development Plan: (working table)[1]

| (1) Crop | Present crops and area | | | Crop area targets | | | | | | |
| | (2) Non-irrigated Acres | (3) Irrigated Acres | (4) Total Acres | Year 1 | | | Year 2 | | | Year 3, etc. |
				(5) Non-irrigated Acres	(6) Irrigated Acres	(7) Total Acres	(8) Non-irrigated Acres	(9) Irrigated Acres	(10) Total Acres	(11)
Association 1										
B.aus (LV)	1,900	-	1,900	1,900	-	1,900	1,900	-	1,900	
T.aman (LV)	1,900	-	1,900	1,900	-	1,900	1,900	-	1,900	
Pineapple	500	-	500	400	-	400	200	-	200	
Arum	1,000	-	1,000	800	-	800	500	-	500	
Jackfruit	200	-	200	300	-	300	400	-	400	
Guava	20	-	20	0	-	50	100	-	100	
Bamboo	500	-	500	600	-	600	700	-	700	
Forest plantation	200	-	200	300	-	300	500	-	500	
Association 2										
B.aus (LV)	300	-	300	200	-	200	150	-	150	
T.aus (LV)	100	-	100	150	-	150	150	-	150	
T.aus (HYV)	100	20	120	150	50	200	150	100	250	
T.aman (LV)	300	-	300	250	-	250	200	-	200	
T.aman (Pajam)	200	-	200	150	-	150	100	-	100	
T.aman (LV)	200	-	200	250	50	300	250	100	350	
Wheat	10	-	10	10	-	10	10	10	20	
Mustard (LV)	30	-	30	15	-	15	-	-	-	
" (HYV)	20	-	20	40	-	40	60	-	60	
Boro (HYV)	-	250	250	-	300	300	-	350	350	
Pineapple	200	-	200	150	-	150	100	-	100	
Arum	300	-	300	200	-	200	100	-	100	
Jackfruit	50	-	50	100	-	100	200	-	200	
Guava	20	-	20	40	-	40	80	-	80	
Bamboo	100	-	100	150	-	150	200	-	200	
Forest plantation	500	-	500	600	-	600	750	-	750	

Note: 1. Hypothetical example. Based on Comilla Kotwali Thana soil survey report soil associations 1 and 2, Tables 7 and 8.

TABLE 23.22
abc Union: 5-Year Agricultural Development Plan: (consolidated)[1]

Crop	Present production						Target production							
	Non-irrigated		Irrigated		Total		Year 1							Year 2, etc.
							Non-irrigated		Irrigated		Total		Production change from last year ± tons	
	Area	Production	Area	Production	Area	Production	Area	Production	Area	Production	Area	Production		
B.aus (LV)	3,000	900			3,000	900	2,800	840			2,800	840		
T.aus (LV)	1,000	400			1,000	400	1,000	400			1,000	400		
T.aus (HYV)	50	40			50	40	200	160			200	160	Aus + 60	
T.aman (LV)	4,000	-1,760			4,000	1,760	3,900	1,716			3,900	1,716		
T.aman (Pajam)	1,000	600			1,000	600	800	480			800	480		
T.aman (HYV)	100	80			100	80	400	320			400	320	Aman + 76	
Boro (HYV)			700	700	700	700			1,200	1,200	1,200	1,200	Boro + 500	
Wheat	10	6			10	6	20	20			20	12	Wheat + 6	
Total cereals					9,860	4,486					10,320	5,128	**+ 642**	
Mustard (LV)	200	50			200	50	150	38			150	38		
Mustard (HYV)	150	50			150	50	250	85			250	85	Mustard + 23	
Pineapple	200				200		150				150			
Arum	200				200		150				150			
Jackfruit	50				50		100				100			
Guava	10				10		20				20			
Bamboo	50				50		60				60			
Forest plantation	50				50		60				60			
Population					25,000						25,625			
Cereals (tons)					4,486						5,128			
% Self-sufficiency					103[2]						115[2]			

Notes: 1. Hypothetical example. For demonstration purposes only.

2. Implies surplus foodgrain production, which can be sold for purchase of other essential goods and services.

Step I20. For each major crop, calculate the addition or reduction of production expected each year as a result of implementing the plan: see the example given in Table 23.22.

Step I21. For each year of the plan, divide the figure for total cereals production by the projected Union population figure for each year in order to determine whether or not the Union is self-sufficient in foodgrains production. Calculate the percentage self-sufficiency by the following formula:

annual production (in tons) × 100 divided by population × 0.174.[36]

Write these figures in the relevant columns at the bottom of the table: see the example given in Table 23.22.

Step I22. Make a list of agricultural schemes identified for inclusion in each year of the 5-Year Plan, together with the area to be benefited, the crops to be grown and the increased production expected. Group the schemes under suitable headings: e.g., expansion of HYV wheat without irrigation; expansion of cash crops; irrigation (by type); drainage; afforestation; etc.

Step I23. Make a Union Agricultural Development Plan map showing:

a. the location of proposed schemes included in the plan, using symbols from relevant chapters of the Union Plan Book;

b. a table giving:

   i. a summary of the area and production targets for major crops for each year of the plan, taken from the completed table illustrated in Table 23.21: (see Steps I18-19);

   ii. the information calculated in Step I20; and

   iii. the information calculated in Step I21.

Step I24. Submit the draft plan and map to the Union Council for review.

Step I25. Make any amendments requested by the Union Council, including consequent revisions of targets. If Union Council members have been adequately consulted during plan preparation, such amendments should not be major ones.

Step I26. The Union Council will submit the final draft Union 5-Year Plan to the Thana Council for review and approval.[37]

Step I27. The TEO, on behalf of the Thana Council, will assemble all the Union plans. He will compile maps and tables for the Thana Agricultural Development Plan summarizing the information given in the Union plans prepared in Steps I1, I9-14 and I19-23, viz.

I1 : make a copy of a Thana map showing soil association boundaries;

I9-14 : make a table showing irrigation potential and targets;

I19 : make a table showing crop area and production targets for each year of the 5-Year Plan;

I20 : calculate the addition or reduction in production during the plan period;

I21 : calculate the percentage self-sufficiency in the Thana;

[36]This formula assumes 15.5 oz consumption per head per day and 10 percent extra production required to cover seed, feed and waste.

[37]From Step I26 onward, the procedures described are those which were in force in 1983 for the submission, review, approval and implementation of schemes in the Thana planning system.

I22   :   make a list of proposed agricultural development schemes;

I23   :   show the position of the proposed development schemes on the Thana map. (If the concentration of symbols is too great to show satisfactorily on a single map, make separate maps for different groups of schemes: e.g., irrigation; drainage; Extension; etc.).[38]

Step I28. The TEO will submit the draft Thana plan to the Thana Council for review.

Step I29. If requested to do so by the Thana Council, the TEO will make any amendments required and resubmit the revised plan to the Council for approval.

Step I30. The Thana Council, after approving the plan, will forward it to the District Council for review and approval.

Step I31. The District Council will refer the Thana Plan to the District Agricultural Development Committee for technical review. That committee will pay particular attention to the following points.

a. Whether or not the irrigation targets are within the limits of water availability set by BWDB on Irrigation Map 2: see Section 23.4.2, Step D5 or Step E5.

b. Whether or not any of the proposed schemes for embankment or drainage would have adverse effects elsewhere in the Thana or in neighbouring Thanas (including Thanas outside the District).

c. Whether or not any of the targets set for foodgrains, cash crop, fodder or forestry production are too ambitious in relation to previous development experience, available resources or available markets.

Step I32. The District Agricultural Development Committee will submit its findings and recommendations to the District Council.

Step I33. The District Council will consider the committee's findings and recommendations, then return the plan to the Thana Council with its approval or with specific recommendations for amendment.

Step I34. If amendments are required, the Thana Council will request the relevant Union Councils to revise their plans accordingly. The TEO and the relevant Block Supervisors will give technical assistance to the Union Councils in making revisions, using the procedures described above in Steps I15-23.

Step I35. When revisions have been completed, the procedures for review, revision, submission and transmittal described in Steps I24-33 will be followed until the Thana Plan and its component Union Plans are approved.

Step I36. The finalized Thana 5-Year Agricultural Development Plan will be placed in the Thana Plan Book. Similarly, the finalized Union 5-Year Plans will be placed in the Union Plan Books.

Step I37. The Thana Council will next request the TEO to assist Union Councils to prepare formal schemes for year 1 of the Plan. The procedures described in relevant chapters of the Union and Thana Plan Books will be followed for submitting, reviewing and approving schemes, releasing funds and implementing schemes.

---

[38]*In Thanas where irrigation development forms an important part of the 5-Year Agricultural Development Plan, it generally will be appropriate to make a separate map showing the location of irrigation schemes proposed for implementation in each year of the plan period. This will become Irrigation Map 3.*

Step I38. In the case of Agricultural Extension programmes, the TEO will prepare an annual plan for year 1 of the 5-Year Plan period, indicating the arrangements to be made to implement the plan. For each crop season, the annual plan should indicate:

a. the kind, number and location of trials and demonstrations;

b. the assistance to be given to BRDB and KSSs in forming new irrigation groups, preparing production programmes and training Model Farmers;

c. the in-service training courses to be organized for Block Supervisors for supporting the Extension programme;

d. the Extension impact points relevant for development schemes in each Union;

e. the arrangements required to ensure the supply of adequate inputs and credit;

f. the arrangements for pest/disease monitoring and management;

g. the arrangements for monitoring and evaluating progress of the programme; and

h. the contingency plans for agricultural rehabilitation in case of disaster: see Annexe 4 to this chapter.

Step I39. The TEO will submit monthly reports to the Union Council describing progress achieved (or not) with implementation of seasonal and annual development plans.

Step I40. The Union Council will review the monthly report and take whatever action it considers necessary to remove any bottlenecks reported, to speed up implementation or to compensate for losses or delays caused by natural disasters or other constraints experienced.

Step I41. The TEO will report monthly to the Thana Council on progress achieved with the implementation of seasonal and annual agricultural development plans.

Step I42. The Thana Council will review the monthly reports and take whatever action may be needed to remove bottlenecks, speed up implementation or compensate for losses or delays.

Step I43. At the end of each crop season, the Thana Council and the Union Council separately will review achievements in order to evaluate results and to make any changes in the following season's or year's plans made necessary by failure to achieve production targets.

Step I44. The measures described in Steps I38-43 will be repeated in year 2 and subsequent years during the 5-Year Plan period.

23.6.3 J. How to prepare an interim extension plan

The simple method for preparing an interim 5-year plan is described in Steps J1-J7 below.

Step J1. The TEO will examine the information given in Tables 23.1, 23.3, 23.12, 23.14 and 23.19 showing crop suitability, irrigation potential and problems in order to find out:

a. what are the main opportunities for agricultural development in the Thana; and

b. what are the main problems and possible solutions.

The TEO will make lists of the opportunities, problems and solutions, side by side.

Step J2. In the list prepared in Step J1, the TEO will underline the opportunities and problems which could be dealt with by Extension activities.

Step J3. The TEO should discuss these possible activities with other Thana technical officials, Block Supervisors, and Thana/Union Council members and add any other possible schemes which they may suggest. The TEO should obtain their ideas on the relative priority of each possible activity. Mark each of the underlined activities H, M or L according to whether they are considered high (H), medium (M) or low (L) priority respectively.

Step J4. Make a table with the headings shown in Table 23.23.

Step J5. Fill in the table as follows.

> **Column 1:** List the activities marked 'H' (= high priority) in Step J3. Below that list, list the activities marked 'M' (= medium priority).
>
> **Column 2:** Against each activity listed in column 1, name the Union (or Unions) in which the activity will be undertaken. If it will be undertaken in every Union, write 'All'.
>
> **Column 3:** Against each activity, give the number (or numbers) of the soil associations in which the activity will be undertaken.
>
> **Columns 4 and 5:** Against each activity, indicate the target to be achieved in each of the next two years. This target usually will be in terms of the area (acres or hectares) expected to benefit, but it may also include the number of new LLPs or tube-wells to be provided.
>
> **Column 6:** Name the person(s) who will be directly responsible for organizing each activity: e.g., TEO; Block Supervisor; SMS; manager of DTW 123.

Step J5. The TEO will take appropriate steps to organize each of the activities listed in column 1 of the table to be carried out in year 1 of the plan. The steps to be taken may include:

a. organizing the training of Block Supervisors for carrying out the activities, and providing relevant impact points;

b. arranging appropriate Extension demonstrations;

c. assisting Union Council members to prepare schemes to be carried out under the Thana Works Programme.

d. assisting cooperative groups to prepare loan applications.

In the case of proposed irrigation schemes, the TEO will endorse or approve only those schemes which are within the limits of the irrigation potential shown on Irrigation Map 2 (which must be kept up-to-date, to ensure that the safe limits of water use are not exceeded).

Step J6. The TEO will monitor the carrying out of the planned activities and take whatever steps may be needed to remove bottlenecks so that planned targets can be achieved.

Step J7. During the course of year 1, the TEO will make whatever amendments may be needed in the targets planned for year 2 so as to keep these targets realistic.[39]

---

[39] *Targets for years 3, 4, and 5 can be made in a similar way to that described in Steps J1-J7. Alternatively, year 1 can be used for preparing a more detailed 5-year plan, using the method described in Steps I1-I44.*

TABLE 23.23

Extension activities in 2-Year Agricultural Development Plan (proforma)

(1) Extension activity	(2) Union(s)	(3) Soil association	Target		(6) Responsible person
			(4) Year 1	(5) Year 2	
High priority					
1.					
2.					
Medium priority					
1.					
2.					
Low priority					
1.					
2.					

Annexe 1

GUIDELINES FOR SITING IRRIGATION EQUIPMENT[40]

1. It is the responsibility of the TEO to ensure that low-lift pumps (LLPs) and tube-wells (DTW, STW, HTW) are sited in such a way that:

   a. they can irrigate at least 25 acres (= 10 ha) per cusec in the case of transplanted paddy and at least 50 acres (= 20 ha) per cusec in the case of dryland crops such as wheat; and

   b. they will not interfere with the rights of other users.

2. In order to achieve these objectives, the TEO will ensure that:

   a. the relief of the proposed command area is suitable for water to be distributed to cover the minimum area specified;

   b. the soils of the proposed command area are suitable for irrigation of the crops the applicant(s) propose to grow;

   c. sufficient water suitable for irrigation is available at the site to irrigate the crops the applicant(s) propose to grow; and

   d. the site is not within the minimum distance from the nearest approved LLP/TW specified for the type of equipment in that particular area.

3. The TEO will satisfy himself that all these requirements are met before he recommends approval for the siting of an LLP or tube-well. In order to satisfy himself on these points, the TEO will adopt the following procedure.

   a. Each applicant for the siting of an LLP or tube-well will attach to the application a map showing:

      i. the precise location (including the mouza plot number) of the site where it is proposed to install the equipment;

      ii. the boundaries of the proposed command area;

      iii. the land type(s) within the proposed command area: i.e., Highland; Medium Highland; Medium Lowland; Lowland; Bottomland;

      iv. the kinds of soil within the proposed command area: i.e., sandy; loamy; clayey loam; clay; and

      v. the position of the highest and lowest land in the vicinity of the proposed command area.

   b. The relevant Block Supervisor will certify on the map that the information given on the map is correct. (The Block Supervisor should, in fact, help the applicant(s) to prepare the map.)

   c. On receipt of the application, the TEO will:

      i. check the application and the accompanying map to find out whether or not the site meets the minimum requirements;

---

[40]*This annexe appeared as Appendix 2 in the original document. See also footnotes 15 and 31 in this chapter.*

   ii. if it does so, locate the site on the Thana soil map to find out in which soil association it is located;

  iii. examine the relevant soil association table and crop suitability map(s) to find out whether the land types and soils indicated in the proposal are suitable for irrigation of the crop(s) proposed;

  iv. locate the proposed site on Irrigation Map 2 to find out from the table on that map whether or not enough surface water or groundwater remains available at the site for the proposed LLP/TW; also, confirms that the proposed site is not within the minimum specified distance from the nearest LLP/TW already in place or approved.[41]

d. If the TEO is satisfied that the proposed site is suitable in all respects, he will recommend approval of the application and will mark the position of the site on Irrigation Map 2 (in pencil until he receives confirmation that the equipment has actually been installed).

e. If the TEO is not satisfied in any respect about the suitability of the proposed site, he will return the application to the relevant Block Supervisor with a request:

   i. to obtain more information (to be specified) about the proposed site;

  ii. to persuade the applicant(s) to select a more suitable site (to be specified); or

  iii. to explain to the applicant(s) that the land/soil/water supply is/are not suitable for irrigation by the kind of equipment applied for.

4. For the satisfactory operation of this procedure, the TEO must ensure that:

a. all existing irrigation sites, and all the sites for which applications have already been approved, are correctly marked on the Irrigation Map 2;

b. all his Extension staff are properly trained in how to select suitable sites for irrigation;

c. suitable impact points are prepared so that farmers can be properly advised about the optimum siting and use of irrigation equipment; and

d. he regularly visits existing potential irrigable areas to check that application maps are being made properly and that equipment is being sited and used according to the approved specifications.

---

[41] *The TEO will also need to check that current proposals do not overlap or exceed available surface/groundwater limits.*

Annexe 2

SYMBOLS FOR USE ON IRRIGATION MAPS[42]

Show existing and potential irrigated areas on Thana Irrigation Maps 1 and 2 as follows.[43]

1. Draw a continuous thin green line around existing irrigated areas on Maps 1 and 2.

2. Draw a dashed green line around potentially irrigable areas on Map 2.

3. For areas irrigated or irrigable by gravity flow from cross-dams or rivers, draw vertical, green, dashed lines across the area. Label separate areas A1, A2, A3, etc.

4. For areas irrigated or irrigable by a single pump directly into existing channels, draw diagonal green lines sloping from right to left across the area. Label separate areas B1, B2, B3, etc.

5. For areas irrigated or irrigable by a single pump but for which a new distribution channel needs to be excavated, draw diagonal green lines sloping from left to right across the area. Label separate areas C1, C2, C3, etc.

6. For areas irrigated or irrigable by double pumping, with or without excavation of a new channel, draw diagonal green lines in both directions (i.e., cross-hatching) across the area. Label separate areas D1, D2, D3, etc.

7. For areas irrigated by deep or shallow tube-wells, draw small green plus (+) signs within the area:
   - labelled Ed1, Ed2, etc., for individual DTW sites;
   - labelled Es1, Es2, etc., for individual STW sites.

8. For areas irrigated by BWDB canal schemes, draw horizontal, green, dashed lines across the area. Label separate areas F1, F2, F3, etc.

9. For areas irrigated by a Thana Irrigation Programme (TIP) scheme where the control structures were designed by BWDB, draw horizontal, green, dashed lines and widely-spaced, vertical, green lines. Label separate areas G1, G2, G3, etc.

10. For areas not irrigated or not irrigable, leave unshaded. Label separate areas H1, H2, H3, etc., if necessary, to distinguish them from irrigated or irrigable areas.

11. For areas irrigated or irrigable by artesian flow, write small, green 'o' signs within the area. Label separate areas I1, I2, I3, etc.

12. For areas irrigated or irrigable by traditional irrigation devices (e.g., don, swing basket), write small, green 'v' signs within the area. Label separate areas J1, J2, J3, etc.

13. For areas irrigated or irrigable by hand tube-wells, write small, green, 'x' signs within the area. Label separate areas K1, K2, K3, etc.

14. For areas irrigated or irrigable by dug wells, write small, green, 'u' signs within the area. Label separate areas L1, L2, L3, etc.

---

[42]*This annexe appeared as Appendix 3 in the original document.*

[43]The symbols for items 3-11 are those illustrated for irrigation maps in the Thana Plan Book. On the scale of the Thana map (1 inch = 1 mile), it may not be possible to show the precise areas occupied by individual small irrigation devices such as those indicated in items 7(Es), 12, 13, and 14. Boundaries should be drawn on the map to indicate the areas within which such devices are used or could be used.

Annexe 3

POSSIBLE WAYS TO OVERCOME AGRICULTURAL PROBLEMS[44]

Possible ways of removing or reducing the 21 problems identified in Table 23.16 are described briefly below. Further information can be obtained from Brammer (1980a, b, 1981a).[45]

1. Water stands in fields after rainfall or irrigation

This problem mainly occurs on loamy and clay soils, especially in fields where the surface is not level and is bare before or soon after sowing. Broadcast aus, broadcast aman and jute are the crops usually affected, mainly at the seedling stage. Wheat and other dryland rabi crops can also be affected, either by late rains or by too-heavy irrigation. Extension advice to farmers is needed to overcome this problem as described below.

   a. Advise farmers to level fields to prevent water standing in pools, and make surface drains to lead surplus water out of the fields.
   b. For soils which are not used for transplanted paddy, also advise farmers to make the soil more permeable by breaking up the ploughpan and by adding more organic matter.
      i. Ploughpan. This can be broken up by deep ploughing or by hand cultivation once every two or three years: e.g., to grow potato, sugarcane, etc.
      ii. Organic matter. There are various ways to add more organic matter to soils:
         • use more farmyard manure, compost or oilcake;
         • leave more straw or other plant residues in the field after cutting crops, and plough this into the soil;
         • use crop residues or weeds (including aquatic weeds such as water hyacinth) as a mulch on dryland crops, and plough this material into the soil before the following crops are sown.
   c. For crops that are easily damaged by surface waterlogging, advise farmers to make ridges or beds (as for growing vegetables or potato) or to grow a crop which is less likely to be damaged by wet conditions.

2. Waterlogging

This problem is caused by the whole soil becoming saturated with rainwater or irrigation water. It can occur on sandy, loamy and clay soils as a result of one or more of the following factors.

   a. Unusually heavy rainfall which brings the water-table close to the soil surface.
   b. Seepage of water from an adjoining field where irrigated transplanted paddy is grown on soils that are too permeable for satisfactory flood irrigation.

---

[44]*This annexe appeared as Appendix 4 in the original document.*

[45]*The Drought Code (Brammer, 1980a) and the Flood and Cyclone Code (Brammer, 1980b) were summarized in Brammer (1999). It is intended to include the publication '17 possible ways to increase agricultural production in Bangladesh' in a future volume of the author's collected works (Brammer, in press).*

c. Seepage of water from higher fields which have been heavily irrigated.

d. Seepage of water from irrigation channels.

e. Blockage of drainage by a road, railway or flood-protection embankment.

f. Changes in river channels accompanied by siltation of minor rivers and khals.

Except for item b and possibly item c, these problems generally are too big for farmers to overcome themselves with Extension advice. In such situations, Extension staff need to:

i. advise farmers to grow other crops, where possible: see paragraphs 2.1 and 2.2 below; and/or

ii. assist farmers to prepare schemes or petitions for drainage improvement.

2.1 Heavy rainfall. In the case of soils which become waterlogged only once in five or ten years, it may not be economical to take any precautions, except to avoid growing tree crops which would be destroyed by waterlogging. In the case of soils which become waterlogged in wet years occurring more often than about once in five years, advise farmers:

a. not to grow crops which would be destroyed by 'wet feet': e.g., kharif maize, summer pulses, kharif groundnut, soyabean, kharif vegetables, cotton; or

b. if such crops are grown, to grow them on ridges or beds so that the root zone does not become waterlogged, especially at the seedling stage.

2.2 Seepage from adjoining fields.

a. Advise farmers on permeable soils not to grow transplanted paddy.

b. Organize farmers to grow irrigated crops in blocks: i.e., not to intermix fields of dryland crops and irrigated paddy.

c. Advise farmers growing dryland crops in fields adjoining irrigated paddy either

i. not to grow a dryland crop in a strip 10-15 feet wide adjoining the paddy field; or

ii. to grow the crops on ridges in this strip (or to transplant paddy in the waterlogged strip).

2.3 Seepage from higher fields. Extension staff should advise and assist farmers with one or more of the following measures.

a. Persuade farmers on the higher land to grow crops needing less irrigation.

b. Assist farmers on the higher land to prepare a scheme for lining irrigation channels.

c. Assist farmers on the waterlogged land to prepare a Works Programme scheme for drainage of their land, if there is a suitable drainage outlet for their area.

d. If the land cannot be drained, advise farmers to grow a suitable paddy or arum (*kochu*) variety, or to make raised beds on which to grow high-value dryland crops (such as vegetables or spices).

2.4 Seepage from irrigation channels. Extension staff should advise or assist farmers with one of the following measures.

a. In the case of waterlogging caused by seepage from LLP or TW irrigation channels, advise the group to maintain the channel better or assist them to prepare a scheme for lining the channels where they pass through permeable soils.

b. In the case of waterlogging caused by seepage from a BWDB irrigation canal, assist the Union or Thana Council to petition BWDB to line the canal in the relevant sections or to provide a drainage ditch and outlet.

2.5 Drainage blocked by an embankment. Extension staff should assist farmers in one of the following ways.

a. In the case of a road, canal or flood-protection embankment made under a Thana or Union Council scheme, assist farmers to prepare a scheme to provide a culvert, regulator, drain, etc., to relieve the problem.

b. In the case of a major road, railway, canal or flood-protection embankment made by a Government department, assist Union or Thana Councils to prepare a petition to the relevant Government agency to provide a culvert, regulator, drain, etc., to relieve the problem.[46]

c. Until such time as the waterlogging problem can be relieved by one of the above measures, advise farmers to grow a suitable paddy or *kochu* variety or to make raised beds on which to grow high-value dryland crops.

2.6 Natural blockage of drainage. The solution to this problem is either:

a. to assist farmers to prepare a scheme for drainage improvements to be effected under the Works Programme or by BWDB; or

b. to advise farmers to grow suitable paddy or *kochu* varieties or to make raised beds on which to grow high-value dryland crops.

3. Early flooding

Early flooding provides a problem in two particular situations: in floodplain basin sites; and on river char land, especially along the Brahmaputra-Jamuna river. In basin sites in the east of the country — e.g., in the Sylhet and Mymensingh haor areas — early flooding can be combined with flash floods. However, flash floods usually recede within a few days, whereas early flooding usually continues and merges with normal seasonal flooding. Extension staff can help farmers to avoid or reduce crop damage from early flooding in three main ways.

a. Advise farmers to grow early-maturing boro varieties in basin sites where there is a risk of early flooding if heavy rainfall occurs in April-May.

b. Assist Union or Thana Councils to prepare a scheme for building a diversion bund and drain or a submersible embankment to protect boro paddy in basin sites (as is practised in some haor areas). Such bunds/embankments should be designed by BWDB.

c. Advise farmers to grow suitable dryland crops which will be harvested before the flood season starts: e.g., barley, wheat, HYV mustard, pulses, tobacco (hookah or snuff types), vegetables, spices, using STWs or hand irrigation if necessary.[47]

---

[46]*An alternative would be to assist affected farmers to seek compensation from the agency for the loss of income resulting from waterlogging.*

[47]*Basin sites subject to early flooding usually have heavy clay soils and stay wet early in the dry season. These characteristics limit the choice of suitable crops. In sites that are not suitable for irrigated boro paddy, one solution may be to make raised beds of water hyacinth and other aquatic weeds as soon as water levels are low enough in November-December and grow suitable fruits and vegetables which can be harvested before the next flood season. Floating gardens might also be suitable: see Chapter 18, Section 18.4.3, last paragraph.*

4.   Flash floods

Flash floods occur on the plains adjoining hill areas following exceptionally heavy rainfall in the hills. They can also occur in valleys within the Madhupur and Barind Tracts, and in neighbouring floodplain basins (especially adjoining the Barind Tract). Damage to crops can be caused in several ways:

a. rapid flow of water over the fields, which may physically up-root plants;
b. burial of the plants by sand or silt; (burial of the fields with raw sand or silt may also reduce crop yields in future years);
c. submergence of seedlings;
d. submergence of plants at the flowering stage;
e. soil waterlogging after the floodwater recedes.

Extension staff can help farmers to avoid or reduce crop damage in four ways.

i. On sites where flash floods cannot be prevented, advise farmers to grow their main crops in the rabi season, preferably with irrigation where suitable surface-water or groundwater supplies are known to exist. Advise farmers which crops to grow, according to soil-crop suitability.
ii. Also on sites where flash floods cannot be prevented, advise farmers to make soil platforms on a part of their land on which to grow suitable rabi (and possibly kharif) dryland crops. The soil platforms must be raised above flash-flood level. Preferably, hand irrigation should be provided for growing high-value crops such as banana, vegetables, spices.
iii. Assist Union and Thana Councils to prepare a petition to BWDB to build a flood-protection embankment, drain or regulator to protect the land from flash floods.
iv. Where appropriate, assist the Thana Council to petition the District Council (and through that Council, central government) to organize soil conservation and afforestation projects in the adjoining hill areas so as to reduce the incidence or severity of flash floods.

5.   Deep flooding

Normal deep flooding of basin land is a problem mainly in that it prevents high-yielding crops from being grown in the kharif season. When combined with a high risk of early flooding, as in many haor areas, it may prevent kharif crops from being grown at all. Until such time as deeply-flooded areas might be included in flood-protection and drainage projects, Extension staff can help farmers to increase production in two main ways.

a. Advise farmers to increase production in the dry season, preferably with irrigation (where suitable water supplies are known to be available).
b. Advise farmers to transplant deepwater aman seedlings, except in basin centres where there is a risk of early flooding or rapid rise of floodwater.

6.   Risk of abnormally high floods

This problem occurs mainly on river char land and river-side land which is not protected by embankments. The solution is for Extension staff to advise farmers to increase crop production in the rabi season, preferably with irrigation (which may have to be by hand methods). Usually, this kind of land is not well suited for transplanted rice. However, where the soils are heavy enough for transplanted rice to be grown, it may be possible to transplant a late-maturing aman variety (or a quick-maturing aus variety) as the floodwater recedes, so long as seedlings can be transplanted before end-September (which means that the seed-beds must be sown on flood-free land by mid-August).

7. River-bank erosion

Normally, there is very little that can be done to prevent river-bank erosion along the major river channels. On small rivers, it may be possible to build spurs which will divert the water-flow away from a threatened section of river-bank, but this may only be worth-while in important places: e.g., to protect a road, bridge or building. Usually, it is not practical to protect agricultural land from river-bank erosion.[48] The role of Extension staff in areas where this problem occurs is to assist the Thana and Union Councils to resettle displaced farmers on new char land when it has become suitable for cultivation: (see item 8 below).

8. Burial by new sediments

Two kinds of land are subject to damage by new sediments:
a. char land and floodplain land close to big river channels; and
b. land near the foot of hills.

This problem often aggravates problems 3-7 above, and it may have to be dealt with at the same time as such problems.

8.1 River char land. There is very little that can be done to prevent new sediments from burying land within and adjoining the major rivers. The effect of burial is particularly serious where a thick layer of sand is deposited. Possible ways to cultivate new alluvium are described in the Flood and Cyclone Code (Bengali edition), Section 6.3.8 (gaw).[49]

8.2 Hill-foot land. Measures taken to control flash floods will also prevent more land from being buried by new alluvium: see item 4 above. Where flash floods cannot be controlled, Extension staff can advise farmers to adopt one of the following measures, whichever is considered appropriate.

a. If a thin layer of sandy alluvium is deposited, either scrape it off the fields, or use hand cultivation methods to mix it into the soil.
b. If the new deposit is too thick to remove or mix into the buried soil, advise farmers which crops it may be suitable to grow, according to the texture of the new material: see the Flood and Cyclone Code (Bengali edition), Section 6.3.8 (gaw).[50]

---

[48] *On small rivers, this is because preventing erosion on one river-bank may cause erosion on the opposite river-bank or downstream. On big rivers, bank protection is so extremely expensive that it may only be justified in order to defend strategic works such as major bridges, irrigation intakes, etc.*

[49] *The methods are described in Brammer (1999), Chapter 15.*

[50] *See footnote 49 above.*

9.   Drought-prone soils

Soils which quickly suffer from lack of moisture when rainfall is below normal are soils with a low moisture-holding capacity. Such soils include:

a. sandy soils;[51]

b. loamy and clay soils which overlie sand at a shallow depth;

c. almost all soils used for transplanted paddy, especially soils on Highland;

d. clay basin soils in the pre-monsoon season, before flooding starts;

e. red and brown clay loams and clays on the Madhupur and Barind Tracts;

f. almost all hill soils.

Extension staff can advise farmers to adopt one or more of the following practices to avoid or reduce the effect of drought on such soils.

i. Provide irrigation. On rapidly-permeable soils (a, b, e, f above), this should be from dug wells or tanks, or by HTWs.

ii. Grow drought-tolerant crops, where feasible: e.g., sorghum, *shama*, *bhurra*, *kaon*, sesamum, pigeon pea.

iii. Cultivate deeply (by hand, if necessary); use more organic manure; mulch the soil under dryland crops with straw or cut weeds; harrow and weed the soil regularly.

For more details of measures to deal with drought-prone soils, see the Drought Code, Chapters 4, 5 and 6.[52]

10.   Shortage of irrigation water

Three kinds of water shortage can occur, in different areas, viz.-

a. no water is available, or water is too saline for irrigation use;

b. only a small amount of water is available; or

c. water is available in the first part of the dry season, but not in the hot season.

Extension staff should first decide which of these conditions exists, and then take appropriate action, as suggested below.

a. **No water**. Three possible remedies should be examined.

i. Can irrigation be provided by building cross-dams, excavating deep tanks or double-lift pumping from a fresh-water river? If so, assist farmers to prepare schemes for funding under the Works Programme or Food-for-Work Programme, or by BWDB. Advise farmers to grow crops as suggested in paragraphs b and c below.

ii. On soils suitable for transplanted paddy, grow-quick-maturing varieties: either t.aus followed by t. aman in the east and centre of the country; or *either* t.aus *or* t.aman in the west and in the saline zone. Transplant aus when reliable rains normally start (in May or early-June).

---

[51]Most of the so-called sandy soils in the north of Dinajpur District (Thakurgaon) are, in fact, deep loams and clay loams. These soils are rapidly permeable and they cannot be puddled properly, so they do not hold water on the surface satisfactorily for transplanted paddy to be grown. However, they have a high moisture-holding capacity which makes them suitable for dryland crops (at times of the year when the soils are not waterlogged).

[52]*This information is summarized in Brammer (1999), Chapter 10. See also Brammer (1997), Chapter 3.*

iii. On soils poorly suited for transplanted paddy, grow kharif and early rabi dryland crops. Use moisture conservation measures: see items 9(ii) and 9(iii) above.

b. **Little water**. If only a small amount of water is available (e.g., in tanks, small rivers, poor aquifers), advise farmers to use it economically so that the greatest benefit can be obtained. Suitable economical methods are:

    i. grow quick-maturing crops;

    ii. give preference to dryland crops in the rabi season;

    iii. use furrow irrigation instead of flood irrigation;

    iv. irrigate only when necessary: for dryland crops, irrigate only when the plants show signs of wilting at mid-day, or when the topsoil is dry down to about 2 inches;

    v. plough or hand-cultivate deeply, so that water and roots can penetrate more deeply into the soil;

    vi. use moisture-conservation practices: see items 9(ii) and 9(iii) above.

c. **Water available only early in the dry season**. Where surface water or groundwater is only available in the cold weather, irrigate wheat, potato, rabi vegetables, spices, tobacco, etc. Give preference to irrigating crops on loamy soils. If heavy soils have to be used (e.g., clays, and soils that have been puddled for transplanted aman):

    i. make ridges or raised beds on which to grow dryland crops;

    ii. irrigate along the furrows or by splashing water over the crop from the ditches between beds; and

    iii. use small amounts of water at frequent intervals to keep soils moist without waterlogging.[53]

11. Puddled soils with strong ploughpan

Soils which are used for transplanted aman typically have a puddled topsoil underlain by a strong ploughpan (a compacted layer which impedes water and root penetration into the subsoil). These layers quickly become dry and hard soon after the end of the rainy season. Silty and clay soils are worst affected; some 'sandy' soils in the north of Dinajpur are not easily puddled and do not develop strong ploughpans.[54] Affected soils do not store sufficient moisture in the topsoil to grow dryland rabi crops, or the growth of such crops (usually khesari or mustard) is stunted and yields are very low. Most such land stays fallow in the dry season (where irrigation is not used or available). Extension staff can advise farmers to use one of three possible measures to grow better rabi crops on such soils.

a. *Provide irrigation*. If there is sufficient water, grow boro paddy. If there is insufficient water to irrigate paddy, use one of the methods described in items 10b and 10c above.

b. *Grow an early-maturing t.aman* (e.g., an HYV) and dibble-sow a pulse crop (lentil, khesari, gram) into the centre of each clump of aman stubble.

c. *Dig small planting holes* at suitable intervals, mix organic manure into the holes, and sow melon, pumpkin, gourds or similar vegetables. Mulch the soil between the

---

[53] *In addition, where water is scarce, as in situations b and c, losses in distribution channels should also be minimized by lining channels (e.g., with plastic sheet) or using plastic pipes.*

[54] See footnote 51 above.

planting holes. Preferably, irrigate by hand from a suitable source during the hot weather.

12. Heavy soils

Heavy clay soils in basin sites are difficult to plough and harrow satisfactorily, especially with weak draught animals. Such soils occur extensively in the coastal tidal zone, in the Sylhet and Mymensingh haor areas and in beel areas elsewhere. Silty soils used for transplanted aman cultivation can also be difficult to plough in the pre-monsoon season if rainfall is below normal. Extension staff can advise farmers to use one or more of the following methods to improve land preparation on heavy soils.

  a. Use buffaloes instead of bullocks (or cows) for ploughing. This would be most appropriate on tidal clay soils and in beel areas near to sugarcane-growing areas where buffaloes are already kept, either for milk production or for transportation.
  b. If it is not feasible to use stronger draught animals, organize farmers to use power-tillers or tractors on a cooperative rental basis.
  c. If possible, plough fields while they are still moist after the kharif season.
  d. Use irrigation to moisten the soil before land preparation.
  e. On silty soils used for transplanted aman, use more organic manure and leave more straw in the fields to be ploughed into the soil.

13. Shortage of draught animals

In areas where there is a shortage of draught cattle due to disease or due to losses caused by a flood or a cyclone, Extension staff can advise farmers to use one or more of the following methods, according to circumstances.[55]

  a. On heavy clays, either:
   i. clear weeds from the soil surface by hoeing, then make planting holes with a strong stick and transplant paddy seedlings (aus, aman or boro, according to the season); or
   ii. clear weeds from the soil surface by hoeing, puddle the soil by foot when the field is wet, then transplant paddy seedlings; or
   iii. organize farmers to use power-tillers or tractors on a cooperative basis.
  b. On silty or loamy soils, either:
   i. cultivate the soil by hand and broadcast sow or transplant crops in the normal way; or
   ii. clear weeds from the soil surface by hoeing, then dibble-sow suitable crops;
   iii. clear weeds from the soil surface by hoeing, make furrows with a hand plough, and sow crops in the furrows; or
   iv. organize farmers to use power-tillers or tractors on a cooperative basis.

14. Irregular relief

Irregular relief makes it difficult to provide irrigation from LLPs, DTWs or STWs in some floodplain areas and on parts of the Madhupur and Barind Tracts. Such areas usually are

---

[55]*The hand methods described could also be used in situations where power-tillers or tractors have been made inoperable by a flood, storm surge or disruption of fuel supplies.*

shown on soil maps or in soil association descriptions as having 'irregular relief phases'. On floodplain land, the problem often is aggravated by the presence of complex soil patterns, with big differences in soil texture and soil-moisture properties within short distances. Irregular relief on floodplain land needs to be considered separately from that on the Madhupur and Barind Tracts.

14.1 Floodplain land. If farmers wish to use irrigation on irregular floodplain relief, Extension staff should either:

    a. advise farmers to use HTWs, dug wells, swing baskets or fractional-horsepower LLPs or STWs to irrigate small command areas; or

    b. assist farmers to prepare schemes for providing pucca distribution channels across permeable soils and narrow depressions, so that bigger command areas can be irrigated by LLPs, STWs or DTWs of conventional sizes.

14.2 Madhupur and Barind Tracts. On deep, permeable, red and brown soils, the methods described above for floodplain soils can be used.

In areas of irregular relief with shallow clay soils, such as exist in many parts of the Madhupur Tract and in the high western part of the Barind Tract, the only way to irrigate the land would be to make terraces (as already exist in many western parts of Rajshahi District). On the Madhupur Tract, terraces could be irrigated from DTWs (or deep-set STWs), using pucca distribution channels and pucca outlets between fields (to prevent erosion). On the High Barind, groundwater generally is not available, and only supplementary irrigation could be provided for t.aus or t. aman crops by:

    a. excavating a network of inter-connected tanks on valley slopes;

    b. providing diversion bunds and channels to lead run-off water into the tanks;

    c. providing each tank with a protected spillway so that the embankment is not breached by overflow during heavy rainfall events; and

    d. providing pucca outlets between fields to prevent gulley erosion.

A pilot scheme to test this technique needs to be organized before Extension can safely recommend it to farmers.[56] Because of the limited amounts of water that could be stored in tanks, water-economical methods of irrigation would need to be used to make best use of the available water, as described in Section 10 above.[57]

15. Sloping hill soils

Hill soils provide four main kinds of problem:

    a. most of them are of low fertility, and heavy rainfall quickly washes nutrients out of the soil (including those in fertilizers);

    b. most of them are droughty in the dry season, especially on slopes that face south or west;

    c. sloping soils are subject to loss of soil by erosion, unless the surface is kept protected against the impact of heavy rainfall; and

    d. many of them occur in remote areas, meaning that farmers have to pay higher prices for input supplies and they receive lower prices for the produce they want to market.

---

[56]*See Chapter 18, Section 18.3.6.*

[57]*See also Brammer (1997), Chapter 8.*

The principles of farming on hill land are described in Chapter 13. In brief, Extension staff should advise farmers and Union/Thana Councils as follows.[58]

   i. Keep the soil surface covered with vegetation or a mulch at all times.

   ii. Preferably, grow tree crops.

   iii. Grow field crops only on level or gently-sloping land.

   iv. Use steep slopes only for forestry

Preferably, Extension staff should organize farmers into groups to manage blocks of land as soil conservation blocks.

16. Soil fertility

Extension staff have an important role to play in monitoring soil fertility in order to identify actual or potential problems that may exist or which might develop under intensive farming systems.

   a. District Subject Matter Specialists should advise TEOs and Thana SMOs:

      i. what kinds of soil fertility problems are likely to occur in their area: e.g., zinc deficiency, sulphur deficiency, iron toxicity, aluminium toxicity (near the Khulna and Chakaria Sunderbans);

      ii. the kinds of land, soil and cropping system where such soil fertility problems are most likely to occur;

      iii. the crops likely to be affected; and

      iv. the crop symptoms to look for.

   b. If a Block Supervisor suspects that any soil fertility problem exists in his work area, he should report this to the TEO (or SMO), bringing a sample of an affected plant and a description of the kind of land, soil and cropping pattern where the problem occurs.

   c. The TEO or SMO will personally check the symptoms in the field. He will take one of the following three actions, whichever he considers is the most appropriate.

      i. If he is certain that a particular deficiency or toxicity problem exists, he will instruct the Block Supervisor on what treatment to recommend to farmers.

      ii. If he suspects that a particular deficiency or toxicity problem exists, but he is not certain about it, he will advise the Block Supervisor to arrange a simple 'look-see' trial on one or more fields to seek confirmation that the problem symptoms have been correctly diagnozed. Where, necessary, he will provide the Block Supervisor with a small dose of the recommended chemical. If the look-see trial confirms the diagnosis, the TEO or SMO will instruct the Block Supervisor on what treatment to recommend to farmers.

      iii. If the TEO or SMO is doubtful about the nature of the problem, he will request assistance from the relevant SMS to solve the problem.

17. Saline soils

Saline soils occur in three areas:

   a. extensively in the coastal tidal zone of Chittagong, Noakhali, Patuakhali and Khulna Districts;

---

[58]*The section given in the original document has been abbreviated since the contents are similar to those given in Chapter 13.*

b. in small patches on floodplain ridges on the Ganges River Floodplain in parts of Jessore and Kushtia Districts; and

c. on land where saline groundwater has been used for irrigation: mainly in Jessore District; locally in eastern parts of Comilla District; but possible also in future in parts of Chittagong, mainland Noakhali, southern Comilla, northern Khulna, Barisal and southern Faridpur Districts.

   a. *Coastal zone*. In this zone, soils are mainly saline in the dry season, but monsoon rainfall washes out the salt so that one or two kharif crops can be grown in most areas. In this situation, Extension staff can advise farmers to reduce the soil salinity problem by using one of the following methods, as may be appropriate:

   i. Maintain embankments and sluices to prevent flooding by saline water.

   ii. Plough the soil quickly after harvesting the transplanted aman crop (if the soil is not too wet or too dry for ploughing at that time).

   iii. On silty soils, either sow a quick-maturing dryland rabi crop which will mature before the topsoil becomes saline, or dibble-sow a salt-tolerant aus variety in February or March if the soils are sufficiently moist for sowing at that time.[59]

   iv. Alternatively, on silty and clay soils, transplant aus in April or May as soon as there has been sufficient rainfall to puddle the topsoil; (in Khulna District, transplant aman at the appropriate time).

   v. Use quick-maturing, salt-tolerant, aus and/or aman varieties.

   vi. Where non-saline water is available, irrigate a quick-maturing boro paddy variety; transplant seedlings as early as possible.

   b. *Floodplain ridges*. Salinity occurs only in the hot weather. It either damages aus or jute seedlings or delays the sowing of these crops. Extension staff can recommend three possible remedies to farmers.

   i. Plough the soil as deeply as possible after harvesting the last kharif crop or rabi crop. If necessary, hand-cultivate the soil (e.g., by ridging or making beds in order to grow sugarcane or vegetables).

   ii. Wait until the rains are well established (end-May or early-June), then transplant aus seedlings.

   iii. If fresh groundwater (or surface water) is available, irrigate wheat, potato or rabi vegetables, followed by aus or jute grown as dryland crops : i.e., irrigate to keep the soil moist, not wet.

   c. *Saline groundwater*. Where tube-well water has become saline and has made the soil saline, heavy rainfall or flooding during the following rainy season will usually be sufficient to wash salt out of the topsoil. If possible, plough or hand-cultivate the soil so that it will absorb rainfall quickly and wash salt out of the topsoil in time for a kharif crop to be grown.

18. Saline flooding

This problem occurs on land outside coastal embankments, and on land within embankments where the embankment or sluices have been damaged. Extension staff can advise farmers

---

[59]*See Chapter 2, Section 2.3.4, Dibbling.*

and Union/Thana Council members to eliminate or reduce the problem in one or other of the following ways.

a. Prepare a request to BWDB to repair an existing embankment or sluice.

b. Prepare a scheme for building an embankment (with sluices) under the Works Programme to protect land outside an existing embankment. This embankment need not be as high as the coastal embankment. Preferably, it should be designed by BWDB. Funds must be provided to maintain the embankment and sluices.[60]

c. Where tidal water is not too saline in the rainy season, plant quick-maturing, salt-tolerant aus or aman varieties as soon as there has been sufficient rainfall to wash salt from the topsoil.

19. Shrimp farming

In order to cultivate shrimps, land-owners in parts of Khulna and Chittagong Districts breach embankments to allow salt water to flood their land in the dry season. This practice either prevents transplanted aman from being grown, or the salt water reduces yields. These practices may also reduce employment opportunities for agricultural labourers — including migrant labour from other Districts — thus increasing poverty.

Extension staff should advise farmers and Union/Thana Councils to organize the shrimp farming in such a way that the catching of shrimps ends on a specified date (probably mid-July) in order to leave sufficient time for the embankment to be repaired and for farmers to plough their land, allow rainfall to reduce soil salinity, and transplant aman seedlings in August.[61] Farmers should use quick-maturing, salt-tolerant, paddy varieties.

20. Poor communications

Extension staff should assist Union or Thana Councils to prepare a scheme (or schemes) for building or improving rural roads (including the provision of culverts or bridges) or for improving boat or ferry services in areas where:

a. poor communications mean that farmers have to pay a higher price for fertilizers, etc.;

b. farmers have difficulty in marketing their produce at a reasonable price; and/or

c. farmers have difficulty in obtaining prompt or regular equipment-repair, Extension services or other services.

21. Land-ownership[62]

In areas where big land-ownership and/or share-cropping prevent improved agricultural practices from being used, Extension staff can adopt one or other of the following practices to increase agricultural production.

a. Concentrate their Extension activities on small or medium farmers who are willing and able to use improved farming methods.

---

[60]*See Chapter 16, Section 16.5.9, subsections 4 and 5.*

[61]*Preferably, sluices should be built in embankments and bunds should be raised around shrimp farms so that the entry of brackish water can be regulated, embankments are not weakened by frequent cutting and saline water does not spread beyond shrimp farms to damage agricultural land not used for shrimp production.*

[62]*See also Chapter 12, Section 12.3, subsection e, footnote 6.*

b. In areas where irrigation is possible, assist small and medium land-owners to obtain HTWs or STWs, or to use tanks or dug wells for irrigation.

c. Assist share-croppers to negotiate *tebagha* tenancy terms, or to lease land on a fixed rental.[63] Then assist such tenants to obtain production credit.

---

[63] *Under traditional share-cropping, the tenant provides all the inputs and receives half the crop. Under tebagha terms, the tenant or the land-owner receives two-thirds of the crop, whichever provides all the inputs.*

Annexe 4

CONTINGENCY PLANS IN CASE OF NATURAL DISASTERS[64]

The TEO must be prepared to handle any kind of natural disaster that may affect agricultural production in his Thana. That means that he must know:

a. what are the kinds of natural disaster most likely to occur;

b. when each kind of disaster is likely to occur;

c. what kinds of land, soils and crops each kind of disaster affects;

d. what is the effect of each kind of disaster on agricultural production (including livestock); and

e. what are the possible remedies which he can recommend to affected farmers to assist them to grow suitable crops again after a disaster.

The disaster-related responsibilities of the TEO, Block Supervisors, Union Councils and Thana Councils are described in detail in Chapters 7-9 of the Drought Code (Brammer, 1980a) and in Chapters 7 and 8 of the Flood and Cyclone Code (Brammer, 1980b). Those codes also describe possible precautionary and rehabilitation measures relating to floods, cyclone and drought for different land and soil types and for individual months of the year.[65]

The TEO will make sure that he is thoroughly familiar with the procedures and information given in the two codes referred to above. He will ensure that his subordinate staff are regularly trained in their duties in relation to disaster management, and that Union and Thana Council members are fully briefed on their responsibilities in relation to the management of disasters affecting agricultural production.

In disaster-prone areas, the TEO will be responsible for the following tasks.

a. Assisting Union and Thana Councils to identify, prepare and implement schemes which will prevent or mitigate the effects of natural disasters: e.g., flood embankments; drains; regulators; irrigation.

b. Demonstrating practices which will reduce the effects of natural disasters and helping farmers to adopt those practices: e.g., quick-maturing crop varieties; supplementary irrigation.

c. Organizing training to ensure that Block Supervisors are kept alert regarding their duties and responsibilities in the event of a natural disaster occurring.

d. After a disaster, reviewing procedures in order to identify what changes could be made to improve the management of future disasters.

e. After a disaster, reviewing observations of farmers' practices for the purpose of identifying those that were most successful in avoiding the disaster, reducing its effects or speeding recovery.

The TEO will prepare a disaster preparedness contingency plan for his Thana. This plan is intended to provide a set of procedures which can be implemented immediately a natural

---

[64]*This annexe is based on Appendix 5 in the original document.*

[65]*This information is also given in Brammer (1999), Chapters 2-5.*

disaster seems imminent or actually occurs, so that no unnecessary time is lost in preparing for action. The plan should consist of three parts, viz.

a. A statement of the responsibilities and duties of each member of the Thana Extension staff in relation to disaster management procedures. This can be taken from the relevant chapters of the Drought Code and the Flood and Cyclone Code, but it should be amended as may be necessary to suit the staffing pattern of the Thana and the kinds of disaster most likely to occur in the Thana.

b. A table showing, in separate columns:

   i. A list of the soil series, phases and land types occurring in each soil association in the Thana, taken from the Thana soil survey report.

   ii. The area occupied by each soil and land type, as shown in Table 23.1.

   iii. Against each soil series, phase and land type, the main crops grown in the kharif-I, kharif-II and rabi seasons; (it usually will be possible to group together soils which have similar land use). Preferably, this information should be given in the form of a calendar showing the normal range of sowing and harvesting dates for each crop. Alternatively, if this information would take up too much space in the table, make a separate calendar for the main crops grown in the Thana.

   iv. For each crop, or group of crops, the action to be taken in case of damage or loss due to a natural disaster occurring in a particular month.[66] This information can be taken from the relevant table for the month, land type, kind of soil and crop given in the Drought Code and the Flood and Cyclone Code: select the method or methods considered suitable for the Thana: see Figure 23.3.

c. A consolidated table for the Thana showing for each crop, or group of crops, a list of any input requirements (such as seed, fertilizers, credit) which may be needed for a rehabilitation programme, where they will come from, and who will be responsible for making then available to farmers. The estimated requirements should be given in per-acre (or hectare) terms, so that the total requirements can quickly be estimated after a disaster occurs when the extent of the damage on different land types in different soil associations is known.

The TEO should review the contingency plan each year in order to ensure that it is kept up-to-date. He should make any amendments he considers necessary in the light of experience gained during any disaster which occurs during his period of office. That experience may be his own, or he may benefit from the experience gained by his colleagues in other Thanas, as reported to him by the District DDA.

---

[66]It may be preferable to give this information in a consolidated form for the whole Thana.

Chapter 24

ZONING OF LAND FOR AGRICULTURE AND URBAN USE IN DHAKA DISTRICT[1]

Criteria are described which can be used for making land use regulations to prevent undue loss of good agricultural land for urban and industrial development.

24.1 INTRODUCTION

The rapid expansion of urban and industrial development around Dhaka poses a serious threat to valuable agricultural land within a wide radius of the city, particularly in areas to the north and west. Already, considerable areas of level Highland have been overwhelmed in the Tejgaon, Dhanmandi, Mohammedpur, Mirpur, Cantonments, Gulshan, Banani, Kurmitola and Tongi areas. Similarly, considerable areas of valuable floodplain land have been lost along the Buriganga and Sitalakhya rivers to the east of Dhaka.

It seems inevitable that further valuable agricultural land will be lost in the Sabhar, Kashimpur and Tongi areas unless official steps are taken to regulate the acquisition of land for urban and industrial development. This chapter draws the attention of both national and District planning authorities to the urgent need for land use zoning regulations which will prevent undue loss of good agricultural land for urban/industrial development and thus encourage further urban/industrial development on land of lower agricultural value.

Figure 24.1 shows the relative potential for agricultural and urban/industrial use of different parts of Dhaka District. Figure 24.2 indicates a number of alternative areas where urban and industrial development could be planned which would minimize losses in agricultural production. It is particularly recommended that an early effort be made to preserve for agricultural use those areas shown in map units 1a and 1b on Figure 24.1 which lie

---

[1] *This chapter reproduces a brief report, originally prepared by the author in 1970 and issued slightly revised in 1975 (Brammer, 1975c). Apart from the recommendations it gave, the report was also prepared as a model for the Soil Survey Department (now SRDI) showing how the information given in District reconnaissance soil survey reports could be used to guide planners in making rational land use decisions. The national priority at that time was to increase food production in order to support the rapidly growing population. For a period in the 1970s, it appeared that the principles advocated in this guide were being followed by the Dhaka Municipal planning authorities. However, urban and industrial sprawl accelerated in the 1980s, apparently unregulated, and substantial losses of valuable agricultural land occurred in the Sabhar and Tongi areas, and in the Dhaka-Narayanganj-Demra irrigation and drainage project area. This chapter describes the situation as it was in 1975: no attempt has been made to up-date the information to accommodate the changes in settlement and land use which took place subsequently. Some of those changes are described in Chapters 4, 5 and 10.*

FIGURE 24.1

Dhaka District: potentials for agricultural and urban land use

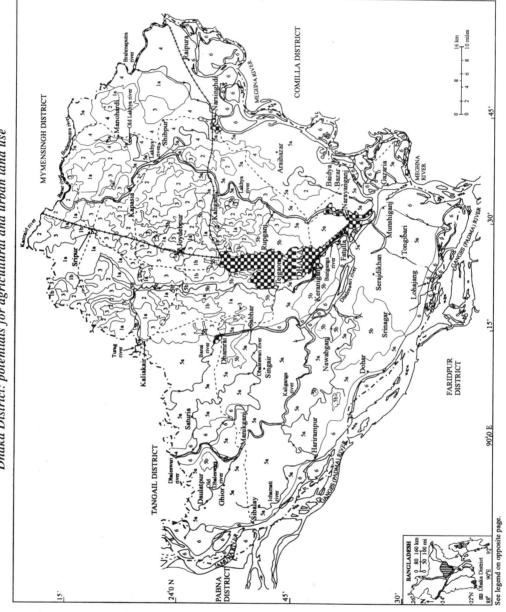

See legend on opposite page.

LEGEND FOR FIGURE 24.1

HIGHLAND

AGRICULTURAL POTENTIAL	URBAN AND INDUSTRIAL USE
High potential	
1a Mainly level, well-drained soils well suited for diversified cropping with irrigation	Well suited, but recommended that this land be preserved for agriculture
1b Mainly level, poorly-drained soils well suited for two HYV rice crops per year with irrigation	Ditto
Moderate potential	
2 Soils similar to 1a together with valley soils well suited for irrigated HYV boro, but occurring on rather broken relief making provision of irrigation less simple than in 1a	Moderately well suited. More difficult to develop because of presence of deep narrow valleys between narrow Highland ridges. Where possible, this land should be preserved for agricultural use
Low potential	
3 Mainly shallow clay soils unsuitable for irrigation on gently undulating to rolling Highland. Soils in narrow valleys moderately well suited for one or two irrigated HYV rice crops per year	Moderately well suited. Generally less broken relief than in unit 2. Where possible, this land should be assigned to urban and industrial development in preference to Highland in units 1 and 2

FLOODPLAIN LAND

AGRICULTURAL POTENTIAL	URBAN AND INDUSTRIAL USE
High potential	
4 Mainly seasonally shallowly-flooded land well suited for diversified cropping on the ridges and for one or two HYV rice crops per year in the basins with irrigation	Ridges well suited; basins poorly suited. Recommended that development be restricted to certain areas of sandy ridge soils of low agricultural value
Moderate potential	
5a Mainly deeply flooded land well suited for HYV boro or aus with irrigation. With flood protection and drainage in addition, well suited for diversified cropping on the ridges and mainly for two HYV rice crops per year in the basins	Poorly suited. Costly earth platforms and embankments needed to raise construction surfaces above flood-level. Where flood protection is provided, this land should be preserved for agricultural use to the fullest possible extent
5b Deeply flooded basins well suited for HYV boro with irrigation. Probably unsuitable for flood protection and drainage	Ditto
Low potential	
6 Mainly deeply flooded land subject to hazard of river erosion and burial by alluvium	Poorly suited because of risk of river erosion

CONVENTIONAL SIGNS

- – · –   District boundary
- —   Mapping unit boundary
- →   Narrow river
- Wide river (non-tidal)
- Wide tidal river
- ┼┼┼   Railway
- - - -   Main road
- ·   Thana HQ
- DHAKA   District town
- ▮▮▮   Urban land

within Sabhar, Tongi and Joydebpur Thanas and the part of Tejgaon Thana that has not yet been overwhelmed by settlements and industry.[2]

24.2 PRIORITY AGRICULTURAL LAND

Land in unit 1a on Figure 24.1 is mainly well-drained level Highland which is well suited for a wide range of crops, in both the wet season and the dry season. With tube-well irrigation, high yields of sugarcane, wheat (and other dryland cereals), oilseeds, potato, vegetables, tobacco, pulses and fodder crops could be obtained, as well as of broadcast paddy. Land with this capability for diversified cropping throughout the year is scarce in Bangladesh. Accordingly, it merits the use of special efforts to keep it in agricultural use.

Land in unit 1b on Figure 24.1 is mainly poorly-drained level Highland and Medium Highland. Most of it produces two paddy crops a year under natural rainfall. Some farmers in the part of unit 1b between Tongi and Joydebpur produce three transplanted paddy crops per year with irrigation from tanks or tube-wells: two HYV crops and a local variety. This land is actually and potentially the best paddy land within a radius of twenty miles of Dhaka city. Accordingly, this land also merits special efforts to keep it in agricultural use.

The level Highland areas in units 1a and 1b undoubtedly provide ideal sites for urban and industrial development. Therefore, without the imposition of some kind of land zoning regulation, it will be impossible to keep this land in agricultural use. Farmers in these areas cannot be blamed for selling their land to urban settlers and industrialists when the prices offered are so high in relation to their present agricultural returns from this land.

Apart from zoning regulations to preserve this land in agricultural use and to ensure that urban and industrial expansion is restricted to areas of lower agricultural value, priority in agricultural development deserves to be given to the areas of good agricultural land. That is not only so that agricultural production could be maximized on this land. It is also as a measure of compensation to farmers on such land who might otherwise be regarded as suffering short-term economic loss by being deprived of the opportunity to sell their land at a high price for urban or industrial use.

Provision of deep tube-wells (DTWs) would be the most appropriate and rapid method of developing the agricultural potential of this land. More than 100 DTWs had already been sunk by 1975 in the parts of units 1a and 1b lying within Sabhar Thana (in the Kashimpur Agricultural Development Estate). Small numbers of DTWs had been provided elsewhere. Experience at Kashimpur and near Joydebpur suggests that groundwater is readily available under the Madhupur Tract, so that the number of DTWs could be greatly expanded in the areas of good agricultural land.[3] When satisfactory progress has been made

---

[2] *Figures 24.1 and 24.2 have been reduced from the 1:250,000 scale used on the original maps. That has required some simplification of the boundaries shown and the omission of Thana boundaries. The original maps were derived from the land capability map in the report on the reconnaissance soil survey of Dhaka District (SRDI, 1967), which was based on information on soils, relief, drainage, hydrology, land use and agricultural potential collected in the field in 1964-65.*

[3] *Subsequent experience showed that groundwater supplies were not readily available in all parts of the Madhupur Tract, especially in the north. Areas close to Dhaka city were also affected by the draw-down of the water-table by big tubewells used to supply water for domestic and industrial use in the city.*

in the Kashimpur Agricultural Development Estate, consideration deserves to be given to creating similar estates in other areas of units 1a and 1b in Dhaka District, especially those areas nearest to Dhaka city or adjacent to new satellite towns that might be planned or established.[4]

In addition to providing tube-wells, other measures that could be taken to stimulate agricultural production include the provision of such facilities as a sugar mill, one or more oilseed-crushing mills, grain-drying plants, improved roads and cooperative marketing arrangements. Such facilities are needed to assure farmers of a ready market for their increased production.

24.3 Urban and Industrial Land

If good agricultural land near Dhaka is to be preserved for agricultural production, specific plans need to be made to allocate alternative areas for urban and industrial use. Undoubtedly, the most suitable large area of land that could be developed for these purposes without undue loss of agricultural production is that shown in unit 3 on Figure 24.1 in the west of Sabhar Thana. This area alongside the Sabhar-Kaliakair road has gently undulating to gently rolling Highland relief interspersed with small valleys. Development costs for land levelling and road construction would be higher than on land in unit 1, but probably appreciably less than on deeply-flooded land in unit 5 which is already being lost rapidly to industry and settlement in the Narayanganj-Demra area. In the Sabhar-Kaliakair area, water for domestic and industrial use probably would be readily available both from DTWs and by pumping from the adjoining Bansi river. The close network of valleys would facilitate drainage.[5]

Other areas of poor or moderate agricultural land which are suitable for urban or industrial development — either as alternatives to, or in addition to, the Sabhar-Kaliakair area — are:

a. *Joydebpur*: areas of unit 3 north-west and south-east of the town, with access to the railway;

b. *Sripur*: the area of unit 3 east of the town, with access to the Dhaka-Mymensingh road and railway, as well as to the Sitalakhya river; and

c. *Ghorasal*: areas of unit 2 along the railway east and west of the Sitalakhya river.

These areas are indicated separately on Figure 24.2. Some of these areas lie within areas of reserved forest. A national-level policy decision will need to be taken whether it is preferable for the national or local economy to surrender the low-value forestry production of such areas or to sacrifice adjoining land of high agricultural potential.

---

[4] *The Kashimpur Agricultural Development Estate was established by the then East Pakistan (later Bangladesh) Agricultural Development Corporation (BADC) to promote the production and marketing of irrigated vegetables by small farmers.*

[5] *One disadvantage of the areas recommended, not referred to in the original publication, is the occurrence of unweathered Madhupur Clay at a shallow depth. The shrink-swell properties of this clay would require that special measures be taken to prevent 'heaving' problems with the foundations of buildings, roads and drains. The impervious nature of this clay would also require that ample provision be made for the safe disposal of storm-water drainage and septic-tank effluent which the soils would not be able to absorb in the same way as the permeable Deep Red-Brown Terrace Soils occurring in units 1a and 1b.*

FIGURE 24.2

Dhaka District: area recommended for agricultural and urban use

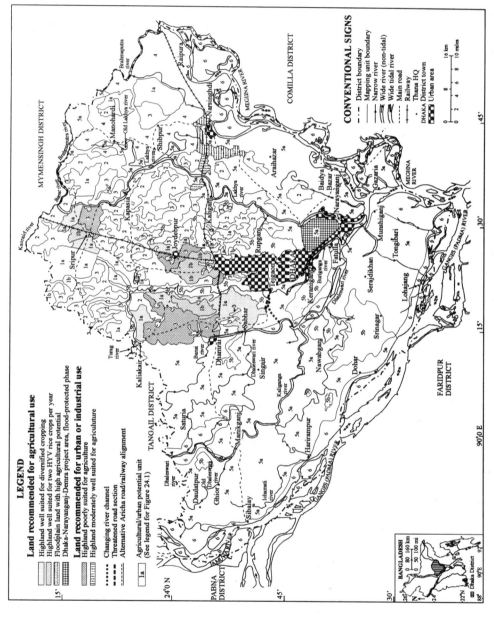

24.4 NEW ROAD ALIGNMENT[6]

If the Sabhar-Kaliakair area is developed for urban and/or industrial use, improved road communications with Dhaka will be needed. A railway link may also be needed. The Dhaka-Aricha and Sabhar-Kaliakair highways provide a satisfactory initial road base. However, the Dhaka-Aricha road is threatened with wash-out due to a change in the course of the Dhaleswari river south of Sabhar Bazar, such that an increasing river flow now impinges directly on the road embankment about 1 mile west of the Mirpur bridge. Either the new river course must be plugged — which might be impractical — or an alternative road alignment must be provided in a safer location further north.

If a new road alignment is needed, airphoto interpretation suggests that the most suitable location would be immediately west of Tongi, so as to join with the Dhaka-Aricha highway where the latter turns west about four miles north of Sabhar Bazar and two miles east of the Nayarhat bridge. This alignment, indicated on Figure 24.2, would require a shorter and lower embankment across the Turag valley than is required for the existing road. The proposed alignment would also be suitable for the Dhaka-Aricha railway, if a decision is taken to proceed with that development.

24.5 DHAKA-NARAYANGANJ-DEMRA PROJECT AREA

In conclusion, attention is drawn to the rapid spread of habitations which has taken place within the flood-protected portion of the Dhaka-Narayanganj-Demra (DND) project area. It must be expected that pressure will continue for expansion of settlements and industrial establishments within this area that was protected for agricultural development. Given the location of this project area on the fringes of the Dhaka-Narayanganj-Demra conurbation, the loss of this land to settlement and industry seems inevitable, sooner or later, unless land zoning regulations are speedily provided and applied.[7]

The DND project area can be regarded as representing in microcosm the much larger areas of Bangladesh where polders will eventually be created: for example, the Chandpur, Dhaka South-west and Belkuchi Project Areas. If the economic benefits of such agricultural development projects are not to be jeopardized by unrestricted sprawl of settlements and

---

[6] *Although the threat to the Dhaka-Aricha road described below eventually diminished, this section is retained as an example of considerations that may need to be taken into account elsewhere in planning urban and rural development in Bangladesh's dynamic physical environment. During a period of high floods in the late 1950s and early 1960s, the Dhaleswari river south of Sabhar Bazar vigorously eroded its east bank and a spill channel formed which connected with the borrow pit on the south side of the Dhaka-Aricha road west of Mirpur. The road embankment at that time formed the west bank of the new channel, and a new river levee formed on the south side of the channel, covering an extensive area with new sediments which buried what had previously been deeply-flooded basin land. In the 1970s, the flow in the Dhaleswari river decreased, the main river channel silted up considerably, and flow into the new spill channel ceased (thereby reducing the threat to the Dhaka-Aricha highway).*

[7] *By the mid-1990s, over half of the area of agricultural land in the DND polder area had been lost to urban and industrial sprawl, further encouraged by the construction of a new section of the Dhaka-Chittagong highway across the middle of the polder in the late-1980s. New buildings within the polder were built with plinth-levels assuming effective flood control, thus making them vulnerable to serious damage and perhaps loss of human lives in the event of the polder embankment being over-topped (as almost occurred in the 1988 and 1998 floods). For contingency planning regulations needed in this situation, see Brammer (1999), Chapter 8.*

industry onto flood-protected land, provision of land zoning regulations within such areas would seem to be essential. It is recommended that provision for land zoning regulations be included in the planning of such projects. Legislation may first be required which would enable Government, a project authority (such as BWDB) or a District Council to regulate land use in the public interest.[8]

---

[8] *See Chapter 10 for a review of the legal aspects of land use regulation.*

References[1]

Ahmad, Q.K., R.A. Warrick, N.J. Ericksen & M.Q. Mirza 1994 A national assessment of the implications of climate change for Bangladesh: a synthesis. Asia Pacific Journal on Environment and Development, Vol. 1, No 1: 46-80.

Aliff International 1981 Special studies of related industries in Bangladesh. Prepared for FAO Village Inventory Project (BGD/78/020). Dhaka.

Andriesse, W. 1982 Changes in land use and soils in major irrigation and drainage project areas in Bangladesh. FAO/UNDP Agricultural Development Adviser Project, Ministry of Agriculture, Dhaka.

Aziz, F.M. 1979 Location of brickfields in Dhaka District. MSc thesis, Dept of Urban and Regional Planning, Bangladesh University of Engineering and Technology, Dhaka.

Bangladesh Bureau of Statistics (BBS) 1981 Report on the Agricultural Census of Bangladesh, 1977, Dhaka.

—— 1984 The Bangladesh Census of Agriculture and Livestock, 1983-84. Dhaka.

Bari, F. 1974 An innovator in a traditional environment. BARD, Comilla.

Blair, G.J. *et. al* 1978 Sulphur nutrition of wetland rice. IRRI Research Paper No 21. IRRI, Los Banos, Philippines.

Bons, A. 1981 Irrigation in Bangladesh. Report to the Government of the Netherlands. The Hague.

Brammer, H 1974a Utilization of soil survey information in agricultural planning and extension. SRDI, Dhaka.

—— 1974b The potential for rainfed HYV rice cultivation in Bangladesh. Ministry of Agriculture, Dhaka.

—— 1974c The contribution of soil survey to agricultural research. Agricultural Research Conference paper. BARC, Dhaka.

—— 1975a Method for determining recommended land use for an area from reconnaissance soil survey reports. SRDI, Dhaka.

—— 1975b The potential for HYV wheat cultivation in Bangladesh. SRDI; Dhaka.

—— 1975c Zoning of land for agriculture and urban use in Dhaka District. (Second edition). SRDI, Dhaka.

—— 1975d Food-for-Work Programme: guidelines for selecting sites for agricultural schemes. Ministry of Agriculture, Dhaka.

—— 1975e Use of tanks for irrigation and fish farming. Ministry of Agriculture, Dhaka.

—— 1976 Use of waste land and fallow land. SRDI, Dhaka.

—— 1977 How to select sites for small water development schemes. SRDI, Dhaka.

—— 1979 Manual on Thana land use planning. Ministry of Local Government, Rural Development and Cooperatives, Dhaka.

—— 1980a Drought Code. Ministry of Agriculture, Dhaka.

---

[1] *The soil survey organization and the Ministry of Agriculture changed names a number of times during the author's period in East Pakistan/Bangladesh. To simplify references, the soils organization is referred to throughout as the Soil Resources Development Institute (SRDI) and the Ministry of Agriculture by that title. Similarly, the capital city is referred to uniformly as Dhaka, not by its former name Dacca.*

——— 1980b Flood and Cyclone Code. Ministry of Agriculture, Dhaka.

——— 1981a Seventeen possible ways to increase agricultural production in Bangladesh. Ministry of Agriculture, Dhaka.

——— 1981b Traditional and modern ways of intensifying crop production in Bangladesh. Ministry of Agriculture, Dhaka.

——— 1982 Agriculture and food production in polder areas. International Symposium on Polders of the World, Lelystad, Netherlands.

——— 1983 Manual on Upazilla agricultural development planning. (Draft edition). Ministry of Agriculture, Dhaka.

——— 1984a Soil and agricultural information needed for improved irrigation planning and management. Paper prepared for Seminar on Improved Irrigation Planning and Management in Bangladesh, Bangladesh University of Engineering and Technology, Dhaka, 27-28 February, 1984.

——— 1984b Land use planning in the tropics. ADAB News, vol. xi.1: 24-26.

——— 1984c Land use planning at the local level. Paper prepared for Seminar on the T & V system of Extension and Management, Graduate Training Institute, Bangladesh Agricultural University, Mymensingh, 11 November 1984.

——— 1985 Trends in fertilizer off-take 1979-80 to 1983-84. FAO/UNDP Agricultural Development Adviser Project (BGD/81/035), Ministry of Agriculture, Dhaka.

——— 1996 The geography of the soils of Bangladesh. UPL, Dhaka.

——— 1997 Agricultural development possibilities in Bangladesh. UPL, Dhaka.

——— 1999 Agricultural disaster management in Bangladesh. UPL, Dhaka.

——— 2000 Agroecological aspects of agricultural research in Bangladesh. UPL, Dhaka.

——— (in press) How to help small farmers in Bangladesh. UPL, Dhaka.

BRRI 1980a Workshop on sulphur nutrition of rice (1978). Joydebpur, Bangladesh.

——— 1980b Proceedings of a Workshop on Zinc Deficiency Problems of Irrigated Rice. (1980). Joydebpur, Bangladesh.

BWDB 1979 Chandpur Irrigation Project. Comprehensive evaluation report. Dhaka.

Castro, R.U. 1977 Zinc deficiency in rice: a review of research at the International Rice Research Institute. IRRI Research Paper No 9. Los Banos, Philippines.

Clay, E.J. 1978 Environment, technology and the seasonal pattern of agricultural employment in Bangladesh. Inst. Dev. Studies, Univ. Sussex, U.K.

Corver, H. (date?) Physical planning and rural planning in the Netherlands. Directorate for Land Use and Fisheries, Ministry of Agriculture and Forests, The Hague.

DDP (Delta Development Project) 1982a Observations, experiments and recommendations on agriculture in Polder 22 (1981/82). The Hague, Netherlands.

——— 1982b Notes on the socio-economic situation in Polder 22. The Hague/Dhaka.

de Datta, S.K. 1978 Fertilizer management for efficient use in wetland rice soils.In Soils and rice. IRRI, Los Banos, Philippines.

EPWAPDA 1967 Soil and agricultural survey of Chandpur Irrigation Project Area (southern Unit). Directorate of Land and Water Use, EPWAPDA. Dhaka.

FAO 1959 Report to the Government of Pakistan on the soil survey of the Ganges-Kobadak Area. Rome.

——— 1971a Soil Survey Project, Bangladesh. Tech. Rpt 2. Agricultural development possibilities. Rome.

——— 1971b Soil Survey Project, Bangladesh. Tech. Rpt 3. Soil resources. Rome.

—— 1971c Legislative principles of soil conservation. Soils Bulletin No 15. Rome.

—— 1980 Report of the Bangladesh Barisal III Project Identification Mission. FAO-World Bank Cooperative Programme (Investment Centre), Rome.

—— 1988 Land resources appraisal for agricultural development in Bangladesh. Report 2: Agroecological regions. Rome.

Flood Plan Coordination Organization (FPCO) 1992a FCD/I agricultural study (FAP12). Final report. Ministry of Irrigation, Water Development and Flood Control, Dhaka.

—— 1992b Operation and maintenance study (FAP13). Vol. I, main report. Ministry of Irrigation, Water Development and Flood Control, Dhaka.

—— 1995 (Final report). Ministry of Irrigation, Water Development and Flood Control, Dhaka.

Forestal International 1966 Soil and land use survey of the Chittagong Hill Tracts. 9 vols. Forestal Forestry and Engineering International, Ltd, Vancouver, Canada.

Gill, G.J. 1981 The impact of mechanized land preparation on production and employment in Bangladesh: a brief summary of conclusions. A/D/C (later Winrock), BARC, Dhaka.

Henle, H.V. 1974 Report on China's agriculture. FAO, Rome.

Hoq, A. & C.D. Grant 1979 First report on frame surveys of the fisheries statistical surveys of Bangladesh. FAO Fisheries Advisory Project (BGD/72/016), Department of Fisheries, Dhaka.

Horst, L. 1978 Ganges-Kobadak Irrigation Project, Kushtia Unit. Mission report, Bangladesh. Ministry of Foreign Affairs, The Hague, Netherlands.

Huizing, H.G.J 1970 An exploratory study of soil moisture relations in East Pakistan soils. SRDI, Dhaka.

Hussain, T. 1982 A study of legal aspects of land use regulation in Bangladesh. Ministry of Agriculture, Dhaka.

Ibrahim, A.Md. 1984 Changes in flood levels in Bangladesh. Agricultural Development Adviser Project (BGD/81/035), Ministry of Agriculture, Dhaka.

IBRD 1975 Appraisal of the Barisal Irrigation Project. Washington D.C., USA.

IECo 1964 Master Plan. East Pakistan Water and Power Development Authority (EPWAPDA), Dhaka.

Islam, A. 1975 Rural land use in Bangladesh. Paper presented at Seminar on Integrated Rural Development. (Series 11, paper 1). Dhaka.

Jager, T. 1982 A study of village lands made derelict by non-agricultural activities. Agricultural Development Adviser Project (BGD/81/035), Ministry of Agriculture, Dhaka.

James, J.R. 1973 Some aspects of town and country planning in Bangladesh. National Physical Planning Project (BGD/72/104). Urban Planning Directorate, Dhaka.

Januzzi, F.T. & J.T. Peach 1980 The agrarian structure of Bangladesh: an impediment to development. Westview Press, Boulder, Colorado, USA.

Joshua, W.D. & M. Rahman 1983a Physical properties of soils in the Ganges floodplain of Bangladesh. SRDI, Dhaka.

—— 1983b Physical properties of soils of the Tista river floodplain and Barind Tract of Bangladesh. SRDI, Dhaka.

Kaplan, A.H. 1980 Report on national physical planning law for Bangladesh. Bangladesh National Physical Planning Project (BGD/72/104), UNDP, Dhaka.

Khan, A.H. 1981 Bengal reminiscences. Vol. I. Food and flood. BARD, Comilla.

—— 1983a The works of Akhter Hameed Khan. Vol. II. Rural development approaches and the Comilla model. BARD, Comilla.

—— 1983b The Works of Akhter Hameed Khan. Vol. III. Rural works and the Comilla cooperative. BARD, Comilla.

Khan, A.R. & F.O. Valera 1982   Promotion of increased fertiliz[...] plot demonstrations. Directorate of Agriculture (Extension & [...] Dhaka.

Leedshill-de Leuw 1968 Coastal Embankment Project. Engineering and Economic evaluation. Vol. I. EPWAPDA, Dhaka.

——— 1969 Feasibility report for Chandpur Irrigation Project. BWDB, Dhaka.

Manalo, E.B. 1976? Agroclimatic survey of Bangladesh. BRRI/IRRI, Dhaka.

Master Plan Organization (MPO) 1986 National Water Plan. 3 vols. Ministry of Irrigation, Water Development and Flood Control, Dhaka.

Nedeco 1980 Report of an irrigation advisory team, Ganges-Kobadak Irrigation Project, Kushtia Unit. Ministry of Foreign Affairs, The Hague, The Netherlands.

Nuruzzaman, K.Md 1979 Physical planning legislation in Bangladesh: a study of proper legislative needs. Master's degree thesis, Univ. of Sheffield, U.K.

Ou, S.H. 1973 A handbook of rice diseases in the tropics. IRRI, Los Banos, Philippines.

Randhawa, N.S. et al. 1978 Micronutrients. **In** Soils and rice. IRRI, Los Banos, Philippines.

Sakai, H. 1979 Report of the IRRI Agronomist on research activities 1977-79. BRRI, Joydebpur, Bangladesh.

Serno, G. 1981 A reconnaissance study of changes in settlement and related non-agricultural land use in Bangladesh. FAO/UNDP Land Use Policy Project (BGD/78/014). Ministry of Agriculture, Dhaka.

Singh, G. 1979 A report on the mango shoot gall psyllid, Apsylla cistellata Buck.: damage in Bangladesh and recommendations for its control. FAO, Rome.

SRDI 1966 Reconnaissance soil survey of Comilla Sadar North and South Subdivisions of Comilla District. SRDI, Dhaka.

——— 1967a Reconnaissance soil survey of Dhaka District. (First edition). SRDI, Dhaka.

——— 1967b Reconnaissance soil survey of Nilphamari and Sadar Subdivisions, Rangpur District. SRDI, Dhaka.

——— 1968 Reconnaissance soil survey of Barisal District. SRDI, Dhaka.

——— 1970a Sabhar Thana: soils information for planning agricultural development. SRDI, Dhaka.

——— 1970b Reconnaissance soil survey of Noakhali District and Sadar North, Sadar South and Chandpur Subdivisions of Comilla District. SRDI, Dhaka.

——— 1972 Reconnaissance soil survey of Bogra and part of Dinajpur Sadar Subdivision. SRDI, Dhaka.

——— 1973a Reconnaissance soil survey of Kushtia District. SRDI, Dhaka.

——— 1973b Reconnaissance soil survey of Sadar and Bagherhat Subdivisions of Khulna District. SRDI, Dhaka.

——— 1975 Sabhar Thana soil guide. (Second edition). SRDI, Dhaka.

——— 1976 Reconnaissance soil survey of Sunamganj and Habiganj Subdivisions of Sylhet District. SRDI, Dhaka.

——— 1977 Reconnaissance soil survey of Jessore District. SRDI, Dhaka.

——— 1981 Reconnaissance soil survey of Dhaka District. (Revised edition). SRDI, Dhaka.

Sultana, P., P.M. Thompson & M.G. Daplyn 1995 Impact of surface water development projects on agriculture in Bangladesh. Project Appraisal, vol. 10, No 4, Dec. 1995: 243-259.

Urban Development Directorate 1979 Policies for urban lands. Urban Housing Policies and Programme, Dhaka.

van der Meulen, A. 1971 Mango growing in South Africa. Leaflet No 48, Subtropical Fruit series No 7, Mango series No 1. Dept of Agricultural Technical Services, Pretoria.

Warrick, R.A. & Q.K. Ahmad (Eds) 1996 The implications of climate and sea-level change for Bangladesh. Kluwer Academic Publishers, Dordrecht.

World Bank 1979 Review of the Bangladesh Water Development Board. Joint document of the Government of Bangladesh and World Bank. Dhaka/Washington D.C.

—— 1980a Project completion report, Bangladesh, Chandpur Irrigation Project. Washington D.C.

—— 1980b The re-assessment and extension of Barisal Irrigation Project. Staff Appraisal Report. Washington D.C.

Yoshida, S. 1981 Fundamentals of rice crop science. IRRI, Los Banos, Philippines.

General Index

The main references are indicated by bold numbers. Crops are listed separately in the Crops index. f = footnote. -(number) = reference continues on next or intermediate pages. ...(number) = references also appear on intermediate pages.

Acid Basin Clay(s)
  crop suitability, 409
  description, **14**, 15, 409
  in Sabhar Thana
    area, 409
    soil series, 409

Acid Sulphate Soil(s)
  description, 13, **14**
  occurrence
    Chakaria Sunderbans, 75
    Ganges Tidal Floodplain, 75
    Gopalganj-Khulna Beels, 353
    Khulna Sunderbans, 352
  reclamation, 352

active/very young (river) floodplain(s)
  and embankments, 61
  flooding by silty water, 9, 64
  occurrence, **8**, 61
  settlements on, 142, 143
  soils on, 13

aerial photographs: *see* airphotos

afforestation: *see* forest

agrarian reform, 24

Agricultural Census
  1977, 193, 204
  1983-84, 26f, 27f, 254f

agricultural development
  constraints, 44
  involvement of farmers, 69
  plan/-ning, *xxi*, *xxii*, 44
    decentralization, 24, 259f
    and the environment, 24
    village: *see* village agricultural development plan(-ning)
    and (water) Master Plan, 67
  in polder areas, **59-78**
  problems, **466**
    ways to overcome, **483-95**
  policy, 274: *see also* agricultural policy

agricultural extension: *see also* Agricultural Extension Department
  demonstrations, optimum production patterns, 275
  farmer-to-farmer, 36
  in hill areas, 277f
  re land use development possibilities, 275
  and planning, *xxii*
  programme(s), 44
  specialists, 77

Agricultural Extension Department/staff
  changes in staff titles, 303f
  role in
    food-for-work schemes, 301-2, 306, 308

overcoming agricultural problems, 483...95
small water development schemes, 311, 336
Thana land use planning, 422...6
village land use planning, 423
training in use of soil survey information, 399f

agricultural markets/-ing: *see* crop, markets/-ing

agricultural planning: *see* agricultural development, plan/-ning

agricultural policy, **271**

agricultural problems: *see* agricultural development, problems

agricultural production, 24
  conflict with urban growth, 237
  increase
    1881-1981, 25
    by small farmers, 24
  intensification
    factors contributing, 25
    by fertilizer use, **35-6**
    pathways, 25
    planning, **43-4**
  measures to increase/stimulate, 271, 503
  riskiness, 274

agricultural research
  and biomass production, 275
  programme(s), 44

Agricultural & Rural Development Council, 264

agricultural/crop statistics
  reliability of, 25, 27, 66...7
    re area not available for cultivation, 133f

agricultural survey(s), **71-2**

agricultural technology, 42-3

agriculture
  in the economy, 16, 60
  in polder areas, **59-78**

Agriculture, Ministry of, 265-6

agroecology/-ical
  region/subregion, **5-9**
    land types in, **11**

Agro-ecological Zones Study/Project, 179, 289

agro-economists, 77

agronomists, 77

ail: see bund

airphoto(s)
  comparison of 1952 and 1974, 133
  comparison of 1963 and 1974, 152
  identification of river channels, 304, 305
  interpretation, 137-9, 287
  non-availability, 136f, 177

stabilized, 43
processing equipment/facilities
    prices, 261
    provision, 43, 264
production
    avoiding adverse impacts, 261
    constraints on, 260, 265
    emphasis on dry-season, 68
    and employment/incomes, 261
    equipment prices, 261
    government policies, 275
    intensification, **23-58**, 265; pathways, **27-37, 39-41**;
    stages, **37-9**; tables, **44-58**
    intensive: modern, 37-8, **39, 40**, 46,48-58; traditional,
    37, **39**, 40, 46, 48-58
    irrigated, 38, 60
    possible improvements, 46, 365, 366
    questionnaire for village development planning, 367-8,
    369-83
    rainfed, 38, 60
    subsistence, 37
    sustained, 260
    targets, 365, 366
    technology, 267
    trials, 412, 417
    ways to increase: on kharif fallow land, 358; on rabi
    fallow land, 356-7; on waste/fallow land, 347-8;
    see also land, reclamation
purchase centres, 43
residues,
    use as fuel, 35, 36
    use as manure, 36
rotation(s): *see also* rotations for individual crops in Crops
index
    in Comilla Kotwali Thana, 447
    on farm holdings, 40
    influence of soil-hydrological conditions, 286
    and land/soil type, **391-8**
    map(s), **444-52**
    with/without irrigation, 333-4, 393-8
and soils, 72
sowing date: *see* crop planting date above
statistics: *see* agricultural statistics
storage, 348
subsistence, 39, 41
suitability
    map(s), 431, **440-6**
    ratings, 433-4, 472f
    table(s), **433-40**; in soil reports, 290
    on reclaimed waste land, 349...55
    with/without irrigation, 330, 333-4, 393-8
testing, 78
threshing, 69, 348
turn-around time between, 450
variety(-ies): *see also* individual crops in Crops index
    change of, **36-7**, 39
    high-yielding (HYV), 39, 45
    new, 48...9, 52...7
    quick-growing/maturing, 26, 39, 45
    selection by farmers, 37f
water-economical, 261
yield(s): *see also* individual crops in Crops index
    in basin sites, 110f
    constraints, **269-71**
    in official statistics, 141f
    potential, 269
    present, 269, 270

cropping intensity
    constraints, 260
    in Districts
      Comilla, 26
      Dinajpur, 26
    double cropping, 26, 68
      mixed aus+aman, 27f
    and employment, 261
    with irrigation/mechanization, 42
    multiple, **29-30**
    in project areas
      BIP, 96, 97, 98
      CIP, 89
      DND, 83...5
      Polder 22, 112
    quadruple cropping, 26
    triple cropping, 26, 68
    and zinc/sulphur deficiency, 113
cropping pattern/system(s)
    adoption rate in project areas, 68
    and climate, 16
    changes, 179f, **183...92**, 291
    demonstrations, 78
    determining factors, **64-5**, 180
    and environmental conditions, 23
    and flooding, **17**, 179f, 180
    intensive
      inducements for, 347
      rate of adoption, 69
    and land type(s), **18**
    mixed, 48
    multiple, **29-30**
      double, 40, 68
      quadruple, 26
      triple, 40, 68
    and natural disasters, **17**
    new, 78
    in project areas
      CIP, 89
      DND, 83
      Polder 22, 110
    and soil conditions, 72
    testing, 78
cropping practices
    intensive/-ification, 21, **29-30**, 41
    intercropping, 29, 33
    multiple: *see* cropping pattern/system(s), multiple above
    relay cropping, 29, 33
    sequence cropping, 29
    traditional, 29, 39
cultivable area, 269
cultivation/tillage: *see also* crop, cropping
    by hand
      instead of animal ploughing, 490
      on Barind Tract, 31
      on *char* soil, 31...2
      ploughing, 490
      instead of tractor ploughing, 490f
    initial, 39
    modern intensive, 37-8, 39, 46
    platform: *see* platform
    practices/techniques
      deep, 118, 417f, 488
      dibble-sowing, 490
      on drought-prone soils, 488

water salinity, 111
project characteristics, **108-110**
salinity
  soil, 109, 110
  water, 108
shrimp cultivation, **112-3**
  conflict with crop cultivation, 112-3
sluice-gates, 108, 110, 111-2
soil(s)
  (kinds of), 106, 108
  analytical data, 109
  conditions affecting land use/productivity, **111-12**
  observation sites, 128-9
studies needed, 111, 113

pole(s)/-wood, 50, 51

pollution
  industrial, 119
  water, 119

population
  density, 60, 140-1, 274, 347
  growth,
    and food production, 21, 25, 28, 61, 77, 221, 237, 269
    and natural resources, 259
    in settlements: *see* settlement(s)
  Hindu, 109
  pressure, 68, 269
  in study Thanas, 140-1: *see* individual study Thanas

post-monsoon season: *see* season

potash
  availability, 64, 85
  (fertilizer): *see* fertilizer type

potential evapo-transpiration (PET)
  v. rainfall, 5

power tiller(s)
  on heavy soils, 490
  labour-displacement, 42
  subsidies, 43f

pre-monsoon season: *see* season

project(s): *see also* drainage/embankment/flood
protection/irrigation/water projects
  design, 73, 78
  economic assessment, 78
    benefit:cost ratio, 68
    implications, 72
    rate of return, 71, 73, 78
  farmers' willingness to pay, 73f
  impact assessment, 72, 78
  land use regulation, 263-4
  monitoring of impacts, 78
  pilot projects, 78
  planning/implementation,
    and farmers, 69, 71, 78
    problem/weaknesses, 67...72, **73-6**, 97
    role of agronomists/soil scientists, 69, 77
    surveys, 71-2
  targets, 69
  zinc/sulphur deficiency, 113-9

Public Works Department
  regulation of building standards, 262

puddling: *see* soil (1)

pulp(-wood), 356

purchasing capacity/power
  and employment/incomes, 43, 275
  for food, 270
  for fuel, 270
  and market prices, 267, 275

rabi (season)
  -1, 371f
  -2, 371f
  crops: *see* Crops index
  definition, 16

railways, economical planning, 263

rainfall
  annual, 5
  and floods/-ing, 3
  with greenhouse warming, 18
  heavy/excessive, 5, 483, **484**
  measurement, 344
  monsoon, 3, 5,
  post-monsoon, 3
  pre-monsoon, 3, 5
  seasonal, 3, 5
  untimely, 5, 17
  variability, 5

rainfed crops/cultivation: *see* crop production

rains/rainy season
  end, 16
  start, 16

raised bed(s): *see also* platform (cultivation)
  in Bogra District, 31
  on Brown Mottled Terrace Soils, 406f
  for crop intensification, 38, 39, 48, 49, 52, 53, 55, 57
  on Deep Red-Brown Terrace Soils, 405f
  on Grey Terrace & Valley Soils, 409
  to improve soil drainage, 356-7, 406f, 483, 484, 485
    using plant material, 485f
  irrigation, 357
  on peaty soils, 33, 330
  in regions
    Arial Beel, 358f
    Barind Tract, 41

Rajshahi District
  mango cultivation
    area/production, 227-8
    orchards, 228-9
  soil platforms, 32
  tanks, 203

Rajshahi (town)
  Engineering College, 207
  Medical College & Hospital, 207
  University, 206-7

Rangpur District, mango area/production, 227-8

reeds, 89, 102

remittances, 60f

relay cropping/sowing, 29, 30, 33, 39, 45, 48, 52

relief, irregular, **490-1**

Relief & Rehabilitation, Ministry of
  role in Thana development planning, 336

rice: *see* Crops index

rice-surplus area(s), 41-2, 260f

ridges (cultivation)
    definition, 419
    to prevent waterlogging, 48, 49, 52, 483, 484
    on puddled paddy soils, **31**, 41, 49, 53, 55, 57

ridges (floodplain): *see* floodplain

river
    bank erosion: *see* erosion
    bank protection, 487
    channel(s)
        changes, 484, 505
        cross-dams, 325
        cutting new, 312, 315
        deepening/widening, 312, 315
        desilting, 303-5, 308, 324, **325**; adverse consequences,
            310
        pumping water into, 315
        sluice-gates, 325
    floodplain: *see* meander floodplain
    international agreements, 67
    irrigation from, 312, 314-5
    loop-cutting, 306, 308, 324, **326**
        adverse consequences, 310, 326
        compensation for loss of land, 325
        creation of reservoir, 325
        technical advice, 326
    low flow records, 456

road(s), 43: *see also* land, non-agricultural; study Thanas
    borrow-pits/ditches, 202-3
        use, 202-3
    economical planning, 263
    embankments, 327
    engineer(s), 316
    provision to stimulate agricultural production, 503
    rural, 494

root-knot: *see* nematodes

rubber plantation(s), 217, 219

run-off,
    (general), 19
    reduction, 261
    in regions
        Barind Tract, 353
        Madhupur Tract, 353

Rural Academy (unspecified): *see also* BARD
    role in village development planning, 365, 366

Rural Development (Ministry): *see* Local Government, Rural
Development & Cooperatives

Sabhar Thana
    agricultural development priorities, **412**
    area, 413
        homesteads & water, 413
    general soil types, 401-16
        agricultural development possibilities, **403-11**
        descriptions, **403-11**
        how to identify, **402-3**
    recommendations for trials, **412**, **417-8**
    soil associations
        area of general soil types, 413
        changes in soils since 1964, 412f
        characteristics, 412, 414-6
        map, 400-1
    soil guide, **399-420**
    urban and industrial development, 412f

salinity
    soil: *see* soil (1)
    water: *see* water salinity

salt (-making), 75

salt-tolerant crops/varieties, 65

Sandwip, crops in, 31

satellite imagery, 146f, 304f

Satla-Baghda
    area, 33
    project, 75

savannah woodland, 49

scrub (vegetation), 48, 50, 51

sea-level, with greenhouse warming, **19**

season
    growing, 16
    monsoon, 3, 16
    post-monsoon, 3
    pre-monsoon, 3, 16
    variability, 16
    winter (cool/dry), 3, 16

sediment deposition on floodplain, 216

seed
    distribution by farmers, 36f
    as cash crop, 49, 53
    germination, 32
    of improved varieties, 43
    rate(s), 45, 348

seed-bed, (paddy), 51

seedling(s)
    distribution by farmers, 36f
    dipping in zinc oxide, 114
    and *ufra* disease, 120

seepage
    from adjoining fields, 483, **484**
    from irrigation canals, 484, **484-5**

settlement(s): *see also* study Thanas (Bahubal, Baidya Bazar,
    Chandina, Dupchanchia, Ghior, Kishoreganj, Mirpur)
    area, 134, 143-4, 193-4
        method of estimating, **134...6**, 152; checking, 137;
        reliability, 137-40
    definition, 136
    expansion **140-5**
        in/around Dhaka city, 246-8
        in Dhaka, Chittagong, Khulna, 141f
        in DND area, 75, 84-5
    encroachment
        on agricultural land, 59, 78, 246-7
        on flood-protected land, 75-6, 78, 264
    and flooding, 133-4, 142-5: *see also* individual study
    Thanas
    housing density, 141: *see also* individual study Thanas
    housing societies, 246-8
    in physiographic units, **142-5**
    on platforms, 134, 139, 142, 152
    and population density, 151f
    population in study Thanas, 141: *see also* individual study
    Thanas
    productive/non-productive land, 137, 204: *see also*
    individual study Thanas
    siting, 16, 133-4, 412

Crops Index

The main references are indicated by bold numbers. -(number) = reference continues on intermediate pages. ...(number) = references also appear on next or intermediate page(s). b = broadcast. f = footnote. t = transplanted. v = versus. + = mixed with. -(crop) = followed by.